서아쌤의 토익 비밀과외

KB184039

최서아 · 시원스쿨어학연구소 지음

어디서도
알려준 적 없는

토익 고득점
비밀과외

RC+LC 실전 모의고사 3회분

서아쌤의
토익
비밀과외

최서아 · 시원스쿨어학연구소 지음

시원스쿨 LAB

서아쌤의 토익 비밀과외

초판 1쇄 발행 2024년 11월 27일

지은이 최서아 · 시원스쿨어학연구소
펴낸곳 (주)에스제이더블유인터내셔널
펴낸이 양홍걸 이시원

홈페이지 www.siwonschool.com
주소 서울시 영등포구 영신로 166 시원스쿨
교재 구입 문의 02)2014-8151
고객센터 02)6409-0878

ISBN 979-11-6150-914-3 13740
Number 1-110701-18230400-08

이 책은 저작권법에 따라 보호받는 저작물이므로 무단복제와 무단전재를 금합니다. 이 책 내용의 전부 또는 일부를 이용하려면 반드시 저작권자와 (주)에스제이더블유인터내셔널의 서면 동의를 받아야 합니다.

머리말

안녕하세요.
시원스쿨랩 토익 대표강사 최서아입니다.

그동안 수많은 학생들과 함께 토익을 공부하며, 실전 경험과 강의 노하우를 꾸준히 쌓아왔습니다. 토익을 준비하는 학생들이 느끼는 막막함과 어려움을 가까이서 보며, 어떻게 보다 효율적으로 고득점을 달성할 수 있을지 끊임없이 고민해 왔습니다. 그 고민이 모이고 모여 시작하게 된 것이 바로 유튜브 채널 <서아쌤의 비밀과외>였습니다. 최신 기출 경향을 반영한 콘텐츠를 통해 많은 학습자들과 소통해왔고, 정말 감사하게도 많은 분들의 뜨거운 호응을 얻을 수 있었습니다. 유튜브를 통한 소통은 저에게 더욱 세밀한 이해를 제공해주었습니다. 이 모든 경험과 노하우를 집약한 「서아쌤의 토익 비밀과외」 도서는 단순히 많은 문제를 푸는 것보다, 실제 시험장에서 고득점을 이루기 위한 핵심 전략과 실전 감각을 길러줄 수 있도록 구성되었습니다.

RC와 LC를 한 권으로 완벽하게 끝낼 수 있도록 만든 통합형 교재로, 이 책을 통해 기본기를 단단히 다질 수 있을뿐만 아니라 더 높은 목표를 향해 나아가실 수 있을 것입니다. 짧은 시간에 고득점을 달성할 수 있도록, RC와 LC 각 15개의 Playlist와 최신 기출 경향을 반영한 실전모의고사 3회분을 수록하여 3주 학습플랜에 맞춰 집중적으로 학습할 수 있습니다. 각 Playlist는 실제 시험에서 가장 자주 출제되는 문제 유형과 출제 의도를 분석하여 빠르고 정확하게 핵심만 학습할 수 있도록 구성했습니다.

토익 공부는 끝이 아닌 시작입니다. 「서아쌤의 토익 비밀과외」를 통해 여러분이 토익을 넘어 더 큰 꿈과 도전으로 나아갈 수 있길 바랍니다. 고득점을 목표로 하는 것도 분명히 중요하지만, 이 과정에서 얻게 될 자기주도적 학습 능력과 스스로 성장해가는 모습이야말로 진정한 보상이 될 것입니다. 시험 준비 과정은 때때로 힘들고 지칠 수 있지만, 그 시간과 노력이 여러분의 성장을 만들어가는 밑거름이 될 것이라고 믿습니다. 이 모든 것이 반드시 좋은 결과로 이어지길 바라며, 함께 걸어갈 이 여정에 저도 작은 힘이 되길 소망합니다.

감사합니다.

최서아 드림

목차

RC

LC

실전모의고사

온라인 부가자료 lab.siwonschool.com

- 본서 음원 MP3
- 실전모의고사 음원 MP3

왜 「서아쌤의 토익 비밀과외」인가?

1 RC + LC + 실전모의고사를 한 권에 !

- [1권] RC 이론 + LC 이론 + 실전모의고사 3회분
- [2권] 정답 및 해설
- 「이론 정리 + 문제집」과 해설서를 분리하여 휴대성 향상

2 3주 완성 커리큘럼으로 토익 고득점 획득 보장

- RC와 LC 이론은 각각 15개의 Playlist로 구성되어 있으며, 각 Playlist는 고득점에 꼭 필요한 최빈출 기출포인트와 토익 만점강사만의 실전 전략 수록
- 15일 만에 이론 학습을 끝내고 매일 1회분씩 총 3회분의 실전모의고사를 푼다면 단 3주 만에 실전 대비 가능

3 13만 토익 유튜버 서아쌤의 고득점 노하우 집약

- 토익 시험을 매회 응시하고 분석하는 서아쌤이 직접 엄선한 고득점 핵심 이론 총정리
- <서아쌤 비밀 Tip>을 통해 추가 포인트뿐만 아니라 실제 시험에 바로 적용할 수 있는 문제풀이 스킬까지 자세히 설명

4 QR코드 스캔으로 편리하게 학습

- 도서 내 QR코드를 찍으면 본서 및 모의고사 음원 바로 재생
- 도서 내 QR코드를 찍으면 실전모의고사 모바일 해설 바로 확인

5 최신 기출 트렌드 완벽 반영

- 최근 크게 어려워진 LC 난이도 반영
- 고득점을 목표로 한다면 반드시 끝까지 풀어야 하는 Part 7 집중 학습

6 QR과 말자막으로 편하게 보는 저자 직강(유료)

- 도서 내 QR코드를 찍으면 강의 바로 재생
- 말자막으로 유튜브 보듯 편하게 보는 토익 강의(이론강의만 해당)
- <서아쌤의 토익 비밀노트> 부교재 특별 증정(강의 패키지 구매 시)
- 서아쌤이 직접 관리하는 실시간 카톡 스터디 서비스 제공(강의 패키지 구매 시)

이 책의 구성과 특징

최빈출 기출포인트

최신 기출 분석을 바탕으로 가장 자주 출제되는 출제 유형들을 수록하였습니다. 각 기출 변형 예문마다 정답과 헷갈릴 수 있는 오답을 같이 제시하여 출제 포인트를 완벽히 이해하고, 실전에서 헷갈리지 않고 빠르게 정답을 고를 수 있도록 하였습니다. LC의 경우, 문제 유형별 정답 패턴과 공통 우회 답변, 빈출 단서 표현 등을 제시하여 실전에 활용할 수 있게 하였습니다.

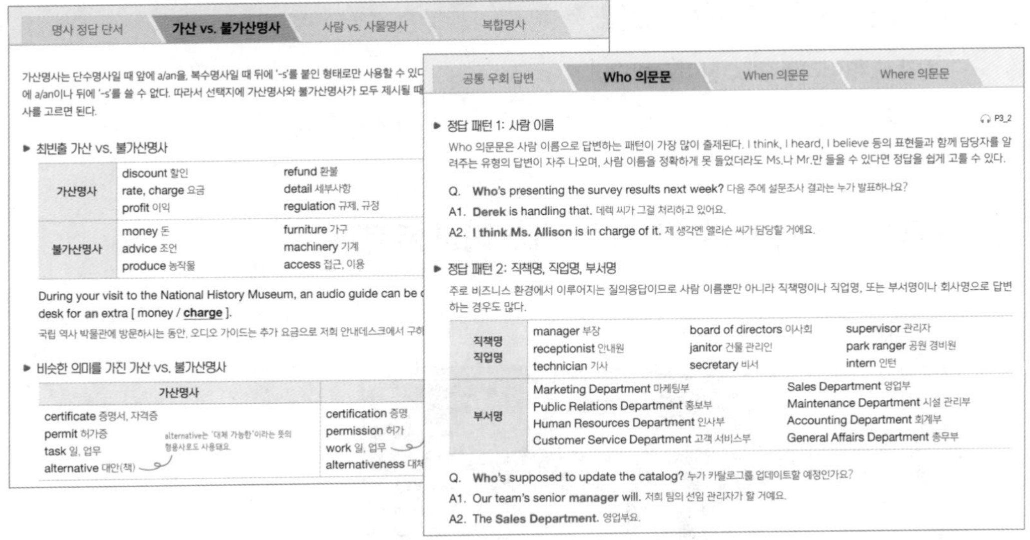

서아쌤 비밀 Tip

기본 학습 내용에서 더 나아가, 반드시 알아야 할 빈출 표현 모음과 고난도 학습 포인트, 그리고 실전에서 바로 적용할 수 있는 서아쌤만의 문제 풀이 전략과 학습법까지 자세히 안내한 코너입니다. 「서아쌤의 토익 비밀과외」 인강에서 더 많은 유용한 팁들을 확인할 수 있습니다.

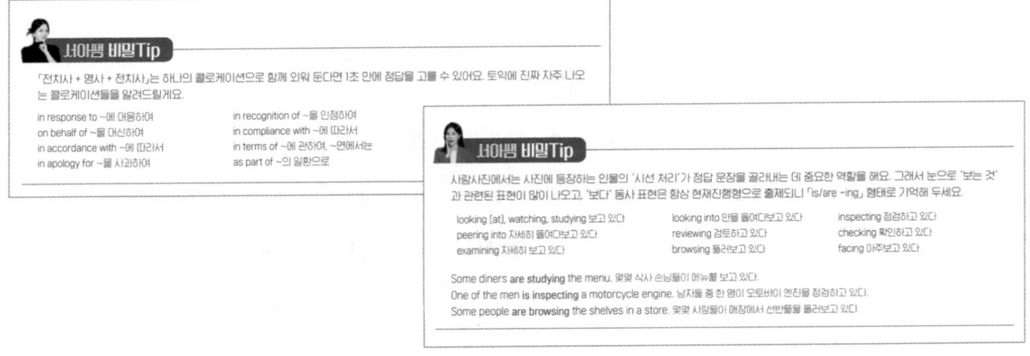

Practice

각 페이지의 이론 학습이 끝나면 간단한 연습 문제를 통해 기출 문제의 정답 포인트를 완벽히 습득할 수 있도록 하였습니다. LC의 경우, 문제의 정답 단서가 되는 포인트를 받아쓰도록 함으로써 학습한 내용을 완벽하게 소화하도록 하였습니다.

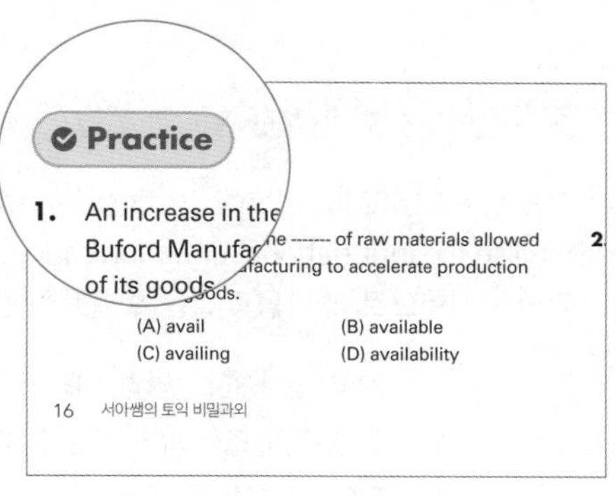

편리한 QR코드

각 Playlist에 있는 QR코드를 통해 본문의 음원을 바로 듣거나 「서아쌤의 토익 비밀과외」 유료 인강을 편리하게 수강할 수 있습니다.

Check-up Test

해당 Playlist의 학습이 끝나면 최신 기출문제를 변형한 실전 문제들을 풀면서 학습이 잘 되었는지 점검합니다. 채점 후, 틀린 문제는 오답노트에 기록하여 취약한 부분은 완전히 복습하고 넘어가야 합니다.

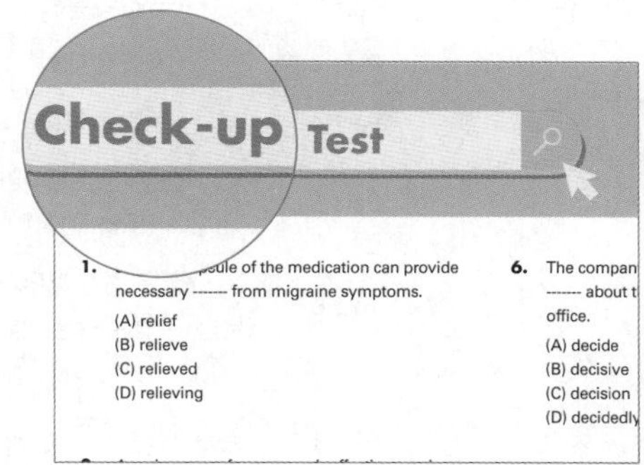

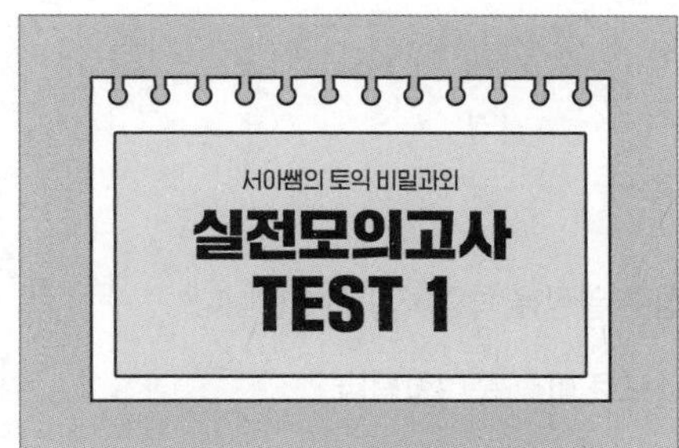

실전모의고사 3회분

최신 기출 경향을 반영한 실전모의고사 3회분을 제공하여 고득점을 완벽하게 대비할 수 있습니다. QR코드를 스캔하여 모의고사 음원을 듣거나 모바일 해설과 해설강의(유료)까지 모두 볼 수 있습니다.

TOEIC이란

토익은 어떤 시험이에요?

TOEIC은 ETS(Educational Testing Service)가 출제하는 국제 커뮤니케이션 영어 능력 평가 시험(Test Of English for International Communication)입니다. 즉, 토익은 영어로 업무적인 소통을 할 수 있는 능력을 평가하는 시험으로서, 다음과 같은 주제를 다룹니다.

기업 일반	계약, 협상, 홍보, 영업, 비즈니스 계획, 회의, 행사, 장소 예약, 사무용 기기
제조 및 개발	공장 관리, 조립 라인, 품질 관리, 연구, 제품 개발
금융과 예산	은행, 투자, 세금, 회계, 청구
인사	입사 지원, 채용, 승진, 급여, 퇴직
부동산	건축, 설계서, 부동산 매매 및 임대, 전기/가스/수도 설비
여가	교통 수단, 티켓팅, 여행 일정, 역/공항, 자동차/호텔 예약 및 연기와 취소, 영화, 공연, 전시

토익은 총 몇 문제인가요?

구성	파트	내용		문항 수 및 문항 번호		시간	배점
Listening Test	Part 1	사진 묘사		6	1-6	45분	495점
	Part 2	질의 응답		25	7-31		
	Part 3	짧은 대화		39 (13지문)	32-70		
	Part 4	짧은 담화		30 (10지문)	71-100		
Reading Test	Part 5	단문 빈칸 채우기 (문법, 어휘)		30	101-130	75분	495점
	Part 6	장문 빈칸 채우기 (문법, 문맥에 맞는 어휘/문장)		16 (4지문)	131-146		
	Part 7	독해	단일 지문	29 (10지문)	147-175		
			이중 지문	10 (2지문)	176-185		
			삼중 지문	15 (3지문)	186-200		
합계				200 문제		120분	990점

토익 시험을 보려고 해요. 어떻게 접수하나요?

- 한국 TOEIC 위원회 인터넷 사이트(www.toeic.co.kr)에서 접수 일정을 확인하고 접수합니다.
- 접수 시 최근 6개월 이내에 촬영한 jpg 형식의 사진이 필요하므로 미리 준비합니다.
- 토익 응시료는 (2024년 11월 기준) 정기 접수 시 52,500원입니다.

시험 당일엔 뭘 챙겨야 하나요?

- 아침 식사를 적당히 챙겨 먹는 것이 좋습니다. 빈속은 집중력을 떨어뜨리고, 과식은 졸음을 유발할 수 있습니다.
- 시험 준비물을 챙깁니다.
  - 신분증 (주민등록증, 운전면허증, 기간 만료 전 여권, 공무원증만 인정. 학생증 안됨. 단, 중고등학생은 국내 학생증 인정)
  - 연필과 깨끗하게 잘 지워지는 지우개 (볼펜이나 사인펜은 안됨. 연필은 뭉툭하게 깎아서 여러 자루 준비)
  - 아날로그 시계 (전자시계는 안됨)
  - 수험표 (필수 준비물은 아님. 수험 번호는 시험장에서 감독관이 답안지에 부착해주는 라벨을 보고 적으면 됨)
- 고사장을 반드시 확인합니다.

시험은 몇 시에 끝나나요?

오전 시험	오후 시험	내용
9:30 - 9:45	2:30 - 2:45	답안지 작성 오리엔테이션
9:45 - 9:50	2:45 - 2:50	수험자 휴식 시간
9:50 - 10:10	2:50 - 3:10	신분증 확인, 문제지 배부
10:10 - 10:55	3:10 - 3:55	리스닝 시험
10:55 - 12:10	3:55 - 5:10	리딩 시험

- 최소 30분 전에 입실을 마치고(오전 시험은 오전 9:20까지, 오후 시험은 오후 2:20까지) 지시에 따라 답안지에 기본 정보를 기입합니다.
- 안내 방송이 끝나고 시험 시작 전 5분의 휴식 시간이 주어지는데, 이때 화장실에 꼭 다녀옵니다.

시험 보고 나면 성적은 바로 나오나요?

- 시험일로부터 9일 후 낮 12시에 한국 TOEIC 위원회 사이트(www.toeic.co.kr)에서 성적이 발표됩니다.

서아쌤의 3주 완성 학습플랜

- 아래의 학습플랜을 참조하여 매일 학습합니다.
- 해당일의 학습을 하지 못했더라도 이전으로 돌아가지 말고 오늘에 해당하는 학습을 하세요. 그래야 끝까지 완주할 수 있습니다.
- 교재를 끝까지 한 번 보고 나면 2회독에 도전합니다. 두 번째 볼 때는 훨씬 빠르게 끝낼 수 있습니다. 토익은 천천히 1회 보는 것보다 빠르게 2회, 3회 보는 것이 훨씬 효과가 좋습니다.

RC부터 시작하는 학습플랜

Day 1	Day 2	Day 3	Day 4	Day 5
월 일	월 일	월 일	월 일	월 일
RC Playlist 1 RC Playlist 2	RC Playlist 3 RC Playlist 4	RC Playlist 5 RC Playlist 6	RC Playlist 7 RC Playlist 8	RC Playlist 9 RC Playlist 1-9 복습
Day 6	**Day 7**	**Day 8**	**Day 9**	**Day 10**
월 일	월 일	월 일	월 일	월 일
RC Playlist 10 RC Playlist 11	RC Playlist 12 RC Playlist 13	RC Playlist 14 RC Playlist 15	LC Playlist 1 LC Playlist 2	LC Playlist 3 LC Playlist 4
Day 11	**Day 12**	**Day 13**	**Day 14**	**Day 15**
월 일	월 일	월 일	월 일	월 일
LC Playlist 5 LC Playlist 6	LC Playlist 7 LC Playlist 8 LC Playlist 9	LC Playlist 10 LC Playlist 11	LC Playlist 12 LC Playlist 13	LC Playlist 14 LC Playlist 15
Day 16	**Day 17**	**Day 18**		
월 일	월 일	월 일		
실전모의고사 TEST 1	실전모의고사 TEST 2	실전모의고사 TEST 3		

RC와 LC를 같이 시작하는 학습플랜

서아쌤 추천!

Day 1	Day 2	Day 3	Day 4	Day 5
월 일	월 일	월 일	월 일	월 일
RC Playlist 1 LC Playlist 1	RC Playlist 2 LC Playlist 2	RC Playlist 3 LC Playlist 3	RC Playlist 4 LC Playlist 4	RC Playlist 5 LC Playlist 5
Day 6	**Day 7**	**Day 8**	**Day 9**	**Day 10**
월 일	월 일	월 일	월 일	월 일
RC Playlist 6 LC Playlist 6	RC Playlist 7 LC Playlist 7	RC Playlist 8 LC Playlist 8	RC Playlist 9 LC Playlist 9	RC Playlist 10 LC Playlist 10
Day 11	**Day 12**	**Day 13**	**Day 14**	**Day 15**
월 일	월 일	월 일	월 일	월 일
RC Playlist 11 LC Playlist 11	RC Playlist 12 LC Playlist 12	RC Playlist 13 LC Playlist 13	RC Playlist 14 LC Playlist 14	RC Playlist 15 LC Playlist 15
Day 16	**Day 17**	**Day 18**		
월 일	월 일	월 일		
실전모의고사 TEST 1	실전모의고사 TEST 2	실전모의고사 TEST 3		

READING
COMPREHENSION

RC

강의 바로보기

1초 만에 명사/대명사 정답 찾는 방법

Part 5

명사 정답 단서 | 가산 vs. 불가산명사 | 사람 vs. 사물명사 | 복합명사

▶ 관사 + ________ + 전치사

StreamWorks has gradually increased **the** [**number** / numbered] **of** advertisements during movies shown on the platform.

스트림웍스 사는 그 플랫폼에서 영화들이 보여지는 동안의 광고 개수를 점진적으로 증가시켰다.

▶ 전치사 + ________ + 전치사

In [respond / **response**] **to** tenants' complaints, the apartment building manager has provided additional free parking.

세입자의 불만사항에 대응하여, 아파트 건물 관리자는 추가적인 무료 주차를 제공했다.

「전치사 + 명사 + 전치사」는 하나의 콜로케이션으로 함께 외워 둔다면 1초 만에 정답을 고를 수 있어요. 토익에 진짜 자주 나오는 콜로케이션들을 알려드릴게요.

in response to ~에 대응하여
on behalf of ~을 대신하여
in accordance with ~에 따라서
in apology for ~을 사과하여
in recognition of ~을 인정하여
in compliance with ~에 따라서
in terms of ~에 관하여, ~면에서는
as part of ~의 일환으로

▶ 관사/소유격 + (부사) + (형용사/분사) + ________

Ms. Young has **a very high** [regarding / **regard**] for the developers of the new fitness mobile application.

영 씨는 새로운 건강 모바일 애플리케이션의 개발자들에 대한 매우 높은 존경심을 가지고 있다.

▶ 타동사 + (형용사/분사) + ________

Use of corporate credit cards **requires full** [approves / **approval**] from the accounting department.

법인카드의 사용은 회계부로부터의 완전한 승인을 필요로 한다.

Practice

1. An increase in the ------- of raw materials allowed Buford Manufacturing to accelerate production of its goods.

(A) avail (B) available
(C) availing (D) availability

2. Our ------- is in charge of ensuring the quality of merchandise before it is shipped to retailers.

(A) divided (B) division
(C) divisive (D) dividing

가산명사는 단수명사일 때 앞에 a/an을, 복수명사일 때 뒤에 '-s'를 붙인 형태로만 사용할 수 있다. 반면에, 불가산명사는 셀 수 없으므로 앞에 a/an이나 뒤에 '-s'를 쓸 수 없다. 따라서 선택지에 가산명사와 불가산명사가 모두 제시될 때, 관사의 유무와 수 일치를 따져 알맞은 명사를 고르면 된다.

▶ 최빈출 가산 vs. 불가산명사

가산명사	discount 할인 rate, charge 요금 profit 이익	refund 환불 detail 세부사항 regulation 규제, 규정	approach 접근법 cost, price 값, 비용 goods, product 상품, 제품
불가산명사	money 돈 advice 조언 produce 농작물	furniture 가구 machinery 기계 access 접근, 이용	information 정보 equipment 장비 merchandise 상품

During your visit to the National History Museum, an audio guide can be obtained from our information desk for **an** extra [money / **charge**].

국립 역사 박물관에 방문하시는 동안, 오디오 가이드는 추가 요금으로 저희 안내데스크에서 구하실 수 있습니다.

▶ 비슷한 의미를 가진 가산 vs. 불가산명사

가산명사	불가산명사
certificate 증명서, 자격증 permit 허가증 task 일, 업무 alternative 대안(책)	certification 증명 permission 허가 work 일, 업무 alternativeness 대체 가능함

alternative는 '대체 가능한'이라는 뜻의 형용사로도 사용돼요.

work가 '작품'으로 해석된다면 가산명사에요.

The city council is considering the construction of an electric monorail as **an** energy-efficient [alternativeness / **alternative**] to current public transportation options.

시 의회는 현재 대중교통 선택지들에 대한 에너지 효율적인 대안으로서 전기 모노레일의 건설을 고려하고 있다.

▶ 암기로만 알 수 있는 -ing형 가산 vs. 불가산명사

가산명사	불가산명사
opening 공석 earnings (복수형) 수익 findings (복수형) 조사 결과	planning 기획 spending 지출 seating 좌석 배치 processing 처리 accounting 회계

Practice

3. Achieving ------- to be a financial advisor typically requires the completion of an intensive course.

(A) certification (B) certificate
(C) certifies (D) certify

4. ------- to this research laboratory is only permitted to employees who have Level 3 security clearance.

(A) Approach (B) Access
(C) Application (D) Association

사람명사는 가산명사로 한 명이면 a/an을, 여러 명이면 '-s'를 붙여야 한다. 반면에, 사물명사 또는 행위명사는 가산명사와 불가산명사 둘 다 가능하다.

▶ 선택지에 함께 제시되는 사람명사 vs. 사물/행위명사

사람명사	사물/행위명사
applicant 지원자	application 지원(서)
architect 건축가	architecture 건축(학)
accountant 회계사	accounting 회계
attendee 참석자	attendance 참석(자의 수)
producer 생산자	production 생산(량)
supplier 공급업자, 공급업체	supply 공급
developer 개발업자, 개발업체	development 개발
expert 전문가	expertise 전문지식
editor 편집자	edition 판, 호
assistant 조수, 보조자	assistance 도움, 지원
supervisor 감독관, 상사	supervision 감독
manager 관리자, 부장	management 관리, 경영
resident 거주자, 주민	residence 거주(지)
founder 설립자	foundation 설립

[Attendee / **Attendance**] at the health and safety training session is mandatory, with no exceptions.
보건과 안전 교육 시간에 대한 참석은 예외 없이 의무적이다.

The questionnaire asks [**residents** / residence] how they normally commute to and from their workplace.
그 설문지는 거주자들이 보통 어떻게 직장으로 통근하는지를 묻는다.

사람명사 vs. 사물/행위명사 문제에서 수 일치로 문제를 풀 수 없다면, 제시된 동사의 뜻을 해석해 의미상 알맞은 명사를 고를 수도 있다.

Mr. Reynolds **has been named** the next [**supervisor** / supervision] now that Ms. Anderson has announced her retirement.
엔더슨 씨가 은퇴를 발표했으므로 레이놀즈 씨가 다음 감독관으로 임명되었다.

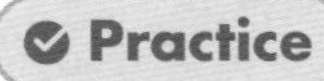

5. Every client account manager employed by the Astreus Financial Services holds a postgraduate qualification in -------.

(A) accountant (B) accounted
(C) accountable (D) accounting

6. Many of the ------- for the vacancy meet the basic job requirements, but Mr. Easton showed the most enthusiasm during the interview stage.

(A) applicants (B) application
(C) applies (D) applied

명사와 명사가 결합하여 하나의 명사 덩어리로 쓰이는 복합명사는 암기를 통해 문제를 푸는 것이 가장 빠르다. 자주 출제되는 복합명사 리스트를 완벽하게 암기한다면, 빈칸 앞 또는 뒤에 위치한 명사와 선택지만 보고도 정답을 바로 고를 수 있다. 또한, 세 개의 명사로 구성된 복합명사도 종종 출제되므로 유의해야 한다.

▶ 토익 최빈출 복합명사

- ☐ application form 지원 양식
- ☐ awards ceremony 시상식
- ☐ sales representatives 영업 사원
- ☐ retail stores 소매점
- ☐ retirement celebration 은퇴 파티
- ☐ customer satisfaction 고객 만족
- ☐ safety regulations 안전 수칙
- ☐ safety standards 안전 기준
- ☐ office supplies 사무용품
- ☐ expiration date 만기일
- ☐ interest rate 이자율
- ☐ supply chain management 공급망 관리
- ☐ job openings 채용 공석
- ☐ registration process 등록 과정
- ☐ food/meal preference 음식/식사 선호도
- ☐ photo identification 사진이 있는 신분증
- ☐ contingency plan 비상 대책
- ☐ performance evaluation 성과 평가
- ☐ employee performance 직원 실적
- ☐ travel expenses 출장 경비
- ☐ safety precautions 안전 예방책
- ☐ security measures 보안 조치
- ☐ employee productivity 직원 생산성
- ☐ recruitment officer role 채용 담당자 직무

Conference attendees are asked to mark their **meal** [**preferences** / preferring] on the sign-in form at the welcome desk.

컨퍼런스 참석자들은 환영 데스크에서 참가 양식에 식사 선호도를 표기하도록 요청받는다.

복합명사 문제는 문법 문제뿐만 아니라 명사 어휘 문제로도 자주 출제되며, 형용사의 '수'에서 단서를 찾아 수 일치로 정답을 고를 수도 있다.

Safety [guideline / **precautions**] must be taken by all restaurant workers while using the grills and deep-fat fryers.

안전 예방책들은 모든 식당 직원들이 그릴과 튀김용 냄비를 사용하는 동안 반드시 취해져야 한다.

Most office [supply / **supplies**] are ordered on the last Friday of each month.

복합명사가 주어 자리에 쓰일 때 뒤에 있는 명사에 동사의 수를 일치시켜요.

대부분의 사무용품들은 매달 마지막 금요일에 주문되어진다.

Practice

7. NutriFirst Inc. sells a wide range of nutritional supplements through its Web site, event vendors, and retail -------.

(A) store (B) stored
(C) storing (D) stores

8. Kensington Department Store has numerous winter job ------- for part-time staff.

(A) opens (B) opened
(C) opening (D) openings

소유격 vs. 소유대명사

▶ 소유격

빈칸 뒤에 명사가 있다면 소유격 인칭대명사가 정답이다.

Highly respected for [his / him] groundbreaking **research** in the field, Professor Danforth is the UK's leading expert on economics.

이 분야에 대한 획기적인 연구로 매우 존경받는 댄포스 교수는 경제학에 대한 영국의 선도적인 전문가이다.

▶ 소유대명사

주로 동사나 전치사의 목적어 자리에 오며, 「소유격 + 명사」의 구조와 동일한 형태로 '~의 것'이라는 뜻을 가진다.

Although John designed an attractive new logo for the company, Ms. Carter used her own design **instead of** [his / him].

비록 존 씨가 회사를 위해 매력적인 새 로고를 디자인했지만, 카터 씨는 그의 것 대신에 그녀 자신의 디자인을 사용했다.

재귀대명사

▶ 재귀용법

주어와 목적어가 동일한 대상일 때 목적어 자리에 올 수 있으며, 목적어로 쓰였기 때문에 생략할 수 없다.

A prominent author of several successful science fiction novels, Ms. Jameson **described** [her / herself] as a curious and imaginative dreamer.

여러 성공적인 공상 과학 소설의 유명 작가인 제임슨 씨는 그녀 자신을 호기심이 많고 상상력이 풍부한 몽상가로 묘사했다.

▶ 강조용법

완전한 구조의 문장에서 부사 자리에 사용할 수 있으며, 주어가 직접 행위를 했다는 것을 강조하기 위해 사용하므로 생략할 수 있다.

The CMO oversaw the development of the marketing campaign [himself / him] to make sure that it would be a success.

최고마케팅경영자는 그 마케팅 캠페인이 성공작이 되는 것을 확실히 하기 위해 그 개발 과정을 직접 감독했다.

지시대명사

▶ anyone who 단수동사 vs. those who 복수동사

지시대명사 문제는 who/전치사구/분사구 앞에 제시된 빈칸에 들어갈 anyone 또는 those를 고르거나, anyone who 또는 those who 뒤에 들어갈 동사의 수 일치 문제로 출제된다.

The successful candidate will be selected among [anyone / those] **who were** able to pass all three stages of the application process.

합격자는 지원 과정의 모든 세 단계를 합격할 수 있는 사람들 중에서 선정될 것이다.

Practice

9. This summer, Audio Events will be hosting ------- fifth music festival in San Francisco.

(A) it (B) themselves
(C) them (D) its

10. For ------- who have first class tickets, Westfield Rail Service provides complimentary beverages and snacks.

(A) those (B) them
(C) whose (D) which

▶ 부정대명사

one	(앞의 명사와 같은) 하나
another	(앞에 제시된 명사와 같은) 또 다른 하나
others	(다른 여러 개) 다른 것들
the others	(범위 내 일부를 제외한) 나머지 전부
each other one another	(둘의 관계) each other (셋 이상의 관계) one another *'서로'라는 뜻으로, 목적어로만 사용된다.

Everyday Reads had been the only **bookstore** in Bellview until a new [**one** / another] opened in February.
에브리데이 리즈 사는 2월에 새로운 서점 하나가 개장하기까지 벨뷰에서 유일한 서점이었다.

The Unlimited Plan is the most popular **membership option** for cinemagoers, but [**others** / the other] are also available.
언리미티드 플랜은 영화팬들에게 가장 인기 있는 회원권이지만, 다른 것들도 이용 가능하다.

▶ 수량 부정대명사

수량 부정대명사는 「수량 부정대명사 + of the 명사」 구조에서 알맞은 수량 부정대명사 또는 of the 뒤에 들어갈 알맞은 명사를 고르는 유형으로 출제된다.

one, each, either, neither + of the 복수명사 + 단수동사
much, (a) little + of the 불가산명사 + 단수동사
all, most, many, some, half, (a) few + of the 복수명사 + 복수동사
all, some, most + of the 불가산명사 + 단수동사

The new musical includes several compositions performed by [**some** / every] **of the best musicians** from the New York Symphony Orchestra.
새로운 뮤지컬은 뉴욕 심포니 오케스트라에서 온 몇몇 최고의 음악가들에 의해 공연되는 여러 곡들을 포함한다.

Designing electronic devices that are both high-quality and affordable is **one of the** hardest [challenge / **challenges**] faced by product developers.
높은 품질과 적정한 가격인 전자기기를 고안하는 것은 제품 개발자들이 직면하는 가장 힘든 도전들 중 하나이다.

Practice

11. The new online chat program allows the company's different departments to stay in close communication with -------.

(A) one another (B) the other
(C) another (D) other

12. ------- of the vendor permit applications received by the city council is extensively reviewed by an official.

(A) All (B) Much
(C) Each (D) Every

Check-up Test

강의 바로보기

1. Just one capsule of the medication can provide necessary ------- from migraine symptoms.
   (A) relief
   (B) relieve
   (C) relieved
   (D) relieving

2. A major ------- of a manager's effectiveness is high employee morale.
   (A) indicate
   (B) to indicate
   (C) indicators
   (D) indication

3. Mr. Astin will create all work schedules ------- until Ms. Tibbs returns from her vacation.
   (A) he
   (B) his
   (C) him
   (D) himself

4. Thanks to thorough -------, the grand opening event at Hereford Department Store was a tremendous success.
   (A) planner
   (B) plan
   (C) planning
   (D) planned

5. To prevent accidents, AG Chemicals enforces rigorous security ------- in all of its production facilities.
   (A) measuring
   (B) to measure
   (C) measure
   (D) measures

6. The company founders have not yet reached a ------- about the potential relocation of the head office.
   (A) decide
   (B) decisive
   (C) decision
   (D) decidedly

7. The registration ------- for the APR Technology Convention takes approximately ten minutes and can be done online.
   (A) deadline
   (B) process
   (C) location
   (D) concept

8. ------- of the two job applicants is experienced in using the Exo9 database software.
   (A) Whatever
   (B) Another
   (C) Neither
   (D) Those

9. In ------- with our policy, returns of defective products must be accompanied by a valid store receipt.
   (A) accordance
   (B) accordingly
   (C) according
   (D) accorded

10. All sales representatives have ------- to participate in the Best Sales seminar if they enroll before December 21.
   (A) permitted
   (B) permission
   (C) permit
   (D) permissive

정답 및 해설 p.3

11. Ms. Hawley will be meeting with ------- regional sales manager to discuss ways to attract new customers.

(A) her
(B) hers
(C) herself
(D) she

12. Dietrich Tool Rental has been a prominent ------- of construction equipment for almost two decades.

(A) supply
(B) supplying
(C) supplier
(D) supplied

13. The manufacturing plant doubled ------- for one week so that it could keep up with consumer demand.

(A) producer
(B) produce
(C) production
(D) productive

14. In the Personal Information section of the application form, applicants were asked to describe ------- in 250 words or less.

(A) they
(B) theirs
(C) themselves
(D) them

15. ------- willing to volunteer at the fundraising event should notify Ms. Hird in general affairs.

(A) Fewer
(B) Another
(C) Whoever
(D) Anyone

16. Based on the report submitted by the financial consultant, Diamond Hotel Group's ------- are down by almost 20 percent.

(A) earnings
(B) earned
(C) earn
(D) earning

17. The HR Director hopes to find a suitable person for the recruitment officer ------- by the end of the week.

(A) production
(B) item
(C) role
(D) view

18. Mr. Pritchard will not open the new manufacturing facility until ------- of the employees have been trained in first aid.

(A) most
(B) already
(C) almost
(D) usually

19. Although our remote employees are located far apart, monthly company gatherings provide an opportunity for them to network with -------.

(A) the same
(B) this
(C) one another
(D) much

20. Ascot Athletic Company has implemented new effective advertising ------- for its wide range of sportswear.

(A) approach
(B) approaches
(C) approached
(D) approaching

Playlist 2

토익 문법의 핵심! 동사 수/태/시제 전쟁을 끝내러 왔다!

Part 5

수 일치 | 태 | 시제 | 복합 동사 문제

▶ 빈칸 앞에 Please/조동사가 있을 때

동사가 들어갈 빈칸 바로 앞에 Please나 조동사가 있는 경우 무조건 동사원형을 정답으로 고른다.

As you do the monthly payroll, **please** [verifies / **verify**] that all employees receive the appropriate overtime rate.
월 급여를 지급하실 때, 모든 직원들이 적절한 초과 근무 수당을 받았는지 확인하십시오.

Call center agents **must** [**handle** / handles] a large number of phone calls per day.
콜센터 직원들은 반드시 하루에 다수의 전화 통화들을 처리해야 한다.

'제안·추천·요구·주장·명령'의 뜻을 가지는 동사 다음에 오는 that절에서는 주어 뒤에 조동사 should가 생략되어 동사 자리에 반드시 동사원형이 와야 해요. 자주 출제되지는 않지만 수동태와 결합되어 나온다면 고난도 문제가 되니 반드시 알고 넘어가세요.

주어 + '제추요주명' 동사 + that + 주어 + (should) + 동사원형		
suggest, propose 제안하다	recommend, advise 추천하다, 권고하다	insist 주장하다
ask, request, require, demand 요청하다	command, order 명령하다	

The Sales Director **recommended that** Mr. Johnson [submits / **submit**] his sales report by Friday, May 30th.
영업 이사는 존슨 씨가 그의 영업 보고서를 5월 30일 금요일까지 제출할 것을 권고했다.

▶ 주어와 동사 빈칸 사이에 거품이 있을 때

주어와 동사가 들어갈 빈칸 사이에 부사, 전치사구, 분사구, to부정사구, 관계대명사절 등의 거품이 있을 때 거품 앞에 위치한 주어에 동사의 수를 맞춘다.

Growth in technology markets throughout Asia [have / **has**] been stronger this year.
아시아 전역에서 기술 시장의 성장이 올해 더 강력해졌다.

The first ever **novel** written by Bruce Harker [**was** / were] available on his Web site until last month.
브루스 하커 씨에 의해 쓰여진 첫 소설은 지난달까지 그의 웹 사이트에서 구매 가능했다.

Practice

1. Quality assurance managers at Zanko Manufacturing ------- the rule that all products be checked twice prior to shipping.
(A) enforcing (B) enforces
(C) enforcement (D) enforce

2. Mr. Richardson has suggested that our company ------- the launch of our new cell phone until the third financial quarter.
(A) postpone (B) postponed
(C) postpones (D) to postpone

▶ 고난도 4형식 수동태

4형식 동사의 사람 목적어(간접목적어)가 주어일 때는 수동태 동사 뒤에 사물 목적어(직접목적어)가 그대로 남아 있고, 사물 목적어가 주어일 때는 수동태 동사 뒤에 전치사(to/for)와 사람 목적어가 남게 된다.

Lancelot Landscaping customers [**are guaranteed** / have guaranteed] **an after-care service and follow-up consultation.**

랜스랏 랜드스케이핑 고객들은 사후 서비스와 후속 상담 서비스를 보장받는다.

After completing the interviews, **an employment offer** [was sending / **was sent**] **to Ms. Pickering** on October 6.

면접이 완료된 후, 채용 제안서가 10월 6일에 피커링 씨에게 전송됐다.

서아쌤 비밀Tip

두 개의 목적어를 가지는 4형식 동사가 수동태로 출제될 때는 한 개의 목적어가 수동태 동사 뒤에 남는 구조가 되므로 능동태라고 착각해 정답을 고를 때 큰 함정이 될 수 있어요. 자주 출제되는 4형식 동사 리스트만 외워두어도 오답 함정에 빠지지 않을 수 있답니다.

give, grant, offer A B A에게 B를 주다, 제공하다
charge A B A에게 B(비용)를 부과하다
guarantee A B A에게 B를 보장하다
award A B A에게 B를 수여하다
send A B A에게 B를 보내다
assign A B A에게 B를 할당하다

▶ 고난도 5형식 수동태

5형식 동사는 주로 빈칸 뒤의 to부정사를 보고 5형식 동사의 수동태를 고르거나, 빈칸 앞에 제시된 5형식 동사의 수동태를 보고 to부정사를 고르는 유형으로 출제된다.

Passengers [require / **are required**] **to store** large carry-on bags in the overhead compartments.

승객들은 머리 위쪽의 짐칸에 큰 기내용 가방을 보관하도록 요구된다.

서아쌤 비밀Tip

5형식 동사는 토익에서 「be + 5형식 동사의 과거분사 + to부정사」의 구조로 자주 출제돼요. 아래 표현들을 익혀두고 문제 또는 선택지에서 5형식 동사만 알아볼 수 있다면 해석을 하지 않고도 정답을 빨리 고를 수 있어요.

be asked [required, invited] to do ~하도록 요청되다, 요구되다
be advised [encouraged] to do ~하도록 권고받다
be expected to do ~할 것으로 예상되다, 기대되다
be allowed to do ~하도록 허용되다

Practice

3. Although Mr. Choi displayed good management potential, the promotion ------- to a more experienced employee.

(A) gives (B) is giving
(C) was given (D) will give

4. Ms. Chalmers ------- to work as the dessert chef at Anatoly Restaurant.

(A) encourages (B) encouragement
(C) is encouraging (D) was encouraged

▶ 현재시제 단서

☐ every 매 (~마다)
☐ regularly 정기적으로
☐ generally, typically 일반적으로
☐ usually, occasionally, frequently 주로, 때때로, 자주

We [updated / **update**] our company brochure with state-of-the-art information.
저희는 최신 정보를 담아 회사 소책자를 업데이트합니다.

어떠한 시제 단서도 없고, 제시된 문장이 일반적인 사실에 대해 언급할 때는 현재 시제를 정답으로 고르세요.

▶ 현재완료시제 단서

☐ since ~ 이래로
☐ recently, lately 최근에
☐ for[over, in] the last[past] + 기간 지난 ~ 동안
☐ already 이미, 벌써

recently는 과거시제 단서로도 쓸 수 있어요.

Mr. Laing [**has been** / is] **employed** by Silas Electronics **over the last 30 years.**
랭 씨는 지난 30년 동안 실라스 일렉트로닉스 사에 고용되어 왔다.

▶ 과거시제 단서

☐ last 지난
☐ yesterday 어제
☐ ago ~ 전에
☐ previously 이전에

Exacta Corporation [announces / **announced**] **yesterday** that it is opening three new production facilities in the United Kingdom.
이그잭타 주식회사는 어제 영국에 세 개의 새로운 생산 시설을 개장할 것이라고 발표했다.

▶ 과거완료시제 단서

☐ By the time + 주어 + 과거동사, 주어 + 과거완료 동사 주어가 ~했을쯤에, 주어는 …했었다
☐ Before + 주어 + 과거동사, 주어 + 과거완료 동사 주어가 ~하기 전에, 주어는 …했었다

Before the health and safety officer **presented** his report, he [conducts / **had conducted**] a thorough inspection of the factory.
보건 안전 담당자는 그의 보고서를 제출하기 전에, 그 공장에 대해 철저한 점검을 수행했었다.

▶ 미래시제 단서

☐ next 다음
☐ tomorrow 내일
☐ soon, shortly 곧
☐ until, by the end of ~까지, ~말까지

by the end of는 미래완료시제 will have p.p.의 단서로도 쓸 수 있어요.

가까운 미래는 현재진행시제를 사용해서도 나타낼 수 있으니 선택지에 will이 없다면 현재진행시제를 정답으로 고르세요.

Mr. Margoy [**is addressing** / had been addressing] the company's disappointing annual sales figures at **tomorrow**'s board meeting.
말고이 씨는 회사의 실망스러운 연 매출 수치를 내일 이사회 회의에서 다룰 것이다.

Practice

5. Acorn Home Furnishings ------- over one hundred retail outlets throughout North America by the end of next year.

(A) will have
(B) has
(C) is having
(D) has had

6. Ms. Reid ------- the need for improved marketing strategies long before the CEO decided to advertise on social media.

(A) stresses
(B) stressing
(C) will stress
(D) had stressed

동사 문법 문제는 보통 수/태/시제를 모두 복합적으로 고려해야 하는 유형으로 출제된다. 따라서 ① 빈칸인 동사 자리를 파악하고, ② 가짜 동사(to부정사/동명사)를 소거한 후, ③ 수 일치, ④ 태(능동태/수동태), ⑤ 시제 순으로 소거하면서 풀어야 한다.

유형 1 수 + 태

The board of directors ------- five staff members for the Employee of the Year award.

(A) nominating
(B) were nominated
(C) has nominated
(D) has been nominated

Step 1 동사 자리 파악
Step 2 가짜 동사 소거 → (   ) 소거
Step 3 수 일치 → (   ) 소거
Step 4 태 → 뒤에 목적어가 있으므로 (   ) 소거
Step 5 정답 → (   )

유형 2 수 + 시제

Those who applied for the position ------- to bring a portfolio of their work to the interview last week.

(A) has encouraged
(B) were encouraged
(C) to encourage
(D) will be encouraged

Step 1 동사 자리 파악
Step 2 가짜 동사 소거 → (   ) 소거
Step 3 수 일치 → (   ) 소거
Step 4 시제 → last week이므로 (   ) 소거
Step 5 정답 → (   )

유형 3 태 + 시제

By the end of the year, the manufacturing plant in Osaka ------- more than 25,000 motor vehicles.

(A) will be produced
(B) has been produced
(C) will have produced
(D) has produced

Step 1 동사 자리 파악
Step 2 태 → (   ), (   ) 소거
Step 3 시제 → (   ) 소거
Step 4 정답 → (   )

유형 4 수 + 태 + 시제

Consumer demand ------- dramatically, and so has our company's rate of production.

(A) are rising
(B) had risen
(C) was risen
(D) has risen

Step 1 동사 자리 파악
Step 2 수 일치 → (   ) 소거
Step 3 태 → (   ) 소거
Step 4 시제 → (   ) 소거
Step 5 정답 → (   )

Check-up Test

강의 바로보기

1. The survey results from Jaket Consulting ------- most passengers find Augustus Airlines' organic meals very delicious.

(A) indicate
(B) indicating
(C) to indicate
(D) indicates

2. The team leader ------- Mr. Davis an additional day off in recognition of his sales performance.

(A) implemented
(B) induced
(C) surprised
(D) granted

3. Bush Street American Diner ------- complimentary soft drink refills since it opened last summer.

(A) is offering
(B) has offered
(C) will be offering
(D) would have been offering

4. The council's Event Planning Department ------- applications for vendor permits soon.

(A) will accept
(B) is accepted
(C) accepted
(D) has been accepted

5. All visitors are ------- to sign in at the security desk before entering the factory.

(A) decided
(B) equipped
(C) assured
(D) required

6. Mr. Song ------- the next workshop with detailed suggestions for further progress.

(A) will close
(B) have closed
(C) to close
(D) closed

7. Because of some unfortunate operational problems, the coffee shop owner ------- any special discounts lately.

(A) was not offered
(B) has not offered
(C) will not offer
(D) had not offered

8. A local journalist will interview volunteers who ------- in planting 50,000 new trees throughout Bramble National Park.

(A) were involved
(B) was involving
(C) involving
(D) will involve

9. The operations manager will lead the tour of the factory next Friday and request that the potential investors ------- him in the reception area.

(A) meet
(B) met
(C) have met
(D) will meet

10. Financial issues ------- Dobson Enterprises to withdraw its bid for the A1 Shopping Mall construction contract.

(A) forcing
(B) forced
(C) forces
(D) are forced

11. The security deposit ------- any damage that may occur in your hotel room during your stay here.

(A) covers
(B) covered
(C) to cover
(D) has covered

12. The new movie starring Robb Flynn that ------- last weekend has already broken several box office records.

(A) to release
(B) was released
(C) releasing
(D) releases

13. In accordance with our policy, all staff members are ------- to treat one another with courtesy and respect.

(A) assumed
(B) confirmed
(C) advised
(D) estimated

14. The height restriction for visitors to Funland Amusement Park ------- according to the type of ride.

(A) vary
(B) be varied
(C) varies
(D) varing

15. By the end of the year, singer-songwriter Niles Longstaff ------- more than 50 albums since his debut single came out two decades ago.

(A) publish
(B) has been published
(C) will have published
(D) has published

16. Before economists predicted a steep rise in unemployment, the President ------- to create hundreds of thousands of new jobs.

(A) had promised
(B) promises
(C) was promised
(D) is promising

17. Though Ms. Gershon is ------- to attend the technology conference in Maine, she may arrive a few hours after the event begins.

(A) explained
(B) expected
(C) contained
(D) continued

18. The installation instructions can ------- on page 3 of the accompanying product information handbook.

(A) finds
(B) be found
(C) findings
(D) have found

19. Ms. Galligan ------- all building residents to come to last Tuesday's meeting even though only those who had purchased an apartment were asked to attend.

(A) to have urged
(B) urged
(C) will have urged
(D) was urged

20. Please ------- Mr. Robertson, the new public relations director, to Altus Enterprises.

(A) welcome
(B) welcomed
(C) welcoming
(D) will welcome

Playlist 3

강의 바로보기

형용사와 부사만 정복해도 문법 문제 절반은 맞힌다!

Part 5

형용사 정답 단서 | 고난도 형용사 | 부사 정답 단서 | 고난도 특수 부사

▶ (관사/소유격/전치사/타동사) + ________ + 명사

The Broxburn Gallery will host an exhibition **of** [**authentic** / authentically] **artwork** from Africa.

브록스번 미술관은 아프리카로부터 온 진품 미술품 전시회를 개최할 것이다.

▶ 부사 + ________ + 명사

Mr. Howden is known to be an **exceptionally** [**thoughtful** / thoughtfully] **manager**.

하우든 씨는 특별히 사려 깊은 관리자로 알려져 있다.

▶ 2형식 동사 + ________

Although demand for solar panels **is** [highly / **high**], only 2 percent of local residences have them installed.

태양열 전지판에 대한 수요가 높음에도 불구하고, 지역 주택들의 오직 2퍼센트만 그것들을 설치했다.

▶ 5형식 동사 + 목적어 + ________

We hope you **find this user manual** [**helpful** / help] when operating the Shinobi Air Fryer.

시노비 에어프라이어를 작동시킬 때 이 사용자 설명서가 도움이 된다고 생각하시길 바랍니다.

서아쌤 비밀Tip

아래 콜로케이션들은 be동사와 전치사 또는 be동사와 to부정사 사이에 들어갈 형용사를 고르는 문제로 자주 출제돼요. 문법 문제로도, 어휘 문제로도 잘 출제되니 꼭 암기하세요!

be responsible for ~에 대한 책임이 있다
be eligible for/to do ~에 대한 자격이 있다, ~할 자격이 있다
be capable of ~을 할 수 있다
be compliant with ~을 준수하다
be willing to do 기꺼이 ~하다
be responsive to ~에 대응하다
be subject to ~하기 쉽다, ~의 영향을 받다
be entitled to do ~할 자격이 있다
be reluctant to do ~하기를 꺼려하다
be comparable in/to ~에 필적하다, ~와 비교할 수 있다

Practice

1. The technology firm usually develops ------- versions of its best-selling software programs to ensure compatibility with various devices.

(A) multiply (B) multiple
(C) multiples (D) multiplicity

2. Books that are returned to the library two days after the due date will be ------- to late fees.

(A) subject (B) entitled
(C) accountable (D) transferable

▶ 헷갈리는 부정대명사 vs. 부정형용사 정리

부정대명사와 부정형용사로 둘 다 쓰일 수 있는 단어도 있고, 부정대명사로만 쓰이는 단어도 있으니 잘 정리해 두어야 한다. 또한, 부정형용사 문제는 ① 빈칸 뒤에 제시된 명사의 수를 보고 알맞은 부정형용사 고르기, ② 빈칸 앞에 제시된 부정형용사를 보고 명사의 수를 일치시키기의 두 가지 유형으로 출제된다.

one	부정대명사	+ 단수동사
	부정형용사	+ 단수명사
another	부정대명사	+ 단수동사
	부정형용사	+ 단수명사
others	부정대명사	+ 복수동사
the others	부정대명사	+ 복수동사

others와 the others는 부정형용사로 쓰이지 않아요.

If [the others / **another**] **vacancy opens up**, you will be notified by e-mail.

만약 또 다른 공석이 열린다면, 귀하께서는 이메일로 연락 받으실 것입니다.

▶ 수량형용사

수량형용사 문제는 부정형용사 출제 패턴과 동일하게 ① 빈칸 뒤에 제시된 명사의 수를 보고 알맞은 수량형용사 고르기, ② 빈칸 앞에 제시된 수량형용사를 보고 명사의 수를 일치시키기의 두 가지 유형으로 출제된다.

each, every, another *every + 숫자 + 복수명사 ~마다 (every 뒤에 숫자 표현이 있으면 반복 주기를 나타내기 때문에 예외적으로 복수명사를 사용할 수 있어요.)	+ 단수명사
several, many, (a) few	+ 복수명사
much, (a) little	+ 불가산명사
all, some, most, other	+ 복수명사 + 불가산명사

Mr. Loomis goes to the national park [**every** / other] **two weeks** to hike and fish.

루미스 씨는 2주마다 등산과 낚시를 하기 위해 국립 공원에 간다.

[Another / **Several**] **mobile phone providers** are offering reasonably priced monthly plans these days.

요즘 여러 휴대전화 제공업체들이 합리적으로 가격이 책정된 월 요금제를 제공하고 있다.

▶ 헷갈리기 쉬운 -ly형 형용사

- ☐ daily, weekly, monthly, yearly 매일의, 주간의, 월간의, 연간의
- ☐ lively 활기 넘치는
- ☐ leisurely 한가한
- ☐ friendly 친절한, 친화적인
- ☐ costly 비싼
- ☐ hourly 매시간의

Practice

3. Starting on May 14, ------- tenants association meetings will be held in the conference room on the first floor.

(A) all (B) every
(C) both (D) anybody

4. To ensure good dental health, patients are encouraged to book a check-up appointment ------- six months.

(A) whenever (B) every
(C) less (D) even

▶ 주어 + ________ + 동사

Because **Mr. Lee** [consists / **consistently**] **meets** targets for sales, he receives a sizable monthly bonus.

이 씨가 매출 목표를 지속적으로 달성하기 때문에, 그는 규모가 있는 월 보너스를 받는다.

▶ 자동사 + ________

Ms. Sanderson makes sure our business operations **run** [smooth / **smoothly**] every step of the way.

샌더슨 씨는 모든 단계에 있어 우리의 사업체 운영을 확실히 순조롭게 진행되게 한다.

▶ 타동사 + 목적어 + ________

Management expects that all landscape gardeners will **clean their equipment** [diligence / **diligently**] and with care.

경영진은 모든 정원사들이 그들의 장비를 성실하고 신중하게 닦을 것이라고 기대한다.

▶ be + ________ + p.p./-ing/형용사

The sofa you expressed an interest in **is** not [current / **currently**] **available** in the size you prefer.

귀하께서 관심을 표하셨던 소파는 현재 선호하시는 사이즈로는 구매 불가능합니다.

▶ 조동사 + ________ + 동사원형

When tour group members arrive, they should report to the hotel lobby, where the front desk staff **will** [**gladly** / be glad] **assist** them.

투어 그룹원들이 도착할 때, 그들은 반드시 호텔 로비에 알려야 하는데, 그곳에서 프론트 데스크 직원들이 그들을 기꺼이 도와줄 것이다.

▶ to + ________ + 동사원형 — to부정사 사이에도 부사가 올 수 있어요.

Ms. Kante says she will not be able **to** [confide / **confidently**] **estimate** this month's projected sales until the advertising campaign goes live.

칸테 씨는 광고 캠페인이 개시될 때까지 이번 달의 예상 매출을 확신을 갖고 추정할 수 없을 것이라고 말한다.

▶ 전치사 + ________ + 동명사

By [innovative / **innovatively**] **incorporating** modern designs into the blueprint, the architect was able to give the building a contemporary style.

청사진에 현대적인 디자인을 혁신적으로 포함시킴으로써, 그 건축가는 건물에 현대의 스타일을 더할 수 있었다.

Practice

5. With approval, employees can obtain company car keys ------- from the manager of the operating department.

(A) direction (B) directly
(C) directness (D) directed

6. Credit and debit cards are ------- accepted in all downtown Chicago taxis.

(A) final (B) finality
(C) finals (D) finally

▶ 증감동사를 수식하는 부사

- ☐ considerably, substantially, significantly 상당히
- ☐ dramatically, sharply 급격히
- ☐ gradually, steadily 점진적으로, 점차
- ☐ slightly 약간

Sales of Firenze Motors automobiles **decreased** [accidentally / **dramatically**] after the manufacturer issued a recall of defective models.

피렌체 모터스 사의 자동차 매출은 제조사가 결함 있는 모델들의 회수를 발표한 후, 급격히 감소했다.

▶ 숫자 표현을 수식하는 부사

- ☐ approximately, nearly, almost, about 약, 대략, 거의
- ☐ over, more than ~가 넘는, ~ 이상의
- ☐ up to 최대 ~까지
- ☐ at least 최소한, 적어도

Mr. Nilsson will need [**approximately** / briefly] **20 minutes** to prepare equipment prior to the product demonstration.

닐슨 씨는 제품 시연 이전에 장비를 준비하기 위해 약 20분이 필요할 것이다.

▶ 명사구를 수식하는 부사

- ☐ largely 주로
- ☐ only, just 단지
- ☐ formerly 이전에, 예전에
- ☐ originally 원래
- ☐ clearly 명백히
- ☐ almost 거의

Odeon Residences was [original / **originally**] **a theater**, but it was transformed into an apartment building five years ago.

오데온 레지던스는 원래 극장이었지만, 5년 전에 아파트 건물로 탈바꿈되었다.

▶ 자체적으로 부정의 의미를 가진 부사

- ☐ hardly, seldom, barely, rarely 거의 ~ 않다

The scratches on the delivery vehicles are [**barely** / exactly] **noticeable** now that the polishing work has been carried out.

광택 작업이 진행되었으므로 배송 차량에 난 긁힌 자국은 거의 눈에 띄지 않는다.

서아쌤 비밀Tip

부사 still은 '아직, 여전히'라는 뜻으로 긍정문/의문문/부정문에 사용할 수 있고, yet은 '아직'이라는 뜻일 때 부정문, '이미, 벌써'라는 의미일 때는 의문문에서 사용할 수 있어요. still과 yet은 not과 함께 쓰일 때 still not 그리고 not yet으로 쓰여 not의 위치로도 구분할 수 있답니다. 특히 yet은 have yet to do(아직 ~하지 않았다) 구문에서 빈칸에 yet을 넣는 유형으로 자주 출제되니 꼭 알아두세요!

Practice

7. It should take ------- two hours to sail from the holiday resort to the remote island of Tijali Dua.

(A) enough (B) somewhat
(C) exceedingly (D) approximately

8. The large space opposite Sugarhill Plaza was ------- a parking lot, but it is now an urban park with several jogging paths.

(A) still (B) costly
(C) enough (D) formerly

Check-up Test

강의 바로보기

1. The new intern deals ------- well with complicated assignments, such as calculating projected expenses for project proposals.
   (A) surprise
   (B) surprisingly
   (C) surprising
   (D) surprised

2. Canary Financial Consultancy provides attractive benefits and incentives to ------- clients.
   (A) regular
   (B) regulars
   (C) regularity
   (D) regularly

3. Istana Kebab began using paper food delivery boxes last month, which had the pleasing effect of decreasing expenses -------.
   (A) great
   (B) greatest
   (C) greater
   (D) greatly

4. Any employee who has worked for more than six months is ------- to enroll in our management training course.
   (A) eligible
   (B) possible
   (C) measured
   (D) relevant

5. Because the majority of employees were ------- of the new dress code policy, the HR manager decided to implement it immediately.
   (A) support
   (B) supportive
   (C) supporter
   (D) supported

6. The Royal Ballet Company recently gave a ------- performance at the newly opened Ewing Concert Hall.
   (A) memory
   (B) memorize
   (C) memorably
   (D) memorable

7. Jackson Marvel will make his new album ------- for digital download early next month.
   (A) availability
   (B) available
   (C) availableness
   (D) availably

8. The director's announcement of the movie sequel ------- excited the audience members at the film festival.
   (A) clearly
   (B) clear
   (C) clearer
   (D) clearest

9. The Amateur Watercolor Contest at Mingus Gallery only includes entries from painters who have ------- to exhibit their work.
   (A) less
   (B) yet
   (C) soon
   (D) very

10. Chef Masako strives to use ------- ingredients in the dishes she prepares at DeSoto Restaurant.
   (A) season
   (B) seasons
   (C) seasonal
   (D) seasonally

11. Ms. Edmonds has decided to remove the kale and apple smoothie from the menu, since ------- customers ever order it.

(A) few
(B) more
(C) other
(D) all

12. It is recommended that patients request diagnoses from ------- two doctors before agreeing to undergo major surgery.

(A) in fact
(B) always
(C) enough
(D) at least

13. Local businesses are encouraged to take an environmentally ------- approach to waste disposal.

(A) friend
(B) friends
(C) friendly
(D) friendship

14. Ms. Singh mentioned that Mr. Harker is ------- punctual with his weekly sales report.

(A) little
(B) near
(C) seldom
(D) well

15. If your rental vehicle is unavailable for any reason, we will provide a different vehicle that is ------- in size and price.

(A) significant
(B) original
(C) comparable
(D) variable

16. ------- responsibility Mr. Neeson has as the head of the IT team is to ensure all company computers are protected from malicious software.

(A) The others
(B) Another
(C) One another
(D) Others

17. The endorsement of our cell phone by the pop star Suzy Lee is certain to ------- boost sales, especially with younger consumers.

(A) strictly
(B) dramatically
(C) punctually
(D) previously

18. The record company has collected the final recordings of the late singer and will ------- release them as a full album.

(A) short
(B) shorter
(C) shorten
(D) shortly

19. Before the highly ------- film premiere, the director and several cast members signed autographs for fans.

(A) anticipate
(B) anticipated
(C) anticipatory
(D) anticipation

20. Marcy's was ------- a shipping warehouse, but it was converted into a five-story department store last year.

(A) originality
(B) original
(C) originals
(D) originally

Playlist 4

강의 바로보기

토익 문법 끝판왕! 전치사와 부사절 접속사 총정리

Part 5

필수 전치사 | 고난도 전치사 | 부사절 접속사 | 전치사 vs. 부접

at/on/in 비교 분석

	시간 전치사		장소 전치사	
at	정확한 시각 시점	at 2 P.M. at the moment	정확한 지점	at the Art Gallery
on	날짜 요일	on September 4 on Friday	접촉한 면	on the second floor
in	월 계절 연도	in April in summer in 2029	행정구역(도시, 국가 등) 3차원 공간 안	in Nelson City in the box

We will provide a full Christmas Dinner buffet at each of the three branch offices you listed [in / **on**] **December 20.**

저희는 귀하께서 기재하신 세 개의 지사 각각에서 12월 20일에 완전한 크리스마스 저녁 뷔페를 제공할 것입니다.

최빈출 전치사

- ☐ during + 기간 명사 ~ 동안에
- ☐ until(지속성) ~까지
- ☐ between(둘), among(셋 이상) ~ 사이에
- ☐ in + 시점 명사 ~ 후에
- ☐ within + 기간 명사/장소 ~ 이내에
- ☐ from + 시작 시점 ~부터
- ☐ for + 숫자 ~ 동안에
- ☐ by(일회성) ~까지
- ☐ throughout + 시간/장소 ~ 내내, ~ 전역에
- ☐ since + 과거 시점 ~ 이래로
- ☐ before + 시점 명사 ~ 전에

Please remember that your Wilshire Leisure Center membership will expire one week [**from** / for] **today.**

귀하의 윌셔어 레저 센터 회원권이 오늘로부터 일주일 후 만료된다는 것이라는 것을 기억하십시오.

Trains delayed by the emergency track maintenance will hopefully leave [of / **within**] **three hours.**

긴급 선로 유지보수 작업에 의해 지연된 기차편이 바라건대 세 시간 이내에 떠날 것입니다.

Practice

1. Employees may take advantage of a 40 percent discount ------- the time of purchase.

(A) as (B) off
(C) into (D) at

2. All magazine articles must be submitted on or ------- January 21 to be included in the February issue.

(A) since (B) until
(C) before (D) along

▶ 고난도 장소 전치사

- ☐ past + 장소 ~을 지나서
- ☐ opposite + 장소 ~ 맞은편에
- ☐ across from + 건너는 시작점 ~의 바로 맞은편에
- ☐ along + 한쪽 면 ~을 따라서
- ☐ across + 건너는 대상 ~을 가로질러, 건너서

The ticket office is situated [**opposite** / across] **the flower shop**, making it easy to locate.
매표소는 찾기 쉽게 꽃집 맞은편에 위치해 있습니다.

▶ 의미로 묶어서 외우는 전치사

~ 때문에	because of, due to, owing to, on account of
~에 관하여	about, on, over, regarding, concerning, pertaining to, as to, as for
~에도 불구하고	despite, in spite of, notwithstanding — notwithstanding은 접속부사로도 쓸 수 있어요.
~뿐만 아니라	besides, in addition to, aside from, apart from
~을 제외하고	besides, except (for), excepting, aside from, apart from

[Due to / **Apart from**] **a few unexpected delays**, the renovation project at Salford Theater **is continuing smoothly**.
몇 가지 예상치 못한 지연을 제외하고, 살포드 극장의 개조 프로젝트는 순조롭게 계속되고 있다.

▶ -ing형 전치사

- ☐ including ~을 포함하여
- ☐ following ~ 후에
- ☐ considering ~을 고려하면
- ☐ starting, beginning ~부터
- ☐ excluding ~을 제외하고

[**Considering** / Upon] **the recent increase** in gas prices, we should start using our bicycles to commute between home and work.
가스비의 최근 인상을 고려하면, 우리는 집과 직장 사이를 통근할 때 자전거를 이용하는 것을 시작해야 한다.

서아쌤 비밀Tip

전치사 관련 표현 문제는 암기를 통해서만 풀 수 있어요. 빈출 전치사 표현들을 미리 익혀 고득점에 좀 더 가까이 가보자구요!

as a result of ~의 결과로
in compliance with, in accordance with ~을 따라서
on behalf of ~을 대신하여
in favor of ~에 찬성하여
in response to ~에 대응하여
in case of, in the event of ~의 경우에 대비하여
by -ing ~함으로써
(up)on -ing ~하자마자

Practice

3. Visitors looking for the sculpture exhibition should walk ------- the information desk and enter the first hall on the right.

(A) between (B) upon
(C) past (D) through

4. Coastline Holiday Resort is always fully booked with guests ------- its poor online reviews.

(A) despite (B) between
(C) except (D) unlike

▶ 부사절 접속사 모아보기

시간	once, as soon as ~하자마자 after, before ~후에, ~전에 when, as ~할 때 while ~하는 동안 since ~이래로 until ~할 때까지
조건	unless ~하지 않는다면 as long as ~하는 한 if, provided (that) 만약 ~라면 only if ~의 경우에만 in case (that), in the event (that) ~하는 경우에 대비하여
이유	because, since, as, now that ~ 때문에, ~이므로
양보	although, though, even though, even if 비록 ~에도 불구하고 (even though와 비슷하게 생긴 as though는 '마치 ~인 것처럼'이라고 해석되는 접속사이니 헷갈리지 마세요.)
목적	so that, in order that ~하기 위해서
대조	while, whereas ~인 반면에
결과	so 형용사/부사 that 너무 ~해서 …하다 (so ~ that 뒤에 제시되는 can/may가 정답 단서인 경우가 많아요.)

We will resume shipping of customer orders [until / **when**] all delivery trucks have passed an annual inspection.
모든 배송 트럭이 연례 점검을 통과했을 때 저희는 고객 주문품의 배송을 재개할 것입니다.

We suggest that you make a copy of this contract [**in case** / unless] you need to check the terms and conditions in the future.
귀하께서 미래에 계약 조건을 확인해야 할 경우에 대비하여 이 계약서의 사본을 만드는 것을 제안드립니다.

Mr. Swanson's farewell letter to staff should be uploaded to the company portal [whereas / **so that**] all employees can view it.
직원들에게 보낸 스완슨 씨의 작별 편지는 모든 직원들이 볼 수 있도록 회사 포털에 게시되어야 한다.

시간이나 조건의 부사절 접속사가 있는 절에서는 미래의 내용을 나타내더라도 현재시제 동사를 사용하는 것을 꼭 잊지 마세요.

Ms. Tibbs **will attend** the product demonstration **if** she [will arrive / **arrives**] at the convention venue on time.
팁스 씨가 컨벤션 행사 장소에 제 시간에 도착한다면 제품 시연회에 참석할 것이다.

Practice

5. ------- her performance attracted more than 10,000 people, Sally Weaver made very little money from the concert.

(A) Nevertheless (B) Although
(C) Even (D) Apart from

6. ------- remodeling of the office space is complete, our staff can set up their new workstations.

(A) Now that (B) Either
(C) Wherever (D) In order that

▶ 의미로 묶어 구분하는 전치사 vs. 부사절 접속사

의미	전치사	부사절 접속사
이유	because of, due to, owing to, on account of ~ 때문에 thanks to ~ 덕분에	because, since, as, now that ~ 때문에, ~이므로
양보	despite, in spite of, notwithstanding 비록 ~일지라도	although, though, even though, even if 비록 ~할지라도
시간	during, for ~동안 following, after ~후에 before, prior to ~ 전에 (up)on -ing ~하자마자 until, by ~까지	while ~하는 동안 after ~한 후에 before ~하기 전에 once, as soon as ~하자마자 until ~할 때까지
조건	in case of, in the event of ~의 경우에 대비하여	in case (that), in the event (that) ~하는 경우에 대비하여
제외	except (for) ~을 제외하고	except (that) ~하는 것을 제외하고
목적	for ~을 위해서	so that, in order that ~하기 위해서
기타	given, considering ~을 고려하면	given that, considering (that) ~하는 것을 고려하면

We will stop several times for refreshment breaks [while / **during**] **the tour** of our local historical buildings.
저희 지역의 역사적인 건물들의 투어 동안 다과 시간을 위해 여러 번 정차할 것입니다.

[**Until** / Due to] **the IT technician arrived** to repair the server, the office had been without Internet for two hours.
IT 기술자들이 서버를 수리하기 위해 도착할 때까지, 사무실은 두 시간 동안 인터넷이 없었다.

Customer complaints have decreased [**since** / before] **training plans were introduced** three months ago.
고객 불만사항이 세 달 전에 교육 계획이 도입된 이후로 감소해왔다.

[**Except for** / Even though] **the occasional delay** during the peak tourism season, the shuttle bus from the airport runs precisely on schedule.
여행 성수기 중에 종종 있는 지연을 제외하고, 공항에서 출발하는 셔틀 버스는 일정대로 정확하게 운영된다.

Practice

7. ------- its value and fragility, the original painting by Vermeer is surrounded by a security barrier.

(A) Because of (B) Along with
(C) In spite of (D) Regarding

8. Mr. Gray plans to look for appropriate accommodation ------- his work transfer is confirmed.

(A) above all (B) as soon as
(C) in addition to (D) other than

Check-up Test

강의 바로보기

1. ------- Mr. Hamed became the CEO of Sportix Beverages, several new workplace safety policies were announced.

(A) So that
(B) As expected
(C) In order that
(D) As soon as

2. St. Mary's Chapel is the oldest historical landmark ------- London after the Blackfriars Monument.

(A) in
(B) on
(C) of
(D) as

3. The fee requested by the business consultant was quite reasonable, ------- his industry background and expertise.

(A) consider
(B) considers
(C) considered
(D) considering

4. Monthly expenses have decreased ------- spending limits were introduced five months ago.

(A) whereas
(B) otherwise
(C) before
(D) since

5. The director of the film accepted the award ------- Martin Olson, who was unable to attend the ceremony due to ill health.

(A) in light of
(B) on condition that
(C) on behalf of
(D) in exchange for

6. Refunds on returned items cannot be issued ------- a valid proof of purchase is presented.

(A) yet
(B) because
(C) unless
(D) whereas

7. In an effort to accommodate more diners during evening hours, Jade Garden is moving to Lotus Road ------- the Habor Heights Mall.

(A) across
(B) opposite
(C) throughout
(D) upon

8. The bell at St. Matthew's Cathedral has been restored to sound normal ------- routine maintenance.

(A) as for
(B) due to
(C) instead of
(D) among

9. The record company presented Marisa Torres with a plaque ------- her debut album sold over two million copies worldwide.

(A) soon
(B) after
(C) toward
(D) besides

10. Mr. Lawton finds that staff productivity increases more ------- he hires experienced workers instead of recent graduates.

(A) over
(B) when
(C) even
(D) while

정답 및 해설 p.12

11. The marketing manager resigned ------- the board members offered him a significant salary increase.

(A) even though
(B) for one thing
(C) as if
(D) lastly

12. Our client, Mr. Kintaro, noted that the flight attendants were so attentive ------- the whole flight to Toronto.

(A) throughout
(B) along
(C) later
(D) underneath

13. Office workers are not permitted to use the fire escape stairs ------- when elevator maintenance is underway.

(A) except
(B) since
(C) against
(D) during

14. ------- the landscaping company Greenfields advertised on local radio, demand for its services has almost tripled.

(A) While
(B) As much as
(C) Besides
(D) Not only

15. Byers Road will be completely reopened ------- replacing the faulty traffic lights.

(A) upon
(B) apart
(C) so that
(D) for instance

16. ------- Dawson Park was once the most sought-after recreation space in the city, Memorial Square has become more popular among residents.

(A) Whereas
(B) Yet
(C) Apart
(D) Since

17. The city council decided to close some streets ------- the town while the concert was taking place.

(A) among
(B) within
(C) besides
(D) between

18. Complimentary bottled water will be available from the refreshment tent ------- the music festival.

(A) during
(B) while
(C) about
(D) when

19. Our newspaper remains as popular as ever ------- an overall decline in national print news readership.

(A) despite
(B) along
(C) like
(D) around

20. Ms. Yamamoto decided to grab a bite to eat before her flight ------- meals were not provided by the budget airline.

(A) unless
(B) in case
(C) whoever
(D) likewise

Playlist 5

강의 바로보기

관계대명사랑 관계부사를 구분해야 된다고?

Part 5

관계대명사 정답 단서 | 고난도 관계대명사 | 관계부사 정답 단서 | 복합관계사

▶ 선행사 + _______ + 동사

관계대명사가 들어갈 자리 뒤에 동사가 있다면 주격 관계대명사가 정답이다. 선행사가 사람이면 who/that을, 사물이면 which/that을 고르면 된다.

The competition offers $500 to **the person** [which / **who**] **designs** the most attractive logo for the city's marketing campaign.

이 대회는 시의 마케팅 캠페인을 위한 가장 매력적인 로고를 디자인한 사람에게 500달러를 제공합니다.

▶ 선행사 + _______ + 주어 + 타동사

관계대명사가 들어갈 자리 뒤에 주어와 타동사가 있다면 목적격 관계대명사가 정답이다. 선행사가 사람이면 whom/that을, 사물이면 which/that을 선택한다.

콤마나 전치사 뒤에 that은 쓸 수 없어요.

In her new **position**, [that / **which**] **she will assume** on March 5, Ms. Anderson will serve as the chief financial officer.

앤더슨 씨가 3월 5일부터 맡을 새 직책에서, 그녀는 최고재무이사로서 근무할 것이다.

▶ 선행사 + _______ + 주어 + 동사 + (목적어/보어)

관계대명사가 들어갈 자리 뒤에 관사 없이 명사가 주어로 제시되어 있고, 동사와 목적어 또는 보어가 있다면 소유격 관계대명사가 정답이다. 이때 선행사의 종류와는 상관없이 whose를 사용하며, whose는 선행사와 주어 사이의 소유 관계를 나타낸다.

The overtime rate is only available to **employees** [that / **whose**] **shifts take place** after 7 P.M. on weekdays or on Sundays.

초과근무수당은 오직 평일 오후 7시 이후 또는 일요일에 교대근무가 있는 직원들에게만 유효할 것이다.

어떤 책에서는 관계대명사를 형용사절 접속사라고 부르기도 하는데, 이름만 다를 뿐 둘 다 같은 것이라고 생각하면 편해요. 둘 모두 절과 절을 연결하는 접속사의 역할을 할 수 있고, 앞에 위치한 선행사인 명사를 꾸며줄 수 있어요. 다만 명사를 수식하기 때문에 형용사의 역할을 하는 접속사라서 형용사절 접속사라고 하기도 하니 헷갈리지 마세요!

Practice

1. Local baseball teams ------- qualify for the state championships will receive sponsorship from Erco Manufacturing.

(A) that (B) they
(C) what (D) whoever

2. Bernard Simmons, ------- achievements as a movie director include winning three Academy Awards, has recently announced his retirement.

(A) whichever (B) whose
(C) who (D) that

▶ 전치사 + 관계대명사

관계대명사는 대명사의 역할도 할 수 있기 때문에 전치사의 목적어 자리에도 올 수 있다. 다만, 전치사 뒤에 사용할 수 있는 관계대명사는 한정적이므로 선행사가 사물이면 which, 사람이면 whom을 정답으로 선택하면 된다.

The names of **branch managers to** [where / **whom**] the monthly financial report should be sent are listed in the management directory.

월간 재무 보고서를 받아야 하는 지사장들의 이름이 경영진 전화번호 안내에 목록화되어 있다.

▶ 수량 표현 + 관계대명사

선택지에 관계대명사가 있고 빈칸 앞에 수량 표현과 of가 제시되어 있다면, 선행사에 따라 which 또는 whom을 정답으로 고른다.

one, both, several, most, some, many, all, each, a few + of	which (사물) whom (사람)

The island boasts over 200 kilometers of scenic **coastline, most of** [**which** / whom] is being purchased by holiday resort developers.

그 섬은 200키로미터가 넘는 경치가 좋은 해안가를 자랑하며, 그것들 중 대부분이 휴양 리조트 개발업자들에 의해 구매되어지고 있다.

This restaurant's kitchen is staffed with 25 **workers, all of** [which / **whom**] are highly qualified and experienced.

이 레스토랑의 주방은 25명의 근무자들로 구성되어 있으며, 그들 모두가 매우 뛰어난 자격을 지니고 있고 경험이 많다.

▶ 관계대명사 what

관계대명사 what은 앞에 선행사가 없는 관계대명사로 빈칸 앞에 선행사가 있다면 다른 관계대명사를 정답으로 골라야 한다. 토익에서 what은 명사절 접속사로 더 많이 출제되지만, 관계대명사 문제의 단골 오답 선택지이므로 함께 알아두는 것이 좋다.

Timmins Accounting is a **company** [**that** / what] strives to exceed the expectations of clients.

티민스 회계법인은 고객들의 기대를 넘기 위해 노력하는 회사이다.

Practice

3. The relocation proposal will be discussed at a meeting during ------- each member of staff will be given a chance to voice their opinion.

(A) through (B) there
(C) which (D) who

4. The job applicants who progressed to the interview stage, some of ------- have extensive industry experience, will be contacted by our HR manager.

(A) whom (B) that
(C) while (D) which

관계부사는 관계대명사처럼 두 개의 절을 연결할 수 있으며, 뒤에 완전한 구조의 문장이 온다. Part 5에서 관계부사는 where과 why만 출제된다. 시간 관계부사 when은 시간 부사절 접속사로, 방법 관계부사 how는 명사절 접속사로 주로 출제된다.

▶ 장소 선행사 + ________ + 완전한 문장

빈칸 앞에 place와 같이 장소 관련 선행사가 있고 뒤에 제시된 문장의 구조가 완벽하다면, 관계부사 where이 정답이다. 빈칸이 장소 관계부사 자리인데 선택지에 where가 없다면 in which를 정답으로 고르면 된다.

The place [which / **where**] **the monthly teambuilding activity is held** has recently been expanded to accommodate larger groups.

월간 팀빌딩 활동이 열리는 장소는 최근 더 많은 사람들을 수용하기 위해 확장되었다.

▶ 이유 선행사 + ________ + 완전한 문장

빈칸 앞에 reason과 같이 이유 관련 선행사가 제시되어 있고 뒤에 완전한 구조의 문장이 있다면, 관계부사 why를 정답으로 선택한다.

The reason [who / **why**] **the grand opening event was postponed** is due to an issue with the building's power supply.

대개장 행사가 연기된 이유는 건물의 전기 공급 문제 때문이다.

관계사 문제의 선택지는 주로 관계대명사와 관계부사가 섞여서 출제되는 경우가 대부분이기 때문에 빈칸 뒤에 제시된 문장 구조를 먼저 파악하는 연습을 해야 해요!

▶ 관계대명사 vs. 관계부사

선택지가 관계사로 구성되어 있고 빈칸 뒤의 문장 구조가 불완전하다면 관계대명사를, 완전하다면 관계부사를 고르면 된다.

The new messaging program, [how / **which**] **was installed** in the second quarter, has significantly improved communication between departments.

이분기에 설치된 새로운 메시지 프로그램은 부서들 간의 의사소통을 상당히 개선시켰다.

The resort [which / **where**] **we stayed** last month was only a 20-minute drive from the airport.

지난달 우리가 머물렀던 리조트는 공항에서 차로 겨우 20분 거리에 있었다.

✔ Practice

5. The invoice attached to your order shows the location code of the retail outlet ------- the products were purchased.

(A) where (B) whose
(C) that (D) which

6. Katherine Mills hosts a radio show ------- she talks about news stories from the entertainment industry.

(A) in which (B) whom
(C) in order to (D) along with

복합관계사는 크게 복합관계대명사와 복합관계부사로 나뉘는데, 앞서 배운 관계대명사와 관계부사 뒤에 -ever만 붙인 것이다. 복합관계사는 관계사와는 다르게 선행사를 꾸며주는 것이 아닌 명사절 접속사 또는 부사절 접속사로 사용된다.

▶ 복합관계대명사

복합관계대명사는 관계대명사와 동일하게 뒤에 불완전한 문장이 와야 하며, 명사절 접속사와 부사절 접속사로 사용할 수 있다.

	명사절 접속사	부사절 접속사
whoever	~하는 누구든	누가 ~할지라도 (= no matter who)
whatever	~하는 무엇이든	무엇을 ~할지라도 (= no matter what)
whichever	~하는 어떤 것이든	어떤 것을 ~할지라도 (= no matter which)

[**Whoever** / Someone] **wishes** to attend next week's sales training workshop should sign their name on the registration sheet.

다음 주 영업 교육 워크숍에 참석하길 희망하는 사람은 누구든 등록 시트에 이름을 서명해야 한다.

▶ 복합관계부사

복합관계부사는 관계부사와 동일하게 뒤에 완전한 구조의 문장이 와야 하며, 부사절 접속사로만 사용된다.

	부사절 접속사
whenever	언제든지 (= no matter when)
wherever	어디든지 (= no matter where)
however	아무리 ~할지라도 (= no matter how) ─ 「However + 형용사/부사 +주어 + 동사」 구조로 쓰여요.

Do not hesitate to speak with your tour guide [**whenever** / whether] **you have any questions** about the places you visit.

귀하께서 방문하실 장소들에 대해 질문이 있다면 언제든지 투어 가이드와 이야기하는 것을 주저하지 마십시오.

however는 특히 별님들이 많이 어려워하는 부분이에요. 복합관계부사로도 접속부사로도 사용되는 however! 제가 완벽하게 정리해 줄게요!

However expensive the tickets are, Mr. Adams is determined to go to the band's reunion concert. [복합관계부사]

입장권이 아무리 비싸더라도, 아담스 씨는 그 밴드의 재결합 콘서트에 가기로 결심했다.

The ferry was scheduled to depart at 2 P.M. **However**, it was delayed due to inclement weather. [접속부사]

그 페리는 오후 2시에 출발할 예정이었다. 하지만, 악천후로 인해 지연되었다.

Practice

7. The manager will close the store early once 20 sales have been made or daily earnings exceed $10,000, ------- occurs first.

(A) whoever (B) either
(C) whichever (D) another

8. It is mandatory for all factory workers to attend safety training sessions regularly, ------- experienced they may be.

(A) very (B) even
(C) likewise (D) however

Check-up Test

강의 바로보기

1. The author acknowledged all ------- helped him with his research while writing the book.

(A) who
(B) them
(C) what
(D) these

2. Yvette LeGrande, ------- books on succeeding in the business world have become bestsellers, will give the keynote speech at this year's literature convention.

(A) who
(B) whom
(C) whoever
(D) whose

3. Learning a foreign language ------- is commonly used in business can help you secure a job.

(A) that
(B) who
(C) them
(D) where

4. Ms. Allenby, ------- is joining us as our new marketing director next month, will take the vacant office on the fourth floor.

(A) which
(B) where
(C) who
(D) whose

5. Please hire ------- provides the best answers to the questions about customer service.

(A) who
(B) whoever
(C) which
(D) whichever

6. The music festival organizers announced that it will open a backstage area, ------- VIP ticket holders can meet some of the performers.

(A) where
(B) such
(C) requiring
(D) as

7. Steelwave Manufacturing has nine assembly lines at the factory, some of ------- are found to be defective.

(A) whose
(B) other
(C) which
(D) either

8. Employees may leave early this Friday or start work at lunchtime on Monday, ------- they prefer.

(A) whose
(B) what
(C) someone
(D) whichever

9. Please inform me of the factory's daily productivity rate ------- it dips below the target level.

(A) likewise
(B) whenever
(C) altogether
(D) including

10. The soundtrack for the new movie by James Goldman contains many impressive songs, several of ------- were composed by Burt Snyder.

(A) which
(B) another
(C) nothing
(D) who

정답 및 해설 p.15

11. The annual Global Motoring Trade Show, ------- will be held in Detroit next April, has increased its number of participating vendors.

(A) who
(B) which
(C) whose
(D) that

12. At the request of the office manager, ------- is the first to arrive at the office each morning should turn on the air conditioner.

(A) which
(B) each
(C) this
(D) whoever

13. Personal vehicles may be parked ------- event attendees can find a space.

(A) whoever
(B) wherever
(C) whatever
(D) whichever

14. Galaxy Software, ------- board members have expressed interest in merging with our firm, has arranged a meeting with our CEO.

(A) whatever
(B) whose
(C) who
(D) which

15. Chef Cussler likes the food ------- he cooks at Indigo Restaurant but would prefer to update the menu.

(A) what
(B) how
(C) which
(D) where

16. The Lennon Accounting Company announced that only office assistants ------- work quickly and efficiently will be promoted.

(A) which
(B) what
(C) whose
(D) who

17. ------- sharply the technology market has decreased within the last quarter, the BlueTech Corporation plans to expand its operations.

(A) However
(B) Notwithstanding
(C) Despite
(D) Even though

18. The Sapphire Shores Resort ------- we stayed last month was only a 10-minute drive from the airport.

(A) whom
(B) in which
(C) whose
(D) when

19. Mr. Thompson is the senior manager with ------- many of our new hires consult for initial training at Global Solutions.

(A) who
(B) whom
(C) which
(D) whose

20. Guests have full access to a business center and other amenities, making the Pacific Hightower a great hotel in ------- to stay during the conference.

(A) what
(B) which
(C) where
(D) whose

Playlist 6

강의 바로보기

명사절 접속사 정답 3초컷 스킬

Part 5

명사절 접속사의 종류 ①　명사절 접속사의 종류 ②

명사절 접속사는 명사와 동일한 역할을 할 수 있으므로 문장 내에서 명사가 들어갈 수 있는 자리에 모두 올 수 있다. 주로 주어, 동사 또는 전치사의 목적어 자리에 알맞은 명사절 접속사를 고르는 유형으로 출제되며, that/whether/if와 Wh-의문사가 명사절 접속사로 사용될 수 있다.

▶ that: ~라는 것

[**That** / With] **the new menu improved diner satisfaction** is clear from our online reviews.

새로운 메뉴가 식사 손님들의 만족도를 향상시켰다는 것은 온라인 후기에서 볼 때 분명하다.

The company **announced** [about / **that**] its new range of energy drinks will be available exclusively in QuickMart convenience stores.

그 회사는 새로운 종류의 에너지 음료를 퀵마트 편의점에서 독점적으로 구매 가능할 것이라는 사실을 발표했다.

▶ whether/if: ~인지 아닌지

if도 명사절 접속사로 사용하지만, 토익에서 조건 부사절 접속사로 대부분 출제돼요.

The issue **of** [after / **whether**] the store will close early on Christmas Eve or not will be addressed by Ms. Kim.

그 매장이 크리스마스 이브에 일찍 문을 닫을 것인지 아닌지에 대한 문제가 김 씨에 의해 다뤄질 것이다.

명사절 접속사 문제는 ① 선택지에 that이나 whether, 다른 품사를 제시해 명사절 접속사를 고르는 유형, ② 동사의 목적어 자리에 쓰일 알맞은 명사절 접속사를 고르는 두 가지 유형으로 출제되는데, 후자의 경우 빈칸 앞에 쓰인 동사와 어울리는 명사절 접속사를 정답으로 고르면 돼요.

that		whether	
announce 발표하다	suggest 제안하다	determine, decide 결정하다	know 알다
indicate, show 나타내다	report 보고하다	ask 묻다	see ~인지 확인하다
request 요청하다	state 명시하다	choose 선택하다, 고르다	find out 알아보다

Lead Pro Solutions employees **will decide** this evening [**whether** / that / about] they will accept the new employment contracts.

리드 프로 솔루션스 사 직원들은 오늘 저녁에 새로운 고용 계약서를 수락할 것인지를 결정할 것이다.

Practice

1. Shenzen Electronics will determine, based on the number of advance orders, ------- the factory will increase its production rate.

(A) whether　(B) who
(C) since　(D) that

2. The inspection indicated ------- almost every machine on the assembly line needs repairs or maintenance.

(A) that　(B) what
(C) those　(D) whose

▶ who, what, which

Wh-의문사 중 명사절 접속사 who, what, which는 뒤에 불완전한 구조의 문장이 와야 한다.

The public relations manager wants to **know** [her / **who**] **will be speaking** at the press conference on Friday.

홍보부장님은 금요일에 있을 기자회견에서 누가 이야기할 예정인지를 알고 싶어 한다.

The itinerary, which will be e-mailed, **describes** [**what** / that] **the participants will see** on the tour.

이메일로 보내질 예정인 그 일정표는 참석자들이 투어에서 무엇을 볼 예정인지를 설명한다.

▶ what, which, whose

Wh-의문사 중 명사절 접속사 what, which, whose는 바로 뒤에 명사를 포함한 완전한 구조의 문장이 올 수 있고, 뒤에 오는 명사를 수식하는 역할을 할 수 있어 의문형용사라고도 한다.

HR employees need to **confirm** [one / **which**] **documents are required** for the staff onboarding process.

인사부 직원들은 어느 서류가 직원 온보딩 과정에 요구되어지는지를 확인해야 한다.

▶ when, where, why, how

Wh-의문사 중 명사절 접속사 when, where, why, how는 뒤에 완전한 구조의 문장이 와야 하며, 특히 빈칸 바로 뒤에 형용사나 부사가 있다면 이를 수식할 수 있는 how가 정답이다.

New medications will be graded based **on** [**how** / only] **well they perform** during clinical trials.

새로운 약물들은 임상 기간 동안 얼마나 잘 작용하는지에 기반해 등급이 매겨질 것이다.

The engineer **explained** [who / **why**] **it's important to clean the air conditioning unit regularly** to ensure efficient performance.

그 기술자는 효율적인 성능을 보장하기 위해 에어컨 기기를 정기적으로 청소하는 것이 왜 중요한지를 설명했다.

명사절 접속사 중 일부는 to부정사와 함께 쓸 수 있어요. 「whether + to부정사」 또는 「how + to부정사」가 주로 이 구조로 출제되고, that/if/why는 to부정사와 함께 쓸 수 없어요.

The new Web-based courses will give students more options in **choosing** [**whether** / while] **to study online** or attend classes in person.

새로운 웹 기반의 교육과정들은 학생들에게 온라인에서 학습할지 또는 직접 수업에 참석할지 고를 수 있는 더 많은 선택사항들을 줄 것이다.

Practice

3. Any staff member who needs to know ------- to use the new photocopier should speak with Ben in the maintenance team.

(A) that (B) why
(C) how (D) whose

4. All event attendees need to decide ------- dishes they would like to eat during the company banquet.

(A) which (B) who
(C) whether (D) where

Check-up Test

강의 바로보기

1. All factory accidents must be recorded in the incident log book, regardless of ------- an employee was injured or not.
   (A) even
   (B) whether
   (C) despite
   (D) that

2. Mr. Murphy, the marketing consultant, suggested ------- all branches send out promotional materials at least once per week.
   (A) whether
   (B) whom
   (C) that
   (D) if

3. Ms. Garland's final decision on expanding the staff cafeteria will be based on ------- many employees are hired over the next three months.
   (A) how
   (B) so
   (C) very
   (D) as

4. Mayor Kisida considered ------- the local residents mentioned at the public debate about the planned airport construction.
   (A) what
   (B) that
   (C) about
   (D) after

5. The management team will gather tomorrow morning to decide ------- pilot projects to invest in this year.
   (A) which
   (B) who
   (C) where
   (D) when

6. Proto Homes is unique because the interior design firm knows ------- to incorporate advanced design features at minimal cost.
   (A) how
   (B) then
   (C) yet
   (D) about

7. ------- Edulite Electronics has sold 300,000 units of its e-book reader device in one month is evidence that demand for e-books is still high.
   (A) For
   (B) If
   (C) With
   (D) That

8. ------- a solar panel is situated on a roof often determines how efficiently it will convert energy into electricity.
   (A) So
   (B) Where
   (C) Since
   (D) When

9. ------- Linton Technologies Inc. launches its new device at the upcoming convention depends on the results of a market research survey.
   (A) Even if
   (B) Consequently
   (C) Whether
   (D) Moreover

10. As soon as the Ministry of Economy and Finance has examined the fund support document, they will determine ------- application will be accepted.
   (A) who
   (B) whom
   (C) whoever
   (D) whose

11. ------- is particularly surprising about this small store on Oakwood Lane is that it has the widest range of electronic devices in the region.

(A) Which
(B) That
(C) Why
(D) What

12. It remains to be seen ------- Robert Miller's new movie will be as highly praised by critics as his previous one.

(A) whereas
(B) regarding
(C) whether
(D) as though

13. Mr. Garibaldi wanted to find out ------- had added his name to the mailing list of the nutritional supplement company.

(A) who
(B) him
(C) himself
(D) when

14. Mr. Horrocks must decide ------- to relocate the company to the vacant lot at Abbey Innovation Park.

(A) whether
(B) whereas
(C) if
(D) unless

15. Idris IT Solutions' employee handbook states ------- items provided to staff members must be returned before they leave the company.

(A) so
(B) that
(C) since
(D) for

16. The HR manager has not yet announced ------- awards employees will receive.

(A) who
(B) which
(C) that
(D) as

17. Mr. Kim contacted the trade show organizers to ask ------- there are accommodations at the convention center.

(A) so
(B) about
(C) whether
(D) of

18. The research study showed ------- almost every graduate of Grandford University was successful in securing long-term employment.

(A) that
(B) what
(C) those
(D) whose

19. The new Greenways Bank mobile app gives customers greater flexibility in choosing ------- to visit the bank.

(A) which
(B) what
(C) while
(D) when

20. Visitors touring BlueArc Fabrication can see ------- our silk fabrics are made in the production lines.

(A) during
(B) about
(C) how
(D) while

Playlist 7

강의 바로보기

점수 상승 보장하는 to부정사 vs. 동명사 구분법

Part 5

to부정사 | 동명사

▶ 3형식 동사의 목적어 역할을 하는 to부정사

- ☐ hope, want 바라다, 원하다
- ☐ need 필요하다
- ☐ intend 의도하다
- ☐ choose 선택하다
- ☐ plan 계획하다
- ☐ promise 약속하다

The accountants **plan** [**to increase** / increasing] revenue by 40 percent over the next two years.
회계사들은 다음 2년 동안 40퍼센트까지 수익을 증가시키는 것을 계획한다.

▶ 5형식 동사 수동태의 목적격 보어 역할을 하는 to부정사

- ☐ be allowed to do ~하도록 허용되다
- ☐ be advised to do ~하도록 권고되다
- ☐ be expected to do ~하는 것이 예상되다
- ☐ be reminded to do ~하도록 상기시켜지다
- ☐ be required[invited, asked] to do ~하는 것이 요구되다, 요청되다

New employees **are required** [making / **to make**] an online profile and complete all training modules.
신입 직원들은 온라인 프로필을 만들고, 모든 교육 모듈을 완료하는 것이 요구된다.

▶ 명사를 수식하는 to부정사

- ☐ plan 계획
- ☐ way 방법
- ☐ effort 노력
- ☐ proposal 제안
- ☐ time 때, 시간
- ☐ decision 결정

Park rangers are installing new trash cans at campsites in an **effort** [cutting / **to cut**] down on litter.
공원 경비원들은 쓰레기를 줄이려는 노력의 일환으로 캠핑장에 새로운 쓰레기통을 설치할 것이다.

▶ 부사의 역할을 하는 to부정사

to부정사는 '~하기 위해서'라는 뜻으로 목적을 나타낼 수 있는데, 토익에서는 이 부사적 용법으로 가장 많이 출제된다. 선택지에 to부정사가 있고, 빈칸 앞에 제시된 문장 구조가 완전하다면 to부정사를 정답으로 고르면 된다.

Place the cardboard packaging on the floor [**to create** / creates] a safe surface for assembly of the product.
(관용적 표현으로 in order to do로 출제되기도 해요.)
제품의 조립을 위한 안전한 표면을 만들기 위해 판지 포장재를 바닥에 놓아주십시오.

Practice

1. Managers with a heavy workflow are allowed ------- our instant messaging software for efficient counseling.

(A) to use (B) should use
(C) using (D) used

2. Sumatra Coffee House launched a limited-edition beverage ------- its 25th year in business.

(A) celebrates (B) to celebrate
(C) celebrated (D) was celebrating

▶ 3형식 동사의 목적어 역할을 하는 동명사

☐ avoid 피하다 ☐ recommend 권고하다 ☐ consider 고려하다
☐ enjoy 즐기다 ☐ suggest 제안하다 ☐ mind 꺼리다

You may come in for a meal at any time, but we **recommend** [to make / **making**] a reservation, as our food is in high demand.

식사를 위해 언제든지 들어오실 수 있지만, 저희 음식이 매우 수요가 높기 때문에 예약하시는 것을 권고 드립니다.

서아쌤 비밀Tip

동명사는 명사의 역할을 할 수 있기 때문에 명사와 동명사를 구분하는 문제가 자주 출제돼요. 문법적 특징으로 아주 쉽게 구분할 수 있으니 꼭 비교해서 알아두세요. 특히 동명사는 training, opening, planning, funding, advertising과 같이 -ing로 끝나는 명사와도 형태가 같으니 꼭 구분할 수 있어야 해요!

	동명사	명사
앞에 관사를 사용할 수 있나요?	NO	YES
뒤에 목적어를 가질 수 있나요?	YES	NO
누구의 수식을 받나요?	부사	형용사

▶ 동명사 관용 표현

☐ be committed[dedicated] to -ing ~에 전념하다, 헌신하다 (동명사는 전치사의 목적어 역할도 할 수 있어요.)
☐ have difficulty (in) -ing ~에 어려움을 겪다
☐ spend 시간/돈 (in) -ing ~하는 데 시간/돈을 소비하다
☐ by -ing ~함으로써
☐ up(on) -ing ~하자마자
☐ look forward to -ing ~을 기대하다, 고대하다 (주로 Part 6 문법 문제로 자주 출제돼요.)

Mr. Archibald **is dedicated to** [**maintaining** / maintain] strong relationships with all business clients.

아치바드 씨는 모든 비즈니즈 고객들과 강력한 관계를 유지하는데 전념한다.

A leave of absence from work may be requested **by** [filled / **filling**] out a holiday request form.

휴가는 휴가 요청 양식을 작성함으로써 요청되어야 한다.

✔ Practice

3. Concertgoers complained about spending too much time ------- for the performance to begin.

(A) wait (B) to wait
(C) waiting (D) waited

4. The CEO of Trident Motors will consider ------- the manufacturing plant to accommodate more staff.

(A) expand (B) expanding
(C) to expand (D) expansion

Check-up Test

강의 바로보기

1. Hotel guests are advised ------- the tourism center for brochures about local attractions and activities.
   (A) visiting
   (B) to visit
   (C) visits
   (D) having visited

2. Many cafés and restaurants now provide reusable metal straws ------- plastic pollution.
   (A) is prevented
   (B) prevent
   (C) to prevent
   (D) prevented

3. The Arctic expedition leader hoped to decrease fatigue among team members by ------- backpack loads.
   (A) light
   (B) lighten
   (C) lightly
   (D) lightening

4. All individuals who have joined the fitness center this month are reminded ------- next week's welcome session.
   (A) to attend
   (B) attended
   (C) be attended
   (D) attending

5. According to the engineer, the security system needs ------- every three years.
   (A) were upgraded
   (B) to be upgraded
   (C) upgrades
   (D) upgrade

6. ------- shifts for staff is one of a manager's most crucial responsibilities at La Belle Bistro.
   (A) Schedules
   (B) Scheduling
   (C) Schedule
   (D) Scheduled

7. Willow Apparel plans ------- 50 to 80 percent discounts on all summer clothing to make storage room for the new winter season stock.
   (A) offering
   (B) to offer
   (C) offers
   (D) be offered

8. The Business 100 course helps those who have difficulty in ------- their skills for a wide variety of positions in business.
   (A) utilizing
   (B) utilize
   (C) to utilize
   (D) utilization

9. For improved performance, avoid ------- the running machine on an uneven surface.
   (A) operated
   (B) operation
   (C) operating
   (D) operates

10. From this November, RX Pharmaceuticals will spend a great deal of time ------- its latest range of quick-relief pain medications.
   (A) test
   (B) testing
   (C) tested
   (D) tests

11. The ferry service in New Zealand is a convenient way for tourists ------- since there are various wineries scattered across small islands.

(A) travel
(B) traveled
(C) to travel
(D) travels

12. Singers and dancers thinking about ------- a career in the entertainment industry are encouraged to sign up with a reputable management agency.

(A) pursuing
(B) pursue
(C) pursues
(D) pursued

13. The financial planner made some suggestions for successfully ------- change in the office maintenance costs.

(A) introducing
(B) introductive
(C) introduces
(D) introduction

14. Even though all motorists are required ------- the traffic laws, many drivers disregard them and cause road accidents.

(A) to obey
(B) obeys
(C) obeyed
(D) obeying

15. Pisa Italian Restaurant will consider ------- its range of pizza toppings in order to provide a greater variety of options for vegan diners.

(A) enlarge
(B) enlargement
(C) enlarging
(D) enlarged

16. Tenants who ------- to finish a property rental contract before the date of expiry must notify their landlord in writing.

(A) renew
(B) preview
(C) intend
(D) initiate

17. The largest domestic airline in Singapore has made a decision ------- its fares as a way of drawing more customers.

(A) reduced
(B) reduction
(C) reduces
(D) to reduce

18. The seminar slides suggest ------- staff incentive programs to increase productivity.

(A) implementing
(B) implementation
(C) to implement
(D) implemented

19. SignalStream Broadcasting is committed to ------- the latest global economic news for stock investment.

(A) delivering
(B) deliver
(C) delivered
(D) delivery

20. Aspire Bank's security software has been providing routine updates ------- strengthen network security.

(A) when
(B) in order to
(C) during
(D) in front of

강의 바로보기

고득점 필수 포인트 분사&분사구문

Part 5

분사 분사구문

▶ 형용사의 역할을 하는 분사

형용사와 분사가 선택지에 둘 다 있다면 형용사가 정답일 확률이 높아요.

분사는 형용사와 동일하게 명사를 수식할 수 있고, 주격 보어와 목적격 보어 자리에 모두 올 수 있다. '~하는'이라는 능동의 의미를 가지면 현재분사(-ing)를, '~되는'이라는 수동의 의미를 가지면 과거분사(p.p.)를 사용한다.

The [revising / **revised**] **assembly process** will be introduced on August 1st.
수정된 조립 과정은 8월 1일에 소개될 것이다.

Azalea Engineering is a **construction firm** [specialization / **specializing**] in swimming pool installation.
아젤리아 엔지니어링 사는 수영장 설치를 전문으로 하는 건설 회사이다.

분사 뒤에 목적어나 전치사구 등이 붙는 경우, 명사 뒤에 위치해 명사를 수식해요.

Convention attendees **found Sigma Corporation's new tablet computer** very [**satisfying** / satisfied].
컨벤션 참석자들은 시그마 주식회사의 새로운 태블릿 컴퓨터가 매우 만족스럽다고 생각했다.

▶ p.p. 형태의 형용사로 굳어진 분사

- ☐ detailed 상세한
- ☐ designated 지정된
- ☐ skilled, experienced 숙련된
- ☐ revised 수정된
- ☐ distinguished 저명한
- ☐ attached 첨부된
- ☐ qualified 적격의
- ☐ reduced 할인된
- ☐ customized 고객 맞춤의
- ☐ preferred 우선의
- ☐ proposed 제안된
- ☐ damaged 손상된
- ☐ limited 한정된
- ☐ advanced 상급의
- ☐ dedicated 헌신하는

Edinburgh Heritage is offering a [**reduced** / reducing] **price** on all city tours to draw more tourists.
에딘버러 헤리티지 사는 더 많은 여행객들을 끌어들이기 위해 모든 도시 투어에 대해 할인된 가격을 제공하고 있다.

▶ -ing 형태의 형용사로 굳어진 분사

- ☐ leading 일류의
- ☐ lasting 지속적인
- ☐ existing 현존의
- ☐ promising 전도유망한
- ☐ remaining 남아 있는, 잔여의
- ☐ demanding 힘든

The entrepreneur made a [lasted / **lasting**] **impression** with her confident presentation.
그 사업가는 자신감 있는 발표로 지속적인 인상을 남겼다.

Practice

1. The main responsibility of our technical safety team is to check for any ------- machine components.

(A) damaging (B) damaged
(C) to damage (D) have damaged

2. Mr. Harris confirmed there is enough money ------- in the business account to fund an excursion for all staff.

(A) remains (B) remainder
(C) remained (D) remaining

분사구문 문제는 아래 두 가지 유형으로 출제되는데, 정답 단서를 찾는 방법이 다르므로 비교해서 학습하는 것을 추천한다.

▶ 빈칸에 알맞은 분사 형태 고르기

분사가 들어갈 빈칸 뒤에 목적어가 있으면 현재분사를, 목적어 없이 전치사구 또는 부사가 있다면 과거분사를 정답으로 고른다.

Before [submitted / **submitting**] **the application form**, ensure that all necessary fields have been completed.

신청 양식을 제출하기 전에, 모든 필요한 영역들이 작성 완료되었는지를 확실히 하십시오.

Although [**reviewed** / reviewing] **regularly**, the sales figures were found to contain several errors.

정기적으로 검토되었음에도 불구하고, 매출 수치는 여러 오류를 포함하고 있는 것으로 밝혀졌다.

▶ 분사구문의 알맞은 시제 고르기

제시된 분사구문을 해석했을 때 주절과 동일한 시제라면 단순시제(-ing/p.p.)가, 주절보다 앞선 시제라면 완료시제(having p.p.)가 정답이다.

[Entering / **Having entered**] the museum 20 minutes before closing time, Mr. Lee **was** pleased to be given one hour to view the exhibits.

마감 시간 20분 전에 박물관에 입장해서, 리 씨는 전시회를 보는 데 한 시간이 주어진 것에 기뻐했다.

서아쌤 비밀Tip

분사구문은 빈칸 뒤에 위치한 분사구문을 이끌 알맞은 접속사를 고르는 부사절 접속사 문제로 활용되어 출제되기도 해요. 이 경우, 해석을 통해 의미상 자연스러운 접속사를 정답으로 선택하면 돼요.

[While / **As**] **stated in his contract**, Josh Meeks will only be expected to work from the office two days per week.

계약서에 명시된 것처럼, 조시 믹스 씨는 일주일에 이틀만 사무실에서 일할 것으로 예상되어진다.

[**After** / If] **evaluating several potential event venues**, Ms. Bertrand decided to hire the banquet hall at Mayfair Hotel.

여러 잠재적인 행사 장소들을 평가한 후에, 버트랜드 씨는 메이페어 호텔에 있는 연회장을 빌리기로 결정했다.

Practice

3. Although ------- numerous awards for her music, Selina Maxwell struggled to sell out many of the venues on her concert tour.

(A) having received (B) receiving
(C) has received (D) received

4. If ------- incorrectly, the solar panel may fail to generate electrical power at an efficient rate.

(A) installation (B) installing
(C) installed (D) installs

Check-up Test

강의 바로보기

1. Due to several recent changes to company policies, all workers will receive a ------- version of the employee handbook.
   (A) revise
   (B) revised
   (C) revising
   (D) revision

2. All kitchen utensils must be ------- before they are used for food preparation.
   (A) sanitizes
   (B) sanitized
   (C) sanitizing
   (D) sanitize

3. The ------- participants in the interview process will be invited to a final evaluation next Friday.
   (A) remains
   (B) remained
   (C) remainders
   (D) remaining

4. Marine Nav Co. is the ------- manufacturer of satellite navigation devices for fishing boats and other vessels.
   (A) leading
   (B) led
   (C) to lead
   (D) leads

5. Glitter Event Planners details ------- options during the initial consultation session.
   (A) customized
   (B) customizing
   (C) customizes
   (D) customize

6. Dixie Park is a poor choice of location for a music festival because of its ------- access to public transportation.
   (A) limitation
   (B) limit
   (C) limited
   (D) limiting

7. All ------- candidates for the security advisor vacancy should have at least four years of experience in a similar role.
   (A) qualifying
   (B) qualified
   (C) qualifies
   (D) qualification

8. While ------- on-the-job training to interns, the assistant office manager will assess their performance.
   (A) providing
   (B) provided
   (C) provide
   (D) provides

9. The user manual has ------- instructions on product assembly and maintenance.
   (A) details
   (B) detail
   (C) detailed
   (D) detailing

10. The enclosed leaflet states all services ------- by Voyager Logistics, and I have marked in red those which you asked about.
   (A) offer
   (B) offering
   (C) offered
   (D) offers

정답 및 해설 p.22

11. In her keynote address, Ms. Julian described the ------- process it took to become a successful entrepreneur.

(A) challenges
(B) challenging
(C) challenge
(D) challenger

12. The ------- employee incentive scheme is designed to improve both staff productivity and workforce morale.

(A) proposed
(B) proposing
(C) proposal
(D) propose

13. Old City Tours encourages tour participants to arrive at the ------- location no later than 10 A.M.

(A) designating
(B) designates
(C) designation
(D) designated

14. Although ------- extra time for event planning, Mr. Lowden failed to meet the expectations of banquet attendees.

(A) having received
(B) be receiving
(C) has received
(D) received

15. The bus terminal's pharmacy is open round the clock, ------- that passengers have access to medical services while waiting for their bus to arrive.

(A) ensure
(B) ensuring
(C) ensured
(D) was ensured

16. Parking spaces ------- with blue lines are reserved for the disabled who are visiting the city council.

(A) highlighting
(B) highlighted
(C) that highlight
(D) are highlighted

17. Premier Realty Group, an ------- Singapore-based company, supports its international employees with residence.

(A) establishes
(B) establish
(C) establishing
(D) established

18. ------- tenants must hand in their parking permit to the apartment building manager on the first floor.

(A) Depart
(B) Departed
(C) Departing
(D) Departure

19. Keep the conference room clean and tidy ------- using it for staff training or meetings.

(A) toward
(B) when
(C) onto
(D) whereas

20. The HarborStone Bank's accounting department has released a financial report ------- its goals for the next quarter.

(A) outline
(B) outlines
(C) outlining
(D) outlined

Playlist 9

강의 바로보기

만점을 부르는 비교구문&가정법 정복하기

Part 5

비교구문 정답 단서 가정법

원급 비교

▶ as + _______ + as: ~만큼 …한/하게

as와 as 사이에 위치한 빈칸에 들어갈 형용사 또는 부사를 골라야 하는 비교구문 유형이다. 문장 내 동사가 1형식이거나 3형식 동사라면 부사를, 2형식 동사일 경우 형용사를 정답으로 고른다.

To create the perfect hot chocolate, the powder **must be mixed** in **as** [quick / **quickly**] **as** possible.

완벽한 핫초코를 만들기 위해, 파우더는 가능한 한 빠르게 섞여져야 한다.

▶ _______ + 복수명사 + as, _______ 불가산명사 + as: ~만큼 많은 수의/양의

빈칸 뒤에 제시되는 「복수명사 + as」를 보고 as many를, 「불가산명사 + as」를 보고 as much를 고르는 유형으로 출제된다.

The city council plans to contact [**as many** / as much] **local residents as** possible to gather feedback about the urban development plan.

시 의회는 도시 개발 계획에 대한 의견을 모으기 위해 가능한 한 많은 지역 주민들에게 연락하는 것을 계획한다.

비교급 비교

▶ (much) _______ + than: ~보다 더/덜 ~한/하게

빈칸 뒤에 제시된 than을 보고 형용사 또는 부사의 비교급 형태를 고르는 비교구문 유형이다.

than 이하가 일반적인 비교 대상을 나타내거나, 문맥상 충분히 유추할 수 있는 경우 생략될 수 있으니 주의!

The newly designed boxes used to ship our merchandise are [rigid / **more rigid**] **than** the old ones.

우리 상품을 배송하는 데 사용되는 새롭게 디자인된 박스들은 예전 것들보다 더 단단하다.

최상급 비교

뒤에 범위가 나오지 않더라도 해석상 자연스럽다면 최상급을 사용해요.

▶ the/소유격 + _______ + (ever) + (of/among/in/during/since 전치사구): 가장 ~한/하게

빈칸 앞에 제시된 the나 소유격을, 빈칸 뒤에 제시된 범위를 나타내는 전치사구를 보고 형용사 또는 부사의 최상급 형태를 고르는 비교구문 유형이다.

Miles Keller was **the** [ambitious / **most ambitious**] **of all the young business entrepreneurs** at the convention.

마일즈 켈러 씨는 총회에서 모든 젊은 비즈니스 사업가들 중에 가장 야망 있었다.

Practice

1. Takealong Industries' commercial propane heaters deliver more warmth to ------- areas.
   (A) wideness (B) widen
   (C) wider (D) widely

2. The Khyber River rose to its ------- level ever during the monsoon season last July.
   (A) high (B) highness
   (C) higher (D) highest

▶ 가정법 과거 — 조건의 의미를 나타내는 가정법 현재는 「If + 주어 + 현재동사~, (please) 동사원형」 구조에서 If를 고르는 유형으로 출제돼요.

☐ If + 주어 + 과거동사 ~, 주어 + would/could/should/might + 동사원형. ~라면, …할 것이다

If we **accepted** your business proposal, you [**would receive** / will receive] an initial investment sum of $5,000.

우리가 귀하의 사업 제안을 수락한다면, 5,000달러의 초기 투자금을 받을 것입니다.

▶ 가정법 과거완료

☐ If + 주어 + had p.p. ~, 주어 + would/could/should/might + have p.p. 만약 ~였다면, ~할 수 있었을 것이다.

If Ms. Hall [completes / **had completed**] the management course last month, she **would have been promoted** to branch supervisor.

만약 홀 씨가 지난달에 관리 교육 코스를 수료했었다면, 지점장으로 승진됐을 것이다.

If Mr. Jenson **had not missed** the appointment to demonstrate our products, he [**could have impressed** / has impressed] the potential investors.

만약 젠슨 씨가 우리 제품을 시연하는 약속을 놓치지 않았더라면, 그는 잠재 투자자들에게 깊은 인상을 남길 수 있었을 것이다.

▶ 가정법 도치

☐ 가정법 현재 도치: Should + 주어 + 동사원형 ~, (please +) 동사원형.
☐ 가정법 과거 도치: 과거동사 + 주어~, 주어 + would/could/should/might + 동사원형.
☐ 가정법 과거완료 도치: Had + 주어 + p.p. ~, 주어 + would/could/should/might + have p.p.

[**Should** / Whenever] the proposed interview arrangement **not work** for you, **notify** Mr. Richardson.

제안된 면접 약속이 귀하에게 맞지 않는다면, 리차드슨 씨에게 알려주십시오.

Had you **informed** us about the press conference earlier, we [**would have prepared** / would prepare] in advance.

만약 기자회견에 대해 저희에게 더 일찍 알려주셨더라면, 저희는 미리 준비할 수 있었을 것입니다.

도치라는 개념이 익숙하지 않죠? 주어와 동사를 서로 바꾸는 것을 '도치'라고 하는데 단지 강조를 위해 하는 것뿐이고, 의미가 달라지지는 않아요! 가정법에서는 도치했다는 것을 확실히 표시하기 위해 If를 삭제한답니다.

Practice

3. If his train from Manchester had arrived on schedule, Mr. Kramer ------- the training workshop's first session.

(A) was attending (B) could have attended
(C) can attend (D) had attended

4. Had Bayview Eagles not offered the promising pitcher a contract, another baseball team ------- so.

(A) should do (B) will be doing
(C) has done (D) would have done

강의 바로보기

Check-up Test

1. Nobody in the Gleetown community fought ------- for the cancellation of the parking lot construction project than Roger Dillon.
   (A) energetic
   (B) more energetic
   (C) energetically
   (D) more energetically

2. Explaining all key points in depth is the ------- aspect of giving a presentation.
   (A) importantly
   (B) more importantly
   (C) most important
   (D) importance

3. The new Vista 8 assembly machine will allow factory workers to complete their tasks much -------.
   (A) more efficient
   (B) most efficiently
   (C) efficient
   (D) more efficiently

4. Ms. Weiss would have been able to participate in the tour of the new factory if her flight ------- on schedule.
   (A) arrives
   (B) will arrive
   (C) had arrived
   (D) arriving

5. Investing in ------- technology companies as possible has proven highly profitable for Ms. Simpson.
   (A) as much
   (B) as many
   (C) so much
   (D) so many

6. Chef Billings prepared one of the most ------- menus the food critic had ever sampled.
   (A) create
   (B) creation
   (C) creative
   (D) creatively

7. North Star Energy trains its call center agents to resolve all customer complaints as ------- as possible.
   (A) quicker
   (B) quickly
   (C) quicken
   (D) quickest

8. Long-term workers may request ------- pay if they feel their skills and experience are of significant value to the company.
   (A) highest
   (B) high
   (C) highly
   (D) higher

9. The government sent workers and emergency supplies to regions where flood relief aid was most -------.
   (A) urgent
   (B) urgency
   (C) urgencies
   (D) urgently

10. The ------- range of properties for sale in Denver can be viewed on Emerald Realty's Web site.
   (A) wide
   (B) width
   (C) widely
   (D) widest

11. In August, Mount Pleasant Amusement Park recorded its ------- monthly attendance figures since opening.

(A) better
(B) good
(C) well
(D) best

12. ------- the stain is still visible after using Vanish Cleanser, consider using our high-strength cleanser, Vanish Plus.

(A) If
(B) So
(C) Even
(D) Such

13. Sales executives should be as ------- as possible when scheduling meetings with potential customers.

(A) flexing
(B) flexed
(C) flexibility
(D) flexible

14. Had flight attendants been aware of the travelers' complaints during the flight, they ------- to change their seats.

(A) could have offered
(B) has offered
(C) is being offered
(D) can be offered

15. The product designers have spent ------- time on user-friendliness as on advanced features for this cell phone.

(A) more than
(B) so many
(C) the most
(D) as much

16. Had Falcon Legal not appointed Mr. Bridges as a senior partner, another law firm ------- so.

(A) does
(B) will do
(C) has done
(D) would have done

17. If Ms. Dixon had not researched the company's goals and philosophy, her interview for the vacancy ------- successful.

(A) has not been
(B) being
(C) would not have been
(D) will not be

18. Lionel Adkins will read excerpts from the ------- book in his Magic Apprentice series.

(A) popularity of
(B) as popular as
(C) most popular
(D) popular than

19. While ------- than anticipated, the overnight snowfall still resulted in many road closures throughout Clark County.

(A) light
(B) lighter
(C) lighted
(D) lightly

20. The world's most ------- technology innovators are expected to attend next month's Robotics&AI Conference in Berlin.

(A) influence
(B) influences
(C) influential
(D) influentially

Playlist 10

강의 바로보기

파트6 접속부사 기술 마스터하기

Part 6

접속부사 | 접속부사의 종류

▶ 접속부사 = '부사'

• 접속사

접속사는 「주어 + 동사」로 구성된 두 개의 절을 연결할 수 있다.

Local residents complained about the traffic congestion [**when** / at that time] **the downtown music festival was held** last weekend.

지역 주민들은 시내 음악 축제가 지난 주말에 개최됐을 때 교통 체증에 대해 불평했다.

• 접속부사

접속부사는 「주어 + 동사 + 목적어 또는 보어」 등으로 구성된 완전한 구조의 두 개의 문장을 의미적으로 연결하는 부사의 역할을 한다.

The marketing campaign for the new TV show **appeared to be very popular** on social media. [Although / **However**], **the number of viewers** for the pilot episode **was disappointing**.

새로운 TV 쇼에 대한 마케팅 캠페인이 소셜 미디어에서 아주 인기인 것처럼 보였다. 하지만, 실험 방송분에 대한 시청자 수는 실망스러웠다.

▶ 접속부사의 위치

접속부사는 부사이기 때문에 문장 내에서 위치가 자유롭다. 따라서 문장의 앞과 뒤, 그리고 문장과 문장 사이에도 올 수 있다.

Even though his work schedule was incredibly busy, Mr. Martinez decided to attend the welcome dinner for new staff [**after all** / so that].

마티네즈 씨의 근무 일정이 놀라울 정도로 바빴음에도 불구하고, 그는 결국 신규 직원들을 위한 환영 저녁식사에 참석하기로 결정했다.

Our interns do not receive the standard employee benefits package and [**therefore** / rather] are not entitled to an employee discount.

우리 인턴들은 표준 직원 복리 후생 제도를 받지 않으므로 직원 할인에 대한 자격이 없다.

Part 6 접속부사 문제는 주로 두 개의 완전한 문장 사이에 있는 빈칸에 알맞은 의미의 접속부사를 고르는 유형으로 출제된다.

Although the latest Spiro washing machine is expensive, it comes with many features. [Likewise / **For example**], the appliance can be controlled directly through a mobile device.

비록 최신 스피로 세탁기가 비싸기는 하지만, 많은 기능들이 딸려 있다. 예를 들어, 그 가전제품은 모바일 기기를 통해 직접 제어될 수 있다.

접속부사 문제는 빈칸 앞과 뒤 문장을 해석해 의미 관계만 파악하면 쉽게 풀 수 있는 유형이지만, 최근에는 지문 전체의 흐름까지 파악해 풀어야 하는 고난도 문제도 출제되고 있으니 다양한 접속부사의 의미를 카테고리별로 분류해서 암기하세요! 이 중에서 However, Therefore, In addition, Additionally, In fact 등은 정답으로 압도적으로 많이 출제되니 시험장에 가기 전에 꼭 알아야 해요.

▶ 대조/양보 접속부사

대조	However 하지만 On the other hand 한편으로는 On the contrary, In contrast 그와 반대로
양보	Nevertheless, Nonetheless, Notwithstanding, Still 그럼에도 불구하고 Even so 그렇기는 하지만 Notwithstanding은 전치사로도 사용할 수 있어요.

▶ 추가/유사/예시/결과/요약 접속부사

추가	Moreover, Besides, In addition, What's more, Additionally, Furthermore 게다가 Also, Plus 또한 Plus는 전치사로도 사용할 수 있어요.
유사	Likewise, Similarly 비슷하게 In the same way 같은 방법으로
예시	For example, For instance 예를 들어
결과	Therefore, Thus 그러므로 As a result 결과적으로 Hence, For that reason 이런 이유로 Accordingly 그에 따라 Consequently, Eventually, After all, Finally, In conclusion 결국, 끝으로 In the end, At last 마침내
요약	In short, In summary, In brief 요컨대

▶ 시간/강조 접속부사

시간	Afterward(s) 나중에 Then 그 때, 그 다음에 Initially 처음에 As always 늘 그렇듯 Previously, Formerly 이전에 So far 지금까지 Since then, After that, Thereafter 그 이후로 At that time 그 당시에
강조	In other words, That is 다시 말해서, 즉 Especially, In particular, Particularly 특히 Absolutely 전적으로 Above all, Best of all 무엇보다도 With that in mind 그 점을 염두에 두고

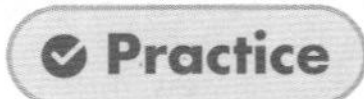

1.

Thank you for your interest in fitness classes at Hardman's Gym. Non-members can attend our aerobics, spinning, and jazzercise classes and pay at the front desk upon arrival. We also run regular pilates and yoga sessions every Thursday and Saturday. -------, those classes are not currently available for non-members.

(A) So that (B) Although (C) Therefore (D) However

2.

At Hong Kong Medical Foundation, our mission is to care for the community using the most comprehensive and connected healthcare system. Our physicians, care teams, and staff demonstrate empathy in every personal interaction and ensure that patients feel understood. -------, we invest in research and pilot programs that lead to better health outcomes for all.

(A) Instead (B) In addition (C) On the contrary (D) Even so

3.

Manchester is the latest city in the United Kingdom to introduce E-scooters. These battery-powered scooters are available to the public and can be used by signing in through a mobile application. They are easy to control and come with advanced GPS technology. -------, E-scooters help to reduce pollution and serve as an environmentally-friendly alternative to traditional forms of transportation.

(A) Best of all (B) For example (C) In any event (D) As always

4.

Originally opened one year ago, Daisy Restaurant has steadily gained an excellent reputation through social media and positive food critic reviews. It is typically packed with delighted customers, no matter what day of the week it is. -------, it is necessary to make a reservation at least one month in advance of your preferred dining date.

(A) Thereafter (B) Additionally (C) For that reason (D) Nevertheless

Check-up Test

강의 바로보기

정답 및 해설 p.27

Questions 1-4 refer to the following article.

Restaurant to Host Event

RIVERDALE (September 15)—Rivertown Bistro, one of the city's most popular dining spots, is inviting food enthusiasts to a special **1.** ------- event on September 28. The restaurant will be offering tastings of its new autumn menu, featuring locally sourced ingredients and seasonal flavors. **2.** -------, diners will have a chance to enter the kitchen and watch the chefs create the food. The event is designed to give patrons a preview of the dishes that will be available throughout autumn. **3.** -------.

Guests who **4.** ------- the event are encouraged to visit the main dining room of Rivertown Bistro's downtown location between 12 P.M. and 8 P.M. No reservations are needed, and dishes will be offered on a first-come, first-served basis.

1. (A) recruiting
(B) sampling
(C) training
(D) fundraising

2. (A) If not
(B) After all
(C) Plus
(D) For now

3. (A) The seasonal menu is scheduled to begin in October.
(B) Most of the chefs have worked in renowned restaurants.
(C) Feedback from diners has been overwhelmingly positive.
(D) The restaurant will reopen in time for the winter season.

4. (A) attending
(B) to attend
(C) attended
(D) are attending

Questions 5-8 refer to the following advertisement.

Harmony Singing Lessons: Find Your Voice

Whether you prefer classical **5.** ------- contemporary styles, consider attending classes with a Harmony Singing instructor to enhance your vocal skills! With a wealth of experience in vocal training, **6.** ------- experienced teachers can help you improve the areas you want to develop. We can provide a personalized learning plan that sets clear goals and addresses the challenges that often lead to frustration. **7.** -------. A Harmony Singing instructor can take you a step further toward singing proficiency!

At Harmony Singing, we believe that singing is a powerful form of self-expression. **8.** -------, we'll help you go beyond basic techniques to find and refine your unique voice. Visit www.harmonysinging.com/lessons to sign up today!

5. (A) is
(B) or
(C) likely
(D) from

6. (A) our
(B) ourselves
(C) ours
(D) us

7. (A) Tickets for performances are provided at a discounted rate.
(B) Singing has been proven to improve health in several ways.
(C) Trying to improve by yourself will have only limited benefits.
(D) It took them several years to become competent singers.

8. (A) So far
(B) With that in mind
(C) On a different note
(D) At that point

Questions 9-12 refer to the following e-mail.

Date: August 13
Subject: Scheduled Maintenance

Dear Mr. Sanderson,

I am writing to inform you of scheduled maintenance to our downtown network. Beginning on August 20 and August 21, network maintenance **9.** ------- performed in your area, which may result in intermittent connectivity between approximately 9:00 P.M. and 5:00 A.M. **10.** -------. Although your **11.** ------- operates outside these hours, please be aware that any overnight tasks that require Internet access might be disrupted. You may **12.** ------- want to consider scheduling critical activities outside this maintenance window. The network will be fully operational by 8:00 A.M., August 21. Thank you for your understanding and cooperation.

Best regards,

Rebecca Tanaka
Network Operations Manager

9. (A) was
(B) will be
(C) can be
(D) has been

10. (A) We are proud to offer the fastest connection speeds in the city.
(B) We look forward to seeing you at the arranged time.
(C) Please refer to the attachment for a precise schedule.
(D) However, all Internet connections will be down during this period.

11. (A) account
(B) vehicle
(C) residence
(D) business

12. (A) fortunately
(B) nevertheless
(C) likewise
(D) therefore

Playlist 11

강의 바로보기

만점강사 시점으로 풀어보는 파트6 문맥파악

Part 6

대명사 | 시제 | 어휘 | 문장삽입

Part 6에서 선택지가 여러 대명사로 구성되어 있다면, 빈칸이 포함된 문장 또는 그 앞에 위치한 문장을 읽고 대명사가 가리키는 대상을 찾아 알맞은 대명사를 골라야 한다. Part 6 대명사 문제로는 인칭대명사와 부정대명사가 출제되는데, 둘 중 인칭대명사의 출제 비중이 훨씬 더 높다.

▶ 인칭대명사를 고르는 경우

he/his/him, she/her, it/its, they/their, we/us/our 등이 주로 정답으로 출제되며, 정답을 고를 때는 ① 대명사가 가리키는 대상의 성별, ② 수, ③ 격까지 반드시 따져야 한다.

> IMPORTANT NOTICE FOR ALL ACCOUNTANTS
>
> Due to the high volume of tax returns this season, several deadlines have been pushed up. As a result, some overtime, including weekend hours, will be necessary. If anyone has an unavoidable commitment that would prevent them from working on a Saturday, please let me know. **Mark Reynolds**, the finance manager, has approved double pay for all weekend shifts. Any questions regarding payment should be directed to [**him** / himself].

▶ 부정대명사를 고르는 경우

one, each, everyone, either, both, some, many, much, all, most 등이 주로 정답으로 출제되며, 정답을 고를 때는 ① 가리키는 대상이 사람 또는 사물인지, ② 단수 또는 복수인지 혹은 불가산명사인지 확인 후 알맞은 부정대명사를 고른다.

> Tired of planning your own events? Dreaming of hosting a party with no stress? Then keep reading! With a wide variety of catering options available, NOW is the perfect time to book! At Gourmet Gatherings Catering, we have a team of **five professional chefs and event planners**, and [everyone / **all**] **have** over 15 years of experience. Our goal is to create the perfect menu to suit your occasion. Call us at 555-123-7840 to start planning your next unforgettable event!

서아쌤 비밀Tip

부정대명사 문제를 풀 때는 문맥상 적절한 것을 선택하는 것도 중요하지만, 부정대명사 자체가 가지고 있는 문법적 특성도 함께 고려해야 정답을 고를 수 있어요.

단수인 대상을 대신하는 부정대명사	one, each, either
복수인 대상을 대신하는 부정대명사	both, several, many, a few, few, all, some, most, everyone
셀 수 없는 대상을 대신하는 부정대명사	much, a little, little, all, some, most

everyone은 복수인 대상을 대신하지만, 단수로 취급해요.

Part 6에서 선택지가 모두 다른 동사의 시제로 구성되어 있다면, 시간 관련 표현을 정답 단서로 잡아 알맞은 시제를 골라야 한다. Part 6 시제 문제는 주로 아래 세 가지 유형으로 출제되므로 유형별 풀이 전략을 비교해서 알아 두면 빠른 문제풀이에 큰 도움이 될 수 있다.

▶ 첫 문장/단락에 시제가 드러난 경우

Dear Mr. Ackerley,

I'm pleased to let you know that the apartment is yours. You [**will pay** / paid] $1,500 per month in rent, along with a security deposit and applicable utilities. The lease is set to begin on Monday, March 20. Please remember to bring a valid form of photo identification when you come to sign the lease. If you have any questions or need further details, feel free to e-mail me at any time.

▶ 지문 유형으로 시제를 알 수 있는 경우

공지(notice), 회람(memo), 공고(announcement) 등의 유형은 앞으로 있을 일들에 대해 알리기 때문에 미래시제가 정답일 확률이 높고, 기사(article)나 후기(review) 유형은 이미 발생한 일에 대해 언급하기 때문에 현재완료시제 또는 과거시제가 정답일 확률이 높다.

Product review

I never **had** a riding lawnmower before. After expanding my garden, I finally **had** enough grass to justify buying a more efficient lawnmower. I **did** a lot of research, and the Mega Mower 5000 **seemed** to be the ideal choice. It **was** more expensive than other models, but all the reviews **were** very positive. So I [decide / **decided**] to treat myself.

특히, 이메일(e-mail)이나 편지(letter) 유형의 지문은 상단의 발신 날짜를 반드시 확인하세요. 이메일과 편지를 보낸 날짜와 지문 내에 제시된 날짜만 단순히 대조해서 시제 문제를 풀 수 있는 경우도 자주 출제돼요.

▶ 단서 없이 시제를 파악해야 하는 경우

빈칸 주변에 시제를 나타내는 시간 표현이 없는 고난도 유형의 경우, 지문 전체적으로 사용된 시제를 정답으로 고르거나 지문의 내용을 파악해 알맞은 시제를 정답으로 골라야 한다.

Dear Mr. Simmons,

I hope this message finds you well. I recently completed my internship with your company and wanted to personally reach out instead of waiting for any official openings to be posted. I [**am writing** / will write] to ask if there might be any current or upcoming opportunities to rejoin your team. Working with you was an invaluable experience, and I would love the chance to continue learning and contributing in the near future.

Part 6에서 선택지가 모두 다른 어휘로 구성되어 있다면, 빈칸에 들어갈 알맞은 의미의 어휘를 고르는 유형이므로 아래 제시된 세 가지 정답 단서 유형을 활용해 문제를 해결하면 된다.

▶ 지시어가 단서로 있는 경우

빈칸이 포함된 문장에 this/these, that/those, the, such, its 등의 지시어가 있는 경우, 빈칸 앞 문장을 살펴 앞에 언급된 대상을 찾으면 된다.

> Dear Sir or Madam,
>
> I purchased a mobile phone from your retail outlet this morning, and I just got home and opened the box. Initially, I was very pleased with the phone's features and appearance. However, upon closer inspection, **I noticed that the screen has a noticeable crack along the bottom edge**. Although I am not seeking a refund, I would be grateful if you could replace **the** [**defective** / discounted] item at no cost.
>
> Thank you for your attention to this matter.

▶ 빈칸 뒤에 단서가 있는 경우

빈칸을 포함한 문장에 지시어나 다른 정답 단서가 없는 경우, 빈칸 뒤 문장에 힌트가 있는 경우도 많다. 특히 첫 문제가 어휘 문제인 경우, 대부분 빈칸 뒤에 위치한 문장에서 단서를 찾을 수 있다.

> ENERGY SOLUTIONS INC.
>
> (November 1) Recent feedback from our customers has shown an overwhelmingly [critical / **positive**] response to the introduction of our new Smart Meters. **Approximately ninety percent of users who provided feedback reported being highly satisfied with the meters' convenience and energy-saving features**. Currently, Smart Meters are installed in around 10,000 households, and we are planning to expand their availability to an additional 15,000 homes by the end of this year.

▶ 전체 지문을 읽어야 하는 경우

특정한 단서가 없어 전체 맥락을 다 읽고 내용을 파악해야 하는 고난도 유형이다. 이 경우, 다른 유형의 문제들을 먼저 풀고 지문의 내용을 이해한 후 가장 마지막으로 푸는 것을 추천한다.

> Bright Children's Hospital **is set to receive a generous donation of $2 million from Sarah Landon,** CEO of Landon Medical Innovations, to support the expansion of its pediatric wing. Ms. Landon, whose contribution will greatly benefit the hospital's future, made the announcement on Tuesday afternoon. **She has committed to personally donating the $2 million, which will be** [**paid** / added] **in three stages, with the first installment scheduled to be transferred to the hospital's board of trustees on October 10.** The board plans to use the initial funds to enlarge the Neonatal Intensive Care Unit(NICU).

Part 6에서 선택지가 문장으로 구성되어 있다면, 문맥을 파악하여 빈칸에 들어갈 알맞은 문장을 골라야 한다.

▶ 선택지의 지시어가 단서인 경우

선택지 문장에 this/these, that/those, the, such, its 등의 지시어가 있는 경우, 빈칸 앞에 위치한 문장에서 해당 지시어가 가리키는 대상을 찾고, 선택지를 해석하여 알맞은 문장을 정답으로 선택한다.

> Subject: Incorrect gym membership charges
>
> Dear Sir/Madam,
>
> I am reaching out again regarding an issue with my gym membership fees for the month of August. After receiving my statement, I noticed an incorrect charge for a late payment from July. When I previously contacted your billing department, I was assured that the incorrect fee would be removed. However, **the latest statement still includes this error.** [**I request that you resolve this matter promptly.** / I will submit the payment immediately.]

▶ 선택지의 접속부사가 단서인 경우

선택지에 접속부사가 포함되어 있는 경우, 접속부사가 정답의 단서일 확률이 매우 높다. 따라서 빈칸 앞에 위치한 문장을 먼저 읽고 접속부사가 포함된 선택지와 의미상 자연스럽게 연결되는지 확인하면 된다.

> CINEMAWORLD MEMBERSHIP RENEWAL OFFER!
>
> **Are you an existing CinemaWorld member wondering whether to renew your annual movie membership?** [In addition, many members have praised our wide range of movies. / **If so, now is the perfect time to take advantage of our exclusive promotion.**] From September 1 to October 31, we are offering additional perks to current members who renew their 1-year or 2-year membership. For instance, you'll receive a 15% discount on your membership fee for the entire term! Reach out to our customer service team at 555-3268 today to renew your membership and continue enjoying unlimited films.

▶ 빈칸 앞뒤를 모두 읽어야 하는 경우

선택지에서 지시어나 접속부사 등의 단서를 찾을 수 없다면, 빈칸 주변을 읽고 정답을 골라야 한다. 쉽게 출제될 경우 빈칸 앞 또는 뒤만 읽어도 문제가 풀리지만, 고난도로 출제될 경우 빈칸의 앞과 뒤를 모두 읽어 문맥을 파악해야만 정답을 찾을 수 있도록 출제된다.

> (London – February 15) A housing research institute reported that property prices have continued to rise steadily for the fourth consecutive year. The primary cause of this is foreign investors purchasing properties at higher prices, driving up demand. As a result, **local buyers are facing tougher competition in the market.** [**A persistent housing shortage is also affecting property prices.** / Construction firms are facing recruitment problems.] **The local government has failed to act on its promise to construct new, low-cost homes for those in need, which increases the value of those houses that are available.**

1.

Hi, everyone,

I have a very big announcement to make about one of the most important members of our team here at Holly Bistro. After 25 years of hard work and dedication, our Head Chef Mauro Materazzi has decided to retire and move back to his hometown in Italy. Our current sous chef, the highly talented Kristi Vennart, ------- Chef Materazzi when he steps down. Chef Materazzi has been mentoring Ms. Vennart since she began working at the restaurant almost nine years ago.

(A) replace (B) was replacing (C) will replace (D) has been replacing

2.

To: All Staff Members
Subject: Customer Service Training

It's time for our annual customer service training workshop. This year, the focus will be on enhancing communication and problem-solving skills. We've introduced new tools to improve how we manage customer inquiries and ensure a positive experience, but it's essential that all staff understands how to use these tools effectively. To accommodate -------, multiple training sessions will be held over the next couple of weeks. You can sign up for a session that suits you by contacting the HR Manager.

(A) itself (B) his (C) whose (D) everyone

3.

In a residential property, homeowners are responsible for ensuring that solar panels are installed efficiently and are regularly inspected to maintain optimal performance. Proper placement is crucial for efficiency. Panels should be positioned in an area free from shade, as obstructions like trees or nearby buildings can reduce their energy production. Also, solar panels should be installed in areas where they can capture the most sunlight. -------. This positioning is key to maximizing exposure to sunlight.

(A) Remember to remove them carefully.
(B) This is typically on a south-facing surface.
(C) Sunlight is known to provide several benefits.
(D) Panels can generate energy in low light.

4.

Thank you for registering for the upcoming Global Pharma Conference. Enclosed is a schedule outlining the times and venues of all keynote speeches and panel discussions. In addition, we are pleased to offer assistance with ------- during the event. In fact, we can arrange shuttle services between the conference center and select hotels at a discounted rate. Should you require this service, please reach out to Lisa Manning, our event coordinator, at 555-7624 for more details.

(A) transportation (B) attendance (C) accommodation (D) transaction

강의 바로보기

Check-up Test

정답 및 해설 p.32

Questions 1-4 refer to the following article.

Horizon Energy Announces Nuclear Project

TOKYO (22 September) – Horizon Energy Corp. **1.** ------- plans to begin construction on a 1,200-megawatt nuclear power plant near Sendai, Japan. **2.** -------. Horizon Energy expects the station to be operational within 36 months and will supply power to national energy provider Nippon Power.

"Our agreement with Nippon Power is a significant step toward achieving **3.** ------- sustainability targets," said Hiroshi Tanaka, CEO of Horizon Energy. "We aim to increase our nuclear capacity to 10 gigawatts within the next decade, supporting Japan's ambitious efforts to **4.** ------- carbon emission goals."

1. (A) announced
(B) announces
(C) will announce
(D) announcing

2. (A) Nuclear power has come under increased scrutiny after several safety concerns.
(B) The facility will utilize advanced nuclear reactors designed to provide low-emission energy.
(C) The move away from nuclear energy signals a notable change in Japan's energy policies.
(D) Almost 10 percent of Japan's energy grid was temporarily without power during the change.

3. (A) we
(B) our
(C) us
(D) ourselves

4. (A) understand
(B) explain
(C) block
(D) reach

Questions 5-8 refer to the following e-mail.

To: Jenna Hartman <jhartman43@snmail.com>
From: Talia Dawson <service@sweetsensationsbakery.com>
Date: 16 February
Subject: Order number 45923

Dear Ms. Hartman,

We received your order for a personalized birthday cake with your daughter's name written on it. We are, of course excited to fulfill your request! **5.** -------, our cake decorator, who specializes in custom designs, will be unavailable for the next two days. Unfortunately, her **6.** ------- means there will be a slight delay in preparing your cake.

7. ------- for the inconvenience, we'd like to offer you a 20 percent discount on this order. Alternatively, we can provide free personalization on your next cake order. **8.** -------. At Sweet Sensations Bakery, customer satisfaction is our top priority!

Sincerely,

Talia Dawson
Customer Service Representative
Sweet Sensations Bakery

5. (A) Accordingly
(B) In brief
(C) However
(D) Then

6. (A) absence
(B) arrival
(C) request
(D) investigation

7. (A) Compensated
(B) To compensate
(C) For compensating
(D) It is compensation

8. (A) So, please let us know your preference.
(B) We guarantee the product will be back in stock soon.
(C) The cake will include several popular cartoon characters.
(D) Above all, our cakes are made with locally sourced ingredients.

Questions 9-12 refer to the following notice.

Dear Staff,

We are pleased to inform you that RBC Enterprises will reimburse employees for relocation and resettlement expenses incurred when transferring to a different company branch. Covered expenses include the **9.** ------- of temporary accommodation, moving services, and any other reasonable requests associated with the move.

To receive reimbursement, please submit an expense report by the first day of the following month. Ensure **10.** ------- item is listed individually with the date, amount, reason for the expense, and a scanned copy of the receipt. Reimbursements should be paid **11.** ------- into your bank accounts on the 7th of each month, alongside your regular salary. **12.** -------.

We appreciate your flexibility and dedication to RBC Enterprises!

Sincerely,

HR Department
RBC Enterprises

9. (A) length
(B) cost
(C) share
(D) content

10. (A) all
(B) which
(C) such
(D) each

11. (A) direct
(B) directs
(C) direction
(D) directly

12. (A) Please remember to include your preferred moving date on the form.
(B) All new employees will receive a $500 resettlement bonus after three months.
(C) Thank you for agreeing to move to our new branch office.
(D) We will inform you in advance if payments are made after this date.

강의 바로보기

만점자들은 무조건 알고 있는 파트7 질문별 특징

Part 7

세부사항 | 추론 | 사실확인 | 주제/목적

Part 7에서 가장 많은 문제 비중을 차지하는 세부사항은 질문에서 물어보는 대상, 날짜, 장소, 방법, 수량, 가격 등의 정보를 찾아내야 하는 유형이다. Wh-의문사와 함께 질문의 키워드를 파악하고, 지문에서 키워드가 제시된 부분을 읽고 문제를 풀면 된다.

▶ 질문 유형

Wh-의문사	**Who** will get **promoted** at the end of **November**? **Whom** did **Mr. Thomas meet** at the technology convention? **What** will **happen** on **Fridays**? **When** do the **employees** plan to **submit** productivity **reports**? **Where** will the **auction** be **held**? **Why** did SkyVally Shopping Mall **undergo renovation**? **How much** will **Ms. MacDonald pay per month** for her **membership**?

세부사항 유형 문제를 정확하게 풀기 위해서는 다음 세 가지 스텝을 따라 질문을 분석하는 것을 추천해요. ① 제시된 Wh-의문사 확인하기 ② 동사를 키워드로 잡기 ③ 문장 가장 마지막에 위치한 명사 위주로 보기! 특히, 전치사 뒤에 제시된 명사의 경우 질문의 키워드 역할을 하는 경우가 정말 많아요. 추가로, 의문사에 따른 정답 단서가 아래 제시된 패턴으로 나오는 경우가 많으니 정리해 두세요.

- Who → Mr., Ms., 사람 이름 찾기
- When → 숫자, day, A.M., P.M. 등 시간 표현 찾기
- Why → Since, Because, Due to 등 이유 접속사/전치사 찾기
- What ~ next? → 지문의 후반부 읽기
- Where → 전치사 + 고유명사, Avenue, Street 등 장소 표현 찾기
- How → By -ing, If you're interested ~, Please ~ 등 방법 찾기

Practice

ROSEWOOD TOWN COUNCIL (Town Planning Office)
Notice for Residents of Rosewood

On May 1, Rosewood's Town Planning Office will close Main Street to all vehicles. The street will be pedestrianized and include new seating areas and food vendors. With this change, the city will attract a greater number of tourists, which will in turn boost the local economy.

1. What change is the Town Planning Office making?

(A) Relocating some businesses
(B) Improving a transportation system
(C) Closing a street to traffic
(D) Enlarging a parking area

2. Why is the new policy being implemented?

(A) To increase local tourism
(B) To lower property prices
(C) To encourage bicycle use
(D) To prevent littering

추론 유형은 지문에 제시되어 있지 않은 내용을 유추해야 하므로 고난도 유형에 속한다. 고득점을 목표로 한다면 틀려서는 안 되는 유형이며, 세부사항 유형과 달리 단서가 직접적으로 나타나지 않으므로 패러프레이징 스킬을 활용하여 정답을 골라야 한다.

▶ 질문 유형

most likely	Where is the leaflet **most likely** found? Where does Ms. Olivia **most likely** work? What did Ms. Hiharu **most likely** want to discuss online? What will **most likely** happen on July 18? For whom is the advertisement **most likely** intended? Who **most likely** is Cory Bullard? When **most likely** will Mr. Kwon meet his clients?
suggested	What is **suggested** about Sweet Home Real Estate?
inferred	What can be **inferred** about the new tenant? — 전치사 about 뒤에 제시된 명사가 질문의 키워드에요.
imply	What does the memo **imply** about the program?
probably	What is **probably** true about Mr. Halliday?

추론 문제는 Part 7에서 난이도가 가장 높은 문제 유형으로, 정답을 맞히려면 지문 전체에 대한 이해가 필요해요. 세트 내의 다른 문제들을 먼저 풀어 자연스럽게 지문의 흐름을 파악한 후 추론 문제를 나중에 푼다면 문제풀이 시간을 크게 줄일 수 있어요. 또, 선택지를 먼저 읽고 소거법과 패러프레이징을 적극 활용한다면 비교적 쉽게 정답을 도출할 수 있답니다!

Spring Fresh Mineral Water

Spring Fresh Mineral Water is the purest and most refreshing mineral water on the market. The water is bottled at its source: a spring in the Scottish Highlands! Many of our clients place bottles of our water in the mini-fridges of their rooms, and the feedback from their guests is highly positive. If you would also like to keep your guests refreshed, consider making your first bulk order today! Visit www.springfreshmineralwater.com to view our pricing and read testimonials from our clients. You can also watch short clips on our Web site, showing how we collect and bottle the water.

3. For whom is the advertisement most likely intended?

(A) Airplane passengers
(B) Hotel owners
(C) Tour members
(D) Event attendees

4. What is NOT indicated as being on a Web site?

(A) Costs
(B) Videos
(C) Discounts
(D) Reviews

사실확인 유형은 일치하는 것을 고르는 일치 유형과 일치하지 않는 것을 고르는 NOT 유형으로 구분할 수 있다. 지문과 선택지의 내용을 하나하나 비교 분석하여 소거법으로 정답을 골라야 하는 고난도 유형이며, 지문의 내용이 선택지에 제시될 때 다른 품사나 동의어 등으로 바뀌어 제시되므로 이에 유의해야 한다.

▶ 질문 유형

일치	What is **true** about Ms. Joan? What is **mentioned** about the presentation materials? What does the e-mail **indicate** about the workshop? What is **stated** about the special offer? What is **included** with the letter?
NOT	What is **NOT true** about EPBN internship programs? What is **NOT mentioned** as an advantage of purchasing Flux Toy? What is **NOT indicated** about The National History Museum? What is **NOT stated** in the form? What information is **NOT included** on the advertisement?

일치 유형과 NOT 유형은 질문에서 주로 about 뒤에 나오는 명사를 키워드로 잡는 것은 동일하지만, 서로 묻는 것이 다르기 때문에 문제를 풀 때는 접근 방법이 달라야 해요. 토익 만점강사인 제가 추천하는 문제풀이 방법은 아래와 같아요.

- 일치 유형: 질문에서 키워드 파악 → 지문에서 키워드 찾기 → 지문에서 키워드 주변 읽기 → 선택지 보고 정답 선택
- NOT 유형: 질문에서 키워드 파악 → 선택지 먼저 읽기 → 지문에서 키워드가 제시된 부분 읽기 → 선택지와 대조하여 정답 선택

Celebrate International Film Week at CinemaFest!

CinemaFest is back, and this year it runs from September 12 to 18. It's the perfect opportunity to experience the magic of cinema in Maplewood for the first time or revisit your favorite local theaters. You might even catch multiple films during this week-long celebration! Ten popular cinemas will offer special screenings of classic and contemporary films, with a special movie pass that includes a movie ticket, popcorn, a drink, and a small treat – all for the reduced price of $12. Booking your passes in advance is highly recommended. CinemaFest attracts hundreds of locals and visitors each year, so don't miss your chance to enjoy great films at a great price. Visit www.maplewoodfilmfest.org for a list of participating theaters and film schedules.

5. What is mentioned about CinemaFest?
(A) It will be held for the first time.
(B) It will take place in one location.
(C) It will be held for one week.
(D) It will be attended by actors.

6. What is NOT included with the movie pass?
(A) A ticket
(B) A beverage
(C) A snack
(D) A poster

주제/목적 유형은 세부사항이나 추론, 사실확인 유형에 비해 많은 출제 비중을 가진 것은 아니지만, 쉽게 출제된다면 지문의 첫 문장 또는 첫 문단에서 정답을 빠르게 고를 수 있는 유형이다. 다만, 고난도로 출제될수록 지문 전체 흐름을 파악해야 글의 주제나 목적을 알 수 있는 경우가 많으므로 첫 문장이나 첫 문단을 읽고 정답을 찾을 수 없다면 다른 문제를 먼저 풀고 마지막으로 푸는 것이 좋다.

▶ 질문 유형

주제	What is the **main topic[subject]** of the letter? What is the memo **mainly about**? What are the writers **mainly discussing**? What does the article **mainly discuss**?
목적	What is the (main) **purpose** of the notice? **Why** was the notice **written[sent]**? **Why** did Mr. Showers **contact** Mr. Ford? **Why** did Ms. Brenson **send** an e-mail?

이 유형의 문제들은 주제 또는 목적을 나타내는 표현들 뒤에 정답이 제시되는 경우가 대부분이니 아래 표현들을 암기해 두고 빠르게 정답을 찾아보세요.

This e-mail is to advise you that ~. 이 이메일은 ~라는 점을 귀하께 권고드리기 위함입니다.
I would like to inquire about ~. ~에 대해 문의드리고 싶습니다.
I'm pleased[delighted] to announce ~. ~을 알리게 되어 기쁩니다.
I was wondering if ~. ~인지 아닌지 궁금합니다.

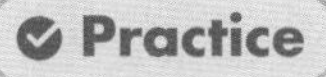

Dear Mr. Grant,

This e-mail is to respond to your inquiry about flower choices for the landscaping project at Parkside Gardens. We recommend planting five flower clusters per designated area for optimal coverage. Our most popular flowers are the lavender, the marigolds, and the daisies. Please note that if you choose lavender, it requires ample sunlight and should not be placed in shaded areas. If you provide us with your flower preferences and detailed instructions on the planting locations, our team can arrange the flowers accordingly without interrupting the park's daily activities.

Emily Hargrove, Blooming Landscapes

7. What is the purpose of the e-mail?
(A) To explain the delay of an order
(B) To present options for a project
(C) To recommend rescheduling some work
(D) To request samples of some flowers

8. What does Ms. Hargrove indicate about the lavender?
(A) It requires an ample amount of moisture.
(B) It is available in several colors.
(C) It should not be planted in dimly lit areas.
(D) It is more expensive than other types of flowers.

문장삽입 유형은 매 시험마다 2문제가 출제되는데, 지문과 문제에 해당 문장이 들어갈 위치를 나타내는 숫자가 있기 때문에 한눈에 알아볼 수 있다. 문장이 들어갈 위치가 지문 전체에 걸쳐 있으므로 제시된 문장을 먼저 읽고 지문의 전체적인 흐름을 파악하면서 다른 문제들과 동시에 푸는 것을 추천한다.

▶ 질문 유형

문장삽입	In which of the positions marked **[1], [2], [3], and [4]** does the following sentence best belong?

문장삽입 유형은 문제에서 따옴표 안에 들어가 있는 문장을 먼저 분석하세요. 제시된 문장의 의미를 파악해야 어느 문단 덩어리에 들어갈 수 있는지 대략적으로라도 알 수 있기 때문인데요. 무엇보다도, 제시된 문장 내에서 정답의 단서가 될 수 있는 힌트를 캐치해 다른 문제를 푸는 동안에도 각 위치에 하나씩 대입하면서 푸는 것이 좋아요. 우리가 활용할 수 있는 정답 단서는 쌤이 정리해 줄게요~!

- 대명사: his, your, her, its, they, our 등
- 지시어: this, that, these, those, such 등
- the + 명사
- 접속부사: Since then, For example, Also, However 등

To: All ClearSight Technologies Staff

On the afternoon of Friday, September 15, we will be hosting an event to unveil our new company innovation, and we hope you will all join us. At this gathering, we will showcase the latest developments and features of our newest cellphone, the M505, emphasizing the collective effort that has driven ClearSight Technologies to this exciting milestone. – [1] –. This event will take place at the Grandview Hotel and will mark the official launch of the M505. – [2] –. In addition to our valued staff, the event will be attended by numerous journalists, our shareholders, and investors. There is no need to request time off from work. – [3] –. We do ask, however, that you inform our HR department if you plan to attend. We look forward to celebrating with you. – [4] –.

Alex Whitman

9. What is the main purpose of the memorandum?

(A) To seek volunteers to organize an event
(B) To express gratitude to staff for their work
(C) To invite workers to a product launch
(D) To announce sales figures for a new product

10. In which of the positions marked [1], [2], [3], and [4] does the following sentence best belong?

"Our offices will be closing at lunchtime."

(A) [1]
(B) [2]
(C) [3]
(D) [4]

의도파악 문제는 온라인 채팅 또는 문자메시지 지문에서 특정 메시지의 숨겨진 의도를 찾아내는 유형이다. 문제를 풀 때 주의할 점은 따옴표 안에 인용된 문장 자체가 나타내는 의미의 선택지를 고르면 오답일 확률이 높고, 해당 메시지 앞 또는 뒤, 혹은 앞뒤 모두를 읽고 문맥 속에서 뜻하는 바를 찾아야 하는 것이다.

▶ 질문 유형

의도파악	**At 4:24 P.M.**, what does Mr. Williams (most likely) mean when he writes, **"That's a great idea"**? **At 10:56 A.M.**, what does Ms. Reynolds imply when she writes, **"Go ahead"**?

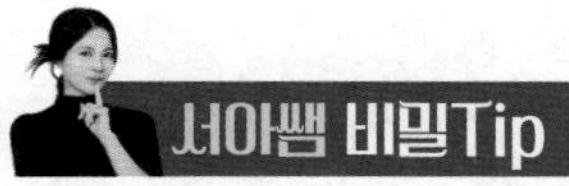

최근 시험에서 의도파악 인용 문장으로 등장했던 표현들을 모아서 보여 줄게요. 대부분의 인용구들은 어려운 단어가 포함되어 있어 해석이 어렵거나 암기로만 뜻을 알 수 있는 숙어는 등장하지 않아요. 주로 짧은 문장으로 출제되고, 제안이나 요청에 대한 수락이나 거절의 표현이 가장 많이 나와요.

Sure thing. 물론이죠.
Ok, go ahead. 알겠어요, 그렇게 하죠.
Good plan. 좋은 계획이에요.
Well, I already tried that. 음, 그건 이미 시도해 봤어요.
I've got it. 이해했어요.
Will do. 그럴게요.
What's your guess? 짐작이 되시는게 있나요?
This is very unusual. 이건 평소와 같지 않아요.

Practice

Ted Garrigan [1:12 P.M.] Hi, Lynne. I'm afraid we won't be able to deliver Mr. Ritter's order today as scheduled. Would you mind calling to let him know?

Lynne Dibbs [1:13 P.M] No problem. He did mention that he needs that order urgently, though. He has new workers starting on Monday, and they all need those work shirts and work pants. When do you think we can get them to him?

Ted Garrigan [1:15 P.M.] The manufacturer is based overseas, and they've had a delay due to inclement weather, so it's hard to say.

Lynne Dibbs [1:17 P.M.] That's too bad. What's your guess?

Ted Garrigan [1:19 P.M.] No later than this Friday.

11. What most likely has Mr. Ritter purchased?
(A) Software
(B) Vehicles
(C) Stationery
(D) Uniforms

12. At 1:17 P.M., what does Ms. Dibbs most likely mean when she writes, "What's your guess?"
(A) She thinks a cost estimate is incorrect.
(B) She needs to calculate the overall cost.
(C) She wants to know a rough delivery date.
(D) She has to check a weather forecast.

동의어 문제는 단일지문과 다중지문에서 모두 출제되는 유형으로, 매 시험마다 1~3문제가 출제된다. 해당 단어가 포함된 문장만 읽어도 빠르게 정답을 고를 수 있는 비교적 쉬운 유형이므로 세트에서 가장 먼저 푸는 것이 좋고, 고득점을 목표로 한다면 반드시 다 맞혀야 한다.

▶ 질문 유형

동의어	The word "**submit**" in **paragraph 1, line 3**, is closest in meaning to In the information, the word "**handle**" in **paragraph 2, line 4**, is closest in meaning to

다중지문에서 동의어 문제가 출제되면, 지문의 종류를 문제에서 꼭 언급하니, 해당 지문을 바로 읽으면 돼요.

▶ 최신 기출 동의어

- ☐ judge = determine 생각하다
- ☐ running = operating, functioning 작동되는, 기능하는
- ☐ top = leading 최고의, 선도적인
- ☐ address = respond to 처리하다
- ☐ suit = satisfy 만족시키다, (수요 등에) 맞다
- ☐ solution = answer 해결책
- ☐ promote = publicize 홍보하다
- ☐ coverage = protection 보장
- ☐ disturbing = interrupting 방해하는
- ☐ driven = caused 유발된
- ☐ reflect = show 보여주다
- ☐ feature = include (특별히) 포함하다
- ☐ cover = report on 보고하다
- ☐ design = create 만들다
- ☐ pass = elapse (시간이) 지나다
- ☐ prepare = get ready 준비되다
- ☐ complimentary = free 무료의
- ☐ fine = skillful 숙련된
- ☐ sole = only 유일한
- ☐ hit = success 성공작
- ☐ temper = moderate 완화시키다
- ☐ exceed = surpass 뛰어넘다

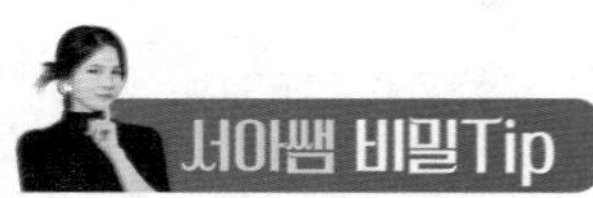

동의어 문제에서 출제되는 단어는 여러 뜻을 동시에 가지고 있는 다의어에요. 따라서 해당 단어가 주로 쓰이는 뜻의 선택지를 고르면 오답일 확률이 매우 높고, 반드시 단어가 속한 문장을 읽어 문맥 속에서 쓰인 의미와 동일한 단어를 정답으로 선택해야 해요. 예를 들어, Our menu can be changed to suit clients' tastes.라는 문장에서 taste의 동의어를 골라야 한다면, 선택지에는 반드시 flavor(맛)가 오답 선택지로 있을 거예요. '고객들의 선호에 맞게 메뉴가 변경될 수 있다'는 문맥을 파악한다면 정답으로는 preference(선호)를 골라야겠죠?

Practice

Elite Events Planning has been creating unforgettable events for over two decades. We utilize the latest techniques to ensure your event is seamless and memorable.

Our expertise spans corporate functions, weddings, and social gatherings. We work closely with you to design every detail. Additionally, we create custom flyers and posters that you can use to promote your event effectively. Contact us today to make your next event extraordinary.

13. What is indicated about Elite Events Planning?

(A) It primarily organizes wedding receptions.
(B) It was established more than 20 years ago.
(C) It has received positive reviews online.
(D) It is currently hiring new employees.

14. The word "promote" in paragraph 2, line 2, is closest in meaning to

(A) publicize
(B) commend
(C) advance
(D) encourage

Check-up Test

강의 바로보기

정답 및 해설 p.37

Questions 1-2 refer to the following notice.

Dr. Joseph Shimizu, DMD
Maintenance Rules for Our Clinic

To maintain the highest standards of care and ensure a clean and welcoming environment for our patients, it is essential to follow consistent practices in facility maintenance. Please review the newly revised guidelines highlighted below.

- Wipe down all surfaces, including chairs, countertops, and any other touchpoints, with approved disinfectants after each patient visit
- Refill supplies, such as gloves, masks, gauze, and disposable bibs, in every treatment room at the end of each shift
- Follow all sterilization and calibration protocols for oral care tools and equipment, like the autoclave, X-ray machines, and dentist's handpieces
- Dispose of any biohazard waste (e.g. sharps, gauze, and other potentially infectious materials) by using a specially designated, leak-proof container
- Immediately notify Dr. Shimizu or a lead technician of any equipment malfunctions, supply shortages, or other issues that could impact patient care

1. For whom is the notice most likely intended for?

(A) Medical students
(B) Dental assistants
(C) Receptionists
(D) Registered nurses

2. What is NOT a stated guideline for maintaining a clinic?

(A) Faulty machinery must be reported.
(B) High-touch surfaces must be sanitized.
(C) Some materials must be discarded separately.
(D) Supplies must be restocked before a shift starts.

Questions 3-4 refer to the following text message chain.

SARA MEYERS [8:12 A.M.]
Hey, Rob... I'm running late for the investor presentation.

ROB KELLER [8:13 A.M.]
Oh no, what happened? It's crucial that you're here—I'm not sure I can handle the pitch alone.

SARA MEYERS [8:15 A.M.]
I'm really sorry. A water pipe burst at my house, and I'm waiting for a plumber to fix it. I'll be there as soon as I can.

ROB KELLER [8:17 A.M.]
Oh, that sounds like a mess! I hope you get it taken care of quickly. No worries, I'll start the presentation and keep them engaged.

SARA MEYERS [8:18 A.M.]
Thanks, Rob. I'll call the head office and let Mr. Johnson know I'll be a bit delayed.

ROB KELLER [8:20 A.M.]
Good plan. Keep me posted. Hope to see you soon!

SARA MEYERS [8:21 A.M.]
Will do. Thanks again, talk to you later.

3. What is suggested about Ms. Meyers?

(A) She will send some slides to Mr. Keller.
(B) She recently invested in a business.
(C) She plans to take a day off work.
(D) She is currently at home.

4. At 8:20 A.M., what does Mr. Keller mean when he writes, "Good plan"?

(A) He thinks that Ms. Meyers has made a poor decision.
(B) He believes Ms. Meyers should get in contact with a colleague.
(C) He would prefer that Ms. Meyers revise a presentation plan.
(D) He is confident that he can lead a presentation by himself.

Questions 5-7 refer to the following article.

GRAND OPENING OF TECH MART'S LARGEST STORE

TORONTO (May 12) –Tech Mart, one of the nation's leading electronic appliance retailers, announced today that it will be celebrating the grand opening of its largest retail location in Toronto next month. The new store, located in the heart of the city's bustling commercial district, spans over 100,000 square feet and will feature a wide range of electronics, from home appliances and smart devices to entertainment systems and personal gadgets.

"This new location will offer customers the latest in cutting-edge technology and home solutions," said Carla Dempsey, CEO of Tech Mart, in a press release. "We're thrilled to bring our largest store yet to Toronto, where customers can enjoy interactive displays, personalized consultations, and exclusive in-store deals."

The grand opening event will take place on Saturday, June 5, from 9:00 A.M. to 9:00 P.M. at the new Toronto Tech Mart Superstore. The event will feature product demonstrations, prize giveaways, and limited-time promotions. Special guests, such as Mike Son from Busan Electronics, are expected to attend, and early visitors will receive exclusive discounts on popular items.

"The opening of this superstore aligns with our goal of providing customers with an unparalleled shopping experience," Dempsey added. "This new location also supports our expansion strategy, following the recent openings of stores in Ottawa and Winnipeg and our plan to open four additional superstores across the country by the end of the year. We are confident that this store will become a key part of the community."

5. What is stated about Tech Mart's new retail location?

(A) It is the company's first physical store.
(B) It will create 100,000 new jobs.
(C) It is scheduled to open in June.
(D) It is situated on the outskirts of Toronto.

6. What is NOT mentioned about the grand opening event?

(A) The benefits offered to attendees
(B) The day and date it will be held
(C) The nearest public transport routes
(D) The name of a special guest

7. What does Ms. Dempsey indicate about Tech Mart?

(A) It has numerous management vacancies.
(B) It will merge with another company.
(C) It is a steadily growing business.
(D) It offers excellent technical support.

Questions 8-11 refer to the following e-mail.

From: sales@zappmarketing.com
To: organizer@summerbeatsfestival.com
Date: May 18
Subject: RE: Flyers and Posters for Festival

Dear Mr. Kane,

I've just spoken with our printing team regarding your request for promotional materials for the Summer Beats Music Festival, which will take place on July 15-17. We recommend printing at least two flyers or posters per expected attendee to cover both promotional distribution and on-site visibility. The estimated cost for printing a set of three designs (flyers, posters, and banners) is approximately $7 to $9 per unit, depending on the sizes and finishes.

Our most requested designs are the lineup flyer, which features all the main stage acts and the festival map, and the schedule poster. These will be printed in vibrant colors to highlight key performers and important details like stage locations and event times.

You mentioned that volunteers would assist with hanging posters and distributing flyers throughout the city. Just remember that some areas might have specific regulations regarding posting flyers in public spaces. If you need help securing permission from certain venues or public spaces, our street team can handle that. Once you finalize the designs, just send us the total number of posters and flyers needed, and we'll ensure everything is printed and delivered to your office.

Best regards,

Jason Matthews
Zapp Marketing Inc.

8. What is the purpose of the e-mail?

(A) To confirm the receipt of a payment
(B) To describe options for an event
(C) To recommend rescheduling a festival
(D) To request samples of some items

9. The word "features" in paragraph 2, line 1, is closest in meaning to

(A) includes
(B) reviews
(C) praises
(D) publishes

10. What does Mr. Matthews indicate about the posters and flyers?

(A) They are made using recycled materials.
(B) They will include the Zapp Marketing logo.
(C) They will be sent to Mr. Kane by e-mail.
(D) They may require permission to post.

11. What information does Mr. Matthews request from Mr. Kane?

(A) The budget for advertising
(B) The main performer at an event
(C) The location of a festival
(D) The number of required items

Questions 12-15 refer to the following brochure.

Garden Retreats Ltd.

Bespoke Garden Summer Houses

If you're dreaming of a personalized outdoor space to enjoy the warmer months, Garden Retreats Ltd. offers the ideal summer house design and installation package. Whether you're seeking a peaceful garden office or an elegant, entertaining area, we'll work with you to create a summer house that perfectly complements your garden. – [1] –.

Here's how our process works:

- First, a design consultant will visit your property to assess the available space, take measurements, and discuss your vision for the summer house.
- During this consultation, you'll also have the opportunity to browse through various design options for exterior finishes, roofing, and interior layouts. – [2] –. We offer a wide range of styles, from traditional wooden structures to sleek, modern designs. If you prefer, you can also come into our showroom to explore materials in person. – [3] –.
- After finalizing your design choices, we will send you a detailed quote, outlining the costs for materials, construction, and installation. This price will be valid for four weeks, giving you ample time to make your decision. Once we receive your approval and deposit, materials will be ordered and typically arrive within two to three weeks.
- Finally, we will schedule an installation date that suits your schedule. Most summer house installations take between one to three days. – [4] –. Simple summer houses can be constructed in approximately five hours!

12. What is the brochure mainly about?

(A) A new product range
(B) An upcoming trade show
(C) A job opportunity
(D) A work process

13. According to the brochure, how can building materials be viewed?

(A) By checking a Web site
(B) By requesting some samples
(C) By visiting a showroom
(D) By browsing a catalog

14. After how many weeks might the total cost provided in a quote change?

(A) One
(B) Two
(C) Three
(D) Four

15. In which of the positions marked [1], [2], [3], and [4] does the following sentence best belong?

"However, this depends on the complexity of the design."

(A) [1]
(B) [2]
(C) [3]
(D) [4]

Playlist 13

강의 바로보기

매번 나오는 파트7 지문별 특징

Part 7

공지/공고/회람 | 광고 | 기사/언론 보도 | 채팅메시지

공지(notice), 공고(announcement), 회람(memorandum) 유형은 회사 내/외부의 사람들에게 특정 정보를 전달하기 위해 사용하며, Part 7에서 가장 많이 출제되는 지문 유형이다. 초반부에는 간단한 인사와 전달사항을, 중반부에는 전달사항에 관한 세부정보나 요청사항들이 이어지며, 후반부에는 추가 정보를 확인할 수 있는 방법으로 마무리된다.

▶ 공지/공고/회람 지문 최빈출 표현

• 지문 초반부

☐ RT Technology will be hosting a conference. RT 테크놀로지 사에서 컨퍼런스를 개최할 것입니다.

☐ We invite you to a tasting event on September 22 at 6 P.M.
저희는 9월 22일, 오후 6시에 귀하를 시식 행사에 초대합니다.

☐ Vernon Plaza is pleased to announce that its new complex will be open for business.
버논 플라자는 영업을 위해 새로운 복합시설을 개장할 것을 알리게 되어 기쁩니다.

• 지문 중반부

☐ Employees are encouraged to find an alternative parking space. 직원들은 대체 주차 공간을 찾도록 권장됩니다.

☐ We offer workshops led by skilled programmers. 저희는 실력 있는 프로그래머들이 이끄는 워크샵을 제공합니다.

☐ This basic course lasts for two months. 이 기본 수업은 두 달 동안 진행됩니다.

• 지문 후반부

☐ Please visit www.blueskyinc.com for more details. 더 많은 세부정보를 위해 www.blueskyinc.com을 방문하십시오.

☐ You can find our schedule and rates on our Web site. 일정과 요금은 저희 웹 사이트에서 확인하실 수 있습니다.

Practice

To: All Sales Team
From: Julia Ramos, Sales Director

I'm pleased to congratulate Emily Davis as she transitions into her new role as a senior account manager in our sales department. Ms. Davis has been an integral part of the team, having worked as a junior sales associate for the past three years. During that time, she has consistently demonstrated exceptional client management skills and helped our client list to grow steadily. Ms. Davis's new responsibilities will begin on Monday, October 2. Please extend your support as she takes on this new challenge!

1. Why did Ms. Ramos send the memo?
(A) To inform employees about an opportunity
(B) To announce a promotion
(C) To introduce a new staff member
(D) To invite staff to an upcoming dinner

2. What is indicated about Ms. Davis?
(A) She has extensive management experience.
(B) She has managed to attract new clients.
(C) She has helped the company reduce expenses.
(D) She will be honored at an event in October.

광고(advertisement) 지문 초반부는 호기심을 유발하는 질문이나 제품/서비스/업체/행사 등에 대한 소개로 시작된다. 중반부에는 광고하는 대상에 대한 특장점이 주로 언급되므로 이에 대한 구체적인 정보를 묻는 세부정보 유형 문제가 출제될 확률이 높다. 특히, 제품 광고는 정해진 기한 내 구매 시 각종 혜택이나 쿠폰, 또는 할인 등을 제공하는 내용 혹은 구매 방법/문의 방법에 대한 안내가 글의 마지막에 제시되는 흐름으로 전개된다.

▶ 광고 지문 최빈출 표현

• 지문 초반부

☐ Do you spend a long time buying meals and refreshments for your guests?
방문객들을 위한 식사와 다과를 구입하는 데 긴 시간을 소비하시나요?

☐ Are you looking for authentic Mexican food using traditional family recipes?
전통적인 가족 요리법을 사용한 진짜 멕시코 음식을 찾으시나요?

☐ During the week of March 15, Browne's Books will be hosting its next book club meet-up.
3월 15일이 있는 주 중에, 브라운 북스가 다음 북클럽 만남 행사를 개최할 예정입니다.

• 지문 중반부

☐ We specialize in remodeling older homes. 저희는 오래된 집을 리모델링하는 것을 전문으로 합니다.

☐ You'll experience the ultimate customized service. 귀하께서는 최상의 맞춤형 서비스를 경험하실 것입니다.

☐ Our products are known for their durability and safety features. 저희 제품들은 내구성과 안전 기능으로 알려져 있습니다.

☐ Try our exclusive content free of charge for 30 days. 30일동안 무료로 저희의 독점 콘텐츠를 이용해 보십시오.

• 지문 후반부

☐ For more information, call our customer support team at 555-0158.
더 많은 정보를 위해서, 555-0158로 고객 지원팀에게 전화주십시오.

☐ Please fill out the form attached to register. 등록하시려면 첨부된 양식을 작성해 주십시오.

☐ Buy one, get one free when you purchase through our online store this week.
이번 주에 저희 온라인 매장을 통해 구입하시면, 하나 구매 시 하나를 무료로 드립니다.

Introduction to Baking Techniques Workshop

Are you aspiring bakers looking to master the essentials of baking? Led by renowned pastry chef, Carla Mendez, you'll learn how to create a variety of breads, cakes, and pastries using professional techniques. Chef Mendez, a graduate of Goldstone Culinary Institute, now teaches full-time and has over a decade of experience in the field. The workshop costs $120 and will be held at Goldstone Culinary Institute on October 14. For more information, e-mail Kelly Jenkins at bakingworkshop@goldstoneculinary.com.

3. The word "master" in paragraph 1, line 1, is closest in meaning to

(A) supervise
(B) understand
(C) exceed
(D) idealize

4. What is indicated about the workshop?

(A) It will include a cooking demonstration.
(B) It will be taught by a former student of the institute.
(C) It will be offered at a discounted rate in October.
(D) It will take place in Ms. Mendez's restaurant.

기사(article)나 언론 보도(press release)는 회사명이나 사람 이름, 지역명 등 고유명사로 된 정보가 많이 포함되어 있기 때문에 다른 지문 유형보다 난이도가 높은 유형에 속한다. 특히, 기업의 인수/합병/신제품 개발 소식, 시 의회의 정책 변경, 지역 매장 이전/확장 소식, 커뮤니티 행사 소개 등의 내용이 출제된다.

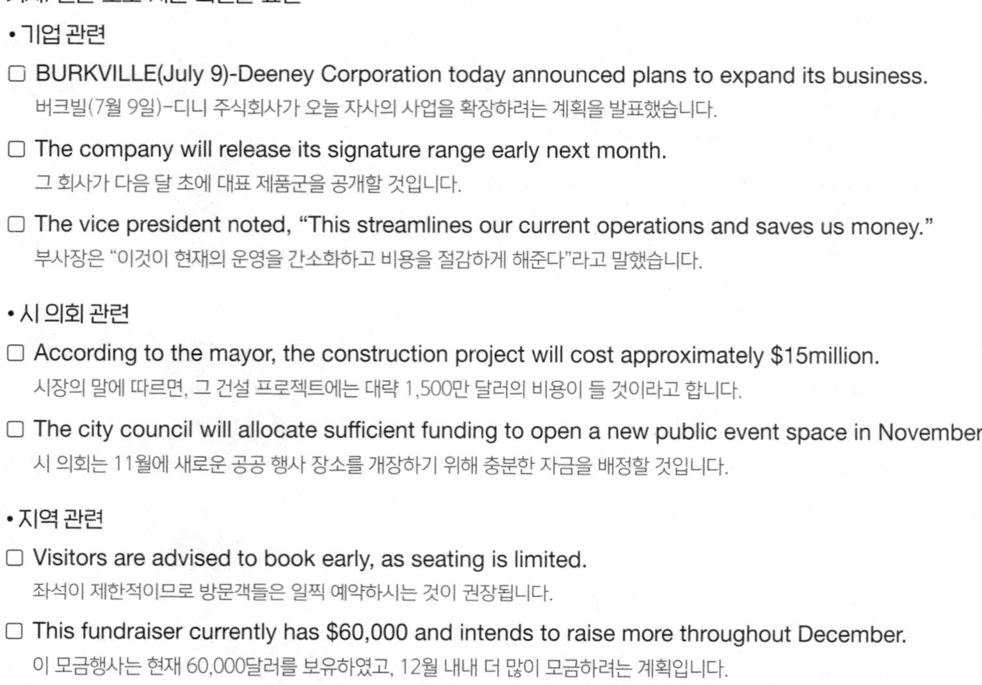

▶ 기사/언론 보도 지문 최빈출 표현

• 기업 관련

☐ BURKVILLE(July 9)-Deeney Corporation today announced plans to expand its business.
버크빌(7월 9일)-디니 주식회사가 오늘 자사의 사업을 확장하려는 계획을 발표했습니다.

☐ The company will release its signature range early next month.
그 회사가 다음 달 초에 대표 제품군을 공개할 것입니다.

☐ The vice president noted, "This streamlines our current operations and saves us money."
부사장은 "이것이 현재의 운영을 간소화하고 비용을 절감하게 해준다"라고 말했습니다.

• 시 의회 관련

☐ According to the mayor, the construction project will cost approximately $15million.
시장의 말에 따르면, 그 건설 프로젝트에는 대략 1,500만 달러의 비용이 들 것이라고 합니다.

☐ The city council will allocate sufficient funding to open a new public event space in November.
시 의회는 11월에 새로운 공공 행사 장소를 개장하기 위해 충분한 자금을 배정할 것입니다.

• 지역 관련

☐ Visitors are advised to book early, as seating is limited.
좌석이 제한적이므로 방문객들은 일찍 예약하시는 것이 권장됩니다.

☐ This fundraiser currently has $60,000 and intends to raise more throughout December.
이 모금행사는 현재 60,000달러를 보유하였고, 12월 내내 더 많이 모금하려는 계획입니다.

☐ Netty's Coffee Shop will participate in the regional food and beverage fair on August 2.
네티스 커피샵은 8월 2일에 지역 식음료 박람회에 참가할 예정입니다.

Practice

WELLFORD (22 July) – In the past few years, businesses across various industries have faced increasing difficulties in retaining staff, now surpassing concerns about competition and customer acquisition. The reasons for this shift are clear. In sectors such as retail and hospitality, labor costs typically account for a significant portion of operational expenses. A high turnover rate not only leads to additional recruitment and training costs but also disrupts day-to-day operations. While companies are trying to mitigate this by offering better benefits and flexible working conditions, the challenge of employee retention continues to impact profitability and overall productivity.

5. What is the article mainly about?
(A) An increase in jobs in the hospitality field
(B) A rise in competition among businesses
(C) The difficulties of attracting customers
(D) The challenges of keeping employees

6. According to the article, what is an effect of high staff turnover?
(A) Increased profitability
(B) Lower training costs
(C) Shift flexibility
(D) Workflow disruption

채팅메시지(text message chain)이나 온라인 채팅(online chat discussion) 유형은 기본적으로 두 명 혹은 세 명 이상의 사람들이 작성한 메시지 및 채팅 내용을 보고 푸는 유형이다. 이 유형의 지문은 의도파악 문제 유형이 항상 포함되어 있으므로 지문의 전체 흐름을 잘 파악하는 것이 매우 중요하다. 특히 다수의 인물이 등장할 경우, 사람 이름에 ○/□/△ 등의 표시를 해 구분하면서 지문을 읽어 내려가는 것을 추천한다.

▶ 채팅메시지/온라인 채팅 지문 최빈출 표현

• 지문 초반부

□ **Hi, I want to talk about the financial reports tomorrow.**
안녕하세요, 내일 재무 보고서와 관련해 이야기하고 싶습니다.

□ **I was wondering if you could bring some flyers to the conference on Friday.**
금요일에 있는 컨퍼런스에 전단지 몇 개를 좀 가져와 주실 수 있는지 여쭤보려고요.

□ **Is there anyone who can check the schedule for me?** 저를 위해 일정표를 확인해 줄 수 있는 분이 계실까요?

• 지문 중반부

□ **As far as I know, you should ask Colin in Personnel.** 제가 알기로는, 인사과의 콜린 씨에게 물어보셔야 할거에요.

□ **Thursday works best for me.** 저는 목요일이 가장 좋습니다.

□ **Is there anything we can do to prepare?** 준비하는데 저희가 할 수 있는 일이 있을까요?

□ **Can you tell me about the details of the company outing?** 제게 회사 야유회에 대한 세부사항을 말씀해 주실 수 있나요?

• 지문 후반부

□ **I'll reach out to the Sales Department and take care of it.** 제가 영업부에 연락해서 그것을 처리할게요.

□ **No problem, Mike. See you there at 5:00 P.M.** 별 거 아닌데요, 마이크 씨. 오후 5시에 그곳에서 봅시다.

□ **Please let me know when you're ready to go.** 나갈 준비가 되면 제게 알려주시기 바랍니다.

□ **Actually, I'm just about to do it.** 사실, 그걸 막 하려던 참이었어요.

Practice

Jamie Tran (2:15 P.M.) I'm almost finished designing our promotional materials for the film festival. I've added the festival dates, location, and the main event lineup to our flyer. Is there anything else I should include before sending it for printing?
Carlos Mendez (2:17 P.M.) Can you also add a section at the bottom about early bird ticket pricing?
Jamie Tran (2:18 P.M.) Sure thing! I'll add that now.
Jamie Tran (2:25 P.M.) By the way, we're running low on color ink for the printers. Should I order more?
Carlos Mendez (2:28 P.M.) Actually, we just got a new batch in. Check the supply room.

7. What does Mr. Tran ask about?
(A) What to include on some flyers
(B) When a festival will take place
(C) How to distribute promotional materials
(D) Where the printing shop is located

8. At 2:28 P.M., what does Mr. Mendez most likely mean when he writes, "Actually, we just got a new batch in"?
(A) Mr. Tran should print additional copies.
(B) Mr. Tran should not order more color ink.
(C) Mr. Tran should tidy up a supply room.
(D) Mr. Tran should train some new employees.

이메일(e-mail)과 편지(letter) 유형은 공지/공고/회람 유형과 더불어 Part 7의 최빈출 지문 유형이며, 싱글지문뿐만 아니라 이중지문과 삼중지문까지 골고루 출제된다. 이메일과 편지는 개인-개인, 회사-회사, 개인-회사 등 다양한 비즈니스 상황에서 주고 받으므로 그 내용이 매우 다양하다. 지문 초반부에서는 안부 인사와 함께 글의 목적이, 중반부에서는 관련 세부 정보가, 후반부에서는 수신인에 대한 요청 사항과 마무리 인사로 주로 전개되므로 지문 구성 패턴이 정해진 편에 속한다.

▶ 이메일/편지 지문 최빈출 표현

• 지문 초반부

☐ Thank you for your proposal regarding our exhibition. 저희 전시회에 관한 제안에 감사드립니다.

☐ I just checked the attached file about the potential suppliers. 잠재적인 공급업체에 대한 첨부파일을 방금 확인했습니다.

☐ I'm writing to confirm that we have received your application successfully.
귀하의 지원서를 성공적으로 받았음을 확인해 드리기 위해 글을 씁니다.

• 지문 중반부

☐ Could you mention this schedule conflict at the meeting? 회의에서 이 일정 충돌을 언급해 주시겠습니까?

☐ To do this, simply input discount code 415285. 이걸 하시려면, 그저 할인 코드 415285만 입력하시면 됩니다.

☐ Unfortunately, I'll be out of town on Thursday. 유감스럽게도, 저는 목요일에 시내를 떠나 있을 예정입니다.

☐ Due to high demand for our service, we've decided to offer two-year internship programs.
저희 서비스의 높은 수요로 인해, 저희는 2년의 인턴십 프로그램을 제공하기로 결정했습니다.

• 지문 후반부

☐ I'd like to meet you to figure out suitable places. 적합한 장소에 대해 알아보기 위해 귀하를 만나고 싶습니다.

☐ If you have any questions, please reply by e-mail. 질문이 있으시면, 이메일로 답장 주십시오.

☐ We look forward to doing business with you. 귀하와 함께 사업을 하는 것을 고대합니다.

Practice

Dear Mr. Hernandez,

I'm writing to confirm the update we discussed over the phone earlier today regarding the delivery on Friday. However, due to unexpected maintenance work in the Maple Room, we've had to change the location of the orientation session. Please ensure that the uniforms are now delivered to the Willow Conference Room at the Eastbrook Training Center instead.

Additionally, it's important that the items arrive by 9:00 A.M. on Friday, as we will be conducting a welcome presentation shortly after and need time to distribute the items to new recruits. If there are any issues, please don't hesitate to reach out to me directly.

Maria Sosa

9. Why did Ms. Sosa send an e-mail to Mr. Hernandez?
(A) To reschedule a staff orientation
(B) To inquire about some maintenance work
(C) To inform him about a job opportunity
(D) To confirm some spoken instructions

10. What does Ms. Sosa expect to receive on Friday morning?
(A) Clothing
(B) Documents
(C) Presentation slides
(D) Office furniture

리뷰(review)는 제품이나 서비스 또는 여행 패키지 등을 경험하고 남긴 후기의 내용을 담은 지문 유형이며, 출장 뷔페 업체에 대한 만족도나, 구매 제품의 사용 후기, 영화/TV 시리즈 시청 후기, 신간 서평 등의 주제로 출제된다. 지문 상단에 review가 아니라 blog review나 testimonial이라는 유형으로 기재될 때도 있으니 함께 알아두는 것이 좋다.

▶ 리뷰 지문 최빈출 표현

• 지문 초반부

- ☐ It was my first time visiting Heaven Scent Candles. 헤븐 센트 캔들스를 방문한 것은 처음이었습니다.
- ☐ With a variety of tours, Happy Bus Tours has offered the best experience by far.
  다양한 투어와 함께, 해피 버스 투어는 지금까지 최고의 경험을 제공해 왔습니다.
- ☐ I'm writing to complain about the quality of your product.
  귀사의 제품 품질에 대해 불만을 제기하기 위해 글을 씁니다.

• 지문 중반부

- ☐ Although some products were expensive, I'm sure they are worth it.
  일부 제품들은 비쌌지만, 그것들이 그만한 가치가 있었다고 확신합니다.
- ☐ The tour guide was very informative and helpful. 여행 가이드는 매우 유익하고 도움이 되었습니다.
- ☐ However, the lack of vegetarian dishes was the sole disappointment.
  그러나, 채식 요리가 부족한 것이 유일한 실망스러운 점이었습니다.

• 지문 후반부

- ☐ I would like to participate in this kind of fair again. 이러한 종류의 박람회에 다음에 또 참여하고 싶습니다.
- ☐ I highly recommend this book to my friends. 제 친구들에게 이 책을 적극 추천합니다.
- ☐ I don't regret the purchase, but I hope you will address this issue in the next update.
  구매를 후회하지는 않지만, 다음 업데이트에서 이 문제를 해결해 주셨으면 좋겠습니다.

Practice

Greenfield Community Garden: A Blossoming Space for All

By Emma Delgado

"Bringing people together through nature and sustainability." That's the guiding principle behind Greenfield Community Garden. With a variety of vegetables, herbs, and flowers, the garden offers a peaceful retreat amid the bustling city life.

The Greenfield Community Garden also features an Education Center located on the south of the property. This center hosts community events like seasonal planting days and children's educational programs. Equipped with a classroom, outdoor demonstration area, and a small greenhouse, the center provides resources for anyone looking to deepen their knowledge of urban gardening. I highly recommend visiting this place to anyone who wants to be a prospective gardener.

11. What is indicated about the Education Center?

(A) It is currently being constructed.
(B) It requires an admission fee.
(C) It hosts events every weekend.
(D) It caters to people of all ages.

12. What is NOT mentioned as a facility in Greenfield Community Garden?

(A) A cafeteria
(B) A demo zone
(C) A classroom
(D) A glasshouse

양식(form) 유형은 영수증이나 송장과 같이 가격 정보가 있는 형태, 출장을 위한 비행기 및 기차 시간표처럼 일정표가 있는 형태, 그리고 지역 축제 또는 무료 강의 등의 행사 일정이 있는 형태 등으로 매우 다양하게 출제된다. 이외에도 티켓 정보나 시상식 개요, 목차, 신청서 등의 형식으로도 나오며, 이중지문과 삼중지문에서 두 번째 또는 세 번째 지문으로 출제된다면 연계문제의 정답 단서를 포함하고 있을 확률이 매우 높으니 먼저 읽는 것을 추천한다.

▶ 양식 지문 문제풀이 전략

❶ 선택지로 만들기 쉬운 4개로 제시되는 정보를 특히 눈 여겨 본다.

❷ ***, NOTE, 글머리 기호(· , –, ▸), 밑줄, 굵은 글씨, 박스, 표 등은 정답의 단서를 포함하고 있을 확률이 높다.

❸ 숫자, 반복되는 고유명사, 금액, 시간 등은 연계문제의 정답 단서로 자주 활용된다.

❹ 영수증이나 청구서의 경우, 비용을 지불하는 사람과 제품을 수령하는 사람이 다를 수 있으므로 꼭 확인한다.

❺ 양식 지문에서 자주 볼 수 있는 약어 표현을 미리 학습하고 암기해 둔다.

양식 지문 유형에서는 우리가 일상생활에서 흔히 볼 수 없는 약어나 용어들이 많이 등장해요. 아는 만큼 지문의 내용을 더 빨리 파악할 수 있으니 꼭 시험 전에 정리하고 가세요~!

VAT(= Value Added Tax) 부가 가치세
RSVP(= Répondez S'il Vous Plaît) 회신 바람
subtotal 소계
installment 할부, 분할 불입금
N/A(= Not Available, Not Applicable) 사용 불가, 해당 없음
ASAP(= As Soon As Possible) 가능한 한 빨리
total 총계
outstanding balance 미불잔고, 미변제잔고

Grover's Farm Store
3829 Ferndale Drive, Brompton
Open 9 A.M. to 4 P.M., Monday to Saturday

August 6	Red Leicester Cheese	$5.50
	Yogurt (4-Pack)	$3.95
	Organic Strawberry Milk	$1.75
	Sales Tax	$1.12
	Total	$12.32

Become a Grover's Farm Store member today!
Members earn points on all farm store transactions and gain benefits such as access to tours and special events at our farm!

13. What was purchased on August 6?
(A) Vegetables
(B) Dairy products
(C) Fresh fruit
(D) Farming equipment

14. What does the receipt indicate about Grover's Farm Store?
(A) It was first opened in August.
(B) It provides discounts to employees.
(C) It offers a membership program.
(D) It is open seven days a week.

기타 지문 유형으로는 소책자(brochure), 초대장(invitation), 구인광고(job posting), 전단지(flyer), 쿠폰(coupon/voucher) 등이 다양하게 출제된다. 소책자/구인광고/전단지/쿠폰 등은 광고의 성격으로, 초대장은 공지의 성격으로 분류하면 문제를 좀 더 수월하게 풀 수 있다.

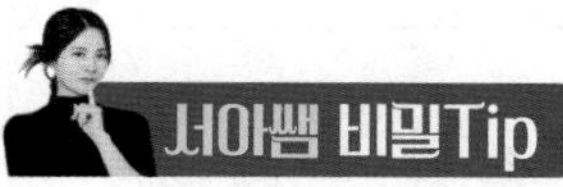

기타 지문 유형별로 자주 출제되는 문장들을 학습하여 고득점을 노려보아요!

소책자 (brochure)	Introducing KMS Auto, where we offer advanced limousines. 고급 리무진을 제공하는, KMS 오토를 소개합니다. Book one of our packages by July 30 and receive a complimentary travel bag. 7월 30일까지 저희 패키지 중 하나를 예약하시고 무료 여행 가방을 받으세요.
초대장 (invitation)	Please let us know if you have any dietary requirements. 식사 요청사항이 있으신 경우 저희에게 알려주시기 바랍니다. Directions to the hotel have been enclosed with this invitation. 호텔로의 길 안내는 이 초대장에 동봉되어 있습니다.
구인광고 (job posting)	We are seeking a graphic designer with experience in promotional materials. 저희는 홍보용 자료에 경력이 있는 그래픽 디자이너를 찾고 있습니다. We offer competitive wages and benefits, including free meals. 저희는 경쟁력 있는 급여와 무료 식사를 포함한 복지들을 제공합니다.
전단지 (flyer)	Don't miss out on our promotional offers happening on November 1. 11월 1일에 진행되는 할인 행사들을 놓치지 마세요. You can get an additional discount with this flyer. 이 전단지로 추가 할인을 받으실 수 있습니다.
쿠폰 (coupon, voucher)	This $30 voucher is valid until December 10. 이 30달러 상품권은 12월 10일까지 유효합니다. Scan this barcode at checkout to redeem the gift certificate. 계산대에서 이 바코드를 스캔해 상품권으로 교환하십시오.

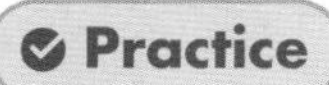

Radiance Beauty Lounge

Pampering the community with expert care for over 15 years

Join us in celebrating the grand reopening of our newly renovated salon on Wilson Street! Book any two beauty treatments and enjoy a complimentary deep-conditioning hair treatment throughout the entire month of October. Valid exclusively at Radiance Beauty Lounge, 225 Wilson Street, Denver, CO. Offer applies to in-salon services only – not to at-home services. Visit our Web site for a full list of services, hours, and additional branches.

15. How can people receive the benefit from the brochure?

(A) By attending a grand opening event
(B) By booking an at-home service
(C) By reserving two treatments
(D) By spending a minimum amount of money

16. What is mentioned about Radiance Beauty Lounge?

(A) It has been in business for two decades.
(B) It operates in multiple locations.
(C) It will reduce its prices in October.
(D) It recently began offering hair treatments.

Check-up Test

Questions 1-2 refer to the following application form.

Dora's Bistro
Job Application Form

Application Date: 3 December

PERSONAL DETAILS

Name: Rafael Pazzi	Telephone: 555-0126
Address: 204 Prince Street, Toronto ON	E-mail: rpazzi@cmail.ca

POSITION APPLYING FOR

Job title	Waiter/Server		
Preferred start date	10 December		
Preferred branch	☐ Rowan Road	☒ Prince Street	☐ Acorn Avenue
Preferred contract	☒ Part-time	☐ Full-time	☐ Flexible

PREVIOUS EMPLOYMENT

Business Name	Job title	Length of Service
Sierra Steakhouse	Kitchen porter	4 years
Marigold Restaurant	Wait staff	2.5 years

EDUCATION

High School/College/University	Qualification Attained
Marley Community College	Certificate in Hospitality
Pine Hills High School	High School Diploma

PERSONAL STATEMENT

I have worked as a waiter for the past two-and-a-half years, and I am a hard-working and reliable individual. My current wait staff job involves a long commute, whereas Dora's Bistro is just two doors along the road from my apartment, which makes it an ideal place for me to work.

1. What is suggested about Dora's Bistro?

(A) It recently opened a new location.
(B) It is located near Marigold Restaurant.
(C) It has several full-time vacancies.
(D) It operates in multiple branches.

2. What is NOT indicated about Mr. Pazzi?

(A) He currently works at Sierra Steakhouse.
(B) He lives on Prince Street.
(C) He has experience serving diners.
(D) He would prefer to work on a part-time basis.

Questions 3-5 refer to the following advertisement.

Greentree Landscaping

Greentree Landscaping is the top choice for homeowners and businesses in the Surrey area who want to transform their outdoor spaces. We specialize in lawn care, garden design, tree trimming, and seasonal maintenance. Our experienced landscapers are skilled in handling projects of all sizes, from simple lawn mowing to complete garden overhauls. Whether you need regular upkeep or a stunning new landscape design, Greentree has you covered.

Our flexible scheduling options make it easy for customers to book an appointment that fits their busy lives. We operate Monday to Saturday, from 7 A.M. to 7 P.M., and on Sunday from 7 A.M. to 3 P.M.

This fall, Greentree is offering a special promotion: 20% off any full-service landscaping package, which includes lawn care, trimming, mulching, and a garden assessment. This offer is available to all brand new customers in Surrey but cannot be combined with other offers. The discount applies to service fees only and does not cover materials or additional custom features.

3. The word "covered" in paragraph 1, line 5, is closest in meaning to

(A) concealed
(B) financed
(C) surrounded
(D) accommodated

4. When can a customer NOT be served by Greentree?

(A) On Monday at 7:00 A.M.
(B) On Wednesday at 7:00 P.M.
(C) On Saturday at 7:00 A.M.
(D) On Sunday at 7:00 P.M.

5. What is true about the promotional offer?

(A) It can be combined with other offers.
(B) It is intended for first-time customers.
(C) It is available to customers outside Surrey.
(D) It covers a variety of custom features.

Questions 6-8 refer to the following notice.

Factory Safety Guidelines and Procedures

Please note that the following guidelines are mandatory. Before starting work on the factory floor, every worker must receive and review our current safety manual. If you were not provided with this, please request one from Ms. Easton.

- Wear appropriate safety gear: This includes hard hats, safety glasses, gloves, steel-toed boots, and any other gear specific to your task.
- Follow machine operation protocols: Ensure that you are trained and authorized to operate any machinery.
- Be aware of emergency stop buttons: Know the location and function of all emergency stops on equipment you are using.
- Report hazards immediately: If you spot any unsafe conditions, defective machinery, or spills, report them to your supervisor immediately.
- Stay clear of moving machinery: Never approach or interfere with running machines unless you are tasked with that duty.
- Emergency exits: Familiarize yourself with all emergency exits and evacuation routes in case of fire or other emergencies.

Adherence to these safety procedures ensures a secure working environment for all employees.

6. Who is the notice most likely intended for?

(A) Safety inspectors
(B) Machine operators
(C) IT technicians
(D) First aid workers

7. Why would Ms. Easton be contacted?

(A) To request a work uniform
(B) To report dangerous conditions
(C) To obtain a required manual
(D) To sign up for a training session

8. What is NOT a stated guideline on the notice?

(A) Wear necessary safety gear
(B) Take breaks when tired
(C) Report equipment faults
(D) Be aware of exit locations

Questions 9-11 refer to the following review.

Sunny Shores Resort: A Perfect Getaway
by Rachel Lin

"Where relaxation meets adventure." That's the tagline featured in the brochure for Sunny Shores Resort, a newly opened holiday destination along the scenic coast of Yarra Bay. Offering a blend of luxurious amenities and fun-filled activities, Sunny Shores promises an unforgettable vacation experience for families, couples, and groups alike. –[1]–.

The resort features beautifully landscaped gardens, wide paths for walking or cycling, and multiple relaxation zones. At the heart of the resort is the central plaza, which houses a beachside café, a seafood restaurant, and several boutiques selling local crafts and souvenirs. –[2]–. The resort's most unique feature is its impressive waterpark, located in the southeastern corner. –[3]–. Complete with twisting water slides, a lazy river, and a wave pool, the waterpark has quickly become the highlight for both kids and adults. "You could easily spend your whole day in the park," said Ellie Peters, Sunny Shores' guest services manager. "It's designed for guests who want a mix of relaxation and thrill." –[4]–.

Tours of the resort's facilities are available for prospective guests. Open days are hosted every weekend from 11:00 A.M. to 3:00 P.M., or you can book a personalized tour by calling 818-555-0192.

9. What is indicated about the waterpark?

(A) It appeals to people of all ages.
(B) It contains several gift shops.
(C) It requires an admission fee.
(D) It is located in the central plaza.

10. How can a prospective guest learn more about Sunny Shores Resort?

(A) By visiting a Web site
(B) By reading a tourist brochure
(C) By participating in a tour
(D) By attending a grand opening event

11. In which of the positions marked [1], [2], [3], and [4] does the following sentence best belong?

"Sunny Shores also has the perfect place for those who wish to stay cool and have fun."

(A) [1]
(B) [2]
(C) [3]
(D) [4]

Questions 12-14 refer to the following article.

GameWorld Expo Set for This Weekend

LOS ANGELES (24 October) – Gaming enthusiasts are in for a treat this weekend as the GameWorld Expo opens at the Mirage Convention Center. Hosted by PixelTech, one of the industry's leading video game publishers, the two-day event promises to showcase the latest in gaming technology, upcoming releases, and exclusive presentations by game developers.

Attendees will have the opportunity to try out unreleased games, explore virtual reality setups, and meet with indie developers displaying their newest projects. Sessions will include live gameplay demos, panel discussions on game design, and tips on breaking into the industry for aspiring developers. The event will also feature e-sports competitions, where visitors can cheer on professional gamers or sign up to participate in tournaments.

For fans of gaming hardware, booths will offer a variety of cutting-edge accessories, from custom controllers to high-performance gaming rigs, available to test and purchase. Industry experts will also be on hand to give advice on building the ultimate gaming setup at home.

Entry to the GameWorld Expo is free, but registration is required due to limited space. To secure your spot and learn more about the event, visit www.gameworldexpo.com.

12. The word "leading" in paragraph 1, line 2, is closest in meaning to

(A) beneficial
(B) prominent
(C) versatile
(D) profitable

13. What is NOT mentioned as something expo attendees can enjoy?

(A) Receiving career advice
(B) Listening to discussions
(C) Testing out hardware
(D) Purchasing discounted games

14. What must people do to attend the expo?

(A) Complete an online sign-up process
(B) Purchase tickets at an event venue
(C) Enter a video game competition
(D) Pay a registration fee

Questions 15-18 refer to the following online chat discussion.

Elena Garcia (2:15 P.M.)
Hey, team. The mayor's office just reached out—they want us to organize a big promotional event at City Hall for his reelection campaign.

David Miller (2:16 P.M.)
Wow, that could be a major project for our firm. What's the deadline?

Elena Garcia (2:17 P.M.)
In about a month. I'm not sure how I feel about this, though. The mayor hasn't done a great job running the city, and I don't agree with how he's handled things.

Sophia Nguyen (2:19 P.M.)
I get that, but we're just here to plan events, not to endorse his policies. This could bring us great exposure.

David Miller (2:20 P.M.)
Exactly. We need the business, especially since it's been slow lately. This could be a great opportunity for us.

Elena Garcia (2:22 P.M.)
Yeah, you're right. It's just business. I guess I'm overthinking it.

Sophia Nguyen (2:23 P.M.)
Definitely. Let's focus on doing what we do best—delivering a top-tier event.

Elena Garcia (2:24 P.M.)
Agreed. Let's get together tomorrow at 9:00 A.M. in our conference room to start figuring out our plan.

15. In what type of business do the writers most likely work?

(A) Event planning
(B) Business recruitment
(C) Financial consulting
(D) Urban development

16. What is indicated about the company the writers work for?

(A) It regularly works with city officials.
(B) It recently implemented new policies.
(C) It is advertising several job opportunities.
(D) It has experienced a decline in business.

17. At 2:19 P.M., what does Ms. Nguyen most likely mean when she writes, "I get that"?

(A) She has received a promotional flyer for an event.
(B) She recognizes that a mayor has underperformed.
(C) She will find out the deadline for a proposed project.
(D) She is aware that Ms. Garcia is running in an election.

18. What will the writers most likely do tomorrow morning?

(A) Start decorating an event space
(B) Contact a mayor's representative
(C) Attend a meeting at City Hall
(D) Begin brainstorming a project

Questions 19-22 refer to the following e-mail.

To: Ethan Ward <eward@customcraft.com>
From: Liam Callahan <lcallahan@globallogistics.com>
Date: February 11
Subject: Business proposal

Dear Mr. Ward,

At Global Logistics Corporation, we understand how important it is for a business like yours to ensure timely and secure delivery of every piece you create. We specialize in providing tailored shipping solutions that meet the unique needs of businesses crafting and delivering high-end custom products.

Whether you are shipping your dining tables and coffee tables locally or internationally, we offer reliable freight options designed to protect your items during transit. Our fleet is equipped with advanced tracking technology, so you and your clients can monitor shipments in real time. We also provide specialized packaging services to ensure that delicate and valuable items are transported without damage.

Additionally, Global Logistics can handle custom delivery schedules and international shipping requirements, including customs clearance and documentation, making the entire process seamless. Our comprehensive logistics network across key markets worldwide allows us to deliver with outstanding care, ensuring that your products arrive exactly as intended.

We would love to discuss how we can further support your business. Please feel free to reach out to me directly at 800-456-7890 or visit our Web site at www.globallogistics.com to explore our full range of services. We look forward to helping you ship your products with confidence.

Sincerely,

Liam Callahan
Head of Operations
Global Logistics

19. What does Mr. Ward's business most likely manufacture?

(A) Appliances
(B) Vehicles
(C) Software
(D) Furniture

20. What is indicated about Global Logistics?

(A) It charges more to ship large items.
(B) It can safely transport fragile merchandise.
(C) It recently opened a new distribution warehouse.
(D) It offers rental of delivery vehicles.

21. The word "outstanding" in paragraph 3, line 3, is closest in meaning to

(A) overdue
(B) excellent
(C) overall
(D) excessive

22. What does Mr. Callahan expect Mr. Ward to do next?

(A) Confirm the destination of an order
(B) Provide samples of some products
(C) Visit Global Logistics in person
(D) Discuss a proposal in more detail

강의 바로보기

이중지문, 이렇게 풀면 만점 받습니다!

Part 7

이중지문　연계문제 전략 연습

이중지문은 두 개의 지문에 다섯 개의 문항이 한 세트로 구성되어 있으며, 총 두 세트가 출제된다. 한 개의 지문이 아닌 두 개의 지문이 한 세트인만큼 두 개의 지문에서 공통적으로 연결되는 부분이 있으므로 이 정보를 취합해서 정답을 도출할 수 있는 연계문제가 나온다는 것이 싱글지문과 구별되는 특징이다.

▶ 이중지문 템플릿

이중지문 상단에 위치한 디렉션에서 지문의 종류를 확인할 수 있으며, 질문에 「According to + 지문 종류」가 제시되어 있다면 해당 지문만 읽고도 문제를 풀 수 있다. 보통 첫 번째 지문을 읽고 1번째 문제를, 두 번째 지문을 읽고 4~5번째 문제를 풀 수 있으므로 2~3번 문제가 연계문제일 확률이 제일 높다.

Questions 176-180 refer to the following e-mail and booking confirmation.

To: Tina Braymer <tbraymer@worldmail.net>
From: Yvonne Gagne <ygagne@evehotels.com>
Subject: Your Room Reservation (#438119)
Date: August 10

Dear Ms. Braymer,

At the end of this month, we will accommodate a large number of presenters and event organizers involved with this year's Skyline Software & Technology Convention. You currently have a room reserved on the second floor, but convention organizers would prefer to book the entirety of that floor for their staff and special guests. Thus, we are contacting you to ask whether you would mind switching to a different room in exchange for a $50 meal coupon. The coupon can be redeemed at any restaurants in any of our hotels, and is valid until the end of this year.

Please look below at the three alternate rooms that we hope you will consider. The first options are the same type of room as you originally reserved, at the same location, but on different floors.

Room 406	Eve Hotel (Porter Road)	Standard Room	Check-in from: 1 P.M., August 28	Check-out by: 11 A.M., August 30
Room 519	Eve Hotel (Porter Road)	Standard Room	Check-in from: 1 P.M., August 28	Check-out by: 11 A.M., August 30

The third option is a Deluxe Room, but this is at our other location, which is a few blocks north from Porter Road. You will be charged at the normal Standard Room rate.

Room 427	Eve Hotel (Clement Street)	Deluxe Room	Check-in from: 2 P.M., August 28	Check-out by: 12 P.M., August 30

If you have no problem with taking one of the suggested rooms, please contact our reservations manager, Harry Henley, at 555-0177. If you wish to keep your originally assigned room, we completely understand. However, we would truly appreciate your cooperation in this matter.

Sincerely,

Yvonne Gagne
Guest Services
Eve Hotel Group

HOTEL BOOKING CONFIRMATION

Reservation #438119) *AMENDED

EVE HOTEL, 387 Clement Street, San Francisco, CA 94105

Guest's Name: Tina Braymer

Reservation Details: Deluxe Room, Check-in: August 28 / Check out: August 30
Complimentary Breakfast Included

Payment Received: $550 (Credit Card No.: 1867-****-****-2878)

Security Deposit Required Upon Check-In: $100

176. What is the purpose of the e-mail?
(A) To encourage a guest to change rooms
(B) To provide a guest with directions to a hotel
(C) To recommend that guests attend a convention
(D) To promote a hotel chain's new location

177. What is indicated about the meal coupon?
(A) It is valid at the Porter Road hotel only.
(B) It must be used by December 31.
(C) It can be exchanged for cash.
(D) It will be mailed to Ms. Braymer.

178. What did Ms. Braymer most likely do after receiving the e-mail?
(A) Contact an event organizer
(B) Make a payment
(C) Respond to the e-mail
(D) Call Mr. Henley

179. What does the booking confirmation indicate about Ms. Braymer's new room reservation?
(A) She paid for her room in cash.
(B) She must pay $550 upon arrival.
(C) She will receive a free meal.
(D) She will stay at the hotel for three nights.

180. By what time should Ms. Braymer check out from the hotel?
(A) 11 A.M.
(B) 12 P.M.
(C) 1 P.M.
(D) 2 P.M.

▶ 이중지문 문제풀이 전략

❶ 첫 번째 지문을 읽고 1번 문제를 푼다. 주제/목적 유형은 보통 지문의 초반부만 보면 되므로 가장 먼저 푼다.

❷ 2번 또는 3번 문제는 연계문제일 확률이 높으므로 문제와 선택지를 가볍게 읽고, 두 번째 지문으로 넘어간다.

❸ 두 번째 지문을 읽으면서 4번과 5번 문항을 푼다. 문제를 풀면서 연계질문에 대한 정답 단서를 찾는다면 함께 해결한다.

❹ 동의어 유형은 지문의 일부분만 보고도 풀 수 있으므로 반드시 풀어야 한다.

❺ 사실확인 유형과 추론 유형은 다른 문제를 먼저 풀면서 지문의 내용을 파악한 후에 가장 마지막으로 푼다.

Question 1 refers to the following announcement and application form.

Evergreen Fitness Center

Evergreen Fitness Center currently serves over 800 members who enjoy our state-of-the-art gym located in the heart of the city. Surrounded by lush greenery, our gym offers a full range of fitness facilities and services for members of all fitness levels.

To join Evergreen Fitness Center, you can choose from one of three membership tiers: Basic, Premium, or Elite. Basic members pay an initial joining fee of $500 and enjoy unlimited access to all gym equipment, group fitness classes, and a personal locker. Premium members, with a $750 joining fee, receive all the benefits of the Basic membership plus access to the sauna, steam rooms, and exclusive wellness workshops. Elite members, with a $1,000 joining fee, enjoy the full range of Premium benefits, plus access to personal training sessions and priority booking for fitness classes.

For more information or to join, please call 555-3456 or e-mail us at membership@evergreenfitness.com.

Membership Application Form

Thank you for your interest in joining Evergreen Fitness Center. Please fill out this form and submit it to the Membership Office located at the front desk of the main gym building.

Date: September 30
Telephone number: 555-3456
Name: Sarah Mitchell
E-mail: smitchell@greenmail.com
Address: 120 Pine Avenue, Calgary, Alberta

I have enclosed a check made payable to Evergreen Fitness Center for the amount of:
__X__ $500.00
_____ $750.00
_____ $1,000.00

1. What benefit will Ms. Mitchell receive?
(A) Personal training sessions
(B) Steam room access
(C) Personal locker space
(D) Wellness workshops

서아쌤 시점
이중지문 연계문제 풀이 ▶

Questions 1-5 refer to the following e-mail and brochure excerpt.

To: James Holcomb <jholcomb@wildlens.com>
From: Sarah Dubois <sarah.dubois@nationalparks.ca>
Subject: Brochure Follow-up
Date: 15 September

Dear Mr. Holcomb,

Thank you so much for the beautiful photos you have provided for our upcoming brochure. The images of the hiking trails and wildlife are stunning and will certainly inspire visitors to explore our park. I especially appreciated the panoramic shot of the lake at sunset—it really captures the serene atmosphere we aim to promote.

I do have one additional request. We would love to include a photo of the newly renovated campground building, which we have spent a lot of time and effort on. We are very proud of the project, and we are confident that visitors to the park will be very impressed with it. A great picture of the building will highlight the improvements we've made for our guests. Please let me know if you can assist with this.

Sincerely,

Sarah Dubois, Communications Coordinator
National Parks Department

Campground Building Opening Soon

We are excited to announce the grand opening of our new campground building at Clearwater National Park, which will be celebrated on Saturday, 7 October. The grand opening event will begin at 10:00 A.M. with remarks from Park Director Lisa Garner, followed by a ribbon-cutting ceremony. Guests will have the opportunity to tour the facility and enjoy refreshments until 1:00 P.M.

The new building, located in the central camping area, has been completely renovated to better serve our visitors. It was originally constructed fifty years ago as a ranger station, and it remained in use for approximately 45 years until it was abandoned due to structural issues. It now features a spacious games room, a fully equipped communal kitchen, modern shower facilities, and comfortable gathering spaces for campers. These improvements reflect our commitment to enhancing the park experience for all.

Campers will be able to use the new facility starting Sunday, 8 October. For more information or to make camping reservations, please visit our Web site or call 555-321-9876.

1. Who most likely is Mr. Holcomb?

(A) A Web designer
(B) A tour guide
(C) A park ranger
(D) A photographer

2. What is indicated about Ms. Dubois?

(A) She is dissatisfied with Mr. Holcomb's work.
(B) She recently participated in a wildlife trail hike.
(C) She is pleased with the conversion of a ranger station.
(D) She has arranged to meet with Mr. Holcomb in person.

3. What will happen at the grand opening event?

(A) Park rangers will provide talks.
(B) Food and beverages will be served.
(C) New trail maps will be unveiled.
(D) Group games will be hosted.

4. In the brochure excerpt, the word "serve" in paragraph 2, line 1, is closest in meaning to

(A) introduce
(B) carry
(C) present
(D) benefit

5. According to the brochure excerpt, what is NOT part of the campground building?

(A) A cooking area
(B) A first aid station
(C) A washing facility
(D) A games room

강의 바로보기

Check-up Test

Questions 1-5 refer to the following online form and e-mail.

Located in Wellington, New Zealand, TechWave Solutions specializes in refurbishing and reselling electronic devices, with a focus on sustainability and reducing e-waste.

Please use the form below to submit your inquiries and offers regarding outdated or unused electronics.

Name: Liam O'Connor
E-mail: loconnor@techglobal.nz
Comment:
I saw your call for outdated equipment on your Web site. I work for a corporate IT firm in Christchurch, and we recently upgraded all our desktop computers and laptops. We now have around 30 older models that are no longer in use. They're fully functional but outdated compared to current industry standards. We have 10 Quasar laptops that are 7 years old, 10 Magna desktop PCs that are only 5 years old, and 10 Photon laptops that are only 4 years old, but are not suitable for our needs. Would TechWave Solutions be interested in purchasing these at a reasonable price? If so, please contact me by e-mail.

To: loconnor@techglobal.nz
From: purchasing@techwavesolutions.co.nz
Date: 16 October
Subject: Your inquiry

Dear Mr. O'Connor,

Thank you for contacting us regarding your surplus of computers and laptops. We're always eager to help reduce e-waste and give used devices a second life. Based on your description, we'd be happy to purchase your Quasar and Magna computers. However, we avoid purchasing Photon models, due to their tendency to malfunction. We bought many of them last year, and we learned our lesson the hard way!

Here's an outline of what we typically pay for items:
Desktop computers (5 years old or newer): NZ $70 per unit
Laptop computers (5 years old or newer): NZ $100 per unit
Older desktops and laptops (6-8 years old): NZ $30 per unit
Non-functional units or severely outdated models: NZ $5 per unit for recycling

At your earliest convenience, please deliver the computers to the loading area at the rear of our store. We will perform a quick evaluation of the items and then pay for them in cash. Our store is open from 9 A.M. until 5 P.M., Monday through Friday.

Thanks for contacting us, and I look forward to meeting you.

Best regards,

Lisa Tremont, Purchasing Manager
TechWave Solutions

1. What motivated Mr. O'Connor to contact TechWave Solutions?

(A) A recent review from a satisfied customer
(B) A Web site post from TechWave Solutions
(C) A magazine article about TechWave Solutions
(D) A phone message from Ms. Tremont

2. What is indicated about Mr. O'Connor?

(A) He specializes in repairing old computers.
(B) He is seeking employment at TechWave Solutions.
(C) His company recently purchased new technology.
(D) His company is interested in merging with TechWave Solutions.

3. According to Ms. Tremont, what happened last year?

(A) Some of her employees were promoted.
(B) Some computers she bought were faulty.
(C) Some prices for buying old computers were increased.
(D) Some devices she paid for were not delivered.

4. What does Ms. Tremont advise Mr. O'Connor to do?

(A) Provide a full list of outdated computers
(B) Contact a different technology business
(C) Buy some devices from TechWave Solutions
(D) Bring some items to TechWave Solutions

5. How much would Ms. Tremont pay Mr. O'Connor for his Quasar computers?

(A) NZ $70 per unit
(B) NZ $100 per unit
(C) NZ $30 per unit
(D) NZ $5 per unit

Questions 6-10 refer to the following article and e-mail.

How to Organize a Successful Charity Event
by Vanessa Givens

Charity events are excellent ways to raise awareness and funds for important causes, but organizing them can be challenging. Not all events achieve their goals, often due to a lack of preparation or understanding of the audience. A successful charity event needs to resonate with participants, motivate donors, and generate publicity. Here are some guidelines to help you create an impactful charity event.

Tip 1! - Maintain Focus. It's tempting to pack your event with a variety of activities, but too much can dilute your message. Focus on a few key activities that will inspire engagement and support for your cause. For example, if you're organizing a fundraiser for a local animal shelter, consider hosting a pet adoption segment alongside a donation drive. This will create a clear, emotional connection between attendees and your mission.

Tip 2! - Manage Your Time. The duration of your event is crucial. A successful charity event should balance entertainment with calls to action. If the event is too short, you may not generate enough momentum for donations; too long, and people may lose interest. Plan breaks to engage with your donors through speeches, videos, or live demonstrations of how their contributions will make a difference.

Tip 3! - Find A Balance. While having charismatic speakers or well-known hosts can attract people, the core focus must always remain on the cause. Choose speakers who not only engage the audience but have been committed to charity work for at least ten years. Make sure that your volunteers and staff understand the cause deeply and can articulate its importance. This will ensure that even casual attendees feel personally connected to the work your charity is doing, leading to increased support.

To: Sophie Andrews <sandrews@charitynetwork.org>
From: Edward Wentworth <ewentworth@charitynetwork.org>
Date: October 13
Subject: Upcoming charity event

Hi, Sophie,

I've attached an article published by Vanessa Givens on October 3 that I think will help as we finalize the plans for our upcoming Charity Network event. The section about being selective with activities really stood out to me. We've planned quite a few, but it might be a good idea to focus on just a couple of key attractions to ensure we hold the audience's attention.

I also wanted to discuss our keynote speaker. Originally, I was thinking of suggesting Paul Stevens, but he'll be unavailable on October 30. I was wondering if Hannah McConnell might be a good replacement. She has experience in our cause area and could really connect with the audience. Furthermore, Tip 3 in the article describes her perfectly. Although Hannah is currently overseas attending some networking workshops, she will be back on October 23, so she would have seven days to prepare.

Regards,

Edward Wentworth, Event Coordinator
Charity Network

6. According to the article, what is one reason that charity events may be unsuccessful?

(A) They are held in inconvenient locations.
(B) They have not been prepared properly.
(C) They focus on causes that are unpopular.
(D) They involve too many guest speakers.

7. Why does the article writer mention a local animal shelter?

(A) To emphasize the importance of charities
(B) To encourage readers to make a donation
(C) To introduce an example of an activity
(D) To suggest a location to hold an event

8. What is NOT indicated in the article about the duration of an event?

(A) Long events may bore attendees.
(B) Events held on multiple days may be more successful.
(C) Scheduled breaks may keep attendees interested.
(D) Short events may generate fewer donations.

9. When most likely is the Charity Network event scheduled to take place?

(A) On October 3
(B) On October 13
(C) On October 23
(D) On October 30

10. What is indicated about Ms. McConnell?

(A) She has made a sizable financial contribution to a charity.
(B) She has served as a keynote speaker at several events.
(C) She has recommended Mr. Stevens for a role.
(D) She has been involved in charity work for over a decade.

Playlist 15

강의 바로보기

삼중지문, 양식부터 분석하면 토익 졸업한다고?

Part 7

삼중지문 연계문제 전략 연습

삼중지문은 세 개의 지문에 다섯 개의 문항이 한 세트로 구성되어 있으며, 총 세 세트가 출제된다. 세 개의 지문이 한 세트인만큼 [첫 번째 지문-두 번째 지문], [첫 번째 지문-세 번째 지문], 또는 [두 번째 지문-세 번째 지문]에서 공통적으로 연결되는 부분들이 있으므로 이 정보를 종합하여 풀 수 있는 연계문제가 적게는 1문제, 많게는 2문제까지 출제된다.

▶ 삼중지문 템플릿

삼중지문 상단에서도 지문의 종류를 파악할 수 있으며, 지문 중 스케줄, 표, 주문서, 영수증, 웹 사이트 등 양식 지문 유형에서 봤던 단어가 다른 지문에서 중복된다면 연계문제의 정답 단서일 확률이 높다. 또한, 나열된 정보가 4개인 경우 선택지로 활용하기 좋으니 유심히 보는 것이 좋다.

Questions 191-195 refer to the following Web page, form, and message board post.

British Bird Watching Message Board
Image Upload Guidelines

1. Please keep your message under 70 words in accordance with our message board policy. This ensures that information is presented concisely and accurately, with no irrelevant details.
2. Image descriptions should adhere to a "Bird species – time – site" format. Our members are all avid bird watchers, so they are particularly interested in being able to quickly scan for details of the images without any fuss. We have a separate page for unidentified bird images.

   Please add a description such as: "Pied Flycatcher – 6 A.M. – At Spurn Point, Yorkshire"

   Please avoid adding vague descriptions such as: "Small brown bird in the countryside"
3. As this is primarily a message board for sharing images, your post should contain at least one image of a bird, and that image must have been taken by you. We will not permit the sharing of images that were not taken personally by you.

British Bird Watching Message Board
New Member Registration Form

Name: Arthur Bedford E-mail: abedford@homenet.com
Years spent bird watching: 10 years
Current employer: Natural World Weekly
Preferred camera: Zenon 650

I am interested in hearing about the quarterly gatherings that are hosted for British Bird Watching members. YES (√) NO ( )

Terms of Image Use:
Please be advised that images uploaded to the message board may be added to the Gallery section of our Web site. Although we reserve the right to use uploaded pictures, we will not permit other companies to use them.

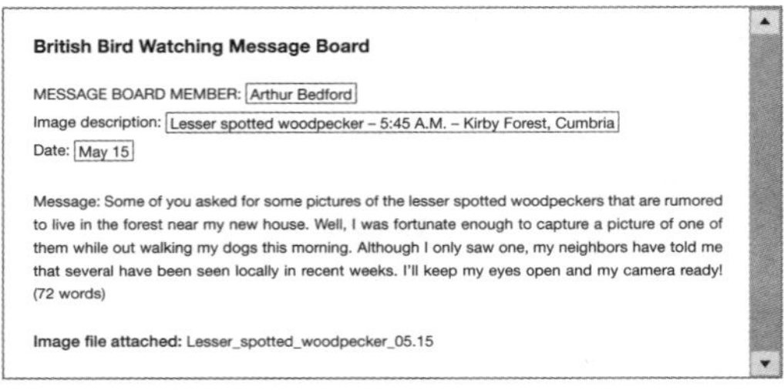
British Bird Watching Message Board

MESSAGE BOARD MEMBER: Arthur Bedford
Image description: Lesser spotted woodpecker – 5:45 A.M. – Kirby Forest, Cumbria
Date: May 15

Message: Some of you asked for some pictures of the lesser spotted woodpeckers that are rumored to live in the forest near my new house. Well, I was fortunate enough to capture a picture of one of them while out walking my dogs this morning. Although I only saw one, my neighbors have told me that several have been seen locally in recent weeks. I'll keep my eyes open and my camera ready! (72 words)

Image file attached: Lesser_spotted_woodpecker_05.15

191. What does the Web page indicate about the message board?
(A) It is used by experienced bird watchers.
(B) It requires members to pay an annual fee.
(C) Members can create their own image gallery.
(D) Videos of certain lengths are permitted.

192. What does the British Bird Watching Message Board promise to its members?
(A) It will not publish images in its Web gallery.
(B) It provides tips on photographing birds.
(C) It holds an event for members once per month.
(D) It does not share images with other businesses.

193. Why did Mr. Bedford post on the message board?
(A) To seek recommendations for bird watching locations
(B) To comment on a member's uploaded image
(C) To respond to requests from other members
(D) To request assistance in identifying a bird

194. How did Mr. Bedford fail to follow the message board rules?
(A) His image description is not detailed enough.
(B) He did not upload the required number of images.
(C) He posted in the wrong section of the board.
(D) His message exceeded a word limit.

195. What is probably true about Mr. Bedford?
(A) He recently moved to a new home.
(B) He just started a new job at a magazine.
(C) He is a moderator of a message board.
(D) He recently purchased a new camera.

▶ 삼중지문 문제풀이 전략

❶ 첫 번째 지문을 읽고 1번 문제를 푼다.
주제/목적 유형이 출제됐다면 우선적으로 풀이하며, 남은 지문을 읽으면서 세부사항 또는 동의어 유형을 푼다.

❷ 2번 또는 3번 문제가 연계문제인 경우 [첫 번째 지문 - 두 번째 지문] 또는 [첫 번째 지문 - 세 번째 지문]을, 4번 또는 5번 문제가 연계문제인 경우 [두 번째 지문 - 세 번째 지문]을 읽고 단서를 조합하여 정답을 고르면 된다.

❸ 주로 연계문제는 사실확인 유형이나 추론 유형으로 출제되므로 다른 문제를 먼저 풀면서 지문의 내용을 파악한 후에 가장 마지막으로 푸는 것이 좋다.

Question 1 refers to the following article, information, and form.

Local Company to Host Community Fair for Charity

Bayside Industries has announced plans to host a community fair on Saturday, August 12, at Riverside Park to raise money for local charities. The event will feature live music, food stalls, games, and a silent auction, with all proceeds going to support organizations like the Children's Shelter and the Hunger Relief Fund. The fair aims to bring the community together for a day of fun while making a positive impact on those in need.

Midford City Council Event Permit Application Process

Event organizers must complete the City Council's event permit application at least 10 days in advance. Once it is submitted, a city safety inspector will visit the proposed event site to perform an evaluation and ensure it meets safety regulations, including crowd management, fire exits, and accessibility. Organizers may be asked to provide additional documentation, such as insurance coverage or a security plan. Upon approval, a permit will be issued, and the event can proceed as scheduled. Fees vary depending on the type of event and are payable at the time of application.

MIDFORD CITY COUNCIL

Event Permit Application Form

Company Name: Bayside Industries
Contact Person: Sarah Thompson
Application Date: August 3
E-mail: sthompson@baysideindustries.com
Event Location: Riverside Park, 1200 Coastal Drive
Proposed Event Date: August 12
Event Setup Start Date/Time: August 11, 8:00 A.M.
Proposed Event End Date/Time: August 12, 6:00 P.M.
Date of Evaluation: August 5

1. What most likely will happen on August 3?

(A) Organizers will begin setting up an event.
(B) A safety inspector will visit Riverside Park.
(C) Ms. Thompson will pay a fee for a permit.
(D) Money will be raised for local charities.

서아쌤 시점
삼중지문 연계문제 풀이 ▶

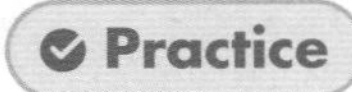

Questions 1-5 refer to the following advertisement, e-mail, and receipt.

Find Your Dream Dress at Elegance Bridal!

Elegance Bridal is excited to announce a change at three of our retail outlets. Starting November 1, our stores in Downtown Ottawa, Vancouver Heights, and Toronto West will remain open until 8 P.M. to better accommodate our customers' busy schedules. Whether you're looking for the perfect wedding gown or bridesmaid dresses, our experienced consultants are ready to assist. Visit one of our beautiful showrooms or call today for more information on availability and pricing.

To: Hanna Wright <hannahwright@email.com>
From: Clara Jones <cjones@elegancebridal.com>
Date: November 12, 10:15 A.M.
Subject: Order EB3039481

Dear Ms. Wright,

I'm reaching out regarding the wedding dress you ordered on November 9. We currently have only one of this specific dress in stock. It has been used as a display sample here in our Toronto West showroom. While the dress has been tried on by other customers, it remains in pristine condition. Our staff has thoroughly inspected it, and there are no visible signs of wear, such as stains or loose stitching.

As you purchased the dress with the expectation that it was brand new, we would like to offer you two options:
- You may cancel the order and receive a full refund immediately.
- If you'd like to keep the sample dress, we will offer you a 15 percent discount on the original price and ship it out today.

Please let us know how you'd like to proceed, and we will make sure the dress is delivered to your preferred location promptly. We apologize for any inconvenience this may have caused.

Sincerely,

Clara Jones
Elegance Bridal

Elegance Bridal - Receipt
Order number: EB3039481
Date: November 13

Description	**Price**
"Serena" Wedding Dress	$1,200.00
15% discount on dress	-$180.00
Shipping and handling	$25.00
Sales tax (7%)	$71.05
Total	**$1,116.05**

Ship to:	Bill to:
Hanna Wright	Hanna Wright
2712 Maple Avenue	2712 Maple Avenue
Calgary, AB T2P 1K2	Calgary, AB T2P 1K2

Visit our Web site at www.elegancebridalonline.ca to view our full range of dresses and store locations.

1. What is the purpose of the advertisement?
(A) To introduce a new range of dresses
(B) To announce a change to business hours
(C) To promote a new retail location
(D) To advertise employment opportunities

2. What is most likely true about the store where Ms. Jones works?
(A) It is open in the evening.
(B) It has expanded its inventory.
(C) It has hired new employees.
(D) It was launched in November.

3. What does the e-mail indicate about the wedding dress?
(A) It requires some alterations.
(B) It has been on display in Ottawa.
(C) It is discounted as part of a seasonal promotion.
(D) It is the only one of that style currently available.

4. What can be inferred about Ms. Wright?
(A) She requested a refund on a dress.
(B) She bought a dress for a friend.
(C) She is getting married in December.
(D) She purchased a display dress.

5. According to the receipt, what is true about Elegance Bridal?
(A) It charges a delivery fee.
(B) It offers free dress repairs.
(C) It has a showroom in Calgary.
(D) It offers discounts on its Web site.

Check-up Test

강의 바로보기

Questions 1-5 refer to the following Web page, schedule, and testimonial.

http://www.titansecuritysolutions.com/aboutus

Titan Security Solutions provides comprehensive security services for large-scale events, with expected attendances of ten thousand people or more, throughout the United States. Whether you're hosting a concert, festival, corporate gathering, or sporting event, our team is equipped to handle all your security needs. We can deploy highly trained security personnel, offer state-of-the-art surveillance equipment, and create tailored security plans to ensure the safety of your guests and staff.

At Titan Security Solutions, our services include crowd control, access point management, VIP protection, and perimeter surveillance. We use cutting-edge approaches, such as drone monitoring and real-time communication systems, to stay ahead of potential threats. Our personnel are licensed, highly experienced, and capable of handling both planned security measures and any on-the-spot challenges. We offer 24/7 support before, during, and after your event to ensure everything runs smoothly.

Let Titan Security Solutions take care of your event's security. Contact us today to learn more about our customizable packages and services!

Titan Security Solutions – Team Assignments

Schedule Date: September 17

Event Details	Event Location	Team Leader
Championship game (baseball)	Mercado Stadium	Steve Arnett
Global food festival	New City Plaza	Mitch Lundgren
Pop music festival	Mayflower Public Park	Jennifer Beale
Comic book convention	Redman Exhibition Hall	Pete Wellford

정답 및 해설 p.56

http://www.titansecuritysolutions.com/testimonials/19829

September 18 –Yesterday, I attended the Soundwave Music Festival, and I have to say, the security provided by Titan Security Solutions was outstanding. Given the size of the crowd and the high-energy atmosphere, I expected long lines and potential chaos at the entrance. Instead, I was impressed by how smoothly everything ran. The security personnel were incredibly efficient and professional. They managed the crowd with ease, kept the lines moving, and ensured everyone felt safe without being overbearing.

What really stood out to me was their attention to detail. Despite the large number of attendees, they handled everything from bag checks to access points seamlessly. I also noticed their use of advanced technology like surveillance drones, which was reassuring. Overall, Titan Security made the entire experience more enjoyable, and I'll definitely feel safer attending future events knowing they're in charge.

Posted by: Leonard Venucci

1. What does the Web page indicate about Titan Security Solutions?

(A) It mainly provides security at sporting events.
(B) It utilizes high-tech technology.
(C) It is currently hiring new personnel.
(D) It provides services outside of the U.S.

2. According to the schedule, who was the security team leader for the baseball game on September 17?

(A) Steve Arnett
(B) Mitch Lundgren
(C) Jennifer Beale
(D) Pete Wellford

3. What is probably true about the event Mr. Venucci attended?

(A) It attracted at least 10,000 attendees.
(B) It did not require an admission fee.
(C) It took place on multiple days.
(D) It was broadcast live on television.

4. Where did Mr. Venucci recently attend an event?

(A) At Mercado Stadium
(B) At New City Plaza
(C) At Mayflower Public Park
(D) At Redman Exhibition Hall

5. What is indicated about the security team in the testimonial?

(A) It was responsible for bag inspections.
(B) It worked on-site for 24 hours.
(C) It asked several people to leave an event.
(D) It ensured a parking area was safe.

Questions 6-10 refer to the following article, e-mail, and attachment.

TechNova Acquires AppEase in $75 Million Deal

SAN FRANCISCO (April 12) – Software giant TechNova announced on Friday that it has acquired AppEase, a fast-growing mobile application developer. This acquisition is part of TechNova's strategic plan to diversify its product portfolio by expanding into the mobile app market. Over the next two years, the company aims to integrate AppEase's app development expertise in human resources applications. Jack Moreno, TechNova's CEO, said that this move is essential for staying competitive in the rapidly evolving tech industry, where mobile platforms are becoming increasingly dominant.

Though headquartered in San Francisco, TechNova has opened offices in New York, Austin, and Seattle to support its expansion. Mr. Moreno noted that he first became aware of AppEase's innovative approach when he used one of their apps during a conference last year. "Their user-friendly design and cutting-edge technology align perfectly with TechNova's mission to deliver superior software solutions," Moreno stated.

From: Michael Trench, Operations Manager
To: All AppEase Staff
Date: April 15
Subject: TechNova Aquisition
Attachment: Current_Overtime_Policy

Hi Team,

As many of you know, with the recent acquisition by TechNova, some company policies will be changing. I'm writing to inform you about TechNova's overtime policies and rates, which will take effect for us starting May 1. To confirm, our overtime policy will be as follows:

- Overtime pay will be calculated at time-and-a-half for hours worked over 40 per week.
- Weekend and holiday work will receive double pay.
- Overtime approval will require direct supervisor sign-off two days in advance.

I have attached AppEase's current policy for your reference. To help clarify any concerns, Melissa Haskin, head of operations at TechNova's headquarters, will host a virtual Q&A session on April 20 at 10 A.M. We expect all of you to attend.

Best regards,

Michael Trench
Operations Manager
AppEase

AppEase
<u>Current Overtime Policy</u>

- Overtime hours are any hours you work in excess of your contracted 40 hours per week. Overtime hours will be paid at a rate of 1.5x your normal hourly rate.
- Occasionally, you will be asked to work over the weekend or on national holidays. Overtime hours in such cases will be paid at a rate of 2x your normal hourly rate based on 40 hours per week.
- If you plan to work overtime, you must receive approval from your line manager at least one day in advance. Your line manager will submit an approval to the accounting department so that your overtime hours are reflected on your next pay slip.

6. According to the article, why is TechNova acquiring AppEase?

(A) To expand its distribution network
(B) To improve workplace productivity
(C) To break into European software markets
(D) To provide a wider range of products

7. What type of mobile applications does AppEase mainly produce?

(A) Human resources
(B) Financial management
(C) Graphic design
(D) Instant messaging

8. Where is Ms. Haskin's office?

(A) In Austin
(B) In Seattle
(C) In New York
(D) In San Francisco

9. What are AppEase's employees expected to do on April 20?

(A) Visit TechNova's headquarters
(B) Attend an online meeting
(C) Sign new employment contracts
(D) Complete a training course

10. How is AppEase's current overtime policy different from TechNova's?

(A) Shorter notice is required for overtime approval.
(B) Employees are contracted to work fewer hours per week.
(C) Overtime rates are higher on weekends and holidays.
(D) Staff are paid less for overtime hours exceeding contracted hours.

서아쌤의 토익 비밀과외

LISTENING COMPREHENSION

LC

Playlist 1

음원 바로듣기 강의 바로보기

만점을 위한 사람사진&고난도 표현의 모든 것!

Part 1

사람사진 필수 문법 상황별 고난도 정답 표현

▶ 현재진행(is/are -ing): ~하고 있다

P1_1

- ☐ The man **is resting** on a wooden bench. 남자가 나무 벤치에서 쉬고 있다.
- ☐ A worker **is inspecting** some machines. 작업자가 몇 대의 기계를 점검하고 있다.
- ☐ A woman **is looking at** a magazine. 여자가 잡지를 보고 있다.
- ☐ Some people **are walking down** some steps. 몇몇 사람들이 몇 개의 계단을 걸어 내려오고 있다.
- ☐ One of the men **is pointing** to a map. 남자들 중 한 명이 지도를 가리키고 있다.
- ☐ They **are boarding** an airplane. 사람들이 비행기에 탑승하고 있다.

▶ 현재진행 수동태(is/are being p.p.): ~되고 있는 중이다

- ☐ Some items **are being placed** on a shelf. 몇몇 상품들이 선반에 놓여지는 중이다.
- ☐ Some potted plants **are being watered.** 몇몇 화분에 심어진 식물들에 물이 뿌려지고 있는 중이다.
- ☐ A rug **is being rolled up.** 러그가 둥글게 말리고 있는 중이다.
- ☐ Some vehicles **are being repaired.** 몇몇 차량들이 수리되고 있는 중이다.
- ☐ A copy machine **is being used.** 복사기가 사용되고 있는 중이다.

사람이 등장하는 사진에서 사람명사 주어를 사용하지 않고, 사물명사를 주어로 사용하여 사진을 묘사할 수 있다는 점을 꼭 명심하세요!

▶ 현재 수동태(is/are p.p.): ~되어 있다

- ☐ A cyclist **is stopped** near some trees. 자전거를 타는 사람이 몇몇 나무 근처에 멈춰 있다.
- ☐ Some people **are seated** in an outdoor dining area. 몇몇 사람들이 야외 식사 구역에 앉아 있다.
- ☐ They **are lined up** at the side of the building. 사람들이 건물 한 쪽 면에 줄지어 있다.

Practice

P1_2

1.

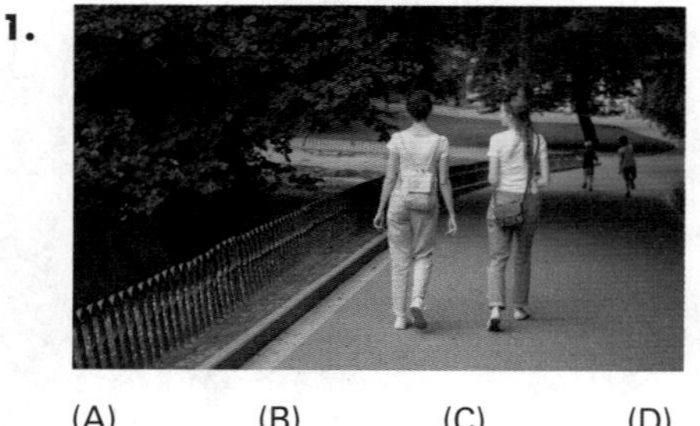

(A) (B) (C) (D)

2.

(A) (B) (C) (D)

▶ 사무실/회의실/실험실

P1_3

- ☐ She **is operating** some machinery. 여자가 몇몇 기계를 작동시키고 있다.
- ☐ The people **are having** a conversation. 사람들이 대화를 하고 있다.
- ☐ A man **is facing** some computer monitors. 남자가 컴퓨터 모니터 몇 대와 마주보고 있다.
- ☐ A woman **is erasing** a whiteboard. 여자가 화이트보드를 지우고 있다.
- ☐ He **is photocopying** a document. 남자가 서류 하나를 복사하고 있다.
- ☐ One of the men **is writing** on a piece of paper. 남자들 중 한 명이 종이 한 장에 쓰고 있다.
- ☐ The man **is using** some laboratory equipment. 남자가 몇몇 실험기구를 사용하고 있다.
- ☐ One of the women **is typing** on a keyboard. 여자들 중 한 명이 키보드로 타자를 치고 있다.
- ☐ A man **is adjusting** the window shade. 남자가 블라인드를 조정하고 있다.
- ☐ The woman **is wearing** safety gloves. 여자가 보호 장갑을 착용한 상태이다.
- ☐ She **is reaching** into a cabinet drawer. 여자가 수납장 서랍에 손을 넣고 있다.
- ☐ Some people **are distributing** papers. 몇몇 사람들이 종이를 나눠주고 있다.

서아쌤 비밀Tip

사람사진에서는 사진에 등장하는 인물의 '시선 처리'가 정답 문장을 골라내는 데 중요한 역할을 해요. 그래서 눈으로 '보는 것'과 관련된 표현이 많이 나오고, '보다' 동사 표현은 항상 현재진행형으로 출제되니 「is/are -ing」 형태로 기억해 두세요.

looking (at), watching, studying 보고 있다	looking into 안을 들여다보고 있다	inspecting 점검하고 있다
peering into 자세히 들여다보고 있다	reviewing 검토하고 있다	checking 확인하고 있다
examining 자세히 보고 있다	browsing 둘러보고 있다	facing 마주보고 있다

Some diners **are studying** the menu. 몇몇 식사 손님들이 메뉴를 보고 있다.
One of the men **is inspecting** a motorcycle engine. 남자들 중 한 명이 오토바이 엔진을 점검하고 있다.
Some people **are browsing** the shelves in a store. 몇몇 사람들이 매장에서 선반들을 둘러보고 있다.

Practice

P1_4

3.

(A) (B) (C) (D)

4.

(A) (B) (C) (D)

▶ 상점/식당

P1_5

- ☐ A man **is examining** the product. 남자가 제품을 자세히 보고 있다.
- ☐ Clothes **are hanging** on racks. 옷들이 옷걸이에 걸려 있다.
- ☐ A man **is paying** at a cash register. 남자가 금전 등록기에서 지불하고 있다.
- ☐ The woman **is weighing** some fruit on a scale. 여자가 저울에 몇몇 과일의 무게를 재고 있다.
- ☐ One of the men **is reaching** for a menu. 남자들 중 한 명이 메뉴판에 손을 뻗고 있다.
- ☐ A woman **is serving** food to a customer. 여자가 손님에게 음식을 서빙하고 있다.
- ☐ A server **is clearing** dishes from a table. 서빙하는 사람이 탁자에서 접시들을 정리하고 있다.
- ☐ A woman **is pushing** a cart filled with some merchandise. 여자가 몇몇 상품으로 채워진 카트를 밀고 있다.

▶ 주방/집안/정원

- ☐ The man **is wiping off** a counter. 남자가 카운터를 닦고 있다.
- ☐ People **are trimming** some bushes. 사람들이 몇몇 덤불을 다듬고 있다.
- ☐ One of the women **is sweeping** the floor. 여자들 중 한 명이 바닥을 쓸고 있다.
- ☐ He **is gripping** a garden tool. 남자가 정원용 기구를 잡고 있다.
- ☐ A woman **is raking** some leaves. 여자가 몇몇 낙엽들을 갈퀴로 모으고 있다.
- ☐ She **is kneeling** on a tile floor. 여자가 타일 바닥에서 무릎을 꿇고 있다.
- ☐ Some people **are bending over** some flowers. 몇몇 사람들이 몇 송이의 꽃 위로 허리를 숙이고 있다.

서아쌤 비밀Tip

사람사진에서 눈으로 보는 것 다음으로 집중해서 봐야 하는 것은 바로 사진에 등장하는 사람의 '손'입니다. Part 1에서 정말 자주 나오는 손 동작과 관련된 표현을 익혀보세요.

holding 들고 있다, 잡고 있다	reaching 손을 뻗고 있다	carrying 나르고 있다, 옮기고 있다
picking up 집어 올리고 있다	pushing 밀고 있다	waving 손을 흔들고 있다
shaking hands 악수하고 있다	pointing at ~을 가리키고 있다	distributing 나눠주고 있다
loading 싣고 있다	putting away 치우고 있다	unloading 내리고 있다

One of the men **is carrying** a suitcase by the handles. 남자들 중 한 명이 손잡이로 여행 가방을 나르고 있다.
Some workers **are unloading** containers from the ship. 몇몇 직원들이 배에서 컨테이너를 내리고 있다.

Practice

P1_6

5.

(A) (B) (C) (D)

6.

(A) (B) (C) (D)

▶ 도심/교통수단/공사 현장 P1_7

☐ A woman **is exiting** a vehicle. 여자가 차에서 내리고 있다.
☐ A wheelbarrow **is being pushed** along a path. 외바퀴 손수레가 도보를 따라 밀려지는 중이다.
☐ They **are stepping down** from a train. 사람들이 기차에서 내리고 있다.
☐ Some passengers **are getting into** a boat. 몇몇 승객들이 배에 탑승하고 있다.
☐ The woman **is leaning over** a brick structure. 여자가 벽돌 구조물에 기대고 있다.
☐ A construction crew **is working on** a machine. 건설 노동자가 기계로 일하고 있다.
☐ The man **is picking up** a shovel to move some soil. 남자가 약간의 흙을 옮기기 위해 삽을 집어 올리고 있다.
☐ A house **is under construction.** 집이 공사 중이다.

서아쌤 비밀Tip

사람사진에서 마지막으로 볼 부분은 '발과 다리'예요. 지금 걷고 있는지, 서 있는지, 내려가거나 올라가고 있는지 등과 같이 사람의 상태나 동작을 나타낼 수 있으므로 발과 다리 관련 동사들을 반드시 암기하세요.

walking 걷고 있다	strolling 산책하고 있다	descending 내려가고 있다
stepping off ~에서 내리고 있다	walking down ~을 내려가고 있다	getting into ~에 탑승하다
stepping onto ~에 오르고 있다	crossing 건너고 있다	climbing (up) (~을) 오르고 있다
getting out of ~에서 내리고 있다	standing 서 있다	passing 지나가고 있다

A man is **descending** some steps. 남자가 몇몇 계단들을 내려가고 있다.
Some pedestrians are **crossing** the street in front of vehicles. 몇몇 보행자들이 차량 앞에서 길을 건너고 있다.

▶ 항구&해변/공원/기타 야외

☐ A man **is stepping onto** a dock. 남자가 부두에 오르고 있다.
☐ Some people **are fishing** from a riverbank. 몇몇 사람들이 강둑에서 낚시를 하고 있다.
☐ Two people **are strolling** along the shore. 두 명의 사람들이 해안을 따라 산책하고 있다.
☐ A woman **is posing** for a photograph. 여자가 사진을 찍기 위해 포즈를 취하고 있다.
☐ Some park maintenance **is being carried out.** 몇몇 공원 유지보수 작업이 진행되고 있다.
☐ Some people **are resting** at a picnic table. 몇몇 사람들이 피크닉 테이블에서 쉬고 있다.
☐ A man **is rowing** a boat. 남자가 배의 노를 젓고 있다.

Practice

P1_8

7.

(A) (B) (C) (D)

8.

(A) (B) (C) (D)

Check-up Test

P1_9

1.

2.

3.

4.

5.

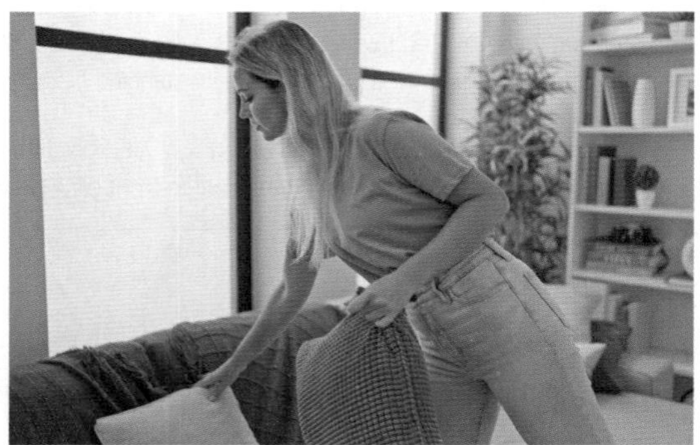

6.

정답 및 해설 p.61

7.

10.

8.

11.

9.

12.

Playlist 2

음원 바로듣기 강의 바로보기

만점을 위한 사물사진&고난도 표현의 모든 것!

Part 1

사물사진 필수 문법 상황별 고난도 정답 표현

▶ 현재 수동태(is/are p.p.): (현재) ~되어 있다

P2_1

- ☐ A pillow **is placed** on a couch. 베개 하나가 소파에 놓여져 있다.
- ☐ Some potted plants **are lined up** in a row. 몇몇 화분에 심어진 식물들이 한 줄로 줄지어 있다.
- ☐ A water fountain **is surrounded** by trees. 분수대가 나무들로 둘러싸여 있다.
- ☐ A picnic area **is covered** by an awning. 피크닉 구역이 차양으로 덮여 있다.
- ☐ A ribbon **is tied** to the fence outside. 리본이 바깥에 있는 울타리에 묶여 있다.

▶ 현재완료 수동태(has/have been p.p.): (과거에서 현재까지) ~되어 있다

현재 수동태와 현재완료 수동태의 의미상 차이는 거의 없어요. 헷갈린다면 Part 1에서는 두 시제가 같다고 생각하고 문제를 풀어도 돼요.

- ☐ Some frying pans **have been turned** over. 몇몇 프라이팬들이 뒤집혀 있다.
- ☐ A vehicle **has been parked** near a curb. 차량이 연석 근처에 주차되어 있다.
- ☐ Window curtains **have been pulled closed.** 창문 커튼들이 닫혀 있다.
- ☐ Some shovels **have been stacked** on the ground. 몇몇 삽들이 땅에 쌓여 있다.
- ☐ Some umbrellas **have been left open** in an outdoor café. 몇몇 파라솔들이 야외 카페에 펼쳐진 채로 있다.

서아쌤 비밀Tip

현재진행 시제(is/are -ing)와 현재진행 수동태(is/are being p.p.) 시제는 사람명사 주어와 함께 주로 사용하지만, 아래 동사들의 경우 예외적으로 사물명사 주어와 함께 사용해 사물의 상태를 나타낼 수 있어요.

Some photographs **are hanging** on the wall. 몇몇 사진들이 벽에 걸려 있다.
A tall building **is overlooking** the city street. 높은 건물이 도시 거리를 내려다보고 있다.
A bus **is crossing** over a bridge. 버스가 다리를 건너고 있다.

Some items **are being displayed** in a shop window. 몇몇 제품들이 매장 유리창에 진열되어 있다.
Sunlight **is being cast** on the porch. 햇살이 현관에 드리워져 있다.

현재진행 수동태(is/are being p.p.)를 썼지만 동작을 나타내지 않는 예외적인 동사 표현이에요.

Practice

P2_2

1.

(A) (B) (C) (D)

2.

(A) (B) (C) (D)

사물사진에서 사물은 주로 사람에 의해 어딘가에 '놓여 있기' 때문에 이와 관련된 동사 표현이 가장 많이 출제되고 있어요.

▶ 주방/집안/정원

P2_3

- ☐ A telephone **is mounted** on a wall. 전화기가 벽에 걸려 있다.
- ☐ The broom **is propped against** the wheelbarrow. 빗자루가 외바퀴 손수레에 기대어져 있다.
- ☐ The vase **is positioned** in a corner. 꽃병이 구석에 위치해 있다.
- ☐ Some eating utensils **have been put** in a drawer. 몇몇 식기들이 서랍 안에 넣어져 있다.
- ☐ Some decorative objects **are suspended** from the ceiling. 몇몇 장식품들이 천장에 매달려 있다.

▶ 항구/공원

- ☐ Some boats **are docked** in a harbor. 몇몇 배들이 항구에 정박해 있다.
- ☐ Some fishing nets **have been left** on a pier. 몇몇 낚시 그물들이 부두에 놓여 있다.
- ☐ Leaves **are scattered** across the grass. 나뭇잎들이 풀밭에 흩어져 있다.
- ☐ Tree branches **are piled** in a field. 나뭇가지들이 들판에 쌓여 있다.
- ☐ Some park benches **are arranged** in a circle. 몇몇 공원 벤치들이 동그랗게 배치되어 있다.

▶ 공사 현장/기타 야외

- ☐ A door **has been taken off** its frame. 문 하나가 틀에서 떨어져 있다.
- ☐ Some materials **have been discarded** in a bin. 몇몇 자재들이 쓰레기통에 버려져 있다.
- ☐ Scaffolding **has been installed** outside the building. 비계가 건물 바깥에 설치되어 있다.
- ☐ Some road signs **have been set up** in a parking lot. 몇몇 도로 표지판들이 주차장에 설치되어 있다.
- ☐ A ladder **has been hung** on a hook at a construction site. 사다리 하나가 건설 현장에 있는 걸이에 걸려 있다.

서아쌤 비밀Tip

사물사진을 묘사할 때 주어로 자주 사용되는 사물명사들이 있는데, 우리에게는 다소 생소한 고난도 어휘들이기 때문에 빠른 해석을 위해 미리 암기해 두는 것이 좋아요.

utensil (가정용) 도구	awning 차양	ramp 경사로	column 기둥
curb 연석	archway 아치형 입구, 길	ferry 배	bush 관목, 덤불
backyard 뒷마당	canopy 천막	deck (배의) 갑판	rack 거치대, 걸이

Bike **racks** are lined up next to a building. 자전거 거치대들이 건물 옆에 줄지어 있다.
Some cooking **utensils** are placed in a sink. 몇몇 요리 도구들이 싱크대 안에 놓여 있다.
A **canopy** is being assembled at a campsite. 천막이 캠핑장에서 조립되어지고 있다.

Practice

P2_4

3.

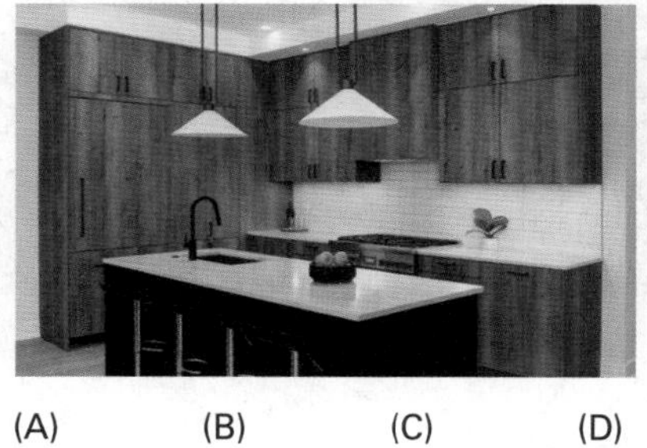

(A) (B) (C) (D)

4.

(A) (B) (C) (D)

Check-up Test

음원 바로듣기 강의 바로보기

P2_5

1.

4.

2.

5.

3.

6.

정답 및 해설 p.63

7.

10.

8.

11.

9.

12.

Playlist 3

시험 전 의문사 의문문 벼락치기 ①

Part 2

공통 우회 답변 | Who 의문문 | When 의문문 | Where 의문문

▶ 모르겠습니다.

P3_1

- ☐ I don't know. I have no idea. Sorry, I'm not quite sure. I am not familiar with that. I don't know what you mean. 잘 모르겠어요.
- ☐ It doesn't make sense to me. 이해가 안 가요.
- ☐ Nobody told me. 아무도 말씀해주시지 않았어요.
- ☐ I haven't heard anything yet. 아직 아무것도 듣지 못했어요.
- ☐ Not as far as I know. Not that I know of. 제가 알기로는 아닙니다.

▶ 아직 결정되지 않았어요.

- ☐ It hasn't been decided yet. The matter is still undecided. 아직 결정되지 않았어요.
- ☐ We're still deciding. 여전히 결정 중입니다.
- ☐ We still need to finalize some details. 여전히 몇 가지 세부사항을 마무리해야 할 필요가 있어요.
- ☐ It's too soon to announce. 발표하기엔 너무 이릅니다.
- ☐ We need time to make a decision. It's going to take some time to decide. 결정하려면 시간이 필요합니다.

▶ 확인해 볼게요. 알아 볼게요. 물어 볼게요. 물어 보세요.

- ☐ Let me check. 확인해 볼게요.
- ☐ I'll find out. 알아 볼게요.
- ☐ I'll look it up. 찾아 볼게요.
- ☐ I'll see what I can find out. 찾을 수 있는지 알아 볼게요.
- ☐ I'll get back to you on that. 그에 관해 알아보고 다시 연락 드릴게요.
- ☐ I'll let you know soon. 곧 알려 드릴게요.
- ☐ You can ask Mr. Steven in the marketing department. 마케팅부의 스티븐 씨에게 물어 보세요.
- ☐ Why don't you ask Mr. Dan in the sales department? 영업부의 댄 씨에게 물어 보시는 게 어때요?
- ☐ Let's ask the waiter. 웨이터에게 물어 보죠.
- ☐ I think Mr. Smith would know. 제 생각엔 스미스 씨가 알 거예요.

▶ 관련 내용으로 되묻기

- ☐ Didn't you check the bulletin board? 게시판 확인 안 하셨나요?
- ☐ Will you be available to discuss that agenda at 2 P.M.? 그 안건을 논의하기 위해 오후 2시에 시간되세요?
- ☐ Haven't you heard that the event was canceled? 행사가 취소된 거 못 들으셨어요?
- ☐ Are you a regular employee? 정규 직원이신가요?

▶ 정답 패턴 1: 사람 이름

P3_2

Who 의문문은 사람 이름으로 답변하는 패턴이 가장 많이 출제된다. I think, I heard, I believe 등의 표현들과 함께 담당자를 알려주는 유형의 답변이 자주 나오며, 사람 이름을 정확하게 못 들었더라도 Ms.나 Mr.만 들을 수 있다면 정답을 쉽게 고를 수 있다.

Q. **Who**'s presenting the survey results next week? 다음 주에 설문조사 결과는 누가 발표하나요?

A1. **Derek** is handling that. 데렉 씨가 그걸 처리하고 있어요.

A2. **I think Ms. Allison** is in charge of it. 제 생각엔 엘리슨 씨가 담당할 거예요.

▶ 정답 패턴 2: 직책명, 직업명, 부서명

주로 비즈니스 환경에서 이루어지는 질의응답이므로 사람 이름뿐만 아니라 직책명이나 직업명, 또는 부서명이나 회사명으로 답변하는 경우도 많다.

직책명 직업명	manager 부장 receptionist 안내원 technician 기사	board of directors 이사회 janitor 건물 관리인 secretary 비서	supervisor 관리자 park ranger 공원 경비원 intern 인턴
부서명	Marketing Department 마케팅부 Public Relations Department 홍보부 Human Resources Department 인사부 Customer Service Department 고객 서비스부	Sales Department 영업부 Maintenance Department 시설 관리부 Accounting Department 회계부 General Affairs Department 총무부	

Q. **Who**'s supposed to update the catalog? 누가 카탈로그를 업데이트할 예정인가요?

A1. Our team's senior **manager** will. 저희 팀의 선임 관리자가 할 거예요.

A2. The **Sales Department**. 영업부요.

▶ 정답 패턴 3: 인칭대명사/부정대명사

두 사람이 주고받는 짧은 대화이므로 보통 I로 시작하는 답변이 정답일 확률이 가장 높다. I 외에도 No one, Nobody, Someone 등의 부정대명사가 포함된 답변이 정답으로 출제되었다.

Q. **Who**'s meeting the representatives at the terminal today? 누가 오늘 터미널에서 직원들을 만나나요?

A1. **I** can take them to our office. 제가 사무실로 그분들을 모시고 올 수 있어요.

A2. **Someone** from the Paris branch. 파리 지사의 누군가가요.

✔ Practice

P3_3

1. Mark your answer on your answer sheet. (A) (B) (C)

2. Mark your answer on your answer sheet. (A) (B) (C)

3. Mark your answer on your answer sheet. (A) (B) (C)

▶ 정답 패턴 1: 같은 시제

P3_4

질문이 미래 시점에 대해 묻는 내용이라면 미래시제를 사용한 답변이, 과거의 일에 대해 묻는다면 과거시제로 답한 문장이 정답일 확률이 매우 높다. 하지만, 고난도로 출제된다면 미래시제로 질문해도 과거시제 또는 현재완료시제가 포함된 답변이 정답인 경우도 있으니 유의해야 한다.

Q. **When** is the ballroom dance performance happening? 사교 댄스 공연이 언제 시작하죠?

A1. It **will** start in about 15 minutes. 약 15분 후에 시작할 거예요. 「in + 시간」은 '~ 후에'라고 해석해요.

A2. We'**ll** need to check the pamphlet tomorrow. 내일 안내책자를 확인해 봐야 해요. 조동사 will 외에도, tomorrow나 next 등의 시간 표현만으로도 미래 시제를 나타낼 수 있어요.

Q. **When** did they purchase the office chairs? 사람들이 사무실 의자들을 언제 구매했나요?

A1. A few months **ago**. 몇 달 전에요.

A2. **Last** Tuesday during the summer sale. 지난주 화요일 여름 세일 중에요.

Q. **When will** the ceiling lights get fixed? 천장 조명이 언제 고쳐질 예정이죠?

A1. Some lightbulbs **were ordered** recently. 몇몇 전구들이 최근에 주문되었어요.

A2. The technician's visit **has been canceled.** 기술자의 방문이 취소됐어요.

▶ 정답 패턴 2: 시간/시점 표현

When 의문문에서 정답으로 자주 들리는 시간과 시점 관련 표현들이 있는데, 이러한 표현들은 듣자마자 해석할 수 있어야 지체 없이 정답을 고를 수 있다. 특히 not until이나 no later than이 포함된 선택지는 해석 시에 시간이 오래 걸리므로 미리 익혀두는 것이 좋다.

Not until ~가 되어서야	Not until the end of next month. 다음 달 말이나 되어서요.
As soon as ~하자마자	As soon as it becomes available. 이용 가능하자마자요.
After/Before ~ 후에/전에	Anytime before lunch. 점심시간 전에 언제든지요.
No later than 늦어도 ~까지	No later than July 17. 늦어도 7월 17일까지요.
Once 일단 ~하면	Once I finish this project. 일단 이 프로젝트를 끝내고 나면요.

Q. **When** will the flooring installation be done? 바닥 설치 작업이 언제 완료되나요?

A1. Right **after** the inspection is passed. 점검이 통과된 직후에요.

A2. **Not until** November. 11월이나 되어서요.

서아쌤 비밀Tip

after나 before 앞에 right가 붙어 '직후에' 또는 '직전에'라는 표현으로 정답이 출제될 수 있어요. Part 5에서도 right 뒤에 들어갈 after나 before를 고르는 문제가 자주 출제되니 함께 기억해 두세요.

Practice

P3_5

4. Mark your answer on your answer sheet. (A) (B) (C)

5. Mark your answer on your answer sheet. (A) (B) (C)

6. Mark your answer on your answer sheet. (A) (B) (C)

▶ 정답 패턴 1: 전치사 + 장소명사

P3_6

Where 의문문은 장소에 대한 질문인 만큼 각종 전치사와 장소명사로 답변하는 유형이 가장 흔하다. 선택지에 장소 전치사가 여러 개 등장할 수 있기 때문에 질문의 내용을 잘 듣고 사람이나 사물이 있을 법한 장소를 언급한 선택지를 정답으로 골라야 하는 것이 포인트이다.

Q. **Where** do you want these boxes to go? 이 박스들이 어디로 가길 원하세요?

A1. **Next to the entrance.** 입구 옆에요.

A2. You can put them **on the desk.** 책상 위에 놓아 주시면 돼요.

서아쌤 비밀Tip

Part 2 Where 의문문의 답변으로 자주 나오는 「전치사 + 장소명사」 조합! 제가 자주 출제되는 표현들만 정리해서 알려 드릴게요.

In a bottom drawer. 아래쪽 서랍 안에요.
Behind the building across the street. 거리 건너편에 있는 건물 뒤에요.
To the sales department. 영업부로요.
Just around the corner. 모퉁이를 돌아서 바로요.
Beside a mailbox. 우체통 옆에요.
On the second floor. 2층에요.
At the registration booth. 등록 부스에서요.
Down the hall. 복도 끝에요.

▶ 정답 패턴 2: 담당자/출처

장소를 물어보는 질문에 대해 사람 이름으로 대답하여 담당자를 알려주거나 정보를 얻게 된 출처로 답할 수도 있는데, 이 경우 주로 웹 사이트나 온라인 검색 또는 프로그램 설치 등으로 답변한 문장이 정답이다.

Q. **Where** can I pick up my business cards? 제 명함을 어디에서 찾을 수 있을까요?

A1. You should ask **Mr. Roper.** 로퍼 씨께 물어 보세요.

A2. **Wilson** in the Human Resources Department has them. 인사부의 윌슨 씨가 가지고 있어요.

Q. **Where**'s last quarter's financial performance analysis? 지난 분기의 재무 성과 분석은 어디에 있나요?

A1. On the company's **Web site.** 회사 웹 사이트에요.

A2. Download the new accounting **software.** 새 회계 소프트웨어를 다운로드하세요.

Practice

P3_7

7. Mark your answer on your answer sheet. (A) (B) (C)

8. Mark your answer on your answer sheet. (A) (B) (C)

9. Mark your answer on your answer sheet. (A) (B) (C)

Check-up Test

음원 바로듣기  강의 바로보기 

정답 및 해설 p.67

P3_8

1. Mark your answer on your answer sheet. (A) (B) (C)
2. Mark your answer on your answer sheet. (A) (B) (C)
3. Mark your answer on your answer sheet. (A) (B) (C)
4. Mark your answer on your answer sheet. (A) (B) (C)
5. Mark your answer on your answer sheet. (A) (B) (C)
6. Mark your answer on your answer sheet. (A) (B) (C)
7. Mark your answer on your answer sheet. (A) (B) (C)
8. Mark your answer on your answer sheet. (A) (B) (C)
9. Mark your answer on your answer sheet. (A) (B) (C)
10. Mark your answer on your answer sheet. (A) (B) (C)
11. Mark your answer on your answer sheet. (A) (B) (C)
12. Mark your answer on your answer sheet. (A) (B) (C)
13. Mark your answer on your answer sheet. (A) (B) (C)
14. Mark your answer on your answer sheet. (A) (B) (C)
15. Mark your answer on your answer sheet. (A) (B) (C)
16. Mark your answer on your answer sheet. (A) (B) (C)
17. Mark your answer on your answer sheet. (A) (B) (C)
18. Mark your answer on your answer sheet. (A) (B) (C)
19. Mark your answer on your answer sheet. (A) (B) (C)
20. Mark your answer on your answer sheet. (A) (B) (C)

MEMO

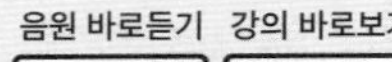

시험 전 의문사 의문문 벼락치기 ②

▶ 정답 패턴 1: 숫자 표현

P4_1

What 의문문은 바로 뒤에 나오는 명사를 집중해서 들어야 한다. What 의문사 뒤에 날짜/금액/시간 명사 등이 키워드로 제시된다면 그에 따른 숫자 표현이 주로 정답으로 출제된다.

Q. **What dates** would you like to reserve your flight tickets for? 어느 날짜로 비행기 티켓을 예약하고 싶으세요?
A1. From **August 19th** to **22nd**, please. 8월 19일부터 22일까지요.
A2. Any dates after the end of this week. 이번 주 말 이후 어느 날짜든지요.

Q. **What's the price** of this coffee vending machine? 이 커피 자판기의 가격은 얼마인가요?
A1. It's **$700** for this week's special price. 이번 주 특가로 700달러입니다.
A2. It's on sale for 800 euros. 800유로로 할인 중입니다.

Q. **What time** does the quarterly budget meeting start? 분기 예산 회의는 몇 시에 시작하나요?
A1. At **9:30 A.M.** sharp. 오전 9시 30분 정각에요.
A2. Usually around **12**. 보통 12시쯤이요.

▶ 정답 패턴 2: 긍정/부정/우회 답변

What 의문문이 「What do you think of/about ~?」으로 나온다면 상대방에게 의견을 물어보는 질문 유형이다. 따라서 긍정적/부정적/우회적 답변으로 말하는 경우가 많으므로 미리 출제 패턴을 익혀두는 것이 좋다. 이 외에도, 「What do you want me to do ~?」와 같은 표현으로 의견을 물을 때도 있다.

Q. **What do you think of** the updated payroll policy? 업데이트된 급여 정책에 대해서 어떻게 생각하시나요?
A1. It'll make our work easier. 우리 업무를 더 쉽게 만들 것 같아요.
A2. I'm worried that it might cause some issues. 몇 가지 문제들을 일으킬 것 같아 걱정되네요.

Q. **What do you want me to do** for the product launch event? 제품 출시 행사에 대해 제가 무엇을 하길 원하세요?
A1. You can contact the catering service. 출장 연회 서비스에 연락해 주시면 됩니다.
A2. It's all set for now, thanks for asking. 지금은 모두 준비되었어요, 물어봐 주셔서 감사합니다.

Practice

P4_2

1. Mark your answer on your answer sheet. (A) (B) (C)
2. Mark your answer on your answer sheet. (A) (B) (C)
3. Mark your answer on your answer sheet. (A) (B) (C)

▶ 정답 패턴 1: The one

P4_3

Which 의문문은 「Which (of) + 명사 ~?」 형태의 질문으로 나와 정해진 범위 내에서 하나를 선택하는 답변을 골라야 하는데, 앞에 언급된 명사를 대신하는 The one이 포함된 문장이 정답으로 가장 많이 출제된다.

Q. **Which projector** was replaced yesterday? 어느 프로젝터가 어제 교체된 거죠?
A1. **The one** next to my desk. 제 책상 옆에 있는 거요.
A2. **The** black **one.** 검정색 거요.

Q. **Which parcel** goes to the Vancouver branch? 밴쿠버 지사로 가는 소포가 어느 것이죠?
A1. **The one** from Okinawa. 오키나와에서 온 거요.
A2. **The one** in the hallway. 복도에 있는 거요.

서아쌤 비밀Tip

Which 의문문이 Part 2에 나오는 의문사 의문문의 출제 비중에서 많은 부분을 차지하는 것은 아니지만, 출제된다면 고득점을 위해 다 맞는 것을 목표로 해야 해요. 혹시 실제 시험에서 제대로 못 들었다면 The one이 들어간 선택지가 정답일 확률이 매우 높으니 The one이 들어가는 문장을 정답으로 골라 보세요.

The one on your left. 당신의 왼쪽에 있는 거요.
The one on the Willow Street. 윌로우 스트리트에 있는 거요.
The same one we used before. 저희가 전에 사용했던 것과 같은 거요.
The one we bought recently. 저희가 최근에 구매했던 거요.
It's the last one on sale. 할인하는 마지막 상품이에요.
I prefer the blue one. 저는 파란색으로 된 것을 선호해요.

▶ 정답 패턴 2: 사람 이름, 직책명, 직업명, 부서명

Which 의문문 다음에 사람명사 또는 회사명이 제시되면 Who 의문문과 동일한 내용을 물어본다고 생각하면 된다. 따라서 사람 이름, 직책명, 직업명, 부서명 등을 정답으로 선택한다.

Q. **Which candidate** has the most experience for the position? 어떤 후보자가 그 직책에 대해 가장 경험이 많나요?
A. **Ms. Maple**'s portfolio seems interesting. 메이플 씨의 포트폴리오가 흥미로워 보여요.

Q. **Which advertising agency** will you hire for the new project?
새로운 프로젝트를 위해 어느 광고 대행사를 고용할 건가요?
A. **Our manager** is still negotiating with the finance team. 저희 부장님이 여전히 재무팀과 협의 중이세요.

Practice

P4_4

4. Mark your answer on your answer sheet. (A) (B) (C)
5. Mark your answer on your answer sheet. (A) (B) (C)
6. Mark your answer on your answer sheet. (A) (B) (C)

▶ 정답 패턴 1: Because, To부정사, For + 명사, So that

P4_5

Why 의문문에 대한 정답은 이유로 답할 수 있는 Because(~ 때문에), To부정사(~하기 위해서), For + 명사 (~을 위해서), So that(~하도록) 4종 세트를 기억하면 된다. 어떤 상황에 대한 이유를 물어봤으니 그에 대한 이유 또는 목적으로 답하는 표현이 주로 정답이다.

Q. **Why** did Mr. Maxim reschedule our monthly meeting? 왜 막심 씨가 우리 월간 회의 일정을 다시 잡았나요?

A1. **Because** all the managers were at the executive meeting. 모든 부장님들이 임원 회의에 계셨기 때문에요.

A2. **To pick** our new clients up from the airport. 공항에서 새 고객님들을 모셔오기 위해서요.

Q. **Why** were you at the office early this morning? 왜 오늘 아침 사무실에 일찍 계셨나요?

A1. **To meet** a project deadline. 프로젝트 마감일을 맞추기 위해서요.

A2. **For an employee training session.** 직원 교육 시간을 위해서요.

Q. **Why** can't I have access to the financial data? 왜 제가 재무 자료를 이용할 수 없죠?

A1. **So that** we can keep the company's information secure. 회사의 정보를 안전하게 유지할 수 있기 위해서요.

A2. Only authorized personnel can see it. 승인 받은 직원만 그걸 볼 수 있어요.

Because를 쓰지 않고 기본 문장으로 이유를 설명을 하는 경우도 출제되고 있으니 문제를 끝까지 들어야 해요.

▶ 정답 패턴 2: 수락/거절

「Why don't you[we] ~?」는 일반적으로 '~하는 게 어때?'라는 제안의 뜻으로 사용되므로 수락과 거절의 답변이 가능하다. 하지만, 종종 '왜 ~하나요?, 왜 ~하지 않나요?'라는 뜻으로 이유를 묻는 고난도 질문으로도 출제되고 있으므로 반드시 소거법을 사용해 정답을 찾아야 한다.

Q. **Why don't we** sign up for the customer support workshop on Monday?
월요일에 있을 고객 지원 워크숍에 등록하는 게 어때요?

A1. That's a great idea. 좋은 생각이에요.

A2. I already did that. 전 이미 했어요.

A3. I'll be in interviews on that day. 저는 그날 계속 면접에 가 있을 겁니다.

Q. **Why didn't you** come to the store's grand opening last night? 왜 지난밤 매장 대개장 행사에 오지 않았나요?

A1. **Because** I had to go to Dallas for a business trip. 출장으로 댈러스에 가야 했기 때문에요.

A2. Didn't Ms. Claudia tell you? 클라우디아 씨가 말씀 안 하셨나요?

A3. I had an urgent deadline to meet. 맞춰야 하는 긴급한 마감이 있었어요.

Why didn't~ 외에도, Why isn't ~?와 Why haven't ~?도 이유를 물어볼 수 있어요.

✔ Practice

P4_6

7. Mark your answer on your answer sheet. (A) (B) (C)

8. Mark your answer on your answer sheet. (A) (B) (C)

9. Mark your answer on your answer sheet. (A) (B) (C)

▶ 정답 패턴 1: 수량, 빈도, 속도, 기간, 거리

P4_7

How 의문문은 How 바로 뒤에 오는 형용사나 부사에 따른 답변이 정해져 있다. 대표적으로 How many/much(얼마나 많이), How often(얼마나 자주), How soon(얼마나 빨리), How long(얼마나 오래), How far(얼마나 멀리) 등이 있다.

Q. **How much** does it cost to repair this refrigerator? 이 냉장고를 고치려면 얼마가 들까요?

A1. Less than **$180.** 180달러 미만이요.

A2. Has the warranty expired? 보증이 만료되었나요?

Q. **How long** will it take to complete the headquarters' remodeling?
본사 리모델링을 완료하는 데 얼마나 오래 걸릴까요?

A1. About **eight months,** but it can take longer. 약 8개월 정도인데, 더 길어질 수도 있어요.

A2. The exact duration was mentioned in the e-mail. 정확한 기간은 이메일에 언급되어 있어요.

▶ 정답 패턴 2: by -ing, through/via, with

How 뒤에 조동사나 동사가 올 경우 '어떻게 ~ 하나요?'라고 해석하며, 관련 방법 또는 수단으로 답변한다.

Q. **How do** I submit a subscription application? 구독 신청서를 어떻게 제출하나요?

A1. **By filling out** this registration form. 이 등록 양식을 작성함으로써요.

A2. You can see all the instructions **through** our Web site. 저희 웹 사이트를 통해 모든 안내사항을 보실 수 있어요.

▶ 정답 패턴 3: 수락/거절

How 의문문이 「How about -ing?」로 사용된다면 '~하는 게 어때요?'라는 뜻으로 제안을 나타낸다. 따라서 이에 대한 응답으로 수락이나 거절 표현이 정답이 될 수 있다. — What about -ing?로도 제안의 의미를 나타낼 수 있어요.

Q. **How about planting** some flowers on the top of the building? 우리 건물 옥상에 꽃을 좀 심는 건 어때요?

A1. That's a good suggestion. 좋은 제안이에요.

A2. There isn't enough budget for that. 그것을 위한 예산이 충분하지 않아요.

서아쌤 비밀Tip

How 의문문은 수량/빈도/속도/기간/거리/방법/수단/제안 외에 의견을 물어볼 때도 사용할 수 있어요. Part 2에서 관용적으로 쓰이는 How 의문문 고난도 표현들을 같이 정리해 볼까요?

How would you like your steak? 스테이크 굽기는 어떻게 해 드릴까요?
How would you like to pay for the purchase? 구매품에 대해 어떻게 지불하길 원하세요?
How did you enjoy your stay? 숙박은 괜찮으셨나요?
How did the presentation go? 발표는 어땠나요?

✔ Practice

P4_8

10. Mark your answer on your answer sheet. (A) (B) (C)

11. Mark your answer on your answer sheet. (A) (B) (C)

12. Mark your answer on your answer sheet. (A) (B) (C)

Check-up Test

음원 바로듣기

강의 바로보기

정답 및 해설 p.71

P4_9

1. Mark your answer on your answer sheet. (A) (B) (C)

2. Mark your answer on your answer sheet. (A) (B) (C)

3. Mark your answer on your answer sheet. (A) (B) (C)

4. Mark your answer on your answer sheet. (A) (B) (C)

5. Mark your answer on your answer sheet. (A) (B) (C)

6. Mark your answer on your answer sheet. (A) (B) (C)

7. Mark your answer on your answer sheet. (A) (B) (C)

8. Mark your answer on your answer sheet. (A) (B) (C)

9. Mark your answer on your answer sheet. (A) (B) (C)

10. Mark your answer on your answer sheet. (A) (B) (C)

11. Mark your answer on your answer sheet. (A) (B) (C)

12. Mark your answer on your answer sheet. (A) (B) (C)

13. Mark your answer on your answer sheet. (A) (B) (C)

14. Mark your answer on your answer sheet. (A) (B) (C)

15. Mark your answer on your answer sheet. (A) (B) (C)

16. Mark your answer on your answer sheet. (A) (B) (C)

17. Mark your answer on your answer sheet. (A) (B) (C)

18. Mark your answer on your answer sheet. (A) (B) (C)

19. Mark your answer on your answer sheet. (A) (B) (C)

20. Mark your answer on your answer sheet. (A) (B) (C)

MEMO

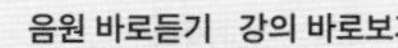

헷갈리기 쉬운 일반/선택/요청&제안 의문문 정리

Part 2

일반 의문문 | 선택 의문문 | 요청&제안 의문문 | 고난도 우회 답변

▶ 정답 패턴 1: Yes/No

P5_1

일반 의문문은 조동사, Be동사, Do/Have 동사 등으로 시작하는 의문문으로, Yes와 No로 답변할 수 있다. 일반 의문문에 not이 붙은 부정 의문문의 경우, 해석할 때 not은 무시하고 '긍정'으로 해석하면 쉽게 답변을 고를 수 있다. 특히, 부정 의문문은 주어와의 연음 때문에 잘 듣지 못할 수 있으니 많은 연습이 필요하다.

Q. **Will** the community center be open tomorrow? 내일 커뮤니티 센터가 문을 여나요?

A1. **Yes**, I checked their notice this morning. 네, 제가 그 공지를 오늘 아침에 확인했습니다.

A2. **No**, it's closed for two weeks. 아니요, 2주 동안 문을 닫습니다.

Q. **Isn't** there an additional discount on this membership? 이 회원권에 대한 추가 할인은 없나요?

A1. **Yes**, there's a 30% discount. 네, 30프로 할인됩니다.

A2. **No**, that sales promotion has ended. 아니요, 그 할인 행사는 종료되었습니다.

질문에 대한 대답이 긍정이면 'Yes', 부정이면 'No'예요. 부정 의문문도 긍정의 뜻을 가진 일반 의문문처럼 해석하면 돼요.

▶ 정답 패턴 2: Yes/No 생략

일반 의문문의 대답에 반드시 Yes나 No가 필수적으로 있어야 하는 것은 아니다. 최근에는 Yes/No가 생략되고 질문에 대한 추가 설명을 하는 유형이 더 많이 출제되고 있어 무작정 Yes/No를 기다리기보다 내용을 듣고 소거법을 통해 정답을 고르는 것이 좋다.

Q. **Have** you always biked to and from work? 자전거로 항상 출퇴근하세요?

A1. I don't have my own car. 저는 자차가 없어요.

A2. It's a convenient way for me to stay fit. 그게 제가 건강을 유지하기 위한 편리한 방법이에요.

Q. **Doesn't** the company pay for taking business courses after work?
퇴근 후 비즈니스 과정을 수강하는 것에 대한 비용을 회사에서 지불해 주시지 않나요?

A1. We do reimburse you all if you keep your original receipts. 원본 영수증을 보유하시면 모두 환급해 드립니다.

A2. Our quarterly budget is not big enough to cover that. 저희 분기별 예산이 그것을 충당하기에 충분히 크지 않습니다.

Practice

P5_2

1. Mark your answer on your answer sheet. (A) (B) (C)
2. Mark your answer on your answer sheet. (A) (B) (C)
3. Mark your answer on your answer sheet. (A) (B) (C)

▶ 정답 패턴 1: 둘 중 하나 선택

P5_3

A나 B 둘 중에 하나를 선택하는 답변이다. 일반적으로 Part 2에서는 질문과 유사한 발음이나 동일한 단어가 들어간 경우 오답의 확률이 높지만, 선택 의문문에서는 예외적으로 정답이 될 확률이 더 높다. 특히 이 유형의 정답 패턴에서는 직접적으로 선택 대상을 언급하기보다 우회적으로 대답하는 경우도 많으니 주의해야 한다.

Q. Should I schedule your presentation for **today or tomorrow in the afternoon?**
당신의 발표 일정을 오늘로 잡을까요, 아니면 내일 오후로 잡을까요?

A1. I'm free this afternoon. 저는 오늘 오후에 시간이 있어요.

A2. I have another project meeting today. 저는 오늘 다른 프로젝트 회의가 있습니다.

Q. **Are you going out to eat with us** for lunch **or did you bring food** from home?
저희와 밖에 나가서 점심 식사를 하실 건가요, 아니면 집에서 도시락을 가져오셨나요?

A1. Which restaurant are you going to? 어느 레스토랑으로 갈 예정이세요?

A2. My salad is in the fridge. 제 샐러드가 냉장고에 있어요.

▶ 정답 패턴 2: 제3의 옵션을 선택

A와 B 둘 중 하나를 선택하지 않고 전혀 다른 제3의 선택지를 요청하거나 제시할 수 있다. 정답으로 둘 중 하나를 선택하는 유형보다 어려운 유형에 속한다.

Q. **Are you walking or taking a bus** to the year-end ceremony?
종무식에 걸어 가시나요, 아니면 버스를 타고 가시나요?

A1. Mr. Hanssen has offered to drive me there. 한센 씨가 저를 그곳에 차로 데려다 주시기로 했어요.

A2. I'm feeling sick today, actually. 사실 저는 오늘 몸이 좋지 않아요.

▶ 정답 패턴 3: 아무거나 괜찮아요.

Q. Would you rather spend time **at a café or the park?**
카페에서 시간을 보내길 원하세요, 아니면 공원에서 보내길 원하세요?

A1. Either will be fine with me. 저는 아무거나 괜찮아요. — I have no preference. I don't mind either (way). Either one is okay.로도 대답할 수 있어요.

A2. Well, it's up to you. 음, 그건 당신에게 달렸어요.

▶ 정답 패턴 4: 둘 다요. 둘 다 아니에요.

Q. Are you going to apply for the internship program **at Eversley Estate or Pendleton Partners?**
에버슬리 에스테이트사 인턴십 프로그램에 지원할 건가요, 아니면 펜들턴 파트너스 사에 지원할 건가요?

A1. I'm considering both. 둘 다 고려하고 있어요.

A2. Neither. I'm not qualified. 둘 다 아니에요. 저는 자격이 되지 않아요. — Neither one appeals to me.로도 대답할 수 있어요.

Practice

P5_4

4. Mark your answer on your answer sheet. (A) (B) (C)

5. Mark your answer on your answer sheet. (A) (B) (C)

6. Mark your answer on your answer sheet. (A) (B) (C)

▶ 정답 패턴 1: 수락

P5_5

Q. **Could you** work the night shift for me instead? 제 밤 근무를 대신 일해주실 수 있나요?

A1. Sure. What day is it? 물론이죠. 무슨 요일이죠?

A2. Of course, I don't have any important plans. 물론이죠, 저는 어떤 중요한 약속도 없어요.

Q. **Why don't we** compare the prices at different landscaping companies?
다른 조경회사들의 가격들을 비교해보는 게 어때요?

A1. That would be really great. 그러면 정말 좋겠어요.

A2. Certainly, I'll do it right now. 그럼요, 제가 지금 바로 할게요.

▶ 정답 패턴 2: 거절

요청이나 제안을 거절하는 경우에는 No라고 단호하게 말하기보다는 우회적으로 거절하거나 관련 내용으로 되묻는 경우가 많다. 이미 요청사항을 완료했거나 선약이 있다는 답변이 자주 출제되고, 사과를 하거나 안타까움을 표현하는 경우 대부분 거절하는 표현으로 보면 된다.

Q. **Would you like me to** order more office furniture? 사무용 가구를 더 주문해 드릴까요?

A1. Thanks, but I already took care of it. 감사합니다만, 제가 이미 처리했습니다.

A2. The management team told us not to. 경영진에서 저희에게 그렇게 하지 말라고 말씀하셨어요.

Q. **Let's** discuss what our clients want to change in the building blueprints.
우리 고객님들이 건물 청사진에서 바꾸고 싶으신 것에 대해 논의합시다.

A1. I'm leaving the office early today for a dental appointment.
저는 오늘 치과 예약을 위해 일찍 퇴근할 예정이에요.

A2. Haven't you seen the e-mail from Ms. Bella yet? 벨라 씨에게서 온 이메일을 아직 못 보셨어요?

서아쌤 비밀Tip

다양한 문장 표현으로 요청이나 제안의 의미를 나타낼 수 있으니 각 질문의 의미와 함께 꼼꼼하게 정리해 두세요~!

요청	제안
Could/Can you ~? ~해 주실 수 있나요?	What[How] about ~? Why don't you[we] ~? ~하는 게 어때요?
Could/Can I ~? 제가 ~해도 될까요?	Would you like me to do? 제가 ~해드릴까요?
Be sure to ~. Please ~. ~해 주세요.	Do you mind ~? ~해도 될까요?
Would you like to do ~? ~하시겠어요?	Let's ~. ~합시다.

Practice

P5_6

7. Mark your answer on your answer sheet. (A) (B) (C)

8. Mark your answer on your answer sheet. (A) (B) (C)

9. Mark your answer on your answer sheet. (A) (B) (C)

P5_7

Part 2를 어렵게 느끼는 이유 중 하나는 '우회 답변'이 출제되기 때문이다. 질문에 대한 직접적인 답변이 정답이 되는 경우도 많지만, 고난도로 출제될수록 간접적으로 돌려서 답변한 응답이 정답일 확률이 높다. 일반 의문문/선택 의문문/요청&제안 의문문에 대한 기본 답변과 고난도 우회 답변을 비교해서 학습해 보자.

Q. Do you usually bring your business cards? 보통 회사 명함을 가지고 다니시나요?

기본 답변 Yes, I use them quite often. 네, 제가 그것들을 꽤 자주 사용합니다.

우회 답변 There are always some in my wallet. 제 지갑에 항상 몇 개가 있습니다.

Q. Doesn't Ashford Hotel offer a shuttle bus to the airport? 애쉬포드 호텔이 공항까지 셔틀 버스를 제공하지 않나요?

기본 답변 Yes, it leaves every 20 minutes. 네, 20분마다 출발합니다.

우회 답변 They already rented several vans for the guests. 그곳은 이미 투숙객들을 위해 승합차 여러 대를 빌렸어요.

Q. Are you interested in buying an apartment in the city? 도시에 있는 아파트를 구매하시는 데 관심이 있으신가요?

기본 답변 No, I just want to take a look. 아니요, 그냥 보기만 하고 싶어요.

우회 답변 It's not in my budget. 제 예산에 맞지 않아요.

Q. Isn't the hallway going to be repainted? 그 현관이 다시 페인트칠될 예정이지 않나요?

기본 답변 Yes, the painters will arrive in an hour. 네, 한 시간 후에 도장공들이 도착할 겁니다.

우회 답변 Who gave the final approval? 누가 최종 승인을 했나요?

Q. Have all the July sales figures been compiled or are we still waiting?
모든 7월 매출 수치가 취합되었나요, 아니면 여전히 기다리고 있나요?

기본 답변 We're still waiting for the data from the Greenwich branch.
저희는 여전히 그린위치 지사의 자료를 기다리고 있어요.

우회 답변 Ms. Charlotte might know well. 샬럿 씨가 아마 잘 알 거예요.

Q. Should I reserve a parking space for the job interview on Monday or Tuesday?
제가 구직 면접을 위해 주차 공간을 월요일에 예약해야 하나요, 아니면 화요일에 예약해야 하나요?

기본 답변 How about Monday? 월요일 어떠세요?

우회 답변 The head of Human Resources will be out of the office on Tuesday.
인사부장님이 화요일에 사무실에 계시지 않을 예정입니다.

Q. Could you please replace the filter in the air purifier? 공기청정기 안에 필터 좀 교체해 주실 수 있나요?

기본 답변 Sure, I can do that for you. 물론이죠, 제가 해 드릴게요.

우회 답변 I have to make an urgent client call. 저는 급한 고객 전화를 해야 해요.

Practice

P5_8

10. Mark your answer on your answer sheet. (A) (B) (C)
11. Mark your answer on your answer sheet. (A) (B) (C)
12. Mark your answer on your answer sheet. (A) (B) (C)

Check-up Test

음원 바로듣기 강의 바로보기

정답 및 해설 p.77

P5_9

1. Mark your answer on your answer sheet. (A) (B) (C)

2. Mark your answer on your answer sheet. (A) (B) (C)

3. Mark your answer on your answer sheet. (A) (B) (C)

4. Mark your answer on your answer sheet. (A) (B) (C)

5. Mark your answer on your answer sheet. (A) (B) (C)

6. Mark your answer on your answer sheet. (A) (B) (C)

7. Mark your answer on your answer sheet. (A) (B) (C)

8. Mark your answer on your answer sheet. (A) (B) (C)

9. Mark your answer on your answer sheet. (A) (B) (C)

10. Mark your answer on your answer sheet. (A) (B) (C)

11. Mark your answer on your answer sheet. (A) (B) (C)

12. Mark your answer on your answer sheet. (A) (B) (C)

13. Mark your answer on your answer sheet. (A) (B) (C)

14. Mark your answer on your answer sheet. (A) (B) (C)

15. Mark your answer on your answer sheet. (A) (B) (C)

16. Mark your answer on your answer sheet. (A) (B) (C)

17. Mark your answer on your answer sheet. (A) (B) (C)

18. Mark your answer on your answer sheet. (A) (B) (C)

19. Mark your answer on your answer sheet. (A) (B) (C)

20. Mark your answer on your answer sheet. (A) (B) (C)

MEMO

Playlist 6

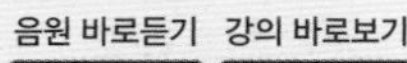

자꾸 어려워지는 평서문/부가 의문문/간접 의문문

Part 2

평서문/부가 의문문 간접 의문문

▶ 정답 패턴 1: 다양한 응답

P6_1

평서문은 의견 제시, 감정 표현, 정보 제공, 문제 상황 공유, 제안 또는 요청 등의 내용으로 골고루 출제된다. 그 내용이 매우 다양하기 때문에 정해진 정답 패턴이 없으므로 반드시 끝까지 듣고 소거법을 통해 정답을 도출해야 한다.

Q. Please let me know when you are ready to make the business proposal presentation.
사업 제안 발표를 하실 준비가 되시면 제게 알려주십시오.

A1. I've been waiting for my manager to come. 저는 부장님이 오시길 기다리는 중이에요.

A2. Certainly. I can start right now. 물론이죠. 저는 지금 시작할 수 있어요.

Q. The coffee machine in the staff break room isn't working. 직원 휴게실에 있는 커피 머신이 작동하지 않아요.

A1. The replacement parts are on their way. 교체 부품들이 오고 있어요.

A2. Let's call Mr. Nicolas in the technical support team. 기술 지원팀의 니콜라스 씨에게 연락합시다.

▶ 정답 패턴 2: 반문하기

평서문의 관련 내용으로 다시 묻거나 다른 의견을 제안, 추가 정보를 요청하는 등의 반문하는 응답이 정답일 확률이 높다.

Q. Our store is going to launch a customer loyalty program. 저희 매장은 고객 보상 프로그램을 출시할 예정입니다.

A1. Okay, have you decided on the date for it? 알겠습니다, 그것을 위한 날짜가 정해졌나요?

A2. Will we need to make a mobile app? 모바일 앱을 만들 필요가 있을까요?

서아쌤 비밀Tip

부가 의문문은 평서문 뒤에 '그렇죠?'의 뜻으로 붙는 의문문을 말하는데, 「평서문, aren't you?」, 「평서문, isn't/hasn't she?」, 「평서문, right/correct?」의 형태가 가장 일반적이에요. 부가 의문문 자체가 큰 의미를 가지고 있지 않기 때문에 뒤에 붙은 꼬리말은 가볍게 무시하고 평서문 부분을 집중해서 듣고 문제를 풀면 돼요.

Q. The Italian food at Cucina Amore Bistro is excellent, **isn't it**? 쿠시나 아모르 비스트로의 이탈리아 음식은 훌륭해요, 그렇죠?

A. Yes, my family likes it a lot. 네, 제 가족도 그곳을 많이 좋아해요.

Practice

P6_2

1. Mark your answer on your answer sheet. (A) (B) (C)

2. Mark your answer on your answer sheet. (A) (B) (C)

3. Mark your answer on your answer sheet. (A) (B) (C)

▶ 정답 패턴 1: Yes/No

P6_3

의문사 의문문 바로 앞에 「Do you know[think]」 또는 「Can you tell me」 등이 붙은 의문문을 간접 의문문이라고 하며, Yes와 No로 시작하는 답변이 정답이 될 수 있다.

Q. **Do you know who** designed the promotional poster? 그 홍보 포스터를 누가 디자인했는지 아세요?

A1. **Yes,** I think Ms. Harris did it. 네, 해리스 씨가 작업한 것 같아요.

A2. **No,** let me connect you to my manager. 아니요, 저희 부장님께 연결해 드릴게요.

Q. **Can you tell me where** the nearest gym is? 가장 가까운 헬스장이 어디에 있는지 알려 주실 수 있나요?

A1. **Yes,** it's just around the corner. 네, 모퉁이를 돌면 바로 있어요.

A2. **No,** I don't live in this area. 아니요, 저는 이 지역에 살지 않습니다.

▶ 정답 패턴 2: Yes/No 생략

간접 의문문은 Yes나 No 없이 부연 설명으로 답변하는 패턴이 훨씬 더 자주 출제된다. 질문에서도 의문사가 포함되지 않고 「Do you know[think]/Can you tell me」 뒤에 「주어 + 동사」, if/whether, 「about + 명사」 등의 다양한 구조가 제시되는 경우도 많다.

Q. **Do you think** I should buy the latest mobile phone? 제가 최신 휴대전화를 사야 한다고 생각하세요?

A1. It has a reasonable price these days. 요즘에 합리적인 가격이에요.

A2. You could just save money for future. 미래를 위해 저금하는 게 좋을 것 같아요.

Q. **Can you tell me if** the employment agency you recommended wants to work with us?
당신이 추천했던 채용 대행사가 저희랑 일하길 원하는지 알려주실 수 있나요?

A1. You can find it in our meeting notes. 저희 회의록에서 찾으실 수 있어요.

A2. I can't remember it at all. 전혀 기억이 안 나요.

A3. Didn't you receive the e-mail? 이메일을 받지 않으셨나요?

서아쌤 비밀Tip

간접 의문문은 상대가 질문에 대한 내용을 알고 있는지 모르고 있는지를 묻는 것보다, Do you know[think] 또는 Can you tell me 뒤에 제시된 정보와 관련된 의견을 간접적으로 요청하는 질문이에요. 따라서 질문에 대한 생각을 직접적으로 얘기하는 답변을 정답으로 고르면 돼요.

Q. Do you think it will snow next week? 다음 주에 눈이 올 것 같나요?

A. Yes, probably. 네 아마도요.

Practice

P6_4

4.	Mark your answer on your answer sheet.	(A)	(B)	(C)
5.	Mark your answer on your answer sheet.	(A)	(B)	(C)
6.	Mark your answer on your answer sheet.	(A)	(B)	(C)

Check-up Test

음원 바로듣기

강의 바로보기

정답 및 해설 p.81

P6_5

1. Mark your answer on your answer sheet. (A) (B) (C)

2. Mark your answer on your answer sheet. (A) (B) (C)

3. Mark your answer on your answer sheet. (A) (B) (C)

4. Mark your answer on your answer sheet. (A) (B) (C)

5. Mark your answer on your answer sheet. (A) (B) (C)

6. Mark your answer on your answer sheet. (A) (B) (C)

7. Mark your answer on your answer sheet. (A) (B) (C)

8. Mark your answer on your answer sheet. (A) (B) (C)

9. Mark your answer on your answer sheet. (A) (B) (C)

10. Mark your answer on your answer sheet. (A) (B) (C)

11. Mark your answer on your answer sheet. (A) (B) (C)

12. Mark your answer on your answer sheet. (A) (B) (C)

13. Mark your answer on your answer sheet. (A) (B) (C)

14. Mark your answer on your answer sheet. (A) (B) (C)

15. Mark your answer on your answer sheet. (A) (B) (C)

16. Mark your answer on your answer sheet. (A) (B) (C)

17. Mark your answer on your answer sheet. (A) (B) (C)

18. Mark your answer on your answer sheet. (A) (B) (C)

19. Mark your answer on your answer sheet. (A) (B) (C)

20. Mark your answer on your answer sheet. (A) (B) (C)

MEMO

음원 바로듣기 강의 바로보기

1번 문제 단골 손님 주제&목적, 신분&직업, 장소

Part 3

주제&목적 | 신분&직업 | 장소 | Paraphrasing

▶ 질문 유형

P7_1

주제	**What** is the main **topic** of the conversation? **What** is the conversation (mainly) **about**? **What** are the speakers (mainly) **discussing**?
목적	**Why** is the woman **calling** (the man)? **What** is the **purpose** of the man's call[visit]? **What** is the **purpose** of the conversation?

▶ 정답 단서 표현

☐ **I'd like to** reserve a table for dinner at 7 tomorrow. → A dining reservation
내일 7시에 저녁을 위해 테이블을 예약하고 싶습니다. 식사 예약

☐ **I'm calling to** confirm your dental visit for next Friday at 2 P.M. → To confirm a schedule
다음 주 금요일 오후 2시 귀하의 치과 방문을 확정하기 위해 전화 드립니다. 일정을 확정하려고

☐ **I'm calling because** I heard you carry a printer I'm looking for. → To inquire about an item
귀하께서 제가 찾고 있는 프린터를 취급하고 계신다는 걸 들어서 전화 드립니다. 제품에 대해 문의하려고

☐ **How's it going with** developing the new payroll software? → Software development
새로운 급여 소프트웨어의 개발은 어떻게 진행되고 있나요? 소프트웨어 개발

☐ **Thank you for** writing up the budget report and sending it to my e-mail. → A budget report
예산 보고서를 작성해 주시고 제 이메일로 보내주셔서 감사합니다. 예산 보고서

서아쌤 비밀Tip

위의 정답 단서 외에도 I want to(~하는 것을 원하다), I hope to(~하는 것을 희망하다), I'm planning to(~할 계획이다), I'm going to(~할 예정이다), I came here to(~하러 왔다), What do you think about[of] ~?(~에 대해 어떻게 생각하시나요?) 등이 Part 3 대화의 주제 또는 목적을 나타내는 결정적 힌트가 될 수 있으니 이러한 표현들을 귀 기울여 들어보세요.

Practice

P7_2

Step 1 질문 유형 파악
Step 2 명사/동사 위주로 선택지 미리 읽기
Step 3 음원 속 단서 표현 노려 듣기
Step 4 Paraphrasing으로 정답 선택

1. What is the main topic of the conversation?
(A) Some store relocations
(B) The launching of a brand
(C) An online advertising campaign
(D) Sustainable materials

▶ 질문 유형

P7_3

신분&직업	**What kind of business** do the speakers **work** for? **Who** (most likely) is the **woman**? **Who** (most likely) are the **men**? **Who** (most likely) are the **speakers**? **What** (most likely) is the man's **job[profession]**? **What** is the woman's **area of expertise**? **What field[industry]** do the speakers (most likely) **work** in?

서아쌤 비밀Tip

Part 3에서는 질문에 언급된 성별의 목소리에만 집중하지 마세요. 여자의 신분이나 직업이 무엇인지 묻는 질문에 대한 정답 단서는 남자의 말에서 나올 수도 있거든요. 또, 자주 나오는 '신분&직업' 단어들을 대화 장소와 묶어서 학습해 놓는다면 실전에서 선택지를 분석할 때 더 빠른 속도를 낼 수 있답니다.

장소	신분&직업		
store 매장	store clerk 매장 직원	sales representative 판매 직원	staff, employee 직원
restaurant 식당	server, waiter 종업원, 웨이터	diner 식사하는 사람	chef 주방장
catering 출장 음식 공급업체	caterer 출장 음식 공급자	deliverer 배달하는 사람	party planner 행사 기획자
hospital 병원	doctor 의사	receptionist 접수원	dentist 치과의사
real estate 부동산	real estate agent 부동산 중개인	tenant 세입자	resident 거주민

▶ 정답 단서 표현

☐ **This is** Mike Tiller, the hotel security guard. → A security guard
호텔 보안 직원 마이크 틸러입니다. 보안 직원

☐ **I'm** a journalist for *Urban Culture* magazine. → A journalist
저는 <어반 컬쳐> 매거진의 기자입니다. 기자

☐ **We oversee** the training of new interns at our law firm. → Training managers
저희는 저희 법률사무소에서 신규 인턴들의 교육을 감독하고 있습니다. 교육 관리자들

☐ **I want to talk about** the layout for the Web site we're making. → Web site designers
저희가 만들고 있는 웹 사이트 레이아웃에 대해 이야기하고 싶습니다. 웹 사이트 디자이너들

☐ **I'm here to** check your Internet system's wiring. → A technical support professional
귀하의 인터넷 시스템 배선 장치를 확인하려고 왔습니다. 기술 지원 전문가

이 한 문장에서 대화의 ① 주제&목적과 ② 신분&직업까지 모두 알 수 있어요. 따라서 화자의 첫 대사를 주의 깊게 잘 들어야 해요.

Practice

P7_4

Step 1 질문 유형 파악
Step 2 명사/동사 위주로 선택지 미리 읽기
Step 3 음원 속 단서 표현 노려 듣기
Step 4 Paraphrasing으로 정답 선택

2. Who most likely is the man?
(A) A food supplier
(B) A tour guide
(C) A flight attendant
(D) A waiter

▶ 질문 유형

P7_5

장소	**Where** does the man (most likely) **work**? **Where** (most likely) are the **speakers**? **Where** do the speakers (most likely) **work**? **Where** does the conversation (most likely) **take place**? **In which department[industry]** do the speakers (most likely) **work**?

▶ 정답 단서 표현

- ☐ **Welcome to** the *Global Economist Weekly*. → At a newspaper company
  <글로벌 이코노미스트 위클리>에 오신 것을 환영합니다. 신문사에서
- ☐ We received your manuscript for review **here at** Finnick's Publishers. → At a publishing firm
  저희가 여기 핀닉 출판사에서 검토를 위해 귀하의 원고를 받았습니다. 출판사에서
- ☐ I booked a flight **through your** travel company homepage. → At a travel agency
  귀하의 여행사 홈페이지를 통해 항공편을 예약했습니다. 여행사에서
- ☐ **I'm looking for** a type of long-grain rice, specifically Jasmine rice. → At a supermarket
  낟알이 긴 쌀의 한 종류를 찾고 있는데, 특히 자스민 쌀이요. 슈퍼마켓에서
- ☐ Ms. Kang, when did the **doctor** say to schedule your next **appointment**? → At a medical office
  강 씨, 의사 선생님께서 다음 예약 일정을 언제로 잡으라고 말씀하셨나요? 진료소에서

대화 장소를 묻는 문제는 문장 내에 제시된 키워드를 조합해서 정답을 고르는 유형으로 많이 출제돼요.

서아쌤 비밀Tip

최근 Part 3에서 정답으로 출제된 장소 중 고난도 장소들을 모아 봤어요. 아래 장소들은 자주 출제되는 식료품점이나 식당 같은 쉬운 장소들이 아니니 꼼꼼히 봐두세요.

At an apartment complex 아파트 단지에서
At a hardware store 철물점에서
At a home improvement store 주택 개조 용품점에서
At a car dealership 자동차 대리점에서
At a nature preserve 자연 보호 구역에서
At an automobile manufacturer 자동차 제조업체에서
At a ceramics studio 도자기 공방에서
At a warehouse 창고에서

Practice

P7_6

Step 1 질문 유형 파악
Step 2 명사/동사 위주로 선택지 미리 읽기
Step 3 음원 속 단서 표현 노려 듣기
Step 4 Paraphrasing으로 정답 선택

3. Where do the speakers most likely work?
(A) At a warehouse
(B) At a post office
(C) At a bookstore
(D) At a hardware store

다음 대화를 읽고 색으로 표시된 단어의 의미와 같은 패러프레이징 표현을 고르시오. P7_7

1. **What** are the speakers **discussing**?

W: We should send out a survey to ask customers what they think about our latest AI-powered smart TVs.
M: Actually, Melissa already **compiled some user feedback** and created a summary.

(A) Collecting reviews (B) Completing a questionnaire

2. **Why** is the man **calling**?

M: Hi, Ms. Hewitt. I'm calling from Minera Dental. Dr. Lee is no longer available this Friday, so I'd like to ask if we can **move your appointment** to next Monday, for the same time.
W: Well, I have an important client meeting that day, but I should be able to make it work.

(A) To postpone an appointment (B) To schedule a client tour

3. **Who** is the **woman**?

W: You've reached Amy **at Perseus Air. How can I help** you today?
M: I have a flight to Kuala Lumpur on June 16, and I'll be carrying some camping gear. Would it be considered oversized baggage?

(A) An aircraft operator (B) An airline agent

4. **In which industry** do the speakers most likely **work**?

M: Suki, how did the meeting with the designers of **our new spring clothing line** go? Any pieces stand out to you in particular?
W: There was a reversible windbreaker that I really liked. It's lightweight and comes in sleek, solid colors, so I'm sure it'd be great for those who like a minimalist style.

(A) Fashion (B) Art

5. **What** is the **purpose** of the woman's call?

W: Hi, is this Greg Collins? My name is Kate Diaz calling from Quantum Tech. I looked over your application for our financial consultant position and decided that **we would like to interview you.**
M: Oh, thank you for reaching out!

(A) To schedule an interview (B) To organize a consultation

6. **Where** do the speakers **work**?

M: Ms. Vega, the director of Yenox Media just called. She confirmed that she can stop by on Tuesday morning at 10 to discuss **our legal services.**
W: Awesome! Yenox is a major leader in online advertisements, so it could be a great opportunity for us.

(A) At an advertising agency (B) At a law firm

Check-up Test

음원 바로듣기 강의 바로보기

P7_8

1. Who are the speakers?
(A) Delivery truck drivers
(B) Front desk receptionists
(C) News reporters
(D) Postal workers

2. What was announced in a flyer?
(A) Some wiring will be repaired.
(B) Some vehicles will be replaced.
(C) A cellular provider will change.
(D) A city official will visit.

3. What is the man concerned about?
(A) How long a battery will last
(B) How far a destination is
(C) How crowded an area will be
(D) How demanding a task is

4. What are the speakers mainly discussing?
(A) A registration process
(B) Employee benefits
(C) An applicant for a new role
(D) A seasonal sales promotion

5. According to the speakers, what has Julianne Shin accomplished?
(A) She secured a business deal.
(B) She obtained a special license.
(C) She increased a company's profitability.
(D) She redesigned a Web site.

6. What does the woman say she will do?
(A) Write a recommendation
(B) Organize a meeting
(C) Distribute some guest passes
(D) Submit some documents

7. Where do the speakers most likely work?
(A) At a fruit orchard
(B) At a nature preserve
(C) At a public reservoir
(D) At a botanical garden

8. What will the speakers do with some samples?
(A) Send them to a laboratory
(B) Store them in a warehouse
(C) Allocate them to various clients
(D) Label them with numbers

9. What does the woman agree to do?
(A) Investigate a location
(B) Check a forecast
(C) Write down some notes
(D) Take some photographs

정답 및 해설 p.86

10. What most likely is the man's job?

(A) A farmer
(B) A chef
(C) A merchant
(D) A server

11. What does the woman suggest?

(A) Restocking an item
(B) Trying a delivery service
(C) Substituting an ingredient
(D) Using a different tool

12. What does the woman say she will do next?

(A) Check a storage room
(B) Process a refund
(C) Ask for a customer's opinion
(D) Visit a supermarket

---

13. Why is the woman calling?

(A) To complain about a bill
(B) To discuss a cost estimate
(C) To ask for some documents
(D) To edit her account information

14. What did the woman do last week?

(A) She bought a new cell phone.
(B) She moved into an apartment.
(C) She traveled abroad.
(D) She took a course.

15. According to the man, what did the woman probably fail to do?

(A) Submit a request
(B) Reach out to an agent
(C) E-mail several pictures
(D) Turn off a device feature

16. Where does the conversation most likely take place?

(A) On a beach
(B) At a sports stadium
(C) At a farm
(D) At a grocery store

17. What does Austin give to Charlie?

(A) Some gloves
(B) Some sunglasses
(C) A set of keys
(D) A notebook

18. According to Austin, what is important?

(A) Drinking water
(B) Wearing a hat
(C) Picking a proper location
(D) Staying within an area

 **Playlist 8**

음원 바로듣기 강의 바로보기

2번 문제는 주로 세부사항과 문제점!

Part 3

세부사항 문제점

▶ 질문 유형

P8_1

대상	**What** does the man **give** the woman? **What** does the woman **say about** the painting? **What** kind of product does the woman **mention**? **What** do the speakers **agree to do**?
이유	**Why** is the man **at** the gallery? **Why was** Mr. Arnold **delayed** yesterday? According to the man, **why** is the workshop **important**? **Why** does the woman suggest **buying** a new computer?
방법 수단	**How** do the men plan to **increase** their sales? **How** did the man **get** a different model? **How** does the woman say she would **send** the document? **How** do the speakers **know** each other?

▶ 정답 단서 표현

□ **M:** I just **hope** she can give us **a cooking demonstration.**
저는 그저 그분이 우리에게 요리 시연을 해 줄 수 있기를 희망합니다.

Q. **What** does the man **hope** the woman will do?
남자는 여자가 무엇을 하기를 희망하는가?

→ Show a demonstration
시연을 보여주는 것

□ **W:** **Since** the report will take a long time, you might want to **get started** right away.
보고서가 시간이 오래 걸릴 것이기 때문에, 귀하께서는 즉시 시작하시면 좋을 겁니다.

Q. **Why** does the woman recommend **beginning** a task soon?
여자는 왜 업무를 곧 시작하는 것을 추천하는가?

→ It is time-consuming.
시간이 걸리기 때문이다.

□ **M:** Wow, I haven't seen you **since you moved out of our neighborhood**!
우와, 우리 지역에서 이사하신 이후로 당신을 본 적이 없어요!

Q. **How** do the speakers **know** each other?
화자들은 서로를 어떻게 아는가?

→ They used to be neighbors.
예전에 이웃이었다.

세부사항 문제의 정답 단서는 의문사와 질문의 키워드예요. 음원에서 질문의 키워드는 주로 패러프레이징되어 제시돼요. 고난도로 출제될 경우, 직접적으로 제시되지 않기도 하니 주의하세요!

Practice

P8_2

Step 1 질문 유형 파악
Step 2 명사/동사 위주로 선택지 미리 읽기
Step 3 음원 속 단서 표현 노려 듣기
Step 4 Paraphrasing으로 정답 선택

1. What do the speakers agree to do?
(A) Hire more personnel for an event
(B) Carry out some refurbishments
(C) Reconfigure a seating layout
(D) Install new safety equipment

▶ 질문 유형

P8_3

문제점	What is the **problem**? What **problem** are the speakers discussing? What **issue** does the man mention? What is the woman **concerned[worried]** about? What **caused** a **delay**?

▶ 정답 단서 표현

- ☐ **I'm concerned about** limited phone reception at the campground. → A weak network signal
  캠핑장에서 제한된 전화 수신에 관해서 걱정됩니다. 약한 네트워크 신호
- ☐ The park rangers restricted access to the trail **due to** flooding. → The conditions are dangerous.
  공원 경비원들이 홍수로 인해 그 산책길에 대한 접근을 제한했습니다. 상황이 위험하다.
- ☐ **Unfortunately**, we have no record of your payment. → A transaction was not processed.
  안타깝게도, 저희는 귀하의 납부 기록이 없습니다. 거래가 처리되지 않았다.
- ☐ **I'm afraid** the printer paper will be too heavy to carry. → The weight of some supplies
  죄송하지만 프린터 종이가 들기에 너무 무거울 것 같습니다. 몇몇 용품의 무게
- ☐ The heater **broke down**, so it's very cold in the office right now. → A heating unit is not working.
  그 히터가 고장나서, 지금 사무실 안이 매우 춥습니다. 난방 기기가 작동하지 않는다.
  문제점을 묻는 문제가 고난도로 출제된다면 대화 속 부정적 의미의 동사를 통해 문제점을 추론해야 해요.

서아쌤 비밀Tip

토익에서는 주로 기술 오류, 예산 부족, 매출 감소, 배송 지연, 상품 파손, 재고 부족, 궂은 날씨 등의 문제점들이 출제돼요. 자주 출제되는 문제점 유형을 정리해두면 음원을 들을 때 미리 예측할 수 있어 더 쉽게 정답을 고를 수 있어요.

최빈출 문제점 유형	정답 단서 표현
기술 오류	The air conditioner is **not working properly**. 에어컨이 제대로 작동하지 않습니다. The Internet connection is **slow**. 인터넷 연결이 느립니다.
예산 부족 매출 감소	We **are not allowed to spend** more than $400. 400달러 넘게 지불하도록 허용되지 않습니다. Product sales **have decreased** since last month. 지난달 이후로 제품 매출이 감소했습니다.
배송 지연	The delivery **was supposed to arrive** today. 배송품이 오늘 도착할 예정이었습니다. A shipment **hasn't been delivered** yet. 수송품이 아직 배송되지 않았습니다.
상품 파손 재고 부족	I found out that two tables **are damaged**. 탁자 두 개가 파손된 것을 발견했습니다. The carpet you ordered is temporarily **out of stock**. 귀하께서 주문하신 카펫이 일시적으로 재고가 없습니다.
궂은 날씨	A **storm** is approaching, so the event **has been postponed**. 폭풍우가 접근 중이어서, 그 행사가 연기되었습니다. Because of the **heavy rain**, the flight **will be delayed**. 폭우 때문에, 비행편이 지연될 것입니다.

Practice

P8_4

Step 1 질문 유형 파악
Step 2 명사/동사 위주로 선택지 미리 읽기
Step 3 음원 속 단서 표현 노려 듣기
Step 4 Paraphrasing으로 정답 선택

2. What is the problem?
(A) A business has shut down.
(B) A bridge is inaccessible.
(C) An order is taking too long.
(D) A road is partly closed.

Check-up Test

음원 바로듣기 강의 바로보기

P8_5

1. What did the woman forget to do?
   (A) Receive a receipt
   (B) Make a reservation
   (C) Bring a coupon
   (D) Write down her name

2. What does the man say about the restaurant?
   (A) There is a change in operating hours today.
   (B) There is an extra fee for large parties.
   (C) The space outdoors is for private events only.
   (D) The business was established recently.

3. What does the woman request?
   (A) A dish recommendation
   (B) A cup of water
   (C) To be seated at one table
   (D) To be seated in a warmer area

---

4. What does the woman propose doing?
   (A) Visiting the local library
   (B) Using a training application
   (C) Developing a marketing strategy
   (D) Recruiting more employees

5. What is the man concerned about?
   (A) A processing time
   (B) Budget limitations
   (C) The cost of a product
   (D) The availability of an item

6. According to the woman, what can be found on a Web site?
   (A) A job description
   (B) Customer reviews
   (C) A discussion forum
   (D) Business hours

7. What is the conversation about?
   (A) Improving in-store sales
   (B) Organizing a product launch
   (C) Preparing for a renovation
   (D) Boosting worker productivity

8. How did the woman get an idea?
   (A) By consulting with an expert
   (B) By listening to a podcast
   (C) By watching a presentation
   (D) By taking an online course

9. What will the speakers probably do?
   (A) Post a sign
   (B) Build some furniture
   (C) Rearrange some merchandise
   (D) Print out some images

정답 및 해설 p.91

10. Who most likely is the woman?
(A) An art collector
(B) A painter
(C) An architect
(D) A restaurant owner

11. What issue does the woman mention?
(A) She cannot start work immediately.
(B) She will need assistance with transportation.
(C) She has been offered a new job.
(D) She is preparing to move abroad.

12. What does the man offer to send?
(A) An invitation
(B) A labor contract
(C) Photographs
(D) Measurement details

---

13. Where are the speakers?
(A) At a print shop
(B) At an electronics store
(C) At a tailor shop
(D) At a clothing store

14. Why is the man at the business?
(A) To pick up an online order
(B) To point out a payment error
(C) To look for a missing item
(D) To exchange a product

15. What does Rhea ask about?
(A) A brand
(B) A color
(C) A design
(D) An address

16. What type of event is the man planning?
(A) A cooking contest
(B) A company retreat
(C) An employee orientation
(D) A professional conference

17. Why was Ms. Huang delayed?
(A) She was in an urgent meeting.
(B) She was returning from a trip.
(C) She was writing up a report.
(D) She was talking on the phone.

18. What does the man inquire about?
(A) Hourly rates
(B) Transportation options
(C) Air conditioning
(D) Internet access

Playlist 9

3번 문제는 요청&제안, 다음에 할 일만 기억하세요!

Part 3

요청&제안 다음에 할 일

▶ 질문 유형

P9_1

요청	**What** does the woman **request**? **What is** the man **asked** to do? — 질문에 be p.p.가 있을 때는 요청을 한 사람과 요청을 받은 사람을 반드시 구분해야 해요. **What** does the woman **remind[tell, ask]** the man to do?
제안	**What** does the woman **recommend**? **What** does the man **suggest** the woman do? **What** does the woman **suggest** (doing)? **What** does the man **offer** to do?

▶ 정답 단서 표현

- ☐ **Could you** show him where the cleaning products are?
  그분에게 청소 제품들이 어디에 있는지를 안내해 주실 수 있나요?
  → Help a customer
  고객을 도와주기
- ☐ **We'd like to** book a room with a nice view.
  좋은 전망을 가진 객실을 예약하고 싶습니다.
  → To stay in a scenic room
  전망이 좋은 객실에 머무는 것
- ☐ **Please** take a seat in the waiting area first.
  우선 대기 구역에 착석해 주십시오.
  → Wait in a certain area
  특정 구역에서 기다리기
- ☐ **Why don't you** partner with the café to collect old books?
  오래된 책들을 수집하기 위해 그 카페와 제휴를 맺는 것이 어때요?
  → Partnering with a business
  한 사업체와 제휴를 맺는 것
- ☐ **How about** passing out a survey to each employee?
  각 직원에게 설문 조사지를 나눠주는 게 어때요?
  → Distributing a survey
  설문 조사지를 배포하는 것
- ☐ Before you leave, **I suggest** you look over the proposal.
  퇴근하시기 전에, 그 제안서를 검토하시는 것을 제안드립니다.
  → Review a document
  서류를 검토하기

서아쌤 비밀Tip

위의 표현 외에도 Do you mind ~?(~해도 괜찮나요?), I want you to(~해주셨으면 좋겠어요), What about ~?(~하는 게 어때요?), I recommend(~을 추천해요), You should(~하셔야 해요), Make sure(~하도록 해 주시기 바랍니다), I can(~ 할 수 있어요) 등의 표현들도 요청과 제안의 내용을 알려주는 정답 단서가 될 수 있으니 반드시 함께 묶어서 기억해 두세요.

Practice

P9_2

Step 1 질문 유형 파악
Step 2 명사/동사 위주로 선택지 미리 읽기
Step 3 음원 속 단서 표현 노려 듣기
Step 4 Paraphrasing으로 정답 선택

1. What does the man suggest?

(A) Changing a color selection
(B) Adding a page to a book
(C) Receiving help from a copy editor
(D) Creating an online catalog

▶ 질문 유형

🎧 P9_3

다음에 할 일	**What** will the woman (most likely[probably]) **do next**? (According to the woman,) **what** will **happen next year**? **What** does the woman **plan to do**? **What** does the man say he **will do (next)**? **What** will Samantha **do on Friday**? **What** is the man **planning to do (tomorrow)**?

▶ 정답 단서 표현

- ☐ **I'll** look into the latest marketing trends for this quarter. → Conduct some research
  제가 이번 분기에 최신 시장 경향을 조사해 보겠습니다. 몇몇 조사를 수행하기
- ☐ **Let me** call the property manager to confirm the dates. → Contact a manager
  날짜를 확정하기 위해 제가 부동산 관리자에게 전화할게요. 관리자에게 연락하기
- ☐ **I'm going to** stop by their headquarters tomorrow. → Visit an office
  제가 내일 그분들의 본사에 들를 예정이에요. 사무실을 방문하기
- ☐ **Why don't I** put together a list of suitable plans for you? → Compile some plan options
  귀하를 위해 제가 적절한 계획들을 목록으로 만들어 드리는 것이 어떨까요? 몇몇 계획 선택사항들을 취합하기
- ☐ **I can** go post the notice in the break room right now. → Hang up a notice
  제가 당장 휴게실에 공지를 게시하러 갈 수 있어요. 공지를 걸기
- ☐ Actually, **I'd be happy** to grab some coffee for everyone. → Pick up some drinks
  사실, 제가 모두를 위해 기꺼이 커피를 좀 가져다 드릴 수 있어요. 몇몇 음료들을 가지러 가기
- ☐ **Could you** stack the chairs after the meeting is over? → Arrange some furniture
  회의가 끝난 후에 의자들을 쌓아 주실 수 있나요? 몇몇 가구를 정리하기

서아쌤 비밀Tip

다음에 할 일을 묻는 문제를 풀 때는 질문 내에 제시된 구체적인 시점에 동그라미를 표시해 놓는 것이 좋아요. 해당 단어를 대화에서 그대로 사용하는 경우가 대부분이니 그 부분을 노려 듣는다면 정답 단서를 놓치지 않을 수 있어요. 또, 질문에서 여자가 할 일에 대해서 묻는다고 여자의 대사만 귀 기울여 들어서도 안 돼요. 앞서 배운 요청&제안 정답 단서 표현을 활용해 대화의 상대방인 남자가 여자가 할 일을 언급할 수도 있기 때문이죠.

Practice

🎧 P9_4

Step 1 질문 유형 파악
Step 2 명사/동사 위주로 선택지 미리 읽기
Step 3 음원 속 단서 표현 노려 듣기
Step 4 Paraphrasing으로 정답 선택

2. What will the woman do next?

(A) Send a Web site link
(B) Give directions
(C) Check an inventory
(D) Call a vendor

Check-up Test

음원 바로듣기 강의 바로보기

P9_5

1. Where are the speakers most likely working?
(A) At a local park
(B) At a vegetable farm
(C) At a science laboratory
(D) At a nature preserve

2. What have the speakers been asked to do?
(A) Build a wooden structure
(B) Place an order for tools
(C) Install a ventilation unit
(D) Gather some damaged crops

3. What does the man offer to do?
(A) Look for some materials
(B) Turn on a machine
(C) Search for information online
(D) Visit a repair shop

---

4. Why is a train platform closed?
(A) Some train cars are being cleaned.
(B) Restrooms are being renovated.
(C) Lighting repairs are being done.
(D) Information displays are being installed.

5. What does the man say he is upset about?
(A) Following incorrect directions
(B) Being late for an appointment
(C) Getting overcharged for a ticket
(D) Transferring at the wrong station

6. What will the man most likely do next?
(A) Visit the help desk
(B) Take a shuttle bus
(C) Call a taxi
(D) Report an issue

7. What does the woman ask the man to do?
(A) Load up a vehicle
(B) Contact a supplier
(C) Take over a coworker's task
(D) Change a delivery date

8. What does the man say he needs?
(A) A list of products
(B) A printed invoice
(C) Some contact information
(D) Directions to a store

9. What does the woman remind the man to do?
(A) Collect a signature
(B) Visit another business
(C) Wait in a certain area
(D) Inform his supervisor

10. Where does the man work?
(A) At an equipment rental facility
(B) At a fitness center
(C) At a home goods store
(D) At a computer store

11. What is the purpose of the woman's visit?
(A) She is registering for a course.
(B) She wants to receive a consultation.
(C) She needs to get an item fixed.
(D) She is interested in a membership.

12. What will the woman probably do next?
(A) Go on a tour
(B) Watch a video
(C) Receive a free gift
(D) Postpone a meeting

---

13. What kind of business do the men most likely work for?
(A) A fencing company
(B) A plumbing service
(C) A hardware supplier
(D) A moving company

14. Why is the woman relieved?
(A) Some damage is minor.
(B) A cost estimate is affordable.
(C) Some staff are available.
(D) The city has issued a permit.

15. What will the woman do on Thursday?
(A) Leave for a business trip
(B) Close her shop temporarily
(C) Pick up some power tools
(D) Install new equipment

16. What does the company produce?
(A) Energy drinks
(B) Cookies
(C) Popcorn
(D) Chocolate

17. What are the speakers mainly discussing?
(A) Production delays
(B) Sales figures
(C) A seasonal promotion
(D) A research study

18. What is the woman asked to do for the next meeting?
(A) Make a product list
(B) Revise a floor plan
(C) Create a poster design
(D) Review a financial statement

음원 바로듣기 강의 바로보기

만점강사는 의도파악 문제를 어떻게 풀까?

Part 3

의도파악 빈출 의도파악 연습

▶ 질문 유형

P10_1

의도파악	**What** does the woman **imply** when she says, "We can discuss it later"? **What** does the man **mean** when he says, "I'm leaving for a holiday tomorrow"? **Why** does the woman **say**, "It won't take more than ten minutes"?

▶ 문제풀이 전략

❶ 문제에 주어진 문장을 먼저 읽는다.

❷ 선택지 (A)-(D)를 읽는다. 이때, 주어진 문장을 곧이 곧대로 해석한 선택지는 오답일 확률이 매우 높으니 주의한다.

❸ 주어진 문장의 바로 앞이나 뒤, 또는 앞뒤 대사에 정답 단서가 제시되므로 대화의 전체적인 흐름을 이해한다.

❹ 대화 흐름을 종합해 주어진 문장의 의도를 나타낸 선택지를 정답으로 고른다.

W: Congratulations on the positive result from your lab experiment!

M: Thank you. I was worried we'd need to run the test at least 8 times or so, but we got the chemical reaction we wanted on our second try!

W: ❸ **There's a form that you'll have to submit with your findings. It should go to our research director, Neha, I believe.**

M: Well, **Neha's last day is this Friday**.

W: ❸ **Oh, really? I'm sad to see her go.** Any idea who will replace her?

M: No, but we definitely need a leader who can coordinate all our operations since we have so many diverse research projects going on.

Q. What does the man imply when he says, ❶ "**Neha's last day is this Friday**"?

❷
(A) He plans to attend a party for Neha.
(B) He will take on a new leadership role.
(C) He will not submit a form to Neha. ❹ 정답
(D) A project deadline cannot be extended.

Practice

P10_2

1. Why does the woman say, "the city does run a commuter shuttle"?

(A) To indicate that a service is free
(B) To correct a mistaken assumption
(C) To provide encouragement
(D) To praise a government policy

2. What does the man mean when he says, "our clients personally requested that flavor"?

(A) Approval has not been received yet.
(B) A change is not possible.
(C) A customer has been loyal for many years.
(D) An order is very urgent.

다음 대화를 읽고 색으로 표시된 문장의 의도와 같은 의미의 표현을 고르시오. P10_3

1. What does the woman imply when she says, **"Isn't this data from a paper by Dr. Seidel"**?

M: Can you quickly look over my slides with me?
W: Of course.
M: I want to make sure I included the proper citations for all my graphs and charts.
W: Let's see... Okay... Ah, hold on! **Isn't this data from a paper by Dr. Seidel?**
M: Oh! Yes, that's right. Thanks for catching that.

(A) A research paper should be helpful. (B) A slide should include some information.

2. What does the man mean when he says, **"it could get really hot in here during the summer"**?

W: Welcome to our newly renovated boardroom. Any thoughts?
M1: It's very spacious, so I think it's perfect for department meetings. I like the views that the large windows provide, too.
M2: Hmm... You know, **it could get really hot in here during the summer.**
W: That's true. Let me ask the building manager if we can get some window blinds installed.

(A) A room gets too much sunlight. (B) A room should be used occasionally.

3. Why does the man say, **"some of our rooftop seats are open"**?

M: Hi, there. Welcome to Ambrose Bistro. Party of two?
W: Yep. How long is the wait time? We have a train to catch in a few hours.
M: It'll be about 20 to 30 minutes for a table inside. **Some of our rooftop seats are open.**
W: Oh... but it's a bit chilly tonight.

(A) To propose an alternative (B) To clarify a misunderstanding

4. What does the man imply when he says, **"That would involve making major adjustments to our booking system"**?

W: Many clients have mentioned they'd like more time with their doctors during their appointments. Currently, doctors and patients only get about 15 minutes to talk. Would it be possible to increase the allotted time per patient?
M: **That would involve making major adjustments to our booking system.** Our institution's board members would need to give final approval, too.

(A) She doubts a change will be implemented. (B) She believes technical support is needed.

음원 바로듣기 강의 바로보기

Check-up Test

P10_4

1. Where are the speakers?

(A) At a job fair
(B) At a trade show
(C) At a workshop
(D) At a fundraising event

2. What does the woman mean when she says, "we have over a hundred workers"?

(A) A product might not be useful for her company.
(B) Some staff have not received sufficient training.
(C) Her company offices will be expanding soon.
(D) She recently became appointed as manager.

3. What does the man give to the woman?

(A) An application form
(B) A business card
(C) A chart
(D) A map

---

4. Where do the speakers most likely work?

(A) At an office cafeteria
(B) At a retail food store
(C) At a warehouse
(D) At a factory

5. What does the man imply when he says, "the trays are usually transferred one by one to the packaging area"?

(A) A device is not practical to use.
(B) A process is time-consuming.
(C) Some shipping fees are unreasonable.
(D) There are not enough personnel.

6. What will the man show the woman?

(A) A project proposal
(B) A cost estimate
(C) A blueprint
(D) A calendar

7. Where do the speakers most likely work?

(A) At a bookstore
(B) At a hospital
(C) At a fitness center
(D) At an aquatics facility

8. Why does the man say, "this region is heavily populated"?

(A) To make a comparison
(B) To disagree with a policy
(C) To warn about long wait times
(D) To explain a decision

9. What does the woman think her business should do?

(A) Hire more employees
(B) Change a marketing strategy
(C) Recruit some volunteers
(D) Purchase a new vehicle

10. What does the man want to discuss?

(A) Guest numbers
(B) Ticket prices
(C) Budget allocations
(D) Snack options

11. What does the woman suggest?

(A) Getting customer feedback
(B) Simplifying a payment process
(C) Building a new attraction
(D) Offering special merchandise

12. What does the woman mean when she says, "Making a draft is pretty easy"?

(A) She has already solved a problem.
(B) She is willing to complete a task.
(C) Some information will be sent out soon.
(D) A report can be created quickly.

---

13. What did the woman recently do?

(A) She picked up swimming as a hobby.
(B) She started growing her own produce.
(C) She built a pool on her property.
(D) She was assigned to decorate a venue.

14. What does the woman imply when she says, "this is my first time buying succulents"?

(A) She is impressed by a selection.
(B) She needs some advice.
(C) She cannot find a certain area.
(D) She wants to know a price.

15. What will the woman most likely do next?

(A) Look through a catalog
(B) Rearrange some items
(C) View an outdoor display
(D) Fill up a storage container

16. What type of event are the speakers attending?

(A) A business conference
(B) A company celebration
(C) A trade exposition
(D) A community fair

17. Why does the woman say, "We should try harder"?

(A) She prefers to try another option.
(B) She is giving the man encouragement.
(C) She wants to change part of a proposal.
(D) She thinks better results can be achieved.

18. What does the man say about the presentation handouts?

(A) They will be sent electronically to all attendees.
(B) They are available near the entrance.
(C) They are included with an information packet.
(D) There are only a few copies left.

Playlist 11

음원 바로듣기 강의 바로보기

파트3에 꼭 나오는 시각자료 연계문제 총정리

Part 3

시각자료 | 빈출 시각자료 ① | 빈출 시각자료 ② | 유형별 필수 어휘

▶ 질문 유형

P11_1

시각자료	**Look at the graphic**. How much will the man most likely pay?

▶ 문제풀이 전략

❶ 문제를 먼저 읽고 키워드를 파악한다. 이때 선택지는 읽을 필요 없다.

❷ 제시된 시각자료를 파악하고, 선택지에 이미 적힌 부분이 아닌 곳에 동그라미 등으로 표시해 둔다.

❸ 대화를 들으면서 눈은 시각자료를 보고 있어야 하는데, 음원에서는 미리 표시해둔 부분이 정답 단서로 들리기 때문에 그 부분에 시선을 둔다.

❹ 대화와 시각자료 사이의 연결고리를 파악해 정답을 고른다.

W: Hi, Fred. Did you get to the airport yet? Highway traffic has been awful, so I'm still about 30 minutes away. I have a feeling I'm going to miss the flight!

M: Hey, Jill. I got here 5 minutes ago, and actually, ❸ **our flight's been delayed by an hour and a half.** So I think you'll be okay.

W: Oh, what luck! In that case, can you contact the airport transfer driver about our new arrival time? That way, he'll know when to pick us up.

❷

Destination	Departure Time	Status
Seattle	15:10	BOARDING
Phoenix	15:30	ON TIME
Albuquerque	16:00	DELAYED – 17:30
San Diego	17:30	DELAYED – 18:00

❸

Q. Look at the graphic. ❶ **Where** are the speakers **going**?

(A) To Seattle

(B) To Phoenix

(C) To Albuquerque ❹ 정답

(D) To San Diego

Practice

P11_2

Monday	4 P.M.	Children's Book Read-Aloud
Tuesday	7 P.M.	Special Talk: Director Calum Pardo
Wednesday	6 P.M.	Movie Screening
Thursday	Closed	---

1. Look at the graphic. When will the man most likely attend a library event?

(A) On Monday

(B) On Tuesday

(C) On Wednesday

(D) On Thursday

P11_3

▶ 시간표

Flight Number	Departure	Arrival
XZ6005	6:20 A.M.	9:45 A.M.
SQ5815	7:05 A.M.	10:30 A.M.
TY8903	8:30 A.M.	11:15 A.M.
GJ4752	9:45 A.M.	12:30 P.M.

W: I don't have an exact time preference, as long as I can get to San Jose around 11:30 A.M.

Q. Look at the graphic. What flight will the woman most likely take?

정답 TY8903

▶ 스케줄

Weekly Delivery Schedule	
Bennington Apartments	April 2
The Glasson Ballroom	April 4
Mercedes Hotel & Suites	April 5
Centerfield Tech Solutions	April 7

M: Actually, I remember The Glasson Ballroom mentioning they can receive their balloons later in the week. Let's squeeze them into April 7 and give that day to HyperEnd Solutions.

Q. Look at the graphic. When will the HyperEnd Solutions delivery most likely be made?

정답 April 4

▶ 가격표

Price Information	
Quantity	**Cost**
100	$75
250	$110
500	$200
1,000	$380 → $340 Sale!

M: Hello, I'd like to make an order for 500 envelopes please. I plan to engrave my company's logo on them.

Q. Look at the graphic. How much will the man's order cost?

정답 $200

▶ 설명서

Step 1. Load paper into main tray
Step 2. Connect power cord
Step 3. Turn on printer
Step 4. Install printer software

W: I have the user guide here. It says we need to download and install the latest printing software. Then, we should be able to start using it right away.

Q. Look at the graphic. Which step does the woman need to do next?

정답 Step 4

▶ 막대 그래프

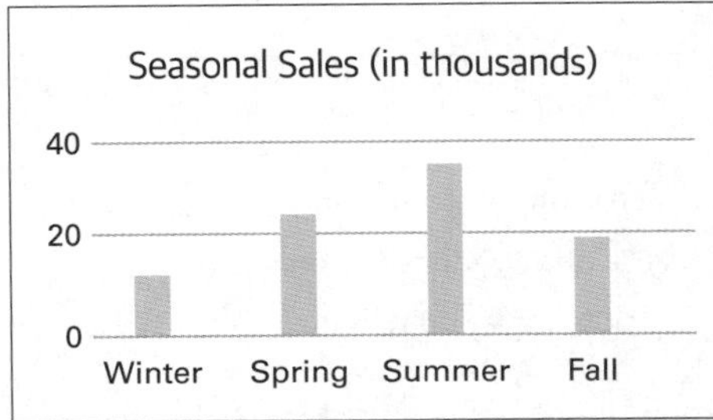

W: Isn't the RazorSpin 3A our most well-known scooter? And we sold 38,000 of them. How did that happen?

Q. Look at the graphic. Which season's sales figures does the woman ask about?

정답 Summer

▶ 원 그래프

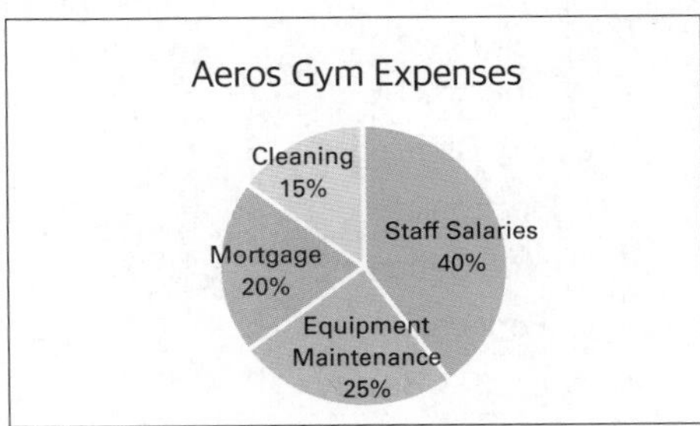

M: Hana, can we discuss the budget for our gym? I ran through our expenses, and I'm worried we're spending too much on equipment maintenance.

Q. Look at the graphic. Which percentage of the budget is the man concerned about?

정답 25%

P11_4

▶ 지도

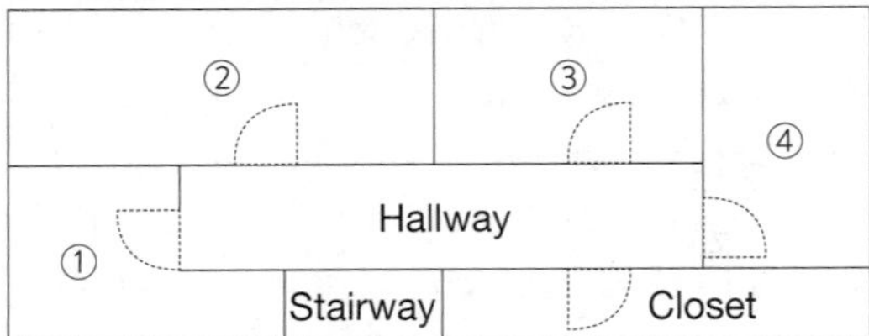

W: Please start with the leather sofa. It's on the second floor, so after going up the stairs, turn right into the hallway. It'll be in the room across from the closet.

Q. Look at the graphic. Which room does the woman refer to?

정답 Room 3

▶ 일기예보

Weather Forecast			
Thursday	**Friday**	**Saturday**	**Sunday**
24°C Cloudy	25°C Partly cloudy	27°C Mostly clear skies	30°C Clear skies

M: Let me pull up the weather forecast. The end of next week looks much better.

W: Yeah. Twenty-seven degrees is pretty warm, and it won't be too cloudy. We can hold the activity then!

Q. Look at the graphic. Which day do the speakers choose?

정답 Saturday

▶ 층별 안내도

Floor	Department
5	Luxury Clothing
4	Electronics
3	Home Goods
2	Footwear
1	Cosmetics & Beauty

W: Hi, I heard you're holding a sale for laptop computers. I was wondering which models are out on display so I can see some in person.

Q. Look at the graphic. Which floor will the woman visit?

정답 Floor 4

▶ 제품 목록

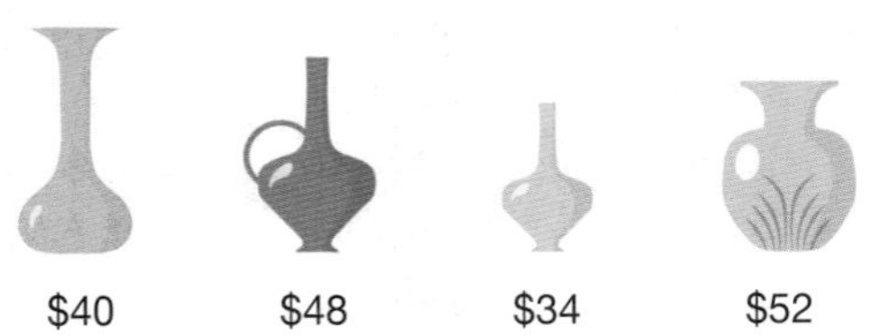

M: The one with the widest neck would be great for displaying lots of flowers!

Q. Look at the graphic. How much is the vase the man wants to buy?

정답 $52

▶ 좌석 배치도

Stage

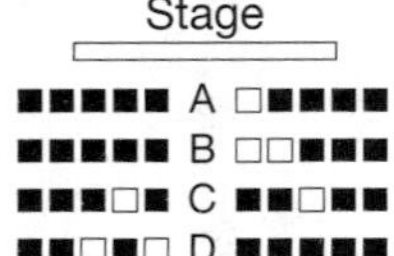

W: One second now... Oh, there is one last pair of seats right next to each other! I can book these for you immediately. May I get your name?

Q. Look at the graphic. Which row will the man purchase tickets for?

정답 Row B

▶ 쿠폰

Summer Blowout Sale!

20% off – Monday only

25% off – Wednesday only

30% off – Friday only

M: You know, if you hold off until Friday to buy it, you could save 30 percent.

W: True, but I have a business trip this week. I guess I'll just have to settle for 20 percent off.

Q. Look at the graphic. On which day is the woman making a purchase?

정답 Monday

P11_5

▶ 시간표/스케줄

- ☐ delay, postpone 연기하다
- ☐ cancel 취소하다
- ☐ departure 출발
- ☐ arrival 도착
- ☐ booked 예약된
- ☐ landed 착륙한
- ☐ on schedule 일정대로
- ☐ on time 정시에
- ☐ carousel 짐 찾는 곳

▶ 가격표

- ☐ payment 납입, 지불
- ☐ withdraw 인출하다
- ☐ receipt 영수증
- ☐ quote 견적
- ☐ inventory 재고 (목록)
- ☐ price list 가격표
- ☐ product code 제품 고유 코드
- ☐ account 계정
- ☐ quantity 수량

▶ 막대/원 그래프

- ☐ proportion 부분, 비율
- ☐ rate 비율
- ☐ The second largest 두번째로 가장 큰
- ☐ The lowest is 가장 낮은 것은
- ☐ The smallest is 가장 작은 것은
- ☐ output 생산량
- ☐ production level 생산 수준
- ☐ capacity 수용력
- ☐ market share 시장 점유율
- ☐ profit 이익

▶ 지도

- ☐ route 노선
- ☐ detour 우회하다
- ☐ be located[situated] 위치하다
- ☐ landmarks 주요 지형지물
- ☐ boulevard 대로
- ☐ intersection 교차로
- ☐ district 구역
- ☐ trail 산책로, 등산길
- ☐ complex 복합건물
- ☐ business center 비즈니스 센터

▶ 일기예보

- ☐ Celsius 섭씨
- ☐ Fahrenheit 화씨
- ☐ temperature 온도
- ☐ chance 가능성
- ☐ weather forecast 일기예보
- ☐ humidity 습도
- ☐ precipitation 강수량
- ☐ wind speed 풍속
- ☐ severe weather 악천후

▶ 층별 안내도

- ☐ level, floor 층
- ☐ extension 내선번호
- ☐ employee directory 직원 안내 책자
- ☐ office directory 사무실 안내도
- ☐ relocate 이전하다

▶ 좌석 배치도

- ☐ layout 배치
- ☐ floor plan 평면도
- ☐ hallway 통로
- ☐ exit 출구
- ☐ entrance 입구
- ☐ reception 접수처
- ☐ copy room 복사실
- ☐ meeting room 회의실
- ☐ row 열

▶ 쿠폰

- ☐ voucher 상품권, 쿠폰
- ☐ valid until ~까지 유효한
- ☐ expiration date 유효 기간
- ☐ ticket holder 티켓 소지자
- ☐ complimentary 무료의

Check-up Test

음원 바로듣기

강의 바로보기

P11_6

Museum Map

Ground Level *Contemporary Art*	**Level 1** *Renaissance Art*
Level 2 *Medieval & Gothic Art*	**Level 3** *18th – 19th Century Art*

1. Look at the graphic. On which floor will the man take a tour?
   (A) Ground Level
   (B) Level 1
   (C) Level 2
   (D) Level 3

2. What will happen at the museum this fall?
   (A) A workshop will be provided.
   (B) A conference will be held.
   (C) Special discounts will be offered.
   (D) Some artists will be giving lectures.

3. Why does the woman suggest using the escalator at the back of the museum?
   (A) It is close to the lobby.
   (B) It was recently built.
   (C) It is faster in speed.
   (D) It is not crowded.

Cumberland Institute Health Fair Fees		
Day 1 Only	Member	$20
	Non-member	$25
Day 2 Only	Member	$22
	Non-member	$30
Day 3 Only	Member	$27
	Non-member	$37

4. What problem does the woman mention?
   (A) A Web site is not working.
   (B) A ticket was not issued.
   (C) Some prices are incorrect.
   (D) Some orders have not been received.

5. Look at the graphic. How much will the woman most likely pay?
   (A) $20
   (B) $22
   (C) $27
   (D) $37

6. What does the man ask the woman to provide?
   (A) Contact information
   (B) A billing address
   (C) A credit card number
   (D) An identification number

정답 및 해설 p.110

GRANDVIEW TOWER BUSINESS SUITES
Fifth Floor Directory

Office 511	Davidson Engineering & Construction
Office 512	Packman Credit Union
Office 513	Karlye & Ledico Legal Services
Office 514	Goldenstein Publishing

7. Look at the graphic. Which office will the man visit?

(A) Office 511
(B) Office 512
(C) Office 513
(D) Office 514

8. What is the man going to do?

(A) Make a deal with a manager
(B) Set up a security system
(C) Replace some water filters
(D) Change some light bulbs

9. Why was the man late?

(A) He misread a schedule.
(B) He could not find some materials.
(C) He had a more urgent request.
(D) His car broke down.

Athletic Sneakers Brand: AeroNova	**Formal Shoes** Brand: Posh Belle
Hiking Boots Brand: Trailblazers	**Beach Sandals** Brand: Bailey Walker

10. Who most likely is the woman?

(A) A sales associate
(B) A product designer
(C) A shoemaker
(D) A sports coach

11. Look at the graphic. Which brand does the man say he likes?

(A) AeroNova
(B) Posh Belle
(C) Trailblazers
(D) Bailey Walker

12. What does the woman offer to do?

(A) Wrap up a package
(B) Check an inventory
(C) Provide a discount coupon
(D) Put an item on hold

음원 바로듣기 강의 바로보기

최빈출 담화 유형 회의발췌/전화메시지

Part 4

회의발췌 전화메시지

Part 4에서 가장 출제 빈도가 높은 유형은 바로 회의발췌(excerpt from a meeting)이다. 사내 이슈 공유, 신제품에 대한 의견 취합, 부서 내 공지, 판매 실적 부진에 대한 해결 방안 요청, 수정된 정책 발표 등의 내용이 자주 출제된다.

▶ 회의발췌 담화 템플릿

P12_1

I'd like to take this time to address one issue that's come up ever since opening this restaurant. ❶ 주제 언급

We've been receiving lots of honest feedback online about our dishes from both local and international customers. Some say our Southeast Asian flavors lack authenticity, so I've contacted a culinary specialist from Thailand to help us out and share expert advice. ❷ 전달사항

He'll come in to train us next Tuesday morning, which means everyone's shifts will start at 10 A.M. that day. Please don't forget to mark your calendars. ❸ 요청사항

▶ 회의발췌 담화 최빈출 표현

• 주제 언급

☐ I want to talk about our new heavy machinery. 저희의 새로운 중장비에 대해 말씀드리고 싶습니다.

☐ As you all know, our company is holding a Hope Charity event.
여러분들 모두 아시다시피, 저희 회사는 희망 자선단체 행사를 개최할 것입니다.

☐ Let's review our previous ads in a video. 영상 안에 있는 자사의 이전 광고들을 검토합시다.

• 전달사항

☐ We should gather the ingredients for tonight's main dish.
오늘 밤의 메인 요리를 위한 재료들을 모아야 합니다.

☐ I'm excited to announce the name of our latest breakfast cereal.
저희 최신 아침 시리얼의 이름을 발표하게 되어 기분이 좋습니다.

☐ We're going to close the business earlier today for repairs. 저희는 수리를 위해 오늘 매장을 더 일찍 닫을 예정입니다.

• 요청사항

☐ Let me know what you're thinking. 어떻게 생각하는지 알려주십시오.

☐ So please sign up for the upcoming technology convention. 그러므로 곧 있을 기술 컨벤션에 등록해 주십시오.

☐ I'd like you to keep working on the brochure until 8 P.M. 오후 8시까지 안내 책자에 대해 계속 작업해 주시기 바랍니다.

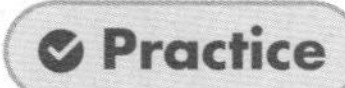

P12_2

1. What type of product has the team developed?

(A) A speaker for radio broadcasting
(B) A scanner for translating foreign text
(C) A display monitor for weather updates
(D) A satellite dish for TV programming

2. What has caused a problem for some users?

(A) Bad weather conditions
(B) Limited streaming services
(C) A lack of space
(D) Complicated set-up procedures

3. What will the listeners most likely do next?

(A) Measure an area
(B) Look up some products
(C) Contact a different supplier
(D) Gather some data

Alright, let's review the product testing feedback for the Astrolink-22V, our ______________________________ ______________________________. The Astrolink-22V is our first satellite dish that can broadcast channels from all over the world. Test users loved having access to a huge variety of content. But, some also reported that when there's ______________________________, the satellite's connection got ______________ sometimes. I think we should create a dish cover that protects the reflector and antenna from any moisture and debris buildup. I'd like you each to take some time to ____________________________________ that can act as a good barrier and, let's reconvene later.

Paraphrasing

satellite TV system → A satellite dish for TV programming
stormy weather → Bad weather conditions
research some durable materials → Look up some products

Part 4에서 회의발췌 다음으로 많이 출제되는 담화 유형은 전화메시지(telephone message)이다. 주로 예약 확인 및 취소, 약속 시간 변경, 일정 조정, 고객 요청사항 전달, 상품/서비스에 대한 문의 등의 내용이 나온다.

▶ 전화메시지 담화 템플릿

P12_3

Good morning, Mr. Lambert. I'm calling about your request to transfer your electricity service to a new address. Just to confirm, you'll be moving out of your current residence on September 21, and the address of your new residence is 577 Bryant Avenue. Also, I have you down as enrolled in paperless billing with automatic bill payments. If you wish to change any of these settings, please visit our Web site. You can also contact me directly at 555-6215.

❶ 회사/부서 소개, 용건 설명
❷ 세부사항/요청사항
❸ 연락 방법 안내 및 마무리 인사

▶ 전화메시지 담화 최빈출 표현

• 회사/부서 소개, 용건 설명

☐ Good afternoon. This is Bruno Ortega (calling) from Benguard Inc.
안녕하세요. 벤가드 사에서 전화드린 브루노 올테가입니다.

☐ I'm calling about my order for your farm's produce. 귀하의 농장 농산물에 대한 제 주문에 관해 전화드립니다.

☐ This is Mike Lopez returning your call. 귀하의 전화에 회신하는 마이크 로페즈입니다.

☐ I am calling to let you know that your prescription is ready.
귀하의 처방전이 준비되었다는 점을 알려드리기 위해 전화드립니다.

☐ I wanted to give you my thoughts. 제 생각을 전달 드리고 싶었습니다.

• 세부사항/요청사항

☐ If you wish to speak with our customer service agent, please continue to hold.
만약 저희 고객 지원 직원과 이야기하길 원하신다면, 끊지 말고 기다리십시오.

☐ But unfortunately, it looks like we made a mistake on one of the changes.
하지만 안타깝게도, 저희가 변경사항들 중 한 곳에 대해 실수를 한 것 같아 보입니다.

☐ Could you forward a copy of the reservation? 예약서 사본 하나를 전달해 주시겠어요?

☐ I'd like you to e-mail the report when you're done. 보고서를 끝내시면 이메일로 보내주시길 바랍니다.

☐ So let me know what you want to do. 귀하께서 무엇을 하고 싶으신지 저에게 알려주십시오.

• 연락 방법 안내 및 마무리 인사

☐ If you go to www.queenparade.com, there's a link. www.queenparade.com으로 가시면, 링크가 있습니다.

☐ You can also contact me directly at 555-0124. 555-0124번으로 제게 직접 연락하실 수도 있습니다.

☐ I'm looking forward to meeting with you. 귀하를 만나 뵙기를 고대하고 있습니다.

☐ Hope to see you there. 거기서 귀하를 뵙기를 원합니다.

☐ I'd really appreciate it. 대단히 감사합니다.

☐ Thanks in advance. 미리 감사드립니다.

☐ If you're interested, please leave a message. 관심이 있으시면, 메시지를 남겨주세요.

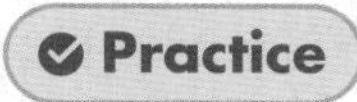

P12_4

1. Why is the speaker calling?
(A) To confirm a reservation
(B) To inquire about an appointment
(C) To express dissatisfaction with a service
(D) To ask for a recommendation

2. What event did the speaker recently participate in?
(A) A dance performance
(B) A community festival
(C) A company workshop
(D) An athletic competition

3. What does the speaker say he will be doing this morning?
(A) Training some employees
(B) Delivering a speech
(C) Visiting some properties
(D) Attending a meeting

Hi, my name is Kyle Chen, and I'm calling to ______________________________ ____________ today. I'm hoping a last-minute slot is available. I played in a ______________________ ________ this past weekend and had no issues the entire time. But, well, come Monday afternoon, I started feeling some discomfort in my right knee. I think I might need to get an x-ray. Could you return this call when you get the chance? I'll be ______________________________ all morning, so if I'm unable to pick up my phone, please just leave a voicemail. Thank you.

Paraphrasing

I'm calling to see if the doctor can see me → To inquire about an appointment
basketball tournament → An athletic competition
be speaking at a conference → Delivering a speech

Check-up Test

강의 바로보기

1. What industry does the speaker most likely work in?
   (A) Accounting
   (B) Entertainment
   (C) Tourism
   (D) Advertising

2. What does the speaker mean when she says, "this assignment is your first"?
   (A) She can provide assistance if needed.
   (B) She is impressed by some work.
   (C) A task will require patience.
   (D) Some information will be lacking.

3. What does the speaker ask the listener to send?
   (A) An invitation
   (B) A timeline
   (C) Some drafts of a report
   (D) Some cost projections

---

4. What industry does the speaker most likely work in?
   (A) Government
   (B) Transportation
   (C) Retail
   (D) Automotive

5. What does the speaker say is a priority?
   (A) Hiring more staff
   (B) Extending business hours
   (C) Attracting more users
   (D) Increasing sales revenue

6. What does the speaker ask the listeners to do?
   (A) Reduce a budget
   (B) Rearrange some work shifts
   (C) Share information about vacancies
   (D) Provide a special training

P12_5

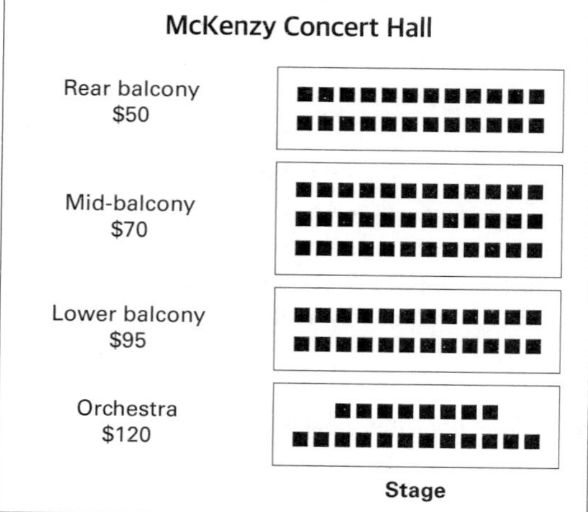

7. Who most likely is the speaker?
   (A) A classical musician
   (B) A hotel clerk
   (C) A sales agent
   (D) A musical actor

8. Look at the graphic. How much do tickets in the available section cost?
   (A) $50
   (B) $70
   (C) $95
   (D) $120

9. What does the listener need to do within 48 hours?
   (A) Log-in to an account
   (B) Go to a front desk
   (C) Respond to an e-mail
   (D) Make a phone call

10. Where does the meeting most likely take place?
(A) At a retail food store
(B) At a coffee shop
(C) At a restaurant
(D) At a food production plant

11. What does the speaker say he is happy about?
(A) Developing a new product
(B) Working with an expert
(C) Expanding a selection
(D) Improving a process

12. What would the speaker like the listeners to do?
(A) Provide some feedback
(B) Move a table display
(C) Practice customer greetings
(D) Update an inventory

---

13. What does the speaker say will happen tomorrow?
(A) A pipe will be replaced.
(B) A machine will be fixed.
(C) A city official will be visiting.
(D) A policy will be updated.

14. Why does the speaker say, "the machinery will be noisy"?
(A) To clarify a misunderstanding
(B) To request assistance
(C) To address an inquiry
(D) To provide a warning

15. What does the speaker say about a permit?
(A) It was issued sooner than expected.
(B) It will be delivered to the listener.
(C) It should be visibly displayed.
(D) It can be used for one month.

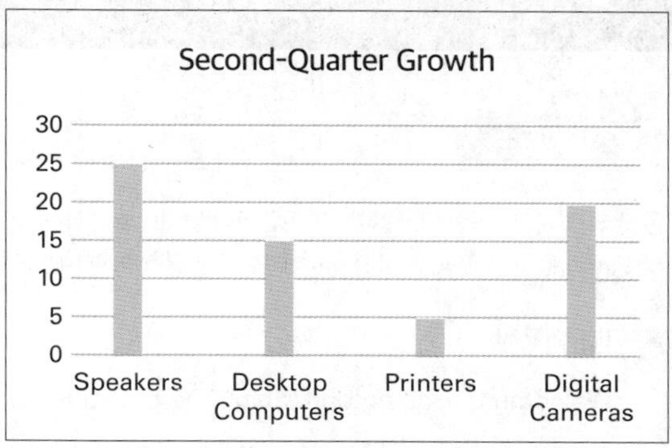

16. Who most likely are the listeners?
(A) Technical support staff
(B) Sales representatives
(C) Event planners
(D) Factory workers

17. Look at the graphic. Which category is the speaker concerned about?
(A) Speakers
(B) Desktop computers
(C) Printers
(D) Digital cameras

18. What has the company decided to do?
(A) Use celebrity endorsements
(B) Open new branch locations
(C) Accept online orders
(D) Lower some prices

음원 바로듣기 강의 바로보기

파트4가 좋아하는 담화/방송 공략법

Part 4

담화 방송

한 명의 화자가 단독으로 말하는 파트인만큼 담화(talk) 유형도 자주 출제되는 유형 중 하나이다. 주로 직원들을 대상으로 한 회의, 각종 외부 행사와 워크숍 진행, 관광지 투어 또는 공장 견학 등의 내용으로 담화가 전개된다.

▶ 담화 템플릿

P13_1

Welcome to Harlington Manor. The previous owner was a renowned carpenter named Ms. Bernice Liu. One unique aspect of this property is that Ms. Liu personally designed the entire estate herself. As we prepare to open the manor as a public park for the first time, we'd like volunteers to help clear fallen branches and debris from the garden paths. Bags and gloves are provided. Also, don't forget to check in with me before heading out — you should each receive a free guest pass, which grants you access to the manor and any events being held throughout the entire summer.

❶ 환영 인사
❷ 전달사항
❸ 요청/당부사항

▶ 담화 최빈출 표현

• 환영 인사

☐ Thank you for attending this supervisors' weekly meeting. 관리자 주간 회의에 참석해 주셔서 감사드립니다.

☐ During today's tour, you'll see beautiful sea animals on the island.
오늘 투어 중, 여러분들은 섬에서 아름다운 해양 동물들을 보게 될 것입니다.

☐ Welcome to the annual CES Technology Convention. 연례 CES 기술 컨벤션에 오신 것을 환영합니다.

• 전달사항

☐ After a coffee break, we'll go into a small group activity.
커피 휴식 시간 이후, 저희는 작은 그룹 활동을 할 예정입니다.

☐ We'd like to offer you a prototype of our new electric car, Mactux 500.
저희의 새로운 전기차 맥턱스 500의 시제품을 여러분들께 제공하고자 합니다.

☐ Be sure to stop by the security office to obtain an access card.
출입 카드를 얻기 위해 보안 사무실에 꼭 들러주세요.

☐ Brighton Catering is looking for people to be taste testers.
브라이튼 케이터링 사는 시식단이 될 분들을 찾고 있습니다.

• 요청/당부사항

☐ Please turn your attention to the screen. 화면에 집중해 주시기 바랍니다.

☐ We want to remind you that we close at 4 P.M. today.
오늘 오후 4시에 폐장한다는 것을 여러분들께 상기시켜드리고 싶습니다.

☐ Also, don't forget to watch a short video on our newly released mobile phone.
또한, 저희의 새롭게 출시된 휴대전화에 관한 짧은 영상을 보시는 것을 잊지 마세요.

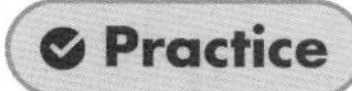

P13_2

1. What industry does the speaker most likely work in?
(A) Education
(B) Healthcare
(C) Media
(D) Telecommunication

2. What is planned for next week?
(A) A new employee orientation
(B) A live video streaming
(C) A security inspection
(D) A tour of a facility

3. Who should send the speaker an e-mail?
(A) Those attending a seminar
(B) Those willing to volunteer
(C) Those wanting to refer candidates
(D) Those traveling for business

I'm really glad that we were able to get the exclusive interview with the governor earlier today. We managed to ____________________ it before all the other ____________! Just a quick reminder that next week we'll be __________________________ for students and jobseekers interested in __________________________. They'll get to check out areas like the production planning desk, our recording studios, and the main operations center. I want to __________________________ __________________________ who can dedicate some of their time to help with this. If you'd like to participate, please send me an e-mail.

Paraphrasing

broadcast, stations → Media
tours for students and jobseekers interested in our line of work → A tour of a facility
a few volunteers who can dedicate some of their time → Those willing to volunteer

방송(broadcast) 담화 유형에서는 지역 뉴스 보도, 일기예보, 교통 방송이 주로 출제된다. 지역 뉴스 보도에서는 기업의 합병, 공사 현황, 행사 소개, 경제 상황 등 도시에서 일어나는 다양한 일들에 대해 언급되는데, 이 때 다소 어려운 어휘들이 사용되어 체감 난이도가 높은 편이다. 일기예보의 경우, 날씨를 알려주는 이미지와 함께 시각자료 문제로 출제될 확률이 높다. 교통 방송은 시내 도로 공사, 재포장 일정, 음악 축제 등의 이유로 인한 우회로 사용 권장 등의 내용이 자주 출제된다.

▶ 방송 담화 템플릿

P13_3

Here's your local weather update. For the remainder of today, you should expect dry and overcast conditions throughout the Sonoma region.	❶ 인사 및 방송 종류 언급
Tomorrow, temperatures are expected to drop again, with chances of light, scattered snowfall. So, make sure to bundle up if you have any outdoor plans. Looking ahead to next week, we'll finally get a small taste of spring.	❷ 전달사항
Now, coming up in just a minute, we'll go over the latest results from our local sports teams, including a major win in football.	❸ 다음 방송 안내 및 마무리 인사

서아쌤 비밀Tip

지역 뉴스 보도에서 나오는 어휘들은 우리가 평소에 접할 기회가 많이 없어 들었을 때 어렵다고 생각할 수 있어요. 자주 출제되는 고난도 어휘 위주로 암기하고, 실전 문제를 풀면서 몰랐던 단어들도 추가해서 단어장에 정리해 보세요!

abandoned 버려진	convert 전환시키다	adjacent 인접한, 가까운
in progress 진행 중인	voice ~의 목소리를 내다	reveal 드러내다
investigate 조사하다	digitalize 디지털화하다	transform 변형하다

▶ 방송 담화 최빈출 표현

• 인사 및 방송 종류 언급

□ In today's GKI News, we're looking into new federal safety regulations.
오늘의 GKI 뉴스에서는, 새 연방 안전 규정들을 살펴보겠습니다.

□ This is your host, Sally Lee. 저는 진행자 샐리 리입니다.

□ I'm Serena Jung with updates for Fairmont residents. 저는 페어몬트 주민들께 새로운 소식을 전하는 세레나 정입니다.

□ Here's your local weather update. 지역 날씨 소식을 전해 드리겠습니다.

• 전달사항

□ You should expect rainy conditions for this weekend. 이번 주말에는 비 오는 날씨를 예상하시면 됩니다.

□ The highly anticipated holiday parade will be held next Sunday.
다음 주 일요일에 많은 기대를 받는 휴일 퍼레이드가 개최될 예정입니다.

□ There's heavy traffic on Highway 30 due to the maintenance work.
유지보수 작업으로 인해 30번 고속도로에 교통 정체가 있습니다.

• 다음 방송 안내 및 마무리 인사

□ We'll go over the latest news about road repairs. 도로 수리에 대한 최신 뉴스에 대해 살펴 보겠습니다.

□ For more information, please visit our Web site. 더 많은 정보를 위해서, 저희 웹 사이트를 방문해 주십시오.

□ Stay tuned after the commercial break for sports news. 스포츠 뉴스를 위해 광고 후 채널을 고정해 주십시오.

P13_4

1. According to the speaker, what happened four years ago?

(A) A building was severely damaged.
(B) A city council was established.
(C) A construction project began.
(D) A business relocated.

2. Who is Alex Santos?

(A) A city inspector
(B) A bank loan officer
(C) A real estate developer
(D) An event planner

3. What will the listeners hear about next?

(A) The weather
(B) New parking laws
(C) A music festival
(D) Traffic updates

This is your host, Carl Kelly. In other news, the old textile factory in the downtown area is finally set to be torn down. The site has been vacant for four years after the ______________________ to a bigger facility located inland. After reviewing several proposals, the city council has decided to sell the run-down property to ______________ Alex Santos, who plans to ______________________ ______________________ that include a dozen contemporary units with an underground parking area. Next up, it seems like the rain is starting to ease up, meaning sunny skies this weekend. Stay tuned after the commercial break for the ______________________ with Hannah.

Paraphrasing

the factory transferred to a bigger facility → A business relocated
developer Alex Santos, who plans to transform the land into residential apartments → A real estate developer
weather forecast → The weather

Check-up Test

음원 바로듣기 강의 바로보기

P13_5

1. What is the podcast episode about?
   (A) Marketing strategies
   (B) Internet security
   (C) Public speaking
   (D) Recent consumer trends

2. What does the speaker say Ms. Gustavson is great at?
   (A) Managing large teams
   (B) Improving workplace efficiency
   (C) Explaining complex ideas
   (D) Helping companies save money

3. What will the speaker discuss next?
   (A) Financial advice
   (B) Survey results
   (C) News updates
   (D) A local sponsor

---

4. What type of photography is the talk about?
   (A) Landscape
   (B) Commercial
   (C) Event
   (D) Travel

5. According to the speaker, what helps a photographer take a good picture?
   (A) Automatic flash
   (B) A camera stand
   (C) A wide lens
   (D) A light source

6. What does the speaker say he will do next month?
   (A) Respond to some questions
   (B) Evaluate some photos
   (C) Post a video
   (D) Give a demonstration

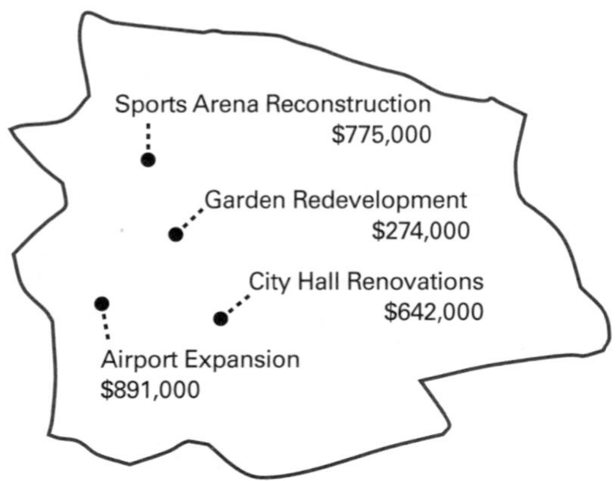

7. What does the speaker say residents have noticed?
   (A) Higher utility costs
   (B) Poor road conditions
   (C) More recreational facilities
   (D) Increased local taxes

8. Look at the graphic. What is the cost of the project currently being worked on?
   (A) $775,000
   (B) $274,000
   (C) $642,000
   (D) $891,000

9. What is scheduled for Thursday?
   (A) A contest
   (B) A forum
   (C) A seminar
   (D) A debate

정답 및 해설 p.121

10. What is the speaker mainly discussing?
(A) Updating a meal selection
(B) Encouraging a vegetarian diet
(C) Promoting sustainability
(D) Collecting food preferences

11. Why does the speaker mention a recent study?
(A) To support her opinion
(B) To introduce a policy
(C) To correct a mistake
(D) To make a comparison

12. Why does the speaker say, "even minor adjustments can make a huge impact"?
(A) To express concern
(B) To reassure the listeners
(C) To propose holding a meeting
(D) To give staff a reminder

---

13. Why is Fullerton Mart hosting a party?
(A) To attract more customers
(B) To celebrate an anniversary
(C) To sell discounted items
(D) To honor a retiring employee

14. According to Sadia Klossner, why is Fullerton Mart successful?
(A) It provides multilingual services.
(B) It has a spacious facility.
(C) It offers foreign products.
(D) It collaborates with other businesses.

15. Why is Sadia Klossner raising funds?
(A) To open more locations
(B) To make a local donation
(C) To expand a selection
(D) To travel abroad

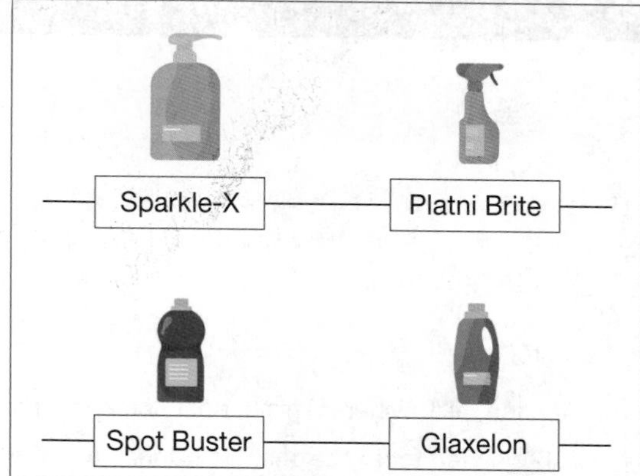

16. What is the purpose of the talk?
(A) To address a problem
(B) To demonstrate some products
(C) To train some employees
(D) To prepare for an event

17. Look at the graphic. Which product does the speaker say is new?
(A) Sparkle-X
(B) Platni Brite
(C) Spot Buster
(D) Glaxelon

18. What happens at 11 o'clock on Wednesdays?
(A) An inspection takes place.
(B) A schedule is posted.
(C) A director makes a visit.
(D) A delivery arrives.

음원 바로듣기 강의 바로보기

공지/광고 담화 절대 안 틀리는 방법

Part 4

공지 광고

공지(announcement) 유형 담화는 비행기나 기차 등의 출발 지연 또는 취소 소식, 쇼핑몰 행사 정보 전달 등의 공공장소 공지와 사내 행사 일정 안내 또는 회사 정책 변경 등의 사내 공지 유형으로 나뉘어 출제된다. 주로 문제 발생에 대한 세부 설명과 이에 대한 해결 방안을 제시하는 흐름으로 출제되고 있다.

▶ 공지 담화 템플릿

P14_1

Attention, all travelers. This announcement is for Sunstream Airways flight DX42 headed for Barcelona.	❶ 환영 인사
Unfortunately, we are experiencing a delay in boarding due to heavy storms in the region. Our local weather station has reported that conditions should improve within the hour.	❷ 세부사항
In the meantime, please take out your boarding passes and have them ready so that we can start the inspection process. Thank you for your patience and for choosing Sunstream Airways.	❸ 다음에 할 일 및 감사 인사

▶ 공지 담화 최빈출 표현

• 환영 인사

☐ We appreciate your attendance to our jazz concert. 저희 재즈 콘서트에 참석해 주셔서 감사합니다.

☐ I'd like to start off the meeting with some good news. 몇몇 좋은 소식들과 함께 이 회의를 시작하고 싶습니다.

☐ Welcome to the Ellerslie Artist's Exhibition. 엘러슬리 아티스트 전시회에 오신 것을 환영합니다.

☐ Attention, all passengers[travelers, shoppers]. 승객[여행객, 쇼핑객] 여러분, 주목해 주십시오.

• 세부사항

☐ I'm happy to announce that a change has been made to the company's time-off policy.
회사 휴가 정책이 변경되었다는 것을 알리게 되어 기쁩니다.

☐ For those interested in starting a new career, please visit our booth.
새로운 경력을 시작하는 데 관심이 있으신 분들은, 저희 부스를 방문하십시오.

☐ Unfortunately, we are experiencing a delay in boarding for train AN 193.
안타깝게도, 저희는 AN 193 열차편에 탑승하는 데 지연을 겪고 있습니다.

☐ In just 10 minutes, we're inviting you to join us for a free fitness class.
단 10분 후, 무료 운동 수업에 참여하시도록 귀하를 초대할 것입니다.

• 다음에 할 일 및 감사 인사

☐ Please remember to pick up some information packets. 몇 개의 정보 묶음집을 가져가시는 것을 기억해 주십시오.

☐ Don't forget to submit your survey forms. 귀하의 설문조사 양식을 제출하시는 것을 잊지 마십시오.

☐ Thank you for your patience and cooperation. 귀하의 인내와 협조에 감사드립니다.

P14_2

1. What does the speaker say she is happy about?
   (A) Expanding an office space
   (B) Winning an award
   (C) Leading a seminar
   (D) Being featured in a publication

2. What kind of business does the speaker work for?
   (A) A movie production agency
   (B) An advertising company
   (C) A financial consulting firm
   (D) A food manufacturer

3. What is planned for February 9?
   (A) An annual dinner
   (B) A product demonstration
   (C) A banquet
   (D) A performance

I'd like to kick off our team meeting with exciting news. I'm happy to announce that the International Marketing Association has chosen our agency to ______________________________! As you may recall, we signed a contract with Big Smile Snacks, our first major client, earlier this year. Our 3D graphics team developed a set of animated _______________ for them. The award will honor the creative animation style that was demonstrated in those ________________________. So, please join our _____________ on February 9, where the award will be presented.

Paraphrasing

receive an award → Winning an award
commercials, ads → An advertising company
our banquet → A banquet

제품, 회사, 서비스 등을 홍보하는 광고(advertisement) 유형은 담화 초반에 호기심을 유발하는 의문문으로 시작하는 경우가 많다. 특히 담화 중반부에서 제품이나 서비스에 대한 특장점이 주로 언급되는데, 이 부분이 세부사항 문제로 출제되는 경우가 많다. 담화 후반부는 광고 대상에 대한 구매를 유도하거나 구매 방법을 안내하는 멘트로 마무리된다.

▶ 광고 담화 템플릿

P14_3

Are you living in a single apartment and looking for furniture? Head over to CozyCorner.com to view our compact recliner! This innovative chair folds neatly into a cushioned box, maximizing your space. When you're ready to use it, simply pull the tab to prop up the sofa. Plus, this month, we have an exclusive offer for our listeners! Use the code 921X at checkout on our Web site, and you'll receive two complimentary pillows with your order. So visit CozyCorner.com today and turn your solo room into a spacious loft!

❶ 제품/서비스 소개
❷ 특장점 및 할인 정보
❸ 구매 유도 및 방법 안내

▶ 광고 담화 최빈출 표현

• 제품/서비스 소개

☐ Are you a small business owner? 소규모 업체 소유주이십니까?

☐ Is it difficult to manage your property? 귀하의 부동산을 관리하기 어려우신가요?

☐ Tired of finding things on your messy desk? 지저분한 책상에서 물건들을 찾는 것이 지겨우신가요?

☐ Here at Union Deliveries, we have the fastest solution to help you.
여기 유니언 딜리버리 사에서, 저희는 귀하를 도와드릴 가장 빠른 해결책을 가지고 있습니다.

☐ Palmerston Gym has everything you need to be healthy!
파머스톤 헬스장은 귀하께서 건강해지기 위해 필요한 모든 것을 갖추고 있습니다!

• 특장점 및 할인 정보

☐ This product comes with two extra batteries. 이 제품은 두 개의 추가 배터리가 함께 나옵니다.

☐ ConnectChat 7.0 is just what you need. 커넥트챗 7.0이 바로 당신이 필요로 하는 것입니다.

☐ Our service is available in over 120 countries. 저희 서비스는 120개국이 넘는 곳에서 이용 가능합니다.

☐ When you donate your used home appliances to us, you'll receive 30% off any purchase.
저희에게 중고 가전제품을 기부하실 때, 어떤 구매에 대해서도 30퍼센트 할인을 받으실 것입니다.

☐ If you order this week, consultation is free of charge. 이번 주에 주문하시면, 상담은 무료입니다.

☐ For a limited time only, we're providing a complimentary dessert.
한정된 기간 동안만, 무료 디저트를 제공합니다.

• 구매 유도 및 방법 안내

☐ Simply sign up for a trial class online. 온라인으로 체험 강좌에 등록하시기만 하면 됩니다.

☐ Call us now at 408-9449. 408-9449번으로 지금 저희에게 연락주세요.

☐ So visit www.chocofactory.com today for a list of all our stores.
그러므로 오늘 전 매장의 목록을 위해 www.chocofactory.com을 방문해 주십시오.

☐ Check out our customer reviews. 저희 고객님들의 후기를 확인해 보십시오.

☐ Interested in giving a try? 한번 해보시는데 관심이 있으신가요?

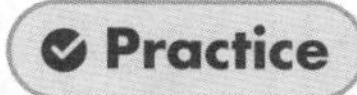

P14_4

1. What type of product is being advertised?

(A) A computer monitor
(B) A storage shed
(C) A dinner table
(D) A desk organizer

2. What special feature does the speaker emphasize?

(A) It is lightweight.
(B) It is adjustable.
(C) It is made of recycled materials.
(D) It comes in various designs.

3. How can the listeners receive a discount?

(A) By calling within a time limit
(B) By visiting a specific Web page
(C) By following a social media account
(D) By texting a keyword to a number

Tired of constantly misplacing items because your space is too messy? If this sounds like you, the Ultimate Storage Organizer is just what you need. Specifically created for busy office workers, this product can ________________ even the most ________________ table into a ________________ workspace. The best part is, it can ________________________________ to fit any amount of area on your desk. Whether you need it slim or wide, you can configure it in just seconds! ________________ us now ____________ ____ to get a 25 percent discount!

Paraphrasing

this product can transform even the most cluttered table into a tidy workspace → A desk organizer
adjust to fit any amount of area → It is adjustable
Call us now within the next 30 minutes → By calling within a time limit

Check-up Test

음원 바로듣기

강의 바로보기

1. What business is being advertised?
(A) A publishing company
(B) An audiobook platform
(C) A sports academy
(D) A recording studio

2. What has the business received an award for?
(A) Its wide selection
(B) Its reasonable rates
(C) Product innovation
(D) Consumer satisfaction

3. What offer does the speaker mention?
(A) A money-back guarantee
(B) Free express shipping
(C) A complimentary product
(D) A membership card

---

4. Why does the speaker say, "some of our speakers are having issues"?
(A) To explain a change in presenters
(B) To ask for product suggestions
(C) To remind the listeners of a policy
(D) To apologize for a delay

5. What are the listeners invited to do?
(A) Donate used items
(B) Become volunteers
(C) Sign up for a newsletter
(D) Enjoy some refreshments

6. Where does the speaker say some information can be found?
(A) On a social media page
(B) At a community office
(C) In a program booklet
(D) On a bulletin board

P14_5

Service Plan	Price
Standard	$120 per hour
Premium	$155 per hour
Ongoing Care	$60 per hour
Elite	$210 per hour

7. What type of business is being advertised?
(A) Roofing
(B) Plumbing
(C) Landscaping
(D) Carpet cleaning

8. According to the speaker, what will probably happen at the end of the month?
(A) Renovations will be completed.
(B) A series of workshops will be held.
(C) New equipment will be installed.
(D) A promotion will end.

9. Look at the graphic. How much does the business's most popular service plan cost?
(A) $120 per hour
(B) $155 per hour
(C) $60 per hour
(D) $210 per hour

정답 및 해설 p.127

10. Who are the listeners?

(A) Tech support staff
(B) Trade show participants
(C) Event organizers
(D) Maintenance crew

11. What does the speaker request that the listeners do?

(A) Take safety precautions
(B) Store boxes in a room
(C) Pick up a free gift
(D) Use a specific path

12. What will take place in the evening?

(A) A musical performance
(B) A banquet dinner
(C) An inspection
(D) A reception

---

13. What is being advertised?

(A) A fitness center
(B) A luxury resort
(C) A housing community
(D) A water park

14. According to the speaker, what sets Riverbend Wellness apart from other businesses?

(A) Its outdoor pool
(B) Its central location
(C) High-speed Internet
(D) Free locker access

15. What does the speaker suggest the listeners do online?

(A) Receive a discount coupon
(B) Take a virtual tour
(C) Make an appointment
(D) Sign up for a membership

Train Number: BX34	
City	**Arrival Time**
Hamburg	4:30 P.M.
Berlin	6:15 P.M.
Dresden	7:45 P.M.
Nuremberg	9:00 P.M.
Munich	10:30 P.M.

16. Why does the speaker apologize?

(A) Some station work is creating noise.
(B) Some arrival times have changed.
(C) A signboard has malfunctioned.
(D) All trains have departed for the night.

17. According to the speaker, why may some listeners need to see an agent?

(A) To print out their ticket
(B) To request luggage service
(C) To ask about a lost item
(D) To buy an annual pass

18. Look at the graphic. When is Train BX34 scheduled to arrive at its next stop?

(A) At 6:15 P.M.
(B) At 7:45 P.M.
(C) At 9:00 P.M.
(D) At 10:30 P.M.

Playlist 15

음원 바로듣기 강의 바로보기

나오면 바로 점수 줍줍! 녹음메시지/소개

Part 4

녹음메시지 소개

녹음메시지(recorded message)는 전화메시지와 유사한 유형으로 담화의 흐름은 유사하지만, 이미 녹음된 ARS 등을 듣고 푸는 유형이다. 주로 해당 업체의 영업시간 안내, 매장의 공사 일정 전달, 예상치 못한 배송 지연이나 주문 취소 등에 대한 해결책 등의 주제가 출제된다.

▶ 녹음메시지 담화 템플릿

P15_1

This is the information line for the Pruneridge Apartments management office.	❶ 인사 및 소속 소개
Please note, the parking lot near the main entrance will undergo resurfacing work on Tuesday, May 19. All Pruneridge residents are asked to move their cars from their assigned parking spaces before 10:00 A.M. on Tuesday. Any vehicles remaining in the lot after this time will be towed at the expense of the owner.	❷ 정보 전달
A map indicating alternative parking locations was e-mailed to residents last week. If you did not receive one, please visit our front desk for a printed copy.	❸ 추가 안내사항 전달

▶ 녹음메세지 담화 최빈출 표현

• 인사 및 소속 소개

☐ You have reached Rockies Asset Management. 로키스 에셋 매니지먼트에 전화 연결되었습니다.

☐ This is the customer support line for Blue Lake Landscaping. 블루 레이크 랜드스케이핑의 고객 지원 전화입니다.

☐ Hello, this message is for Jack Talcom. 안녕하세요, 이 메시지는 잭 탈콤 씨를 위한 것입니다.

☐ Thank you for calling Redwood Robotics. 레드우드 로보틱스에 전화 주셔서 감사합니다.

• 정보 전달

☐ Please note, we're under renovation from November 11 to December 12.
저희가 11월 11일부터 12월 12일까지 보수 공사 중이라는 점에 유의하시기 바랍니다.

☐ We've finalized a promotional video for our autumn clothing collection.
저희 가을 의류 컬렉션을 위한 홍보 비디오를 마무리했습니다.

☐ If you're calling about operating hours, our office is open Monday through Saturday, 9 A.M. to 7 P.M.
저희 운영 시간에 대해 전화하셨다면, 저희 사무실은 월요일부터 토요일, 오전 9시부터 오후 7시까지 열려 있습니다.

☐ All applications will take 10 business days to process. 모든 지원서는 처리하는 데 영업일로 10일이 걸릴 것입니다.

• 추가 안내사항 전달

☐ Please visit our Web site to submit a registration form. 등록 양식을 제출하기 위해 저희 웹 사이트를 방문해 주십시오.

☐ Let me know whether this time is convenient for you. 이 시간이 귀하께 편하신지 알려주십시오.

☐ We'd like to apologize for all of the delays due to a staffing shortage.
직원 부족으로 인한 모든 지연에 대해 사과드리고 싶습니다.

☐ Simply enter your order number in the link. 그저 링크에 귀하의 주문번호를 입력해 주십시오.

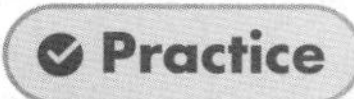

P15_2

1. What kind of business recorded the message?
   (A) An electronics store
   (B) A software development firm
   (C) A utility company
   (D) An Internet service provider

2. What does the speaker say will happen by 2 P.M.?
   (A) A problem will be resolved.
   (B) A new Web site will be published.
   (C) Some staff will return to the office.
   (D) Some areas will become closed off.

3. What does the speaker say is available on a Web site?
   (A) Shipping policies
   (B) Work order forms
   (C) A list of rates
   (D) A feedback survey

Hello there. You have reached Golden ________________________, the leading ____________________ in the Bay Area. Please stay on the line for the next available agent. If you're calling about the ______________________ in Santa Clara County, we can confirm that our technicians have been dispatched, and ______________________________ ____________ by 2 P.M. If you've recently changed residences and need to start, stop, or transfer your service, please visit our Web site to ______________________ for your ____________ ______. Thank you.

Paraphrasing

Golden Gas and Electric, energy provider → A utility company
power outages, services will be back to normal → A problem will be resolved
a form for your work order → Work order forms

소개(introduction) 유형은 상을 수상하는 인물이나 새로 입사한 직원을 소개하는 등의 인물 소개와 세미나나 은퇴 파티 등의 이벤트를 소개하는 행사 소개로 나뉘어 출제된다. 행사 소개보다 인물 소개에 대한 출제 비율이 더 높은 편이며, 보다 다양한 주제를 다루는 방송 등의 유형보다는 한정된 주제로 담화가 구성되므로 비교적 쉬운 난이도로 출제된다.

▶ 소개 담화 템플릿

P15_3

Thank you all for attending today's conference! It's a relief that many of you were able to find this room. I apologize for any confusion – I thought the new location had been updated on the schedule, but I guess that wasn't the case. Now, I'd like to introduce our first speaker: Amelia Clement. Ms. Clement teaches communication courses at Stratford University. She is an expert on effective teamwork strategies, and her lectures highlight different ways that individuals can work better as a team. I'm sure we all know how important strong collaborative skills are. Let's welcome Ms. Clement to the stage!

❶ 인물/행사 소개
❷ 관련 정보 전달
❸ 마무리 멘트

▶ 소개 담화 최빈출 표현

• 인물/행사 소개

☐ Thank you for attending The Future Leaders Conference. 퓨처 리더스 컨퍼런스에 참석해 주셔서 감사합니다.

☐ I'd like to introduce our first guest speaker. 저희의 첫 연사를 소개하고 싶습니다.

☐ Welcome, everyone, to this retirement party for Ms. Sage. 세이지 씨를 위한 은퇴 파티에 오신 모두를 환영합니다.

☐ I'm excited to introduce our keynote speaker, Maria Sanchez.
저희의 기조연설자이신 마리아 산체스 씨를 소개하게 되어 기쁩니다.

• 관련 정보 전달

☐ Mr. Everett is going to tell us about international trade strategies.
에버렛 씨가 국제 무역 전략에 대해 말씀해 주실 것입니다.

☐ Quinn Garcia has been dedicated to this company for over 20 years.
퀸 가르시아 씨는 이 회사에서 20년 넘게 헌신해 오셨습니다.

☐ Ophelia River is the founder of Marble Accounting. 오펠리아 리버 씨는 마블 어카운팅 사의 창립자이십니다.

☐ Rowan will share what it's like to work at Verdant Innovations.
로완 씨가 벌덴트 이노베이션 사에서 일하는 것이 어떤지 공유해 주실 것입니다.

• 마무리 멘트

☐ Before I let Ms. Celine start, just a reminder to turn off your mobile phones.
셀린 씨께서 시작하시도록 하기 전에, 휴대전화 전원을 꺼주시길 당부드립니다.

☐ So please give a round of applause for the award winner. 수상자를 위해 박수갈채를 보내주십시오.

☐ There'll be time to ask Dr. Avan any questions about it.
에반 박사님께 그 부분에 대한 어떤 질문들도 여쭤보실 수 있는 시간이 있을 것입니다.

☐ Let's welcome Mr. Lucian to the stage. 루시안 씨를 무대로 모셔 환영합시다.

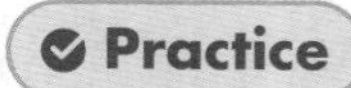

P15_4

1. Where does the introduction take place?

(A) At a science exhibition
(B) At a fundraising event
(C) At a professional conference
(D) At a company celebration

2. According to the speaker, what is Clara Griffin known for?

(A) Founding a nature conservation area
(B) Developing marketing strategies
(C) Her work with ocean pollution
(D) Her international travel experience

3. What are the listeners asked to do?

(A) Select a meal for lunch
(B) Check their information packets
(C) Read a news article
(D) Reserve their own bus tickets

Welcome everyone to the 20th Global Marine Science ____________________. We're delighted to have Clara Griffin from the Port Costa Research Institute with us to give an opening statement. Dr. Griffin is ________________ for her ________________ on ____________________________ and has collaborated extensively with researchers across the globe to develop initiatives for ocean conservation. Before I let her start, please take a moment to ______________________________ ______________________________ to ensure you have a ticket for lunch. Several attendees have mentioned that their packets didn't have one.

Paraphrasing

Global Marine Science Symposium → At a professional conference
Dr. Griffin is well-known for her studies on marine pollution → Her work with ocean pollution
flip through your informational materials → Check their information packets

Check-up Test

1. What does Harmond Industries sell?
   (A) Printer paper
   (B) Dining chairs
   (C) Cleaning supplies
   (D) Computer parts

2. According to the speaker, what problem is the company experiencing?
   (A) Supply shortages
   (B) Shipping delays
   (C) A Web site error
   (D) A power outage

3. What will arrive in an e-mail?
   (A) A refund form
   (B) A delivery schedule
   (C) A discount code
   (D) A revised invoice

---

4. Where is the introduction probably taking place?
   (A) At an employee retreat
   (B) At a sports competition
   (C) At an awards ceremony
   (D) At a corporate reception

5. What kind of business does Hayley Kim own?
   (A) A sporting goods store
   (B) A hair salon
   (C) A health food store
   (D) A fitness center

6. How does Ms. Kim help others stay healthy?
   (A) She gives lectures on nutrition.
   (B) She provides free classes.
   (C) She runs a community garden.
   (D) She developed a wellness application.

P15_5

Daily Schedule – Monday, Oct 11th Employee: Tom Quimby	
9:00	Fall promotion meeting
10:10	Client consultation
11:00	Video conference call (w/ ARD Co.)
11:45	Department check-in meeting
12:30	Lunch (w/ Marissa B.)

7. What does the speaker want to talk about with the listener?
   (A) Including an image on a pamphlet
   (B) Visiting a production factory
   (C) Donating samples to local stores
   (D) Changing a marketing strategy

8. What does the speaker say he will attend after lunch?
   (A) A management meeting
   (B) A business seminar
   (C) A training session
   (D) A sales conference

9. Look at the graphic. At what time will the speaker and the listener most likely meet?
   (A) 9:00
   (B) 10:10
   (C) 11:00
   (D) 12:30

정답 및 해설 p.133

10. What is the purpose of the session?
(A) To attract more customers
(B) To celebrate an accomplishment
(C) To announce an expansion
(D) To recruit new employees

11. Who is Mr. Yamagishi?
(A) A creative director
(B) An industrial designer
(C) An online magazine editor
(D) A Human Resources supervisor

12. What will take place after Mr. Yamagishi's talk?
(A) A panel discussion
(B) An autograph session
(C) A product demonstration
(D) An inquiry session

---

13. What kind of products does the business most likely sell?
(A) Arts and crafts supplies
(B) Beauty products
(C) Party decorations
(D) Clothing accessories

14. According to the speaker, what has been extended?
(A) A submission deadline
(B) A promotional event
(C) A free shipping offer
(D) A return policy

15. Why does the speaker apologize?
(A) Some prices have increased.
(B) Some deliveries are delayed.
(C) A parking area is unavailable.
(D) A wait time might be long.

Foundation	Mission
The Great Dipper	Music education
The Springtime Initiative	Ecological conservation
Home is Here	Community restoration
Blooming Season	Youth development

16. What type of event is taking place?
(A) An awards celebration
(B) A fundraising gala
(C) A press conference
(D) A companywide workshop

17. Look at the graphic. Which foundation did Crescent Studio most likely work with?
(A) The Great Dipper
(B) The Springtime Initiative
(C) Home is Here
(D) Blooming Season

18. What will the listeners probably do next?
(A) Watch a video
(B) Greet each other
(C) Take some photos
(D) Enter a raffle

시원스쿨 LAB

★ ★ ★

서아쌤의 토익 비밀과외

온라인 강의

< RC/LC/실전모의고사 >

13만 유튜버 서아쌤!
유튜브를 인강에 녹여
말자막으로
편하게 학습!

토익시험을 매회 응시하는
토익 만점강사 서아쌤의
최신 고득점 기출포인트
집약!

RC+LC+실전모의고사
3주 완성
All-in-One 커리큘럼으로
토익 고득점 달성!

시원스쿨LAB(lab.siwonschool.com)에서 유료 강의를 수강하실 수 있습니다.

★Special Event★ 서아쌤의 토익 비밀과외 학습 지원!

SIWONSCHOOL LAB

서아쌤 토익
단과 1만원 할인쿠폰

쿠폰번호 : **서아쌤토익1**

COUPON

SIWONSCHOOL LAB

서아쌤 토익
프리패스 2만원 할인쿠폰

쿠폰번호 : **서아쌤토익2**

COUPON

* 시원스쿨LAB(lab.siwonschool.com)에서 쿠폰번호 등록 후 사용가능합니다. / *쿠폰 유효기간 : 등록일로부터 3일간

서아쌤만의 비밀과외 노하우 방출
초밀착 케어까지!

서아쌤 토익 프리패스

토익 3주 초단기 완성을 위한
서아쌤 토익 프리패스의 특별혜택

1

RC+LC 3주 종결 가능
서아쌤 토익 강의/교재 포함

2

기본기에 필요한 알짜 강의
처음토익 LC/RC 무료증정

3

토익 기초체력 마스터
기초영문법 토익 VOCA 교재 포함

4

점수 달성 보장
수강기간 90일씩 무한 연장
*목표점수 미달성시

토익 한 번에 끝내줄
서아쌤 스터디 자료 3종 무료 제공

6

토익+취업까지 책임지는
취업영어 강의 무료 제공

시원스쿨LAB(lab.siwonschool.com)에서 프리패스를 신청하실 수 있습니다.
제공하는 혜택은 기간에 따라 다를 수 있습니다.

과목별 스타 강사진 영입, 기대하세요!

시원스쿨LAB 강사 라인업

20년 노하우의 토익/토스/오픽/지텔프/텝스/아이엘츠/토플/SPA/듀오링고
기출 빅데이터 심층 연구로 빠르고 효율적인 목표 점수 달성을 보장합니다.

시험영어 전문 연구 조직

시원스쿨어학연구소

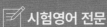

 시험영어 전문

 기출 빅데이터

264,000시간

히트브랜드 토익·토스·오픽 인강 1위

시원스쿨LAB 교재 라인업

*2020-2024 5년 연속 히트브랜드대상 1위 토익·토스·오픽 인강

시원스쿨 토익 교재 시리즈

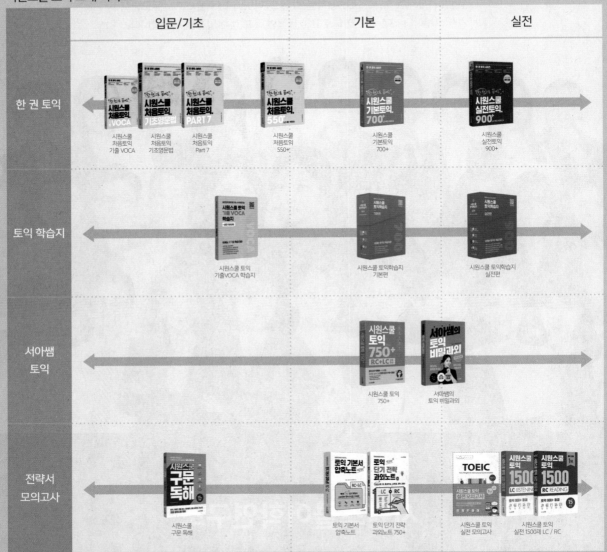

	입문/기초	기본	실전
한 권 토익	시원스쿨 처음토익 기출 VOCA / 시원스쿨 처음토익 기초영문법 / 시원스쿨 처음토익 Part 7 / 시원스쿨 처음토익 550+	시원스쿨 기본토익 700+	시원스쿨 실전토익 900+
토익 학습지	시원스쿨 토익 기출VOCA 학습지	시원스쿨 토익학습지 기본편	시원스쿨 토익학습지 실전편
서아쌤 토익		시원스쿨 토익 750+ / 서아쌤의 토익 비밀과외	
전략서 모의고사	시원스쿨 구문 독해	토익 기본서 압축노트 / 토익 단기 전략 과외노트 750+	시원스쿨 토익 실전 모의고사 / 시원스쿨 토익 실전 1500제 LC / RC

시원스쿨 토익스피킹·오픽 교재 시리즈

10가지 문법으로 시작하는 토익스피킹 기초영문법

28시간에 끝내는 토익스피킹 START

5일 만에 끝내는 토익스피킹 실전모의고사

15개 템플릿으로 끝내는 토익스피킹 필수전략서

멀티캠퍼스X시원스쿨 오픽 진짜학습지 IM 실전

멀티캠퍼스X시원스쿨 오픽 진짜학습지 IH 실전

멀티캠퍼스X시원스쿨 오픽 진짜학습지 AL 실전

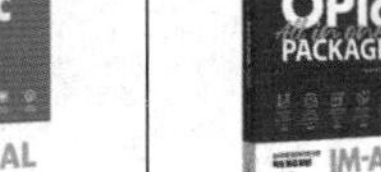
OPIc All in one PACKAGE IM-AL

서아쌤의 토익 비밀과외

실전모의고사
TEST 1

MP3 바로듣기

해설 바로보기

강의 바로보기

시작 시간 ________시 ________분

종료 시간 ________시 ________분

서아쌤의 토익 비밀과외
실전모의고사 TEST 1

LISTENING TEST

In the Listening test, you will be asked to demonstrate how well you understand spoken English. The entire Listening test will last approximately 45 minutes. There are four parts, and directions are given for each part. You must mark your answers on the separate answer sheet. Do not write your answers in your test book.

PART 1

Directions: For each question in this part, you will hear four statements about a picture in your test book. When you hear the statements, you must select the one statement that best describes what you see in the picture. Then find the number of the question on your answer sheet and mark your answer. The statements will not be printed in your test book and will be spoken only one time.

Statement (D), "They are taking photographs," is the best description of the picture, so you should select answer (D) and mark it on your answer sheet.

1.

2.

GO ON TO THE NEXT PAGE

3.

4.

5.

6.

GO ON TO THE NEXT PAGE →

PART 2

Directions: You will hear a question or statement and three responses spoken in English. They will not be printed in your test book and will be spoken only one time. Select the best response to the question or statement and mark the letter (A), (B), or (C) on your answer sheet.

7. Mark your answer on your answer sheet.

8. Mark your answer on your answer sheet.

9. Mark your answer on your answer sheet.

10. Mark your answer on your answer sheet.

11. Mark your answer on your answer sheet.

12. Mark your answer on your answer sheet.

13. Mark your answer on your answer sheet.

14. Mark your answer on your answer sheet.

15. Mark your answer on your answer sheet.

16. Mark your answer on your answer sheet.

17. Mark your answer on your answer sheet.

18. Mark your answer on your answer sheet.

19. Mark your answer on your answer sheet.

20. Mark your answer on your answer sheet.

21. Mark your answer on your answer sheet.

22. Mark your answer on your answer sheet.

23. Mark your answer on your answer sheet.

24. Mark your answer on your answer sheet.

25. Mark your answer on your answer sheet.

26. Mark your answer on your answer sheet.

27. Mark your answer on your answer sheet.

28. Mark your answer on your answer sheet.

29. Mark your answer on your answer sheet.

30. Mark your answer on your answer sheet.

31. Mark your answer on your answer sheet.

PART 3

Directions: You will hear some conversations between two or more people. You will be asked to answer three questions about what the speakers say in each conversation. Select the best response to each question and mark the letter (A), (B), (C), or (D) on your answer sheet. The conversations will not be printed in your test book and will be spoken only one time.

32. What are the speakers preparing for?
(A) A job interview
(B) A product presentation
(C) A training session
(D) A company luncheon

33. What did the man just do?
(A) He cleaned a storage space.
(B) He sent out some invitations.
(C) He printed some documents.
(D) He set up some chairs.

34. According to the woman, why should the man participate in an event?
(A) To meet new colleagues
(B) To present some awards
(C) To make a retirement speech
(D) To announce his promotion

35. Why is the man calling?
(A) To ask for directions to a restaurant
(B) To increase the size of a table
(C) To inquire about menu options
(D) To change the location of a booking

36. What does the woman warn the man about?
(A) A reservation change fee
(B) A parking policy
(C) A change to a menu
(D) A restaurant closing time

37. What will the man most likely do next?
(A) Check a list of locations
(B) Visit a restaurant
(C) Share a confirmation text
(D) Organize some transportation

38. Where most likely are the speakers?
(A) At a campground
(B) At a gym
(C) At a hotel
(D) At a bus company

39. According to the man, what can be found in the Edenville neighborhood?
(A) Shopping centers
(B) Outdoor sports facilities
(C) Budget accommodations
(D) Dining establishments

40. What does the woman say she will look into?
(A) Vehicle rentals
(B) Discount vouchers
(C) Transportation options
(D) Training courses

41. What is the conversation about?
(A) An overdue payment
(B) A shipping delay
(C) A misplaced invoice
(D) A damaged product

42. What does the man offer?
(A) A voucher
(B) A complimentary item
(C) Next-day delivery
(D) A promotional code

43. Why will the woman visit a Web site?
(A) To view some product details
(B) To submit a complaint
(C) To make a payment
(D) To update an address

GO ON TO THE NEXT PAGE

44. What are the speakers organizing?

(A) A shareholder meeting
(B) A staff orientation
(C) A grand opening event
(D) A product launch

45. What does the woman offer to do?

(A) Post an advertisement
(B) Compare some rates
(C) Visit an event venue
(D) Contact some employees

46. What information will the man gather?

(A) Employee feedback
(B) Customer reviews
(C) Budget allocations
(D) Product specifications

---

47. Where do the speakers most likely work?

(A) At a health clinic
(B) At a warehouse
(C) At a sporting goods store
(D) At a gym

48. What does the woman ask the man to do?

(A) Order some devices
(B) Lead a class
(C) Assemble a machine
(D) Perform some repairs

49. What does the woman hand to the man?

(A) A work schedule
(B) An instruction manual
(C) A promotional pamphlet
(D) An identification tag

---

50. What industry does the woman most likely work in?

(A) Pharmaceutical
(B) Telecommunications
(C) Automotive
(D) Construction

51. What is the woman asked to provide a photograph of?

(A) A new product
(B) A management team
(C) A company's headquarters
(D) A business logo

52. What will be the focus of the magazine article?

(A) Environmental impact
(B) Increased production
(C) Workplace safety
(D) Innovative technology

---

53. What does the woman say she would like to do?

(A) Develop new products
(B) Relocate a head office
(C) Reduce business expenses
(D) Attract more customers

54. Why does the man say, "that is one of my strengths"?

(A) To accept praise for some work
(B) To show interest in a job vacancy
(C) To correct the woman's error
(D) To reassure the woman

55. According to the man, what will be the focus of his evaluation?

(A) Materials
(B) Shipping
(C) Advertising
(D) Recruitment

---

56. Where most likely are the speakers?

(A) At a clothing store
(B) At a dental office
(C) At a modeling agency
(D) At a photography studio

57. What does the woman discuss?

(A) A safety procedure
(B) A new product
(C) Some costs
(D) Some images

58. What will the woman do next?

(A) Perform an examination
(B) Check a schedule
(C) Take a photo
(D) Make a phone call

---

59. What type of food does the man's company sell?

(A) Sandwiches
(B) Fruit smoothies
(C) Baked goods
(D) Fresh vegetables

60. What is the woman being sent in a text message?

(A) A delivery address
(B) A Web site link
(C) A photograph
(D) A contact e-mail

61. Why does the man say, "We'd prefer to use our own packaging"?

(A) To express agreement
(B) To praise a service
(C) To reject an offer
(D) To ask for assistance

Area of Interest	Influencer Name
Food & Beverages	Gillian Hubert
Music & Film	Olly Gunn
Fashion & Beauty	Lydia Sparks
Fitness & Sports	Chad Benning

62. Where did the speakers meet?

(A) At an orientation
(B) At a seminar
(C) At a board meeting
(D) At a product launch

63. Why is the man calling?

(A) To ask for information
(B) To offer a job opportunity
(C) To fulfill a request
(D) To finalize a schedule

64. Look at the graphic. Which influencer will the woman probably contact?

(A) Gillian Hubert
(B) Olly Gunn
(C) Lydia Sparks
(D) Chad Benning

GO ON TO THE NEXT PAGE

Community Event	Date	Location
Independence Day Parade	July 4th	Main Street
Annual Boat Show	July 12th	Wiltshire Pier
Arts & Crafts Fair	July 21st	Merrydale Park
Local Farmers Market	August 2nd	Robinson Park

65. What does the woman ask the man to do?

(A) Create a Web site
(B) Visit a community center
(C) Check some details
(D) Make an announcement

66. Look at the graphic. Which event will be canceled?

(A) Independence Day Parade
(B) Annual Boat Show
(C) Arts & Crafts Fair
(D) Local Farmers Market

67. What will the speakers most likely do next?

(A) Distribute promotional flyers
(B) Visit a public park
(C) Attend a community meeting
(D) Select some decorations

Wilderness Lodge
$265 per night
Fir Trail Lodge
$295 per night
Seven Peaks Lodge
$365 per night
Lakefront Lodge
$475 per night

68. What industry do the speakers most likely work in?

(A) Tourism
(B) Film
(C) Real estate
(D) Music

69. Look at the graphic. What rate will the speakers pay to rent a lodge?

(A) $265 per night
(B) $295 per night
(C) $365 per night
(D) $475 per night

70. What will the man most likely do next?

(A) Reschedule a trip
(B) Contact a national park
(C) Load up a vehicle
(D) Repair some equipment

PART 4

Directions: You will hear some talks given by a single speaker. You will be asked to answer three questions about what the speaker says in each talk. Select the best response to each question and mark the letter (A), (B), (C), or (D) on your answer sheet. The talks will not be printed in your test book and will be spoken only one time.

71. Who is the speaker?
(A) A recruitment agent
(B) A marketing manager
(C) A web designer
(D) A financial advisor

72. What feature does the speaker mention?
(A) Next-day delivery
(B) Enhanced security
(C) Employee benefits
(D) Customer rewards

73. What does the speaker say she expects to happen?
(A) Job opportunities will become available.
(B) Business profits will increase.
(C) New retail outlets will open.
(D) Product reviews will be positive.

---

74. Where is the speaker?
(A) At a street parade
(B) At a business conference
(C) At a music festival
(D) At an art exhibition

75. What has caused a problem?
(A) A ticketing system error
(B) A scheduling conflict
(C) Transportation delays
(D) Inclement weather

76. What does the speaker say he has tried to do?
(A) Obtain a refund
(B) Talk to an official
(C) Reschedule an event
(D) Interview a performer

---

77. What type of event is taking place?
(A) A birthday celebration
(B) A grand opening event
(C) An anniversary party
(D) A retirement dinner

78. According to the speaker, what has Ms. Silver helped the company with?
(A) Providing technical support
(B) Improving brand recognition
(C) Reducing annual expenses
(D) Developing innovative products

79. What is on the speaker's wall?
(A) Client photographs
(B) Business proposals
(C) Work schedules
(D) Industry awards

---

80. Why does the speaker want to hold an event?
(A) To attract potential customers
(B) To improve staff relationships
(C) To celebrate achieving a target
(D) To welcome new employees

81. Why does the speaker say, "the location is quite far from the office"?
(A) To recommend a different location
(B) To justify a previous request
(C) To ask for driving directions
(D) To suggest rescheduling an event

82. What does the speaker say she would like to do by Friday?
(A) Post an announcement
(B) Send out invitations
(C) Place an advertisement
(D) Hold a staff meeting

GO ON TO THE NEXT PAGE →

83. Who is Mr. Russo?

(A) A research scientist
(B) A high school teacher
(C) A renowned author
(D) A university president

84. What topic will next week's show focus on?

(A) Advances in online education
(B) Advice on securing employment
(C) Tips on creating study plans
(D) Reductions to college enrollment fees

85. What does the speaker encourage the listeners to do on a Web site?

(A) Take advantage of a limited-time offer
(B) Recommend guests for future broadcasts
(C) Listen to recordings of previous shows
(D) Submit questions for a guest

---

86. Why is the speaker in Philadelphia?

(A) To train some staff
(B) To inspect a factory
(C) To negotiate a contract
(D) To interview for a job

87. Which department does George Chan most likely work in?

(A) Purchasing
(B) Human Resources
(C) Advertising
(D) Technical Support

88. Why does the speaker say, "My return is scheduled for Friday"?

(A) To ask for assistance
(B) To apologize for a delay
(C) To agree to a request
(D) To reschedule a meeting

---

89. What does the speaker say took place last night?

(A) A movie premiere
(B) A sporting event
(C) An art exhibition
(D) An outdoor concert

90. According to the speaker, what addition is being made to a building?

(A) A merchandise store
(B) A bus terminal
(C) A shopping mall
(D) A ticket office

91. What will the listeners hear next?

(A) A weather forecast
(B) A special guest interview
(C) A traffic report
(D) A product advertisement

---

92. Who most likely is the speaker?

(A) A gym manager
(B) A renovation worker
(C) A real estate agent
(D) A health advisor

93. What does the speaker mean when he says, "it's on the east side of town"?

(A) A business is popular.
(B) An event will be well attended.
(C) A location is inconvenient.
(D) A property price is high.

94. What does the speaker ask Ricardo to do?

(A) Update a business Web site
(B) Make some phone calls
(C) Change a work schedule
(D) Visit a community center

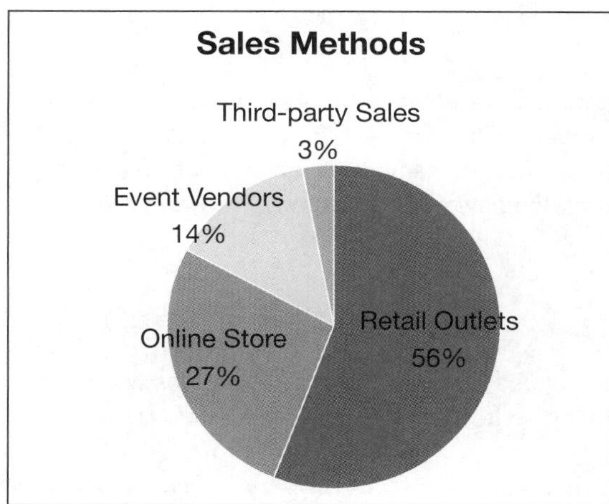

EXOTICA COFFEE COMPANY	
PRODUCT NAME	**UNIT PRICE (Per Bag)**
Dark Blend	$25.99
Java Roast	$29.99
Barista's Choice	$35.99
Colombia Deluxe	$39.99

95. What type of product does the speaker's company sell?
(A) Fruit beverages
(B) Vegetarian meals
(C) Health supplements
(D) Organic snacks

96. Look at the graphic. Which sales method does the speaker want to focus on?
(A) Retail Outlets
(B) Online Store
(C) Event Vendors
(D) Third-party Sales

97. What does the speaker want to do?
(A) Offer customer discounts
(B) Reduce product prices
(C) Hire more employees
(D) Create an advertisement

98. What is the purpose of the telephone call?
(A) To make an inquiry
(B) To place an order
(C) To make a complaint
(D) To confirm a payment

99. Look at the graphic. Which unit price has recently increased?
(A) $25.99
(B) $29.99
(C) $35.99
(D) $39.99

100. Who most likely is the speaker?
(A) A delivery driver
(B) An office manager
(C) A coffee bean farmer
(D) A restaurant owner

This is the end of the Listening test. Turn to Part 5 in your test book.

READING TEST

In the Reading test, you will read a variety of texts and answer several different types of reading comprehension questions. The entire Reading test will last 75 minutes. There are three parts, and directions are given for each part. You are encouraged to answer as many questions as possible within the time allowed. You must mark your answers on the separate answer sheet. Do not write your answers in your test book.

PART 5

Directions: A word or phrase is missing in each of the sentences below. Four answer choices are given below each sentence. Select the best answer to complete the sentence. Then mark the letter (A), (B), (C), or (D) on your answer sheet.

101. Realdek Corporation is seeking a spacious venue ------- its annual company banquet.

(A) hosting
(B) to host
(C) hosted
(D) will host

102. The new online chat program will make it ------- for staff from different departments to communicate.

(A) bigger
(B) easier
(C) richer
(D) busier

103. Urgent road ------- in Sandford caused major traffic congestion this morning.

(A) repaired
(B) repairer
(C) repairs
(D) repairable

104. Each branch's sales data should be compiled ------- 4:30 P.M. every day.

(A) by
(B) on
(C) in
(D) with

105. After almost two years of development, Mr. Yamal ------- launched his mobile application.

(A) finalization
(B) finalized
(C) final
(D) finally

106. Ms. Deringer intends to form a ------- to choose award nominees for this year's Cartwright Prize.

(A) supervisor
(B) suggestion
(C) notification
(D) committee

107. ------- a two-hour delay, passengers were invited to board the train to Birmingham.

(A) Additionally
(B) Although
(C) Following
(D) Furthermore

108. In his best-selling book, Leon Clemence provides effective strategies for ------- online marketing campaigns.

(A) optimize
(B) optimally
(C) optimizing
(D) optimization

109. The customer service workshop ------- the most common complaints made by our customers.

(A) covering
(B) covers
(C) to cover
(D) cover

110. Our server at the restaurant was very ------- but was not knowledgeable enough about the dishes on the menu.

(A) friendly
(B) neutral
(C) possible
(D) frequent

111. To ensure that we stand out from our competitors, ------- clients of our beauty salon receive additional treatments for free.

(A) regular
(B) regularly
(C) regularize
(D) regularity

112. Because Midwest Rail Company ------- its ticket prices, we were able to travel to Albertville for only 9 dollars.

(A) guarantees
(B) advises
(C) requires
(D) delays

113. New employees who were trained by Ms. Beck and Mr. Atkinson will meet with ------- regularly during the probation period.

(A) they
(B) their
(C) theirs
(D) them

114. Thanks to our new shuttle bus service, passengers with connecting flights can transfer ------- between our terminals.

(A) quickly
(B) anymore
(C) quite
(D) shortly

115. Today's press conference at company headquarters will be ------- for next Monday morning.

(A) planned
(B) maintained
(C) heard
(D) rescheduled

116. By partnering with Litmus IT Solutions, we have ------- improved our technical support services.

(A) great
(B) greatly
(C) greater
(D) greatest

117. Mr. Loomis reminded all employees at the morning meeting that ------- unauthorized breaks is unacceptable.

(A) taken
(B) takers
(C) takes
(D) taking

118. Guests ------- wish to order room service may press 5 on the room phone to speak directly to the kitchen.

(A) who
(B) whom
(C) whose
(D) which

119. All of our steaks come with a baked potato and mushrooms or a side salad and sweet potato fries, ------- you prefer.

(A) whoever
(B) either
(C) whichever
(D) another

120. The music festival organizer ------- it would take approximately two days to clean up the site after the event.

(A) designed
(B) managed
(C) estimated
(D) installed

GO ON TO THE NEXT PAGE

121. ------- hotel room is equipped with a secure safe in which guests can store their valuables and travel documents.

(A) Each
(B) All
(C) Some
(D) Most

122. ------- Ms. Embolo planned to have her business proposal completed last week, her heavy workload made that impossible.

(A) Therefore
(B) Following
(C) Although
(D) Nevertheless

123. The health clinic administrator prepared a comprehensive set of ------- related to the handling of patients' personal information.

(A) guided
(B) guidelines
(C) guidance
(D) guiding

124. Tenants of the Brookfield Apartment Building are reminded to ------- all corridors and communal areas clean at all times.

(A) check
(B) monitor
(C) stay
(D) keep

125. The proposal to build a casino in Shepford City received a ------- negative response from local residents.

(A) considering
(B) consider
(C) considerably
(D) consideration

126. Recycling bins in the reception area are ------- marked with the appropriate types of items that should be placed in them.

(A) recently
(B) clearly
(C) easily
(D) widely

127. According to the CEO, sales of Astrid Sportswear's running shoes have increased ------- the past few weeks.

(A) even
(B) only
(C) yet
(D) over

128. Mr. Ortega must take the 7 A.M. train to Boston, or he will ------- being late for the technology conference.

(A) risk
(B) protect
(C) hold
(D) cancel

129. Any meal deals purchased during our special promotion this month ------- an additional portion of chicken wings and a beverage upgrade.

(A) includes
(B) will include
(C) including
(D) had included

130. ------- most workers at Engleford Corporation eat their meals in the staff canteen, Ms. Phillips prefers to eat a packed lunch in the nearby park.

(A) Once
(B) Whereas
(C) In spite of
(D) Unless

PART 6

Directions: Read the texts that follow. A word, phrase, or sentence is missing in parts of each text. Four answer choices for each question are given below the text. Select the best answer to complete the text. Then mark the letter (A), (B), (C), or (D) on your answer sheet.

Questions 131-134 refer to the following e-mail.

To: Dalton Gym <contact@daltongym.com>
From: John Davis <jdavis@intermail.net>
Subject: Gym membership suspension
Date: May 18th

Hello,

My name is John Davis, and I have been a dedicated member of your gym for over three years. I truly ------- (**131.**) the facilities and the supportive environment your gym provides. I am writing to inquire about the possibility of suspending my year-long membership for two months. Due to an important overseas business -------, (**132.**) I will be unable to use the gym from June 1st to July 31st. Could you please inform me if it is possible to temporarily freeze my membership ------- (**133.**) this period and guide me through the process? I look forward to resuming my fitness routine upon my return.

-------. (**134.**)

Best regards,

John Davis

131. (A) enjoy
(B) enjoyed
(C) will enjoy
(D) enjoying

132. (A) location
(B) expense
(C) trip
(D) colleague

133. (A) after
(B) until
(C) among
(D) during

134. (A) I expect to receive confirmation of the cancellation.
(B) I would be happy to extend my membership for another year.
(C) I hope you will be able to accommodate my request.
(D) I want to thank you for changing my fitness schedule.

GO ON TO THE NEXT PAGE

Questions 135-138 refer to the following advertisement.

Sweet Treats Summer Ice Cream Promotion!

Cool down this August with our special summer promotion at Sweet Treats Ice Cream Shop! Throughout the entire month, enjoy a double scoop of your favorite ice cream for the ------- **135.** of a single scoop. That's right! Two scoops for only $1.75!

------- **136.**. We are thrilled to introduce our brand-new flavor, Summer Berry, launching on August 1st. This delightful blend of fresh berries and creamy goodness is sure to become your new favorite. To celebrate, we ------- **137.** free samples of Summer Berry on the launch day.

Don't miss out ------- **138.** this fantastic deal and the chance to try our latest creation. Visit Sweet Treats Ice Cream Shop this August for double the flavor and double the fun at half the price.

Sweet Treats Ice Cream Shop – Where every scoop is a smile!

135. (A) number
(B) cost
(C) budget
(D) profit

136. (A) Our new location could not be more convenient.
(B) Spaces at the grand opening event are limited.
(C) Meanwhile, we have several positions to fill.
(D) Also, we have more good news to share.

137. (A) are offering
(B) will be offered
(C) had been offering
(D) are offered

138. (A) for
(B) in
(C) to
(D) on

Questions 139-142 refer to the following memorandum.

To: All Marketing Department Staff
From: Jane Scanlon, Office Manager
Date: May 14
Subject: Reminder

Dear Team,

-------. As such, your usual workspace will be inaccessible from May 20th to May 24th. Please
139.
ensure that all personal belongings and work materials are removed from your desks and -------
140.
to the temporary workspace on the fifth floor by the end of this Friday, May 19th.

The remodeling will include installing new carpeting, upgrading the lighting, and repainting the walls. These ------- will create a more comfortable and efficient work environment, enhancing
141.
both our productivity and overall well-being.

Thank you for your cooperation and understanding. ------- you have any questions or need
142.
assistance with the move, please feel free to contact me.

Best regards,

Jane Scanlon, Office Manager

139. (A) We are delighted to announce the acquisition of a rival company.
(B) All staff should note the changes to the staff parking space allocation.
(C) I would like to remind you that a shareholder meeting will be held tomorrow.
(D) Please remember that renovation work will be carried out next week.

140. (A) transferring
(B) will transfer
(C) transferred
(D) transfer

141. (A) expenditures
(B) ventures
(C) calculations
(D) modifications

142. (A) Would
(B) Should
(C) Because
(D) Unless

GO ON TO THE NEXT PAGE

Questions 143-146 refer to the following instructions.

Using WonderGro Grass Seed and After-Care

Start by clearing the area of weeds, rocks, and debris. Loosen the soil to a depth of 2-3 inches using a rake. Next, ------- **143.** spread the grass seed with a tool or by hand for smaller patches, aiming for consistent coverage.

Lightly rake the soil to cover the seeds with a thin layer of soil. Immediately water the area gently ------- **144.** the soil. Keep the soil consistently moist by watering lightly twice daily until the seeds germinate, which typically takes 7-14 days.

------- **145.** the grass begins to grow, reduce watering to once daily, then gradually to twice a week. Avoid heavy foot traffic on the new grass. Mow the grass when it reaches 3-4 inches high, cutting no more than one-third of its height. ------- **146.**.

143. (A) extremely
(B) evenly
(C) equally
(D) eventually

144. (A) moistens
(B) is moistening
(C) to moisten
(D) will moisten

145. (A) Once
(B) Still
(C) Yet
(D) Later

146. (A) Lawnmower repairs should only be performed by a technician.
(B) These steps will help you achieve and maintain a healthy lawn.
(C) The flowers should bloom within four or five weeks of planting.
(D) Always keep your gardening tools in a safe and secure place.

PART 7

Directions: In this part you will read a selection of texts, such as magazine and newspaper articles, e-mails, and instant messages. Each text or set of texts is followed by several questions. Select the best answer for each question and mark the letter (A), (B), (C), or (D) on your answer sheet.

Questions 147-148 refer to the following invitation.

You are invited to attend a special workshop here at Riverside College.

Special Guest Speaker:
Dr. Lisa Warren
Esteemed Environmental Scientist and Award-Winning Author of
Sustainable Practices in Modern Agriculture

Subject: Environmental Sustainability
Date: June 15, 2:00-4:00 P.M.
Venue: Greenfield Auditorium

This workshop is open only to Riverside College faculty who are involved in teaching and research. Space is limited to 70 individuals. Call Mr. John Franklin at Extension 115 to reserve a seat.

147. For whom is the invitation most likely intended?

(A) Recent graduates
(B) Environmental scientists
(C) Postgraduate students
(D) College researchers

148. How can interested individuals secure a place at the event?

(A) By filling out a form
(B) By visiting a Web site
(C) By contacting Mr. Franklin
(D) By purchasing a book

GO ON TO THE NEXT PAGE

Questions 149-150 refer to the following e-mail.

From:	Emily Carter <ecarter@techinnovators.com>
To:	Alex Morrison <amorrison@allmail.com>
Date:	August 10
Subject:	Re: Convention arrangements

Dear Mr. Morrison,

Thank you for your recent e-mail outlining your specific needs for your presentation at the Tech Innovators Convention in Austin. We would be happy to fulfill these requirements in gratitude for your participation. You will be given access to a private room, which will be stocked with sparkling water and fruit, as you requested. You are scheduled to speak at 10 a.m. sharp, and our team will make sure that all your equipment and additional refreshments are set up on stage beforehand.

Additionally, I am still awaiting a draft of your presentation content. It is essential for us to review this to ensure it aligns with our convention's standards and guidelines. Please include this as an attachment when you respond.

Best regards,

Emily Carter, Senior Event Planner
Tech Innovators Convention

149. What is the purpose of the e-mail?
(A) To extend an invitation
(B) To outline a schedule change
(C) To agree to some requests
(D) To negotiate a business contract

150. What is Mr. Morrison asked to do?
(A) Present a special award
(B) Share some presentation materials
(C) Check a changed schedule
(D) Review some guidelines

Questions 151-152 refer to the following text message chain.

(2:15 P.M.) Sarah Nichols
Jake, are you heading back to the kitchen?

(2:16 P.M.) Jake Thompson
Yes, I just finished meeting a client. What's going on?

(2:17 P.M.) Sarah Nichols
Our delivery of catering supplies is delayed, and I urgently need some large serving trays and disposable cutlery for tonight's event. We don't have any left.

(2:18 P.M.) Jake Thompson
Do you know where I can find those nearby?

(2:19 P.M.) Sarah Nichols
Yes, the shop on Elm Street.

(2:20 P.M.) Jake Thompson
There's more than one shop on Elm Street.

(2:21 P.M.) Sarah Nichols
Of course! It's next to the bakery, close to the Main Street junction.

(2:23 P.M.) Jake Thompson
Oh, I think I remember seeing that place. Does it have a yellow sign?

(2:24 P.M.) Sarah Nichols
You've got it! Thanks, Jake. I'll reimburse you when you return.

151. Where most likely do the writers work?

(A) At a catering firm
(B) At a moving company
(C) At an appliance store
(D) At a manufacturing plant

152. At 2:20 P.M., what does Mr. Thompson imply when he writes, "There's more than one shop on Elm Street"?

(A) He is too far away from Elm Street.
(B) He requires a precise location.
(C) He would like to buy additional items.
(D) He is unfamiliar with a neighborhood.

GO ON TO THE NEXT PAGE

Questions 153-154 refer to the following instructions.

Welcome to Parkview Apartments in Boston! To ensure a smooth transition into your new home, please follow the guidelines below:

✔ Collect your apartment keys and welcome packet from the main office located on the first floor.

✔ Set up your utility accounts by contacting Boston Utilities at www.bostonutilities.com. You will need your lease agreement and identification.

✔ Register your vehicle for parking by visiting the management office. Complete the parking registration form and obtain your parking permit.

✔ Access our tenant portal at www.parkviewtenants.com to submit maintenance requests, pay rent, and access community announcements.

✔ Schedule an orientation meeting with our Tenant Relations Manager, Ms. Emma Wright, by calling 555-4507. This meeting will cover building amenities, security procedures, and community guidelines.

153. For whom are the instructions most likely intended?

(A) Event participants
(B) Parking attendants
(C) New tenants
(D) Real estate agents

154. What is the reader encouraged to do?

(A) Keep an area clean
(B) Park behind the building
(C) Contact Ms. Wright by e-mail
(D) Visit a Web site

Questions 155-157 refer to the following form.

Service Agreement

Greenfield Landscaping

E-mail: support@greenfieldlandscaping.com

Phone: 555-7890

Web site: http://www.greenfieldlandscaping.com

Client's Name: Olivia Martinez

Service Location: 1025 Highland Street, Sparfield

Type of Service: Residential Landscaping and Maintenance

Service Date/Time: April 25, 8:00 A.M. - 4:00 P.M.

Cost Breakdown of Services Performed:

Spring Lawn Treatment and Fertilization: $300.00

Installation of Flower Beds and Rose Planting: $450.00

Pruning and Tree Trimming: $275.00

Total Amount Due: $1,025.00

Deposit (Received on April 18): $600.00

Balance Due Upon Completion: $425.00

155. What is indicated about the work?
(A) It will require several days of work.
(B) It will be completed by two workers.
(C) It will be carried out at Ms. Martinez's home.
(D) It will take place on a weekend.

156. What type of work will NOT be performed?
(A) Tree maintenance
(B) Decking installation
(C) Grass fertilization
(D) Flower planting

157. What payment amount will Greenfield Landscaping receive on April 25?
(A) $275.00
(B) $425.00
(C) $600.00
(D) $1,025.00

GO ON TO THE NEXT PAGE

Questions 158-160 refer to the following press release.

FOR THE ATTENTION OF THE PRESS
Contact: Jennifer Braun <jbraun@e-move.de>

Berlin (March 15) - E-Move is excited to announce the launch of its new and improved e-scooters at various rental hubs across central Berlin. – [1] –. Initially, the fleet will comprise 50 advanced e-scooters, with plans to triple this number within the next eighteen months.

Each e-scooter is equipped with state-of-the-art GPS navigation, a robust frame designed for comfort, and an automatic balancing system. The scooters feature enhanced battery life for longer rides, ergonomic handles, and built-in phone holders for convenience. – [2] –. Additionally, every e-scooter is outfitted with a small lockbox where you can keep your wallet, keys, or other valuables.

Our e-scooters are environmentally friendly and come with full insurance coverage. – [3] –. Riders can also benefit from the lower costs of charging compared to refueling traditional petrol-powered scooters.

We invite you to visit our Berlin hubs and explore our extensive fleet of e-scooters. – [4] –. For those interested in test riding one of our new e-scooters before renting, please send an e-mail to jgrosser@e-move.de.

158. What most likely is E-Move?

(A) A tour organization
(B) A mobile app developer
(C) A moving company
(D) A vehicle manufacturer

159. What is indicated about the e-scooters?

(A) They should be charged every hour.
(B) They are suitable for two riders.
(C) They include a space for storage.
(D) They are made from lightweight materials.

160. In which of the positions marked [1], [2], [3], and [4] does the following sentence best belong?

"One of our experienced employees would be happy to give you a demonstration."

(A) [1]
(B) [2]
(C) [3]
(D) [4]

Questions 161-163 refer to the following notice.

PRIVATE LOCKER USAGE GUIDELINES - ACCESS RULES

Use of private lockers is exclusively for UberFit Gym members. Lockers can be rented on a long-term basis and require a signed rental agreement. We also offer daily-use lockers for short-term convenience during your gym visits.

- Long-term locker rentals are assigned to members upon request and can be renewed along with their gym membership. To request or renew a locker rental, please check the appropriate box on your membership application or renewal form. Each locker comes with a unique combination lock for added security.
- Daily-use lockers are available at the main entrance and can be accessed by obtaining a key from the front desk. These lockers must be emptied and the key returned by the end of the day to avoid additional charges.
- Any long-term locker found without a valid rental agreement or daily-use locker left occupied overnight will have its contents removed and securely stored. Members will need to pay a $50 fine to retrieve their belongings from the administration office.

For any questions or assistance with locker rentals, please contact our front desk staff.

161. What is the purpose of the notice?

(A) To attract new members to a gym
(B) To outline the rules of locker usage
(C) To announce a change to membership plans
(D) To remind members about gym safety

162. What is indicated about long-term lockers?

(A) They cost $50 per month to rent.
(B) They are located at the gym's main entrance.
(C) They come with a secure locking device.
(D) They are smaller than daily-use lockers.

163. According to the notice, why might gym members need to pay a fine?

(A) Because they used their own lock on a gym locker
(B) Because they stored prohibited items in a locker
(C) Because they failed to pay their membership fees
(D) Because they left belongings in a locker overnight

GO ON TO THE NEXT PAGE

Questions 164-167 refer to the following online chat discussion.

Julia Reynolds [11:15 A.M.]	Hi, everyone. I'm moving to Manchester next month, so I need some advice from you locals. I'm trying to decide which neighborhood to rent an apartment in and have narrowed it down to Maplewood, Brookside, or Pinecrest. Any thoughts?
Liam Carter [11:22 A.M.]	We live in Pinecrest, and my family loves it here. The community is very friendly.
Julia Reynolds [11:25 A.M.]	I've read good reviews about Pinecrest, too. I noticed there's a shuttle service for downtown commuters, but I'm thinking about driving myself. What do you all think?
Ava Thompson [11:34 A.M.]	I used the shuttle when we first moved to Maplewood, and it was very convenient. They have several pick-up points throughout the neighborhood.
Julia Reynolds [11:36 A.M.]	Is the shuttle service reasonably priced, Ava?
Liam Carter [11:39 A.M.]	Driving yourself means you're in control of your schedule. I prefer driving, especially since I can drop my kids off at school on the way.
Ava Thompson [11:44 A.M.]	The shuttle was quite affordable. It's about $30 per week.
Emma Johnson [11:48 A.M.]	Julia, Brookside isn't as far from downtown as the other neighborhoods. It's about a 15-minute drive without traffic.
Julia Reynolds [11:55 A.M.]	That's good to know, Emma. And Liam, that's a great point!
Emma Johnson [12:00 P.M.]	Just be sure to avoid Woolcroft Street during rush hour. Everyone around here knows that it's always packed with commuters.
Julia Reynolds [12:05 P.M.]	That's enough to get me started! I'll give it some more thought. Thanks, everyone!

164. With whom is Ms. Reynolds most likely chatting?

(A) People who work at her company
(B) People who are renting apartments
(C) People who have traveled overseas
(D) People who reside in Manchester

165. What benefit of the shuttle service is mentioned by Ms. Thompson?

(A) It has numerous pick-up locations.
(B) It travels past local schools.
(C) It stops in the Brookside neighborhood.
(D) It is free for local residents.

166. According to Ms. Johnson, why should Ms. Reynolds avoid Woolcroft Street?

(A) It is temporarily closed.
(B) It has very limited parking space.
(C) It is known for traffic congestion.
(D) It does not connect to the downtown area.

167. At 12:05 P.M., what does Ms. Reynolds most likely mean when she writes, "That's enough to get me started"?

(A) She is happy with a transportation fee.
(B) She appreciates the advice she received.
(C) She will rent an apartment in Brookside.
(D) She plans to hire a car in Manchester.

Questions 168-171 refer to the following article.

(April 25) - An exciting new project is underway in Eastside. The project will commence with the transformation of a long-abandoned warehouse located near the intersection of Maple Street and Orchard Avenue into a vibrant entertainment venue. This new space will feature a state-of-the-art concert hall, art galleries, and a variety of dining options to rejuvenate the local cultural scene.

However, the warehouse has suffered considerable neglect over the years, raising concerns about the structural integrity of the building. If the foundation is found to be too compromised, it could pose a significant safety risk to future patrons of the venue. Heavy rains and occasional flooding have also been a regular concern for this part of Eastside. The renovation plans include measures to improve drainage and fortify the structure against future water damage. Local officials are optimistic that these enhancements will not only safeguard the venue but also improve overall infrastructure resilience.

To mitigate these concerns, the Eastside Urban Renewal Committee has enlisted the help of Simonsen Solutions, a renowned engineering firm, to perform a detailed assessment of the warehouse. The firm will begin its evaluation in the first week of May, conducting thorough inspections and stress tests. If the building is deemed sound, the renovation phase is slated to begin in mid-June.

The transformation of this warehouse into an entertainment venue marks a pivotal step in Eastside's revitalization efforts, promising to breathe new life into the community and attract visitors from across the region.

168. What is the article mainly about?

(A) The relocation of a popular concert hall
(B) The construction of new roads in Eastside
(C) The need for recreational facilities in Eastside
(D) The conversion of an empty warehouse

169. What is suggested about Eastside?

(A) It has numerous entertainment venues.
(B) It is preparing to host a music festival.
(C) It receives frequent inclement weather.
(D) It is highly regarded for its dining options.

170. What has Simonsen Solutions been hired to do?

(A) Construct an entertainment complex
(B) Conduct a survey of residents
(C) Evaluate the safety of a building
(D) Develop a budget for a project

171. What is expected to happen in June?

(A) A new venue will be opened.
(B) An inspection will be carried out.
(C) Renovation work will begin.
(D) Building permits will be issued.

GO ON TO THE NEXT PAGE

Questions 172-175 refer to the following letter.

August 22

Dear Ms. Janek,

We are excited to confirm your participation as the lead instructor for our upcoming advertising workshop at the Creative Marketing Forum. – [1] –. Your renowned expertise in contemporary advertising strategies will greatly benefit our attendees. Your session, "Innovative Advertising in the Digital Age," is scheduled for 11 a.m. on September 15th, the opening day of our two-day forum. – [2] –. Due to increasing interest, we have relocated the event to the Grand River Exhibition Hall, anticipating a turnout of approximately 8,000 participants. – [3] –.

To ensure a smooth experience on the day of your workshop, you will be supported by David Morgan, one of my most reliable assistants. Mr. Morgan will greet you at the main entrance of the exhibition hall and escort you to the speakers' preparation area, where you can unwind and make any final adjustments to your presentation. – [4] –. He will be available to assist with any logistical needs, including practicing your presentation, printing materials, or technical setup.

Included with this letter is a premium parking pass. To activate your pass and secure a convenient parking spot, please visit our forum Web site, go to the "Speaker Access" section, and enter the unique code found on your pass under the "Parking Registration" tab.

We are delighted to have you with us and look forward to the invaluable insights you will bring to the Creative Marketing Forum. Your workshop is sure to be a key highlight of the event.

Warm regards,

Alexander Greene
Event Director
Creative Marketing Forum

Enclosure

172. What aspect of Ms. Janek's workshop session is NOT mentioned?

(A) The topic covered during the session
(B) The location of the session
(C) The duration of the session
(D) The date of the session

173. What does the letter indicate about Mr. Morgan?

(A) He is one of Mr. Greene's employees.
(B) He will lead one of the workshop sessions.
(C) He has purchased a ticket for the workshop.
(D) He will provide transportation for Ms. Janek.

174. What is Ms. Janek required to do before the workshop?

(A) Update her Web site profile
(B) Submit her presentation materials
(C) Activate a parking permit
(D) Attend a public forum

175. In which of the positions marked [1], [2], [3], and [4] does the following sentence best belong?

"This is almost double the attendance figures recorded at last year's event."

(A) [1]
(B) [2]
(C) [3]
(D) [4]

GO ON TO THE NEXT PAGE →

Questions 176-180 refer to the following leaflet and e-mail.

Unlock Your Career Potential with Elevate Recruitment Agency

Over the past 15 years, Elevate Recruitment Agency has seen a consistent increase in membership, and we currently support more than 750,000 members throughout Canada. We understand that job hunting can be a daunting process. That's why we offer personalized support tailored to your unique needs. Our services include résumé and cover letter assistance to help you craft compelling documents that highlight your strengths. We also provide job matching, using our extensive network of employers to connect you with opportunities that align with your career goals. Additionally, our team offers interview preparation, providing coaching and resources to ensure you are fully prepared for interviews.

We offer three levels of membership to suit different needs and budgets. The Basic Membership, at $49 per month, grants access to job listings, résumé and cover letter templates, and a monthly newsletter with job search tips. The Premium Membership, priced at $99 per month, includes all Basic Membership benefits plus personalized résumé and cover letter reviews and priority job matching. For those seeking a comprehensive package, our Elite Membership costs $199 per month and includes all Premium Membership benefits along with one-on-one career coaching, exclusive job opportunities, and a guaranteed interview within the first three months.

Joining Elevate Recruitment Agency is simple. Visit our Web site, select your desired membership level, complete the registration form, and upload your résumé to get started. To maximize your chances of success, keep your résumé concise, ideally 1-2 pages, and use bullet points to highlight your achievements and responsibilities clearly. Tailor your résumé for each job application to adjust the job description and include industry-specific keywords to pass through applicant tracking systems.

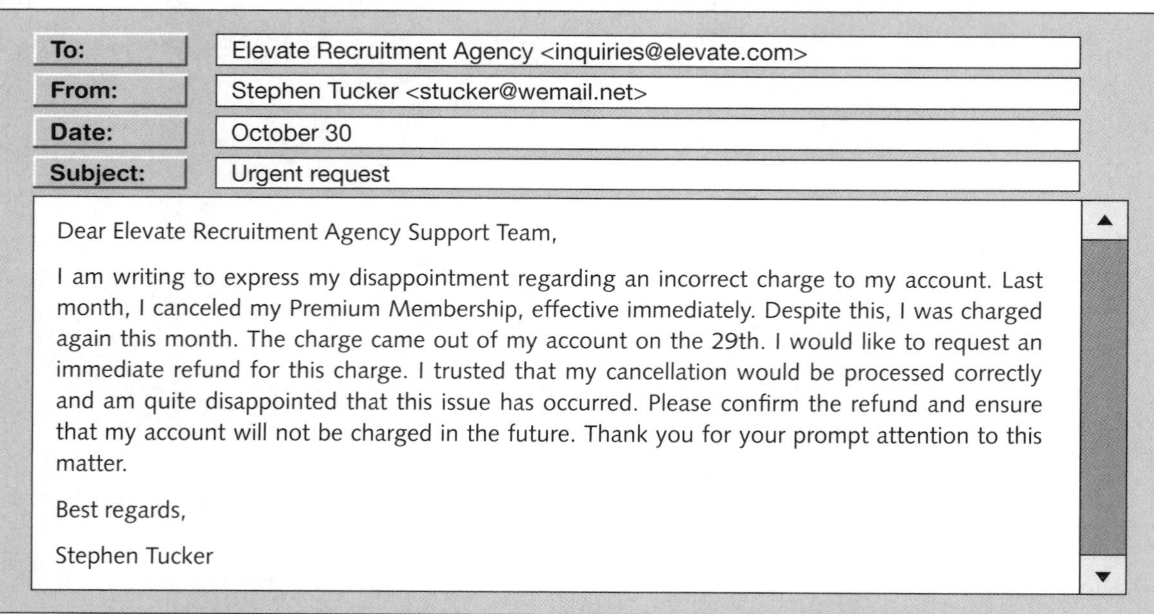

To:	Elevate Recruitment Agency <inquiries@elevate.com>
From:	Stephen Tucker <stucker@wemail.net>
Date:	October 30
Subject:	Urgent request

Dear Elevate Recruitment Agency Support Team,

I am writing to express my disappointment regarding an incorrect charge to my account. Last month, I canceled my Premium Membership, effective immediately. Despite this, I was charged again this month. The charge came out of my account on the 29th. I would like to request an immediate refund for this charge. I trusted that my cancellation would be processed correctly and am quite disappointed that this issue has occurred. Please confirm the refund and ensure that my account will not be charged in the future. Thank you for your prompt attention to this matter.

Best regards,

Stephen Tucker

176. What is suggested about Elevate Recruitment Agency?

(A) It was established less than a decade ago.
(B) It has members all over the world.
(C) It has received several industry awards.
(D) It has steadily grown since its founding.

177. What is NOT mentioned in the leaflet as a service provided by Elevate Recruitment Agency?

(A) Job recommendations
(B) Tips on writing cover letters
(C) Invitations to job fairs
(D) Interview coaching

178. What recommendation is made in the leaflet regarding résumés?

(A) Ensure they are brief
(B) Make multiple copies of them
(C) Submit them by e-mail
(D) Add contact details to them

179. Why did Mr. Tucker send the e-mail?

(A) To renew his membership
(B) To complain about an error
(C) To request an upgraded service
(D) To provide some suggestions

180. What amount does Mr. Tucker expect to be refunded?

(A) $29
(B) $49
(C) $99
(D) $199

GO ON TO THE NEXT PAGE

Questions 181-185 refer to the following e-mails.

E-Mail Message

To: Apollo Car Rental <support@apollo.com>
From: Rick Walker <rwalker@globenet.com>
Subject: Car Rental
Date: August 13

Dear Customer Service Team,

I am writing to seek further information regarding my vehicle booking for my upcoming trip to Chicago, scheduled from September 4 to September 7. Unfortunately, the confirmation email I received lacked certain crucial details about the vehicle. My booking reference number is 58233.

Firstly, as I am not well acquainted with the Chicago area, I would like to verify whether the vehicle includes a satellite navigation system. Having a satnav would be indispensable for navigating the city efficiently and ensuring timely arrivals at my various client appointments.

Secondly, I am worried about the size of the vehicle's trunk. Could you please provide specifics on how many suitcases the trunk can accommodate? I will be traveling with a considerable amount of luggage, and it is essential to know if the vehicle can comfortably fit all my belongings.

Best regards,

Rick Walker

To: Rick Walker <rwalker@globenet.com>
From: Karen Randall <support@apollo.com>
Subject: Re: Car Rental
Date: August 14

Dear Mr. Walker,

Based on the information you provided in your e-mail, I can see that you rented an Altus V5 vehicle. I can confirm that the Altus V5 does come equipped with a satellite navigation system. And, regarding the trunk, the vehicle can comfortably fit up to three large suitcases and two smaller bags. This should provide ample space for your luggage during the trip.

Additionally, I have attached the vehicle's manual to this e-mail. It includes detailed information about the car's features, operation, and safety guidelines, which you may find useful. We hope you have a successful and stress-free trip. Thank you for choosing our car rental service.

Best regards,

Karen Randall, Customer Service Team
Apollo Car Rental

181. What is indicated about Mr. Walker?

(A) He has rented vehicles from Apollo before.
(B) He wishes to cancel his car rental.
(C) He is planning to move to Chicago.
(D) He will go on a business trip in September.

182. What aspect of the vehicle is Mr. Walker concerned about?

(A) Its gas mileage
(B) Its insurance coverage
(C) Its storage capacity
(D) Its safety features

183. How most likely did Ms. Randall find out what type of vehicle Mr. Walker has rented?

(A) By checking a booking number
(B) By consulting a colleague
(C) By looking in a brochure
(D) By making a phone call

184. In the second e-mail, the word "regarding" in paragraph 1, line 3, is closest in meaning to

(A) considering
(B) observing
(C) including
(D) concerning

185. What did Ms. Randall attach to her e-mail?

(A) An invoice
(B) A discount voucher
(C) A map of Chicago
(D) A user manual

GO ON TO THE NEXT PAGE

Questions 186-190 refer to the following article, e-mail, and online review.

Developer Seeks Funding for Innovative Mobile App

(March 4) - John Anderson, a talented mobile app developer, is seeking funding to bring his next idea to life. Anderson's journey in app development began with the creation of "FitLife Tracker," his first and only app to date. Launched just a year ago, FitLife Tracker has gained significant traction, amassing over 10 million downloads and earning high praise for its user-friendly design and comprehensive fitness tracking capabilities.

Following the success of FitLife Tracker, Anderson is now looking to expand his horizons with a new venture. He is currently in discussions with two prominent potential investors: Sarah Thompson and Michael Harris. Thompson, a seasoned venture capitalist, has a track record of backing successful tech start-ups, including the popular social media app "ChatterBox." Harris, on the other hand, is a former tech entrepreneur who sold his cybersecurity firm to a major corporation and now focuses on mentoring and investing in innovative tech ideas.

The funding Anderson seeks will be directed towards developing a groundbreaking mobile app called "WellNest." This new app aims to revolutionize mental wellness by providing users with personalized mindfulness exercises, mood tracking, and virtual therapy sessions. WellNest will leverage artificial intelligence to tailor recommendations based on user behavior and preferences, making mental health support more accessible and effective.

E-Mail Message

To: Michael Harris <mharris@zensecurity.com>
From: John Anderson <janderson@fitwell.com>
Subject: Thanks For Your Support!
Date: August 11

Dear Mr. Harris,

I wanted to take a moment to express my sincere gratitude for your support and belief in my vision for WellNest. Your encouragement has been incredibly motivating as we move forward with this exciting project.

I am thrilled to share that we are on track for the WellNest app's launch. My team is working diligently to finalize the app's features, ensuring that it meets the highest standards of functionality and user experience. We aim to enter the beta testing phase by early October, allowing us to gather valuable user feedback and make necessary improvements. Following the beta phase, we plan to officially launch WellNest in December. We are also preparing a comprehensive marketing strategy to create buzz and ensure a successful rollout.

Thank you once again for your invaluable support. I look forward to keeping you updated on our progress and sharing more details as we approach the launch date.

Best regards,

John Anderson, Founder, WellNest

ONLINE TECH REVIEWS

Name: Raymond Khan
Date: December 29

Comments: As an avid user and fan of John Anderson's first app, I was eagerly anticipating the release of WellNest. After a few weeks of using the app, it has exceeded all my expectations!

The personalized mindfulness exercises are fantastic. The app uses AI to tailor sessions based on my mood and preferences, making each one feel uniquely suited to me. The mood tracking feature is another standout, providing insightful analytics that help me understand patterns in my mental health. The virtual therapy sessions are a game-changer, offering professional support directly through the app. The sessions are well structured, and the therapists are compassionate and knowledgeable. The only downside is that, due to high demand, it takes around a week to get an appointment.

Overall, WellNest is an exceptional app that combines user-friendly design with powerful tools for mental wellness, and I highly recommend WellNest to anyone looking to improve their mental health.

186. What is the purpose of the article?
(A) To highlight advances in mobile apps
(B) To announce a business merger
(C) To discuss Mr. Anderson's next project
(D) To announce the launch of FitLife Tracker

187. In the article, the word "backing" in paragraph 2, line 3, is closest in meaning to
(A) turning
(B) considering
(C) reversing
(D) supporting

188. What is suggested about Mr. Harris?
(A) He has helped to design a mobile application.
(B) He will meet with Mr. Anderson in October.
(C) He played a role in the success of the Chatterbox app.
(D) He accepted Mr. Anderson's request for funding.

189. What is indicated about Mr. Khan?
(A) He is a qualified mental health therapist.
(B) He was impressed with the FitLife Tracker app.
(C) He was involved in the beta testing of WellNest.
(D) He has been using WellNest for two months.

190. What aspect of WellNest was Mr. Khan disappointed with?
(A) The lack of personalization features
(B) The wait time to consult a therapist
(C) The accuracy of the mood tracking software
(D) The design of the user interface

GO ON TO THE NEXT PAGE

Questions 191-195 refer to the following e-mails and invitation.

To:	Kurt Stenson <kstenson@ima.org>
From:	Lillian Lambert <llambert@ima.org>
Subject:	Event Invitations
Date:	April 23

Hi Kurt,

I hope you're doing well. I've attached the first draft of the invitation for the 10th Annual IMA Awards Ceremony. Could you please take a look at it and make a few changes to the format and style?

Also, please note that the live performance will only last for one hour, so the finishing time needs to be adjusted accordingly.

Thank you for your help with this. I'm looking forward to your feedback.

Best regards,

Lillian Lambert

The International Music Association (IMA)

We would be delighted for you to attend
The 10th Annual IMA Awards Ceremony
@The Grand Palace Hotel, 789 Harmony Lane, New York City
Saturday, July 20th

6:00 P.M. ~ 6:30 P.M. – Introduction Speech (IMA President, Linda Harris)
6:30 P.M. ~ 7:30 P.M. – Gourmet Buffet (Prepared by Chef Antonio Ramirez)
7:30 P.M. ~ 9:00 P.M. – Award Presentations (Hosted by David Kingston)
9:00 P.M. ~ 10:30 P.M. – Performance of Songs (Jackson Tyler & Band)

Important Award Winners:
Best Album - *Echoes of Tomorrow* (Sunrise Records)
Best Artist - Rachel Martinez (Midnight Sun)
Best Song - "Whispering Winds" (Luminous Sound)
Best New Artist - Lucas Quinn (Rising Star)

To: Kurt Stenson <kstenson@ima.org>
From: Lillian Lambert <llambert@ima.org>
Subject: Great Work!
Date: April 26

Hi Kurt,

Thank you so much for making the changes to the invitation and schedule. It looks great! I need some additional assistance with the design of the event program. Since the same individual has been selected as the Best Artist award three years in a row, we're planning to feature a 4-page tribute to her music, life, and contributions to the industry. Could you help source some photographs that we can use for this? Please send them to me by within the next couple of hours, if possible. Your help with this is greatly appreciated. Thanks again for all your hard work!

Best regards,

Lillian Lambert

191. Why did Ms. Lambert send the first e-mail?

(A) To extend an invitation to an event
(B) To announce a new venue location
(C) To request changes to a document
(D) To nominate an individual for an award

192. Which time will most likely be changed on the invitation?

(A) 6:30 P.M.
(B) 7:30 P.M.
(C) 9:00 P.M.
(D) 10:30 P.M.

193. What is indicated about The 10th Annual IMA Awards Ceremony?

(A) Ms. Lambert will give a speech at the event.
(B) Lucas Quinn will present one of the awards.
(C) Attendees will be provided with food.
(D) Award winners will attend a press conference.

194. What is suggested about Ms. Martinez?

(A) She will perform songs live at the event.
(B) She will attend her first IMA Awards Ceremony.
(C) She has a record deal with Sunrise Records.
(D) She has won awards at previous events.

195. What will Mr. Stenson most likely do after receiving the second e-mail?

(A) Revise the schedule for an event
(B) Compile a set of photographs
(C) Send invitations to IMA members
(D) Write an article for an event program

GO ON TO THE NEXT PAGE

Questions 196-200 refer to the following form, e-mail, and Web site.

StreamMaster
Your premier choice for an unparalleled streaming experience!

Please complete the form below if you have any comments or suggestions for how StreamMaster can improve its service or content.

Name: Edwin Malen
Address: 492 Fir Trail Road, Bracebridge, ON P1J 1TL
Email: edwinmalen@maplemail.ca
Comments/Suggestions:
As a regular user of StreamMaster, I have enjoyed numerous movies and TV shows on your platform for several years now, and I am typically very happy with the quality and variety of content you offer. In particular, I exclusively use StreamMaster for my weekend movie nights. Friends and family often comment on how much they love the selection and streaming quality. However, the last few weeks have been disappointing. Many shows seem to buffer more frequently, and some of the latest releases have been lacking in variety and quality. I hope StreamMaster will take steps to address these issues.

To: Edwin Malen <edwinmalen@maplemail.ca>
From: Sheryl Lewis <customersupport@streammaster.com>
Subject: Your Recent Feedback
Date: July 12

Dear Mr. Malen,

We are sorry to hear about the streaming issue you have encountered. Our technical team has been working diligently to address the problem that you mentioned. We are confident that this issue will be resolved shortly, ensuring a smoother streaming experience. Regarding the variety and quality of new releases, we are in the process of negotiating new content deals to bring a wider and more diverse range of movies and shows to our platform. We appreciate your patience as we work to enhance our content library.

We have heard similar feedback from numerous customers, and we take such matters seriously. As a token of our appreciation for your loyalty and understanding, we would like to offer you a 3-month free trial of our newest add-on StreamMaster service, which typically costs $35.99 per month. To redeem your free trial, please use the code PREMIUM3FREE after logging into your account on our Web site or app.

Sheryl Lewis, StreamMaster Customer Service

http://www.streammaster.com/extraservices

STREAMMASTER ADD-ON SERVICES

StreamMaster Kids
Includes: Exclusive access to the latest animated movies, beloved animated classics, and early access to new animated releases.
Price: $14.99 per month
StreamMaster Indie
Includes: Award-winning independent films, festival favorites, and critically acclaimed indie dramas and documentaries.
Price: $19.99 per month
StreamMaster International
Includes: A diverse selection of foreign films, including critically acclaimed dramas, comedies, and arthouse cinema from around the world.
Price: $24.99 per month
StreamMaster Classics
Includes: Timeless films from Hollywood's Golden Age, iconic dramas, classic comedies, and vintage thrillers.
Price: $35.99 per month

196. What does Mr. Malen mention in the form?
(A) The cost of a service is too high.
(B) The installation of hardware is difficult.
(C) The variety of movies is worsening.
(D) The customer support is lacking.

197. What is the main purpose of the e-mail?
(A) To request additional information
(B) To confirm a membership upgrade
(C) To address a customer's concerns
(D) To explain a change in service fees

198. What is indicated about StreamMaster's technical team?
(A) It has recently been expanded.
(B) It can be contacted by customers directly.
(C) It will upgrade Mr. Malen's Internet speed.
(D) It is aware of a buffering problem.

199. What can be inferred about StreamMaster from Ms. Lewis's e-mail?
(A) It is more affordable than other streaming services.
(B) It values the opinions of its customers.
(C) It offers discounted rates to long-term customers.
(D) It offers a technical support live chat service.

200. Which streaming service will Mr. Malen receive for free for a limited time?
(A) StreamMaster Kids
(B) StreamMaster Indie
(C) StreamMaster International
(D) StreamMaster Classics

Stop! This is the end of the test. If you finish before time is called, you may go back to Parts 5, 6, and 7 and check your work.

서아쌤의 토익 비밀과외

실전모의고사 TEST 2

MP3 바로듣기

해설 바로보기

강의 바로보기

시작 시간 ________ 시 ________ 분

종료 시간 ________ 시 ________ 분

서아쌤의 토익 비밀과외

실전모의고사 TEST 2

LISTENING TEST

In the Listening test, you will be asked to demonstrate how well you understand spoken English. The entire Listening test will last approximately 45 minutes. There are four parts, and directions are given for each part. You must mark your answers on the separate answer sheet. Do not write your answers in your test book.

PART 1

Directions: For each question in this part, you will hear four statements about a picture in your test book. When you hear the statements, you must select the one statement that best describes what you see in the picture. Then find the number of the question on your answer sheet and mark your answer. The statements will not be printed in your test book and will be spoken only one time.

Statement (D), "They are taking photographs," is the best description of the picture, so you should select answer (D) and mark it on your answer sheet.

1.

2.

GO ON TO THE NEXT PAGE

3.

4.

5.

6.

GO ON TO THE NEXT PAGE

PART 2

Directions: You will hear a question or statement and three responses spoken in English. They will not be printed in your test book and will be spoken only one time. Select the best response to the question or statement and mark the letter (A), (B), or (C) on your answer sheet.

7. Mark your answer on your answer sheet.

8. Mark your answer on your answer sheet.

9. Mark your answer on your answer sheet.

10. Mark your answer on your answer sheet.

11. Mark your answer on your answer sheet.

12. Mark your answer on your answer sheet.

13. Mark your answer on your answer sheet.

14. Mark your answer on your answer sheet.

15. Mark your answer on your answer sheet.

16. Mark your answer on your answer sheet.

17. Mark your answer on your answer sheet.

18. Mark your answer on your answer sheet.

19. Mark your answer on your answer sheet.

20. Mark your answer on your answer sheet.

21. Mark your answer on your answer sheet.

22. Mark your answer on your answer sheet.

23. Mark your answer on your answer sheet.

24. Mark your answer on your answer sheet.

25. Mark your answer on your answer sheet.

26. Mark your answer on your answer sheet.

27. Mark your answer on your answer sheet.

28. Mark your answer on your answer sheet.

29. Mark your answer on your answer sheet.

30. Mark your answer on your answer sheet.

31. Mark your answer on your answer sheet.

PART 3

Directions: You will hear some conversations between two or more people. You will be asked to answer three questions about what the speakers say in each conversation. Select the best response to each question and mark the letter (A), (B), (C), or (D) on your answer sheet. The conversations will not be printed in your test book and will be spoken only one time.

32. Why are the speakers planning a luncheon?
(A) To bid farewell to a colleague
(B) To celebrate the launch of a business
(C) To entertain a new client
(D) To celebrate reaching a sales target

33. What does the woman say she likes about Berryfield Bistro?
(A) Its affordable prices
(B) Its distance from a workplace
(C) Its experienced staff members
(D) Its extensive menu

34. What does the man offer to do?
(A) Speak with employees
(B) Check a weather forecast
(C) Make a reservation
(D) Post an announcement

---

35. What problem does the woman mention?
(A) A vehicle has broken down.
(B) A delivery driver is absent.
(C) A customer has complained.
(D) A device has been misplaced.

36. Why does the man apologize?
(A) He forgot to send an e-mail.
(B) He was late in making an order.
(C) He provided the wrong information.
(D) He is not qualified to perform a task.

37. What will the woman most likely do?
(A) Update a schedule
(B) Make a phone call
(C) Print some business cards
(D) Visit an auto shop

---

38. What type of business do the speakers most likely work for?
(A) A home furnishings store
(B) A catering company
(C) An interior design firm
(D) A cleaning service

39. What does the woman ask the man to do?
(A) Speak to a client
(B) Wear a name tag
(C) Label some items
(D) Check a guest list

40. According to the woman, what will happen tomorrow?
(A) A business will be closed.
(B) A celebration will take place.
(C) A carpet will be replaced.
(D) An invoice will be issued.

---

41. Where do the speakers most likely work?
(A) At a supermarket
(B) At a pizza restaurant
(C) At a manufacturing plant
(D) At an engineering company

42. Who does the man say he will call?
(A) A store supervisor
(B) A repair technician
(C) A sales representative
(D) A customer service agent

43. What does the woman say she will do next?
(A) Install an appliance
(B) Mop a floor
(C) Schedule a delivery
(D) Relocate some products

GO ON TO THE NEXT PAGE

44. What most likely was the topic of yesterday's seminar?
(A) Social media
(B) Product development
(C) Graphic design
(D) Real estate

45. According to the woman, what problem did she encounter?
(A) Some information was incorrect.
(B) Some equipment malfunctioned.
(C) An event venue was too small.
(D) An invitation was not sent by e-mail.

46. What does the man want to do?
(A) Gather feedback from attendees
(B) Revise some data
(C) Arrange another seminar
(D) Postpone an event

---

47. Who most likely is the woman?
(A) An art critic
(B) A painter
(C) A gallery employee
(D) A guest speaker

48. What do the men ask the woman about?
(A) The location of an exhibit
(B) The price of a painting
(C) The opening hours of a building
(D) The availability of prints

49. What will the men most likely do next?
(A) Listen to a talk
(B) Visit a gift shop
(C) Join a tour
(D) Purchase a ticket

---

50. Who most likely is the man?
(A) A racing driver
(B) A tour operator
(C) A car salesperson
(D) A vehicle rental agent

51. What does the man imply when he says, "It's lacking a lot of features"?
(A) A vehicle has disadvantages.
(B) A car needs to be repaired.
(C) A finance plan should be amended.
(D) A Web site will be improved.

52. What will the woman probably do next?
(A) View some alternative options
(B) Test drive a vehicle
(C) Receive a refund
(D) Complete some paperwork

---

53. Where does the man most likely work?
(A) At a clothing store
(B) At a fitness center
(C) At a printing shop
(D) At an event planning agency

54. What does the man say about Angel Sports?
(A) It will move to a new location.
(B) It has several local branches.
(C) It is currently having a sale.
(D) Its merchandise is high-quality.

55. What does the man recommend?
(A) Placing a bulk order
(B) Considering a different size
(C) Choosing a specific color
(D) Using a discount code

---

56. What product is the woman selling?

(A) Training courses
(B) Office furniture
(C) Business software
(D) Health insurance

57. What is David concerned about?

(A) A change of office location
(B) A decrease in productivity
(C) The size of some products
(D) The cost of an order

58. What does the woman anticipate will happen in a few months?

(A) Staff complaints will decrease.
(B) New clients will be secured.
(C) Product prices will rise.
(D) Company profits will increase.

---

59. How do the speakers most likely know each other?

(A) They work at the same business.
(B) They organized an event together.
(C) They met at last month's workshop.
(D) They grew up in the same neighborhood.

60. What does the woman say she wanted to do after a group activity?

(A) Check out some food
(B) Submit some feedback
(C) Register for an event
(D) Speak with attendees

61. What does the man imply when he says, "I brought a packed lunch with me"?

(A) He intends to cancel a lunch reservation.
(B) He has some food allergies.
(C) He will give vouchers to the woman.
(D) He received a welcome pack.

Toronto Central Rail Station - Delayed Trains

Train No.	Destination	Delay
Z314	Ottawa	1 hour
Y217	Montreal	30 minutes
Z374	Kingston	1 hour
Y291	Barrie	2 hours

62. Look at the graphic. What is the woman's train number?

(A) Z314
(B) Y217
(C) Z374
(D) Y291

63. What does the woman ask the man to do?

(A) Print some handouts
(B) Reschedule an event
(C) Give a presentation
(D) Make an announcement

64. What does the man ask about?

(A) Who will demonstrate a product
(B) What time the woman will arrive
(C) Where to host an event
(D) How to access a computer

GO ON TO THE NEXT PAGE

Document 1	Guest List
Document 2	Seating Plan
Document 3	Dietary Preferences
Document 4	Guest Program

65. What kind of event are the speakers discussing?
(A) A shareholder meeting
(B) A retirement dinner
(C) An awards ceremony
(D) A trade show

66. Why does the man ask for the woman's help?
(A) She knows the local area well.
(B) She has relevant work experience.
(C) She attended a similar event in the past.
(D) She is acquainted with a special guest.

67. Look at the graphic. Which document does the man mention?
(A) Document 1
(B) Document 2
(C) Document 3
(D) Document 4

EZ Eats Meal Plans

Meal Plan	Monthly Fee	Ideal for
EZ Basic	$50	Value
EZ Asian	$75	Spice lovers
EZ Health	$90	Dieting
EZ Exquisite	$110	Fancy food

68. What did the man recently do?
(A) He remodeled his kitchen.
(B) He purchased a property.
(C) He joined a gym.
(D) He started a new job.

69. Look at the graphic. Which meal plan will the man probably sign up for?
(A) EZ Basic
(B) EZ Asian
(C) EZ Health
(D) EZ Exquisite

70. What does the woman offer to do?
(A) Send a sample
(B) Provide express delivery
(C) Apply a discount
(D) Customize a plan

PART 4

Directions: You will hear some talks given by a single speaker. You will be asked to answer three questions about what the speaker says in each talk. Select the best response to each question and mark the letter (A), (B), (C), or (D) on your answer sheet. The talks will not be printed in your test book and will be spoken only one time.

71. What is the main topic of the broadcast?
(A) A new subway system
(B) A road construction plan
(C) A bike-riding incentive
(D) A city clean-up project

72. According to the speaker, what will happen in June?
(A) Some streets will be closed.
(B) Some vehicles will be modified.
(C) Some businesses will be relocated.
(D) Some council members will meet.

73. What does the city council intend to do?
(A) Launch a marketing campaign
(B) Survey local residents
(C) Reduce public transport fares
(D) Provide discount vouchers

---

74. Who is the speaker?
(A) A gym employee
(B) A restaurant owner
(C) An event planner
(D) A musician

75. According to the speaker, what is the benefit of a location?
(A) It has good access to public transportation.
(B) It receives a lot of visitors.
(C) It is close to a catering facility.
(D) It has low property prices.

76. What does the speaker ask the listener about?
(A) The number of guests
(B) The date of a celebration
(C) Some menu choices
(D) A budget estimate

---

77. What field does Caroline most likely work in?
(A) Online sales
(B) Staff recruitment
(C) Information technology
(D) Financial consulting

78. Why does the speaker say, "It was an easy choice"?
(A) To request assistance
(B) To recommend a client
(C) To praise an employee
(D) To express surprise

79. What will most likely happen next?
(A) Caroline will talk to the listeners.
(B) Caroline will receive an award.
(C) Caroline will tour a new office.
(D) Caroline will meet her new coworkers.

---

80. According to the speaker, what happened in March?
(A) New products were introduced.
(B) Customers provided some feedback.
(C) Employees attended a training course.
(D) A remodeling project was completed.

81. What type of business do the listeners most likely work for?
(A) An interior design firm
(B) A hotel company
(C) A restaurant chain
(D) A fitness center

82. According to the speaker, what aspect of the business may need to be changed soon?
(A) Its lighting
(B) Its seating
(C) Its booking process
(D) Its heating system

GO ON TO THE NEXT PAGE

83. What event is the speaker calling about?
(A) A product launch
(B) A grand opening
(C) A training workshop
(D) A company outing

84. What does the speaker imply when he says, "it's not within our budget"?
(A) He thinks a document contains some errors.
(B) He will ask a manager for additional funding.
(C) The listener's suggestion cannot be approved.
(D) An event may need to be postponed.

85. What does the speaker ask the listener to do?
(A) Receive a delivery
(B) Update a schedule
(C) Send some invitations
(D) Make a payment

---

86. What is the main topic of the talk?
(A) A landscaping project
(B) An urban development plan
(C) An annual community event
(D) An advertising campaign

87. What does the speaker say the city council hopes to do?
(A) Improve transportation
(B) Lower property rates
(C) Increase tourism
(D) Build public parks

88. According to the speaker, what can the listeners do on a Web site?
(A) View some designs
(B) Participate in a survey
(C) Register for an event
(D) Check a schedule

---

89. Where most likely are the listeners?
(A) On a train
(B) On an airplane
(C) On a bus
(D) On a ferry

90. What does the speaker say about the ticket?
(A) It should be presented to an official.
(B) It can be downloaded to mobile devices.
(C) It includes a discount code.
(D) It can be used to order food.

91. What will the listeners soon be able to see?
(A) A cathedral
(B) A theater
(C) A bridge
(D) A port

---

92. What type of product does the speaker's company make?
(A) Appliances
(B) Furnishings
(C) Construction tools
(D) Jewelry

93. According to the speaker, what will titanium improve about a product?
(A) Its affordability
(B) Its versatility
(C) Its durability
(D) Its appearance

94. Why does the speaker say, "the material is very lightweight"?
(A) To suggest an alternative
(B) To praise the listeners
(C) To disagree with some feedback
(D) To make the listeners less worried

First Meeting Location (3 P.M.)

Team 1	Room 312
Team 2	Room 313
Team 3	Room 314
Team 4	Room 315

95. What will the listeners do at 2:30?

(A) Watch a presentation
(B) Tour a building
(C) Fill out a form
(D) Enjoy some refreshments

96. What is the seminar most likely about?

(A) Customer service
(B) Accounting
(C) Product design
(D) Marketing

97. Look at the graphic. Which team's first meeting location has changed?

(A) Team 1
(B) Team 2
(C) Team 3
(D) Team 4

STORE MAP – ADDISON'S CLOTHING

98. Why is the business currently closed?

(A) A street is temporarily inaccessible.
(B) The store is moving to a new location.
(C) Staff members are being trained.
(D) Remodeling work is being carried out.

99. Look at the graphic. Which section of the store will be relocated?

(A) Men's Clothing
(B) Sportswear
(C) Fashion Accessories
(D) Undergarments

100. What does the speaker say she will be working on?

(A) Cleaning an office
(B) Taking an inventory
(C) Calculating payments
(D) Scheduling deliveries

This is the end of the Listening test. Turn to Part 5 in your test book.

READING TEST

In the Reading test, you will read a variety of texts and answer several different types of reading comprehension questions. The entire Reading test will last 75 minutes. There are three parts, and directions are given for each part. You are encouraged to answer as many questions as possible within the time allowed. You must mark your answers on the separate answer sheet. Do not write your answers in your test book.

PART 5

Directions: A word or phrase is missing in each of the sentences below. Four answer choices are given below each sentence. Select the best answer to complete the sentence. Then mark the letter (A), (B), (C), or (D) on your answer sheet.

101. Former Mayfair Bistro Head Chef John Browning spoke about ------- signature dishes.

(A) him
(B) he
(C) himself
(D) his

102. First-class passengers who are taking a ------- international flight may use the terminal shuttle bus.

(A) connecting
(B) connects
(C) connectivity
(D) connect

103. Ripe and ------- organic produce is available every Saturday morning at the Kirktown Farmers Market at an affordable price.

(A) free
(B) tasty
(C) eaten
(D) open

104. Aztec Sportswear manufactures the most extensive range of ------- in Europe.

(A) events
(B) stadiums
(C) apparel
(D) coupons

105. One responsibility of the project manager is to make sure all employees are keeping ------- client records.

(A) update
(B) updating
(C) updated
(D) updates

106. It is recommended to check the software's compatibility ------- installing it on an operating system.

(A) like
(B) so
(C) before
(D) how

107. The city council expects that residents will ------- embrace any new eco-friendly transportation systems.

(A) enthusiasm
(B) enthused
(C) enthusiastically
(D) enthusiastic

108. Assembly line testing and machine ------- are a major part of our monthly safety review.

(A) inspector
(B) inspections
(C) inspected
(D) inspects

109. Our special summer range of ice cream flavors is now available ------- August 31.

(A) until
(B) while
(C) yet
(D) into

110. Expansion of our business into overseas markets has been ------- this year.

(A) assorted
(B) limited
(C) separate
(D) willing

111. Mr. Kane will be receiving ------- from several suppliers of computer parts on Monday morning.

(A) delivered
(B) deliver
(C) deliverable
(D) deliveries

112. The Sapi Valley Park Association does not have the right to ------- camping in woodland areas.

(A) hike
(B) prohibit
(C) bother
(D) maintain

113. The Mediterranean Salad on our lunch menu will be ------- unavailable due to a shortage of ingredients.

(A) recently
(B) collectively
(C) competitively
(D) temporarily

114. Mark's Delicatessen stocks a wide variety of locally produced foods, ------- dairy products to fruit jams.

(A) under
(B) from
(C) against
(D) on

115. Office intern Archie Munro has proven to be extremely ------- with responding to customer inquiries.

(A) helpfulness
(B) helpful
(C) help
(D) helpfully

116. Crispy Chicken employees will receive extra training ------- the week beginning July 20th at all branches.

(A) during
(B) onto
(C) between
(D) above

117. The custom-made decorations and lights were not received ------- enough to be installed at the wedding party venue.

(A) soon
(B) far
(C) almost
(D) very

118. With his background in events management, Mr. Howard would succeed in the role of concert -------.

(A) organized
(B) organizational
(C) organizer
(D) organizes

119. Rizuko Electronics Inc. is ------- for strategies to reach younger consumers through social media.

(A) seeing
(B) leaning
(C) looking
(D) promoting

120. King Culinary Institute can arrange a cooking course that suits your life and schedule -------.

(A) perfectly
(B) perfects
(C) perfect
(D) perfection

GO ON TO THE NEXT PAGE

121. The promotional flyers were ------- discarded, but Ms. Haim was able to order replacements from the printing shop.

(A) accidents
(B) accident
(C) accidental
(D) accidentally

122. The manager of Vitality Gym believes that membership will double over the ------- six months.

(A) with
(B) next
(C) now
(D) which

123. Any building tenant who still ------- to complete a feedback form should do so before the end of this week.

(A) were needing
(B) needing
(C) needs
(D) has needed

124. Several new signings have ------- begun to transform Huntingdon Hornets into one of the league's best teams.

(A) exactly
(B) closely
(C) hardly
(D) already

125. The employee manual describes the high ------- that customer service representatives must adhere to.

(A) recommendations
(B) experts
(C) standards
(D) accounts

126. Because ------- of the downtown streets are too narrow, the city's parade will take place in the Richmond neighborhood.

(A) everyone
(B) some
(C) those
(D) any

127. The urban development plan ------- the involvement of numerous companies and government agencies.

(A) decided
(B) passed
(C) performed
(D) required

128. We cannot use the new company logo on our promotional materials until it ------- by the CEO.

(A) will be approved
(B) has been approved
(C) is approving
(D) approves

129. ------- the unexpected retirement of Ms. Baskin, we are urgently seeking a replacement for the marketing director position.

(A) Just as
(B) In spite of
(C) According to
(D) In light of

130. The ------- information included on the city map helps tourists to find local transportation and accommodations.

(A) superfluous
(B) potential
(C) arbitrary
(D) supplemental

PART 6

Directions: Read the texts that follow. A word, phrase, or sentence is missing in parts of each text. Four answer choices for each question are given below the text. Select the best answer to complete the text. Then mark the letter (A), (B), (C), or (D) on your answer sheet.

Questions 131-134 refer to the following announcement.

Come to the Riverdale Science Center and discover innovative ways to recycle and reduce waste in your community. -------. We will teach you creative recycling techniques, transforming everyday waste into useful and beautiful items.
131.

Learn how to upcycle household items into unique home décor and practical tools, minimizing waste and maximizing creativity. Our instructors will also cover advanced composting methods and how to properly recycle different types of materials ------- they are repurposed effectively.
132.

By attending, you will learn that recycling is not only easy but also fun and interesting. -------, innovative recycling practices contribute to a more sustainable and eco-friendlier lifestyle. Among other things, ------- help conserve natural resources and reduce pollution.
133. **134.**

To register, visit www.riverdale-sciencecenter.org.

131. (A) The clean-up project will cover several neighborhoods in Riverdale.
(B) Find out how businesses can go paperless to reduce waste.
(C) This coming Sunday at 10 A.M., we are hosting a public workshop.
(D) Our new exhibition is specifically designed to appeal to children.

132. (A) ensures
(B) ensured
(C) are ensuring
(D) to ensure

133. (A) As a matter of fact
(B) Best of all
(C) For example
(D) In any event

134. (A) they
(B) we
(C) both
(D) yours

GO ON TO THE NEXT PAGE

Questions 135-138 refer to the following letter.

July 1

Kwame Addo
Ashforth Road Studios
Daytona

Dear Mr. Addo,

I wanted to express my gratitude for your ------- help in assisting me with the grand opening of **135.** my art exhibition at Daytona Gallery. Things could not have gone better at the event, and it was a pleasure to collaborate with you. I know that our attendees are avid followers of your work, and they were thrilled with the designs you contributed for this event.

Your background music and lighting garnered significant ------- from the attendees. The **136.** atmosphere you created was a perfect match for the artworks I displayed. -------. **137.** I acknowledge that I made several last-minute requests for changes, and you were always happy to accommodate me.

My fundraiser ------- underprivileged children in Daytona is coming up soon, and I truly hope you **138.** will be interested in lending your support to that event as well.

Sincerely,

Haruto Tanaka

135. (A) amazingly
(B) amazing
(C) amazement
(D) amazed

136. (A) proposals
(B) innovation
(C) attention
(D) criticism

137. (A) I was particularly impressed by the improvement in your paintings.
(B) It may be more effective to use a different style of music.
(C) Several local artists exhibited their latest artworks at the event.
(D) Your adaptability in planning the event was much appreciated.

138. (A) benefits
(B) will benefit
(C) benefiting
(D) has benefited

Questions 139-142 refer to the following e-mail.

From: Membership Services <membership@blueridgecountryclub.org>
To: Robert Miller <miller.r98@crestwoodhills.com>
Subject: Membership Expiration Notification
Date: April 5

Dear Mr. Miller,

We are writing to notify you that your Blue Ridge Country Club membership will expire on May 5. To continue enjoying your membership benefits in the coming year, ------- **139.** must be renewed. ------- **140.** You can renew your membership at the member services desk at the country club. ------- **141.** you choose to renew, no further action is required. Your membership privileges will automatically end if the renewal is not completed by the ------- **142.** deadline. If you would like to contact us directly regarding this notification or our club services in general, you can reach us by calling 555-0992.

Best regards,

Membership Services
Blue Ridge Country Club

139. (A) you
(B) each
(C) it
(D) ours

140. (A) We look forward to welcoming you as a new member of our club.
(B) Thank you for your inquiry regarding membership fees.
(C) Membership renewal rates have decreased in recent years.
(D) Please ensure that the process is completed promptly.

141. (A) Although
(B) Because
(C) Also
(D) Unless

142. (A) specificity
(B) specified
(C) specifics
(D) specifically

GO ON TO THE NEXT PAGE

Questions 143-146 refer to the following letter.

May 20

Sophia Caldwell
98 Harbor Lane
East Haven, CT 06512

Dear Ms. Caldwell,

My name is Jamal Thompson, and I am the owner of WebWave Design. -------. **143.** We offer a comprehensive range of web design services for businesses like yours. We specialize in ------- **144.** visually appealing and highly functional Web sites that enhance your online presence.

WebWave Design spares no effort in delivering superior digital solutions. -------, **145.** our professional-grade tools, creative design techniques, and attention to detail allow us to highlight the best aspects of your business. And once the initial design is complete, every Web site ------- **146.** rigorous testing and optimization. All these services are included in every package.

Please visit our Web site to view our portfolio and pricing. I hope to hear from you soon to discuss a potential business arrangement.

Sincerely,

Jamal Thompson
WebWave Design

143. (A) We are looking forward to collaborating with you on the project.
(B) I am writing to describe how my company could help you.
(C) Web design companies typically provide an ideal work-life balance.
(D) I would like to tell you about our current promotional discounts.

144. (A) displaying
(B) purchasing
(C) creating
(D) researching

145. (A) Indeed
(B) Otherwise
(C) By comparison
(D) If not

146. (A) had to receive
(B) is receiving
(C) receives
(D) had received

PART 7

Directions: In this part you will read a selection of texts, such as magazine and newspaper articles, e-mails, and instant messages. Each text or set of texts is followed by several questions. Select the best answer for each question and mark the letter (A), (B), (C), or (D) on your answer sheet.

Questions 147-148 refer to the following information.

IMPORTANT INFORMATION - PLEASE READ

We hope you will be happy with this item you have purchased!

Before you begin assembly of this product, please ensure that all parts are present and place them in a secure location to prevent any loss or damage. Assemble the product outdoors to prevent any damage to your carpet or flooring.

Follow the instructions carefully, starting with the main frame, and then the grass collection component. Take care when attaching the blades, as these are very sharp. For maintenance tips and to register your product for warranty coverage, please visit our Web site: www.ezhardware.com.

147. Where is the information most likely found?

(A) In a brochure
(B) On a notice board
(C) On a Web site
(D) In a box

148. What kind of product is most likely discussed?

(A) A paddling pool
(B) A power drill
(C) A lawnmower
(D) A sprinkler

GO ON TO THE NEXT PAGE

Questions 149-150 refer to the following memorandum.

All London employees are encouraged to have this schedule at their workstations for easy reference when organizing meetings or conference calls with our new client. Ideally, schedule these meetings and calls within the highlighted times(*), specifically between 5:00 P.M. and 8:00 P.M.

London	Vancouver
4:00 P.M.	8:00 A.M.
5:00 P.M. (*)	9:00 A.M.
6:00 P.M. (*)	10:00 A.M.
7:00 P.M. (*)	11:00 A.M.
8:00 P.M. (*)	12:00 P.M.
9:00 P.M.	1:00 P.M.

149. What is suggested by the memorandum?

(A) A staff member will go on a business trip.
(B) A company has taken on a client in Vancouver.
(C) A firm is planning to relocate to London.
(D) Some meeting rooms are currently unavailable.

150. What is indicated about 9:00 P.M. London time?

(A) It is the preferred time for a client meeting.
(B) It is when workers in Vancouver start work.
(C) It is not a suitable time for a conference call.
(D) It is when the London company opens for business.

Questions 151-152 refer to the following brochure.

Rosehill Manor is one of the most sought-after wedding venues in our region. Perched on a gentle rise, it features large windows that offer breathtaking views of the surrounding rose gardens and nearby lake. Originally built in 1905, it served as the residence of the Whitmore family until its transformation into a premier event space two years ago. Now, the venue can host up to 250 guests, making it perfect for weddings. With its polished hardwood floors, vaulted ceilings, and exquisite artwork, Rosehill Manor is the perfect setting for your special occasion.

Le Jardin, our on-site bistro introduced a decade ago, provides catering for weddings and operates as an independent eatery. This sophisticated establishment, led by Chef Antonio De Luca, caters to all dietary preferences and has become a cornerstone of the local culinary scene. Locals know to book well in advance to secure a table.

For inquiries regarding reservation prices and services provided, please call us at 310-555-0789.

151. What is indicated about Rosehill Manor?

(A) It will soon plant a rose garden for visitors.
(B) It offers guided tours all year round.
(C) It has undergone renovation work.
(D) It is the current home of the Whitmore family.

152. What is suggested about Le Jardin?

(A) It uses only locally grown ingredients.
(B) It recommends advance reservations.
(C) It was first established in the early 1900s.
(D) It provides a national food delivery service.

GO ON TO THE NEXT PAGE

Questions 153-154 refer to the following online chat discussion.

May Ryerson (1:44 P.M.)	Hi Joseph, are you almost done with your sales report? We're waiting to go downstairs to the new bakery's grand opening.
Joseph Mandel (1:45 P.M.)	Sorry, May. You and Ms. Kwon will need to try out the free samples without me. There was a problem with the data, and I'm going to have to start over.
May Ryerson (1:54 P.M.)	That's too bad! We could grab you a few things, if you'd like.
Joseph Mandel (1:58 P.M.)	I'd love to try their bagels!
May Ryerson (1:59 P.M.)	Sure thing, Joseph. See you in a bit.

153. At 1:59 P.M., what does Ms. Ryerson most likely mean when she writes, "Sure thing, Joseph"?

(A) She will review some sales data for Mr. Mandel.
(B) She will bring food samples for Mr. Mandel.
(C) Some bakery items have been selling well.
(D) Some employees can help with a report.

154. What will happen next?

(A) Mr. Mandel will attend a grand opening.
(B) Ms. Kwon will place a food delivery order.
(C) Ms. Ryerson will go to Mr. Mandel's office.
(D) Ms. Ryerson and Ms. Kwon will visit a bakery.

Questions 155-157 refer to the following notice.

This summer's favorable weather conditions have resulted in a bumper crop of flowers, often exceeding what local florists can sell. Those interested in donating excess blooms to charitable organizations can do so by visiting Bloomfield Community Center's Web site (www.bloomfield communitycenter.org), which includes details for drop-off points.

If you require pickup services, please get in touch with us. We will coordinate with one of the many volunteer couriers who have offered to transport and promptly distribute your floral donations to various groups in need. Visit our Web site listed above for additional details on this service and for various tips on floral care and arranging.

155. For whom is the notice most likely intended?

(A) Community leaders
(B) Event planners
(C) Flower distributors
(D) Charity members

156. What does the notice suggest about the summer weather?

(A) It caused an increase in flower prices.
(B) It was ideal for flower growth.
(C) It broke previous annual records.
(D) It resulted in shipping delays.

157. According to the notice, what can be found on a Web site?

(A) Approximate delivery times
(B) News about new types of flowers
(C) Locations of retail outlets
(D) Advice on flower arrangement

Questions 158-160 refer to the following notice.

We are thrilled to welcome you to our grand opening day. – [1] –. To ensure everyone enjoys the event, please follow these guidelines.

Before attending one of our free classes, please make sure that you change into clean, comfortable indoor shoes. – [2] –. In the event that you forget to bring a pair of shoes to change into, we will provide you with a pair of non-slip socks.

Clutter in workout areas can pose a safety risk. Please place your belongings on the shelves at the rear of the exercise room. Bags that are too large to fit on the shelves can be stored in one of our lockers for just $1. – [3] –. Our staff will be happy to assist you with locker arrangements.

– [4] –. We hope you enjoy the event!

158. Where most likely is the notice posted?
(A) In a college
(B) In a gym
(C) At a shopping mall
(D) At a sports store

159. What is indicated about oversized bags?
(A) They should be left at home.
(B) They can be purchased at the event.
(C) They will undergo an inspection.
(D) They should be kept in a locker.

160. In which of the positions marked [1], [2], [3], and [4] does the following sentence best belong?

"It is important that we keep our floors free from dirt."

(A) [1]
(B) [2]
(C) [3]
(D) [4]

Questions 161-163 refer to the following product review.

Fantastic Air Fryer!

I had always wanted to get an air fryer, but I simply did not have enough room on my countertop. After redesigning my kitchen, I eventually had space for one. I did some reading about air fryers, and the AirWave Pro 2000 had the best ratings on several Web sites. Even though it was more expensive than other models, I figured it would be worth it, based on what other consumers had said. I have had the air fryer for two weeks now, and I know that I made the right choice. Regardless of what type of food I cook, it comes out perfectly crispy, without being overly dry inside. Also, the appliance runs so quietly that you barely notice it's on. Lastly, it is far more energy efficient than a conventional kitchen oven, and this is a huge plus for me. I would wholeheartedly recommend this air fryer to everyone.

Reviewed by: Grant Bagshaw
Date: April 26

161. Why did Mr. Bagshaw choose the AirWave Pro 2000?

(A) It came with several accessories.
(B) It is a brand he has used before.
(C) It was cheaper than other models.
(D) It received positive reviews online.

162. The word "runs" in paragraph 1, line 7, is closest in meaning to

(A) operates
(B) moves
(C) charges
(D) transforms

163. What is indicated about Mr. Bagshaw?

(A) He recently purchased a new house.
(B) He bought the appliance in March.
(C) He cares about conserving energy.
(D) He regularly hosts dinner parties.

GO ON TO THE NEXT PAGE

Questions 164-167 refer to the following e-mail.

To:	Toby Jarvis <tjarvis@bridgercorp.com>
From:	Angela Martinez <amartinez@culinarycreations.com>
Date:	October 14
Subject:	Upcoming Event
Attachment:	Culinary Creations Order Form

Dear Mr. Jarvis,

Thank you for choosing Culinary Creations to cater Bridger Corporation's annual office Christmas party. We are delighted to be a part of your celebration for the third year running!

On December 15, we will provide a variety of holiday-themed dishes for the ten venues you specified. These include a roast turkey with cranberry sauce, honey-glazed ham, and a selection of festive side dishes like garlic mashed potatoes and roasted Brussels sprouts. We will also deliver the Christmas dessert you ordered, based on your specifications. You will be billed on December 14. Please review the attached order form, and if everything is to your satisfaction, sign and return it to me as soon as possible.

Our head chef has already prepared a sample of the dessert you ordered – a rich Chocolate Yule Log with peppermint cream filling. Although this is the first time we have ever used peppermint flavoring in this type of dessert, we found it to be absolutely delightful during our tasting session and are confident that you and your team will love it.

Angela Martinez, Owner
Culinary Creations

164. What is the main purpose of the e-mail?
(A) To suggest a business partnership
(B) To announce some new menu options
(C) To ask for confirmation of an order
(D) To extend an invitation to an event

165. What is suggested about Bridger Corporation?
(A) It will be billed for an order on December 15.
(B) It is celebrating the opening of a new business location.
(C) It has ordered from Culinary Creations before.
(D) It will host a party at a restaurant.

166. What is indicated about the Chocolate Yule Log?
(A) It is Culinary Creations' most popular dessert.
(B) It boasts a unique flavor combination.
(C) It will be sampled on December 14.
(D) It comes with a fruit sauce.

167. The word "found" in paragraph 3, line 3, is closest in meaning to
(A) uncovered
(B) located
(C) sought
(D) determined

Questions 168-171 refer to the following information.

Florida Funland currently has a workforce of more than 2,000 staff members from diverse backgrounds. Our amazing theme park is expanding rapidly, and we have numerous job openings. – [1] –. So, no matter your experience and academic level, we can likely offer you a spot on our team! Florida Funland employees receive several benefits. – [2] –. For instance, our employee discount program offers heavily discounted park entry and ride passes. We provide opportunities for career advancement, access to free training courses, discounts on affiliated hotels, and a competitive compensation package. – [3] –. Each worker is allocated 25 paid leave days per year to ensure a healthy work-life balance. It is no surprise that Florida Funland has been named "Top Amusement Park Employer" by *Adventure Today* magazine for five consecutive years. – [4] –.

168. Who is the target audience of the information?

(A) Potential investors
(B) Current job seekers
(C) Florida Funland visitors
(D) Florida Funland employees

169. In the information, what is NOT mentioned as a benefit of employment?

(A) Annual paid leave
(B) Training opportunities
(C) Accommodation discounts
(D) Free park entry

170. What is mentioned about Florida Funland?

(A) It is planning to introduce new rides.
(B) It is building an on-site hotel.
(C) It is the largest theme park in Florida.
(D) It has been recognized by a publication.

171. In which of the positions marked [1], [2], [3], and [4] does the following sentence best belong?

"The positions we are seeking to fill require a wide range of skills."

(A) [1]
(B) [2]
(C) [3]
(D) [4]

GO ON TO THE NEXT PAGE

Questions 172-175 refer to the following text message chain.

Mike Brown (9:03 A.M.)
Good morning. The construction proposal for the new shopping mall is nearly ready for submission to the appropriate government departments. We are on track to submit it next Wednesday.

Gary Falco (9:04 A.M.)
How is it looking so far?

Mike Brown (9:07 A.M.)
There are still a few components that need to be added.

Miranda Song (9:08 A.M.)
We mainly need the traffic and environmental impact studies. We should receive those reports from the engineering office by Friday.

Gary Falco (9:09 A.M.)
Yes, we can't do without those. And if there's any concern about the reports not arriving by Friday, please contact Lisa Andrews and remind her that it is urgent.

Mike Brown (9:10 A.M.)
Assuming we receive the summary in time to integrate its findings into the construction proposal, should the three of us schedule a review session on Monday or Tuesday?

Gary Falco (9:11 A.M.)
Let's aim for Monday afternoon. That way, we still have Tuesday to make any necessary adjustments.

Miranda Song (9:12 A.M.)
Works for me. I'm available after 1 P.M.

172. What is indicated about the construction proposal?

(A) It will be submitted ahead of schedule.
(B) It will be received by multiple departments.
(C) It is Mr. Brown's first project of this kind.
(D) It includes an adjustment to a budget.

173. At 9:09 A.M., what does Mr. Falco most likely mean when he writes, "we can't do without those"?

(A) Traffic congestion has been increasing.
(B) More staff are required for a project.
(C) Findings from some studies are crucial.
(D) The approval of a supervisor is required.

174. Who most likely is Ms. Andrews?

(A) An environmental scientist
(B) A construction site supervisor
(C) An engineering office manager
(D) A safety inspector

175. When do the writers plan to meet to review a building blueprint?

(A) On Monday
(B) On Tuesday
(C) On Wednesday
(D) On Friday

GO ON TO THE NEXT PAGE →

Questions 176-180 refer to the following press release and review.

Linda James, Media Contact
PureStyle Hair
ljames@purestylehair.com

FOR IMMEDIATE RELEASE

MIAMI (10 July) – PureStyle Hair and award-winning hairdresser Ethan Roberts are teaming up to offer clients a premium hair care experience. Ethan Roberts, celebrated for his creative flair and owner of salons in both Miami and New York City, including the recently opened Hair Couture, is bringing his expertise to a new line of signature hairdressing tools and products.

"My aim with these products is to make professional hair care accessible at home," said Roberts. "Each item is designed to help you achieve salon-quality results effortlessly, allowing you to recreate your favorite styles with ease."

Megan Foster, vice president of PureStyle Hair, expressed her enthusiasm for the partnership. "We're thrilled to collaborate with Ethan Roberts and introduce his innovative hair care tools and products to our customers." PureStyle Hair offers a comprehensive selection of hair care products and styling tools, including eco-friendly options. Customers can choose from various bundles, and products will be available for purchase both online and in-store at Ethan Roberts' salons.

For more information, visit the PureStyle Hair Web site at www.purestylehair.com.

http://www.eastcoastbeauty.com

A friend recommended that I visit Hair Couture while I was in Miami for a business trip. Their appointments book up fast; you might need to schedule months ahead for a slot. I asked for a weekday morning appointment, and luckily there had been a cancellation. The experience was fantastic, and the hair products they used made my hair look and feel incredible. Plus, they offer head massages to all customers! It was a worthwhile treat before heading back to Boston.

Emily Chan

176. What is the purpose of the press release?

(A) To congratulate an award winner
(B) To introduce a new range of shampoo
(C) To announce a business collaboration
(D) To promote the opening of a hair salon

177. In the press release, the word "achieve" in paragraph 2, line 2, is closest in meaning to

(A) collect
(B) aspire
(C) succeed
(D) accomplish

178. What is indicated about PureStyle Hair?

(A) It is headquartered in New York City.
(B) It offers various packages of products.
(C) It is run by several famous hairstylists.
(D) It provides free product samples to customers.

179. What is most likely true about Ms. Chan?

(A) She receives regular orders from PureStyle Hair.
(B) She is a former coworker of Ms. Foster.
(C) She visited Mr. Roberts' salon.
(D) She recently relocated to Miami.

180. What did Ms. Chan suggest about Hair Couture in the review?

(A) It is currently hiring hairstylists.
(B) It is located near a massage parlor.
(C) It will open a location in Boston.
(D) It accepts advance bookings.

GO ON TO THE NEXT PAGE →

Questions 181-185 refer to the following e-mail and ticket.

E-Mail Message

To: Niall Hirst <nhirst@allmans.org>
From: Beverley Swank <beverley@swankdesign.com>
Date: July 6
Subject: RE: Receipt of order

Dear Mr. Hirst,

I appreciate your suggestions regarding the delivery of your order. Although delivery by truck or you coming to Edinburgh to collect the items are both good ideas, I actually have an even better idea! It turns out that I will be visiting Dundee with my assistant on July 11, so I can drop off your items in person. I am planning to meet with a potential collaborator in nearby Newport to discuss a project. Before I take a bus over to Newport, I will take a taxi to your house and hand over the items to you safely myself.

To be honest, this arrangement is preferable to me, as I have had too many orders damaged by careless delivery drivers. Quite often my items are placed in the back of a van, and they move around a lot during transport. Given the nature of my items, this can quite easily result in breakages.

At your earliest convenience, please let me know your home address. I look forward to seeing you on July 11.

Best regards,

Beverley Swank
Swank Design Ltd.

Tay Lothian Travel Company

Date of Issuance: July 7
Passenger Name: Beverley Swank

Departing Edinburgh: Saturday, July 11, 8:32 A.M. (Platform 2)
Arriving at Dundee: Saturday, July 11, 9:44 A.M. (Platform 3)

Baggage: 1 personal bag, 2 oversized packages (1 oil painting, 1 sculpture)

Standard Adult Ticket: £18.00

Please sit in your assigned seat for your journey.
Carriage: D
Seat: 23

181. What is the purpose of the e-mail?

(A) To apologize for a delay
(B) To suggest a delivery company
(C) To propose a solution
(D) To extend an invitation

182. Why will Ms. Swank travel from Dundee to Newport?

(A) To attend a meeting
(B) To deliver an order
(C) To visit some relatives
(D) To purchase supplies

183. What is indicated in the e-mail?

(A) Mr. Hirst recently traveled to Edinburgh.
(B) Ms. Swank has visited Mr. Hirst's home before.
(C) Mr. Hirst's ordered items are fragile.
(D) Ms. Swank will contact a delivery company.

184. What is most likely true about Mr. Hirst?

(A) He will meet Ms. Swank in Newport.
(B) He made a change to his original order.
(C) He recently purchased some artworks.
(D) He collaborated with Ms. Swank on a project.

185. How is Ms. Swank traveling to Dundee on July 11?

(A) By bus
(B) By taxi
(C) By train
(D) By van

GO ON TO THE NEXT PAGE

Questions 186-190 refer to the following advertisement, online forum posting, and outline.

Canadian Filmmaking Institute (CFI) - Empowering Your Creative Journey!

Highlighted in the latest *Creative Arts Canada* magazine, the Canadian Filmmaking Institute (CFI) stands as a premier training provider in North America. Our diverse range of online courses bring the art of filmmaking directly to your home. All courses feature personalized instruction and are taught by industry-renowned experts in their respective crafts. By completing any course, you will receive a letter of accreditation from the CFI, a valuable asset for any aspiring filmmaker. To browse a full list of class courses and fees, visit our Web site at www.cfifilmmaking.ca. Here are some of our most popular courses.

Introduction to Cinematography (CFI101): Taught by award-winning cinematographer Ethan Blake, this class equips you with essential techniques for capturing stunning visuals on film.

Screenwriting for Beginners (CFI202): Acclaimed screenwriter Jessica Lee provides expert guidance on crafting compelling stories and writing scripts that sell.

Editing Masterclass (CFI303): Veteran film editor Michael Chen shares advanced editing techniques and practical tips for assembling your footage into a cohesive narrative.

Directing Actors (CFI404): Esteemed director Ava Thompson teaches you how to effectively communicate with actors and bring out their best performances.

Canadian Filmmaking Institute Class CFI202 – Student Online Forum

Date of post: 15 July, 10:30 A.M.
Message posted by: Emma Cartwright
Subject: Online Profiles

Looking at the list of students who have also signed up for this class, I recognize a few names from the March cinematography course. I'm excited to collaborate and learn with all of you again! I just wanted to share a useful tip I received while having my first meeting with Ms. Lee. During our discussion, I asked for ways to improve my CFI online profile to make it more appealing to potential collaborators and employers. She advised that I include information about things that inspire my creativity in filmmaking. I thought this was excellent advice, so I updated my profile accordingly.

Hopefully this tip is useful to the rest of you!

Canadian Filmmaking Institute (CFI) Online Profile

Course Member's Name: Emma Cartwright
Section A: Educational Background
Section B: Notable Skills & Certifications
Section C: Creative Inspiration & Motivation
Section D: Filmmaking Ambitions & Career Goals

186. What is indicated about the CFI?
(A) It was established by a renowned film director.
(B) Its courses are led by experienced professionals.
(C) It has teaching locations throughout North America.
(D) It has produced several successful films.

187. According to the advertisement, what does the CFI provide to those who complete a course?
(A) A membership to the CFI
(B) An employment opportunity
(C) A savings on future courses
(D) A beneficial certificate

188. What is most likely true about Ms. Cartwright?
(A) She has auditioned for a role in a film.
(B) She has been contacted by a potential employer.
(C) She is the moderator of an online forum.
(D) She has taken a CFI course before.

189. What CFI course is Ms. Cartwright currently enrolled in?
(A) Introduction to Cinematography
(B) Screenwriting for Beginners
(C) Editing Masterclass
(D) Directing Actors

190. Which section of Ms. Cartwright's profile was updated after she talked with Ms. Lee?
(A) Section A
(B) Section B
(C) Section C
(D) Section D

GO ON TO THE NEXT PAGE

Questions 191-195 refer to the following article, review, and e-mail.

A Taste of Asia

By Liam Walters

SAN FRANCISCO (November 11) - Lotus Blossom Catering has been delighting clients with an array of Asian flavors and a team of professional servers for the past eight months. Under the management of Ming Zhao, this dynamic catering company has quickly become a favorite among San Francisco's event planners and food enthusiasts.

The dedicated catering team is always eager to assist customers in choosing from the diverse offerings on the expansive menu, which features dishes such as Thai green curry, Korean BBQ beef, and Vietnamese pho. However, the company's most renowned dish is the Peking duck. This succulent dish, prepared with a meticulous marinating process that lasts 48 hours and served with sides of steamed buns and hoisin sauce, is a steal at $18 per serving.

For a special treat, book their services for an event of at least 75 people and enjoy a live sushi-making demonstration by their skilled sushi chef.

Posted on 12 December by Chloe Tan, ctan@calmail.com

Lotus Blossom Catering: ★★☆☆☆

Having read an enthusiastic article about Lotus Blossom Catering by Liam Walters, I was excited to try their service for my company's holiday party. I booked their services for a 3 P.M. event yesterday, hoping to enjoy a live sushi-making demonstration along with our dinner.

Unfortunately, the demonstration was canceled at the last minute. Despite this setback, we decided to proceed with the event and ordered the Peking duck for our main course. While the duck was flavorful and well prepared, the accompanying steamed buns were disappointingly bland. Additionally, the portion sizes were smaller than expected, prompting us to request additional appetizers to ensure our guests were satisfied.

The senior event coordinator personally came out to apologize and was very courteous, but given the overall experience, it is unlikely that we would use Lotus Blossom Catering again for future events.

To: Chloe Tan <ctan@calmail.com>
From: Ming Zhao <ming@lotusblossom.com>
Subject: Recent Review
Date: December 14

Dear Ms. Tan,

Thank you for using our service at your workplace recently. I spoke with Marcus Elmore, our senior event coordinator, about the issues you mentioned in your review. Before I address the issues, I would like to apologize for the unsatisfactory service we provided and offer you a $100 voucher that can be redeemed on any future services. I truly hope you will give us another chance.

On the day of your event, our sushi chef, Hiroto Tanaka, was unfortunately unavailable due to a personal issue. As a gesture of goodwill, Mr. Tanaka has offered to visit your workplace to provide a sushi demonstration and tasting session at your convenience. Also, with regard to our steamed buns, we ran out of a vital ingredient that day, and I can assure you that this will not happen again.

Sincerely,

Ming Zhao, Owner
Lotus Blossom Catering

191. What does the article mention about Lotus Blossom Catering?
(A) It was originally founded in Asia.
(B) It opened earlier this year.
(C) It recently appointed new staff.
(D) It employs several award-winning chefs.

192. According to the article, what is the most popular dish provided by Lotus Blossom Catering?
(A) Thai green curry
(B) Korean BBQ beef
(C) Vietnamese pho
(D) Peking duck

193. What is suggested about Ms. Tan's work event?
(A) It took place during a weekend.
(B) It was postponed until a later date.
(C) It included at least 75 individuals.
(D) It was held in a restaurant.

194. What is a purpose of the e-mail?
(A) To confirm an upcoming service
(B) To seek feedback on some dishes
(C) To respond to an inquiry
(D) To provide an explanation

195. Whom did Ms. Tan meet at Lotus Blossom Catering?
(A) Mr. Walters
(B) Mr. Elmore
(C) Mr. Tanaka
(D) Ms. Zhao

GO ON TO THE NEXT PAGE →

Questions 196-200 refer to the following invoice, notice, and e-mail.

Ferrydale Shipping

Customer Name: Ryan Hargreaves
Customer Account Number: #3837
Invoice Date: August 9
Customer Request: Please ensure these items are shipped promptly as I need to make repairs to my apartment as soon as possible.

Product Purchased	Cost
EZ Spirit Level	$15
3-Pack Screwdrivers	$25
Rykon Power Drill	$75
Drill Bit Case (40 Pieces)	$30
Subtotal	$145
Discount (5%)	-$7.25
Shipping Fee	$10
Amount Due	$147.75

Please allow up to 3 days for delivery. We have attached an important notice regarding changes to your invoices.

Ferrydale Shipping

Dear Esteemed Clients,

Please be advised that the system we have used to create and distribute invoices for the past 10 years will be changing. Since the establishment of Ferrydale Shipping, we have maintained the same invoicing system. We are excited to announce a significant upgrade to our electronic invoicing process. Starting September 15, you will receive an automatically generated invoice each month, and this will be e-mailed to you directly.

Please note that our valued discounts and benefits remain unchanged:

- A 5% discount for orders exceeding $100
- A 15% discount for non-profit organizations
- Free delivery within a 10-mile radius of our distribution locations
- Complimentary samples for members of our Loyalty Program

For additional details on our new automatic electronic invoicing, please visit our Web site. We greatly value your continued patronage and support.

To:	Polly Bell <pbell@ferrydale.com>
From:	Wendy Weghorst <wweghorst@ferrydale.com>
Subject:	Account #2829
Date:	November 22

Hi Polly,

I just read an e-mail that was sent by Manuel Vasquez at Vasquez Decorators. He is wondering why he did not receive his invoice for the month of October.

Mr. Vasquez has been one of our best customers since the day our company was founded. He is a member of our Loyalty Program, and he often posts positive reviews about us online. So, as you can imagine, we need to help him to the best of our abilities. Otherwise, he will choose to work with one of our competitors. I already apologized to him and explained that we are still fixing some issues with our automatic invoice system.

I would like you to find out what the problem was and make sure you send Mr. Vasquez his October invoice with a polite and detailed explanation.

Wendy

196. What does the invoice suggest about Mr. Hargreaves?

(A) He will receive his items on August 9.
(B) He is the owner of a construction company.
(C) He intends to do some DIY jobs at home.
(D) He recently moved into a new property.

197. Why most likely did Mr. Hargreaves receive a discount?

(A) He works at a non-profit organization.
(B) He spent more than $100 on his order.
(C) He is a member of a company's Loyalty Program.
(D) He used a gift voucher to make a purchase.

198. According to the notice, what is changing at Ferrydale Shipping?

(A) The way it rewards customers
(B) The way it packages products
(C) The way it issues invoices
(D) The way it handles complaints

199. What is suggested about Mr. Vasquez?

(A) He has requested a meeting with Ms. Weghorst.
(B) He ordered some power tools from Ferrydale Shipping.
(C) He has been a Ferrydale Shipping customer for around ten years.
(D) He did not receive some merchandise purchased in October.

200. What does Ms. Weghorst ask Ms. Bell to do?

(A) Arrange a training session
(B) Provide express shipping
(C) Investigate a problem
(D) Issue a refund

Stop! This is the end of the test. If you finish before time is called, you may go back to Parts 5, 6, and 7 and check your work.

서아쌤의 토익 비밀과외

실전모의고사 TEST 3

MP3 바로듣기

해설 바로보기

강의 바로보기

시작 시간 ________시 ________분

종료 시간 ________시 ________분

서아쌤의 토익 비밀과외

실전모의고사 TEST 3

LISTENING TEST

In the Listening test, you will be asked to demonstrate how well you understand spoken English. The entire Listening test will last approximately 45 minutes. There are four parts, and directions are given for each part. You must mark your answers on the separate answer sheet. Do not write your answers in your test book.

PART 1

Directions: For each question in this part, you will hear four statements about a picture in your test book. When you hear the statements, you must select the one statement that best describes what you see in the picture. Then find the number of the question on your answer sheet and mark your answer. The statements will not be printed in your test book and will be spoken only one time.

Statement (D), "They are taking photographs," is the best description of the picture, so you should select answer (D) and mark it on your answer sheet.

1.

2.

GO ON TO THE NEXT PAGE

3.

4.

5.

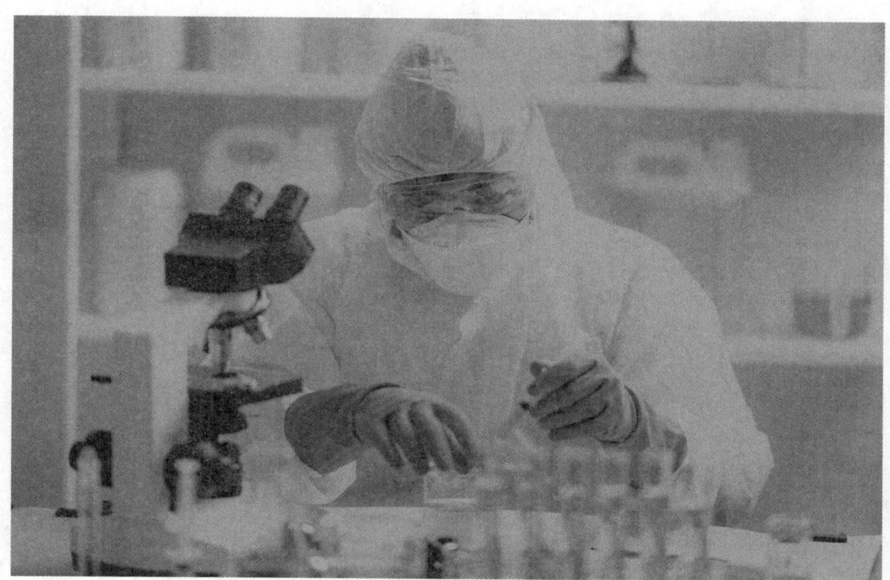

6.

GO ON TO THE NEXT PAGE

PART 2

Directions: You will hear a question or statement and three responses spoken in English. They will not be printed in your test book and will be spoken only one time. Select the best response to the question or statement and mark the letter (A), (B), or (C) on your answer sheet.

7. Mark your answer on your answer sheet.

8. Mark your answer on your answer sheet.

9. Mark your answer on your answer sheet.

10. Mark your answer on your answer sheet.

11. Mark your answer on your answer sheet.

12. Mark your answer on your answer sheet.

13. Mark your answer on your answer sheet.

14. Mark your answer on your answer sheet.

15. Mark your answer on your answer sheet.

16. Mark your answer on your answer sheet.

17. Mark your answer on your answer sheet.

18. Mark your answer on your answer sheet.

19. Mark your answer on your answer sheet.

20. Mark your answer on your answer sheet.

21. Mark your answer on your answer sheet.

22. Mark your answer on your answer sheet.

23. Mark your answer on your answer sheet.

24. Mark your answer on your answer sheet.

25. Mark your answer on your answer sheet.

26. Mark your answer on your answer sheet.

27. Mark your answer on your answer sheet.

28. Mark your answer on your answer sheet.

29. Mark your answer on your answer sheet.

30. Mark your answer on your answer sheet.

31. Mark your answer on your answer sheet.

PART 3

Directions: You will hear some conversations between two or more people. You will be asked to answer three questions about what the speakers say in each conversation. Select the best response to each question and mark the letter (A), (B), (C), or (D) on your answer sheet. The conversations will not be printed in your test book and will be spoken only one time.

32. Where do the speakers most likely work?
(A) At a hardware store
(B) At a magazine company
(C) At a dry cleaner
(D) At a pharmacy

33. What does the woman compliment the man on?
(A) His quickness
(B) His politeness
(C) His record keeping
(D) His problem solving

34. What does the woman give the man advice about?
(A) Using a database
(B) Talking with customers
(C) Delivering products
(D) Logging into a Web site

35. Where do the speakers most likely work?
(A) At a fitness center
(B) At a manufacturing plant
(C) At an electronics store
(D) At an amusement park

36. What task is the woman assigned?
(A) Reserving a meeting room
(B) Scheduling customer orders
(C) Creating an advertising campaign
(D) Rearranging a stockroom

37. What does the man expect to do by the end of the day?
(A) Clean some windows
(B) Test a new product
(C) Calculate some expenses
(D) Put up some posters

38. What did the man recently do?
(A) He started a new company.
(B) He purchased a new property.
(C) He designed some furniture.
(D) He moved overseas.

39. What does the woman ask the man about?
(A) A delivery address
(B) A shipping date
(C) Some room dimensions
(D) Some material preferences

40. What is the man concerned about?
(A) Meeting a deadline
(B) Using a discount coupon
(C) Assembling some items
(D) Cleaning a product

41. Why is the man calling?
(A) To buy exhibition tickets
(B) To apply for a position
(C) To inquire about a price
(D) To find out an artist's name

42. Where does the woman work?
(A) At an art supply shop
(B) At a college
(C) At an art gallery
(D) At a window cleaning company

43. Who most likely is Richard Bachman?
(A) A sales executive
(B) A journalist
(C) A famous painter
(D) An art collector

GO ON TO THE NEXT PAGE

44. What problem does the woman mention?
(A) Her cellphone screen is cracked.
(B) Her mobile device has frozen.
(C) She has forgotten a password.
(D) She has purchased the wrong product.

45. What does the man recommend that the woman do?
(A) Avoid visiting certain Web sites
(B) Purchase some accessories
(C) Update some software
(D) Keep a device in a protective case

46. What will the woman probably do next?
(A) Enjoy a beverage
(B) Browse some products
(C) Visit another business
(D) Complete a form

---

47. Why is the man calling?
(A) To accept a job offer
(B) To register for a course
(C) To schedule an interview
(D) To extend an event invitation

48. What does the woman tell the man to bring?
(A) A security pass
(B) A form of identification
(C) A list of references
(D) A payment method

49. What does the woman say can be found on a Web site?
(A) Staff profiles
(B) Branch locations
(C) Employee benefits
(D) Current vacancies

---

50. Where do the men most likely work?
(A) At a sports store
(B) At a fitness center
(C) At a health clinic
(D) At a library

51. What problem do the speakers mainly discuss?
(A) A membership fee increase
(B) An incorrect address
(C) A faulty keycard
(D) A temporary closure

52. What service does the woman ask about?
(A) Repairs
(B) Transportation
(C) Refreshments
(D) Internet

---

53. What problem does the woman have?
(A) She is unable to attend a meeting.
(B) She cannot contact a client.
(C) She has misplaced a phone number.
(D) She has never been to Macclesfield before.

54. What will be discussed during a meeting?
(A) Product designs
(B) Machine installations
(C) A marketing campaign
(D) A building blueprint

55. Why does the man say, "safety is our main concern"?
(A) To remind the woman to look after herself
(B) To disagree with the woman's suggestion
(C) To emphasize the need for changes
(D) To recommend delaying a project

---

56. What type of work do the speakers do?
(A) Event planning
(B) Talent seeking
(C) Book publishing
(D) Movie producing

57. What will Rodney do this afternoon?
(A) Tour a workplace
(B) Review a document
(C) Attend an interview
(D) Visit a client

58. What does Meredith ask Rodney to accept?
(A) A lunch reservation
(B) A contract amendment
(C) A social media request
(D) A meeting invitation

---

59. In which industry do the speakers most likely work?
(A) Architecture
(B) Retail
(C) Web design
(D) Farming

60. What does the woman say she will send the man?
(A) An e-mail attachment
(B) A business plan
(C) A product image
(D) A list of team members

61. What does the man imply when he says, "I'm leaving at 3 for an appointment"?
(A) He will contact a client directly.
(B) He plans to change his appointment time.
(C) He will be unable to attend a meeting.
(D) He needs more time to complete a task.

62. Why does the woman apologize?
(A) She lost a contact telephone number.
(B) She provided the wrong event location.
(C) She was late in responding to an e-mail.
(D) She is unable to participate in an event.

63. What type of food does the man sell?
(A) Baked goods
(B) Fresh produce
(C) Fast food
(D) Dairy products

64. Look at the graphic. Where will the man sell his product?
(A) Stall 2
(B) Stall 4
(C) Stall 6
(D) Stall 7

GO ON TO THE NEXT PAGE

Voicemail Options

1. Press 1 to delete this message
2. Press 2 to save this message
3. Press 3 to listen to this message again
4. Press 4 to hear the date and time of this message

65. Who most likely are the speakers?

(A) Graphic designers
(B) Appliance installers
(C) Sales representatives
(D) Computer technicians

66. Look at the graphic. What voicemail option does the man use?

(A) Option 1
(B) Option 2
(C) Option 3
(D) Option 4

67. What does the woman suggest doing?

(A) Offering a refund
(B) Expediting a delivery
(C) Returning a call
(D) Checking an e-mail

Oliver's Weekly Work Schedule

Monday 2P.M. - 5P.M.	Board meeting
Tuesday 9A.M. - 3:30P.M.	Staff evaluations
Wednesday 1P.M. - 4P.M.	Interviews
Thursday 10A.M. - 11:30A.M.	Product demonstration

68. What did the man's team recently develop?

(A) An exercise machine
(B) A kitchen appliance
(C) A mobile phone
(D) A construction tool

69. Look at the graphic. When does the man suggest testing out a prototype?

(A) On Monday
(B) On Tuesday
(C) On Wednesday
(D) On Thursday

70. What will the speakers discuss next?

(A) Potential product names
(B) Upcoming job vacancies
(C) Changes to a design
(D) New company policies

PART 4

Directions: You will hear some talks given by a single speaker. You will be asked to answer three questions about what the speaker says in each talk. Select the best response to each question and mark the letter (A), (B), (C), or (D) on your answer sheet. The talks will not be printed in your test book and will be spoken only one time.

71. What is being advertised?

(A) An apartment building
(B) An entertainment complex
(C) A holiday resort
(D) A shopping mall

72. According to the speaker, what will local residents appreciate about Shangri-La?

(A) An exclusive discount
(B) A rise in property value
(C) Employment opportunities
(D) Improved transportation

73. What does the speaker suggest the listeners do online?

(A) View some images
(B) Register for an event
(C) Claim a complimentary gift
(D) Reserve a parking space

---

74. What type of journalism is the talk about?

(A) Current affairs
(B) Sports
(C) Entertainment
(D) Politics

75. According to the speaker, what helps a journalist create an interesting article?

(A) Unique vocabulary
(B) Accompanying photos
(C) Extensive research
(D) Interview quotes

76. What does the speaker say he will do next week?

(A) Publish a book
(B) Evaluate some writing
(C) Reschedule a class
(D) Assign group projects

---

77. Where does the speaker most likely work?

(A) At a travel agency
(B) At a magazine company
(C) At a food delivery firm
(D) At an Internet service provider

78. What will the listener do on November 2?

(A) Make a payment
(B) Cancel a subscription
(C) Attend a staff orientation
(D) Travel to a different country

79. What will the speaker send to the listener?

(A) A partial refund
(B) A feedback form
(C) A confirmation e-mail
(D) A monthly invoice

---

80. Where is the speech being given?

(A) At a conference
(B) At an investor meeting
(C) At a career fair
(D) At a press conference

81. How is the speaker's business different from its competitors?

(A) Its products are free.
(B) It offers higher salaries.
(C) Its staff all work remotely.
(D) It donates money to charity.

82. Why does the speaker say, "It only takes a few minutes"?

(A) To excuse himself for a short break
(B) To praise the work of employees
(C) To persuade the listeners to apply
(D) To emphasize a product's performance

GO ON TO THE NEXT PAGE

83. What will take place this weekend?

(A) A street parade
(B) A sporting event
(C) A music festival
(D) A trade show

84. Why does the speaker recommend checking social media?

(A) To purchase a ticket
(B) To enter a competition
(C) To view some video clips
(D) To check a schedule

85. According to the speaker, what will some attendees receive for free?

(A) A gift certificate
(B) An item of clothing
(C) A ticket upgrade
(D) A selection of snacks

---

86. What is the speaker mainly discussing?

(A) Changing a route
(B) Increasing subway fares
(C) Remodeling a station
(D) Launching a travel card

87. What does the speaker mean when he says, "we don't expect any change"?

(A) A budget will be used up completely.
(B) The listeners will still need to undergo training.
(C) Departure times will remain the same.
(D) The listeners will not have to work overtime.

88. According to the speaker, what are available in the HR office?

(A) Tools
(B) Uniforms
(C) Application forms
(D) Work schedules

---

89. Who most likely is the speaker?

(A) A council member
(B) An event organizer
(C) A food vendor
(D) A musician

90. What advantage does the speaker mention about Primrose Park?

(A) It is located in a residential area.
(B) It has good access to public transportation.
(C) It includes a large parking area.
(D) It can be rented free of charge.

91. What will the speaker most likely do next?

(A) Lead a tour of a site
(B) Distribute some handouts
(C) Answer some questions
(D) Present some slides

---

92. What type of work will take place at the Newcastle branch?

(A) Some flooring will be replaced.
(B) Some appliances will be installed.
(C) Some light fixtures will be modified.
(D) Some furniture will be removed.

93. Why does the speaker prefer to hire Workman Solutions?

(A) It charges affordable prices.
(B) It provides a free consultation.
(C) It can carry out work on weekends.
(D) It has received good online reviews.

94. Why does the speaker say, "the store will close for a public holiday on August 5"?

(A) To cancel a meeting
(B) To make a suggestion
(C) To confirm a request
(D) To correct an error

Platform 1	Trains to: Downtown, Theater District
Platform 2	Trains to: Historic Old Town, Waterfront
Platform 3	Trains to: Business District, Glenburg
Platform 4	Trains to: Hadley Hills, Hollyvale

95. What item has an employee found?
(A) A ticket
(B) A computer
(C) A backpack
(D) A cellphone

96. Look at the graphic. Which platform is temporarily closed?
(A) Platform 1
(B) Platform 2
(C) Platform 3
(D) Platform 4

97. Why has the train station extended its hours?
(A) A special event is taking place.
(B) A renovation project will begin.
(C) An inspection will be carried out.
(D) A training session is being held.

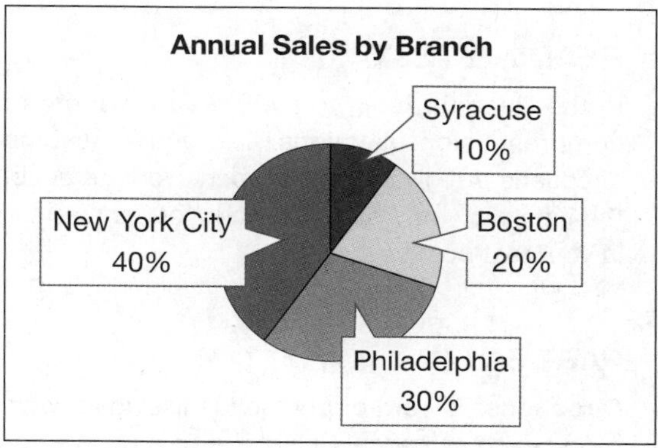

98. What type of product does the company sell?
(A) Office supplies
(B) Garden equipment
(C) Home furnishings
(D) Business software

99. Look at the graphic. Which branch does the speaker work at?
(A) New York City
(B) Philadelphia
(C) Boston
(D) Syracuse

100. According to the speaker, what is the first step of a sales strategy?
(A) To arrange product demonstrations
(B) To hire experienced employees
(C) To adjust product prices
(D) To provide training to staff

This is the end of the Listening test. Turn to Part 5 in your test book.

READING TEST

In the Reading test, you will read a variety of texts and answer several different types of reading comprehension questions. The entire Reading test will last 75 minutes. There are three parts, and directions are given for each part. You are encouraged to answer as many questions as possible within the time allowed. You must mark your answers on the separate answer sheet. Do not write your answers in your test book.

PART 5

Directions: A word or phrase is missing in each of the sentences below. Four answer choices are given below each sentence. Select the best answer to complete the sentence. Then mark the letter (A), (B), (C), or (D) on your answer sheet.

101. Local journalist Veronica Briggs spoke about ------- interview with the mayor.

(A) hers
(B) she
(C) her
(D) herself

102. People who are pursuing an ------- career may be interested in the institute's new course.

(A) acting
(B) acts
(C) act
(D) activity

103. ------- Mr. Patel started working with our firm, he has effectively grown our list of clients.

(A) When
(B) Before
(C) Whereas
(D) Since

104. Ms. Stone will return ------- the office following a two-week leave of absence.

(A) over
(B) to
(C) with
(D) as

105. One of the team leader's tasks is to ensure that employees are creating ------- folders for the files.

(A) organizes
(B) organizing
(C) organized
(D) organize

106. Albany Hotel ------- cut its water usage by installing low-flow shower heads in all bathrooms.

(A) drastically
(B) exactly
(C) tightly
(D) mutually

107. Be sure to input the correct department's billing code ------- placing office supply orders.

(A) within
(B) when
(C) this
(D) from

108. Properly storing all laboratory equipment can reduce ------- and ensure a safer workplace.

(A) accidentally
(B) accident
(C) accidental
(D) accidents

109. Each staff member was assigned a spending ------- for business trips to keep costs down.

(A) route
(B) distance
(C) limit
(D) status

110. In its ------- showroom, Clayton Autos has over thirty different vehicle models on display.

(A) spacious
(B) precise
(C) relative
(D) impartial

111. The Vaccari Bridge was designed to ------- heavy traffic loads and severe weather.

(A) prevent
(B) eliminate
(C) prohibit
(D) withstand

112. It is a ------- misconception that only large companies benefit from using specialized software.

(A) fragile
(B) stable
(C) common
(D) narrow

113. Passengers' seat belts must be ------- fastened before the airplane takes off.

(A) securely
(B) secure
(C) securing
(D) security

114. Mr. Mason ------- some cash from his account in order to visit the farmer's market.

(A) oversaw
(B) noticed
(C) withdrew
(D) devoted

115. Inquiries regarding communication with media outlets should be handled by the ------- of the project.

(A) coordinate
(B) coordinator
(C) coordinated
(D) coordinating

116. Site manager Levi Wilhelm warned team members to be very ------- with the glass doors.

(A) care
(B) carefully
(C) carefulness
(D) careful

117. Because of increases in energy prices, overhead costs are ------- this quarter than last quarter.

(A) greatest
(B) greater
(C) great
(D) greatly

118. Crane Clothing's new product line is ------- priced thanks to bulk purchasing and efficient production processes.

(A) competitively
(B) absently
(C) formally
(D) constantly

119. The recycling truck parked in the middle of the road, ------- the flow of traffic temporarily.

(A) was restricted
(B) restricts
(C) had restricted
(D) restricting

120. ------- he prepares a presentation, Mr. Ling thoroughly checks all data for errors.

(A) Following
(B) Either
(C) Whenever
(D) Already

GO ON TO THE NEXT PAGE

121. Those who still ------- to apply for the financial analyst position should complete the online forms by Friday.

(A) wish
(B) wishing
(C) were wishing
(D) have wished

122. Please ------- the sales pitch to take the cultural differences of the client into account.

(A) modifies
(B) modified
(C) modify
(D) modifications

123. Owing to her impressive educational background and experience, Ms. Rinaldi is the ------- candidate for this role.

(A) perfection
(B) perfect
(C) perfectly
(D) perfects

124. ------- the city council meeting, residents can submit topics that they believe should be addressed.

(A) As long as
(B) Prior to
(C) Except for
(D) On behalf of

125. If ------- of the conference delegates do not speak English, an interpreter can be provided.

(A) any
(B) those
(C) everyone
(D) another

126. The project funding was achieved largely due to the unexpected ------- of several anonymous donors.

(A) figure
(B) eligibility
(C) opposition
(D) generosity

127. As soon as everyone ------- a password, we can move on to the next stage of the tutorial.

(A) has created
(B) is creating
(C) created
(D) to create

128. ------- the software issues, Kemberly Tech Solutions completed the upgrades in a timely manner.

(A) Now that
(B) Ever since
(C) In spite of
(D) Just as

129. There are specific ------- that must be met before the rental agreement will be signed.

(A) authorities
(B) assortments
(C) conditions
(D) backgrounds

130. Mr. Norris accepted the job offer, ------- it required relocating to a different city.

(A) not only
(B) even though
(C) as a result of
(D) so that

PART 6

Directions: Read the texts that follow. A word, phrase, or sentence is missing in parts of each text. Four answer choices for each question are given below the text. Select the best answer to complete the text. Then mark the letter (A), (B), (C), or (D) on your answer sheet.

Questions 131-134 refer to the following press release.

FOR IMMEDIATE RELEASE
Contact: Shandra Escobar, 555-2087

Piedmont Inc. is pleased to announce the appointment of Surya Viswan as our new Chief Operating Officer. Ms. Viswan brings over 25 years of experience, having ------- (**131.**) led teams at Ayaar Enterprises and CY Industries. Her expertise in enhancing operational efficiency will be ------- (**132.**) as Piedmont Inc. continues to grow and innovate.

Ms. Viswan is eager to take the business to the next level, stating, "My vision is to optimize our operations and drive sustainable growth, ------- (**133.**) will ensure long-term stability."

We are excited about the positive changes Ms. Viswan will bring to our company. ------- (**134.**).

131. (A) successfully
(B) succeeded
(C) successful
(D) succeeding

132. (A) exclusive
(B) considerate
(C) instrumental
(D) abstract

133. (A) what
(B) whose
(C) that
(D) which

134. (A) The headquarters building has modern facilities.
(B) We look forward to achieving new objectives together.
(C) Ms. Viswan will respond to them after reviewing the details.
(D) The production rate has declined over the past year.

GO ON TO THE NEXT PAGE →

Questions 135-138 refer to the following e-mail.

To: Meg Holm <holm.meg@inboxpro.com>
From: Ana Nealy <orders@lanzalife.com>
Date: July 27
Subject: Your purchase

Dear Ms. Holm,

Thank you for your order from Lanza Life! We are pleased to confirm your purchase of a charcoal gray sweater, a floral-print dress, and a pair of black jeans. Your ------- (**135.**) will arrive within 3 days. Rest assured, all items are thoroughly inspected for defects such as ------- (**136.**) threads and other issues before dispatch. We also ensure that each item is properly folded and packaged to prevent ------- (**137.**) during shipping. If you have any questions, please don't hesitate to reach out to our customer service agents. ------- (**138.**).

Sincerely,

Ana Nealy
Shipping Supervisor, Lanza Life

135. (A) devices
(B) apparel
(C) furniture
(D) dishes

136. (A) loosest
(B) loosely
(C) loosen
(D) loose

137. (A) damage
(B) to damage
(C) is damaging
(D) damaging

138. (A) They are available around the clock.
(B) I thought it was a pleasure to meet you.
(C) You can view it in the latest catalog.
(D) The Web site contained pricing errors.

Questions 139-142 refer to the following letter.

Leigh Tristan
4202 Ash Street
Oakland, NJ 07436

Dear Ms. Tristan,

Congratulations on your new catering business! At GV Accounting, we understand that this is an exciting yet challenging time. -------. **139.** Our professional bookkeeping services will ------- **140.** your financial management, allowing you to have more time to focus on your business.

We provide comprehensive services, including expense tracking, invoicing, payroll management, and financial reporting. -------, **141.** our expertise ensures accuracy and compliance, giving you peace of mind.

We would love ------- **142.** how we can support your business. Please feel free to contact me anytime to schedule a meeting.

Sincerely,

Douglas Keenan
GV Accounting

139. (A) The loan was approved by our committee.
(B) We can help you manage the accounting side of your startup.
(C) The feedback from customers is still being analyzed.
(D) Our team is interested in food for an upcoming event.

140. (A) streamline
(B) accept
(C) obtain
(D) compensate

141. (A) Along with
(B) Therefore
(C) In addition
(D) Otherwise

142. (A) discuss
(B) discusses
(C) to discuss
(D) will discuss

GO ON TO THE NEXT PAGE

Questions 143-146 refer to the following advertisement.

Find your next pair of glasses at Starz Eyewear!

Steven Pool, ------- (143.) of Starz Eyewear, has been providing exceptional service and quality for over twenty years. The knowledgeable Starz Eyewear staff ------- (144.) at helping you find the ideal frames that suit both your style and face shape. Whether you're seeking a classic look or a trendy update, we have a wide selection to meet your needs. And you can shop with confidence thanks to our guarantee. -------. (145.) Visit us today and see why we are ------- (146.) the region's leading eyewear providers.

143. (A) founded
(B) found
(C) founding
(D) founder

144. (A) excels
(B) pursues
(C) fulfills
(D) practices

145. (A) For example, wide frames can help to reduce the appearance of length.
(B) The clearance sale has been extended to a full month.
(C) If you change your mind, you can return your purchase within 30 days.
(D) Therefore, we are seeking team members for part-time shifts.

146. (A) onto
(B) throughout
(C) among
(D) toward

PART 7

Directions: In this part you will read a selection of texts, such as magazine and newspaper articles, e-mails, and instant messages. Each text or set of texts is followed by several questions. Select the best answer for each question and mark the letter (A), (B), (C), or (D) on your answer sheet.

Questions 147-148 refer to the following coupon.

Berlin City Tours!

We are delighted to announce our brand new city tour: Berlin By Bicycle! Book one ticket for the Berlin By Bicycle tour and receive a second ticket free of charge! The tour starts opposite the Intercontinental Hotel and includes numerous important sites. Simply enter the coupon code below when booking a spot on the tour. This coupon is single-use and valid for one month.

Visit Berlin City Tours online at www.berlincitytours.com to view all of our tour options, available seven days a week and suitable for all age groups.

Coupon Code: 39280

Date: April 2

147. What must people do to use the coupon?

(A) Reserve a tour this week
(B) Visit a ticket office
(C) Book a specific tour
(D) Stay at a certain hotel

148. What is indicated about Berlin City Tours?

(A) It has received positive reviews.
(B) It was recently founded.
(C) It operates tours on Sundays.
(D) Its tours are unsuitable for children.

GO ON TO THE NEXT PAGE

Questions 149-150 refer to the following e-mail.

To:	Miranda Sinclair <msinclair@lapoint.com>
From:	Courtney Becker <membership@zenithgym.net>
Date:	September 5
Subject:	Silver Package

Dear Ms. Sinclair,

Thank you for signing up for Zenith Gym's Silver Package. A charge of $720.00 for your one-year membership has been made to your credit card ending in 8941. Please note that this reflects the ten percent Refer a Friend discount for both you and the member who signed you up. Your membership gives you unlimited use of our swimming pool, fitness equipment, and weight room. You will also receive a monthly class pass, with which you can attend up to 10 group classes in any combination. Classes exceeding ten in the same month will be charged at the usual rate. We are glad to welcome you aboard, and we wish you all the best in achieving your fitness goals.

Sincerely,

Courtney Becker
Membership Services
Zenith Gym

149. Why did Ms. Sinclair receive a discount on her membership?

(A) She paid all of her fees in advance.
(B) She signed up for a two-year contract.
(C) She was referred by a gym member.
(D) She completed a feedback survey.

150. What does the e-mail explain about classes?

(A) They are free to a certain point each month.
(B) They must be booked in advance.
(C) They should all be of the same type.
(D) They change their schedule each month.

Questions 151-152 refer to the following text message chain.

Carl Rowe (11:25 A.M.)
Hi, Angela. Are you on your way to Ms. Dorsey's house with the bricks? We want to finish the walkway today so we can take photographs of the entire backyard.

Angela Flemming (11:26 A.M.)
I'm afraid I can't get away. I'm waiting for a delivery. I'll have to ask Wendall if he can do it for me.

Carl Rowe (11:27 A.M.)
That's too bad. Let me know what he says.

Angela Flemming (11:28 A.M.)
I will. And could you please e-mail me the photos when you're done?

Carl Rowe (11:29 A.M.)
Of course.

151. What most likely will happen next?

(A) Ms. Flemming will ask Wendall for a favor.
(B) Mr. Rowe will reschedule a project.
(C) Ms. Flemming will order some supplies.
(D) Mr. Rowe will give Wendall a ride.

152. At 11:29 A.M., what does Mr. Rowe most likely mean when he writes, "Of course"?

(A) He will deliver some bricks to Ms. Flemming.
(B) He will edit Ms. Flemming's photos.
(C) He will send some images of a garden.
(D) He will e-mail a copy of a contract.

GO ON TO THE NEXT PAGE

Questions 153-154 refer to the following invitation.

You're Invited to a Tax Preparation and Planning Workshop

Help your small business by getting clear and accurate advice at our workshop. You will get in-depth insights into maximizing your tax deductions and credits, ensuring compliance with the latest tax regulations, and strategically planning for future tax liabilities. Learn from experienced tax professionals who will guide you through practical exercises and real-world scenarios. Attendees will also receive a tax planning software program (a $49.99 value) and a one-on-one consultation with a tax expert. Don't miss this opportunity to gain the knowledge and tools necessary to optimize your tax strategy and protect your business's financial future.

Date & Time: October 19, 1 P.M. to 5 P.M.
Location: Lecture Hall B, The Atwood Center*
Confirm Your Attendance: www.protaxsupport.net/Oct19

*Please use the Linden Street lot only, as the Reza Avenue lot is undergoing repairs.

153. What is NOT indicated about the workshop?
(A) It includes an individual consultation.
(B) Its fees can be credited to a future session.
(C) Its information is up to date.
(D) Its participants will receive a free software.

154. What is suggested about the Atwood Center?
(A) Its staff frequently leads workshops.
(B) It is near public transportation.
(C) Its interior is being renovated.
(D) It has two parking areas.

Questions 155-157 refer to the following product review.

A nice iron at a fair price!

I bought the Balson-45 steam iron about two months ago, and I am very pleased with its performance so far. I go on a lot of business trips, so I wanted something that didn't take up much room in my suitcase. This iron is definitely right for me. Despite its size, it is surprisingly powerful, heating up quickly and producing plenty of steam. It also features a steam burst function, which is excellent for removing stubborn wrinkles in my clothing.

I especially appreciate the auto-shutoff feature, which provides peace of mind in knowing that the iron will turn off automatically if left unattended. This safety feature is crucial for me, as I am often in a rush. The Balson-45 comes with a one-year warranty, and I believe that it is well worth the price.

Eva Jensen

155. Why did Ms. Jensen select the Balson-45 iron?

(A) It has a long cord.
(B) It is compact.
(C) It has a modern look.
(D) It is energy efficient.

156. The word "right" in paragraph 1, line 3, is closest in meaning to

(A) genuine
(B) ideal
(C) valid
(D) accurate

157. What is suggested about Ms. Jensen?

(A) She plans to change jobs.
(B) She highly values safety.
(C) She owns many appliances.
(D) She cares about the environment.

GO ON TO THE NEXT PAGE

Questions 158-160 refer to the following e-mail.

To:	Undisclosed Recipients
From:	Vista Voyages Team <contact@vista-voyages.com>
Date:	August 20
Subject:	Sightseeing Tour

Thank you for signing up for the August 26 Vista Voyages sightseeing tour. We hope you will have a great time exploring the area. The tour bus will depart from the main entrance of the Charack Hotel at 8:30 A.M. so that we may get to our first stop, the Dekalb History Museum, right when it opens at 9:00 A.M. – [1] –. Please arrive at the departure point thirty minutes before departure to allow time for check-in and seating arrangements. – [2] –.

Bottled water and a variety of snacks will be available throughout the tour. – [3] –. In addition, we will have lunch at a charming local restaurant known for its delicious regional cuisine. The highlight of the tour will be the visit to Croft Cave. – [4] –. We will supply helmets, gloves, and knee pads for your safety. You may, however, wish to bring an extra layer because it can get very cold in the cave.

We look forward to seeing you on August 26!

Sincerely,

The Vista Voyages Team

158. What is the purpose of the e-mail?

(A) To request a payment for a tour
(B) To encourage customers to upgrade a tour
(C) To apologize for a tour schedule change
(D) To help participants prepare for a tour

159. When are the e-mail recipients asked to arrive on August 26?

(A) At 7:30 A.M.
(B) At 8:00 A.M.
(C) At 8:30 A.M.
(D) At 9:00 A.M.

160. In which of the positions marked [1], [2], [3], and [4] does the following sentence best belong?

"There is no need to bring any protective clothing."

(A) [1]
(B) [2]
(C) [3]
(D) [4]

Questions 161-163 refer to the following notice.

NOTICE TO SPENCER TOWER TENANTS

The water to the entire building will be temporarily shut off on Monday, May 12, from 8 A.M. to approximately 3 P.M. This is due to replacing our old water heaters with new ones, which will provide a higher volume of hot water while also being more energy efficient. To ensure minimal inconvenience, please prepare by filling bottles or pots with water for drinking and cooking needs. It is also advisable to complete any urgent laundry, dishwashing, or cleaning beforehand. Additionally, look into your options for nearby water facilities should you need them. After the water flow is restored, please contact the rental office if you notice that your water has an unusual color or cloudiness. Thank you for your cooperation.

161. How will the change help tenants?

(A) By ensuring quieter operation
(B) By repairing some water heaters' damage
(C) By removing toxic substances
(D) By providing more hot water

162. What is NOT mentioned as a preparation step?

(A) Checking the water pressure
(B) Filling containers with water
(C) Doing household chores
(D) Researching alternative facilities

163. According to the notice, what should be reported?

(A) A strange odor in the water
(B) Water that is discolored
(C) Drips from the water tap
(D) External water leaks

GO ON TO THE NEXT PAGE

Questions 164-167 refer to the following information.

Blakely's is a leading retail company that specializes in home improvement products and services, aimed at both professional contractors as well as homeowners making changes to their property. – [1] –. Thanks to unprecedented growth, we are currently seeking to expand our workforce. We offer competitive wages, on-the-job training, and employee discounts on merchandise. – [2] –. So, there is sure to be something to fit your schedule.

– [3] –. We truly care about our staff and customers. Our extensive range of goods includes tools, materials, and fixtures, and we host regular workshops and demonstrations to help customers use our products. Additionally, our flooring team visits customers on site to measure spaces and provide recommendations. We also hold monthly collections of hazardous waste such as old paint.

With the Mayfield branch recently opened and the Bridgeton branch undergoing an exciting building expansion, there's never been a better time to join our team. Become a part of a dynamic and supportive work environment where your skills and enthusiasm for home improvement will be valued and appreciated. – [4] –. Visit www.blakelys.com for more information.

164. For whom is the information intended?
(A) Homeowners
(B) Potential job applicants
(C) Professional builders
(D) Blakely's employees

165. What is NOT indicated as a service offered by Blakely's?
(A) In-person measurements
(B) Tool repairs
(C) Product demonstrations
(D) Waste collection

166. What is true about the Bridgeton branch?
(A) It is the Blakely's headquarters.
(B) Its business hours will be extended.
(C) It is a newly opened location.
(D) Its building is being made larger.

167. In which of the positions marked [1], [2], [3], and [4] does the following sentence best belong?

"We need coverage for a variety of shifts, including evenings and weekends."

(A) [1]
(B) [2]
(C) [3]
(D) [4]

Questions 168-171 refer to the following online chat discussion.

Beth Ellis (9:10 A.M.)	Good morning. There are a few things to do that have come up since our meeting. Lorraine, do you have anything urgent this morning?
Lorraine Brown (9:11 A.M.)	I'm meeting the Hoffmans at 10:30 to show them around the Englewood Street property. They've already seen it twice, so I think they may make an offer today.
Beth Ellis (9:12 A.M.)	That's fantastic news! I need you to handle a consultation at one o'clock with Josie Wright this afternoon. She's hoping to put her house on the market next month.
Lorraine Brown (9:13 A.M.)	Certainly. I'll be back before then.
Beth Ellis (9:15 A.M.)	Thanks. Jacob, please call Adam about fixing the bathroom's leaky faucet and the broken banister in the house on Cedar Avenue.
Jacob Baldwin (9:16 A.M.)	I'll take care of that as soon as possible, as the open house is on Saturday.
Beth Ellis (9:17 A.M.)	Exactly. Jacob, also make sure the owners know that the place has to be cleaned thoroughly.
Jacob Baldwin (9:18 A.M.)	Got it. By the way, Mr. McBride agreed to June 3 for his open house. I'm working on the flyer now.
Beth Ellis (9:19 A.M.)	Alright. I'd like to see a version of it before it goes to the printer.
Jacob Baldwin (9:20 A.M.)	By all means.

168. Why does Ms. Ellis contact her colleagues?
(A) To discuss a complaint
(B) To postpone a meeting
(C) To assign some tasks
(D) To update a policy

169. For what kind of business do the writers most likely work?
(A) A cleaning company
(B) A job recruitment firm
(C) A landscaping service
(D) A real estate agency

170. What is indicated about the Cedar Avenue site?
(A) It is near the writers' office.
(B) It is in need of repairs.
(C) It will be visited by the Hoffmans.
(D) It is owned by Ms. Wright.

171. At 9:20 A.M., what does Mr. Baldwin most likely mean when he writes, "By all means"?
(A) He will explain a process.
(B) He will confirm Ms. Ellis's schedule.
(C) He will print an agreement.
(D) He will show Ms. Ellis a draft.

GO ON TO THE NEXT PAGE

Questions 172-175 refer to the following e-mail.

E-Mail Message

To: Sienna Latimer <latimers@mesamail.com>

From: Isaac Khan <dot@madison.gov>

Date: February 26

Subject: Application #58924

Attachment: G258924.doc

Dear Ms. Latimer,

Your Residential Parking Permit (RPP) has been activated. You can begin using it immediately by downloading the attached temporary permit, and you will receive the standard permit in the mail within one week. The RPP is exclusively for Zone G2, so please park only within this designated area to avoid a parking ticket. You can find a map of the parking zones on our Web site. Should changes to the zones be made, you will be informed by both e-mail and text.

The RPP is assigned specifically to the vehicle with the license plate number you provided. Additionally, it must be prominently displayed on your dashboard at all times. Your RPP will expire twelve months from today's date. One month before the expiration of your permit, you will be contacted regarding your renewal, as you will need to submit documents to re-verify your residency.

Sincerely,

Isaac Khan
Parking Authority
Madison Department of Transportation

172. What is the purpose of the e-mail?

(A) To explain why a parking application was rejected
(B) To request payment for a parking ticket
(C) To confirm the activation of a parking permit
(D) To provide directions to a parking facility

173. What is indicated about the RPP?

(A) It will be sent by overnight mail.
(B) It can only be used in a specific area.
(C) It has restricted hours on weekends.
(D) It can be printed for multiple vehicles.

174. According to the e-mail, why would Ms. Latimer receive a text?

(A) If a price has increased
(B) If a payment is late
(C) If a vehicle is damaged
(D) If a zone has changed

175. What will Ms. Latimer be asked to do in eleven months?

(A) Get a new license plate
(B) Have her vehicle inspected
(C) Renew her driver's license
(D) Provide some paperwork

GO ON TO THE NEXT PAGE

Questions 176-180 refer to the following e-mail and article.

To:	All Manager Staff <managerlist@yakimaairlines.com>
From:	Ethan Webster <e.webster@yakimaairlines.com>
Date:	August 3
Subject:	Feedback

Dear Managers,

Last month, we sent out a questionnaire to all Yakima Airlines customers, 20 percent of which responded. Within that group, only 48 percent reported that they were pleased with the service they received. As for complaints, 63 percent of respondents rated our communication regarding flight changes as "poor", and 27 percent said that it was difficult to find the information they needed. I think that improving our smartphone app will help with some of these issues. I've scheduled a meeting with the team leader of the mobile application development project on August 15 to discuss how to proceed. I will update you on this matter soon.

All the best,

Ethan Webster

Yakima Airlines Aiming High

By Diana Trevino

In response to customer feedback, Yakima Airlines is rolling out significant improvements to its services, focusing particularly on its smartphone app. CEO Melinda Dunning commented, "We are committed to enhancing the travel experience for our customers. These improvements are part of our broader strategy to provide more convenience and efficiency."

Victor Russell, who is leading the team in making changes to the app, added, "We are integrating advanced technology to ensure our app is user-friendly and meets the needs of today's travelers."

Travelers are looking forward to additional features and better functionality. "I fly frequently for work," said Katie Adkins, "and I pick my flights based on not only cost but also the quality of the airline. An easy-to-use app is a big plus for me."

The updates are expected to strengthen Yakima Airlines' position in the market, which is facing heavy competition where it operates. For example, Corbett Air and Scanlon Airlines have recently opened more flights in the northwest. Further information is available at www.yakimaairlines.com/news.

176. What is the purpose of the e-mail?

(A) To recommend investing in staff training
(B) To request feedback on a smartphone app
(C) To provide details about a survey
(D) To ask for suggestions about a plan

177. According to the e-mail, what percentage of respondents were satisfied with the airline?

(A) 20 percent
(B) 27 percent
(C) 48 percent
(D) 63 percent

178. Who most likely did Mr. Webster meet on August 15?

(A) Melinda Dunning
(B) Diana Trevino
(C) Victor Russell
(D) Katie Adkins

179. In the article, the word "pick" in paragraph 3, line 2, is closest in meaning to

(A) choose
(B) shift
(C) gather
(D) catch

180. What is suggested about Yakima Airlines?

(A) Most of its flights are in the northwest.
(B) It has recently changed its CEO.
(C) Some of its airplanes must be replaced.
(D) It plans to expand its range of routes.

GO ON TO THE NEXT PAGE

Questions 181-185 refer to the following schedule and e-mail.

The Gilbert Brothers: September Tour Schedule

Enjoy a unique show featuring hilarious jokes, creative scenes, and songs performed with unusual instruments. You might even be one of the lucky ones to come up on stage and join in the show!

Date	City	Venue	Times
September 5	San Antonio, Texas	Rio Comedy Club	7 P.M., 10 P.M.
September 13	Houston, Texas	Ruby's Show	6 P.M., 8 P.M.
September 19	Los Angeles, California	Electric Groove	7 P.M., 10 P.M.
September 27	Palm Springs, California	Laugh Lounge	7 P.M., 11 P.M.

To: Brandon Gilbert <brandon@gilbertbroscomedy.com>
From: Kai Harrison <kaiharrison@pattoninv.com>
Date: September 30
Subject: Booking

Dear Mr. Gilbert,

I went to your September 13 show, and I had a great time. Having seen all of your TV specials, I was pleasantly surprised that there was so much fresh content. And, of course, it was very funny.

I am interested in booking the Gilbert Brothers for a private performance at Patton Investments' annual corporate retreat in Los Angeles. We would like to include some lighthearted activities to make the retreat more enjoyable for everyone, so your group would be ideal. The retreat is scheduled for December 2 to 4, so there is some flexibility regarding the dates, as no other outside groups have been booked yet. At your earliest convenience, could you please let me know if you are free on any of these days? Our finance team has already tentatively approved the fees listed on your Web site.

Kind regards,

Kai Harrison
Patton Investments

181. What is NOT mentioned about the Gilbert Brothers' show?

(A) It includes audience participation.
(B) It has two performances per city.
(C) It contains live music.
(D) It has been praised by critics.

182. Where did Mr. Harrison attend a Gilbert Brothers' show?

(A) In San Antonio
(B) In Houston
(C) In Los Angeles
(D) In Palm Springs

183. What is suggested about the Gilbert Brothers?

(A) They have made TV appearances.
(B) They plan to go into retirement.
(C) They currently live in California.
(D) They have performed for Patton Investments' before.

184. What is true about Patton Investments?

(A) It holds a company retreat each year.
(B) It will relocate to Los Angeles.
(C) Its retreat will last for two days.
(D) It has more than one branch.

185. What does Mr. Harrison ask Mr. Gilbert to provide?

(A) A list of proposed fees
(B) Images from a stage show
(C) A sample of a contract
(D) Information about availability

GO ON TO THE NEXT PAGE →

Questions 186-190 refer to the following e-mails and receipt.

E-Mail Message

From: Rishu Dalavi <rdalavi@parnellit.com>
To: Work-Max Supplies <contact@workmaxsupplies.com>
Subject: Order #12795
Date: March 10, 10:25 A.M.

To Whom It May Concern:

I made a purchase on your Web site yesterday, order #12795, but I've just realized that I ordered navy blue folding chairs when I actually wanted black. They looked very similar on my computer screen. Is it too late to change this? We don't mind if this delays the original delivery date.

In addition, I am responsible for ordering supplies on behalf of my company, but I don't always work on site. It is inconvenient for the deliveries to arrive on days when I'm not in the office. So, I'm wondering if it is possible to book a specific day for delivery.

Thank you,

Rishu Dalavi, Administrative Assistant
Parnell IT

From: Claudia Matthews <cmatthews@workmaxsupplies.com>
To: Rishu Dalavi <rdalavi@parnellit.com>
Subject: RE: Order #12795
Date: March 10, 3:12 P.M.

Dear Mr. Dalavi,

As your order has already been dispatched, we cannot make any changes to it. However, you can return the items after you receive them and reorder them. Please note that you purchased the chairs while they were on sale, but they have now returned to the original price. I have generated a special code that will give you the discounted price that you paid. Input CD8305 in the "Vouchers/Codes" box on the order page. I also noticed that you were supposed to receive a free spare light bulb with each of your desk lamps, but these were not included in the order. I will have those sent to you right away. Regarding your delivery inquiry, it is not possible at this time, but we plan to change delivery partners in June. So, it might be an option after that.

Thank you for your patronage,

Claudia Matthews, Customer Services
Work-Max Supplies

Work-Max Supplies

Order #12795
Date of Order: March 9

Item #	Description	Price	Quantity	Subtotal
1542	Metal file cabinet (black)	$70.00	3	$210.00
2689	Padded folding chair (navy blue)	$45.00	12	$540.00
4093	Wooden desk (60" x 24" x 30")	$225.00	1	$225.00
6745	Desk lamp (white)	$30.00	5	$150.00
				TOTAL CHARGE: $1,125.00

Returns: Log into your account and select the item(s) to return from the Order History page. Download and print the return shipping label. Attach the label to your package and drop it off at your nearest shipping location.

186. What is true about Mr. Dalavi?
(A) He was overcharged for an item.
(B) He ordered the wrong color.
(C) He received broken items.
(D) He used an incorrect address.

187. Why did Ms. Matthews send a code to Mr. Dalavi?
(A) To give him a sale price
(B) To apologize for an error
(C) To reset his account
(D) To thank him for his feedback

188. Which item should have included a free gift?
(A) Item 1542
(B) Item 2689
(C) Item 4093
(D) Item 6745

189. According to Ms. Matthews, what may be available in the future?
(A) Tracking delivery items
(B) Choosing a delivery day
(C) Accessing delivery lockers
(D) Arranging same-day delivery

190. What is one step required for a return?
(A) Completing a return form
(B) Providing a copy of a receipt
(C) Printing a shipping label
(D) E-mailing customer service

GO ON TO THE NEXT PAGE →

Questions 191-195 refer to the following report, letter, and article.

Annual Seafood Consumption in Seneca Bay (per person)

People living in Seneca Bay consume an average of 50 pounds of seafood annually, 73% of which is caught in Seneca Bay. This is higher than the national average of 19 pounds. The most-consumed types are as follows:

Shrimp: 15 pounds
Blue Crab: 12 pounds
Oysters: 10 pounds
Red Snapper: 7 pounds

Prepared by the Seneca Bay Economic Development Agency, January 1

Seneca Bay Nature Alliance
1244 Gerald Street
Seneca Bay, WA 98357

January 18

Archer Preston, Director
Seneca Bay Economic Development Agency
461 Perine Avenue
Seneca Bay, WA 98357

Dear Mr. Preston,

I am the president of the Seneca Bay Nature Alliance (SBNA), a local environmental group. Having read the January 1 report on seafood consumption in Seneca Bay, I note that there has been a decline in all categories compared to last year. We believe this is due to growing concerns about the pollution levels in the bay. The SBNA is actively working to address this issue. Our research shows that local, state, and federal laws have not kept up with industrial practices. Therefore, we are pushing for stronger regulations and enforcement against waste dumping. Additionally, we have applied for a government grant to purchase 10 acres of land for wetland restoration near the bay, which will aid in natural filtration.

I would appreciate the opportunity to meet with you to discuss how we can collaborate to improve the area. Your support and partnership would be invaluable to our efforts.

Warmest regards,

Isabelle Godina, President
SBNA

Seneca Bay Nature Alliance Honored by City

SENECA BAY (April 4)—The Seneca Bay Nature Alliance (SBNA) was presented with the city's Community Contributor Award in recognition of its positive impact on Seneca Bay. The group has purchased a ten-acre section of land with the aim of restoring wetlands near the bay. Additionally, the SBNA hosts monthly cleanups as well as community education programs, both online and in person. The group works diligently to preserve Seneca Bay's natural beauty as well as foster community involvement and awareness. New volunteers are always needed. To find out how you can help, visit www.sbna.org.

191. What does the report indicate about Seneca Bay?

(A) The most popular seafood item to eat is blue crab.
(B) Tourists visit the area because of its fresh seafood.
(C) About seventy-three percent of revenue comes from seafood.
(D) The majority of its seafood is sourced locally.

192. What is one purpose of the letter?

(A) To give advice on following new regulations
(B) To explain efforts to resolve a problem
(C) To remind Mr. Preston to renew a membership
(D) To correct an error in a report

193. What is true about oyster consumption in Seneca Bay?

(A) It may be banned by the Economic Development Agency.
(B) It was more than ten pounds per person on average last year.
(C) It has been the most negatively affected by water pollution.
(D) It experienced a decrease last year.

194. What is suggested about the Seneca Bay Nature Alliance?

(A) It offers educational opportunities in person only.
(B) It has the mayor of Seneca Bay as a member.
(C) It will select a new president soon.
(D) It received a grant from the government.

195. According to the article, why should people visit the SBNA Web site?

(A) To view a schedule of upcoming fundraisers
(B) To sign up for a discounted membership
(C) To get information on volunteer opportunities
(D) To make a financial donation to a project

GO ON TO THE NEXT PAGE

Questions 196-200 refer to the following advertisement, Web post, and document.

Give your podcast a boost with help from Pod-Trainer!

Following ten years of creating popular podcasts, Jack Brandt launched Pod-Trainer three years ago to help podcasters reach their full potential. Class participants get access to our exclusive resource library. They are also invited to virtual events throughout the year where they can network with other podcasters. After completing a class, participants can add a link and description of their podcast to our promotional page so that others can find out more about it.

Visit pod-trainer.com to register for one of the August classes below:

Podcast Planning and Scripting [A102]
Learn how to structure your podcast from concept to completion. Shane Willard will cover how to develop engaging content, create a compelling script, and outline episodes effectively.

Audio Recording and Editing [A225]
Master the technical aspects of production. Taught by Jia Chen, you'll gain experience with using audio recording equipment, editing, and enhancing sound quality.

Effective Interview Techniques [A437]
Kelvin Rivera will give you strategies for asking engaging questions, maintaining flow, and making guests feel comfortable, helping to create interviews that resonate with their audience.

Podcast Promotion and Marketing [A590]
Tricia Hoyt will show you how to use effective marketing strategies, such as social media promotion, search engine optimization, and audience engagement techniques.

Pod-Trainer: Student Discussion Forum

Posted by: Keira Elliot, August 15, 2:25 P.M.
Subject: Small business loan

I changed from full-time to part-time in my office job a few weeks ago, so I am devoting more time to my podcast. I'm enjoying the class so far, and I can see a great improvement in my editing skills already. I'm applying for a small business loan for some equipment and the hosting fees for my podcast's Web site. I spoke with Ms. Chen after yesterday's class to get some advice about the business overview for my application. She suggested adding a sector about the audience I intend to reach with my podcast, as it demonstrates my understanding of the market. I thought this was a great tip, so I wanted to pass it along.

Keira Elliot: Business Overview

Sector 1: Personal and educational background
Sector 2: Podcast genre and description
Sector 3: Information about target audience
Sector 4: Summary of equipment needed and cost estimates
Sector 5: Revenue generation plans and projections

196. What is true about Pod-Trainer?

(A) It hosts networking events.
(B) It was opened ten years ago.
(C) Its program takes three years to complete.
(D) Its instructors have published books.

197. According to the advertisement, what can students do after completing a class?

(A) Get a discount on the next Pod-Trainer class they take
(B) Receive an official certificate of completion by mail
(C) Be entered into a prize drawing for some equipment
(D) Promote their podcast on the Pod-Trainer Web site

198. What is true about Ms. Elliot?

(A) She has not selected a podcast topic yet.
(B) She recently reduced her hours at work.
(C) She has previously taken a Pod-Trainer class.
(D) She hopes to start a group project.

199. What class is Ms. Elliot most likely taking?

(A) A102
(B) A225
(C) A437
(D) A590

200. Which sector did Ms. Elliot probably add based on an instructor's advice?

(A) Sector 2
(B) Sector 3
(C) Sector 4
(D) Sector 5

Stop! This is the end of the test. If you finish before time is called, you may go back to Parts 5, 6, and 7 and check your work.

시원스쿨 LAB

서아쌤의 토익 비밀과외

정답 및 해설

시원스쿨 LAB

READING

Playlist 1
1초 만에 명사/대명사 정답 찾는 방법

Practice

1. (D)	2. (B)	3. (A)	4. (B)	5. (D)
6. (A)	7. (D)	8. (D)	9. (D)	10. (A)
11. (A)	12. (C)			

1.

해석 원자재의 이용 가능성의 증가는 버포드 매뉴팩처링 사가 자사의 상품들의 생산을 가속화할 수 있도록 했다.

해설 빈칸 앞에 관사와 빈칸 뒤에 전치사가 있으므로 빈칸은 명사 자리이다. 따라서 (D) availability가 정답이다.

어휘 **raw material** 원자재 **accelerate** ~을 가속화하다 **avail** ~에 도움이 되다, 효력이 있다

2.

해석 우리 부서는 상품이 소매업체들에게 배송되기 전에 그것의 품질을 보증하는 것을 담당하고 있다.

해설 빈칸 앞에 소유격이 있으므로 빈칸은 명사 자리이다. 따라서 (B) division이 정답이다.

어휘 **in charge of** ~을 담당하는, 책임지는 **retailer** 소매업체 **divisive** 구분하는, 분열을 초래하는

3.

해석 재정 고문이 되기 위한 증명을 해내는 것은 일반적으로 집중 과정의 수료를 필요로 한다.

해설 빈칸 앞에 타동사의 동명사가 있으므로 빈칸은 이 동명사의 목적어 역할을 할 명사 자리인데, (A) certification과 (B) certificate 중 빈칸 앞에 관사가 없으므로 불가산명사 (A) certification이 정답이다.

어휘 **advisor** 고문, 자문 **intensive** 집중의 **certify** ~을 증명하다

4.

해석 이 연구소에 대한 접근은 레벨 3 보안 인가 등급을 가진 직원들에게만 허용된다.

해설 빈칸 앞에 관사가 없으므로 빈칸은 불가산명사 또는 복수명사 자리인데, 선택지에 복수명사가 없고 특정 보안 인가 등급을 가진 직원들에게 연구소를 대상으로 허용되는 것은 '접근, 이용'의 뜻을 가진 (B) Access가 정답이다.

어휘 **security clearance** 보안 인가 등급

5.

해석 에스트레우스 파이낸셜 서비스 사에 의해 고용된 모든 고객 계정 관리자는 회계에 대한 대학원 자격을 보유하고 있다.

해설 빈칸 앞에 전치사가 있으므로 빈칸은 명사 자리인데, 빈칸 앞에 관사가 없고 사람명사 (A) accountant는 가산 단수 명사이므로 사물명사 (D) accounting이 정답이다.

어휘 **postgraduate** 대학원 **accountable** 책임이 있는

6.

해석 그 공석에 대한 많은 지원자들이 기본적인 직무 필수요건을 충족하지만, 이스턴 씨는 면접 단계 동안 가장 큰 열정을 보여주었다.

해설 빈칸 앞에 관사와 빈칸 뒤에 전치사가 있으므로 빈칸은 명사 자리인데, 기본적인 직무 필수요건을 충족하는 대상은 지원자이므로 사람명사 (A) applicants가 정답이다.

어휘 **requirement** 필수요건 **enthusiasm** 열정 **stage** 단계

7.

해석 뉴트리퍼스트 사는 다양한 종류의 영양 보충제를 자사의 웹사이트, 행사 판매처, 그리고 소매점을 통해 판매한다.

해설 빈칸에는 빈칸 앞에 제시된 명사들과 함께 회사가 보충제를 판매하는 장소들 중 하나를 나타내야 하고 빈칸 앞에 관사가 없으므로 retail과 함께 '소매점'이라는 뜻의 복합명사로 쓸 수 있는 복수명사 (D) stores가 정답이다.

어휘 **nutritional** 영양의 **supplement** 보충제

8.

해석 켄싱턴 백화점은 아르바이트 직원에 대한 수많은 겨울 채용 공석들이 있다.

해설 빈칸은 빈칸 앞에 위치한 명사 job과 함께 동사 has의 목적어 역할을 하는 명사 자리이며, 백화점이 소유할 수 있는 대상을 나타내야 한다. 따라서 (C) opening과 (D) openings 중 정답을 골라야 하는데, 빈칸 앞에 numerous라는 복수를 나타내는 수량형용사가 있으므로 복수명사 (D) openings가 정답이다.

9.

해석 이번 여름, 오디오 이벤트 사는 샌프란시스코에서 자사의 다섯 번째 음악 축제를 개최할 것이다.

해설 빈칸 앞에는 동사가, 빈칸 뒤에 명사가 있으므로 명사 앞에 사용할 수 있는 소유격 (D) its가 정답이다.

10.

해석 1등석 티켓을 가진 사람들을 위해, 웨스트필드 레일 서비스 사는 무료 음료와 다과를 제공한다.

해설 빈칸 앞에 전치사가, 빈칸 뒤에 who 관계대명사절이 있으므로 빈칸은 전치사의 목적어 역할을 할 대명사 자리인데, who의 수식을 받을 수 있는 것은 지시대명사이므로 (A) those가 정답이다.

11.

해석 새로운 온라인 채팅 프로그램은 회사의 다른 부서들이 서로 밀접한 의사소통 상태로 있도록 해준다.

해설 빈칸 앞에 전치사가 있으므로 전치사의 목적어 역할을 할 수 있는 유일한 부정대명사 (A) one another이 정답이다.

어휘 **stay** ~인 상태로 있다

12.

해석 시 의회에 의해 접수된 각각의 판매 허가 지원서는 담당 공무원에 의해 광범위하게 검토된다.

해설 빈칸 뒤에 「of the 복수명사」와 단수동사가 있으므로 이 구조와 함께 쓰일 수 있는 단수 수량 부정대명사 (C) Each가 정답이다.

어휘 **extensively** 광범위하게, 두루 **official** (담당) 공무원

Check-up Test

1. (A)	**2.** (D)	**3.** (D)	**4.** (C)	**5.** (D)
6. (C)	**7.** (B)	**8.** (C)	**9.** (A)	**10.** (B)
11. (A)	**12.** (C)	**13.** (C)	**14.** (C)	**15.** (D)
16. (A)	**17.** (C)	**18.** (A)	**19.** (C)	**20.** (B)

1.

해석 그 약 한 알만으로 편두통 증상으로부터 필요한 완화 효과를 제공할 수 있습니다.

해설 빈칸 앞에 타동사와 형용사가 있으므로 빈칸은 명사 자리이다. 따라서 (A) relief가 정답이다.

어휘 **capsule** (알약의) 캡슐 **migraine** 편두통 **relief** (고통의) 완화, 경감 **relieve** ~을 경감시키다, 없애 주다

2.

해석 관리자 유효성의 주요한 징후는 높은 직원의 사기이다.

해설 빈칸 앞에 관사와 형용사가 있으므로 빈칸은 명사 자리이다. 따라서 (C) indicators와 (D) indication 중에 정답을 골라야 하는데, 빈칸 앞에 관사 A가 있으므로 단수명사 (D) indication이 정답이다.

어휘 **effectiveness** 유효(성), 효과적임 **morale** 사기, 의욕 **indicator** 지표, 계기 **indication** 징후, 표시

3.

해석 에스틴 씨는 팁스 씨가 휴가에서 돌아올 때까지 직접 모든 근무 일정을 고안할 것이다.

해설 빈칸 앞에 완전한 문장이, 빈칸 뒤에 부사절이 있으므로 빈칸은 부사의 역할을 하는 자리이다. 따라서 재귀대명사 (D) himself가 정답이다.

4.

해석 철저한 기획 덕분에, 히어포드 백화점에서의 대개장 행사는 엄청난 성공이었다.

해설 빈칸 앞에 형용사가 있어 빈칸이 명사 자리이므로 (A) planner와 (B) plan, 그리고 (C) planning 중에 정답을 골라야 하는데, 빈칸 앞에 관사가 없고 (A)와 (B)는 가산명사이므로 -ing형의 불가산명사 (C) planning이 정답이다.

어휘 **thorough** 철저한, 완전한 **tremendous** 엄청난, 굉장한

5.

해석 사고를 방지하기 위해, AG 케미칼 사는 모든 생산 시설에서 엄격한 보안 조치를 시행한다.

해설 빈칸에는 빈칸 앞에 위치한 명사와 함께 기업이 사고 방지를 위해 시행하는 대상을 나타내야 하므로 security와 함께 '보안 조치'라는 뜻의 복합명사를 구성해야 한다. 따라서 (C) measure과 (D) measures 중에 정답을 골라야 하는데 빈칸 앞에 관사가 없으므로 복수명사 (D) measures가 정답이다.

어휘 **enforce** ~을 시행하다, 집행하다 **rigorous** 엄격한

6.

해석 그 회사 창립자들은 아직 본사의 잠재적인 이전에 대해 결정을 내리지 못했다.

해설 빈칸 앞에 관사가, 빈칸 뒤에 전치사가 있으므로 빈칸은 명사 자리이다. 따라서 (C) decision이 정답이다.

어휘 **decisive** 결정적인 **decidedly** 확실히, 분명히

7.

해석 APR 테크놀로지 컨벤션 등록 과정은 약 10분 정도 소요되며, 온라인으로 할 수 있다.

해설 빈칸에는 빈칸 앞에 제시된 registration과 함께 복합명사를 구성해 주어 역할을 할 수 있으면서 일정 시간이 소요되는 특성을 지닌 일을 나타낼 명사가 필요하므로 '과정'을 뜻하는 (B) process가 정답이다.

8.

해석 두 명의 구직 지원자 모두 Exo9 데이터베이스 소프트웨어를 사용해 본 경험이 없다.

해설 빈칸 바로 뒤에 「of the + 복수명사」 구조가 있으므로 이 구조와 쓰일 수 있는 수량 부정대명사 (C) Neither가 정답이다.

9.

해석 우리 정책에 따라서, 결함이 있는 제품들의 반품은 반드시 유효한 매장 영수증이 동반되어야 한다.

해설 빈칸 앞뒤에 전치사가 있으므로 빈칸은 명사 자리이다. 따라서 In 및 with와 함께 '~에 따라서'라는 의미를 구성하는 (A) accordance가 정답이다.

어휘 **accompany** ~을 동반하다 **accordance** 일치, 합치 **accord** ~에 부합하다, 일치하다

10.

해석 모든 영업사원들은 12월 21일 전에 등록한다면 베스트 세일즈 세미나에 참가할 허가를 갖는다.

해설 빈칸 앞에 타동사가 있으므로 빈칸은 타동사의 목적어 역할을 할 명사 자리이다. 따라서 (B) permission과 (C) permit 중에서 정답을 골라야 하는데 빈칸 앞에 관사 a가 없으므로 불가산명사 (B) permission이 정답이다.

11.

해석 호리 씨가 신규 고객들을 끌어들이기 위한 방법들을 논의하기 위해 지역 영업부장과 만날 것이다.

해설 빈칸 앞에 전치사가, 빈칸 뒤에 명사가 있으므로 빈칸은 소유격 인칭대명사 자리이다. 따라서 (A) her가 정답이다.

12.

해석 다이트리지 툴 렌탈 사는 거의 20년 동안 건설 장비 공급업체로 유명하다.

해설 빈칸 앞에 관사와 형용사가 있으므로 빈칸은 명사 자리이다. 따라서 (A) supply와 (C) supplier 중에 정답을 골라야 하는데, 회사명과 동격을 이룰 수 있는 것은 공급업체이므로 (C) supplier가 정답이다.

어휘 **prominent** 유명한, 중요한

13.

해석 그 제조 공장은 소비자 수요에 발맞출 수 있도록 일주일 동안 생산량을 두 배로 늘렸다.

해설 빈칸은 타동사의 목적어 역할을 해야 하므로 명사 자리이다. 따라서 (A) producer과 (B) produce, 그리고 (C) production 중에 정답을 골라야 하는데 제조 공장에서 두 배로 늘릴 수 있는 대상은 '생산(량)'이므로 행위명사 (C) production이 정답이다.

어휘 **keep up with** (진행, 속도 등) ~와 발맞추다, ~을 따라가다

14.

해석 지원서의 개인 정보 작성란에, 지원자들은 250자 이하로 자신을 설명하도록 요청 받았다.

해설 빈칸은 to부정사로 쓰인 타동사 describe의 목적어 자리이며, 동사의 목적어로서 설명 대상이 되는 것은 주어인 applicants 자신이어야 하므로 재귀대명사 (C) themselves가 정답이다.

어휘 **or less** (숫자 뒤에서) ~ 이하로

15.

해석 모금 행사에서 기꺼이 자원봉사를 할 사람은 누구든지 총무부의 허드 씨에게 알려야 한다.

해설 빈칸 뒤에 분사구와 문장의 동사가 있으므로 빈칸에는 분사구의 수식을 받을 수 있는 지시대명사 (D) Anyone이 정답이다.

어휘 **willing to do** 기꺼이 ~하는

16.

해석 재무 컨설턴트에 의해 제출된 보고서를 기반으로, 다이아몬드 호텔 그룹의 수익은 거의 20퍼센트까지 떨어진다.

해설 빈칸 앞에 소유격이, 빈칸 뒤에 문장의 동사가 있으므로 빈칸은 명사 자리이다. 따라서 (A) earnings와 (D) earning 중에서 정답을 골라야 하는데 명사 earning은 가산명사이고, 빈칸 앞에 관사가 없으므로 가산 복수명사 (A) earnings가 정답이다.

17.

해석 인사부장은 이번 주 말까지 채용 담당관 직무에 적합한 사람을 찾기를 바라고 있다.

해설 빈칸 앞에 이미 복합명사의 형태로 쓰여 있는 recruitment officer와 어울리는 또 다른 명사가 빈칸에 쓰여야 하므로 '채용 담당관 직무'라는 의미로 복합명사를 구성할 수 있는 (C) role이 정답이다.

어휘 **suitable** 적합한, 어울리는

18.

해석 프릿차드 씨는 직원 대부분이 응급 처치에 대해 교육을 받고 나서야 신규 제조 시설을 개장할 것이다.

해설 빈칸 뒤에 「of the + 복수명사」 구조가 있으므로 이 구조와 함께 쓰일 수 있는 수량 부정대명사 (A) most가 정답이다.

어휘 **first aid** 응급 처치

19.

해석 원격으로 근무하는 직원들이 멀리 떨어져 있음에도 불구하고, 월간 회사 모임은 그들에게 서로 인적 네트워크를 쌓을 기회를 제공한다.

해설 빈칸 앞에 전치사가 있으므로 전치사의 목적어 역할을 할 수 있으면서 '서로'라는 뜻으로 셋 이상의 관계를 나타내는 (C) one another이 정답이다.

어휘 **remote** 원격의 **apart** 떨어진, 분리된 **gathering** 모임

20.

해석 에스콧 애틀레틱 컴퍼니는 자사의 다양한 종류의 스포츠 의류들을 위한 새로운 효과적인 광고 접근법을 시행해왔다.

해설 빈칸 앞에 위치한 명사 advertising과 함께 회사가 시행하는 대상을 나타낼 또 다른 명사가 빈칸에 와야 한다. 따라서 (A) approach와 (B) approaches 중에 정답을 골라야 하는데, 빈칸 앞에 관사가 없으므로 복수명사 (B) approaches가 정답이다.

Playlist 2
토익 문법의 핵심! 동사 수/태/시제 전쟁을 끝내러 왔다!

Practice

1. (D)	**2.** (A)	**3.** (C)	**4.** (D)	**5.** (A)
6. (D)				

1.

해석 잰코 매뉴팩처링 사의 품질 보증 관리자들은 모든 제품들이 배송 이전에 두 번 점검되어야 한다는 규칙을 시행한다.

해설 빈칸 앞에 주어와 전치사구, 빈칸 뒤에 목적어가 있으므로 빈칸은 문장의 동사 자리인데, 주어가 Quality assurance managers로 복수이므로 복수동사 (D) enforce가 정답이다.

어휘 **assurance** 보증, 보장

2.

해석 리차드슨 씨는 우리 회사가 3분기 금융분기까지 새로운 휴대전화의 출시를 연기할 것을 제안했다.

해설 빈칸 앞뒤에 that절의 주어와 명사 목적어가 있으므로 빈칸은 타동사 has suggested의 목적어 역할을 하는 that절의 동사 자리이다. 빈칸 앞에 제안의 의미를 나타내는 동사 has suggested가 있으므로 동사원형 (A) postpone이 정답이다.

3.

해석 비록 최 씨가 훌륭한 관리 잠재 능력을 보여주었지만, 승진은 더 경험 많은 직원에게 주어졌다.

해설 선택지가 4형식 동사 give로 구성되어 있고, 빈칸 뒤에 목적어 없이 전치사와 사람 목적어가 제시되어 있으므로 수동태 (C) was given이 정답이다.

4.

해석 차머스 씨는 아나톨리 레스토랑에서 디저트 쉐프로서 일하도록 권고 받았었다.

해설 빈칸 앞에 주어가, 빈칸 뒤에 to부정사가 제시되어 있으므로 빈칸은 5형식 동사의 수동태 자리이다. 따라서 (D) was encouraged가 정답이다.

5.

해석 에이콘 홈 퍼니싱스 사는 내년 말까지 북미 전역에 백 개가 넘는 소매 판매점을 보유할 것이다.

해설 빈칸 뒤에 by the end of next year라는 미래시제 단서가 제시되어 있으므로 (A) will have가 정답이다.

6.

해석 레이드 씨는 대표이사가 소셜 미디어에 광고하기로 결정하기 오래 전에 개선된 마케팅 전략들에 대한 필요성을 강조했었다.

해설 빈칸 뒤에 before과 과거시제 동사 decided가 제시되었으므로 레이드 씨가 필요성을 강조한 시점은 과거시제보다 더 과거여야 한다. 따라서 과거완료시제 (D) had stressed가 정답이다.

어휘 **long before** ~하기 오래 전에 **stress** ~을 강조하다

복합 동사 문제

1. (C)	**2.** (B)	**3.** (C)	**4.** (D)

1.

해석 이사회는 올해의 직원 사을 위해 다섯 명의 직원들을 지명했다.

해설 빈칸이 동사 자리이므로 가짜 동사 (A) nominating을 소거, 주어가 단수이므로 복수동사 (B) were nominated를 소거, 빈칸 뒤에 목적어가 있으므로 수동태 (D) has been nominated를 소거한다. 따라서 (C) has nominated가 정답이다.

어휘 **nominate** (후보자로) 지명하다, 추천하다, 임명하다

2.

해석 그 직책에 지원했던 사람들은 지난주 면접에 그들의 작업에 대한 포트폴리오를 가져오도록 권고되었다.

해설 빈칸이 동사 자리이므로 가짜 동사 (C) to encourage를 소거, 주어가 복수이므로 단수동사 (A) has encouraged를 소거, 빈칸 뒤에 last week라는 과거시점이 있으므로 미래시제 (D) will be encouraged를 소거한다. 따라서 (B) were encouraged가 정답이다.

3.

해석 올해 말까지, 오사카에 있는 제조 공장은 25,000대 이상의 자동차를 생산할 것이다.

해설 빈칸이 동사 자리이고, 빈칸 뒤에 목적어가 있으므로 수동태 (A) will be produced와 (B) has been produced를 소거, 빈칸 앞에 By the end of the year이라는 미래시점이 있으므로 현재완료시제 (D) has produced를 소거한다. 따라서 (C) will have produced가 정답이다.

4.

해석 소비자 수요가 급격하게 증가했으므로 우리 회사의 생산율도 증가했다.

해설 빈칸이 동사 자리이고, 주어가 단수이므로 복수동사 (A) are risen을 소거, 선택지에 제시된 동사 rise는 자동사이므로 수동태 (C) was risen을 소거, 빈칸 뒤에 현재완료시제가 T였으므로 과거완료 (B) had risen도 소거한다. 따라서 (D) has risen이 정답이다.

어휘 **dramatically** 급격하게 **rate of production** 생산율

Check-up Test

1. (A)	**2.** (D)	**3.** (B)	**4.** (A)	**5.** (D)
6. (A)	**7.** (B)	**8.** (A)	**9.** (A)	**10.** (B)
11. (A)	**12.** (B)	**13.** (C)	**14.** (C)	**15.** (C)
16. (A)	**17.** (B)	**18.** (B)	**19.** (B)	**20.** (A)

1.

해석 자켓 컨설팅 사의 설문조사 결과는 대부분의 승객들이 어거스터스 항공사의 유기농 식사가 매우 맛있다고 생각한다는 것을 나타낸다.

해설 빈칸 앞에 주어와 전치사구가, 빈칸 뒤에 목적어 역할을 하는 명사절이 위치해 있으므로 빈칸은 문장의 동사 자리인데, 주어 The survey results가 복수명사이므로 복수동사 (A) indicate가 정답이다.

2.

해석 팀 리더는 데이비스 씨의 영업 성과를 인정하여 그에게 추가 휴가를 주었다.

해설 빈칸 뒤에 사람 명사와 사물 명사가 목적어로 제시되어 있으므로 빈칸은 4형식 동사 자리이다. 따라서 (D) granted가 정답이다.

어휘 **day off** 휴가 **in recognition of** ~을 인정하여 **induce** ~을 설득하다, 유발하다

3.

해석 부시 스트리트 아메리칸 다이너는 지난 여름에 개업한 이후로 무료 청량 음료 리필 서비스를 제공해 오고 있다.

해설 빈칸 뒤에 과거시제 동사와 함께 접속사 since가 있으므로 과거에서 현재까지 이어져 온 일을 나타내는 현재완료시제 (B) has offered가 정답이다.

어휘 **soft drink** 청량 음료 **would have p.p.** ~했었을 것이다

4.

해석 의회의 행사 기획부는 곧 노점상 허가증에 대한 신청서를 받을 것이다.

해설 빈칸 뒤에 목적어가 있으므로 빈칸에는 능동태 동사가 와야 하고, 빈칸 뒤 soon이라는 미래시점이 제시되어 있으므로 미래시제 (A) will accept가 정답이다.

5.

해석 모든 방문객들은 공장에 들어가기 전에 보안검색대에서 서명하도록 요청된다.

해설 빈칸 앞뒤로 be동사 및 to부정사가 있으므로 이 구조와 함께 쓰일 수 있으면서 '~하도록 요청되다'라는 의미를 나타낼 때 사용하는 (D) required가 정답이다.

어휘 **assure** ~에게 장담하다, 보장하다

6.

해석 송 씨는 추가적인 발전을 위한 상세한 제안사항들을 제시하면서 다음 워크숍을 마칠 것이다.

해설 빈칸 앞뒤에 주어와 목적어가 있으므로 빈칸은 동사 자리이며, 빈칸 뒤에 next가 있으므로 워크숍이 앞으로 개최될 것임을 알 수 있다. 따라서 미래시제인 (A) will close가 정답이다.

어휘 **progress** 발전, 진척, 진전

7.

해석 몇몇 불운한 운영상의 문제들로 인해, 그 커피 매장 소유주는 최근에 특별 할인 서비스를 제공하지 못했다.

해설 빈칸 뒤에 lately가 있으므로 이 부사와 어울릴 수 있는 현재완료시제 (B) has not offered가 정답이다.

어휘 **unfortunate** 불운한, 운이 없는

8.

해석 지역 기자는 브램블 국립 공원 전역에 50,000개의 새로운 나무를 심는데 참여한 자원봉사자들을 인터뷰할 것이다.

해설 빈칸 앞에 관계대명사 who와 빈칸 뒤에 전치사 in이 있으므로 빈칸은 관계대명사절의 동사 자리인데, 선행사가 복수명사 volunteers이므로 복수동사가 와야 한다. 또한, 빈칸 뒤에 목적어가 없으므로 수동태 (A) were involved가 정답이다.

9.

해석 그 운영부장은 다음 주 금요일에 공장 견학을 이끌 예정이며, 잠재적인 투자자들은 그를 안내 구역에서 만나야 한다고 요청할 것이다.

해설 빈칸 앞에 등위접속사 and로 이어지는 또 다른 절의 동사가 '요청'의 뜻을 나타내는 request이므로 이 동사의 목적어 역할을 하는 that절의 동사는 동사원형이 와야 한다. 따라서 (A) meet이 정답이다.

10.

해석 재정 문제는 돕슨 엔터프라이시스 사가 A1 쇼핑몰 건설 공사 계약에 대한 입찰을 철회하도록 했다.

해설 빈칸 앞에 주어가, 빈칸 뒤에 목적어가 있으므로 빈칸은 능동태 동사 자리이다. 또한, 주어가 Financial issues로 복수명사이므로 (B) forced가 정답이다.

어휘 **withdraw** ~을 철회하다 **bid** 입찰

11.

해석 보증금은 여기서 숙박하시는 동안 귀하의 객실에서 발생될 수 있는 어떠한 손상에 대해서 그 비용을 충당합니다.

해설 빈칸 앞에 주어가, 빈칸 뒤에 목적어가 있으므로 빈칸은 능동태 동사 자리인데, 보증금이 객실에서 발생되는 손상에 대한 비용을 충당하는 것은 사실에 해당되므로 현재시제 (A) covers가 정답이다.

12.

해석 지난 주말에 개봉한 롭 플린 씨가 출연하는 새로운 영화가 이미 여러 박스 오피스 기록을 경신했다.

해설 빈칸은 주어 The new movie를 수식하는 that 관계대명사절의 동사 자리인데, 새로운 영화는 사람에 의해 개봉되는 것이므로 수동태 (B) was released가 정답이다.

어휘 **star A** A가 출연하다 **break a record** 기록을 경신하다

13.

해석 우리 정책에 따라, 모든 직원들은 예의와 존중으로 서로를 대하도록 권고 받는다.

해설 빈칸에는 빈칸 앞뒤에 위치한 be동사와 to부정사와 함께 어울리면서 이와 같은 구조와 함께 '~하도록 권고 받는다'라는 의미를 나타내는 (C) advised가 정답이다.

어휘 **in accordance with** ~에 따라 **treat** ~을 대하다, 다루다, 치료하다 **courtesy** 예의 (바름), 공손함, 정중함 **assume** ~라고 생각하다, 가정하다, (책임 등) ~을 맡다

14.

해석 펀랜드 놀이공원을 방문하는 이용객들의 신장 제한은 놀이기구 유형에 따라 다르다.

해설 빈칸 앞에는 주어와 전치사구가, 빈칸 뒤에 전치사구가 있으므로 빈칸은 동사 자리임을 알 수 있다. 또한, 선택지에 제시된 vary는 목적어가 필요 없는 자동사이고, 주어 The height restriction이 단수이므로 단수동사 (C) varies가 정답이다.

어휘 **height** 키, 신장 **ride** 놀이 기구 **vary** 다르다, 다양하다

15.

해석 올 연말쯤이면, 가수 겸 작곡가인 닐스 롱스태프 씨는 20년 전에 자신의 데뷔 싱글이 나온 이후로 50개가 넘는 앨범들을 내게 된다.

해설 주어 singer-songwriter가 단수이므로 선택지 중 복수동사 (A) publish를 소거하고, 빈칸 뒤에 목적어가 있으므로 수동태 (B) has been published를 소거한다. 마지막으로 콤마 앞에 미래시제 단서인 By the end of가 있으므로 미래완료시제 (C) will have published가 정답이다.

어휘 **publish an album** 앨범을 내다, 출시하다, 공개하다

16.

해석 경제 전문가들이 실업률의 급격한 증가를 예측하기 전에, 대통령은 수십 만 개의 새로운 일자리를 창출해 내겠다고 약속했다.

해설 빈칸 앞에는 부사절과 주어가, 빈칸 뒤에 목적어 역할을 하는 to부정사구가 있으므로 빈칸은 주절의 동사 자리이다. 또한, 빈칸 뒤 to부정사구를 목적어로 취해야 하므로 능동태가 와야 하며, 대통령이 약속한 시점이 경제 전문가들이 실업률의 증가를 예측하기 전이므로 과거완료시제 (A) had promised가 정답이다.

어휘 steep 급격한 unemployment 실업(률) hundreds of thousands 수십 만 개, 수십 만 명

17.

해석 걸숀 씨가 메인에서 기술 컨퍼런스에 참석하는 것이 예상됨에도 불구하고, 그녀는 행사가 시작한 후 몇 시간 뒤에 도착할지도 모른다.

해설 빈칸 앞뒤에 be동사와 to부정사가 있으므로 빈칸은 이 구조와 함께 사용할 수 있는 (B) expected가 정답이다.

18.

해석 설치 작업 안내사항은 첨부된 제품 정보 안내서의 3 페이지에서 찾아보실 수 있습니다.

해설 빈칸 앞에 조동사가 있으므로 빈칸에는 동사원형이 와야 하므로 선택지 (B) be found 또는 (D) have found 중에서 정답을 골라야 하는데, 빈칸 뒤에 목적어가 아닌 전치사구가 있고, 설치 작업 안내사항은 사람에 의해 찾아지는 대상이므로 수동태 (B) be found가 정답이다.

어휘 accompanying 첨부된, 동반된

19.

해석 아파트를 매매했던 사람들만 참석하도록 요청되었지만, 갈리건 씨는 모든 건물 입주자들이 지난 화요일 회의에 오도록 강력히 권고했다.

해설 빈칸 앞에 주어가, 빈칸 뒤에 명사 목적어가 있으므로 빈칸은 문장의 동사 자리이며, 능동태가 와야 한다. 또한, 아파트 매매자들만 회의에 참석하도록 요청 받은 시점과 거주자들이 참석하도록 권고 받은 시점이 모두 과거이므로 과거시제 (B) urged가 정답이다.

20.

해석 알터스 엔터프라이스 사의 신임 홍보이사인 로버트슨 씨를 환영해 주십시오.

해설 빈칸 바로 앞에 Please가 있으므로 빈칸에는 동사원형이 와야 한다. 따라서 (A) welcome이 정답이다.

Playlist 3
형용사와 부사만 정복해도 문법 문제 절반은 맞힌다!

Practice

1. (B)	**2.** (A)	**3.** (A)	**4.** (B)	**5.** (B)
6. (D)	**7.** (D)	**8.** (D)		

1.

해석 그 기술 회사는 보통 다양한 기기들과의 호환성을 보장하기 위해 가장 잘 팔리는 소프트웨어 프로그램의 다양한 버전을 개발한다.

해설 빈칸 앞에 타동사가, 빈칸 뒤에 명사가 있으므로 빈칸은 명사를 수식할 형용사 자리이다. 따라서 (B) multiple이 정답이다.

어휘 compatibility with ~와의 호환성 multiply ~을 크게 증가시키다 multiplicity 다수, 다양성

2.

해석 반납일 이틀 후에 도서관에 반납된 도서들은 연체료의 영향을 받을 것이다.

해설 빈칸 앞에 be동사가, 빈칸 뒤에 전치사 to가 있으므로 이와 어울리면서 '늦게 반납된 책이 연체료의 영향을 받을 것'이라는 의미가 자연스러우므로 be동사 및 전치사 to와 함께 '~의 영향을 받다, ~하기 쉽다'라는 뜻의 (A) subject가 정답이다.

어휘 late fee 연체료 entitled 자격이 있는 accountable 책임이 있는 transferable 이동 가능한

3.

해석 5월 14일부터, 모든 세입자 연합회 회의는 1층에 있는 컨퍼런스 회의실에서 개최될 것이다.

해설 빈칸 뒤에 복수명사 tenants association meetings가 있으므로 이를 수식할 수 있는 수량형용사 (A) all이 정답이다.

어휘 starting on + 날짜 ~부터

4.

해석 좋은 치아 건강을 보장하기 위해, 환자들은 여섯 달마다 검진 예약을 잡는 것이 권고된다.

해설 빈칸 뒤에 six months라는 숫자 표현이 있으므로 '~마다'라는 뜻을 가져 반복 주기를 나타낼 수 있는 수량형용사 (B) every가 정답이다.

5.

해석 승인과 함께, 직원들은 운영부의 부장님으로부터 직접 법인 차량 키를 받을 수 있다.

해설 빈칸 앞에 타동사와 목적어가, 빈칸 뒤에 전치사구가 있으므로 빈칸은 타동사를 수식할 부사 자리이다. 따라서 (B) directly가 정답이다.

어휘 directness 직접적임, 솔직함

6.

해석 신용카드와 직불카드가 마침내 모든 시카고 시내 택시에서 수락된다.

해설 빈칸 앞에 be동사가, 빈칸 뒤에 과거분사가 있으므로 빈칸은 이 사이에서 과거분사를 수식할 부사 자리이다. 따라서 (D) finally가 정답이다.

어휘 **debit card** 직불카드

7.

해석 휴양지 리조트에서 외딴 섬 티잘리 두아까지 항해하는 데 약 2시간이 걸린다.

해설 선택지가 모두 부사로 구성되어 있고, 빈칸 뒤에 숫자 표현이 제시되어 있으므로 이를 수식할 수 있는 (D) approximately가 정답이다.

어휘 **sail** 항해하다 **remote** 외딴, 떨어진 **somewhat** 다소 **exceedingly** 매우, 극도로

8.

해석 슈가힐 플라자 반대편의 넓은 공간은 이전에 주차장이었지만, 현재는 여러 조깅 길들이 있는 도심 공원이다.

해설 빈칸 앞에 be동사가, 빈칸 뒤에 명사구가 있으므로 이 명사구를 수식할 수 있는 (D) formerly가 정답이다.

Check-up Test

1. (B)	**2.** (A)	**3.** (D)	**4.** (A)	**5.** (B)
6. (D)	**7.** (B)	**8.** (A)	**9.** (B)	**10.** (C)
11. (A)	**12.** (D)	**13.** (C)	**14.** (C)	**15.** (C)
16. (B)	**17.** (B)	**18.** (D)	**19.** (B)	**20.** (D)

1.

해석 그 신입 인턴 직원은 프로젝트 제안에 대한 예상 지출 비용을 계산하는 일과 같은 복잡한 할당 업무를 놀라울 정도로 잘 처리한다.

해설 자동사 deals 뒤에 빈칸과 부사 well이 있으므로 빈칸은 자동사를 수식할 수 있는 부사 자리이다. 따라서 (B) surprisingly가 정답이다.

어휘 **assignment** 할당 업무, 배정된 일 **calculate** ~을 계산하다 **projected** 예상된

2.

해석 카나리 파이낸셜 컨설턴시 사는 단골 고객들에게 매력적인 혜택 및 보상책을 제공하고 있다.

해설 빈칸이 전치사와 명사 사이에 위치해 있으므로 빈칸은 명사를 수식할 형용사 자리이다. 따라서 (A) regular가 정답이다.

어휘 **regularity** 정기적임, 규칙적임

3.

해석 이스타나 케밥은 지난달에 종이로 만든 음식 배달 상자를 사용하기 시작했으며, 이는 비용을 크게 줄이는 만족스러운 효과를 낳았다.

해설 전치사 of 뒤에 타동사와 목적어가 있으므로 빈칸은 타동사를 수식할 부사 자리이다. 따라서 (D) greatly가 정답이다.

어휘 **have the effect of** ~하는 효과를 낳다

4.

해석 6개월 이상 일한 직원들은 누구든지 우리 경영 관리 교육 코스에 등록할 자격이 있다.

해설 빈칸 앞뒤에 be동사와 to부정사가 있으므로 이 구조와 쓰일 수 있으면서 6개월 이상 근무하는 것이 교육 코스에 등록하는 자격에 해당되므로 be동사 및 to부정사와 함께 '~할 자격이 있다'라는 의미를 구성하는 (A) eligible이 정답이다.

5.

해석 대다수의 직원들이 새 복장 규정 정책을 지지했기 때문에, 인사부장은 그 정책을 즉시 시행하기로 결정했다.

해설 빈칸 앞에 2형식 동사가, 빈칸 뒤에 전치사구가 있으므로 빈칸은 주격 보어 역할을 할 수 있는 형용사 자리이다. 따라서 (B) supportive가 정답이다.

어휘 **supportive** 지지하는, 지원하는

6.

해석 로열 발레 컴퍼니는 새롭게 문을 연 이윙 콘서트장에서 최근에 기억에 남을 만한 공연을 했다.

해설 빈칸 앞뒤에 타동사와 명사가 있으므로 이 명사를 수식할 수 있는 형용사가 빈칸에 와야 한다. 따라서 (D) memorable이 정답이다.

어휘 **memorable** 기억에 남을 만한

7.

해석 잭슨 마블 씨는 다음 달 초에 그의 새 앨범을 디지털 다운로드용으로 이용 가능하게 만들 것이다.

해설 빈칸 앞에 5형식 동사와 목적어가 있으므로 빈칸은 목적격 보어 자리이다. 따라서 명사와 형용사가 빈칸에 올 수 있는데, 목적어인 his new album이 명사 (A) availability 그리고 (C) availableness와 동격의 관계가 아니므로 형용사 (B) available이 정답이다.

어휘 **availableness** 쓸모 있음 **availably** 쓸모 있게

8.

해석 그 영화 속편에 대한 감독의 발표는 영화제에 참석한 관객들을 분명히 신이 나게 했다.

해설 빈칸 앞에 주어와 전치사구가, 빈칸 뒤에 타동사와 목적어가 있으므로 빈칸은 타동사를 수식할 부사 자리이다. 따라서 (A) clearly가 정답이다.

어휘 **sequel** 속편 **audience member** 관객, 청중, 독자

9.

해석 민구스 갤러리에서 열리는 아마추어 수채화 대회는 아직 작품을 전시한 적이 없는 화가들의 출품작들만 포함한다.

해설 빈칸 앞뒤에 have와 to부정사가 있으므로 빈칸은 이 구조와 함께 쓰일 수 있으면서 '아직 ~하지 않다'라는 뜻을 구성할 수 있는 부사 (B) yet이 정답이다.

어휘 **entry** 출품작, 참가작

10.

해석 요리사 마사코 씨는 데소토 레스토랑에서 자신이 준비하는 여러 요리에 제철 재료만을 사용하기 위해 애쓴다.

해설 빈칸 앞뒤에 타동사와 명사가 있으므로 빈칸은 이 명사를 수식할 형용사 자리이다. 따라서 (C) seasonal이 정답이다.

어휘 **strive to do** ~하기 위해 애쓰다 **seasonally** 계절적으로

11.

해석 에드몬즈 씨는 메뉴에서 케일 애플 스무디를 없애기로 결정했는데, 그것을 주문하는 고객이 한번이라도 거의 없기 때문이다.

해설 빈칸 뒤에 복수명사 customers가 있으므로 이 명사를 수식할 형용사가 필요한데, 상품이 메뉴에서 빠지는 이유와 관련되어야 하므로 '주문하는 고객이 거의 없다'라는 의미를 나타내는 수량형용사 (A) few가 정답이다.

어휘 **ever** (부정문에서) 한번이라도

12.

해석 환자들은 큰 수술을 거치도록 합의하기에 앞서 적어도 두 명의 의사로부터 받는 진단을 요청하도록 권장된다.

해설 빈칸 뒤에 숫자 표현이 있으므로 '적어도, 최소한'이라는 의미를 나타내는 부사 (D) at least가 정답이다.

어휘 **diagnose** 진단 **undergo** ~을 거치다, 겪다

13.

해석 지역 업체들은 폐기물 처리에 대해 친환경적인 접근 방식을 취하도록 권고된다.

해설 빈칸이 부사와 명사 사이에 위치해 있으므로 빈칸은 부사의 수식을 받으면서 명사를 수식할 형용사 자리이다. 따라서 (C) friendly가 정답이다.

어휘 **waste disposal** 폐기물 처리

14.

해석 싱 씨는 하커 씨가 주간 매출 보고서에 대해 거의 시간을 엄수하지 않는다고 언급했다.

해설 빈칸이 be동사와 형용사 보어 사이에 위치해 있으므로 빈칸은 부사 자리인데, '거의 시간을 엄수하지 않는다'는 부정적 의미가 되어야 자연스러우므로 (C) seldom이 정답이다.

어휘 **punctual** 시간을 엄수하는

15.

해석 귀하의 대여 자전거가 어떠한 이유로든 이용할 수 없다면, 저희가 크기와 가격에 필적하는 다른 자전거를 제공해 드릴 것입니다.

해설 빈칸 앞뒤에 be동사와 전치사 in이 있으므로 이 구조와 함께 사용할 수 있는 (C) comparable이 정답이다.

어휘 **variable** 변화할 수 있는, 변동이 심한

16.

해석 IT 팀장으로서 니슨 씨의 또 다른 책무는 모든 회사 컴퓨터들이 악성 소프트웨어로부터 보호받는 것을 확실하게 하는 것이다.

해설 빈칸 뒤에 단수명사 responsibility가 있으므로 이를 수식할 수 있는 수량형용사 (B) Another이 정답이다.

어휘 **malicious** 악성의, 악의적인

17.

해석 우리 휴대전화에 대한 팝 스타 수지 리 씨의 광고가 특히 젊은 소비자들 사이에서 급격히 매출을 증대해 줄 것이 분명하다.

해설 빈칸 뒤에 증가의 의미를 나타내는 동사 boost가 있으므로 이 앞에서 증가 정도를 나타낼 수 있는 부사 (B) dramatically가 정답이다.

어휘 **endorsement** (유명인이 나오는) 광고 **punctually** 시간을 엄수하여

18.

해석 그 음반회사에서 사망한 그 가수의 마지막 녹음 자료를 수집했으며, 곧 온전한 앨범의 형태로 출시할 것이다.

해설 빈칸 앞뒤로 조동사와 동사가 있으므로 빈칸에는 동사를

수식할 수 있는 부사가 와야 한다. 따라서 (D) shortly가 정답이다.

어휘 late 이미 사망한, 고인이 된

19.

해석 높은 기대를 받았던 영화 시사회 전에, 감독과 여러 명의 출연진이 팬들을 위해 사인을 해주었다.

해설 빈칸 앞뒤에 부사와 명사가 있으므로 빈칸은 부사의 수식을 받으면서 명사를 수식할 수 있는 형용사 자리이다. 따라서 (B) anticipated와 (D) anticipatory 중에서 정답을 골라야 하는데 해석상 '높은 기대를 받았던 영화 시사회'가 자연스러우므로 (B) anticipated가 정답이다.

어휘 **film premiere** 영화 시사회 **cast members** 출연진 **anticipatory** 앞지른, 예측의

20.

해석 마시스는 원래 배송 창고였지만, 작년에 5층짜리 백화점으로 개조되었다.

해설 빈칸 앞에 be동사가, 빈칸 뒤에 명사구가 있으므로 빈칸은 명사구를 수식할 부사 자리이다. 따라서 (D) originally가 정답이다.

어휘 **convert** ~을 개조하다, 변형시키다 **originality** 독창성

Playlist 4
토익 문법 끝판왕! 전치사와 부사절 접속사 총정리

Practice

1. (D)	**2.** (C)	**3.** (C)	**4.** (A)	**5.** (B)
6. (A)	**7.** (A)	**8.** (B)		

1.

해석 직원들은 구매 시점에 40퍼센트의 할인을 이용할 수 있다.

해설 빈칸 뒤에 the time이라는 시점이 제시되어 있으므로 시간 전치사 (D) at이 정답이다.

2.

해석 모든 잡지 기사들은 2월호에 포함되기 위해 1월 21일 또는 그 전에 제출되어야 한다.

해설 빈칸 뒤에 제시된 January 21는 2월호에 수록되기 위해 기사가 제출되어야 하는 시점을 나타내므로 '~ (이)전에'라는 뜻의 전치사 (C) before이 정답이다.

3.

해석 조각품 전시회를 찾는 방문객들은 안내데스크를 걸어서 지나고 오른쪽에 위치한 첫 번째 홀에 입장해야 한다.

해설 빈칸 뒤에 information desk라는 장소가 제시되어 있고, 이는 방문객들이 전시회를 보기 위해 지나야 하는 곳이므로 '~을 지나서'라는 뜻의 장소 전치사 (C) past가 정답이다.

4.

해석 코스트라인 홀리데이 리조트는 좋지 않은 온라인 후기에도 불구하고 항상 투숙객들로 가득 예약되어 있다.

해설 빈칸 앞에는 투숙객들로 예약되어 있다는 내용이, 빈칸 뒤에는 좋지 않은 후기라는 내용이 있으므로 '~에도 불구하고'의 의미를 가진 전치사 (A) despite이 정답이다.

5.

해석 샐리 위버 씨의 공연이 10,000명 이상의 사람들을 끌여들였음에도 불구하고, 그녀는 콘서트로 거의 돈을 벌지 못했다.

해설 빈칸 뒤에 두 개의 절이 있으므로 빈칸은 부사절 접속사 자리이다. 또한, 콤마 앞에는 많은 사람들을 끌여들였다는 내용이, 뒤에는 돈을 거의 벌지 못했다는 내용이 있으므로 '비록 ~임에도 불구하고'라는 의미의 양보 부사절 접속사 (B) Although가 정답이다.

6.

해석 사무실의 리모델링이 완성되었으므로, 우리 직원들은 그들의 새로운 작업 장소를 설치할 수 있다.

해설 빈칸 뒤에 두 개의 절이 있으므로 빈칸은 부사절 접속사 자리이다. 또한, 리모델링이 완료된 것이 작업 장소를 설치할 수 있는 이유에 해당되므로 '~이므로, ~ 때문에'라는 의미의 이유 부사절 접속사 (A) Now that이 정답이다.

어휘 **workstation** 작업 장소

7.

해석 버미어 씨의 진품 그림의 가치와 취약함 때문에, 그것은 보안 벽으로 둘러 쌓여 있다.

해설 그림의 가치와 취약함은 그림이 보안 벽으로 둘러 쌓인 이유에 해당되므로 '~ 때문에'라는 뜻의 (A) Because of가 정답이다.

어휘 **fragility** 취약함, 섬세함 **surround** ~을 둘러 싸다 **barrier** (장)벽

8.

해석 그레이 씨는 직장 전근이 확정되자마자 적절한 숙박시설을 찾는 것을 계획한다.

해설 빈칸 앞뒤로 두 개의 절이 있으므로 빈칸은 부사절 접속사 자리이다. 따라서 선택지 중 유일한 부사절 접속사인 (B)

as soon as가 정답이다.

Check-up Test

1. (D)	**2.** (A)	**3.** (D)	**4.** (D)	**5.** (C)
6. (C)	**7.** (B)	**8.** (B)	**9.** (B)	**10.** (B)
11. (A)	**12.** (A)	**13.** (A)	**14.** (A)	**15.** (A)
16. (A)	**17.** (B)	**18.** (A)	**19.** (A)	**20.** (B)

1.

해석 하메드 씨가 스포틱스 베버리지 사의 대표이사가 되자마자, 몇 가지 새로운 작업장 안전 규정이 발표되었다.

해설 빈칸 뒤에 두 개의 절이 있으므로 빈칸은 부사절 접속사 자리인데, 새로운 정책을 발표한 시점이 대표이사가 된 시점보다 뒤에 발생되어야 하므로 '~하자마자'라는 의미의 시간 부사절 접속사 (D) As soon as가 정답이다

2.

해석 성모 마리아 성당은 런던에서 블랙프라이어스 기념비 다음으로 오래된 역사적인 건축물이다.

해설 빈칸 뒤에 London이라는 행정구역이 있으므로 '~(안)에서'라는 의미의 장소 전치사 (A) in이 정답이다.

어휘 **chapel** 성당 **landmark** (가장 눈에 띄는) 건축물, 유적, 명소 **monument** 기념비, 기념관

3.

해석 사업 컨설턴트가 요청한 수수료는 그의 업계 이력과 전문지식을 고려할 때 꽤 적절한 편이다.

해설 빈칸 앞에 절이, 빈칸 뒤에 명사구가 있으므로 빈칸은 전치사 자리이다. 따라서 전치사 (D) considering이 정답이다.

어휘 **industry background** 업계 이력

4.

해석 지출 제한이 5개월 전에 도입된 이래로 월간 비용이 감소하였다.

해설 빈칸 앞뒤에 두 개의 절이 있으므로 빈칸은 부사절 접속사 자리이다. 또한, 월간 비용이 줄어든 시점이 지출 제한을 도입한 시점 이후이므로 '~이래로'라는 뜻의 시간 부사절 접속사 (D) since가 정답이다.

5.

해석 그 영화의 감독이 좋지 않은 건강 상태로 인해 시상식에 참석할 수 없었던 마틴 올슨 씨를 대신하여 상을 받았다.

해설 빈칸 뒤에 명사구가 있으므로 빈칸은 전치사 자리인데, 영화 감독이 시상식에 참석하지 못한 사람을 대신하여 상을 받았다는 의미가 자연스러우므로 '~을 대신해'라는 뜻의 (C) on behalf of가 정답이다.

어휘 **ill** 건강이 좋지 않은, 아픈 **in light of** ~에 비추어 보아

6.

해석 반품된 상품의 환불금은 유효한 구매 증거가 제시되지 않으면 지급될 수 없습니다.

해설 빈칸 앞에는 환불금이 지급될 수 없다는 내용이, 빈칸 뒤에는 유효한 구매 증거를 제시한다는 내용이 있으므로 구매 증거를 제시하는 것은 환불금을 받기 위한 조건임을 알 수 있다. 따라서 '~하지 않는다면'의 뜻인 조건 부사절 접속사 (C) unless가 정답이다.

7.

해석 저녁 시간 동안 더 많은 식사 손님들을 수용하기 위한 노력의 일환으로, 제이드 가든은 하버 하이츠 몰 맞은편에 있는 로투스 로드로 이전할 것이다.

해설 빈칸 뒤에 장소가 제시되어 있으므로 빈칸에는 장소 전치사가 와야 하는데, 해석상 '하버 하이츠 몰 맞은편에 있는 로투스 로드로'라는 의미가 자연스러우므로 '~ 맞은편에'라는 뜻의 (B) opposite이 정답이다.

8.

해석 정기적인 유지보수 작업으로 인해 성 메튜 성당의 종이 정상적으로 소리를 낼 수 있도록 복원되었다.

해설 성당의 종이 소리를 낼 수 있었던 이유가 정기적인 유지보수 작업 때문이므로 '~로 인해, ~ 때문에'라는 뜻의 전치사 (B) due to가 정답이다.

어휘 **restore** ~을 복원하다, 복구하다

9.

해석 그 레코드 회사는 마리사 토레스 씨의 데뷔 앨범이 세계적으로 200만장 넘게 판매된 후에 그녀에게 기념패를 제공했다.

해설 빈칸 앞뒤로 두 개의 절이 있으므로 빈칸은 이 절들을 연결할 부사절 접속사 자리이다. 따라서 선택지에서 유일한 접속사인 (B) after가 정답이다.

어휘 **plaque** 기념패, 감사패

10.

해석 로튼 씨는 최근 졸업생 대신 경험 많은 직원들을 고용할 때 직원 생산성이 더 높아진다고 생각한다.

해설 빈칸 앞뒤로 두 개의 절이 있으므로 빈칸은 부사절 접속사 자리인데, 직원 생산성이 높아지는 시점이 경험 많은 직원들을 고용할 때이므로 '~할 때'라는 뜻의 시간 부사절 접속

사 (B) when이 정답이다.

11.

해석 이사회에서 상당한 연봉 인상을 제안했음에도 불구하고 마케팅 부장은 사임했다.

해설 빈칸 앞뒤로 두 개의 절이 위치해 있으므로 빈칸은 부사절 접속사 자리이다. 또한 '이사회에서 연봉 인상을 제안했음에도 불구하고 마케팅 부장이 사임했다'와 같은 의미가 되어야 자연스러우므로 '~임에도 불구하고'를 뜻하는 양보 부사절 접속사 (A) even though가 정답이다.

어휘 **for one thing** 우선 첫째로, 한 가지는

12.

해석 저희 고객이신 킨타로 씨께서 승무원들이 토론토로 가는 전체 비행 시간 내내 아주 세심했다고 특별히 언급해 주셨습니다.

해설 빈칸이 속한 that절에서 주격 보어 attentive 뒤로 빈칸과 명사구가 있으므로 빈칸은 이 명사구를 목적어로 취할 전치사가 필요한 자리이다. 또한 빈칸 뒤에 제시된 the whole flight는 승무원들이 세심하게 행동한 기간에 해당되므로 '~ 동안 내내'라는 의미로 기간 명사 앞에 사용하는 전치사 (A) throughout이 정답이다.

어휘 **attentive** 세심한, 배려하는 **underneath** ~ 밑에, 아래에

13.

해석 사무실 직원들은 엘리베이터 유지 관리 작업이 진행 중인 때를 제외하고 화재 대피용 계단을 이용하도록 허용되지 않는다.

해설 선택지가 모두 전치사의 역할을 할 수 있으므로 빈칸 뒤의 when절은 명사절임을 알 수 있으며, 이 when절은 직원들이 화재 대피용 계단을 이용할 수 있는 특정한 상황을 나타내고 있다. 이는 허용되지 않는 대상에서 제외되는 상황에 해당되므로 '~을 제외하고'를 뜻하는 전치사 (A) except가 정답이다.

어휘 **fire escape stairs** 화재 대피용 계단 **underway** 진행 중인

14.

해석 조경회사인 그린필즈 사가 지역 라디오에 광고했던 동안에, 그 회사의 서비스에 대한 수요가 거의 세 배로 늘었다.

해설 콤마 앞뒤로 절이 하나씩 위치해 있으므로 빈칸에는 부사절 접속사가 필요하다. 따라서 선택지에서 유일한 접속사인 (A) While이 정답이다.

어휘 **triple** v. 세 배로 늘다, 세 배가 되다 **as much as** ~만큼 많이

15.

해석 결함이 있는 교통 신호등이 교체되자마자 바이어스 로드가 완전히 재개방될 것이다.

해설 빈칸 앞에는 절이, 빈칸 뒤에는 동명사구가 있으므로 빈칸은 이 동명사구를 목적어로 취할 전치사 자리이다. 또한, 도로가 재개방되는 시점이 결함 있는 신호등이 교체된 직후이므로 동명사와 함께 '~하자마자'를 뜻하는 전치사 (A) upon이 정답이다.

16.

해석 도슨 공원은 한때는 시에서 가장 인기있는 오락 공간이었던 반면에, 메모리얼 스퀘어가 주민들 사이에서 더 인기 있어지고 있다.

해설 콤마를 기준으로 두 개의 절이 있으므로 빈칸은 부사절 접속사 자리인데, '한 때는 인기 있었던 반면에, 다른 곳이 더 인기 있어 졌다'는 뜻으로 해석하는 것이 자연스러우므로 '~인 반면에'라는 뜻의 대조 부사절 접속사 (A) Whereas가 정답이다.

어휘 **recreation space** 오락 공간

17.

해석 시 의회는 콘서트가 진행되는 동안 도시 내의 몇몇 도로들을 폐쇄하기로 결정했다.

해설 행사가 진행되는 동안에 폐쇄되는 도로는 시내 안에 위치해 있으므로 '~ 이내에'라는 뜻의 전치사 (B) within이 정답이다.

18.

해석 병에 담긴 무료 생수가 그 음악 축제 진행 기간 동안 간식 제공 텐트에서 이용 가능할 것이다.

해설 빈칸 뒤에 제시된 음악 축제가 무료 생수를 이용할 수 있는 기간에 해당되므로 '~ 동안'이라는 뜻의 전치사 (A) during이 정답이다.

19.

해석 우리 신문은 전국적인 인쇄 매체 뉴스 독자층의 전반적인 감소에도 불구하고 여느 때처럼 여전히 인기 있는 상태이다.

해설 빈칸 앞에는 신문이 여전히 인기 있다는 내용이, 빈칸 뒤에는 독자층의 전반적인 감소라는 명사구가 있으므로 '독자층 감소에도 불구하고 여전히 인기 있다'와 같은 의미가 되어야 자연스럽다. 따라서 '~에도 불구하고'라는 뜻의 전치사 (A) despite이 정답이다.

어휘 **as A as ever** 여느 때처럼 A한 **overall** 전반적인 **print news** 인쇄 매체 뉴스 **readership** 독자층

20.

해석 야마모토 씨는 그 저가 항공사에 의해 식사가 제공되지 않을 경우에 대비해 항공편 탑승 전에 간단히 식사하기로 결정했다.

해설 빈칸 앞뒤로 절들이 위치해 있으므로 빈칸은 부사절 접속사 자리이다. '식사가 제공되지 않을 경우에 대비해 탑승 전에 간단히 식사하기로 결정했다'와 같은 의미가 되어야 자연스러우므로 '~할 경우에 (대비해)'라는 의미로 쓰이는 조건 부사절 접속사 (B) in case가 정답이다.

어휘 **grab a bite to eat** 간단히 식사하다 **budget airline** 저가 항공사

Playlist 5
관계대명사랑 관계부사를 구분해야 된다고?

Practice

1. (A)	**2.** (B)	**3.** (C)	**4.** (A)	**5.** (A)
6. (A)	**7.** (C)	**8.** (D)		

1.

해석 주 선수권 대회 참전에 자격이 있는 지역 야구팀들은 에르코 메뉴팩쳐링 사로부터 후원을 받을 것이다.

해설 빈칸 뒤에 문장의 동사 will receive가 있으므로 빈칸부터 championships까지가 관계사절로 주어 Local baseball teams를 수식해야 한다. 따라서 빈칸 뒤에 동사가 있으므로 주격 관계대명사 (A) that이 정답이다.

어휘 **championship** 선수권 대회 **sponsorship** 후원

2.

해석 영화감독으로서 세 개의 아카데미상을 수상한 성과를 가진 버나드 시몬스 씨는 최근 은퇴를 발표했다.

해설 빈칸 뒤에 문장의 동사 has announced가 있으므로 콤마 사이에 위치한 절은 주어인 Bernard Simmons를 수식하는 관계사절이 되어야 한다. 빈칸 뒤에 주어와 동사 그리고 목적어가 있으므로 소유격 관계대명사 (B) whose가 정답이다.

3.

해석 이전에 대한 제안이 각 직원들이 그들의 의견에 대해 목소리를 낼 기회를 받게 될 회의에서 논의될 것이다.

해설 빈칸 앞뒤에 두 개의 완전한 절이 있으므로 빈칸은 접속사 역할을 할 수 있어야 하는데, 빈칸 앞에 전치사가 있으므로 전치사의 목적어 역할을 할 수 있는 관계대명사 (C) which가 정답이다.

어휘 **voice** v. ~에 대한 목소리를 내다

4.

해석 면접 단계로 나아간 구직 지원자들이 있는데, 이들 중 몇몇은 광범위한 업계 경험을 가지고 있으며 우리 인사부장님께 연락 받을 것이다.

해설 빈칸 앞에 수량 표현 some과 전치사 of가 있으므로 빈칸은 관계대명사 자리인데, 빈칸에 들어갈 관계대명사의 선행사가 job applicants이므로 (A) whom이 정답이다.

어휘 **progress** (앞으로) 나아가다, 진행되다

5.

해석 귀하의 주문서에 첨부된 송장은 상품이 구매되어진 소매 할인점의 위치 코드를 보여준다.

해설 빈칸 앞뒤에 완전한 절이 있으므로 빈칸은 관계부사 자리인데, 선행사가 retail outlet이므로 장소 관계부사 (A) where이 정답이다.

6.

해석 캐서린 밀스 씨는 연예 산업에서의 새로운 이야기들에 대해 얘기하는 라디오쇼를 진행한다.

해설 빈칸 앞뒤에 완전한 절이 있으므로 빈칸은 관계부사 자리인데, 선행사가 radio show이므로 장소 관계부사가 와야 한다. 따라서 where을 대신해 쓸 수 있는 (A) in which가 정답이다.

7.

해석 그 관리자는 20개의 매출이 발생하거나 일일 수익이 10,000달러를 넘는다면, 어느 것이 먼저 발생하든지 매장 문을 일찍 닫을 것이다.

해설 빈칸 앞에 완전한 구조의 문장이 있으므로, 빈칸부터 first까지가 부사절의 역할을 해야 하는데, 빈칸 뒤 문장 구조가 불완전하고, 두 가지 조건 중 하나를 선택하는 의미를 나타내므로 복합관계대명사 (C) whichever이 정답이다.

어휘 **exceed** ~을 넘다, 초과하다

8.

해석 모든 공장 근로자들은 경험이 아무리 많더라도 안전 교육 시간에 정기적으로 참석해야 하는 것은 의무적이다.

해설 빈칸 앞에 완전한 구조의 문장이 있으므로, 빈칸부터 be까지가 부사절의 역할을 해야 하는데, 빈칸 뒤에 형용사가 있으므로 이를 수식할 수 있는 복합관계부사 (D) however이 정답이다.

어휘 **mandatory** 의무적인

Check-up Test

1. (A)	**2.** (D)	**3.** (A)	**4.** (C)	**5.** (B)
6. (A)	**7.** (C)	**8.** (D)	**9.** (B)	**10.** (A)
11. (B)	**12.** (D)	**13.** (B)	**14.** (B)	**15.** (C)
16. (D)	**17.** (A)	**18.** (B)	**19.** (B)	**20.** (B)

1.

해석 그 작가는 책을 쓰는 동안 자신의 조사에 도움을 준 모든 사람들에게 감사를 표했다.

해설 빈칸 앞에 '모든 사람들'이라는 뜻의 부정대명사 all과 빈칸 뒤에 동사가 있으므로 주격 관계대명사 (A) who가 정답이다.

어휘 **acknowledge** ~에게 감사의 뜻을 표하다

2.

해석 비즈니스계에서 성공하는 것에 관한 책이 베스트셀러가 된 이베트 르그란데 씨가 올해의 문학 총회에서 기조연설을 하실 것입니다.

해설 콤마 사이에 위치한 절 앞에 주어가, 절 뒤에 동사가 있으므로 삽입절은 사람 선행사를 수식할 관계대명사절이다. 또한, 빈칸 뒤에 위치한 명사 books는 Yvette LeGrande 씨가 소유한 것이므로 소유격 관계대명사인 (D) whose가 정답이다.

어휘 **literature** 문학

3.

해석 비즈니스에서 일반적으로 사용되는 외국어를 배우는 것이 일자리를 얻는 데 도움이 될 수 있다.

해설 빈칸 뒤에 문장의 동사 can help가 있으므로 빈칸부터 business까지가 선행사인 a foreign language를 수식해야 하고, 빈칸 바로 뒤에 동사가 있으므로 주격 관계대명사 (A) that이 정답이다.

어휘 **secure** ~을 얻다, 고정시키다

4.

해석 다음 달에 신임 마케팅 이사로 우리 회사에 합류할 예정인 앨런비 씨는 4층에 있는 빈 사무실을 이용할 것이다.

해설 빈칸 앞에 사람 주어가, 빈칸 뒤에 문장의 동사 will take가 있으므로 빈칸부터 next month까지가 주어를 수식하는 관계대명사절이 되어야 한다. 따라서 빈칸 바로 뒤에 동사가 있고, 사람 선행사를 수식할 수 있는 주격 관계대명사 (C) who가 정답이다.

5.

해석 고객 서비스에 대한 질문에 대해 최고의 답변을 한 사람은 누구든지 채용하도록 하십시오.

해설 빈칸 앞에 동사가 있으므로 빈칸부터 문장 끝까지가 목적어 역할을 하는 명사절이 되어야 하는데, 빈칸 바로 뒤에 불완전한 절이 있으므로 '~하는 사람은 누구든'이라는 의미로 명사절 접속사 역할을 할 수 있는 복합관계대명사 (B) whoever가 정답이다.

6.

해석 그 음악 축제 주최자들은 무대 뒤쪽 구역을 개방할 것이라고 발표했으며, 이곳에서 VIP 입장권 소지자들이 일부 공연자들을 만날 수 있다.

해설 빈칸 앞뒤에 완전한 구조의 문장이 있으므로 관계부사 (A) where와 부사절 접속사 (D) as 중에서 정답을 골라야 한다. 그런데 빈칸 뒤의 절은 빈칸 앞에 위치한 장소 명사구 a backstage area를 수식하는 역할을 해야 자연스러우므로 (A) where가 정답이다.

7.

해석 스틸웨이브 메뉴팩처링 사는 공장에 9개의 조립 라인이 있는데, 그것들 중 몇 개는 결함이 있는 것으로 밝혀졌다.

해설 빈칸 앞에 수량 표현과 of가 있으므로 빈칸에는 관계대명사가 들어가야 하는데, 관계대명사가 대신하는 것이 assembly lines라는 사물이므로 (C) which가 정답이다.

8.

해석 직원들은 이번 주 금요일에 일찍 퇴근하거나 월요일 점심시간에 근무를 시작할 수 있으며, 어느 쪽이든 선호하는 것으로 할 수 있다.

해설 빈칸 앞뒤에 두 개의 절이 있으므로 빈칸은 접속사 자리이다. 빈칸 뒤에 위치한 절은 앞서 언급된 두 가지 근무 형태에 대한 선택의 의미를 나타내야 하므로 '~하는 어느 것이든'이라는 의미로 쓰이는 복합관계대명사 (D) whichever가 정답이다.

9.

해석 공장의 일일 생산률이 목표 수준보다 아래로 떨어질 때마다 제게 알려 주시기 바랍니다.

해설 빈칸 앞뒤로 두 개의 완전한 구조의 절이 있으므로 빈칸은 접속사 자리이다. 따라서 선택지 중 유일하게 접속사 역할을 할 수 있는 복합관계부사 (B) whenever가 정답이다.

어휘 **dip below** ~보다 아래로 떨어지다 **target level** 목표 수준 **altogether** 완전히, 전적으로, 모두 합쳐

10.

해석 제임스 골드만 씨의 새 영화를 위한 영화 음악은 많은 인상적인 노래들을 포함하는데, 그것들 중 여러 곡은 버트 시나이더 씨에 의해 작곡되었다.

해설 빈칸 바로 앞에 수량 표현과 of가 있으므로 빈칸에는 관계대명사가 들어가야 한다. 따라서 (A) which가 정답이다.

어휘 **soundtrack** 영화 음악, 사운드트랙 **compose** ~을 작곡하다

11.

해석 내년 4월 디트로이트에서 개최될 예정인 연례 글로벌 모터 무역 박람회는 참가하는 판매사의 수를 늘렸다.

해설 콤마로 된 삽입절 내에 있는 빈칸 앞에 사물명사가, 빈칸 뒤에 동사가 있으므로 빈칸은 사물 선행사를 수식할 수 있는 주격 관계대명사 (B) which가 정답이다.

12.

해석 사무실 관리자의 요청으로, 사무실에 매일 아침 가장 먼저 도착하는 사람은 누구든 에어컨을 켜야 한다.

해설 빈칸 뒤로 주어 없이 동사 is와 보어, to부정사구가 있고, 그 뒤로 또 다른 동사 should turn이 곧바로 이어지고 있으므로 빈칸에서부터 morning까지가 주어 역할을 하는 명사절이 되어야 한다. 또한, 사무실에 도착해 에어컨을 켜는 주체는 사람이어야 하므로 명사절의 역할을 할 수 있는 복합관계대명사 (D) whoever가 정답이다.

13.

해석 행사 참석자들이 어디든지 공간을 찾을 수 있다면 개인 차량들은 주차되어질 수 있다.

해설 빈칸 앞뒤에 완전한 구조의 절이 있으므로 빈칸은 복합관계부사 자리이다. 따라서 선택지에서 유일한 복합관계부사인 (B) wherever이 정답이다.

14.

해석 이사회 임원들이 우리 회사와 합병하는 것에 관심을 표현한 갤럭시 소프트웨어 사는 우리 대표이사와 회의를 잡았다.

해설 콤마로 된 삽입절 내에 있는 빈칸 앞에 사물명사가, 빈칸 바로 뒤에 주어와 동사, 그리고 목적어가 있으므로 빈칸은 소유격 관계대명사 자리이다. 따라서 (B) whose가 정답이다.

어휘 **merge with** ~와 합병하다

15.

해석 요리사 쿠슬레 씨는 자신이 인디고 레스토랑에서 요리하는 음식을 마음에 들어 하지만, 메뉴를 업데이트하고 싶어한다.

해설 빈칸 앞에 완전한 구조의 절이, 빈칸 뒤에 주어와 동사 그리고 전치사구로 구성된 불완전한 절이 있으므로 빈칸부터 Restaurant까지가 food를 수식하는 관계대명사절이 되어야 한다. 빈칸 뒤 절에 목적어가 없으므로 목적격 관계대명사 (C) which가 정답이다.

16.

해석 레논 어카운팅 사는 오직 신속하고 효율적으로 일하는 사무 보조 직원들만이 승진될 것이라고 공지했다.

해설 빈칸에 쓰일 관계사는 사람명사인 office assistants를 수식하면서 동사 work의 주어 역할을 해야 하므로 주격 관계대명사 (D) who가 정답이다.

17.

해석 기술 시장이 지난 분기 내에 아무리 급격하게 감소되었더라도, 블루테크 주식회사는 자사의 사업을 확장할 계획이다.

해설 콤마를 기준으로 완전한 구조의 절 두개가 연결되어 있으므로 빈칸이 속한 절은 부사의 역할을 해야 한다. 빈칸 뒤에 부사가 있으므로 '아무리 ~할지라도'라는 뜻을 가진 복합관계부사 (A) However이 정답이다.

18.

해석 우리가 지난달에 머물렀던 사파이어 쇼어 리조트는 공항에서 차로 10분밖에 걸리지 않는다.

해설 빈칸 뒤에 완전한 구조의 절과 문장의 동사 was가 있으므로 빈칸부터 last month까지가 주어인 The Sapphire Shores Resort를 수식하는 관계부사절이 되어야 한다. 선행사가 장소이므로 관계부사 where과 동일하게 사용할 수 있는 (B) in which가 정답이다.

19.

해석 톰슨 씨는 글로벌 솔루션스 사에서 우리의 많은 신입사원들에게 초기 교육을 위한 상담을 하는 선임 부장이다.

해설 빈칸 앞에 사람 선행사와 전치사가, 빈칸 뒤에 주어와 동사, 그리고 전치사구가 있으므로 사람 선행사를 수식하면서 전치사의 목적어 역할을 할 수 있는 목적격 관계대명사 (B) whom이 정답이다.

20.

해석 투숙객들은 비즈니스 센터와 다른 편의시설에 대한 완전한 이용권을 가지는데, 이는 퍼시픽 하이타워를 컨퍼런스 동안 머물기에 훌륭한 호텔로 만들어 준다.

해설 선택지가 관계사로 구성되어 있고, 빈칸 앞에 전치사 in이

있으므로 전치사의 목적어 역할을 할 수 있는 목적격 관계 대명사 (B) which가 정답이다.

Playlist 6
명사절 접속사 정답 3초컷 스킬

Practice

1. (A)	2. (A)	3. (C)	4. (A)

1.

해석 선전 일렉트로닉스 사는 선주문의 수에 기반해 자사 공장의 생산율을 증가시킬 것인지 결정할 것이다.

해설 빈칸 앞에 타동사 will determine과 전치사구가, 빈칸 뒤에 완전한 구조의 절이 있으므로 이 절이 동사의 목적어 역할을 하는 명사절이 되어야 한다. 동사 determine은 명사절 접속사 whether과 어울리므로 (A) whether가 정답이다.

2.

해석 그 점검은 조립 라인의 거의 모든 기계가 수리나 유지보수 작업을 필요로 한다는 것을 나타냈다.

해설 빈칸 앞에 타동사 indicated가, 빈칸 뒤에 완전한 구조의 절이 있으므로 이 절이 동사의 목적어 역할을 할 명사절이 되어야 한다. 따라서 빈칸에는 명사절 접속사가 필요한데 동사 indicate는 명사절 접속사 that과 어울리므로 (A) that이 정답이다.

3.

해석 새로운 복사기를 사용하는 방법을 알 필요가 있는 어떤 직원이든 유지보수팀의 벤 씨와 이야기하면 된다.

해설 빈칸 앞에 타동사 know가 있고, 빈칸 뒤에 to부정사가 있으므로 빈칸부터 photocopier까지가 동사 know의 목적어 역할을 해야 하는데 '새로운 복사기의 사용 방법에 대해 알고 싶은 직원'이라고 해석하는 것이 자연스러우므로 (C) how가 정답이다.

4.

해석 모든 행사 참석자들은 회사 연회 중에 그들이 먹고 싶어하는 것이 어떤 요리인지 결정할 필요가 있다.

해설 빈칸 앞에 타동사 decide가 있고, 빈칸 뒤에 명사가 있으므로 명사를 수식할 수 있으면서 동사의 목적어 역할을 할 수 있는 명사절 접속사 (A) which가 정답이다.

Check-up Test

1. (B)	2. (C)	3. (A)	4. (A)	5. (A)
6. (A)	7. (D)	8. (B)	9. (C)	10. (D)
11. (D)	12. (C)	13. (A)	14. (A)	15. (B)
16. (B)	17. (C)	18. (A)	19. (D)	20. (C)

1.

해석 공장 내의 모든 사고들은 직원들이 부상을 입든지 아니든지와 상관 없이 반드시 사고 일지에 기록되어야 한다.

해설 빈칸 앞에 전치사가 있고, 빈칸 뒤에 절이 있으므로 빈칸에는 전치사의 목적어 역할을 할 수 있으면서 절을 이끌 수 있는 명사절 접속사가 와야 한다. 따라서 (B) whether가 정답이다.

어휘 **incident log book** 사고 일지 **regardless of** ~에 상관없이

2.

해석 마케팅 컨설턴트 머피 씨는 모든 지사들이 적어도 한 주에 한 번씩 홍보 자료를 발송할 것을 제안했다.

해설 빈칸 앞에 동사 suggested가 있고, 빈칸 뒤에 완전한 구조의 절이 있으므로 빈칸부터 문장 끝까지가 타동사의 목적어 역할을 할 명사절이 되어야 한다. 따라서 빈칸은 명사절 접속사 자리인데, '발송할 것을 제안했다'라는 뜻이 되어야 자연스러우므로 '~라는 것'의 뜻을 가진 (C) that이 정답이다.

어휘 **send out** ~을 발송하다, 보내다

3.

해석 직원 카페테리아를 확장하는 것에 대한 갈랜드 씨의 최종 결정은 다음 3개월 동안 얼마나 많은 수의 직원들이 고용될 것인지에 기반할 것이다.

해설 빈칸 앞에 전치사가 있고, 빈칸 뒤에 완전한 구조의 절이 있으므로 빈칸부터 문장 끝까지가 전치사의 목적어 역할을 할 명사절이 되어야 하는데 빈칸 바로 뒤에 형용사 many가 있으므로 명사절 접속사 (A) how가 정답이다.

4.

해석 키시다 시장은 지역 주민들이 계획된 공항 건설에 대해 공청회에서 언급한 것에 대해 고려했다.

해설 빈칸 앞에 타동사 considered가 있고, 빈칸 뒤에 불완전한 절이 있으므로 빈칸에는 동사의 목적어 역할을 하면서 절을 이끌 수 있는 명사절 접속사 (A) what이 정답이다.

어휘 **mayor** 시장 **public debate** 공청회

5.

해석 경영진은 올해 어느 시범 사업에 투자할 것인지 결정하기 위해 내일 오전에 모일 것이다.

해설 빈칸 앞에 타동사 decide가 있고, 빈칸 뒤에 명사가 있으므로 동사의 목적어 역할을 할 수 있으면서 명사를 수식할 수 있는 (A) which가 정답이다.

어휘 **pilot project** 시범 사업

6.

해석 프로토 홈즈가 특별한 이유는 이 인테리어 디자인 회사가 최소 비용으로 고급의 디자인 특징들을 포함하는 방법을 알고 있기 때문이다.

해설 빈칸 앞에 타동사 knows가, 빈칸 뒤에 to부정사가 있으므로 동사의 목적어 역할을 하면서 뒤에 위치한 to부정사와 결합 가능한 (A) how가 정답이다.

어휘 **incorporate** ~을 포함하다, 통합하다

7.

해석 에듀라이트 전자가 한 달에 300,000대의 전자책 리더기 기기를 판매했다는 것은 전자책의 수요가 여전히 높다는 증거이다.

해설 빈칸 뒤에 완전한 구조의 절과 문장의 동사 is가 있으므로 빈칸부터 one month까지가 주어 역할을 해야 한다. 따라서 명사절을 이끌 수 있는 명사절 접속사 (D) That이 정답이다.

어휘 **unit** (기기의) 대

8.

해석 옥상 어디에 태양열 전지판이 위치하는지가 종종 얼마나 효율적으로 에너지를 전기로 변환할지를 결정한다.

해설 빈칸 뒤로 타동사 determines와 목적어 역할을 하는 명사절이 나오므로 빈칸부터 roof까지는 주어 역할을 하는 명사절이 되어야 한다. 빈칸 뒤에 절이 완전한 구조이고, 태양열 전지판이 위치하는(situated) 상태는 장소와 밀접한 관련이 있으므로 장소를 나타내는 명사절 접속사 (B) Where가 정답이다.

어휘 **solar panel** 태양열 전지판 **convert A into B** A를 B로 변환하다

9.

해석 린튼 테크놀로지 사가 다가오는 컨벤션에서 자사의 새로운 기기를 공개할 것인지는 시장 설문 조사 결과에 달려 있다.

해설 빈칸 뒤에 두 개의 동사가 있으므로 빈칸부터 convention까지가 주어의 역할을 하는 명사절이 되어야 한다. 따라서 명사절 접속사 (C) Whether가 정답이다.

어휘 **consequently** 결과적으로

10.

해석 재정부가 자금 지원 서류를 검토하자마자, 그들은 누구의 지원서가 수락되었는지 결정할 것이다.

해설 빈칸 앞에 타동사 determine이, 빈칸 뒤에 명사 주어와 동사가 있으므로 빈칸부터 끝까지가 determine의 목적어 역할을 해야 한다. 따라서 명사 바로 앞에 쓸 수 있는 명사절 접속사 (D) whose가 정답이다.

어휘 **Ministry of Economy and Finance** 재정부

11.

해석 오크우드 레인에 있는 이 작은 매장에 대해 특별히 놀라운 것은 그곳이 지역에서 가장 다양한 전자기기를 갖고 있다는 것이다.

해설 빈칸부터 문장의 동사 is까지 두 개의 동사가 있으므로 빈칸부터 Oakwood Lane까지가 주어 역할을 할 수 있는 명사절이 되어야 하는데, 빈칸 뒤에 불완전한 절이 있고 '~하는 것'으로 해석하는 것이 자연스러우므로 (D) What이 정답이다.

12.

해석 로버트 밀러 씨의 새로운 영화가 그의 이전 영화처럼 비평가들에 의해 높게 평가되는지는 지켜봐야 한다.

해설 빈칸 앞에 주어와 동사가 있으므로 빈칸부터 문장 끝까지가 목적어 역할을 해야 한다. 따라서 빈칸은 명사절 접속사 자리이므로 선택지 중 유일한 명사절 접속사 (C) whether이 정답이다.

어휘 **it remains to be seen** ~하는지 지켜봐야 한다, 두고봐야 한다 **praised** 평가된, 칭찬 받는

13.

해석 가리발디 씨는 누가 그의 이름을 영양 보충제 회사의 우편물 목록에 추가했는지 알아내고 싶어했다.

해설 빈칸 앞에 타동사 find out이 있고, 빈칸 뒤에 불완전한 절이 있으므로 빈칸은 동사의 목적어 역할을 할 명사절 접속사 자리이다. 따라서 (A) who가 정답이다.

어휘 **mailing** 우편물 **nutritional** 영양의 **supplement** 보충(제)

14.

해석 호록스 씨는 에비 이노베이션 파크에 있는 비어 있는 부지로 회사를 이전할지를 결정해야만 한다.

해설 빈칸 앞에 동사 decide가, 빈칸 뒤에 to부정사가 있으므로 빈칸은 to부정사와 함께 타동사의 목적어 역할을 할 수 있

어야 한다. 따라서 명사절 접속사 (A) whether이 정답이다.

어휘 lot 부지, 특정 지역

15.

해석 아이디리스 IT 솔루션즈 사의 직원 안내서는 직원들에게 제공된 물품들이 회사를 떠나기 전에 반납되어야 한다는 것을 명시한다.

해설 빈칸 앞에 동사 states가, 빈칸 뒤의 완전한 절이 있으므로 빈칸부터 문장 끝까지가 타동사의 목적어 역할을 하는 명사절이 되어야 한다. 따라서 명사절 접속사 (B) that이 정답이다.

16.

해석 그 인사부장은 아직 어떤 상을 직원들이 받게 될지 발표하지 않았다.

해설 빈칸 앞에 동사 has not announced가 있고, 빈칸 바로 뒤에 명사와 절이 있으므로 타동사의 목적어 역할을 할 수 있으면서 명사를 수식할 수 있는 명사절 접속사 (B) which가 정답이다.

17.

해석 김 씨는 컨벤션 센터에 숙박시설이 있는지 문의하기 위해 무역 박람회 주최자들에게 연락했다.

해설 빈칸 앞에 타동사 ask가 있고, 빈칸 뒤에 완전한 구조의 절이 있으므로 빈칸부터 문장 끝까지가 목적어 역할을 할 수 있는 명사절이 되어야 하므로 ask와 어울리는 명사절 접속사 (C) whether이 정답이다.

18.

해석 그 연구는 그랜포드 대학의 거의 모든 졸업생들이 장기 고용 계약을 획득하는 데 성공했다는 것을 보여주었다.

해설 빈칸 앞에 동사 showed가, 빈칸 뒤에 완전한 구조의 절이 있으므로 빈칸부터 문장 끝까지가 타동사의 목적어 역할을 하는 명사절이 되어야 한다. 또한, '연구가 ~한 것을 보여주었다'는 뜻이 되어야 자연스러우므로 '~라는 것'이라는 뜻의 명사절 접속사 (A) that이 정답이다.

19.

해석 새로운 그린웨이즈 은행 모바일 앱은 고객들에게 언제 은행을 방문할지에 대해 선택할 수 있다는 점에서 더 많은 유연성을 준다.

해설 빈칸 앞에 동명사 형태의 동사 choosing이 있고, 빈칸 뒤에 to부정사가 있으므로 빈칸은 명사절 접속사 자리인데 모바일 앱으로 은행 방문 시간을 정할 수 있다고 해석하는 것이 자연스러우므로 명사절 접속사 (D) when이 정답이다.

어휘 flexibility 유연성

20.

해석 블루아크 직물회사를 투어하는 방문객들은 자사의 실크 직물들이 생산 라인에서 어떻게 만들어지는지를 볼 수 있다.

해설 빈칸 앞에 타동사 see가 있고, 빈칸 뒤에 완전한 구조의 절이 있으므로 빈칸부터 문장 끝까지가 동사의 목적어 역할을 해야 한다. 또한, 공장 방문객들이 생산 라인에서 볼 수 있는 것은 직물이 만들어지는 방법이므로 (C) how가 정답이다.

어휘 fabric 직물

Playlist 7
점수 상승 보장하는 to부정사 vs. 동명사 구분법

Practice

1. (A) **2.** (B) **3.** (C) **4.** (B)

1.

해석 효율적인 조언을 위해 많은 업무량이 있는 부장들은 우리의 즉석 메시지 소프트웨어를 사용하도록 허용된다.

해설 빈칸 앞에 제시된 are allowed는 5형식 동사의 수동태이므로 to부정사를 목적격 보어로 가진다. 따라서 (A) to use가 정답이다.

어휘 workflow 업무량, 업무 속도 counseling 조언, 상담

2.

해석 수마트라 커피 하우스는 영업 25주년을 기념하기 위해 한정판 음료를 출시했다.

해설 빈칸 앞에 완전한 구조의 절이 있고, 빈칸 뒤에 명사구 목적어와 전치사구가 있으므로 빈칸부터 문장 끝까지가 부사의 역할을 해야 한다. 따라서 부사적 용법의 (B) to celebrate가 정답이다.

어휘 in business 영업 중인

3.

해석 콘서트 방문객들은 그 공연이 시작되는 것을 기다리는데 너무 많은 시간을 소비한 것에 대해 불평했다.

해설 빈칸 앞에 「spend + 시간」 표현이 있으므로 빈칸은 동명사 자리이다. 따라서 (C) waiting이 정답이다.

어휘 concertgoer 콘서트 방문객

4.

해석 트리덴트 모터스 사의 대표이사는 더 많은 직원들을 수용하기 위해 제조 공장을 확장하는 것을 고려할 것이다.

해설 빈칸 앞에 있는 동사 consider는 동명사를 목적어로 가지는 동사이므로 (B) expanding이 정답이다.

Check-up Test

1. (B)	**2.** (C)	**3.** (D)	**4.** (A)	**5.** (B)
6. (B)	**7.** (B)	**8.** (A)	**9.** (C)	**10.** (B)
11. (C)	**12.** (A)	**13.** (A)	**14.** (A)	**15.** (C)
16. (C)	**17.** (D)	**18.** (A)	**19.** (A)	**20.** (B)

1.

해석 호텔 손님들은 지역 명소들과 활동들에 관한 안내책자를 위해 관광 안내 센터를 방문하는 것이 권고된다.

해설 빈칸 앞에 위치한 are advised는 5형식 동사 수동태이므로 목적격 보어 역할을 할 수 있는 to부정사 (B) to visit이 정답이다.

2.

해석 많은 카페와 레스토랑들이 현재 플라스틱 오염을 방지하기 위해 재활용 가능한 금속 빨대를 제공하고 있다.

해설 빈칸 앞에 완전한 구조의 문장이 있으므로 빈칸부터 문장 끝까지가 부사의 역할을 해야 한다. 따라서 재활용 가능한 금속 빨대를 제공하는 목적을 나타내는 to 부정사 (C) to prevent가 정답이다.

어휘 **reusable** 재활용 가능한 **straw** 빨대

3.

해석 북극 탐험대장은 배낭의 짐을 덜어 줌으로써 대원들 사이에 피로를 줄일 수 있기를 바랐다.

해설 빈칸 앞에 전치사 by가, 빈칸 뒤에 명사구가 있으므로 빈칸은 전치사의 목적어 역할을 하면서 그 뒤에 위치한 명사구를 목적어로 취해야 한다. 따라서 동명사 (D) lightening이 정답이다.

어휘 **the Arctic** 북극 **expedition** 탐험대, 원정대 **fatigue** 피로 **load** 짐의 양, 적재량 **lighten** v. ~을 덜어 주다, 가볍게 해 주다

4.

해석 이번 달에 피트니스 센터에 가입한 모든 사람들은 다음 주 환영 시간에 참석하도록 상기시켜졌다.

해설 빈칸 앞에 위치한 are reminded는 5형식 동사의 수동태이므로 목적격 보어 역할을 할 수 있는 to부정사 (A) to attend가 정답이다.

5.

해석 그 엔지니어에 따르면, 보안 시스템은 3년마다 업그레이드 되어야 한다.

해설 빈칸 앞에 제시된 동사 needs는 to부정사를 목적어로 취하는 동사이므로 (B) to be upgraded가 정답이다.

6.

해석 직원들의 교대근무 일정을 짜는 것은 라 벨레 비스트로에서 관리자의 가장 중요한 책무 중 하나이다.

해설 빈칸 뒤에 명사와 전치사구, 그리고 문장의 동사 is가 있으므로 빈칸부터 staff까지가 주어의 역할을 해야 하는데, 빈칸 뒤 명사를 목적어로 취할 수 있어야 하므로 동명사 (B) Scheduling이 정답이다.

7.

해석 윌로우 어패럴 사는 새로운 겨울 시즌 재고를 위한 창고 공간을 만들기 위해 모든 여름 의류에 대해 50퍼센트에서 80퍼센트 할인을 제공하는 것을 계획한다.

해설 빈칸 앞에 제시된 동사 plans는 to부정사를 목적어로 가지는 동사이므로 (B) to offer이 정답이다.

8.

해석 비즈니스 100 강의는 비즈니스 상의 아주 다양한 직책들을 위한 능력을 활용하는 데 어려움이 있는 사람들에게 도움을 준다.

해설 빈칸 앞에 have difficulty in이 있으므로 빈칸에는 전치사 in의 목적어 역할을 할 수 있으면서, 빈칸 뒤에 제시된 명사구를 목적어로 가질 수 있는 동명사 (A) utilizing이 정답이다.

9.

해석 향상된 성능을 위해, 평평하지 않은 지면에서 러닝머신을 운행하는 것을 피하십시오.

해설 빈칸 앞에 제시된 동사 avoid는 동명사를 목적어로 가지는 동사이므로 (C) operating이 정답이다.

어휘 **uneven** 평평하지 않은, 울퉁불퉁한 **surface** 지면, 표면

10.

해석 이번 11월부터, RX 제약회사는 빠른 효과가 있는 최신 진통제 제품군을 테스트하는데 많은 시간을 보낼 것이다.

해설 빈칸 앞에 「spend + 시간」 표현이 있고, 빈칸 뒤에 명사구가 있으므로 빈칸에는 이 구조와 함께 쓰이면서 뒤의 명사구를 목적어로 취할 수 있는 동명사가 와야 한다. 따라서

(B) testing이 정답이다.

어휘 **quick-relief** 빠른 효과가 있는, 즉효가 있는 **pain medication** 진통제

11.

해석 작은 섬들을 가로질러 흩어져 있는 다양한 와이너리들이 있기 때문에 뉴질랜드의 페리 서비스는 관광객들이 여행하기 편리한 방법이다.

해설 빈칸 앞에 명사 way가 있으므로 이 명사를 수식할 수 있는 to부정사 (C) to travel이 정답이다.

어휘 **winery** 와이너리, 양조장 **scattered** 흩어져 있는

12.

해석 연예계에서의 경력을 추구하는 것에 대해 생각하고 있는 가수와 댄서들은 명성 있는 기획사와 계약하도록 권고된다.

해설 빈칸 앞에 전치사 about이, 빈칸 뒤에 명사구가 있으므로 전치사의 목적어 역할을 하면서 명사구를 목적어로 취할 수 있는 동명사 (A) pursuing이 정답이다.

어휘 **reputable** 명성 있는, 평판이 좋은 **management agency** 기획사 **pursue** ~을 추구하다

13.

해석 재무 설계사는 사무실 유지보수 비용에 대한 변동사항을 성공적으로 도입하기 위해 몇 가지 제안을 했다.

해설 빈칸 앞에 전치사 for와 부사가, 빈칸 뒤에 명사가 있으므로 전치사의 목적어 역할을 하면서 부사의 수식을 받을 수 있는 동명사 (A) introducing이 정답이다.

어휘 **introductive** 초입의

14.

해석 모든 운전자들이 교통법규를 지키도록 요구됨에도 불구하고, 많은 운전자들은 그것들을 무시하고 교통사고를 유발한다.

해설 빈칸 앞에 5형식 동사의 수동태 are required가 있으므로 빈칸에는 목적격 보어 역할을 할 수 있는 to부정사가 와야 한다. 따라서 (A) to obey가 정답이다.

어휘 **motorist** 운전자 **disregard** ~을 무시하다

15.

해석 피사 이탈리아 레스토랑은 채식 식사 손님들에게 더욱 다양한 선택권을 제공하기 위해 피자 토핑 종류에 대한 확대를 고려할 것이다.

해설 빈칸 앞에 위치한 consider는 동명사를 목적어로 가지는 동사이므로 (C) enlarging이 정답이다.

어휘 **enlarge** ~을 확대하다, 확장하다 **enlargement** 확대, 확장

16.

해석 만료일 전에 부동산 임대 계약을 끝낼 계획인 임차인은 반드시 그들의 임대인에게 서면으로 알려야 한다.

해설 빈칸 앞에 관계대명사 who가, 빈칸 뒤에 to부정사가 있으므로 빈칸에는 관계대명사절의 동사 역할을 하면서 to부정사를 목적어로 가질 수 있는 동사가 필요하다. 따라서 (C) intend가 정답이다.

어휘 **expiry** 만료, 만기 **in writing** 서면으로

17.

해석 싱가포르에서 가장 큰 국내선 항공사는 더 많은 고객들을 끌어들일 방법으로서 자사의 요금을 줄이기로 결정했다.

해설 빈칸 앞에 명사 decision이 있고, 빈칸 뒤에 명사구가 있으므로 이 명사구를 목적어로 취할 수 있으면서 명사 decision을 꾸며줄 수 있는 to부정사 (D) to reduce가 정답이다.

어휘 **domestic** 국내(선)의

18.

해석 그 세미나 슬라이드들은 생산성을 높이기 위해 직원 보상 프로그램을 시행할 것을 제안한다.

해설 빈칸 앞에 동사 suggest가, 빈칸 뒤에 명사구가 있으므로 빈칸에는 이 명사구를 목적어로 취할 수 있는 동명사 (A) implementing이 정답이다.

어휘 **implement** ~을 시행하다, 실행하다

19.

해석 시그널스트림 방송사는 주식 투자를 위한 최신 세계 경제 뉴스를 전달하는 데 전념하고 있다.

해설 빈칸 앞에 is committed to가, 빈칸 뒤에 명사구가 있으므로 빈칸에는 전치사 to의 목적어 역할을 하면서 이 명사구를 목적어로 취할 수 있는 동명사 (A) delivering이 정답이다.

어휘 **broadcasting** 방송사 **stock** 주식

20.

해석 에스파이어 은행의 보안 소프트웨어는 네트워크 보안을 강화하기 위해 정기적인 업데이트를 제공해왔다.

해설 빈칸 앞에 완전한 구조의 문장이 있고, 빈칸 바로 뒤에 동사원형이 있으므로 빈칸부터 문장 끝까지가 부사의 역할을 해야 한다. 따라서 목적을 나타내는 to부정사 관용 표현 (B) in order to가 정답이다.

어휘 **routine** 정기적인, 일상의 **strengthen** ~을 강화하다

Playlist 8
고득점 필수 포인트 분사&분사구문

Practice

1. (B)	**2.** (D)	**3.** (A)	**4.** (C)

1.

해석 우리 기술 안전팀의 주요 책무는 어떤 손상된 기계 부품에 대해 확인하는 것이다.

해설 빈칸 뒤에 명사구가 있으므로 빈칸에는 이를 수식할 수 있는 형용사가 와야 한다. 따라서 이러한 역할을 할 수 있으면서 과거분사 형태로 굳어져 사용하는 (B) damaged가 정답이다.

어휘 **component** 부품, 구성품

2.

해석 해리스 씨는 전 직원들을 위한 야유회에 자금을 조달하기 위해 사업 계좌에 돈이 충분히 남아 있는지 확인했다.

해설 빈칸 앞에 완전한 구성의 절이 있으므로 빈칸부터 account까지가 분사구로서 명사 money를 수식하는 구조가 되어야 한다. 따라서 이러한 역할을 할 수 있으면서 현재분사 형태로 굳어진 (D) remaining이 정답이다.

어휘 **excursion** 야유회, 소풍

3.

해석 셀리나 멕스웰 씨는 그녀의 음악으로 수많은 상을 받아왔음에도 불구하고, 그녀는 콘서트 투어를 하는 많은 곳을 다 팔려고 분투했다.

해설 빈칸 앞에 접속사가, 빈칸 뒤에 명사구가 있으므로 빈칸은 이 명사구를 목적어로 취할 수 있는 현재분사 자리이다. 그런데 콤마 뒤에 있는 주절의 동사의 시제가 과거이고, 셀리나 맥스웰 씨가 상을 받아 온 시점은 콘서트 투어 자리를 판매하기 전이므로 완료시제 (A) having received가 정답이다.

어휘 **struggle to do** ~하려고 분투하다 **sell out** ~을 다 팔다

4.

해석 부정확하게 설치된다면, 태양광 전지판은 효율적인 속도로 전기를 생성하는 데 실패할 지도 모른다.

해설 빈칸 앞에 접속사가, 빈칸 뒤에 목적어 없이 부사가 있으므로 과거분사 (C) installed가 정답이다.

Check-up Test

1. (B)	**2.** (B)	**3.** (D)	**4.** (A)	**5.** (A)
6. (C)	**7.** (B)	**8.** (A)	**9.** (C)	**10.** (C)
11. (B)	**12.** (A)	**13.** (D)	**14.** (A)	**15.** (B)
16. (B)	**17.** (D)	**18.** (C)	**19.** (B)	**20.** (C)

1.

해석 회사 정책에 대한 최근의 여러 변화로 인해, 모든 직원들이 개정된 버전의 직원 안내서를 받을 것이다.

해설 빈칸이 관사와 명사 사이에 위치해 있으므로 빈칸은 명사를 수식할 형용사 또는 분사가 쓰일 자리인데, 안내서는 사람에 의해 개정되므로 과거분사인 (B) revised가 정답이다.

2.

해석 모든 주방기구는 음식 준비를 위해 사용되기 전에 반드시 살균 처리되어야 한다.

해설 빈칸 앞에 be동사가 있으므로 be동사와 결합 가능한 과거분사 (B) sanitized와 현재분사 (C) sanitizing 중에서 정답을 골라야 한다. 그런데 sanitize가 타동사이고, 빈칸 뒤에 목적어가 없으므로 수동태를 구성할 수 있는 과거분사 (B) sanitized가 정답이다.

어휘 **kitchen utensils** 주방용품 **sanitize** ~을 살균하다

3.

해석 면접 과정에서 남은 참가자들은 다음 주 금요일에 있을 최종 평가에 참석하도록 요청받을 것이다.

해설 빈칸이 관사와 명사 사이에 위치해 있으므로 빈칸은 명사를 수식할 형용사 또는 분사 자리이다. 선택지에 형용사가 없으므로 분사를 골라야 하는데, remain은 현재분사 형태로 굳어져 사용하므로 (D) remaining이 정답이다.

어휘 **remain** 남아있다, 유지되다 **remainder** 나머지

4.

해석 마린 네비 주식회사는 낚싯배와 다른 선박들을 위한 위성 네비게이션 기기의 선도적인 제조사이다.

해설 빈칸이 관사와 명사 사이에 위치해 있으므로 빈칸에는 형용사 또는 분사가 와야 하는데, 선택지에 제시된 동사 lead는 현재분사 형태로 굳어져 사용하므로 (A) leading이 정답이다.

어휘 **satellite** 위성 **vessel** (대형) 선박, 배

5.

해석 글리터 이벤트 플래너스 사는 첫 상담 시간 동안 고객 맞춤

의 선택사항들에 대해 상세히 설명해준다.

해설 빈칸 뒤에 명사가 위치해 있으므로 빈칸은 형용사 역할을 할 분사 자리인데, options는 사람에 의해 맞춤 제작되는 대상에 해당되므로 과거분사 (A) customized가 정답이다.

6.

해석 디시 공원은 제한적인 대중교통 이용 문제 때문에 음악 축제 장소로 좋지 못한 선택지이다.

해설 빈칸이 소유격과 명사 사이에 위치해 있으므로 빈칸은 명사를 수식할 수 있는 분사 자리이다. 대중교통에 대한 이용은 사람에 의해 제한되기 때문에 과거분사 (C) limited가 정답이다.

7.

해석 보안 자문 공석에 대한 자격을 갖춘 모든 후보자들은 유사한 직무에서 최소 4년간의 경력을 지녀야 한다.

해설 빈칸에는 빈칸 뒤에 위치한 명사를 수식할 형용사 또는 분사가 와야 하므로 '자격을 갖춘, 적격인'이라는 의미로 쓰이면서 과거분사 형태로 굳어져 사용하는 (B) qualified가 정답이다.

8.

해석 차장님이 인턴들에게 실무 교육을 제공하는 동안 그들의 업무 능력을 평가할 것이다.

해설 빈칸 앞에 접속사가, 빈칸 뒤에 주어 없이 명사구가 있으므로 빈칸에는 명사구를 목적어로 취할 현재분사가 와야 한다. 따라서 (A) providing이 정답이다.

어휘 **on-the-job** 실무의, 현장의 **assistant office manager** 차장

9.

해석 사용자 안내서는 제품 조립과 유지보수에 대한 상세한 안내사항을 담고 있다.

해설 빈칸 앞에 동사가, 빈칸 뒤에 명사가 있으므로 빈칸에는 명사를 수식할 수 있는 분사가 와야 하는데, 안내사항은 사람에 의해 설명되는 것이므로 과거분사 (C) detailed가 정답이다.

10.

해석 동봉된 안내책자는 보야저 로지스틱스 사에 의해 제공되는 모든 서비스들을 명시하고 있고, 귀하께서 문의하신 것들에 대해 제가 빨간색으로 표시해 놓았습니다.

해설 빈칸 앞에 명사 목적어가, 빈칸 뒤에 전치사구가 있으므로 빈칸에는 이 전치사구와 함께 명사를 뒤에서 수식할 수 있는 과거분사 (C) offered가 정답이다.

어휘 **leaflet** 안내책자, 전단지 **state** ~을 명시하다, 언급하다 **mark** ~을 표시하다

11.

해석 줄리안 씨의 기조 연설에서, 그녀는 성공적인 사업가가 되기 위해 취해 온 과정들을 설명했다.

해설 빈칸 앞에 관사가, 빈칸 뒤에 명사가 있으므로 빈칸에는 명사를 수식할 수 있는 분사가 필요하다. 따라서 (B) challenging이 정답이다.

어휘 **keynote address** 기조 연설 **entrepreneur** 사업가, 기업가

12.

해석 제안된 직원 인센티브 제도는 직원 생산성과 노동자들의 사기 둘 모두를 향상시키기 위해 고안된 것이다.

해설 빈칸이 관사와 명사구 사이에 위치해 있으므로 빈칸은 명사구를 수식할 분사 자리이다. 그런데 employee incentive scheme은 사람에 의해 제안되는 대상이므로 과거분사 (A) proposed가 정답이다.

어휘 **scheme** 제도, 계획 **morale** 사기, 의욕

13.

해석 구시가 투어는 투어 참가자들이 늦어도 오전 10시까지는 지정된 장소에 도착할 것을 권고한다.

해설 빈칸 앞에 관사가, 빈칸 뒤에 명사가 있으므로 빈칸에는 명사를 수식할 수 있는 분사가 필요한데, 투어 참가자들이 모여야 하는 장소는 사람에 의해 정해진 것이므로 과거분사 (D) designated가 정답이다.

어휘 **no later than** 늦어도 ~까지는 **designate** ~을 지정하다 **designation** 지정

14.

해석 행사 기획을 위한 추가 시간을 받았음에도 불구하고, 로우든 씨는 연회 참석자들의 기대치를 맞추는 데 실패했다.

해설 빈칸 앞에 접속사가, 빈칸 뒤에 주어 없이 명사구가 있으므로 빈칸에는 분사가 와야 하는데, 행사 기획을 위한 추가 시간을 받은 시점이 기대치를 맞추는 데 실패한 시점보다 과거이므로 (A) having received가 정답이다.

15.

해석 버스 터미널의 약국은 24시간 열려 있는데, 이는 탑승객들이 버스가 도착하는 것을 기다리는 동안 의료 서비스를 이용할 수 있도록 보장한다.

해설 빈칸 앞에 완전한 구조의 문장이, 빈칸 뒤에 that절이 있으

므로 이 that절을 목적어로 취하면서 접속사 없이 절을 연결할 수 있는 현재분사 (B) ensuring이 정답이다.

어휘 **open round the clock** 24시간 열려 있는

16.

해석 파란 선들로 강조된 주차 공간은 시 의회를 방문하는 장애인들을 위해 따로 남겨져 있다.

해설 빈칸 앞에 명사구가, 빈칸 뒤에 전치사구가 있으므로 빈칸에는 이 전치사구와 함께 뒤에서 명사구를 수식해줄 수 있는 과거분사가 와야 한다. 따라서 (B) highlighted가 정답이다.

어휘 **reserve** (자리 등을) 따로 남겨두다, 잡아두다 **the disabled** 장애인, 몸이 불편한 사람 **highlight** ~을 강조하다

17.

해석 싱가폴에 본사가 있는 인정 받는 회사인 프리미어 부동산 그룹은 외국인 직원들에게 주거 서비스에 대한 지원을 하고 있다.

해설 빈칸 앞에 관사가, 빈칸 뒤에 명사구가 있으므로 빈칸에는 명사구를 수식할 분사가 와야 하는데, 회사는 사람들에 의해 인정 받는 것이므로 과거분사 (D) established가 정답이다.

18.

해석 떠나는 세입자들은 반드시 1층에 있는 아파트 건물 관리자에게 주차 허가증을 제출해야 한다.

해설 빈칸 뒤에 명사가 있으므로 빈칸에는 명사를 수식할 수 있는 분사가 와야 하는데, 세입자는 스스로 떠나는 주체이므로 능동의 의미의 현재분사 (C) Departing이 정답이다.

19.

해석 직원 교육이나 회의를 위해 사용할 때 대회의실을 깨끗하고 잘 정돈된 상태로 유지하십시오.

해설 빈칸 앞에 명령문인 완전한 구조의 절이 있고, 빈칸 뒤에 현재분사로 시작하는 분사구문이 있으므로 빈칸에는 접속사가 와야 한다. 따라서 (B) when과 (D) whereas 중에 정답을 골라야 하는데, 대회의실을 깨끗하고 정돈된 상태로 유지해야 하는 시점은 교육이나 회의를 위해 대회의실을 사용할 때이므로 '~할 때'라는 뜻의 (B) when이 정답이다.

어휘 **tidy** 잘 정돈된, 말끔한

20.

해석 하버스톤 은행의 회계부는 다음 분기를 위한 자사의 목표들을 간략히 서술한 재무 보고서를 발표했다.

해설 빈칸 앞에 주어와 동사 그리고 명사구 목적어가, 빈칸 뒤에 명사구가 있으므로 빈칸은 명사구를 목적어로 가지면서 빈칸 앞 명사구를 수식해줄 수 있는 현재분사 자리이다. 따라서 (C) outlining이 정답이다.

Playlist 9
만점을 부르는 비교구문&가정법 정복하기

Practice

1. (C)	**2.** (D)	**3.** (B)	**4.** (D)

1.

해석 테이크얼롱 인더스트리 사의 상업 프로판 히터는 더 넓은 구역에 더 많은 온기를 전달한다.

해설 빈칸 뒤에 명사가 있으므로 빈칸에는 형용사가 와야 하는데, 의미상 '더 넓은 구역에 더 많은 온기를 전달한다'고 해석하는 것이 자연스러우므로 비교급 (C) wider가 정답이다.

어휘 **warmth** 온기, 따뜻함 **wideness** 넓이, 폭

2.

해석 카이버 강이 지난 7월 장마철 동안 여태껏 가장 높은 수위로 올라갔다.

해설 빈칸 뒤에 명사가 있으므로 빈칸은 형용사 자리인데, 빈칸 앞에 소유격이 있고 의미상 '특정 기간 내 가장 수위가 높았다'고 해석하는 것이 자연스러우므로 최상급 (D) highest가 정답이다.

어휘 **monsoon season** 장마철

3.

해석 맨체스터로부터의 크래머 씨의 기차가 일정대로 도착했다면, 그는 교육 워크숍의 첫 시간에 참석할 수 있었을 것이다.

해설 빈칸 앞에 If와 과거완료시제 had arrived가 있으므로 (B) could have attended가 정답이다.

어휘 **on schedule** 일정대로

4.

해석 베이뷰 이글스가 전망이 있는 그 투수에게 계약을 제안하지 않았다면, 다른 야구팀이 그렇게 했을 것이다.

해설 빈칸 앞에 If가 생략되어 도치된 과거완료시제 Had not offered가 있으므로 (D) would have done이 정답이다.

어휘 **pitcher** 투수

Check-up Test

1. (D)	**2.** (C)	**3.** (D)	**4.** (C)	**5.** (B)
6. (C)	**7.** (B)	**8.** (D)	**9.** (A)	**10.** (D)
11. (D)	**12.** (A)	**13.** (D)	**14.** (A)	**15.** (D)
16. (D)	**17.** (C)	**18.** (C)	**19.** (B)	**20.** (C)

1.

해석 글리타운 커뮤니티에서 로저 딜런 씨보다 더 활동적으로 주차장 공사 프로젝트의 철회를 위해 싸운 사람은 없었다.

해설 빈칸 앞에 자동사 fought가, 빈칸 뒤에 전치사구가 있으므로 빈칸은 부사 자리인데, 뒤에 제시된 than과 어울려야 하므로 비교급 (D) more energetically가 정답이다.

어휘 **energetically** 활동적으로, 열성적으로

2.

해석 모든 핵심 요점들을 심도 있게 설명하는 것이 발표의 가장 중요한 측면이다.

해설 빈칸 앞에 정관사가, 빈칸 뒤에 명사가 있으므로 빈칸은 형용사 자리이다. 또한 정관사 the와 어울리면서 의미상 '~하는 것이 가장 중요하다'라고 해석하는 것이 자연스러우므로 최상급이 빈칸에 와야 한다. 따라서 (C) most important가 정답이다.

어휘 **in depth** 심도 있게, 깊이

3.

해석 새로운 비스타 8 조립 기계는 공장 근로자들이 그들의 업무를 훨씬 더 빠르게 완료하도록 할 것이다.

해설 빈칸 앞에 완전한 구조의 to부정사가 있으므로 빈칸은 to부정사로 쓰인 동사 complete을 수식할 부사 자리인데, 빈칸 앞에 제시된 much의 수식을 받을 수 있어야 한다. 따라서 비교급 (D) more efficiently가 정답이다.

4.

해석 와이스 씨의 항공편이 일정대로 도착했었다면 그녀는 새 공장 견학에 참가할 수 있었을 것이다.

해설 주절의 동사가 would have p.p.일 경우, if절의 동사는 가정법 과거완료를 나타내는 had p.p.여야 하므로 (C) had arrived가 정답이다.

5.

해석 가능한 한 많은 기술 회사들에 투자하는 것은 심슨 씨에게 매우 수익이 높은 것으로 증명되었다.

해설 빈칸 뒤에 복수명사와 as가 있으므로 이 원급 비교 표현과 함께 쓰일 수 있는 (B) as many가 정답이다.

6.

해석 요리사 빌링스 씨는 그 음식 평론가가 맛을 봤던 것 중에서 가장 창의적인 메뉴 중의 하나를 준비했다.

해설 빈칸 앞에 위치한 the most와 어울려 최상급 표현을 구성해야 하는데, 빈칸 뒤에 제시된 명사구를 수식해야 하므로 형용사 (C) creative가 정답이다.

어휘 **critic** 평론가 **sample** v. ~을 한 번 맛 보다, 시식하다 **creation** 창작(품)

7.

해석 노스 스타 에너지 사는 모든 고객 불만사항을 가능한 한 빠르게 해결하기 위해 자사의 콜센터 직원들을 교육시킨다.

해설 빈칸 앞뒤에 as가 제시되어 있으므로 원급 (B) quickly가 정답이다.

8.

해석 장기 근로자들은 각자의 능력과 경험이 회사에 중요한 가치를 지닌다고 생각할 경우에 더 높은 급여를 요구할지도 모른다.

해설 빈칸 앞에 타동사가, 빈칸 뒤에 명사 목적어와 if 부사절이 있으므로 빈칸은 명사를 수식할 형용사 자리이다. 또한, 장기 근무한 직원들이 기존 급여보다 더 높은 급여를 요구할 수 있다는 비교의 의미가 되어야 자연스러우므로 비교급 형용사 (D) higher가 정답이다.

어휘 **of significant value** 중요한 가치를 지니는

9.

해석 정부는 홍수 구호 활동이 가장 긴급한 지역에 인력과 비상 물품을 보냈다.

해설 빈칸 앞에 be동사와 최상급 표현 most가 있으므로 빈칸에는 most와 함께 최상급을 구성할 수 있는 형용사가 와야 한다. 따라서 (A) urgent가 정답이다.

어휘 **emergency supplies** 비상 물품, 긴급 보급품 **flood** 홍수 **relief aid** 구호 활동 **urgency** 긴급(함)

10.

해석 덴버에서 판매되는 가장 다양한 부동산을 에메랄드 부동산 웹 사이트에서 보실 수 있습니다.

해설 빈칸 앞에 정관사가, 빈칸 뒤에 명사가 있으므로 빈칸에는 형용사가 와야 하는데 빈칸 앞에 the와 빈칸 뒤에 범위를 나타내는 in 전치사구가 있으므로 최상급 (D) widest가 정답이다.

11.

해석 8월에, 마운트 플리샌트 놀이동산은 개장 이후로 최고 월간

입장객 수치를 기록했다.

해설 빈칸 앞에 소유격이, 빈칸 뒤에 명사구가 있으므로 빈칸에는 명사구를 수식할 수 있는 형용사가 와야 하는데, 월간 입장객 수치를 비교하는 기간이 개장 이후부터이므로 '최고의'이라는 뜻의 최상급 (D) best가 정답이다.

12.

해석 '바니시 클렌저'를 사용한 이후에도 여전히 얼룩이 보인다면, 저희의 가장 강력한 세제인 '바니시 플러스'를 사용하는 것을 고려해 보십시오.

해설 빈칸 뒤에 완전한 구조의 절이, 콤마 뒤에 명령문이 있으므로 빈칸에는 접속사가 필요하다. 해석상 '~라면, …하십시오'라는 의미가 자연스러우므로 가정법 현재를 나타낼 수 있는 (A) If가 정답이다.

어휘 **stain** 얼룩 **visible** 눈에 보이는

13.

해석 영업 임원들은 잠재 고객들과 회의 일정을 잡을 때 가능한 한 융통성 있어야만 한다.

해설 빈칸 앞뒤로 as가 있으므로 원급 (D) flexible이 정답이다.

14.

해석 승무원들이 비행 도중 여행객들의 불만사항을 알고 있었다면, 그들의 좌석을 바꿔주는 것을 제안할 수 있었을 것이다.

해설 콤마 앞에 가정법 과거완료의 도치 문장 Had been이 있으므로 주절에 「조동사 + have p.p.」가 와야 한다. 따라서 (A) could have offered가 정답이다.

15.

해석 제품 디자이너들은 이 휴대전화를 위해 발전된 기능에 많은 시간을 소비하는 것만큼 사용자 친화성에도 많은 시간을 쓴다.

해설 빈칸 뒤에 불가산명사 time과 as가 있으므로 이 원급 비교와 함께 사용할 수 있는 (D) as much가 정답이다.

어휘 **user-friendliness** 사용자 친화성

16.

해석 팔콘 법무법인이 브릿지스 씨를 선임 파트너로 임명하지 않았더라면, 다른 로펌이 그렇게 했을 것이다.

해설 빈칸 앞에 가정법 과거완료 도치 구문을 나타내는 Had not appointed가 있으므로 주절에 「조동사 + have p.p.」가 와야 한다. 따라서 (D) would have done이 정답이다.

어휘 **appoint A as B** A를 B로 임명하다

17.

해석 만약 딕슨 씨가 그 회사의 목표와 철학에 대해 연구하지 않았다면, 공석인 자리에 대한 그녀의 면접이 성공적이지 못했을 것이다.

해설 콤마 앞에 가정법 과거완료 구문이 제시되어 있으므로 주절에는 「조동사 + have p.p.」가 와야 한다. 따라서 (C) would not have been이 정답이다.

어휘 **philosophy** 철학

18.

해석 리오넬 엣킨스 씨가 자신의 <매직 어프렌티스> 시리즈에서 가장 인기 있는 책의 발췌본을 낭독할 것이다.

해설 빈칸 앞뒤에 정관사와 명사가 있으므로 빈칸은 명사를 수식할 형용사 자리인데, 뒤에 범위를 나타내는 in 전치사구가 제시되어 있으므로정관사 the와 함께 최상급 형용사를 구성하는 (C) most popular가 정답이다.

어휘 **excerpt** 발췌(본)

19.

해석 예상보다 더 약하기는 했지만, 간밤의 강설량이 여전히 클라크 카운티 전역에 걸쳐 많은 도로 폐쇄를 야기했다.

해설 빈칸에는 빈칸 바로 뒤에 위치한 than과 어울리는 비교급 표현이 와야 하므로 (B) lighter가 정답이다.

어휘 **overnight** 밤사이의, 야간의 **snowfall** 강설(량) **lighted** 불이 붙은, 불이 켜진

20.

해석 세계에서 가장 영향력 있는 기술 혁신가들이 다음 달에 베를린에서 열리는 로봇&인공지능 컨퍼런스에 참석할 것으로 예상된다.

해설 빈칸 앞에 소유격과 most가, 빈칸 뒤에 명사구가 있으므로 빈칸에는 이 명사구를 수식할 수 있는 형용사가 와야 한다. 또한, most와 어울려 최상급 표현을 구성해야 알맞으므로 (C) influential이 정답이다.

Playlist 10
파트6 접속부사 기술 마스터하기

Practice

1. (D) **2.** (B) **3.** (A) **4.** (C)

1.

하드만스 짐에서 열릴 운동 수업에 대한 여러분들의 관심에 감사드립니다. 비회원분들도 저희 에어로빅, 스피닝, 재즈 체

조 수업에 참석하실 수 있으며, 도착하시자마자 프론트 데스크에서 비용을 지불하시면 됩니다. 저희는 또한 매주 목요일과 토요일에 정기적인 필라테스와 요가 수업을 운영하고 있습니다. **하지만**, 이러한 수업들은 현재 비회원분들이 이용하실 수 없습니다.

해설 빈칸 앞에는 비회원들도 특정 운동 수업에 참석할 수 있으며 정기적인 필라테스와 요가 수업도 운영한다는 내용이, 빈칸 뒤에는 이러한 수업들(필라테스와 요가 수업)은 현재 비회원들이 이용할 수 없다는 상반된 내용이 제시되어 있으므로 대조 접속부사 (D) However이 정답이다.

어휘 **upon arrival** 도착하자마자 **run** 운영하다

2.

홍콩 메디컬 재단에서, 저희의 사명은 가장 포괄적이고 일관된 건강 관리 시스템을 이용하여 지역사회를 돌보는 것입니다. 저희 내과 의사들, 의료팀, 그리고 직원들은 모든 개인적인 상호 작용에 공감력을 보여주고, 환자분들이 이해를 받는다고 느끼도록 보장합니다. **게다가**, 저희는 모두를 위해 더 나은 건강 결과로 이어지는 연구와 시범 사업들에 투자합니다.

해설 빈칸 앞에는 의료 재단의 소개와 재단 내 구성원들이 보장하는 서비스에 대한 설명이, 빈칸 뒤에는 재단이 환자들을 위해 하는 투자에 대한 내용이 제시되어 있다. 따라서 유사한 내용을 덧붙이는 추가 접속사 (B) In addition이 정답이다.

3.

맨체스터는 영국에서 전기스쿠터를 도입한 가장 최신의 도시입니다. 이러한 배터리로 동력을 얻는 스쿠터들은 대중들이 이용 가능하며, 모바일 애플리케이션을 통해 등록함으로써 사용될 수 있습니다. 스쿠터들은 제어하기 쉬우며, 발전된 GPS 기술이 딸려 있습니다. **무엇보다도**, 전기스쿠터는 오염을 줄이는 데 도움이 되며 교통수단의 전통적인 형태에 대한 환경 친화적인 대안으로서의 역할을 합니다.

해설 빈칸 앞에는 전기스쿠터의 일반적인 장점들이 나열되어 있고, 빈칸 뒤에는 기존 교통 수단에 대한 친환경적인 대체제로서의 역할을 할 수 있다는 내용이 제시되어 있다. 따라서 빈칸에는 앞서 언급한 장점을 넘는 환경적인 측면에서의 이점을 강조하고 있으므로 강조 접속부사 (A) Best of all이 정답이다.

어휘 **come with** ~이 딸려 있다 **serve as** ~로서의 역할을 하다

4.

애초에 1년 전에 개장한 데이지 레스토랑은 소셜 미디어와 긍정적인 음식 비평가들의 후기를 통해 꾸준히 훌륭한 평판을 얻어 왔습니다. 그곳은 일반적으로 한 주에 어떤 날이든 상관없이 기쁨이 넘치는 고객들로 가득 차 있습니다. **이런 이유로**, 선호하는 식사 날짜보다 적어도 한 달 일찍 예약하는 것은 필수적입니다.

해설 빈칸 앞에는 특정 식당이 꾸준히 좋은 평가를 받고 있어 언제든 고객들로 가득 차 있다는 내용이, 빈칸 뒤에는 원하는 날짜에 식사를 하고 싶다면 미리 예약을 해야 한다는 내용이 제시되어 있다. 따라서 앞서 언급된 평판에 의해 미리 예약하는 것이 필수적이라는 결과가 발생되었으므로 결과 접속부사 (C) For that reason이 정답이다.

어휘 **be packed with** ~로 가득 차 있다

Check-up Test

1. (B)	**2.** (C)	**3.** (A)	**4.** (D)	**5.** (B)
6. (A)	**7.** (C)	**8.** (B)	**9.** (B)	**10.** (C)
11. (D)	**12.** (D)			

1-4.

행사를 주최하는 레스토랑

리버데일 (9월 15일) - 시에서 가장 인기 있는 식사 장소들 중 한 곳인, 리버타운 비스트로가 9월 28일에 음식 애호가들을 특별 **1 시식** 행사에 초대합니다. 이 레스토랑은 가을 신메뉴에 대한 시식 서비스를 제공할 것이며, 지역에서 공급 받는 재료와 계절적인 맛들을 특징으로 합니다. **2 추가로**, 식사 손님들이 주방에 들어가 요리사들이 음식을 만들어 내는 모습을 지켜 볼 기회도 있을 것입니다. 이 행사는 손님들에게 가을 내내 이용 가능하게 될 요리들에 대한 사전 공개 시간을 제공하기 위한 것입니다. **3 이 계절 메뉴는 10월에 시작될 예정입니다.**

이 행사에 **4 참석하는** 손님들은 오후 12시부터 오후 8시 사이에 리버타운 비스트로 시내 지점의 주 식사 공간을 방문하도록 권장됩니다. 예약은 필요하지 않으며, 요리는 선착순으로 제공될 것입니다.

어휘 **enthusiast** 애호가, 열광적인 팬 **tasting** 시식, 시음 **source** ~을 공급 받다 **preview** 사전 공개, 시사회, 예고편 **on a first-come, first-served basis** 선착순으로

1.

해설 빈칸 뒤에 위치한 문장에 가을 신메뉴에 대한 시식 서비스를 제공한다는 말이 쓰여 있어 event와 함께 이러한 특징을 나타낼 행사명을 구성해야 하므로 '시식, 시음'을 뜻하는

(B) sampling이 정답이다.

어휘 **sampling** 시식, 시음

2.

해설 빈칸 앞에는 가을 신메뉴 시식 서비스를 제공한다는 말이, 빈칸 뒤에는 손님들이 주방에서 요리사들이 음식을 만드는 모습을 보게 된다는 말이 각각 쓰여 있다.
이는 시식 행사의 진행과 관련된 두 가지 세부 정보에 해당하므로 '추가로' 등의 의미로 유사 정보를 추가할 때 사용하는 추가 접속부사 (C) Plus가 정답이다.

어휘 **if not** 그렇지 않다면 **after all** 결국, 어쨌든

3.

(A) 이 계절 메뉴는 10월에 시작될 예정입니다.
(B) 대부분의 요리사들이 유명 레스토랑에서 근무한 바 있습니다.
(C) 식사 손님들의 의견이 압도적으로 긍정적이었습니다.
(D) 이 레스토랑이 겨울철에 맞춰 재개장될 것입니다.

해설 앞 문장에 손님들에게 가을 내내 이용 가능할 요리들에 대한 사전 공개를 목적으로 하는 행사라는 말이 쓰여 있다. 따라서, 그 가을 요리들을 The seasonal menu로 지칭해 해당 계절 메뉴가 시작되는 시점을 알리는 (A)가 정답이다.

어휘 **overwhelmingly** 압도적으로 **in time for** ~하는 때에 맞춰

4.

해설 주격 관계대명사 who 다음은 who절의 동사 자리이며, 앞 단락에 미래시제 동사를 통해 미래 시점에 있을 행사와 관련해 설명하고 있어 동일한 미래 시점에 참석하는 일을 의미해야 알맞다. 따라서, 미래를 대신할 수 있는 현재진행시제 동사 (D) are attending이 정답이다.

5-8.

하모니 싱잉 레슨: 여러분의 목소리를 찾아 보세요

여러분께서 고전적인 스타일을 선호하시든, **5 아니면** 현대적인 스타일을 선호하시든 상관없이, 여러분의 보컬 능력을 향상시켜 드릴 하모니 싱잉 강사와 함께 하는 강좌에 참석하시는 것을 고려해 보십시오! 보컬 트레이닝에 있어 풍부한 경험을 지니고 있는, **6 저희** 경험 많은 선생님들께서 발전시키기를 원하시는 부분들을 향상시키시는 데 도움을 드릴 수 있습니다. 저희는 명확한 목표를 설정해 드리면서 흔히 좌절로 이어지는 어려움들을 해결해 드리는 개인 맞춤 학습 계획을 제공해 드릴 수 있습니다. **7 혼자 향상되려 노력하시는 것은 오직 제한적인 이점만 있을 뿐입니다.** 하모닝 싱잉 강사께서 노래 숙련도를 한 단계 더 끌어 올려 드릴 수 있습니다!

저희 하모니 싱잉에서는, 노래가 자기 표현의 한 가지 강력한 방식이라고 생각합니다. **8 이를 염두에 두고**, 저희는 여러분께서 기본적인 기술을 뛰어넘어 고유의 목소리를 찾고 개선하실 수 있도록 도와 드릴 것입니다. 오늘 www.harmonysinging.com/lessons을 방문하셔서 등록해 보십시오!

어휘 **contemporary** 현대의, 동시대의 **enhance** ~을 향상시키다, 강화하다 **a wealth of** 풍부한 **frustration** 좌절 **take A a step further** A를 한 단계 더 끌어 올리다 **proficiency** 숙련(도), 능숙 **go beyond** ~을 뛰어넘다 **refine** ~을 개선하다, 개량하다

5.

해설 빈칸 앞뒤에 위치한 두 개의 형용사가 'A이든, 아니면 B이든 상관없이'를 뜻하는 'Whether A or B'의 구조로 나열되어야 알맞으므로 (B) or가 정답이다.

어휘 **likely** 가능성 있는, 있을 법한

6.

해설 빈칸 뒤에 명사구 주어 experienced teachers와 동사가 이어져 있어 명사구를 앞에서 수식할 단어가 빈칸에 필요하므로 소유격 인칭대명사 (A) our가 정답이다.

7.

(A) 공연 입장권이 할인된 요금으로 제공됩니다.
(B) 노래가 여러 면에서 건강을 향상시켜 주는 것으로 입증되었습니다.
(C) 혼자 향상되려 노력하시는 것은 오직 제한적인 이점만 있을 뿐입니다.
(D) 그분들이 유능한 가수가 되시는 데 여러 해가 걸렸습니다.

해설 빈칸 앞에는 개인에게 맞춰진 학습 계획을 제공해 줄 수 있다는 말이, 빈칸 뒤에는 소속 강사가 노래 숙련도를 한 단계 더 끌어 올려 줄 수 있다는 말이 각각 쓰여 있다. 따라서, 하모닝 싱잉에서 강사를 통해 노래를 배우는 것과 관련된 문장이 필요하므로 혼자 노력하는 것의 한계를 언급한 (C)가 정답이다.

어휘 **competent** 유능한, 능숙한

8.

해설 빈칸 뒤에 고유의 목소리를 찾고 개선하도록 도와 주겠다는 말이 쓰여 있는데, 이는 빈칸 앞에서 노래가 자기 표현의 강력한 방식이라고 말한 것에 따른 일종의 교육 방향에 해당한다. 따라서, '이를 염두에 두고'라는 의미로 어떤 일의 방향성과 관련해 언급할 때 사용하는 강조 접속부사 (B) With that in mind가 정답이다.

어휘 **on a different note** (대화의) 분위기를 바꿔서, 화제를

바꿔서 at that point 그 당시에, 그 시점에

9-12.

날짜: 8월 13일
제목: 예정된 유지보수 작업

샌더슨 씨께,

저희 시내 지역 네트워크에 대해 예정된 유지보수 작업을 알려 드리고자 이메일을 씁니다. 8월 20일부터 8월 21일까지, 네트워크 유지보수 작업이 귀하의 구역에서 **9** **실시될 것이며**, 이는 대략 오후 9시부터 오전 5시 사이에 간헐적인 연결을 초래할 수 있습니다. **10** **정확한 일정은 첨부 문서를 참조하시기 바랍니다.** 비록 귀하의 **11** **업체**가 이 시간대를 벗어나 운영되고 있기는 하지만, 인터넷 접속을 필요로 하는 모든 야간 업무가 지장을 받을지도 모른다는 점에 유의하시기 바랍니다. **12** **그러므로** 귀하께서는 이 유지보수 작업 시간대를 피해 중요한 활동의 일정을 잡으시는 것을 고려하시기 원하실 수도 있습니다. 이 네트워크는 8월 21일 오전 8시까지 전면 가동될 것입니다. 귀하의 이해와 협조에 감사 드립니다.

안녕히 계십시오.

레베카 타나카
네트워크 운영 책임

어휘 intermittent 간헐적인 connectivity 연결(성) disrupt ~에 지장을 주다, ~을 방해하다 window 시간대

9.

해설 빈칸 앞에 작업이 실시되는 날짜로 쓰여 있는 August 20 and August 21가 지문 상단의 이메일 작성 날짜 Date: August 13보다 미래 시점이므로 미래시제 (B) will be가 정답이다.

10.

(A) 저희는 시에서 가장 빠른 연결 속도를 제공하는 것이 자랑스럽습니다.
(B) 예정된 시간에 귀하를 뵐 수 있기를 고대합니다.
(C) 정확한 일정은 첨부 문서를 참조하시기 바랍니다.
(D) 하지만, 모든 인터넷 연결이 이 기간 중에 작동하지 않을 것입니다.

해설 빈칸 앞에 네트워크 유지 관리 작업이 실시되는 날짜 및 간헐적인 연결이 이뤄지는 대략적인 시간대가 언급되어 있다. 따라서, 그러한 작업 진행 일정과 관련해 정확한 정보를 파악할 수 있는 방법을 알리는 (C)가 정답이다.

어휘 arranged 예정된, 조치된, 마련된 precise 정확한 down (기계 등이) 작동하지 않는, 멈춘

11.

해설 빈칸 뒤에 위치한 동사 operates와 어울려 운영의 주체가 될 수 있는 어휘가 필요하며, 주절에 야간 업무가 지장을 받을지도 모른다는 말이 쓰여 있으므로 사업체를 뜻하는 (D) business가 정답이다.

12.

해설 빈칸 뒤에 유지보수 작업 시간대를 피해 중요한 활동의 일정을 잡도록 권하는 말이 쓰여 있는데, 이는 앞선 문장에서 언급한 '모든 야간 업무가 지장을 받는 일'이라는 원인에 따른 결과로서 제안하는 조치이다. 따라서, '그러므로' 등의 의미로 결과를 말할 때 사용하는 결과 접속부사 (D) therefore가 정답이다.

Playlist 11
만점강사 시점으로 풀어보는 파트6 문맥파악

대명사

모든 회계 담당자들에게 알리는 중요 공지

이번 시즌 다량의 소득세 신고로 인해, 여러 마감 기한이 앞당겨졌습니다. 그 결과, 주말 시간을 포함해, 일부 초과 근무가 필수적일 것입니다. 어느 분이든 토요일에 근무하시는 데 방해가 될 만한 불가피한 일이 있으실 경우, 제게 알려 주시기 바랍니다. 마크 레이놀즈 재무부장님께서 모든 주말 교대 근무에 대해 두 배의 급여를 승인해 주셨습니다. 급여 지급과 관련된 모든 질문은 그분께 전달되어야 합니다.

어휘 tax return 소득세 신고 push up ~을 앞당기다 unavoidable 불가피한, 피할 수 없는 commitment 일, 공헌 direct v. ~에게 전달하다

여러분만의 행사를 계획하시는 게 지겨우신가요? 스트레스 없는 파티를 주최하시는 것을 꿈 꾸고 계신가요? 그러시면 계속 읽어 보세요! 아주 다양한 출장 요리 선택사항들이 이용 가능한 상태인, '지금'이 예약하시기에 완벽한 때입니다! 저희 고메 개더링스 케이터링 사는, 다섯 분의 전문 요리사 및 행사 기획 담당자로 구성된 팀을 보유하고 있으며, 모두 15년이 넘는 경험을 지니고 계십니다. 저희 목표는 여러분의 행사에 적합한 완벽한 메뉴를 만들어 내는 것입니다. 555-123-7840번으로 저희에게 전화 주셔서 여러분의 다음 번 잊지 못할 행사를 계획하기 시작하십시오!

시제

애컬리 씨께,

그 아파트가 귀하의 것이라는 사실을 알려 드리게 되어 기쁩니다. 귀하께서는 임대 보증금 및 해당 공과금과 함께 임대료로 매달 1,500달러를 지불하시게 될 것입니다. 임대 계약은 월요일인 3월 20일부터 시작될 예정입니다. 임대 계약서에 서명하러 오실 때 사진을 포함한 유효 신분증을 하나 지참하고 오셔야 한다는 점을 기억하시기 바랍니다. 어떤 질문이든 있으시거나 추가 상세 정보가 필요하실 경우, 부담 갖지 마시고 언제든지 제게 이메일을 보내 주시기 바랍니다.

제품 후기

저는 전에 한 번도 타고 다니는 잔디 깎기 기계를 구입한 적이 없었습니다. 저희 정원을 확장한 후에, 마침내 더 효율적인 잔디 깎기 기계 구입을 정당화할 정도로 충분한 잔디가 생겼습니다. 제가 조사를 많이 했는데, 메가 모우어 5000이 이상적인 선택인 것 같았습니다. 다른 모델들보다 더 비싸긴 했지만, 모든 후기가 아주 긍정적이었습니다. 그래서 제 자신에게 한턱 내기로 결정했습니다.

어휘 lawnmower 잔디 깎기 기계 justify ~을 정당화하다 treat oneself ~에게 한턱 내다

시몬스 씨께,

이 메시지가 잘 전달되기를 바랍니다. 저는 최근 귀사에서 인턴 프로그램을 완료했으며, 어떤 공식적인 공석이든 게시되기를 기다리는 대신 직접 연락 드리고 싶었습니다. 현재 또는 곧 귀하의 팀에 재합류할 기회가 있을 수도 있는지 여쭤 보고자 글을 씁니다. 귀하와 함께 일했던 것은 매우 귀중한 경험이었으며, 가까운 미래에 계속 배우고 기여할 수 있는 기회가 꼭 있었으면 합니다.

어휘

담당자께,

제가 오늘 아침에 귀하의 소매점에서 휴대전화기를 한 대 구입했는데, 막 집에 도착해서 상자를 개봉했습니다. 처음에는, 이 전화기의 특징 및 외관에 대해 아주 기뻤습니다. 하지만, 더 자세히 점검해 보자마자, 화면에 아래쪽 가장자리를 따라 눈에 띄는 균열 부분이 있다는 것을 알게 되었습니다. 제가 환불을 받으려고 하는 건 아니지만, 결함이 있는 제품을 무료로 교체해 주실 수 있다면 감사하겠습니다.

이 문제에 대한 귀하의 관심에 감사 드립니다.

어휘 noticeable 눈에 띄는 crack 균열 matter 문제, 일

에너지 솔루션즈 주식회사

(11월 1일) 우리 고객들의 최근 의견은 우리의 새로운 스마트 미터스의 도입에 대해 압도적으로 긍정적인 반응을 보여주었습니다. 의견을 제공해 주신 사용자들 중 대략 90퍼센트가 이 계량기의 편의성 및 에너지 절약 기능에 매우 만족하고 있다고 보고했습니다. 현재, 스마트 미터스는 약 10,000곳의 가정에 설치되어 있으며, 우리는 올 연말까지 추가로 15,000곳의 주택에 그 이용 가능성을 확대할 계획을 세우고 있습니다.

어휘 overwhelmingly 압도적으로 energy-saving 에너지 절약의

브라이트 아동 병원이 랜던 메디컬 이노베이션즈의 새라 랜던 대표이사로부터 2백만 달러라는 너그러운 기부금을 받아 소아과 병동의 확장 공사를 지원할 예정입니다. 랜던 씨는 그 기부로 이 병원의 미래에 크게 혜택을 제공해 줄 것이며, 화요일 오후에 그 내용을 발표했습니다. 랜던 씨는 개인적으로 2백만 달러를 기부하겠다고 약속했는데, 이는 세 단계로 지불될 것이며, 그 첫 번째 분할금은 10월 10일에 병원 이사회로 송금될 예정입니다. 이사회는 신생아 집중 치료 시설(NICU)을 확장하기 위해 그 첫 자금을 사용할 계획입니다.

어휘 pediatric 소아과의, 소아학의 installment 분할금, 할부금

문장삽입

제목: 부정확한 체육관 회비 청구

담당자께,

8월 한 달 동안에 대한 제 체육관 회비 문제와 관련해 다시 연락 드립니다. 제 내역서를 받은 후, 7월 연체금에 대한 부정확한 청구 요금을 알게 되었습니다. 제가 전에 귀사의 청구서 발급 담당 부서에 연락했을 때, 이 부정확한 요금이 삭제될 거라고 보장 받았습니다. 하지만, 최신 내역서는 여전히 이 오류를 포함하고 있습니다. 이 문제를 즉시 해결해 주시기를 요청 드립니다.

어휘 billing department 청구서 발급 담당 부서 promptly 즉시, 지체 없이

시네마월드 회원 자격 갱신 제공 혜택!

기존의 시네마월드 회원이시면서 연간 영화 회원 자격을 갱신하실 것인지 궁금해 하고 계신가요? 그러시다면, 지금 바로 저희 독점 판촉 행사를 이용하십시오. 9월 1일부터 10월 31일까지, 1년 또는 2년 기간의 회원 자격을 갱신하시는 현재의 회원들께 추가 특혜를 제공해 드립니다. 예를 들어, 전체 기간에 대해 회비에서 15퍼센트 할인을 받으실 것입니다! 오늘 555-3268번으로 저희 고객 서비스팀에 연락하셔서 회원 자격을 갱신하시고 계속 무제한 영화를 즐겨 보시기 바랍니다.

어휘 **exclusive** 독점의 **perk** 특혜, 혜택

(런던 – 2월 15일) 한 부동산 연구 기관은 부동산 가격이 4년 연속으로 꾸준히 계속 상승해 온 것을 보고했습니다. 이에 대한 주된 원인은 더 높은 가격에 부동산을 매입하면서, 수요를 끌어올린 외국인 투자자들입니다. 그 결과, 국내 구매자들이 시장에서 더 치열한 경쟁에 직면하고 있습니다. 끊임없이 지속되는 주택 부족 문제도 부동산 가격에 영향을 미치고 있습니다. 지역 정부는 도움이 필요한 사람들을 위해 새로운 저가형 주택을 건설하겠다는 약속을 이행하지 못했으며, 이는 이용 가능한 그 주택들의 가치를 끌어올리고 있습니다.

어휘 **consecutive** 연속의 **drive up** ~을 끌어올리다 **tougher** 더 치열한, 더 힘든 **persistent** 지속적인 **act on** ~을 이행하다

Practice

1. (C) **2.** (D) **3.** (B) **4.** (A)

1.

안녕하세요, 여러분,

이곳 홀리 비스트로의 우리 팀에서 가장 중요한 일원들 중 한 분과 관련해 전해 드릴 아주 중대한 발표가 있습니다. 25년 동안의 노고와 헌신 끝에, 우리 마우로 마테라치 주방장님께서 은퇴하신 다음, 이탈리아에 있는 고향으로 돌아가시기로 결정하셨습니다. 우리의 현 부주방장으로서, 뛰어난 능력을 지니고 계신, 크리스티 베나트 씨께서 마테라치 주방장님께서 물러나시면 후임자가 되실 것입니다. 마테라치 주방장님께서는 베나트 씨께서 거의 9년 전에 레스토랑에서 근무하기 시작하신 이후로 계속 멘토의 역할을 해 주시고 계십니다.

어휘 **sous chef** 부주방장 **step down** (자리 등에서) 물러나다, 사퇴하다

해설 지문의 첫 문장에 공지를 한다는 내용이 제시되었으므로 부주방장인 크리스티 베나트 씨가 후임자가 되는 시점은 미래임을 알 수 있다. 또한, 접속사 when이 이끄는 시간 부사절의 동사가 현재시제일 때, 주절에 미래시제 동사를 함께 사용하므로 (C) will replace가 정답이다.

2.

수신: 전 직원
제목: 고객 서비스 교육

연례 고객 서비스 교육 워크숍 시간이 다가왔습니다. 올해는, 의사 소통 능력 및 문제 해결 능력을 향상시키는 데 초점이 맞춰질 것입니다. 우리가 고객 문의 사항을 처리하고 긍정적인 경험을 보장하는 방법을 개선하기 위해 새로운 수단을 도입한 바 있지만, 모두가 이 수단을 효과적으로 이용하는 방법을 이해하는 것이 필수적입니다. 모두를 수용하기 위해, 다수의 교육 시간이 앞으로 몇 주 동안에 걸쳐 개최될 것입니다. 인사부장님께 연락하셔서 여러분께 적합한 시간에 등록하실 수 있습니다.

해설 to부정사로 쓰인 타동사 accommodate의 목적어로서 수용 대상을 나타낼 대명사가 필요한데, 빈칸 뒤에 다수의 교육 시간이 개최된다는 말이 쓰여 있어 모든 직원을 수용하기 위한 방법임을 알 수 있으므로 '모두'를 뜻하는 부정대명사 (D) everyone이 정답이다.

3.

주거용 건물에서, 주택 소유주들은 최적의 성능을 유지할 수 있게 태양열 전지판을 효율적으로 설치하고 주기적으로 점검받도록 보장하는 일에 대한 책임이 있습니다. 적합한 배치는 효율성을 위해 매우 중요합니다. 전지판은 그늘이 없는 구역에 위치해야 하는데, 나무나 근처의 건물 같은 장애물이 에너지 생산량을 감소시킬 수 있기 때문입니다. 또한, 태양열 전지판은 가장 많은 햇빛을 포착할 수 있는 구역에 설치되어야 합니다. 이는 일반적으로 남쪽을 향해 있는 표면입니다. 이 위치 선정이 햇빛에 대한 노출을 극대화하는 데 핵심입니다.

(A) 그것들을 신중히 제거하셔야 한다는 점을 기억하십시오.
(B) 이는 일반적으로 남쪽을 향해 있는 표면입니다.
(C) 햇빛은 여러 혜택을 제공해 주는 것으로 알려져 있습니다.
(D) 전지판은 낮은 조도로 에너지를 생산할 수 있습니다.

어휘 **optimal** 최적의 **proper** 적합한, 제대로 된 **placement** 배치, 위치 선정 **obstruction** 장애물 **capture** ~을 포착하다, 사로잡다 **south-facing** 남쪽을 향해 있는 **surface** 표면

해설 빈칸 앞뒤에 태양열 전지판이 설치되어야 하는 위치의 특성 및 위치 선정의 중요성을 알리는 문장들이 쓰여 있다. 따라서, 전지판 설치 위치와 관련된 정보를 담은 문장이 빈칸에 쓰여야 흐름상 자연스러우므로 (B)가 정답이다.

4.

다가오는 세계 제약 컨퍼런스에 등록해 주셔서 감사합니다. 동봉해 드린 것은 모든 기조 연설 및 패널 토론회의 시간과 장소를 간략히 설명해 드리는 일정표입니다. 추가로, 행사 중에 **교통편**에 대한 지원을 제공해 드리게 되어 기쁘게 생각합니다. 실제로, 저희가 컨퍼런스 센터와 할인된 요금으로 엄선된 호텔들 사이를 오가는 셔틀 버스 서비스를 마련해 드릴 수 있습니다. 이 서비스가 필요하신 경우, 추가 상세 정보를 위해 555-7624번으로 저희 행사 진행 책임자인 리사 매닝 씨께 연락하시기 바랍니다.

어휘 **Enclosed is A** 동봉해 드린 것은 A입니다 **select** a. 엄선된 **coordinator** 진행 책임자, 조정 담당자

해설 빈칸이 속한 문장 뒤에 셔틀 버스 서비스를 마련할 수 있다는 내용이 제시되어 있어 빈칸이 속한 문장은 행사 중에 차량 제공과 관련된 지원을 제공한다는 의미를 나타내야 알맞으므로 '교통(편)'을 뜻하는 (A) transportation이 정답이다.

Check-up Test

1. (A)	**2.** (B)	**3.** (B)	**4.** (D)	**5.** (C)
6. (A)	**7.** (B)	**8.** (A)	**9.** (B)	**10.** (D)
11. (D)	**12.** (D)			

1-4.

호라이즌 에너지 사, 원자력 프로젝트를 발표하다

도쿄 (9월 22일) – 호라이즌 에너지 주식회사가 일본 센다이 근처에 1,200 메가와트 원자력 발전소에 대한 건설 공사를 시작할 계획을 **1 발표했습니다. 2 이 시설은 저공해 에너지를 제공하도록 고안된 고급 원자로를 활용할 것입니다.** 호라이즌 에너지 사는 이 발전소가 36개월 내에 가동될 것으로 예상하고 있으며, 전국적인 에너지 제공업체인 니폰 파워 사에 전력을 공급할 것입니다.

"니폰 파워 사와의 합의는 **3 저희의** 지속 가능성 목표를 달성하기 위한 중요한 발걸음입니다,"라고 호라이즌 에너지 사의 대표이사인 히로시 타나카 씨가 밝혔습니다. "저희는 향후 10년 내로 저희 원자력 생산량을 10 기가와트로 늘려, 탄소 배출량 목표에 **4 도달하기** 위한 일본의 야심 찬 노력을 뒷받침하는 것을 목표로 하고 있습니다."

어휘 **nuclear power** 원자력 **sustainability** 지속 가능성 **capacity** 생산량, 용량, 수용력 **ambitious** 야심 찬 **carbon** 탄소 **emission** 배출(량)

1.

해설 지문의 종류가 기사글이고, 지문의 제목과 첫 문장에서 원자력 발전소 건설에 대한 계획을 이미 발표한 것을 알 수 있으므로 과거시제 (A) announced가 정답이다.

2.

(A) 원자력은 여러 안전 관련 우려 후에 정밀 조사를 더 많이 받아 왔습니다.

(B) 이 시설은 저공해 에너지를 제공하도록 고안된 고급 원자로를 활용할 것입니다.

(C) 원자력 에너지에서 벗어나려는 움직임은 일본 에너지 정책의 주목할 만한 변화를 시사합니다.

(D) 일본 에너지 공급망의 거의 10퍼센트가 그 변화 중에 일시적으로 전력이 끊긴 상태였습니다.

해설 빈칸 앞뒤 문장에 원자력과 관련된 무언가를 건설하기 시작할 계획이라는 말과 36개월 내에 가동될 것으로 예상한다는 말이 쓰여 있다. 따라서, 새롭게 건설되는 것을 '시설'을 뜻하는 The facility로 지칭해 그곳의 특징을 언급하는 (B)가 정답이다.

어휘 **come under scrutiny** 정밀 조사를 받다 **nuclear reactor** 원자로 **low-emission** 저공해의 **signal** v. ~을 시사하다, ~의 조짐을 보이다 **grid** 공급망

3.

해설 전치사 toward 뒤에 위치한 동명사 achieving과 명사 목적어 sustainability targets 사이에 위치한 빈칸은 명사를 수식할 단어가 필요한 자리이므로 소유격 인칭대명사 (B) our가 정답이다.

4.

해설 빈칸 뒤에 '탄소 배출량 목표'를 뜻하는 명사구 carbon emission goals가 쓰여 있어 그러한 목표에 도달하기 위한 노력을 의미해야 알맞으므로 '~에 도달하다, 이르다'를 뜻하는 (D) reach가 정답이다.

어휘 **block** ~을 차단하다, 가로막다

5-8.

수신: 제나 하트먼 <jhartman43@snmail.com>
발신: 탈리아 도슨 <service@sweetsensationsbakery.com>
날짜: 2월 16일
제목: 주문 번호 45923

하트먼 씨께,

따님의 이름이 위에 쓰여지는 개인 맞춤형 생일 케이크에 대한 귀하의 주문을 접수했습니다. 저희는, 당연히, 귀하의 요청 사항을 이행해 드리게 되어 기쁩니다! **5 하지만**, 주문

제작 디자인을 전문으로 하시는 저희 케이크 장식 전문가께서 앞으로 이틀 동안 시간이 나지 않으실 것입니다. 유감스럽게도, 이분의 **6 부재**는 귀하의 케이크를 준비해 드리는 데 있어 약간의 지연이 있을 것임을 의미합니다.

이러한 불편함에 대해 **7 보상해 드리기 위해**, 이 주문품에 대해 20퍼센트 할인을 제공해 드리고자 합니다. 또는, 귀하의 다음 번 케이크 주문에 대해 무료 맞춤 제작 서비스를 제공해 드릴 수 있습니다. **8 그러므로, 귀하의 선호 사항을 저희에게 알려 주시기 바랍니다.** 저희 스위트 센세이션즈 베이커리에서는, 고객 만족이 최우선사항입니다!

안녕히 계십시오.

탈리아 도슨
고객 서비스 직원
스위트 센세이션즈 베이커리

어휘 **decorator** 장식가 **custom** 주문 제작의 **alternatively** (대안을 말할 때) 또는, 그렇지 않으면 **priority** 우선사항

5.

해설 빈칸 앞에는 주문을 받게 되어 기쁘다는 내용이, 빈칸 뒤에는 케이크 장식 전문가가 특정 기간 동안 시간이 나지 않는다는 상반된 내용이 제시되어 있으므로 대조 접속부사 (C) However가 정답이다.

6.

해설 빈칸 앞에 위치한 her는 앞선 문장에서 언급하는 our cake decorator를 가리키며, 빈칸 뒤에는 지연 문제가 발생할 것이라고 알리는 말이 쓰여 있다. 따라서, 앞선 문장에서 그 사람이 시간이 나지 않는다고 언급한 것에 따른 문제임을 알 수 있으므로 그러한 상태를 가리킬 수 있는 어휘로서 '부재, 결근' 등을 뜻하는 (A) absence가 정답이다.

어휘 **absence** 부재, 결근, 결석

7.

해설 빈칸 뒤에 주문품에 대해 20퍼센트 할인을 제공해 주겠다고 제안하는 말이 쓰여 있는데, 이는 앞서 언급한 지연에 대한 보상 조치에 해당한다. 따라서, 빈칸은 '불편함에 대해 보상하기 위해'라는 의미로 목적을 나타내야 알맞으므로 to 부정사 (B) To compensate이 정답이다.

8.

(A) 그러므로, 귀하의 선호 사항을 저희에게 알려 주시기 바랍니다.
(B) 그 제품이 곧 다시 재고로 있을 것임을 보장해 드립니다.
(C) 그 케이크가 여러 인기 만화 캐릭터들을 포함할 것입니다.
(D) 아시다시피, 저희 케이크는 지역에서 공급 받는 재료로 만들어집니다.

해설 빈칸 앞에 위치한 문장들을 읽어 보면, 보상 조치로서 주문품에 대한 20퍼센트 할인과 다음 번 케이크 주문에 대한 무료 맞춤 제작 서비스라는 두 가지 방법이 언급되어 있다. 따라서, 둘 중 한 가지 방법에 대한 선택을 요청하는 의미를 나타내는 (A)가 정답이다.

어휘 **be in stock** 재고로 있다 **cartoon** 만화

9-12.

직원 여러분께,

우리 RBC 엔터프라이즈 사는 회사의 다른 지사로 전근하실 때 발생되는 이전 및 재정착 비용에 대해 직원 여러분께 환급해 드릴 것이라는 사실을 알려 드리게 되어 기쁩니다. 충당되는 지출 비용은 임시 숙소와 이사 서비스, 그리고 해당 이전과 연관된 다른 모든 합리적인 요청에 대한 **9 비용**을 포함합니다.

환급을 받으시려면, 익월 첫째 날까지 지출 비용 보고서를 제출해 주시기 바랍니다. 반드시 **10 각각의** 항목이 날짜와 금액, 해당 비용에 대한 사유, 그리고 스캔한 영수증 사본과 함께 개별적으로 기재되도록 해 주시기 바랍니다. 환급은 정규 급여와 함께, 매달 7일에 여러분의 계좌로 **11 곧바로** 지급될 것입니다. **12 이 날짜 후에 지급이 이뤄지는 경우에 여러분께 미리 알려 드릴 것입니다.**

여러분의 유연성 및 우리 RBC 엔터프라이즈에 대한 헌신에 감사 드립니다!

안녕히 계십시오.

인사부
RBC 엔터프라이즈

어휘 **reimburse** ~을 환급해 주다 **resettlement** 재정착 **incur** (비용) ~을 발생시키다 **associate with** ~와 연관된 **alongside** ~와 함께 **flexibility** 유연성, 탄력성

9.

해설 빈칸에 쓰일 명사는 동사 include의 목적어로서 주어 Covered expenses가 의미하는 '충당되는 지출 비용'의 범주에 속하는 금전적인 요소를 나타내야 하므로 '비용'을 뜻하는 (B) cost가 정답이다.

어휘 **share** 몫, 할당, 부분, 주식

10.

해설 빈칸과 item은 동사 Ensure의 목적어 역할을 하는 that절(that은 빈칸 앞에 생략)의 주어이므로 빈칸은 명사를 수식

하는 형용사 자리이다. 또한, 단수명사 item과 어울리는 수량형용사가 필요하며, 보고서에 개별적으로 기재되는 항목을 나타내야 하므로 '각각의'라는 의미로 단수명사를 수식하는 (D) each가 정답이다.

11.

해설 수동태 동사와 전치사 사이에 위치한 빈칸은 수동태 동사 또는 전치사를 수식할 부사가 필요한 자리이므로 (D) directly가 정답이다.

12.

(A) 해당 양식에 선호하시는 이전 날짜를 포함하셔야 한다는 점을 기억해 주십시오.
(B) 모든 신입 사원들은 3개월 후에 500달러의 재정착 보너스를 받을 것입니다.
(C) 저희 신규 지사 사무실로 옮기시는 데 동의해 주셔서 감사합니다.
(D) 이 날짜 후에 지급이 이뤄지는 경우에 여러분께 미리 알려 드릴 것입니다.

해설 빈칸 앞 문장에 매달 7일에 계좌로 지급된다는 말이 쓰여 있어 그러한 방식과 관련된 정보를 담은 문장이 쓰여야 자연스러우므로 그 날짜를 this date로 지칭해 그 이후에 지급되는 경우에 취하는 조치를 설명하는 (D)가 정답이다.

Playlist 12
만점자들은 무조건 알고 있는 파트7 질문별 특징

Practice

1. (C)	**2.** (A)	**3.** (B)	**4.** (C)	**5.** (C)
6. (D)	**7.** (B)	**8.** (C)	**9.** (C)	**10.** (C)
11. (D)	**12.** (C)	**13.** (B)	**14.** (A)	

1-2.

> **로즈우드 시 의회 (도시 기획실)**
> **로즈우드 주민들께 전하는 공지**
>
> 5월 1일에, **1** 로즈우드의 도시 기획실이 모든 차량을 대상으로 메인 스트리트를 폐쇄할 것입니다. 이 거리는 보행자 전용으로 만들어지고 새로운 좌석 구역과 음식 판매업체들을 포함할 것입니다. 이러한 변화와 함께, 시에서는 **2** 결과적으로 지역 경제를 활성화시켜 줄 더 많은 관광객들을 끌어들일 것입니다.

어휘 **pedestrianize** ~을 보행자 전용으로 만들다 **in turn** 결과적으로, 결국

1. 도시 기획실에서 어떤 변화를 만들어 내고 있는가?
(A) 몇몇 업체들을 이전하는 일
(B) 교통 체계를 향상시키는 일
(C) 차량들을 대상으로 거리를 폐쇄하는 일
(D) 주차 구역을 확대하는 일

해설 지문 초반부에 로즈우드의 도시 기획실이 모든 차량을 대상으로 메인 스트리트를 폐쇄할 것이라고 밝히는 내용이 쓰여 있으므로 (C)가 정답이다.

2. 새로운 정책이 왜 시행되는가?
(A) 지역 관광 산업을 증진하기 위해
(B) 부동산 가격을 낮추기 위해
(C) 자전거 이용을 권장하기 위해
(D) 쓰레기 투기를 방지하기 위해

해설 지문 후반부에 정책의 변화에 따른 결과로 지역 경제를 활성화시키는 일이 언급되어 있으므로 (A)가 정답이다.

어휘 **littering** 쓰레기 투기

3-4.

> **스프링 프레시 생수**
>
> 스프링 프레시 생수는 시중에 나와 있는 가장 순수하고 가장 신선한 미네랄 워터입니다. 이 물은 공급원인 스코틀랜드 고지대의 한 수원지에서 병에 담깁니다! **3** 많은 저희 고객들께서 객실에 있는 소형 냉장고에 저희 생수 병을 놓아 두고 계시며, 그분들의 손님들께서 전하시는 의견은 대단히 긍정적입니다. 여러분께서도 손님들을 상쾌한 기분으로 유지시켜 드리기를 원하실 경우, 오늘 첫 대량 주문을 하시는 것을 고려해 보십시오! www.springfreshmineralwater.com을 방문하셔서 **4(A)** 저희 가격도 확인해 보시고 **4(D)** 저희 고객들의 추천 후기도 읽어 보시기 바랍니다. 저희 웹 사이트에서 저희가 어떻게 물을 모아 병에 옮겨 담는지 보여 드리는 **4(B)** 짧은 동영상도 보실 수 있습니다.

어휘 **refreshing** 신선한, 상쾌하게 해 주는 **bottle** v. ~을 병에 담다 **spring** 수원지, 샘 **bulk** a. 대량의 **pricing** 가격 (책정) **testimonials** 고객 추천 후기 **clip** 동영상

3. 광고는 누구를 대상으로 할 것 같은가?
(A) 항공기 승객들
(B) 호텔 소유주들
(C) 투어 구성원들
(D) 행사 참석자들

해설 지문 초반부에 많은 고객들이 객실에 있는 소형 냉장고에 생수 병을 놓아 둔다는 점과 그곳의 손님들이 전하는 의견이 언급된 부분을 통해 호텔을 운영하는 사람이 대상인 것으로 볼 수 있으므로 (B)가 정답이다.

4. 웹 사이트에 있는 것으로 언급되지 않는 것은 무엇인가?
(A) 비용
(B) 동영상
(C) 할인
(D) 후기

해설 지문 후반부에 웹 사이트 주소와 함께 그곳에서 볼 수 있는 정보로 our pricing과 testimonials from our clients, 그리고 short clips가 언급되고 있으므로 (A)와 (D), 그리고 (B)를 확인할 수 있다. 하지만 할인과 관련된 정보는 제시되어 있지 않으므로 (C)가 정답이다.

5-6.

시네마페스트에서 해외 영화 주간을 기념해 보세요!

시네마페스트가 돌아왔으며, **5 올해는 9월 12일부터 18일까지 진행됩니다.** 이 행사는 처음으로 메이플우드에서 영화의 마술을 경험해 보시거나 여러분께서 가장 좋아하시는 지역 영화관들을 재방문하실 수 있는 완벽한 기회입니다. 심지어 **5 이 일주일 기간의 기념 행사** 중에 다수의 영화를 관람하실 수도 있습니다! 열 곳의 인기 영화관들이 고전 영화 및 현대 영화에 대한 특별 상영회를 제공해 드릴 것이며, **6(A) 영화 입장권과 6(C) 팝콘, 6(B) 음료**, 그리고 작은 특별 선물까지, 이 모두를 할인된 가격 12달러에 포함하는 특별 무비 패스가 있습니다. 미리 여러분의 입장권을 예매하시는 것이 매우 권장됩니다. 시네마페스트가 매년 수백 명의 지역 주민과 방문객들을 끌어들이고 있으므로, 훌륭한 가격에 훌륭한 영화들을 즐기실 수 있는 기회를 놓치지 마시기 바랍니다. 참여 영화관 목록 및 상영 일정표를 보시려면 www.maplewoodfilmfest.org를 방문하십시오.

어휘 **catch** (영화·TV 프로그램 등) ~을 보다 **screening** 상영(회) **contemporary** 현대의, 동시대의 **treat** 특별 선물, 대접, 한턱 **in advance** 미리, 사전에

5. 시네마페스트와 관련해 언급된 것은 무엇인가?
(A) 처음으로 개최될 것이다.
(B) 한 곳에서 개최될 것이다.
(C) 일주일 동안 개최될 것이다.
(D) 배우들이 참석할 것이다.

해설 지문 초반부와 중반부에 9월 12일부터 18일까지 개최된다는 점과 일주일 기간의 행사라는 말이 언급되어 있으므로 (C)가 정답이다.

6. 무비 패스에 포함되지 않는 것은 무엇인가?
(A) 입장권
(B) 음료
(C) 간식
(D) 포스터

해설 지문 중반부에 특별 무비 패스에 포함되는 것으로 movie ticket과 popcorn, 그리고 drink가 언급되어 있으므로 (A)와 (C), 그리고 (B)를 확인할 수 있다. 하지만 포스터는 제시되어 있지 않으므로 (D)가 정답이다.

7-8.

그랜트 씨께,

이 이메일은 파크사이드 가든의 조경 프로젝트에 필요한 꽃 선택과 관련된 귀하의 문의사항에 답변해 드리기 위한 것입니다. 저희는 최적의 적용 범위를 위해 지정 구역 한 곳마다 5개의 화단을 설치하도록 권해 드립니다. **7 가장 인기 있는 저희 꽃들은 라벤더와 매리골드, 그리고 데이지입니다. 8 라벤더를 선택하시는 경우, 충분한 햇빛이 필요하며, 그늘진 곳에 놓아 두시면 안 된다는 점에 유의하시기 바랍니다.** 선호하시는 꽃과 심는 장소에 관한 상세 설명을 저희에게 제공해 주시면, 저희 팀이 공원의 일일 활동에 지장을 주지 않고 그에 따라 꽃들을 배치해 드릴 수 있습니다.

에밀리 하그로브, 블루밍 랜드스케이프

어휘 **landscaping** 조경 (작업) **cluster** 집단, 무리 **designated** 지정된 **optimal** 최적의 **ample** 충분한 **shaded** 그늘진 **accordingly** 그에 따라, 그에 맞게 **without -ing** ~하지 않고 **interrupt** ~에 지장을 주다, ~을 방해하다

7. 이메일의 목적은 무엇인가?
(A) 주문품의 지연 문제를 설명하는 것
(B) 프로젝트에 대한 선택권을 제시하는 것
(C) 일부 작업 일정의 재조정을 추천하는 것
(D) 몇몇 꽃들의 샘플을 요청하는 것

해설 조경 작업을 위한 화단 설치를 권하면서 지문 중반부에 선택 가능한 꽃들을 언급하고 있다. 이는 조경 프로젝트를 위한 선택권을 제시하는 것과 같으므로 (B)가 정답이다.

8. 하그로브 씨가 라벤더와 관련해 언급하는 것은 무엇인가?
(A) 충분한 양의 수분을 필요로 한다.
(B) 여러 색상으로 이용 가능하다.
(C) 어둡게 빛이 비치는 구역에 심어져서는 안된다.
(D) 다른 종류의 꽃들보다 더 비싸다.

해설 지문 중반부에 라벤더는 충분한 햇빛이 필요하고 그늘진 곳에 놓아 두면 안 된다는 점에 유의하라는 말이 쓰여 있으므로 (C)가 정답이다.

어휘 **moisture** 수분, 습기 **dimly lit** 어둡게 빛이 비치는

9-10.

> **9** 수신: 클리어사이트 테크놀로지 전 직원
>
> **9** **9월 15일, 금요일 오후에, 우리 회사의 새로운 혁신 제품을 공개하는 행사를 주최할 예정이므로, 여러분 모두 함께 하시길 바랍니다.** 이 모임에서, 우리는 최근의 발전상 및 최신 휴대전화기 M505의 특징들을 선보이면서, 이 흥미로운 중대 시점에 이르도록 우리 클리어사이트 테크놀로지에게 원동력이 되어 준 공동의 노력을 강조하게 될 것입니다. - [1] -. 이 행사는 그랜드뷰 호텔에서 개최될 것이며, M505의 공식 출시를 기념할 것입니다. - [2] -. 소중한 우리 직원들뿐만 아니라, 이 행사에는 수많은 기자와 우리 주주들, 그리고 투자자들까지 참석하실 것입니다. **10** **휴무를 신청하실 필요는 없습니다.** - [3] -. 하지만, 여러분께서 참석하실 계획이시면 우리 인사부에 알리시도록 분명히 요청 드립니다. 여러분과 함께 기념할 수 있기를 고대합니다. - [4] -.
>
> 알렉스 휘트먼

어휘 unveil ~을 공개하다 developments 발전상, 진전된 사항들 collective 공동의, 집단적인 milestone 중대 시점, 획기적인 사건, 이정표 mark ~을 기념하다, ~에 해당하다 time off 휴무, 휴가

9. 회람의 주 목적은 무엇인가?
(A) 행사를 주최하기 위해 자원 봉사자를 찾는 것
(B) 직원들에게 노고에 대해 감사의 뜻을 표하는 것
(C) 직원들을 제품 출시 행사에 초대하는 것
(D) 신제품 판매 수치를 알리는 것

해설 상단에 수신인이 소속 회사 전 직원으로 쓰여 있고, 지문 시작 부분에 자사의 새로운 혁신 제품을 공개하는 행사에 모두 함께 하시길 바란다고 알리고 있어 제품 출시 행사에 직원들을 초대하는 것이 목적임을 알 수 있으므로 (C)가 정답이다.

10. [1], [2], [3], 그리고 [4]로 표기된 위치들 중에서, 다음 문장이 들어가기에 가장 적절한 곳은 어디인가?
"우리 사무실은 점심 시간에 문을 닫을 예정입니다."
(A) [1]
(B) [2]
(C) [3]
(D) [4]

해설 제시된 문장은 사무실이 점심 시간에 문을 닫는다는 의미를 지니고 있다. 이는 업무가 진행되지 않는다는 뜻으로서, 휴무를 신청할 필요가 없다고 밝히는 문장 뒤에 위치한 [3]에 들어가 휴무를 신청하지 않아도 되는 이유를 언급하는 흐름이 되어야 알맞으므로 (C)가 정답이다.

11-12.

> **테드 개리건 [오후 1:12]** 안녕하세요, 린 씨. 유감스럽게도 우리가 오늘 예정대로 리터 씨의 주문품을 배송해 드릴 수 없을 겁니다. 그분께 전화 드려서 알려 주시겠어요?
> **린 딥스 [오후 1:13]** 알겠습니다. 하지만, 그분께서 그 주문품이 급히 필요하시다고 분명히 언급하셨어요. 월요일에 근무를 시작하는 신입 직원들이 있는데, **11** **모두 그 근무용 셔츠와 바지가 필요하시거든요.** **12** **우리가 언제 전해 드릴 수 있다고 생각하세요?**
> **테드 개리건 [오후 1:15]** **12** **제조사가 해외에 본사가 있는데, 악천후로 인해 지연 문제를 겪었기 때문에, 말씀 드리기 어렵습니다.**
> **린 딥스 [오후 1:17]** 너무 아쉽네요. 짐작이 되시는 게 있나요?
> **테드 개리건 [오후 1:19]** **12** **늦어도 이번 주 금요일까지요.**

어휘 though (문장 끝이나 중간에서) 하지만 get A to B A를 B에게 갖다 주다 inclement weather 악천후 no later than 늦어도 ~까지

11. 리터 씨가 무엇을 구입했을 것 같은가?
(A) 소프트웨어
(B) 차량
(C) 문구류
(D) 유니폼

해설 딥스 씨가 1시 13분에 리터 씨의 주문품을 설명하면서 리터 씨의 신입 직원들이 근무용 셔츠와 바지가 필요하다는 사실을 밝히고 있으므로 (D)가 정답이다.

12. 오후 1시 17분에, 딥스 씨가 "짐작이 되시는 게 있나요?"라고 쓸 때 무엇을 의미할 것 같은가?
(A) 비용 견적서가 부정확하다고 생각한다.
(B) 전체적인 비용을 계산해야 한다.
(C) 대략적인 배송 날짜를 알고 싶어 한다.
(D) 일기 예보를 확인해 봐야 한다.

해설 1시 13분에 딥스 씨가 리터 씨의 주문품을 언제 전해 줄 수 있는지 묻는 것에 대해 개리건 씨가 말하기 어렵다고 밝히자, 딥스 씨가 '짐작이 되시는 게 있나요?'라고 묻고 있고, 개리건 씨는 대략적인 미래 시점으로 답변하는 흐름이다. 따라서, 딥스 씨가 리터 씨의 주문품 전달과 관련해 짐작이 되는 시점을 궁금해했다는 사실을 알 수 있으므로 (C)가 정답이다.

13-14.

저희 엘리트 행사 기획사는 **13** **20년 넘게 잊지 못할 행사들을 계속 만들어 오고 있습니다.** 저희는 반드시 여러분의 행사가 매끄럽게 진행되고 기억에 남을 만한 것이 될 수 있도록 최신 기술을 활용하고 있습니다.

저희 전문 지식은 기업 행사와 결혼식, 그리고 사교적 모임의 범위에 이릅니다. 저희는 여러분과 밀접하게 협업해 모든 세부 요소를 고안합니다. 추가로, 저희는 여러분께서 행사를 효과적으로 **14** **홍보하시는** 데 이용하실 수 있는 맞춤 제작 전단지와 포스터를 만듭니다. 오늘 저희에게 연락하셔서 여러분의 다음 번 행사를 특별하게 만들어 보십시오.

어휘 **unforgettable** 잊지 못할 **seamless** 매끄럽게 진행되는 **span** ~의 범위에 이르다, ~에 걸쳐 있다 **function** 행사, 의식 **flyer** 전단지 **extraordinary** 특별한, 특출한, 예사롭지 않은

13. 엘리트 행사 기획사와 관련해 언급된 것은 무엇인가?
(A) 주로 결혼식 피로연을 마련한다.
(B) 20년도보다 더 이전에 설립되었다.
(C) 온라인에서 긍정적인 평가를 받았다.
(D) 현재 신입 직원을 고용하고 있다.

해설 첫 단락에 엘리트 행사 기획사가 20년 넘게 잊지 못할 행사들을 계속 만들어 오고 있다는 말이 쓰여 있어 설립된 지 20년이 넘은 회사임을 알 수 있으므로 (B)가 정답이다.

어휘 **reception** 피로연, 축하 연회

14. 두 번째 단락, 두 번째 줄의 단어 "promote"와 의미가 가장 가까운 것은 무엇인가?
(A) 홍보하다
(B) 칭찬하다
(C) 진급시키다
(D) 장려하다

해설 promote이 속한 that절이 전단지와 포스터를 의미하는 flyers and posters를 수식하는 that절인 것으로 볼 때, 목적어 your event 및 부사 effectively와 함께 '효과적으로 행사를 홍보하는 데 이용할 수 있는 전단지와 포스터'를 의미해야 자연스러우므로 '홍보하다'를 뜻하는 (A) publicize가 정답이다.

Check-up Test

1. (B)	**2.** (D)	**3.** (D)	**4.** (B)	**5.** (C)
6. (C)	**7.** (C)	**8.** (B)	**9.** (A)	**10.** (D)
11. (D)	**12.** (D)	**13.** (C)	**14.** (D)	**15.** (D)

1-2.

의사 조셉 시미즈, DMD
우리 진료소를 위한 유지 관리 규약

1 **가장 높은 기준의 치료와 우리 환자분들을 위해 깔끔하고 환영하는 환경을 보장하기 위해, 시설 유지 관리에서의 일관성 있는 관행을 따르는 것은 필수적입니다. 아래 강조된 새롭게 개정된 지침들을 검토해 주십시오.**

- **2(B)** **각 환자가 방문하신 후, 의자, 작업대, 그리고 어떤 다른 접촉된 지점들을 인가된 소독약으로 모든 표면들을 닦으십시오.**
- 각 근무의 종료 시점에 모든 치료실에서 장갑, 마스크, 거즈, 그리고 일회용 턱받이와 같은 용품들을 다시 채워 넣으십시오.
- 멸균 처리기, 엑스레이 기기, 그리고 치과의사의 손잡이 기구와 같이 구강 치료 기구들과 장비를 위해 모든 살균과 교정 관리 규약을 따르십시오.
- **2(C)** **특별히 지정되고 새지 않는 용기를 사용함으로써 생물학적 위험이 있는 폐기물들(예시: 날카로운 물건, 거즈, 그리고 다른 잠재적인 감염 물질)을 처리하십시오.**
- **2(A)** **각 장비의 오작동, 용품 부족 또는 환자 치료에 영향을 끼칠 수 있는 다른 문제들에 대해 즉시 시미즈 선생님 또는 선임 치과 기술자분께 알리십시오.**

어휘 **care** 치료, 돌봄, 주의 **consistent** 일관성 있는 **practice** 관행, 실행 **wipe down** ~을 닦다 **countertops** 작업대, 조리대 **touchpoints** 접촉된 지점, 접점, 터치포인트 **disinfectant** 소독약 **disposable** 일회용의 **bib** 턱받이, 앞치마의 가슴 부분 **sterilization** 살균, 멸균 **calibration** 교정 **protocol** 관리 규약 **oral** 구강의 **autoclave** 멸균 처리기 **handpieces** 손잡이 기구 **dispose of** ~을 처리하다, 버리다 **biohazard** 생물학적 위험이 있는 **waste** 폐기물 **sharps** 날카로운 물건 **infectious** 감염의 **malfunctions** 오작동

1. 공지는 누구를 대상으로 할 것 같은가?
(A) 의대생
(B) 치과 조무사
(C) 접수 안내원
(D) 공인된 간호사

해설 첫 단락 시작 부분에 치료와 환자들을 위해 준수해야 할 필수 지침들을 확인해 보도록 당부하는 말과 함께 치과 진료소 내에서의 상세 규칙을 설명하고 있다. 이는 치과에서 일하는 사람을 대상으로 하므로 (B)가 정답이다.

2. 진료소를 유지 관리하기 위해 명시된 지침이 아닌 것은 무엇인가?

(A) 결함이 있는 기계는 보고되어야 한다.
(B) 사람이 접촉되는 표면들은 살균되어야 한다.
(C) 몇몇 물질들이 분리되어 버려져야 한다.
(D) 용품들이 근무가 시작되기 전에 다시 채워져야 한다.

해설 두 번째 단락 마지막 항목의 Immediately notify Dr. Shimizu or a lead technician of any equipment malfunctions에서 (A)를, 첫 번째 항목의 any other touchpoints, with approved disinfectants after each patient visit에서 (B)를, 그리고 네 번째 항목의 Dispose of any biohazard waste (e.g. sharps, gauze, and other potentially infectious materials) by using a specially designated, leak-proof container에서 (C)를 각각 확인할 수 있다. 하지만, 용품들이 채워지는 시점은 근무가 끝난 후라고 언급되어 있으므로 (D)가 정답이다.

3-4.

새라 마이어스 [오전 8:12]
안녕하세요, 롭 씨... 제가 투자자 발표회에 늦고 있어요.
롭 켈러 [오전 8:13]
아, 이런, 무슨 일 있으셨어요? 당신이 이곳에 계시는 게 아주 중요한데, 저 혼자 권유 연설을 감당할 수 있을지 잘 모르겠어요.
새라 마이어스 [오전 8:15]
정말 죄송해요. **3 저희 집에서 수도관이 파열되었는데, 그걸 고치려고 배관공을 기다리고 있어요.** 가능한 한 빨리 그곳으로 갈게요.
롭 켈러 [오전 8:17]
아, 엉망진창일 것 같네요! 빨리 그 일이 처리되도록 하시기를 바랍니다. 걱정 마세요, 제가 발표회를 시작해서 그분들 관심을 사로잡아 놓고 있을게요.
새라 마이어스 [오전 8:18]
고마워요, 롭 씨. **4 본사에 전화해서 존슨 씨에게 제가 좀 지체될 거라고 알려 드릴게요.**
롭 켈러 [오전 8:20]
좋은 계획입니다. 저한테 계속 알려 주세요. 곧 뵙기를 바랍니다!
새라 마이어스 [오전 8:21]
그럴게요. 다시 한 번 고마워요, 이따 얘기해요.

어휘 **be running late for** ~에 늦다, 지각하다 **pitch** (구매 등을 유도하는) 권유 연설, 설득 **burst** 파열되다, 터지다 **mess** 엉망진창, 어수선함 **engaged** 관심이 사로잡힌, 몰두한

3. 마이어스 씨와 관련해 암시된 것은 무엇인가?
(A) 켈러 씨에게 몇몇 슬라이드를 보낼 것이다.
(B) 최근에 한 업체에 투자했다.
(C) 회사 일을 하루 쉴 계획이다.
(D) 현재 집에 있다.

해설 마이어스 씨가 8시 15분에 작성한 메시지에 집에서 수도관이 파열되어 그걸 고치기 위해 배관공을 기다리고 있다고 쓰여 있다. 따라서, 현재 집에서 기다리는 상황임을 알 수 있으므로 (D)가 정답이다.

어휘 **take A off work** 회사 일을 ~만큼 쉬다

4. 오전 8시 20분에, 켈러 씨가 "좋은 계획입니다"라고 쓸 때 무엇을 의미하는가?
(A) 켈러 씨는 마이어스 씨가 좋지 못한 결정을 내렸다고 생각한다.
(B) 켈러 씨는 마이어스 씨가 동료 직원에게 연락해야 한다고 생각한다.
(C) 켈러 씨는 마이어스 씨가 발표 계획을 변경하기를 원한다.
(D) 켈러 씨는 혼자 발표를 진행할 수 있다고 확신하고 있다.

해설 마이어스 씨가 8시 18분에 본사에 전화해서 존슨 씨에게 자신이 좀 지체될 거라고 알리겠다고 말하자, 켈러 씨가 '좋은 계획입니다'라고 대답하는 흐름이다. 이는 그렇게 연락해서 알리는 것을 지지한다는 뜻이므로 (B)가 정답이다.

5-7.

테크 마트의 최대 규모 매장 개장식

5 토론토 (5월 12일) - 전국 최고의 전자기기 소매점들 중 하나인, 테크 마트가 다음 달에 토론토에서 자사 최대 규모의 소매 판매점 대개장을 기념할 예정이라고 오늘 발표했습니다. 도시 내 북적이는 상업 지구의 중심부에 위치하는, 이 신규 매장은 10만 평방 피트가 넘는 규모에 이르며, 가전 제품과 스마트 기기에서부터 엔터테인먼트 시스템과 개인용 소형 기기에 이르기까지, 아주 다양한 전자기기를 특징으로 할 것입니다.

"이 신규 지점은 고객들께 최첨단 기술 및 가정 내 해결책에 있어 최신 제품을 제공해 드릴 것입니다,"라고 테크 마트의 칼라 뎀프시 대표이사가 보도 자료를 통해 밝혔습니다. "저희는 지금까지 중에서 저희의 가장 큰 매장을 토론토에 제공해 드리게 되어 대단히 기쁘게 생각하며, 이곳에서 **6(A) 고객들께서 대화형 디스플레이, 개인 맞춤형 상담, 그리고 매장 내 독점 구매 거래를 즐기실 수 있습니다.**"

6(B) 대개장 기념 행사는 6월 5일, 토요일, 오전 9시부터 오후 9시까지, 새로운 토론토 테크 마트 슈퍼스토어에서 개최될 것입니다. 이 행사는 제품 시연회, 경품 증정, 그리고 기간 한정 판촉 행사를 특징으로 할 것입니다. **6(D) 부산 일렉트로닉스의 마이크 손 씨 같은 특별 초대 손님들께서도 참석**하실 것으로 예상되며, 조기 방문객들께서는 인기 제품에 대해 독점 할인을 받으시게 됩니다.

"이 슈퍼스토어의 개장은 고객들께 비교할 수 없는 쇼핑 경험을 제공해 드리겠다는 저희 목표와 방향이 일치합니다,"라고 뎀프시 씨가 덧붙였습니다. "이 신규 지점은 또한 **7** **최근 있었던 오타와와 위니펙에서의 매장 개장 및 연말까지 전국에 걸쳐 네 곳의 추가 슈퍼스토어를 개장하려는 저희 계획 끝에** 나타난 저희의 확장 전략을 뒷받침해 줍니다. 저희는 이 매장이 지역 사회의 핵심적인 일부분이 될 것으로 확신합니다."

어휘 **bustling** 북적이는, 부산한 **span** (범위, 기간 등) ~에 이르다, ~에 걸쳐 이어지다 **gadget** 소형 기기 **cutting-edge** 최첨단의, 최신의 **interactive** 대화형의, 상호 작용하는 **deal** 구매 거래 (제품) **giveaway** 증정(품) **align with** ~와 방향이 일치하다, ~에 맞춰 조정하다 **unparalleled** 비교할 수 없는

5. 테크 마트의 신규 소매점과 관련해 언급된 것은 무엇인가?
(A) 그 회사 최초의 물리적인 매장이다.
(B) 10만 개의 새로운 일자리를 창출할 것이다.
(C) 6월에 개장할 예정이다.
(D) 토론토 교외 지역에 자리잡고 있다.

해설 첫 단락에 테크 마트가 다음 달에 토론토에서 자사 최대 규모의 소매 판매점을 개장한다고 발표한 사실이 쓰여 있고, 기사 작성 날짜가 5월 12일로 표기되어 있어 6월 개장한다는 것을 알 수 있으므로 (C)가 정답이다.

어휘 **physical** 물리적인, 신체적인 **outskirts** 교외, 변두리

6. 개장 기념 행사와 관련해 언급되지 않은 것은 무엇인가?
(A) 참석자들에게 제공되는 혜택
(B) 개최되는 요일과 날짜
(C) 가장 가까운 대중 교통 노선
(D) 특별 초대 손님의 이름

해설 두 번째 단락의 where customers can enjoy interactive displays에서 참석자 대상 혜택을 언급한 (A)를, 세 번째 단락의 The grand opening event will take place on Saturday, June 5와 Special guests such as Mike Son에서 (B)와 (D)를 각각 확인할 수 있다. 하지만, 대중 교통과 관련된 정보는 제시되어 있지 않으므로 (C)가 정답이다.

7. 뎀프시 씨가 테크 마트와 관련해 언급하는 것은 무엇인가?
(A) 다수의 관리직 공석이 있다.
(B) 다른 회사와 합병할 것이다.
(C) 꾸준히 성장하는 업체이다.
(D) 훌륭한 기술 지원 서비스를 제공한다.

해설 네 번째 단락에 최근 오타와와 위니펙에서 매장을 개장한 사실 및 연말까지 네 곳의 추가 슈퍼스토어를 개장하려는 계획이 언급되어 있다. 이는 회사가 계속 성장하고 있음을 의미하므로 (C)가 정답이다.

8-11.

발신: sales@zappmarketing.com
수신: organizer@summerbeatsfestival.com
날짜: 5월 18일
제목: 회신: 축제용 전단 및 포스터

케인 씨께,

7월 15일부터 17일까지 개최되는, 써머 비츠 뮤직 페스티벌의 홍보용 물품에 대한 귀하의 요청과 관련해 저희 인쇄팀과 막 이야기 나눴습니다. **8** **저희는 홍보를 위한 배부 및 현장에서의 가시성 둘 모두를 충족할 수 있도록 예상 참석자 1인당 최소 두 장의 전단 또는 포스터를 인쇄하시기를 권해 드립니다.** 일련의 세 가지 디자인(전단, 포스터, 그리고 현수막)을 인쇄하시는 데 대한 견적가는 개당 약 7달러에서 9달러이며, 크기 및 마감 처리에 따라 다를 수 있습니다.

저희가 가장 많이 요청 받는 디자인은 주요 무대 출연 그룹 전체를 **9** **특징으로 하는** 라인업 전단과 페스티벌 안내도, 그리고 일정일을 나타낸 포스터입니다. 이것들은 주요 공연자들 및 무대 위치와 행사 시간대 같은 중요 상세정보를 강조하기 위해 생동감 있는 색상으로 인쇄될 것입니다.

귀하께서는 자원 봉사자들이 시 전역에서 포스터를 게시하고 전단을 배부하는 데 도움을 줄 것이라고 언급하셨습니다. **10** **일부 지역에서는 공공 장소에서 전단을 게시하는 것과 관련된 특정 규정이 있을 수도 있다는 점만 기억해 주시기 바랍니다.** 특정 행사장 또는 공공 장소로부터 허가를 받으시는 데 도움이 필요하실 경우, 저희 거리 담당팀이 그 부분을 처리해 드릴 수 있습니다. 디자인을 최종 확정하시는 대로, **11** **필요하신 포스터 및 전단의 총 수량만 저희에게 보내 주시면**, 모든 것이 인쇄되어 귀하의 사무실로 배송되도록 보장해 드리겠습니다.

안녕히 계십시오.

제이슨 매튜스
잽 마케팅 주식회사

어휘 **on-site** 현장의, 부지 내의 **visibility** 가시성, 눈에 잘 보임 **estimated** 견적의, 추정되는 **banner** 현수막 **finish** n. 마감 (처리) **act** (공연 등의) 그룹, 팀 **vibrant** 생동감 있는, 생생한

8. 이메일의 목적은 무엇인가?
(A) 결제 비용의 수납을 확인해 주는 것
(B) 행사에 필요한 선택사항을 설명하는 것
(C) 축제 일정을 재조정하도록 권하는 것
(D) 일부 제품의 샘플을 요청하는 것

해설 첫 단락에 홍보를 위한 배부 및 현장에서의 가시성 둘 모두를 위해 예상 참석자 1인당 최소 두 장의 전단 또는 포스터를 인쇄하기를 권한다고 언급한 뒤로, 전단 및 포스터와 관련해 설명하고 있으므로 (B)가 정답이다.

9. 두 번째 단락, 첫 번째 줄의 단어 "features"와 의미가 가장 가까운 것은 무엇인가?
(A) 포함하다
(B) 검토하다
(C) 칭찬하다
(D) 출간하다

해설 features가 포함된 which절 바로 앞에는 선행사로 lineup flyer가, features 뒤에는 주요 무대 출연 그룹 전체를 뜻하는 명사구가 쓰여 있다. 따라서, features가 전단이 그러한 정보를 특징으로 한다는 의미를 나타내는 동사임을 알 수 있는데, 이는 포함하고 있다는 말과 같으므로 (A) includes가 정답이다.

10. 매튜스 씨가 포스터 및 전단과 관련해 언급하는 것은 무엇인가?
(A) 재활용 물품을 이용해 만들어진다.
(B) 잽 마케팅 사의 로고를 포함할 것이다.
(C) 이메일로 케인 씨에게 보내질 것이다.
(D) 게시하는 데 허가가 필요할 수도 있다.

해설 세 번째 단락에 일부 지역에서는 공공 장소에서 전단을 게시하는 것과 관련된 특정 규정이 있을 수도 있다고 언급하면서 허가를 받는 일과 관련해 이야기하고 있으므로 (D)가 정답이다.

11. 매튜스 씨가 케인 씨에게 어떤 정보를 요청하는가?
(A) 광고에 필요한 예산
(B) 행사의 주요 공연자
(C) 축제 장소
(D) 필요한 물품의 수

해설 세 번째 단락에 디자인을 최종 확정하는 대로 필요한 포스터 및 전단의 총 수량을 보내 달라고 요청하고 있으므로 (D)가 정답이다.

12-15.

가든 리트리츠 주식회사
맞춤형 정원 여름 별장

따뜻한 기간을 즐기실 수 있는 개인 맞춤형 옥외 공간을 꿈꾸고 계시는 분이라면, 저희 가든 리트리츠 주식회사가 이상적인 여름 별장 디자인 및 설치 패키지 서비스를 제공해 드립니다. 평화로운 정원 사무실을 찾고 계시든, 아니면 고급스러운 오락 공간을 찾고 계시든 상관없이, 여러분의 정원을 완벽히 보완해 드리는 여름 별장을 만들어 드리기 위해 여러분과 협업할 것입니다. - [1] -.

12 다음은 저희 처리 과정이 진행되는 방식입니다.
► 첫 번째로, 디자인 컨설턴트가 귀하의 건물을 방문해 이용 가능한 공간을 평가하고, 치수를 측정한 다음, 여름 별장에 대한 귀하의 비전을 논의할 것입니다.
► 이 상담 시간 중에, 외부 마감 처리, 지붕 공사, 그리고 실내 배치에 대한 다양한 디자인 선택사항들을 두루 살펴 보실 수 있는 기회도 갖게 되실 것입니다. - [2] -. 저희는 전통적인 목재 구조물에서부터 매끈하고 현대적인 디자인에 이르기까지, 아주 다양한 스타일을 제공해 드립니다. **13 원하실 경우, 저희 전시장으로 오셔서 직접 자재들도 살펴 보실 수 있습니다.** - [3] -.
► 디자인 선택사항들을 최종 확정하시고 나면, 자재와 공사, 그리고 설치 작업에 대한 비용을 개괄적으로 보여 드리는, **14 상세 견적서를 보내 드릴 것입니다. 이 가격은 4주 동안 유효하므로**, 귀하께 결정을 내리실 수 있는 충분한 시간이 되실 것입니다. 저희가 귀하의 승인 및 선금을 받는 대로, 자재가 주문될 것이며, 일반적으로 2~3주 내로 도착합니다.
► 마지막으로, 저희가 귀하의 일정에 적합한 설치 날짜에 대한 일정을 잡을 것입니다. **15 대부분의 여름 별장 설치 작업은 1~3일 사이로 소요됩니다.** - [4] -. 단순한 여름 별장은 약 5시간 내로 지어질 수도 있습니다!

어휘 **bespoke** 맞춤형의, 맞춤 주문의(= personalized) **complement** ~을 보완하다 **browse through** ~을 두루 살펴 보다, 훑어 보다 **roofing** 지붕 공사 **sleek** 매끈한 **explore** ~을 살펴 보다 **ample** 충분한

12. 안내책자는 주로 무엇에 관한 것인가?
(A) 신규 제품군
(B) 다가오는 무역 박람회
(C) 구직 기회
(D) 업무 처리 과정

해설 첫 단락에서 여름 별장과 관련된 서비스를 간단히 언급한 다음, 두 번째 단락에서 공사를 진행하기 위한 과정을 순서대로 상세히 설명하고 있으므로 (D)가 정답이다.

13. 안내책자에 따르면, 건축 자재를 어떻게 볼 수 있는가?
(A) 웹 사이트를 확인함으로써
(B) 일부 샘플을 요청함으로써
(C) 전시장을 방문함으로써
(D) 카탈로그를 훑어 봄으로써

해설 두 번째 단락 두 번째 항목에 원할 경우에 전시장으로 가서 직접 자재들도 살펴 볼 수 있다고 설명하고 있으므로 (C)가 정답이다.

14. 몇 주가 지나면 견적서에 제공된 총액이 변경될 수도 있는가?
(A) 1주
(B) 2주
(C) 3주
(D) 4주

해설 두 번째 단락 세 번째 항목에 상세 견적서를 보내는 것과 관련해 그 가격이 4주 동안 유효하다는 사실을 밝히는 정보가 제시되어 있다. 이는 4주 후에 해당 가격이 변동될 수도 있다는 뜻이므로 (D)가 정답이다.

15. [1], [2], [3], 그리고 [4]로 표기된 위치들 중에서, 다음 문장이 들어가기에 가장 적절한 곳은 어디인가?
"하지만, 이는 디자인의 복잡성에 따라 다릅니다."
(A) [1]
(B) [2]
(C) [3]
(D) [4]

해설 제시된 문장은 특정 대상을 this로 지칭해 그것이 디자인의 복잡성에 따라 다르다는 의미를 나타내고 있다. 따라서, 대부분의 설치 작업이 소요되는 기간을 언급하는 문장 뒤에 위치한 [4]에 들어가 그 기간이 변동될 수 있는 조건을 알리는 흐름이 되어야 자연스러우므로 (D)가 정답이다.

어휘 complexity 복잡성

Playlist 13
매번 나오는 파트7 지문별 특징

Practice

1. (B)	**2.** (B)	**3.** (B)	**4.** (B)	**5.** (D)
6. (D)	**7.** (A)	**8.** (B)	**9.** (D)	**10.** (A)
11. (D)	**12.** (A)	**13.** (B)	**14.** (C)	**15.** (C)
16. (B)				

1-2.

수신: 영업팀 전 직원
발신: 줄리아 라모스, 영업 이사

1 **에밀리 데이비스 씨가 우리 영업부 선임 고객 관리자로서 새로운 역할로 전환됨에 따라 축하 인사를 전해 드리게 되어 기쁩니다.** 데이비스 씨는 우리 팀의 필수적인 일원으로서, 지난 3년 동안 사원급 영업 직원으로 근무해 왔습니다. 그 기간 중에, 데이비스 씨는 지속적으로 뛰어난 고객 관리 능력을 보여 주셨으며, **2** **우리의 고객 목록이 꾸준히 늘어나는 데 도움을 주셨습니다.** 데이비스 씨의 새로운 책무는 10월 2일, 월요일에 시작될 것입니다. 데이비스 씨가 이 새로운 도전 과제를 맡으시는 과정에서 여러분의 지지를 보내 주시기 바랍니다!

어휘 transition into ~로 전환하다, 이행되다 integral 필수적인 consistently 지속적으로 exceptional 뛰어난, 이례적인 extend (인사 · 지원 · 친절 등) ~을 보내다, 베풀다 take on (책임 등) ~을 맡다

1. 라모스 씨는 왜 회람을 보냈는가?
(A) 직원들에게 한 가지 기회에 관해 알리기 위해
(B) 승진을 발표하기 위해
(C) 한 신입 직원을 소개하기 위해
(D) 직원들을 곧 있을 저녁 회식에 초대하기 위해

해설 지문 상단에 수신인이 영업팀 전 직원으로 쓰여 있고, 첫 문장에서 에밀리 데이비스 씨가 영업부 선임 고객 관리자로서의 새로운 역할을 맡게 되었음을 알리면서 데이비스 씨와 관련해 간략히 소개하고 있으므로 (B)가 정답이다.

2. 데이비스 씨와 관련해 언급된 것은 무엇인가?
(A) 폭넓은 관리 경력을 지니고 있다.
(B) 신규 고객들을 끌어들이는 일을 해냈다.
(C) 회사가 지출을 줄이는 데 도움을 주었다.
(D) 10월에 있을 한 행사에서 상을 받을 것이다.

해설 지문 중반부에 고객 목록이 꾸준히 늘어나는 데 도움을 주었다는 말이 쓰여 있는데, 이는 새로운 고객을 끌어들이는 역할을 훌륭히 해냈음을 의미하므로 (B)가 정답이다.

어휘 manage to do (어떻게든) ~해내다 honor ~에게 상을 주다, 영예를 주다

3-4.

제과제빵 기술 워크숍 소개

제과제빵의 정수를 **3** **완벽히 터득하기**를 바라시는 제과제빵사 지망생이신가요? **4** **유명 패스트리 요리사, 칼라 멘데즈 씨의 지도를 받아**, 여러분께서는 전문 기술을 이용해 다양한 빵과 케이크, 그리고 패스트리를 만드는 방법을 배우시게 될 것입니다. **4** **골드스톤 요리 학교 졸업생이신, 요리사 멘데즈 씨**께서는 현재 정규직으로 가르치고 계시며, 이 분야에서 10년이 넘는 경력을 보유하고 계십니다. 이 워크숍은 비용이 120달러이며, 10월 14일에 골드스톤 요리 학교에서 개최될 것입니다. 추가 정보를 원하시면, bakingworkshop@goldstoneculinary.com으로 켈리 젠킨스 씨께 이메일을 보내시기 바랍니다.

어휘 aspiring ~을 지망하는, 장차 ~가 되려는 look to do ~하기를 바라다 master v. ~을 완벽히 터득하다 essential n. 정수, 필수적인 것, 핵심

3. 첫 번째 단락, 첫 번째 줄의 단어 "master"와 의미가 가장 가까운 것은 무엇인가?
(A) 감독하다
(B) 이해하다
(C) 초과하다
(D) 이상화하다

해설 master 뒤에 목적어로 '제과제빵의 정수'를 뜻하는 명사구가 쓰여 있어 master는 제과제빵사 지망생이 그러한 요소들을 터득하거나 갖춘다는 의미를 나타내는 것으로 볼 수 있다. 이는 이해하는 것과 같은 의미로 생각할 수 있으므로 (B) understand가 정답이다.

4. 워크숍과 관련해 언급된 것은 무엇인가?
(A) 요리 시연회를 포함할 것이다.
(B) 해당 학교의 이전 학생이 가르칠 것이다.
(C) 10월에 할인된 비용으로 제공될 것이다.
(D) 멘데즈 씨의 레스토랑에서 개최될 것이다.

해설 지문 중반부에 유명 패스트리 요리사인 칼라 멘데즈 씨가 가르치는 워크숍임을 설명하면서 멘데즈 씨가 골드스톤 요리 학교의 졸업생임을 밝히고 있으므로 (B)가 정답이다.

5-6.

웰포드 (7월 22일) - 지난 몇 년 동안, **5** **다양한 업계 전체에 걸쳐 업체들이 직원을 유지하는 데 있어 점점 더 많은 어려움에 직면해 오면서**, 현재 경쟁 및 고객 확보와 관련된 우려를 뛰어넘었습니다. 이러한 변화에 대한 이유는 명확합니다. 소매업 및 접객업 같은 분야에서는, 인건비가 일반적으로 운영비의 상당한 부분을 차지합니다. 높은 이직률은 추가적인 채용 및 교육 비용으로 이어질 뿐만 아니라 **6** **일상적인 운영에도 지장을 줍니다.** 회사들이 더 나은 혜택 및 탄력적인 근무 조건을 제공하는 방법으로 이를 완화하기 위해 노력하고 있기는 하지만, 직원 유지의 까다로움은 수익성 및 전반적인 생산성에 지속적으로 영향을 미치고 있습니다.

어휘 **retain** ~을 유지하다 **surpass** ~을 뛰어넘다, 능가하다 **shift** 변화 **hospitality** 접객(업) **labor costs** 인건비 **account for** (비율 등) ~을 차지하다 **turnover rate** 이직률 **mitigate** ~을 완화하다 **flexible** 탄력적인, 유연한 **retention** 유지, 보유 **overall** 전반적인

5. 기사는 주로 무엇에 관한 것인가?
(A) 접객업 분야에서의 일자리 증가
(B) 업체들 사이에서의 경쟁 증가
(C) 고객 유치의 어려움
(D) 직원 유지의 까다로움

해설 첫 단락 시작 부분에 다양한 업계에 나타나는 직원 유지의 어려움을 먼저 언급한 다음, 그 이유와 영향 등에 관해 이야기하고 있으므로 (D)가 정답이다.

6. 기사의 내용에 따르면, 높은 직원 이직률의 영향은 무엇인가?
(A) 높아진 수익성
(B) 더 낮은 교육 비용
(C) 교대 근무의 탄력성
(D) 업무 흐름상의 지장

해설 두 번째 단락에 높은 이직률로 인해 나타나는 것들 중의 하나로 일상적인 운영에 지장을 준다는 문제가 언급되어 있으므로 (D)가 정답이다.

7-8.

제이미 트랜 (오후 2:15) 영화제에 필요한 우리 홍보 자료 디자인 작업을 거의 끝마쳤습니다. **7** **우리 전단에 영화제 날짜와 장소, 그리고 주요 행사 목록을 추가했습니다. 인쇄를 위해 보내기 전에 제가 포함해야 하는 다른 어떤 것이라도 있을까요?**
칼로스 멘데즈 (오후 2:17) 얼리 버드 티켓 가격에 관한 부분도 하단에 추가해 주실 수 있으세요?
제이미 트랜 (오후 2:18) 물론입니다! 지금 그 부분을 추가하겠습니다.
제이미 트랜 (오후 2:25) 그건 그렇고, **8** **프린터용 컬러 잉크가 다 떨어져 가고 있어요. 제가 더 주문할까요?**
칼로스 멘데즈 (오후 2:28) 실은, 새 배송 물량이 막 들어왔어요. **8** **물품 보관실을 확인해 보세요.**

어휘 **lineup** (출연자나 행사 등의) 목록, 명단, 예정표 **by the way** (화제 전환 시) 그건 그렇고, 그런데 **run low on** ~이 다 떨어지다, 부족해지다 **batch** (일괄 처리되는) 1회분, 분량

7. 트랜 씨는 무엇에 관해 묻는가?
(A) 일부 전단에 포함할 것
(B) 축제가 개최되는 때
(C) 홍보용 자료를 배포하는 방법
(D) 인쇄소가 위치해 있는 곳

해설 첫 번째 메시지에 트랜 씨가 전단에 몇 가지 정보를 추가한 사실과 함께 인쇄를 위해 보내기 전에 포함해야 하는 다른 어떤 게 또 있는지 묻고 있으므로 (A)가 정답이다.

8. 오후 2시 28분에, 멘데즈 씨가 "실은, 새 배송 물량이 막 들어왔어요"라고 쓸 때 무엇을 의미할 것 같은가?
(A) 트랜 씨가 추가 사본을 인쇄해야 한다.
(B) 트랜 씨가 추가 컬러 잉크를 주문하지 말아야 한다.
(C) 트랜 씨가 물품 보관실을 말끔히 치워야 한다.
(D) 트랜 씨가 일부 신입직원을 교육해야 한다.

해설 2시 25분에 트랜 씨가 컬러 잉크가 다 떨어져 가고 있다고

언급하면서 추가로 주문해야 하는지 묻자, 멘데즈 씨가 '실은, 새 배송 물량이 막 들어왔어요'라고 대답하면서 물품 보관실을 확인해 보라고 알리고 있다. 이는 이미 물품을 받았기 때문에 주문할 필요가 없다는 뜻이므로 (B)가 정답이다.

어휘 tidy up ~을 말끔히 치우다

9-10.

> 에르난데즈 씨께,
>
> **9 오늘 아까 전화상에서 이야기했던 금요일 배송과 관련된 최신 정보를 확인해 드리기 위해 글을 씁니다.** 하지만, 메이플 룸의 예기치 못한 유지 관리 작업으로 인해, 오리엔테이션 시간의 장소를 변경해야 했습니다. **10 유니폼들이 이제 이스트브룩 교육 센터의 윌로우 컨퍼런스 룸으로 대신 전달되도록 확실히 해 주시기 바랍니다.**
>
> 추가로, **10 제품들이 금요일 오전 9시까지 도착하는 것이 중요한데**, 저희가 직후에 환영 발표회를 실시할 예정이라서 그 제품들을 신입직원들에게 나눠 줄 시간이 필요할 것이기 때문입니다. 어떤 문제든 있을 경우, 주저하지 마시고 제게 직접 연락 주시기 바랍니다.
>
> 마리아 소사

어휘 unexpected 예기치 못한 conduct ~을 실시하다 shortly after 직후에

9. 소사 씨는 왜 에르난데즈 씨에게 이메일을 보냈는가?
(A) 직원 오리엔테이션 일정을 재조정하기 위해
(B) 일부 유지 관리 작업에 관해 문의하기 위해
(C) 취업 기회와 관련해 알려 주기 위해
(D) 말로 했던 일부 설명을 확인해 주기 위해

해설 첫 단락 시작 부분에 오늘 아까 전화상에서 이야기했던 금요일 배송과 관련된 정보를 확인해 주기 위해 글을 쓴다는 말로 목적을 밝히고 있으므로 (D)가 정답이다.

10. 소사 씨가 금요일 오전에 무엇을 받을 것으로 예상하는가?
(A) 의류
(B) 서류
(C) 발표 슬라이드
(D) 사무용 가구

해설 첫 단락에서 유니폼을 배송할 장소를 확인해 준 다음, 두 번째 단락에서 그 제품들이 금요일 오전 9시까지 도착하는 것이 중요하다고 밝히고 있으므로 (A)가 정답이다.

11-12.

> **그린필드 커뮤니티 가든: 모두를 위한 꽃이 피는 공간**
> *작성자, 엠마 델가도*
>
> "자연과 지속 가능성을 통해 사람들을 화합시키는 것." 이것이 바로 그린필드 커뮤니티 가든의 이면에 존재하는 운영 지침입니다. 다양한 채소와 허브, 그리고 꽃들과 함께, 저희 가든은 북적거리는 도시의 삶의 한가운데에서 평화로운 휴양 시간을 제공해 드립니다.
>
> 저희 그린필드 커뮤니티 가든은 또한 부지 내 남쪽에 위치해 있는 교육 센터를 특징으로 합니다. 이 센터는 계절 식목일 및 **11 아동 교육 프로그램 같은 지역 사회 행사를 주최합니다. 12 강의실과 옥외 시연 구역, 그리고 작은 온실이 갖춰져 있는**, 이 센터는 **11 도시에서의 원예에 대한 지식에 깊이를 더하기를 바라시는 모든 분을 위해 자원을 제공해 드립니다.** 잠재적인 원예 애호가가 되고 싶으신 분들께 이 공간을 방문하는 것을 매우 추천합니다.

어휘 blossoming 꽃을 피우는 bring A together A를 화합시키다, 한데 모으다 sustainability 지속 가능성 guiding principle 운영 지침, 지도 원칙 retreat 휴양, 야유회 amid ~하는 가운데 bustling 북적거리는 planting 식목, 식수 look to do ~하기를 바라다 deepen ~을 깊이 있게 만들다 prospective 잠재적인

11. 교육 센터와 관련해 언급된 것은 무엇인가?
(A) 현재 지어지고 있는 중이다.
(B) 입장료를 필요로 한다.
(C) 주말마다 행사를 주최한다.
(D) 모든 연령대에 속한 사람들의 구미를 충족한다.

해설 두 번째 단락에 아동 교육 프로그램 같은 행사도 언급되어 있고, 원예 관련 지식에 깊이를 더하기를 바라는 모든 사람에게 자원을 제공한다는 정보가 제시되어 있어 모든 연령대의 사람을 대상으로 한다는 것을 알 수 있으므로 (D)가 정답이다.

어휘 cater to ~의 구미를 충족하다

12. 그린필드 커뮤니티 가든에서의 시설로 언급되지 않은 것은 무엇인가?
(A) 카페테리아
(B) 시연 구역
(C) 강의실
(D) 온실

해설 두 번째 단락 중반부에 강의실, 옥외 시연 구역, 그리고 작은 온실이 갖춰져 있다고 쓰여 있고, 카페테리아는 언급되지 않았으므로 (A)가 정답이다.

어휘 glasshouse 온실

13-14.

그로버스 팜 스토어 펀데일 드라이브 3829번지, 브럼튼 월요일부터 토요일, 오전 9시에서 오후 4시까지 영업		
13 8월 6일	레드 레스터 치즈	$5.50
	요거트 (4팩)	$3.95
	유기농 딸기 우유	$1.75
	판매세	$1.12
	총액	$12.32
14 오늘 그로버스 팜 스토어의 회원이 되어 보세요! 회원들께서는 모든 팜 스토어 거래에 대해 포인트도 받고 저희 농장 내 견학 및 특별 행사에 대한 출입 권한 같은 혜택도 얻습니다!		

어휘 transaction 거래 access 출입 (권한), 이용 (권한)

13. 8월 6일에 무엇이 구입되었는가?
(A) 채소
(B) 유제품
(C) 신선한 과일
(D) 농기구

해설 지문 중반부의 8월 6일 구매 제품 항목에 치즈와 요거트, 그리고 우유가 표기되어 있으므로 (B)가 정답이다.

14. 영수증에서 그로버스 팜 스토어와 관련해 언급하는 것은 무엇인가?
(A) 8월에 처음 개장했다.
(B) 직원들에게 할인을 제공한다.
(C) 회원 프로그램을 제공한다.
(D) 일주일에 7일 문을 연다.

해설 지문 하단에 회원이 되도록 권하는 말과 함께 회원에게 주어지는 혜택을 간략히 설명하고 있으므로 (C)가 정답이다.

15-16.

래디언스 뷰티 라운지
15년 넘게 전문적인 관리 서비스로 지역사회를
소중히 가꿔왔습니다

저희와 함께 새롭게 개조한 저희 월슨 스트리트 미용실의 재개장을 기념해 보시기 바랍니다! **15 10월 한 달 내내 어느 것이든 미용 트리트먼트 서비스 두 가지를 예약하시고 무료 집중 컨디셔닝 헤어 트리트먼트를 즐겨 보세요.** 오직 콜로라도 주, 덴버, 월슨 스트리트 225번지, 래디언스 뷰티 라운지에서만 유효합니다. 이 제공 혜택은 오직 매장 내 서비스에 대해서만 적용되며, 자택 서비스는 해당되지 않습니다. 서비스와 시간대, 그리고 **16 추가 지점들**에 대한 전체 목록을 보시려면 저희 웹 사이트를 방문하시기 바랍니다.

어휘 pamper ~을 소중히 가꾸다, 애지중지하다 valid 유효한 exclusively 오직, 독점적으로 apply to ~에 적용되다

15. 사람들이 어떻게 안내책자에 나온 혜택을 받을 수 있는가?
(A) 대개장 기념 행사에 참석함으로써
(B) 자택 서비스를 예약함으로써
(C) 두 가지 트리트먼트를 예약함으로써
(D) 최소한의 금액을 소비함으로써

해설 지문 중반부에 어느 것이든 미용 트리트먼트 서비스 두 가지를 예약하면 무료 집중 컨디셔닝 헤어 트리트먼트를 받는 혜택이 언급되어 있으므로 (C)가 정답이다.

16. 래디언스 뷰티 라운지와 관련해 언급된 것은 무엇인가?
(A) 20년 동안 영업해 왔다.
(B) 다양한 곳에서 운영되고 있다.
(C) 10월에 가격을 인하할 것이다.
(D) 최근에 헤어 트리트먼트를 제공하기 시작했다.

해설 지문 후반부에 추가 지점들을 확인해 볼 수 있는 방법이 쓰여 있어 여러 곳에서 운영되고 있음을 알 수 있으므로 (B)가 정답이다.

Check-up Test

1. (D)	**2.** (A)	**3.** (D)	**4.** (D)	**5.** (B)
6. (B)	**7.** (C)	**8.** (B)	**9.** (A)	**10.** (C)
11. (B)	**12.** (B)	**13.** (D)	**14.** (A)	**15.** (A)
16. (D)	**17.** (B)	**18.** (D)	**19.** (D)	**20.** (B)
21. (B)	**22.** (D)			

1-2.

도라스 비스트로
입사 지원서

지원 날짜: 12월 3일
개인 상세 정보

성명: 라파엘 파찌	전화번호: 555-0126
주소: 프린스 스트리트 204번지, 토론토 ON	이메일: rpazzi@cmail.ca

지원 직책

직위	웨이터/종업원
선호 근무 시작일	12월 10일

1 선호 지점	☐ 로완 로드	**2(B)** ☒ 프린스 스트리트	☐ 에이콘 애비뉴
2(D) 선호 근무 계약	☒ 시간제	☐ 정규직	☐ 유연 근무

과거 근무 경력

회사명	직위	근무 기간
시에라 스테이크하우스	주방 보조	4년
매리골드 레스토랑	종업원	2.5년

학력

고등학교/전문대/4년제	취득 자격
말리 커뮤니티 칼리지	접객 분야 자격증
파인 힐즈 고등학교	고교 졸업장

자기 소개

2(C) **저는 지난 2년 반 동안 종업원으로 근무해 왔으며,** 성실히 일하고 신뢰할 수 있는 사람입니다. 현재의 종업원 일자리가 긴 통근 시간을 포함하는 반면, **2(B)** **도라스 비스트로는 제 아파트에서 도로를 따라 불과 두 집 건넌 곳에 있어서,** 제가 근무하기 이상적인 장소입니다.

어휘 **flexible** 유연한, 탄력적인 **attain** ~을 얻다, 획득하다 **hospitality** 접객업 **diploma** 졸업장, 수료증 **reliable** 신뢰할 수 있는 **commute** 통근, 통학

1. 도라스 비스트로와 관련해 암시된 것은 무엇인가?
(A) 최근에 신규 지점을 열었다.
(B) 매리골드 레스토랑 근처에 위치해 있다.
(C) 여러 정규직 공석이 있다.
(D) 다수의 지점에서 운영되고 있다.

해설 두 번째 항목에 선호 근무 지점이 세 곳 제시되어 있어 여러 지점을 보유한 업체임을 알 수 있으므로 (D)가 정답이다.

2. 파찌 씨와 관련해 언급되지 않은 것은 무엇인가?
(A) 현재 시에라 스테이크하우스에서 근무하고 있다.
(B) 프린스 스트리트에 살고 있다.
(C) 식사 손님들에게 서비스를 제공한 경험이 있다.
(D) 시간제를 바탕으로 근무하고 싶어 한다.

해설 지문 하단의 자기 소개 항목에 도라스 비스트로와 두 집 떨어진 곳에 살고 있다는 말이 쓰여 있고 두 번째 항목에 프린스 스트리트로 선호 지점이 표기되어 있어 (B)를 확인할 수 있다. 또한, 2년 반 동안 종업원으로 일해 왔다고 밝히는 부분에서 (C)를, 두 번째 항목에 시간제 근무로 선호 계약이 표기된 부분에서 (D)를 각각 확인할 수 있다. 하지만, 시에라 스테이크하우스는 과거의 근무지 중 한 곳으로 쓰여 있으므로 (A)가 정답이다.

어휘 **on a part-time basis** 시간제를 바탕으로

3-5.

그린트리 랜드스케이핑

저희 그린트리 랜드스케이핑은 옥외 공간을 탈바꿈시키고자 하시는 서레이 지역 주택 소유주 및 업체들에게 있어 최고의 선택입니다. 저희는 잔디 관리와 정원 디자인, 나무 손질, 그리고 계절별 유지 관리를 전문으로 하고 있습니다. 경험 많은 저희 조경사들은 단순한 잔디 깎기에서부터 완전한 정원 정비에 이르기까지, 모든 규모의 프로젝트를 처리하는 데 능숙합니다. 주기적인 유지 관리가 필요하시든, 아니면 아주 멋진 새 조경 디자인이 필요하시든 상관없이, 저희 그린트리가 모두 **3** **해결해** 드립니다.

탄력적인 저희 일정 관리 선택권으로 인해 고객들께서 바쁜 생활에 적합한 예약을 하시기가 수월합니다. 저희는 월요일부터 토요일까지는 오전 7시부터 오후 7시까지, 그리고 **4** **일요일에는 오전 7시부터 오후 3시까지 영업합니다.**

올 가을, 저희 그린트리는 모든 전체 서비스 조경 패키지에 대해 20퍼센트가 할인되는 특별 판촉 행사를 제공해 드리며, 이는 잔디 관리와 손질, 뿌리 덮개 작업, 그리고 정원 평가를 포함합니다. **5** **이 제공 서비스는 서레이 지역에 계신 완전히 새로운 모든 고객들께서 이용 가능하지만,** 다른 제공 서비스들과 결합될 수 없습니다. 이 할인은 서비스 요금에 대해서만 적용되며, 자재 또는 추가적인 맞춤 제공 특징들은 포함하지 않습니다.

어휘 **transform** ~을 탈바꿈시키다, 변모시키다 **specialize in** ~을 전문으로 하다 **trimming** 손질, 다듬기 **maintenance** 유지 관리, 시설 관리(= upkeep) **mowing** 풀 깎기, 풀 베기 **overhaul** 정비, 점검 **stunning** 아주 멋진, 굉장히 아름다운 **have A covered** A를 위해 모두 해결하다, A의 문제를 처리하다 **mulching** 뿌리 덮개 작업

3. 첫 번째 단락, 다섯 번째 줄의 단어 "covered"와 의미가 가장 가까운 것은 무엇인가?
(A) 감춰진
(B) 자금이 제공된
(C) 둘러싸인
(D) 수용된

해설 해당 문장의 Whether절이 '주기적인 유지 관리가 필요하든, 아니면 아주 멋진 새 조경 디자인이 필요하든 상관없이'를 뜻하므로 has you covered가 그린트리라는 업체에서 고객들을 위해 그런 일들이 해결되도록 해 준다는 의미임을

알 수 있다. 이는 고객들의 요구가 수용되는 것과 같으므로 (D) accommodated가 정답이다.

4. 고객이 언제 그린트리의 서비스를 받을 수 없는가?
(A) 월요일 오전 7시에
(B) 수요일 오후 7시에
(C) 토요일 오전 7시에
(D) 일요일 오후 7시에

해설 두 번째 단락에 일요일에는 오전 7시부터 오후 3시까지 영업한다고 쓰여 있어 이 시간대에 해당되지 않는 (D)가 정답이다.

어휘 serve ~에게 서비스를 제공하다

5. 판촉을 위한 제공 서비스와 관련해 사실인 것은 무엇인가?
(A) 다른 제공 서비스와 결합될 수 있다.
(B) 첫 방문 고객들을 대상으로 한다.
(C) 서레이 외부 지역의 고객들이 이용할 수 있다.
(D) 다양한 맞춤 제공 특징들을 포함한다.

해설 판촉 행사 혜택이 언급되는 세 번째 단락에 서레이 지역에 사는 완전히 새로운 모든 고객들이 이용할 수 있다는 정보가 제시되어 있으므로 (B)가 정답이다.

어휘 be intended for ~을 대상으로 하다 a variety of 다양한

6-8.

공장 안전 가이드라인 및 절차

다음 가이드라인이 의무라는 점에 유의하기 바랍니다. 6 **공장 작업 현장에서 근무를 시작하기 전에, 모든 작업자는 반드시 현 안전 설명서를 받아 살펴 봐야 합니다.** 7 **이를 제공 받지 못한 경우, 이스턴 씨께 요청하기 바랍니다.**

- 8(A) **적절한 안전 장비를 착용하기 바랍니다**: 이는 안전모, 보호 안경, 장갑, 발가락 부분이 강철로 보강된 부츠, 그리고 각자의 업무에 특화된 모든 다른 장비를 포함합니다.
- 기계 조작 규정을 준수하기 바랍니다: 어떤 기계든 조작하려면 반드시 교육 및 승인을 받아야 합니다.
- 비상용 정지 버튼을 인지하기 바랍니다: 이용하고 있는 모든 장비에서 비상용 정지 버튼의 위치 및 기능을 알아 두십시오.
- 위험 요소는 즉시 보고하기 바랍니다: 8(C) **어떤 안전하지 못한 상태나 결함이 있는 기계, 또는 유출물이든 발견하는 경우, 즉시 상사에게 보고하십시오.**
- 작동 중인 기계에서 벗어나 있기 바랍니다: 해당 업무를 담당하는 경우가 아니라면 절대 작동 중인 기계에 접근하거나 개입하지 마십시오.
- 비상구: 화재 또는 기타 비상 상황이 발생될 경우에 대비해 8(D) **모든 비상구 및 대피 경로를 숙지해 두십시오.**

이 안전 절차에 대한 준수가 모든 직원들에게 안전한 작업 환경을 보장해 줍니다.

어휘 mandatory 의무적인 appropriate 적절한, 해당하는 gear 장비 steel-toed 발가락 부분이 강철로 보강된 specific to ~에 특화된 protocol 규정, 규약 authorize ~에게 승인하다, 권한을 부여하다 hazard 위험 (요소) spill 유출(물), 엎지름, 쏟음 stay clear of ~에서 벗어나 있다, ~을 멀리 하다 interfere with ~에 개입하다, ~을 방해하다 be tasked with ~을 담당하다, 맡다 evacuation 대피, 피난 adherence to ~의 준수, 고수

6. 공지는 누구를 대상으로 할 것 같은가?
(A) 안전 점검 담당자들
(B) 기계 운전자들
(C) IT 기술자들
(D) 응급 처치 직원들

해설 첫 단락에 공장 작업 현장에서 근무를 시작하기 전에 모든 작업자가 반드시 받아서 살펴 봐야 하는 안전 설명서임을 밝히는 내용이 제시되어 있으므로 (B)가 정답이다.

7. 왜 이스턴 씨에게 연락하게 될 것인가?
(A) 작업용 유니폼을 요청하기 위해
(B) 위험한 상태를 보고하기 위해
(C) 필수 설명서를 얻기 위해
(D) 교육 시간에 등록하기 위해

해설 첫 단락에 반드시 해당 안전 설명서를 살펴 봐야 한다고 알리면서 제공 받지 못한 경우에 이스턴 씨에게 요청하라고 알리고 있으므로 (C)가 정답이다.

8. 공지에 명시된 지침이 아닌 것은 무엇인가?
(A) 필수 안전 장비를 착용할 것
(B) 피곤할 때 휴식을 취할 것
(C) 장비 결함을 보고할 것
(D) 비상구 위치를 알아 둘 것

해설 두 번째 단락에서, 안전 장비 착용과 관련해 설명하는 첫 번째 항목에서 (A)를, 결함이 있는 기계 등과 관련해 즉시 보고하도록 요청하는 네 번째 항목에서 (C)를, 그리고 비상구와 관련해 설명하는 여섯 번째 항목에서 (D)를 각각 확인할 수 있다. 하지만, 휴식 시간과 관련된 정보는 제시되어 있지 않으므로 (B)가 정답이다.

어휘 fault 결함, 흠

9-11.

써니 쇼어스 리조트: 완벽한 휴가지

작성자, 레이첼 린

"휴식과 모험이 만나는 곳." 이것이 바로 야라 베이의 경치 좋은 해안을 따라 새롭게 개장한 휴양지, 써니 쇼어스 리조트의 안내책자에 특징으로 언급된 표어입니다. 조화를 이룬 고급 편의 시설과 즐거움 가득한 활동을 제공하는, 써니 쇼어스는 가족들과 연인들, 그리고 단체 고객들에게 모두 똑같이 잊지 못할 휴가 경험을 약속합니다. - [1] -.

이 리조트는 아름답게 조경된 정원들, 산책 또는 자전거 타기를 위한 넓은 이동로, 그리고 다수의 휴식 구역들을 특징으로 합니다. 리조트의 한복판에는 중앙 광장이 있으며, 이곳은 해변 카페와 해산물 레스토랑, 그리고 지역 공예품과 기념품을 판매하는 몇몇 양품점이 들어서 있습니다. - [2] -. 11 **이 리조트의 가장 독특한 특징은 남동쪽 구석에 위치해 있는 인상적인 워터파크입니다.** - [3] -. 구불구불한 워터 슬라이드와 유수풀, 그리고 파도풀이 완비되어 있는, 9 **이 워터파크는 아이들과 어른들 모두에게 빠르게 하이라이트가 되었습니다.** "저희 워터파크에서는 쉽게 하루 종일을 보내실 수 있어요,"라고 써니 쇼어스의 엘리 피터스 고객 서비스 관리부장이 밝혔습니다. "이곳은 휴식과 스릴의 조화를 원하시는 고객들을 위해 고안된 곳입니다." - [4] -.

10 **이 리조트 시설에 대한 견학이 잠재 고객들을 대상으로 이용 가능합니다.** 개방일 행사가 매주 주말 오전 11시에서 오후 3시까지 주최되며, 818-555-0192번으로 전화하셔서 개인 맞춤 투어를 예약하셔도 됩니다.

어휘 **getaway** 휴가(지) **relaxation** 휴식 **tagline** 표어, 구호 **blend** 조화, 조합 **A-filled** A로 가득한 **A, B, and C alike** A와 B, 그리고 C 모두 똑같이 **craft** 공예품 **prospective** 잠재적인, 장차 ~가 되려는

9. 워터파크와 관련해 언급된 것은 무엇인가?

(A) 모든 연령대의 사람들에게 매력적이다.

(B) 여러 선물 매장을 포함하고 있다.

(C) 입장료를 필요로 한다.

(D) 중앙 광장에 위치해 있다.

해설 두 번째 단락에 아이들과 어른들 모두에게 빠르게 하이라이트가 되었다는 내용이 쓰여 있어 모든 연령대의 사람들이 좋아하는 곳임을 알 수 있으므로 (A)가 정답이다.

어휘 **appeal to** ~에게 매력적이다, ~의 마음을 끌다 **admission** 입장(료)

10. 잠재 고객이 어떻게 써니 쇼어스 리조트에 관해 더 많이 알 수 있는가?

(A) 웹 사이트를 방문함으로써

(B) 관광객 안내책자를 읽음으로써

(C) 견학 시간에 참가함으로써

(D) 대개장 기념 행사에 참석함으로써

해설 마지막 단락에 해당 리조트에 관해 더 많이 알아 볼 수 있는 방법으로서 잠재 고객들을 대상으로 하는 견학과 관련된 정보가 제시되어 있으므로 (C)가 정답이다.

11. [1], [2], [3], 그리고 [4]로 표기된 위치들 중에서, 다음 문장이 들어가기에 가장 적절한 곳은 어디인가?

"써니 쇼어스는 시원함을 유지하면서 즐거운 시간을 보내기를 바라는 분들에게 완벽한 장소도 보유하고 있습니다."

(A) [1]

(B) [2]

(C) [3]

(D) [4]

해설 제시된 문장은 시원함을 유지하면서 즐거운 시간을 보내기를 바라는 사람들에게 완벽한 장소도 있다는 의미를 나타낸다. 따라서, 워터파크에 관해 설명하기 시작하는 문장 앞에 위치한 [2]에 들어가 그 설명의 도입 문장과 같은 역할을 하는 흐름이 되어야 자연스러우므로 (B)가 정답이다.

12-14.

이번 주말로 예정된 게임월드 박람회

로스앤젤레스 (10월 24일) - 게임월드 박람회가 미라지 컨벤션 센터에서 개막함에 따라 게임 애호가들에게 이번 주말은 특별 선물이 될 것입니다. 업계 내 12 **선도적인** 비디오 게임 공급업체들 중 한 곳인, 픽셀테크 사가 주최하는, 이틀간의 이 행사에서는 최신 게임 기술력과 다가오는 출시작들, 그리고 게임 개발업체들의 독점 발표회를 선보이게 될 가능성이 있습니다.

참석자들은 미발매 게임을 체험해 보고, 가상 현실 환경을 탐사하며, 최신 프로젝트들을 공개하는 독립 개발사들을 만나 볼 기회가 있을 것입니다. 행사 시간들은 라이브 게임 플레이 시연과 13(B) **게임 설계에 관한 패널 토론**, 그리고 13(A) **개발자 지망생을 위한 업계 진출 관련 팁을 포함할 것입니다.** 이 행사는 또한 e-스포츠 경기 대회도 특징으로 할 것이며, 방문객들은 프로 게이머들을 응원하거나 토너먼트 참가 신청을 할 수 있습니다.

게임 하드웨어를 좋아하는 팬들을 위해, 부스마다 맞춤 제작 컨트롤러에서부터 고성능 장비에 이르기까지, 다양한 최신식 부대용품을 제공하게 되며, 13(C) **테스트 및 구매가 가능합니다.** 업계 전문가들 또한 자택 내 최상의 게임 환경 구축에 관한 조언을 제공하기 위해 현장에 있을 것입니다.

게임월드 박람회 입장은 무료이지만, 14 **공간 제한으로 인해 등록이 필수입니다. 자리를 확보하고 행사에 관해 더 많**

은 것을 알아 보시려면, www.gameworldexpo.com을 방문하시기 바랍니다.

어휘 set for 시점 ~로 예정된 enthusiast 애호가, 열성적인 팬 be in for a treat 특별한 선물이 되다, 멋진 경험을 하게 되다 exclusive 독점적인, 전용의 unreleased 미발매된 virtual reality 가상 현실 setup 환경 break into ~을 진출하다 aspiring ~을 지망하는, 장차 ~가 되려는 cutting-edge 최신의, 최첨단의 high-performance 고성능의 rig 장비, 장치 on hand 현장에 있는, 준비된 ultimate 최상의, 궁극적인

12. 첫 번째 단락, 두 번째 줄의 단어 "leading"과 의미가 가장 가까운 것은 무엇인가?
(A) 유익한
(B) 중요한
(C) 다재다능한
(D) 수익성 있는

해설 해당 문장에서 one of the industry's leading video game publishers는 행사를 주최하는 업체로 언급된 PixelTech 뒤에서 동격의 역할을 하는 명사구이다. 행사를 주최할 수 있는 업체는 업계를 이끌어 가거나 업계 내에서 중요한 위치를 차지하는 곳으로 볼 수 있으므로 '중요한'을 뜻하는 (B) prominent가 정답이다.

13. 박람회 참석자들이 즐길 수 있는 것으로 언급되지 않은 것은 무엇인가?
(A) 진로 관련 조언을 받는 일
(B) 토론 내용을 듣는 일
(C) 하드웨어를 체험해 보는 일
(D) 할인된 게임을 구입하는 일

해설 두 번째 단락에 패널 토론 및 개발자 지망생을 위한 업계 진출 관련 팁이 언급되어 있어 (B)와 (A)의 내용을 차례로 확인할 수 있으며, 하드웨어에 관해 설명하는 세 번째 단락에 테스트해 볼 수 있다고 쓰여 있어 (C)의 내용도 확인 가능하다. 하지만, 게임 제품 할인과 관련된 정보는 제시되어 있지 않으므로 (D)가 정답이다.

14. 사람들이 박람회에 참석하려면 무엇을 반드시 해야 하는가?
(A) 온라인 등록 과정을 완료하는 일
(B) 행사 개최 장소에서 입장권을 구입하는 일
(C) 비디오 게임 경기대회에 참가하는 일
(D) 등록비를 지불하는 일

해설 마지막 단락에 공간 제한으로 인해 등록이 필수라는 말과 함께 자리를 확보하기 위해 웹 사이트를 방문하는 방법이 제시되어 있으므로 (A)가 정답이다.

15-18.

엘레나 가르시아 (오후 2:15)
안녕하세요, 팀원 여러분. 시장님 집무실에서 방금 연락이 왔는데, **15 우리에게 시장님의 재선 운동을 위해 시청에서 대규모 홍보 행사를 조직해 달라고 하시네요.**
데이빗 밀러 (오후 2:16)
우와, 그럼 우리 회사에겐 대형 프로젝트가 될 수 있겠네요. 마감 기한이 언제인가요?
엘레나 가르시아 (오후 2:17)
약 한 달 후에요. 하지만, 저는 이걸 어떻게 받아 들여야 할지 잘 모르겠어요. **17 시장님께서는 우리 시를 운영하시는 일을 훌륭히 해내시지 못했는데, 그분께서 일을 처리해 오신 방식이 공감되지 않아요.**
소피아 은구옌 (오후 2:19)
무슨 말씀이신지 알아요, 하지만 **15 우리는 그저 여기서 행사를 기획하면 됩니다,** 그분 정책을 홍보하는 게 아니고요. 이 일은 우리에게 엄청난 노출 효과를 가져 올 수 있어요.
데이빗 밀러 (오후 2:20)
맞습니다. 우리는 그 비즈니스가 필요해요, **16 특히 최근에 상황이 좋지 못했으니까요.** 이 일은 우리에게 아주 큰 기회가 될 수 있어요.
엘레나 가르시아 (오후 2:22)
네, 옳은 말씀입니다. 그저 비즈니스일 뿐이죠. 제가 지나치게 생각하고 있는 것 같네요.
소피아 은구옌 (오후 2:23)
분명 그렇습니다. 우리가 가장 잘 하는 것을 하는 데에만 집중하죠, 최고 수준의 행사를 전하는 것 말이에요.
엘레나 가르시아 (오후 2:24)
동감입니다. **18 우리 계획을 파악하기 시작할 수 있도록 내일 오전 9시에 우리 대회의실에서 모입시다.**

어휘 reelection 재선 campaign (사회적·정치적) 운동, 활동 get that (앞선 말에 대해) 그 말을 이해하다, 무슨 말인지 알아듣다 endorse (유명인 등이) ~을 홍보하다, 광고하다 slow 경기가 침체된 overthink ~을 지나치게 생각하다 top-tier 최고 수준의, 최상급의 figure out ~을 파악하다, 알아내다

15. 메시지 작성자들이 어떤 종류의 업체에 근무하고 있을 것 같은가?
(A) 행사 기획
(B) 사업체 모집
(C) 재무 컨설팅
(D) 도시 개발

해설 가르시아 씨의 2시 15분 메시지와 은구엔 씨의 2시 19분 메시지에 홍보 행사를 조직하는 일과 행사를 기획하는 일이 언급되어 있으므로 (A)가 정답이다.

16. 메시지 작성자들이 근무하는 회사와 관련해 언급된 것은 무엇인가?
(A) 주기적으로 시 관계자들과 협업한다.
(B) 최근 새로운 정책을 시행했다.
(C) 여러 취업 기회들을 광고하고 있다.
(D) 사업상의 부진을 경험했다.

해설 밀러 씨가 2시 20분에 작성한 메시지에 최근에 회사 상황이 좋지 못했던 경험을 언급하는 말이 쓰여 있어 사업이 부진했음을 알 수 있으므로 (D)가 정답이다.

17. 오후 2시 19분에, 은구옌 씨가 "무슨 말씀이신지 알아요"라고 쓸 때 무엇을 의미할 것 같은가?
(A) 한 행사의 홍보용 전단을 받았다.
(B) 시장이 저조한 성과를 냈음을 인정하고 있다.
(C) 제안된 한 프로젝트에 대한 마감기한을 알아낼 것이다.
(D) 가르시아 씨가 선거에 출마한다는 사실을 알고 있다.

해설 2시 17분 메시지에 가르시아 씨가 시장이 시를 운영하는 일을 잘하지 못한 사실을 언급하는 것에 대해 은구옌 씨가 '무슨 말씀이신지 알아요'라고 반응하는 흐름이다. 이는 가르시아 씨의 의견에 동의한다는 뜻으로서 시장의 저조한 성과를 인정하는 말에 해당하므로 (B)가 정답이다.

어휘 **flyer** 전단 **underperform** 저조한 성과를 내다, 실적이 기대를 밑돌다 **run in an election** 선거에 출마하다

18. 메시지 작성자들이 내일 오전에 무엇을 할 것 같은가?
(A) 행사 공간을 장식하기 시작하는 일
(B) 시장의 대변인에게 연락하는 일
(C) 시청에서 열리는 회의에 참석하는 일
(D) 한 프로젝트에 대한 아이디어 회의를 시작하는 일

해설 2시 24분 메시지에 가르시아 씨가 계획을 파악하기 시작할 수 있도록 내일 오전 9시에 대회의실에서 모이자고 제안하고 있다. 이는 계획을 세우기 위한 아이디어 회의를 하자는 뜻이므로 (D)가 정답이다.

19-22.

수신: 이선 워드 <eward@customcraft.com>
발신: 리엄 캘러핸 <lcallahan@globallogistics.com>
날짜: 2월 11일
제목: 사업 제안

워드 씨께,

저희 글로벌 로지스틱스 주식회사에서는, 귀사와 같은 업체가 회사에서 제작하는 모든 제품에 대해 때맞춘 안전한 배송을 보장하는 일이 얼마나 중요한지 알고 있습니다. 저희는 고급 주문 제작 제품을 만들어 배송하는 업체들의 특별한 요구사항을 충족하는 맞춤 배송 해결책을 제공해 드리는 것을 전문으로 합니다.

19 귀사의 식탁과 커피 테이블을 국내로 배송하시든, 아니면 해외로 배송하시든 상관없이, 저희는 운송 중에 제품을 보호하도록 고안된 신뢰할 수 있는 화물 운송 선택권을 제공해 드립니다. 저희가 보유한 전체 운송 수단은 고급 추적 기술 장치를 갖추고 있으므로, 귀사 및 귀사의 고객들께서 실시간으로 배송품을 관찰하실 수 있습니다. **20 저희는 또한 취약하고 귀중한 제품이 반드시 손상 없이 운송되도록 해 드리기 위해 특수 포장 서비스도 제공해 드립니다.**

추가로, 저희 글로벌 로지스틱스는 통관 수속 및 서류 작업을 포함해, 맞춤 배송 일정 및 국제 배송 요건을 처리해 드림으로써, 전체 과정을 매끄럽게 만들어 드릴 수 있습니다. 전 세계적으로 여러 중요 시장에 걸친 종합적인 저희 물류 운송망으로 인해 **21** 뛰어난 관리와 함께 배송해 드릴 수 있으므로, 귀사의 제품이 의도대로 정확히 도착하도록 보장해 드립니다.

22 저희가 어떻게 더 깊이 있게 귀사를 지원해 드릴 수 있는지 꼭 논의해 보고자 합니다. 언제든지 800-456-7890번으로 제게 직접 연락 주시거나 저희 웹 사이트 www.globallogistics.com을 방문하셔서 모든 종류의 저희 서비스를 살펴 보시기 바랍니다. 귀사에서 확신을 갖고 제품을 배송하시는 데 도움을 드릴 수 있기를 고대합니다.

안녕히 계십시오.

리엄 캘러핸
운영부장
글로벌 로지스틱스

어휘 **craft** (공들여) ~을 만들다 **high-end** 고급의 **custom** 주문 제작의 **reliable** 신뢰할 수 있는 **freight** 화물 (운송) **transit** 운송 **fleet** (한 업체가 보유한 차량이나 항공기 등의) 전체 운송 수단 **in real time** 실시간으로 **delicate** 취약한, 섬세한 **customs clearance** 통관 (수속) **seamless** (진행 등이) 매끄러운 **logistics** 물류 (수송)

19. 워드 씨의 업체가 무엇을 제조할 것 같은가?
(A) 가전기기
(B) 차량
(C) 소프트웨어
(D) 가구

해설 두 번째 단락에 워드 씨의 회사에서 만드는 제품의 종류로 식탁과 커피 테이블이 언급되어 있으므로 (D)가 정답이다.

20. 글로벌 로지스틱스와 관련해 언급된 것은 무엇인가?
(A) 대형 물품을 배송하는 데 더 많은 요금을 청구한다.
(B) 취약한 상품을 안전하게 운송할 수 있다.
(C) 최근 새 유통 창고를 열었다.
(D) 배송 차량 대여 서비스를 제공한다.

해설 두 번째 단락에 취약하고 귀중한 제품이 반드시 손상 없이 운송되도록 하기 위해 특수 포장 서비스를 제공한다고 알리는 내용이 제시되어 있으므로 (B)가 정답이다.

어휘 fragile 취약한, 깨지기 쉬운

21. 세 번째 단락, 세 번째 줄의 단어 "outstanding"과 의미가 가장 가까운 것은 무엇인가?

(A) 기한이 지난
(B) 훌륭한
(C) 전반적인
(D) 과도한

해설 해당 문장에서 with outstanding care는 전 세계적으로 종합적인 물류 운송망으로 인해 어떤 관리 상태로 물품을 운송하는지를 나타낸다. 바로 뒤에 정확히 도착하도록 보장한다는 말이 쓰여 있어 뛰어난 배송 관리를 나타낸다는 것을 알 수 있으므로 유사한 의미로 쓰이는 (B) excellent가 정답이다.

22. 캘러핸 씨는 워드 씨가 곧이어 무엇을 할 것으로 기대하는가?

(A) 한 가지 주문사항의 도착지를 확인해 주는 일
(B) 몇몇 제품의 샘플을 제공해 주는 일
(C) 글로벌 로지스틱스를 직접 방문하는 일
(D) 제안을 더 상세히 논의하는 일

해설 마지막 단락에 어떻게 더 깊이 있게 워드 씨의 회사를 지원할 수 있는지 꼭 논의해 보고 싶다는 뜻을 나타내면서 연락 방법 등을 알려 주고 있으므로 (D)가 정답이다.

Playlist 14
이중지문, 이렇게 풀면 만점 받습니다!

연계문제 전략 연습

에버그린 피트니스 센터

현재 저희 에버그린 피트니스 센터는 도심 지역에 위치해 있는 저희 최신식 체육관을 즐기시는 800명이 넘는 회원들께 서비스를 제공해 드리고 있습니다. 무성한 녹지 공간으로 둘러싸여 있는, 저희 체육관은 모든 운동 수준의 회원들을 대상으로 모든 종류의 피트니스 시설과 서비스를 제공해 드리고 있습니다.

저희 에버그린 피트니스 센터에 가입하시려면, 세 가지 회원 등급인 베이직, 프리미엄, 그리고 엘리트 중 하나를 선택하시면 됩니다. **베이직 회원들께서는 500달러의 초기 가입비를 지불하시며, 모든 체육관 장비와 단체 피트니스 강좌, 그리고 개인 사물함에 대한 무제한 이용 권한을 누리시게 됩니다.** 프리미엄 회원들께서는 750달러의 가입비가 있으며, 베이직 회원권의 모든 혜택과 더불어 사우나와 한증탕, 그리고 전용 건강 워크숍에 대한 이용 권한도 얻으시게 됩니다. 엘리트 회원들께서는 1,000달러의 가입비가 있으며, 모든 종류의 프리미엄 등급 혜택과 더불어, 개인 훈련 시간 및 피트니스 강좌 우선 예약에 대한 이용 권한을 누리시게 됩니다.추가 정보가 필요하시거나 가입하시려면, 555-3456번으로 전화하시거나 membership@evergreenfitness.com으로 저희에게 이메일 보내시기 바랍니다.

회원 가입 신청서

에버그린 피트니스 센터 가입에 대한 귀하의 관심에 감사 드립니다. 이 양식을 작성하신 다음, 체육관 본관의 프론트 데스크에 위치한 회원 관리실로 제출해 주시기 바랍니다.

날짜: 9월 30일
전화번호: 555-3456
성명: 새라 미첼
이메일: smitchell@greenmail.com
주소: 파인 애비뉴 120번지, 캘거리, 앨버타

저는 다음 금액에 대해 에버그린 피트니스 센터로 지불 가능한 상태로 된 수표를 동봉했습니다.

__X__ $500.00
_____ $750.00
_____ $1,000.00

1. 미첼 씨는 어떤 혜택을 받을 것인가?

(A) 개인 훈련 시간
(B) 한증탕 이용
(C) 개인 사물함 공간
(D) 건강 워크숍

Practice

1. (D)	**2.** (C)	**3.** (B)	**4.** (D)	**5.** (B)

1-5.

수신: 제임스 홀컴 <jholcomb@wildlens.com>
발신: 새라 두보이스 <sarah.dubois@nationalparks.ca>
제목: 안내책자 관련 후속 조치
날짜: 9월 15일

홀컴 씨께,

1 **곧 나올 저희 안내책자를 위해 제공해 주신 아름다운 사진들에 대해 대단히 감사 드립니다.** 등산로와 야생 동물 이미지가 굉장히 아름다워서 방문객들에게 저희 공원을 살펴보도록 영감을 줄 것이 분명합니다. 저는 특히 해질녘의 호수

전경 사진이 감사했는데, 저희가 홍보하는 것을 목표로 하는 고요한 분위기가 정말 잘 담겨 있습니다.

한 가지 추가로 꼭 요청 드리고 싶은 것이 있습니다. **2** **저희가 새롭게 개조된 캠핑장 건물 사진을 꼭 포함했으면 하는데, 저희가 그곳에 많은 시간과 노력을 들였습니다. 저희는 이 프로젝트를 매우 자랑스럽게 여기고 있으며,** 공원을 찾으시는 방문객들께서 그곳에 아주 깊은 인상을 받으실 것으로 확신합니다. 그 건물을 담은 훌륭한 사진이 저희가 고객들을 위해 이룬 개선사항들을 강조해 줄 것입니다. 이 부분을 도와 주실 수 있는지 제게 알려 주시기 바랍니다.

안녕히 계십시오.

새라 두보이스, 홍보 진행 책임
국립 공원 관리국

어휘 **follow-up** 후속 조치 **stunning** 굉장히 아름다운, 아주 멋진 **inspire A to do** A에게 ~하도록 영감을 주다 **panoramic** 전경이 보이는 **capture** (사진·그림 등으로) ~을 담아내다, 포착하다 **serene** 고요한, 평화로운 **atmosphere** 분위기

곧 개장하는 캠핑장 건물

저희는 클리어워터 국립 공원의 새 캠핑장 건물의 대개장을 알려 드리게 되어 기쁘게 생각하며, 이는 10월 7일, 토요일에 기념될 것입니다. 대개장 기념 행사는 오전 10시에 리사 가너 공원 관리국장님의 말씀과 함께 시작되어, 그 후 개장식이 이어질 것입니다. 손님들께서는 오후 1시까지 시설물도 둘러 보시고 **3** **다과도 즐기실 수 있는 기회를 가지시게 됩니다.**

이 새로운 건물은 중앙 캠핑 구역에 위치해 있으며, 저희 방문객들께 더 나은 **4** **서비스를 제공해 드릴** 수 있도록 완전히 개조되었습니다. **2** **이곳은 50년 전에 공원 감시 초소로 처음 지어졌으며,** 구조적 문제로 인해 버려질 때까지 약 45년 동안 계속 이용되던 상태였습니다. **5** **이곳은 이제 널찍한 게임 공간, 모든 설비가 갖춰진 공용 주방, 현대적인 샤워 시설, 그리고 캠핑객들을 위한 편안한 모임 장소를 특징으로 합니다.** 이러한 개선사항들은 모든 분들을 대상으로 공원 경험을 향상시키기 위한 저희의 헌신을 반영합니다.

캠핑객들께서는 10월 8일, 일요일부터 새로운 시설을 이용하실 수 있을 것입니다. 추가 정보가 필요하시거나 캠핑 예약을 하시려면, 저희 웹 사이트를 방문하시거나 555-321-9876번으로 전화 주시기 바랍니다.

어휘 **remark** 말, 발언 **followed by A** A가 뒤에 이어지는 **ribbon-cutting ceremony** 개장식, 개관식 **serve** ~에게 서비스를 제공하다 **ranger station** 공원 감시 초소 **abandon** ~을 버리다, 버리고 떠나다 **communal** 공용의, 공동의 **gathering** 모임

1. 홀컴 씨는 누구일 것 같은가?
(A) 웹 디자이너
(B) 여행 가이드
(C) 공원 경비대원
(D) 사진가

해설 첫 지문 첫 단락에 곧 나올 안내책자를 위해 아름다운 사진들을 제공해 준 것에 대한 감사의 인사말이 쓰여 있어 사진가임을 알 수 있으므로 (D)가 정답이다.

2. 두보이스 씨와 관련해 언급된 것은 무엇인가?
(A) 홀컴 씨의 작품에 대해 만족하지 못하고 있다.
(B) 최근에 야생 동물 이동로 하이킹에 참가했다.
(C) 공원 감시 초소의 개조에 만족하고 있다.
(D) 직접 홀컴 씨와 만나기 위해 조치했다.

해설 첫 지문 두 번째 단락에 두보이스 씨는 새롭게 개조된 캠핑장 건물과 관련해 그 프로젝트를 매우 자랑스럽게 여기고 있다고 언급하고 있다. 두 번째 지문 두 번째 단락에는 그 건물이 50년 전에 공원 감시 초소로 처음 지어졌다는 사실이 쓰여 있어 두보이스 씨가 개조 공사에 만족하고 있다는 것을 알 수 있으므로 (C)가 정답이다.

어휘 **conversion** 개조, 전환 **arrange to do** ~하기 위해 조치하다 **in person** 직접 (가서)

3. 대개장 기념 행사에서 무슨 일이 있을 것인가?
(A) 공원 경비대원들이 이야기를 제공해 줄 것이다.
(B) 음식과 음료가 제공될 것이다.
(C) 새로운 등산로 안내도가 공개될 것이다.
(D) 단체 게임이 주최될 것이다.

해설 두 번째 지문 첫 단락에 대개장 기념 행사 중에 다과를 즐길 수 있는 기회가 있을 것이라는 내용이 제시되어 있으므로 (B)가 정답이다.

어휘 **unveil** ~을 공개하다, 선보이다

4. 안내책자 발췌문에서, 두 번째 단락, 첫 번째 줄의 단어 "serve"와 의미가 가장 가까운 것은 무엇인가?
(A) 소개하다
(B) 옮기다
(C) 제시하다
(D) 유익하다

해설 to better serve 앞에는 새로운 건물이 완전히 개조되었다는 말이 쓰여 있고, serve 뒤에는 방문객들을 뜻하는 명사구가 목적어로 쓰여 있다. 따라서, 건물 개조가 방문객들에게 더 나은 시설을 제공하기 위한 조치였음을 알 수 있는데, 이는 방문객들에게 유익한 것과 같으므로 (D) benefit가 정답이다.

5. 안내책자 발췌문에 따르면, 캠핑장 건물의 일부가 아닌 것은 무엇인가?
(A) 요리 구역
(B) 응급 치료소
(C) 씻을 수 있는 시설
(D) 게임 공간

해설 두 번째 지문 두 번째 단락에 건물 내 시설로 게임 공간과 공용 주방, 샤워 시설, 그리고 캠핑객들을 위한 모임 장소가 있다고 쓰여 있다. 하지만 응급 치료와 관련된 시설은 언급되어 있지 않으므로 (B)가 정답이다.

Check-up Test

1. (B)	**2.** (C)	**3.** (B)	**4.** (D)	**5.** (C)
6. (B)	**7.** (C)	**8.** (B)	**9.** (D)	**10.** (D)

1-5.

뉴질랜드의 웰링턴에 위치한, 저희 테크웨이브 솔루션즈는 지속 가능성 및 전자 제품 폐기물의 감소에 초점을 맞춰, 전자 기기를 재정비해 재판매하는 것을 전문으로 하고 있습니다.

아래의 양식을 이용해 노후하거나 사용하지 않는 전자제품에 관한 문의 및 제안 사항을 제출해 주시기 바랍니다.

성명: 리엄 오코너
이메일: loconnor@techglobal.nz
의견:
1 귀사의 웹 사이트에서 노후 장비에 대한 요청을 확인했습니다. 저는 크라이스트처치에 위치한 IT 법인 회사에서 근무하고 있으며, **2 저희가 최근에 모든 데스크톱 컴퓨터와 노트북 컴퓨터를 업그레이드했습니다.** 현재 더 이상 사용하지 않는 약 30대의 더 오래된 모델이 있습니다. 이것들이 온전히 기능하기는 하지만 현재의 업계 기준에 비해서는 낡은 상태입니다. 저희는 **5 7년된 퀘이사 노트북 10대**와 5년밖에 되지 않은 매그너 데스크톱 PC 10대, 그리고 4년밖에 되지 않은 포튼 노트북 컴퓨터 10대를 갖고 있는데, 저희가 필요로 하는 부분에 적합하지 않습니다. 테크웨이브 솔루션즈 사에서 이것들을 합리적인 가격에 매입하시는 데 관심이 있으실까요? 그러실 경우, 이메일로 제게 연락 주시기 바랍니다.

어휘 **refurbish** ~을 재정비하다, 재단장하다 **sustainability** 지속 가능성 **e-waste** 전자 제품 폐기물 **outdated** 노후한, 낡은, 구식의 **functional** 기능하는

수신: loconnor@techglobal.nz
발신: purchasing@techwavesolutions.co.nz
날짜: 10월 16일
제목: 귀하의 문의

오코너 씨께,

여분의 컴퓨터 및 노트북 컴퓨터와 관련해 저희에게 연락 주셔서 감사합니다. 저희는 항상 전자제품 폐기물을 줄이는 데에도 도움이 되고 중고 기기에게도 두 번째 삶을 제공해 주기를 간절히 바라고 있습니다. 귀하의 설명 내용을 바탕으로 볼 때, 저희가 기꺼이 퀘이사 컴퓨터와 매그너 컴퓨터들을 매입하겠습니다. 하지만, **3 저희가 포튼 모델 매입은 피하고 있는데, 그것의 오작동 경향 때문입니다. 저희가 작년에 그것들을 많이 매입했는데, 실수를 통해 비싼 교훈을 얻었습니다!**

다음은 저희가 일반적으로 제품들에 대해 지불하는 비용의 개요입니다.
데스크톱 컴퓨터(사용 연수 5년 이하): 개당 70 뉴질랜드 달러
노트북 컴퓨터(사용 연수 5년 이하): 개당 100 뉴질랜드 달러
5 더 오래된 데스크톱 컴퓨터 및 노트북 컴퓨터(사용 연수 6-8년): 개당 30 뉴질랜드 달러
기능하지 않는 기기 또는 심각하게 구식인 모델: 개당 5 뉴질랜드 달러로 재활용 처리

4 가급적 빨리, 해당 컴퓨터들을 저희 매장 뒤쪽의 하역장으로 전달해 주시기 바랍니다. 저희가 제품들에 대해 간단한 평가를 실시한 다음, 현금으로 비용을 지불해 드릴 것입니다. 저희 매장은 월요일부터 금요일, 오전 9시부터 오후 5시까지 영업합니다.

저희에게 연락 주셔서 감사 드리며, 만나 뵐 수 있기를 고대합니다.

안녕히 계십시오.

리사 트레몬트, 구매부장
테크웨이브 솔루션즈

어휘 **surplus** 여분, 과잉 **tendency to do** ~하는 경향 **malfunction** 오작동하다 **learn one's lesson the hard way** 실수를 통해 비싼 교훈을 얻다 **non-functional** 기능하지 않는 **severely** 심각하게, 극심하게 **loading area** 하역장

1. 무엇이 테크웨이브 솔루션즈에 연락하도록 오코너 씨에게 동기를 부여했는가?
(A) 만족한 고객의 최근 후기
(B) 테크웨이브 솔루션즈의 웹 사이트 게시물
(C) 테크웨이브 솔루션즈에 관한 잡지 기사
(D) 트레몬트 씨의 전화 메시지

해설 첫 지문 하단의 의견 항목에 웹 사이트에서 노후 장비에 대한 요청을 확인했다고 밝히면서 매각하려는 장비와 관련해 설명하고 있으므로 (B)가 정답이다.

2. 오코너 씨와 관련해 언급된 것은 무엇인가?
(A) 오래된 컴퓨터를 수리하는 일을 전문으로 한다.
(B) 테크웨이브 솔루션즈에서 일자리를 찾고 있다.
(C) 그의 회사가 최근에 새로운 기술 장비를 구입했다.
(D) 그의 회사가 테크웨이브 솔루션즈와 합병하는 데 관심이 있다.

해설 첫 지문 하단의 의견 항목에 오코너 씨의 회사가 최근에 모든 데스크톱 컴퓨터와 노트북 컴퓨터를 업그레이드한 사실과 함께 기존의 장비와 관련해 설명하고 있으므로 (C)가 정답이다.

어휘 merge with ~와 합병하다

3. 트레몬트 씨의 말에 따르면, 작년에 무슨 일이 있었는가?
(A) 자신의 직원들 중 몇몇이 승진되었다.
(B) 자신이 구입한 몇몇 컴퓨터가 결함이 있었다.
(C) 오래된 컴퓨터를 구입하는 데 대한 몇몇 가격이 인상되었다.
(D) 자신이 비용을 지불한 몇몇 기기가 배송되지 않았다.

해설 두 번째 지문 첫 단락에 포튼 모델이 오작동하는 경향이 있다고 밝히면서 작년에 그것들을 많이 매입한 것이 실수를 통해 비싼 교훈을 얻은 일이었다고 알리고 있으므로 (B)가 정답이다.

4. 트레몬트 씨가 오코너 씨에게 무엇을 하도록 조언하는가?
(A) 노후 컴퓨터의 전체 목록을 제공하는 일
(B) 다른 기술 업체에 연락해 보는 일
(C) 테크웨이브 솔루션즈에서 몇몇 기기를 구입하는 일
(D) 테크웨이브 솔루션즈로 몇몇 제품을 가져가는 일

해설 두 번째 지문 세 번째 단락에 트레몬트 씨가 오코너 씨에게 가급적 빨리 컴퓨터들을 자신의 매장 뒤쪽에 있는 하역장으로 전달해 달라고 요청하는 말이 쓰여 있으므로 (D)가 정답이다.

5. 트레몬트 씨가 퀘이사 컴퓨터에 대해 오코너 씨에게 얼마를 지불할 것인가?
(A) 개당 70 뉴질랜드 달러
(B) 개당 100 뉴질랜드 달러
(C) 개당 30 뉴질랜드 달러
(D) 개당 5 뉴질랜드 달러

해설 첫 지문 하단의 의견 항목에 7년된 퀘이사 노트북 10대가 있다고 언급되어 있고, 두 번째 지문 두 번째 단락에 6~8년된 데스크톱 컴퓨터 및 노트북 컴퓨터에 대해서는 개당 30 뉴질랜드 달러에 매입한다는 정보가 제시되어 있으므로 (C)가 정답이다.

6-10.

성공적인 자선 행사를 주최하는 방법
작성자, 바네사 기븐스

자선 행사는 중요한 대의를 위해 인식을 드높이고 기금을 마련할 수 있는 훌륭한 방법이지만, 그것을 주최하는 일은 까다로울 수 있습니다. 6 **모든 행사가 그 목적을 달성하는 것은 아니며, 이는 흔히 준비 부족 또는 사람들에 대한 이해 부족으로 인한 것입니다.** 성공적인 자선 행사는 참가자들에게 반향을 불러 일으키며, 기부자들에게 동기를 부여하고, 홍보 효과를 만들어 냅니다. 다음은 영향력 있는 자선 행사를 만들어 내는 데 도움이 되는 몇몇 지침들입니다.

1번 팁! – 초점을 유지하십시오. 행사를 다양한 활동들로 가득 채우는 것이 솔깃한 일이기는 하지만, 너무 많으면 그 메시지를 희석시킬 수 있습니다. 7 **여러분의 대의를 위한 참여와 지지를 불러 일으키는 몇 가지 핵심적인 활동에 초점을 맞추십시오. 예를 들어, 지역 동물 보호소를 위한 모금 행사를 주최하는 경우**, 기부 운동과 함께 반려동물 입양 부문을 주최하시는 것을 고려해 보십시오. 이는 참석자들과 여러분의 사명 사이에서 명확하고 감정적인 연관성을 만들어 낼 것입니다.

2번 팁! – 시간을 관리하십시오. 행사 지속 시간은 아주 중요합니다. 성공적인 자선 행사는 오락적 요소와 행동 촉구 사이에서 균형을 유지해야 합니다. 8(D) **행사가 너무 짧으면, 기부를 위한 충분한 추진력을 만들어 내지 못할 수도 있는 반면,** 8(A) **너무 길면, 사람들이 관심을 잃을 수 있습니다.** 8(C) **기부금이 어떻게 변화를 가져올 것인지에 대한 연설과 동영상, 또는 라이브 시연회를 통해 여러분의 기부자들과 교류할 수 있도록 휴식 시간을 계획하십시오.**

3번 팁! – 균형감을 찾으십시오. 카리스마 있는 연사 또는 잘 알려진 진행자가 사람들을 끌어들일 수 있기는 하지만, 핵심이 되는 초점은 반드시 언제나 그 대의에 맞춰진 상태로 유지되어야 합니다. 10 **사람들을 사로잡을 뿐만 아니라 최소 10년 동안 자선 사업에도 전념해 오신 연사를 선택하십시오.** 반드시 여러분의 자원 봉사자와 직원들이 그 대의를 깊이 이해하고 그 중요성을 분명히 표현할 수 있도록 하십시오. 이는 심지어 가볍게 참석하시는 분들조차 여러분의 자선 단체가 하고 있는 일과 개인적으로 공감대를 형성하는 것을 보장해, 지원 증가로 이어줄 것입니다.

어휘 raise awareness 인식을 드높이다 cause 대의, 이유, 원인 audience 사람들, 청중, 시청자들 resonate with ~에게 반향을 불러 일으키다 donor 기부자 publicity 홍보 (효과) tempting 솔깃한, 유혹적인 dilute ~을 희석시키다, 묽게 하다 inspire ~을 불러 일으키다, 불어넣다 engagement 참여, 관여 adoption 입양, 채택 segment 부문, 부분 drive (조직적) 운동 call to action

행동 촉구 **momentum** 추진력, 탄력 **core** 핵심적인 **articulate** ~을 분명히 표현하다

> **수신:** 소피 앤드류스 <sandrews@charitynetwork.org>
> **발신:** 에드워드 웬트워스 <ewentworth@charitynetwork.org>
> **날짜:** 10월 13일
> **제목:** 다가오는 자선 행사
>
> 안녕하세요, 소피 씨,
>
> 10월 3일에 바네사 기븐스 씨에 의해 실린 기사 하나를 첨부해 드렸는데, 다가오는 우리 채리티 네트워크 행사를 위한 계획을 최정 확정하는 과정에서 도움이 될 것으로 생각합니다. 활동에 대해 선별적인 것에 관한 부분이 정말로 제 눈에 띄었습니다. 우리가 꽤 여러 가지 계획하긴 했지만, 반드시 우리가 사람들의 관심을 유지할 수 있도록 두어 가지 핵심적인 인기 행사에만 초점을 맞추는 게 좋은 생각일지도 모릅니다.
>
> **10 우리의 기조 연설자 문제도 논의하고 싶었습니다. 9 원래, 폴 스티븐스 씨를 제안해 드릴 생각이었지만, 이분께서 10월 30일에 시간이 나지 않으실 겁니다. 10 저는 한나 맥코넬 씨가 좋은 대체자가 되실 수 있을지 궁금했습니다.** 이분께서 우리의 대의에 해당하는 분야에서 경력을 보유하고 계셔서 사람들과 정말로 교감하실 수 있을 것입니다. 더욱이, **10 기사에 제시된 3번 팁은 이분을 완벽하게 설명해 줍니다.** 한나 씨께서 몇몇 인적 교류 워크숍에 참석하시느라 현재 해외에 계시기는 하지만, **9 10월 23일에 돌아오실 것이므로, 준비하시는 데 7일의 시간이 있으실 것입니다.**
>
> 안녕히 계십시오.
>
> 에드워드 웬트워스, 행사 진행 책임
> 채리티 네트워크

어휘 **selective** 선별적인 **stand out to** ~의 눈에 띄다, ~에게 두드러져 보이다 **attraction** 인기 있는 것, 관심을 끄는 것 **keynote speaker** 기조 연설자 **replacement** 대체(자) **networking** 인적 교류, 인적 관계 형성

6. 기사 내용에 따르면, 자선 행사가 성공할 수 없는 한 가지 이유는 무엇인가?
(A) 불편한 곳에서 개최된다.
(B) 적절히 준비되지 않았다.
(C) 인기 없는 대의에 초점을 맞춘다.
(D) 너무 많은 초청 연사와 관련되어 있다.

해설 첫 지문 첫 단락에 자선 행사가 목적을 달성하지 못하는 이유로 준비 부족 또는 사람들에 대한 이해 부족이 언급되어 있으므로 준비 부족 문제에 해당하는 (B)가 정답이다.

7. 기사 작성자가 왜 지역 동물 보호소를 언급하는가?
(A) 자선 단체의 중요성을 강조하기 위해
(B) 독자들에게 기부하도록 권장하기 위해
(C) 한 가지 활동의 예시를 소개하기 위해
(D) 한 행사를 개최할 장소를 제안하기 위해

해설 첫 지문 두 번째 단락에 몇 가지 핵심적인 활동에 초점을 맞추라는 조언과 함께 그에 대한 예시로 지역 동물 보호소를 위한 모금 행사의 주최를 언급하고 있으므로 (C)가 정답이다.

어휘 **emphasize** ~을 강조하다

8. 기사에서 행사 지속 시간과 관련해 언급되지 않은 것은 무엇인가?
(A) 장시간의 행사는 참석자들을 지루하게 만들 수 있다.
(B) 며칠 동안 개최되는 행사가 더 성공적일 수 있다.
(C) 예정된 휴식 시간이 참석자들을 관심 있는 상태로 유지해 줄 수 있다.
(D) 짧은 행사는 더 적은 기부를 만들어 낼 수 있다.

해설 첫 지문 세 번째 단락에 행사가 너무 짧거나 너무 길게 진행되는 경우에 사람들에게 미치는 영향과 관련된 단점과 함께 휴식 시간 계획에 관한 조언이 언급되어 있으므로 (D)와 (A), 그리고 (C)를 각각 확인할 수 있다. 하지만, 며칠 동안 개최되는 행사가 더 성공적일 가능성과 관련된 정보는 제시되어 있지 않으므로 (B)가 정답이다.

어휘 **bore** ~을 지루하게 만들다

9. 채리티 네트워크 행사는 언제 개최될 예정일 것 같은가?
(A) 10월 3일에
(B) 10월 13일에
(C) 10월 23일에
(D) 10월 30일에

해설 두 번째 지문 두 번째 단락에 기조 연설자로 추천하는 한나 맥코넬 씨가 해외에서 10월 23일에 돌아온다는 말과 함께 그 사람이 연설을 준비하는 데 7일의 시간이 있다는 정보가 제시되어 있다. 또한, 원래 기조 연설자로 제안하려고 했던 폴 스티븐스 씨가 10월 30일에 시간이 나지 않을 것이라는 내용도 언급되어 있으므로 해당 행사가 10월 30일에 개최되는 행사임을 알 수 있다. 따라서 (D)가 정답이다.

10. 맥코넬 씨와 관련해 언급된 것은 무엇인가?
(A) 한 자선 단체에 상당한 액수의 금전적 기부를 했다.
(B) 여러 행사에서 기조 연설자의 역할을 한 적 있다.
(C) 한 가지 역할에 대해 스티븐스 씨를 추천했다.
(D) 10년 넘게 자선 사업에 관여해 왔다.

해설 두 번째 지문 두 번째 단락에 기조 연설자로 추천하는 사람의 한 명으로 한나 맥코넬 씨가 언급되어 있다. 이 연설자와 관련해, 첫 지문 마지막 단락에 사람들을 사로잡을 뿐만 아

니라 최소 10년 동안 자선 사업에도 전념해 온 연사를 선택하라는 말이 쓰여 있어 맥코넬 씨가 10년 넘게 자선 사업에 관여해 온 사람임을 알 수 있으므로 (D)가 정답이다.

어휘 sizable (금액·크기 등) 상당한 be involved in ~에 관여하다, 관련되다

Playlist 15
삼중지문, 양식부터 분석하면 토익 졸업한다고?

연계문제 전략 연습

자선을 위한 지역 축제 마당을 주최하는 지역 회사

베이사이드 인더스트리 사는 지역 자선 단체들을 위한 기금을 마련하기 위해 8월 12일, 토요일, 리버사이드 공원에서 지역 축제 마당을 주최하는 계획을 발표했습니다. 이 행사는 라이브 음악과 식품 가판대, 게임, 그리고 입찰식 경매를 특징으로 할 것이며, 모든 수익금은 아동 보호소와 기아 구제 기금 같은 단체들을 후원하는 데 쓰입니다. 이 축제 마당은 즐거움이 있는 하루 동안 지역 사회를 화합하게 함과 동시에 도움이 필요한 분들에게 긍정적인 영향을 미치는 것을 목표로 합니다.

미드포드 시 의회 행사 허가증 신청 과정

행사 주최측은 반드시 최소 10일 전에 미리 시 의회의 행사 허가증 신청서를 작성 완료해야 합니다. 일단 그것이 제출되면, 시 안전 조사관이 제안된 행사 부지를 방문해 평가를 실시하고 군중 관리, 화재 비상구, 그리고 접근 용이성을 포함한, 안전 규정을 반드시 충족하도록 할 것입니다. 주최측은 보험 적용 범위 또는 보안 계획 같은, 추가 서류를 제공하도록 요청받을 수 있습니다. 승인 즉시, 허가증이 발급될 것이며, 해당 행사는 예정대로 진행될 수 있습니다. **수수료는 행사 종류에 따라 상이하며, 신청 시에 지불 가능합니다.**

미드포드 시 의회
행사 허가증 신청서

회사명: 베이사이드 인더스트리
연락 담당자: 새라 톰슨
신청일: 8월 3일
이메일: sthompson@baysideindustries.com
행사 장소: 리버사이드 공원, 코스털 드라이브 1200번지
제안된 행사 날짜: 8월 12일
행사장 설치 시작일/시간: 8월 11일, 오전 8:00
제안된 행사 종료일/시간: 8월 12일, 오후 6:00
평가일: 8월 5일

1. 8월 3일에 무슨 일이 있을 것 같은가?

(A) 주최측에서 행사장을 설치하기 시작할 것이다.
(B) 안전 조사관이 리버사이드 공원을 방문할 것이다.
(C) 톰슨 씨가 허가증에 필요한 수수료를 지불할 것이다.
(D) 지역 자선 단체를 위한 기금이 마련될 것이다.

Practice

1. (B)	**2.** (A)	**3.** (D)	**4.** (D)	**5.** (A)

1-5.

엘레강스 브라이덜에서 꿈에 그리던 드레스를 찾아 보십시오!

1 2 저희 엘레강스 브라이덜은 세 곳의 저희 소매 판매점에서 있을 변화를 알려 드리게 되어 기쁩니다. **11월 1일부터, 오타와 시내와 밴쿠버 하이츠, 그리고 토론토 웨스트에 위치한 저희 매장들이 고객 여러분의 바쁜 일정을 더 잘 수용하기 위해 오후 8시까지 계속 영업할 것입니다.** 완벽한 웨딩 드레스를 찾고 계시든, 아니면 신부 들러리 드레스를 찾고 계시든 상관없이, 경험 많은 저희 상담 전문가들이 도와드릴 준비가 되어 있습니다. 구매 가능성 및 가격에 관한 추가 정보를 원하시면 아름다운 저희 상품 진열실 중 한 곳을 방문하시거나 오늘 전화 주시기 바랍니다.

어휘 retail 소매 outlet 판매점, 할인점 bridesmaid 신부 들러리 pricing 가격 (책정)

수신: 한나 라이트 <hannahwright@email.com>
2 발신: 클라라 존스 <cjones@elegancebridal.com>
2 날짜: 11월 12일, 오전 10:15
제목: 주문 번호 EB3039481

라이트 씨께,

귀하께서 11월 9일에 주문하신 웨딩 드레스와 관련해 연락 드립니다. **3 저희가 현재 이 특정 드레스를 오직 한 벌만 재고로 보유하고 있습니다. 2 4 이 제품은 이곳 저희 토론토 웨스트 상품 진열실에서 샘플 진열품으로 이용되어 왔습니다.** 이 드레스가 다른 고객들께서 착용해 보셨던 것이기는 하지만, 새 것 그대로의 상태로 유지되고 있습니다. 저희 직원이 철저히 점검해 왔으며, 얼룩이나 헐거워진 바느질 같이, 눈에 보이는 마모의 흔적이 전혀 없습니다.

귀하께서는 완전히 새로운 것이라는 기대감을 갖고 이 드레스를 구입하셨기 때문에, 저희가 두 가지 선택사항을 제안해 드리고자 합니다.
- 주문을 취소하신 후, 즉시 전액 환불을 받으실 수 있습니다.
- **4 샘플 드레스를 소유하고자 하시는 경우, 원가에서 15퍼센트 할인을 제공해 드리고 오늘 발송해 드리겠습니다.**

어떻게 진행하시고자 하는지 저희에게 알려 주시기 바라며, 반드시 드레스가 선호하시는 곳으로 즉시 전달되도록 해 드릴 것입니다. 이 문제가 초래했을 수도 있는 모든 불편함에 대해 사과 드립니다.

안녕히 계십시오.

클라라 존스
엘레강스 브라이덜

어휘 specific 특정한, 구체적인 pristine 새 것 그대로의, 원래 그대로의 visible 눈에 보이는 wear n. 마모, 닳음 stain 얼룩 loose 헐거워진, 느슨한 stitching 바느질 proceed 진행하다

엘레강스 브라이덜 - 영수증
주문 번호: EB3039481
날짜: 11월 13일

설명	**가격**
"세레나" 웨딩 드레스	$1,200.00
4 15% 드레스 할인	-$180.00
5 배송 취급 수수료	$25.00
판매세 (7%)	$71.05
총액	**$1,116.05**

배송 주소:	청구 주소:
4 한나 라이트	한나 라이트
메이플 애비뉴 2712번지	메이플 애비뉴 2712번지
캘거리, ABT2P 1K2	캘거리, ABT2P 1K2

저희 웹 사이트 www.elegancebridalonline.ca를 방문하셔서 모든 종류의 드레스 및 매장 위치 정보를 확인해 보시기 바랍니다.

어휘 handling 취급 (수수료)

1. 광고의 목적은 무엇인가?
(A) 새로운 드레스 제품군을 소개하는 것
(B) 영업 시간의 변경을 알리는 것
(C) 새로운 소매 지점을 홍보하는 것
(D) 취업 기회를 광고하는 것

해설 첫 지문 초반부에 매장에 있을 변화를 언급하면서 11월 1일부터 오후 8시까지 영업한다는 사실을 알리고 있으므로 (B)가 정답이다.

2. 존스 씨가 근무하는 매장과 관련해 무엇이 사실일 것 같은가?
(A) 저녁 시간대에 영업한다.
(B) 재고를 확대했다.
(C) 신입사원을 고용했다.
(D) 11월에 개장했다.

해설 두 번째 지문 상단에 이메일 발신 날짜가 11월 12일이고, 발신자가 존스 씨임을 알 수 있다. 또한, 첫 단락에는 토론토 웨스트 매장 소속이라고 언급되어 있는데, 이곳은 첫 지문에서 11월 1일부터 오후 8시까지 영업한다고 밝힌 매장들 중 하나이므로 (A)가 정답이다.

3. 이메일에서 해당 웨딩 드레스와 관련해 언급하는 것은 무엇인가?
(A) 일부 수선을 필요로 한다.
(B) 오타와에서 진열되어 있었다.
(C) 계절 판촉 행사의 일환으로 할인된다.
(D) 현재 구매 가능한 동일 스타일의 유일한 제품이다.

해설 두 번째 지문 첫 단락에 상대방이 구입한 특정 드레스를 오직 한 벌만 재고로 보유하고 있다는 말이 쓰여 있으므로 (D)가 정답이다.

어휘 alteration 수선, 변형 as part of ~의 일환으로

4. 라이트 씨와 관련해 유추할 수 있는 것은 무엇인가?
(A) 드레스에 대해 환불을 요구했다.
(B) 친구를 위해 드레스를 구입했다.
(C) 12월에 결혼한다.
(D) 진열품 드레스를 구입했다.

해설 두 번째 지문 첫 단락에 주문한 드레스가 상품 진열실에서 샘플 진열품으로 이용된 것이라는 정보가 언급되어 있고 두 번째 단락에 샘플 드레스를 소유하고자 하는 경우 원가에서 15퍼센트 할인을 제공해 준다는 내용이 제시되어 있다. 이와 관련해 세 번째 지문 영수증 설명에 '15% 드레스 할인' 항목과 배송/청구 주소가 모두 한나 라이트 씨로 되어 있으므로 라이트 씨가 진열품 드레스를 구입했음을 알 수 있다. 따라서 (D)가 정답이다.

5. 영수증 내용에 따르면, 엘레강스 브라이덜과 관련해 사실인 것은 무엇인가?
(A) 배송비를 청구한다.
(B) 무료 드레스 수선 서비스를 제공한다.
(C) 캘거리에 상품 진열실이 있다.
(D) 웹 사이트에서 할인을 제공해 준다.

해설 세 번째 지문 두 번째 단락에 '배송 취급 수수료' 항목과 그 액수가 기재되어 있어 배송비를 청구한다는 것을 알 수 있으므로 (A)가 정답이다.

Check-up Test

1. (B)	**2.** (A)	**3.** (A)	**4.** (C)	**5.** (A)
6. (D)	**7.** (A)	**8.** (D)	**9.** (B)	**10.** (A)

1-5.

http://www.titansecuritysolutions.com/aboutus

4 저희 타이탄 시큐리티 솔루션즈는 미국 전역에 걸쳐 참석자 수가 1만 명 이상으로 예상되는 대규모 행사를 대상으로 종합적인 보안 서비스를 제공해 드리고 있습니다. 콘서트나 축제, 기업 모임을 주최하시든, 아니면 스포츠 행사를 주최하시든 상관없이, 저희 팀은 모든 보안 요구 사항을 처리해 드릴 수 있도록 준비되어 있습니다. 저희는 고도로 훈련된 보안 인력을 배치해 드릴 수 있고, 최신 감시 장비를 제공해 드릴 수 있으며, 맞춤 보안 계획을 만들어 손님과 직원들의 안전을 보장해 드립니다.

저희 타이탄 시큐리티 솔루션즈에서, 저희 서비스는 군중 통제, 출입 지점 관리, VIP 보호, 그리고 주변 구역 감시를 포함합니다. **1 저희는 잠재 위협보다 한발 앞서 있는 상태를 유지하기 위해 드론 감시와 실시간 통신 시스템 같은, 최첨단 접근법을 이용하고 있습니다.** 저희 직원들은 면허를 소지하고 있고, 대단히 경험이 많으며, 계획된 보안 조치 및 현장의 모든 어려움 두 부분 모두를 처리할 수 있는 능력이 있습니다. 저희는 행사 전후와 진행 중에 하루 24시간 지원 서비스를 제공해 모든 것이 순조롭게 운영되도록 보장해 드립니다.

저희 타이탄 시큐리티 솔루션즈가 여러분 행사의 보안을 처리해 드리겠습니다. 오늘 저희에게 연락 주셔서 맞춤 제공 가능한 저희 패키지 및 서비스에 관해 더 많은 것을 알아 보시기 바랍니다.

어휘 comprehensive 종합적인, 포괄적인 large-scale 대규모의 be equipped to do ~할 준비가 되어 있다, ~하도록 갖춰져 있다 deploy ~을 배치하다 state-of-the-art 최신의, 최첨단의 surveillance 감시 tailored 맞춰진 perimeter 주변, 주위 cutting-edge 최첨단의 threat 위협 on-the-spot 현장의 customizable 맞춤 제공 가능한, 주문대로 만들 수 있는

타이탄 시큐리티 솔루션즈 - 팀별 업무 배정

2 일정표 날짜: 9월 17일

행사 세부 사항	행사 장소	2 팀장
2 *챔피언 결정전 (야구)*	메르카도 경기장	2 스티브 아넷
세계 식품 축제	뉴 시티 플라자	미치 룬드그렌
4 *팝 음악 축제*	4 메이플라워 공원	제니퍼 비일
만화책 컨벤션	레드먼 전시홀	피트 웰포드

어휘 assignment 배정(되는 것), 할당(되는 것)

http://www.titansecuritysolutions.com/testimonials/19829

9월 18일 – **3 4 어제, 저는 사운드웨이브 뮤직 페스티벌에 참석했는데, 꼭 말씀 드리고 싶은 것은, 타이탄 시큐리티 솔루션즈에서 제공한 보안이 뛰어났다는 점입니다.** 군중의 규모와 열기 가득한 분위기를 고려해 볼 때, 저는 입구에서의 긴 줄들과 잠재적 혼란을 예상했습니다. 대신, 저는 모든 것이 얼마나 순조롭게 운영되었는지에 대해 깊은 인상을 받았습니다. 보안 직원들께서는 믿을 수 없을 정도로 효율적이고 전문적이셨습니다. 이분들께서는 수월하게 군중을 관리해 주셨고, 줄을 선 사람들을 계속 움직이게 해 주셨으며, 강압적이지 않으면서 모든 사람이 안전하게 느끼도록 보장해 주셨습니다.

정말로 제 눈에 띄었던 부분은 세부 요소에 대한 이분들의 주의력이었습니다. 많은 참석자의 수에도 불구하고, **5 이분들께서는 가방 검색대에서부터 출입 지점에 이르기까지 모든 것을 매끄럽게 처리해 주셨습니다.** 저는 또한 이분들께서 감시용 드론 같은 고급 기술 장비를 이용하신다는 점도 알게 되면서, 안심이 되었습니다. 전반적으로, 타이탄 시큐리티 사는 전체적인 경험을 더욱 즐겁게 만들어 주었으며, 이분들께서 담당하고 계신다는 사실을 알고 앞으로의 행사에 참석한다면 분명 더 안전하게 느낄 것입니다.

게시자: 레오나르도 베누치

어휘 outstanding 뛰어난, 우수한 given ~을 고려해 (볼 때) atmosphere 분위기 chaos 혼란, 혼돈 with ease 수월하게 overbearing 강압적인, 위압적인 stand out to ~의 눈에 띄다 seamlessly 매끄럽게 reassuring 안심시키는 in charge 담당하는, 책임지는

1. 웹 페이지에서 타이탄 시큐리티 솔루션즈와 관련해 언급하는 것은 무엇인가?
(A) 주로 스포츠 행사에서 보안 서비스를 제공한다.
(B) 첨단 기술 장비를 활용한다.
(C) 현재 신입직원을 고용하고 있다.
(D) 미국 외의 지역에서 서비스를 제공한다.

해설 첫 지문 두 번째 단락에 드론 감시와 실시간 통신 시스템 같은 최첨단 접근법을 이용하고 있다는 내용이 제시되어 있으므로 이러한 기술력과 관련된 장점에 해당하는 (B)가 정답이다.

2. 일정표에 따르면, 누가 9월 17일 야구 경기의 보안 팀장이었는가?
(A) 스티브 아넷
(B) 미치 룬드그렌
(C) 제니퍼 비일

(D) 피트 웰포드

해설 두 번째 지문의 첫 번째 줄에 Championship game (baseball)으로 표기된 야구 경기 행사의 팀장 이름이 Steve Arnett으로 표기되어 있으므로 (A)가 정답이다.

3. 베누치 씨가 참석한 행사와 관련해 무엇이 사실일 것 같은가?

(A) 최소 1만 명의 참석자들을 끌어들였다.
(B) 입장료를 필요로 하지 않았다.
(C) 며칠 동안 개최되었다.
(D) 텔레비전에서 생방송되었다.

해설 세 번째 지문 첫 단락에 베누치 씨가 참석한 행사에서 타이탄 세큐리티 솔루션즈가 보안을 제공한 사실이 쓰여 있다. 이 보안 업체와 관련해, 첫 지문 첫 단락에 참석자 수가 1만 명 이상으로 예상되는 대규모 행사를 대상으로 보안 서비스를 제공하는 곳이라고 소개되어 있어 베누치 씨가 참석한 행사에도 최소 1만 명의 사람들이 찾은 것으로 볼 수 있으므로 (A)가 정답이다.

4. 베누치 씨가 최근 어디에서 행사에 참석했는가?

(A) 메르카도 경기장에서
(B) 뉴 시티 플라자에서
(C) 메이플라워 공원에서
(D) 레드먼 전시홀에서

해설 세 번째 지문 첫 단락에 어제 사운드웨이브 뮤직 페스티벌에 참석한 사실이 쓰여 있다. 두 번째 지문의 세 번째 줄에 Pop music festival로 표기된 행사가 이 음악 축제에 해당하며, 그 장소는 Mayflower Public Park로 쓰여 있으므로 (C)가 정답이다.

5. 고객 추천 후기에서 보안팀과 관련해 언급된 것은 무엇인가?

(A) 가방 점검에 대한 책임이 있었다.
(B) 24시간 동안 현장에서 근무했다.
(C) 여러 사람에게 행사에서 떠나도록 요청했다.
(D) 주차 공간이 안전하도록 보장해 주었다.

해설 세 번째 지문 두 번째 단락에 해당 보안팀이 가방 검색대에서부터 출입 지점에 이르기까지 모든 것을 매끄럽게 처리해 주었다는 말이 쓰여 있어 가방 점검에 대한 책임이 있었다는 사실을 알 수 있으므로 (A)가 정답이다.

6-10.

테크노바, 7천 5백만 달러 계약으로 앱이즈를 인수하다

샌프란시스코 (4월 12일) – 거대 소프트웨어 기업 테크노바가 빠르게 성장하고 있는 모바일 애플리케이션 개발사 앱이즈를 인수했다고 금요일에 발표했습니다. **6** **이 인수는 테크노바가 모바일 앱 시장으로 사업을 확장함으로써 자사의 제품 포트폴리오를 다양화하려는 전략적 계획의 일환입니다.** 앞으로 2년 동안에 걸쳐, **7** **이 회사는 인적 자원 애플리케이션 분야에서 앱이즈가 보유한 앱 개발 전문 지식을 통합하는 것을 목표로 하고 있습니다.** 테크노바의 대표이사 잭 모레노 씨는 모바일 플랫폼이 점점 더 지배적으로 변하면서, 빠르게 발전하고 있는 기술 업계에서 경쟁력을 유지하는 데 필수적이라고 밝혔습니다.

8 **비록 샌프란시스코에 본사를 두고 있기는 하지만, 테크노바는 자사의 사업 확장을 뒷받침하기 위해 뉴욕과 오스틴, 그리고 시애틀에 사무실을 열었습니다.** 모레노 씨는 작년에 한 컨퍼런스 행사 중에 앱이즈의 앱 중 하나를 이용했을 때 그곳의 혁신적인 접근 방식을 처음 알게 되었다고 언급했습니다. "이곳의 사용자 친화적인 디자인과 첨단 기술은 우수한 소프트웨어 해결책을 전해 드리기 위한 저희 테크노바의 사명과 완벽히 방향이 일치합니다."라고 모레노 씨가 밝혔습니다.

어휘 **acquire** ~을 인수하다, 획득하다 **diversify** ~을 다양화하다, 다각화하다 **integrate** ~을 통합하다 **evolving** 발전하는, 진화하는 **dominant** 지배적인 **headquartered in** ~에 본사를 둔 **note that** ~라고 언급하다, ~라는 점에 주목하다 **user-friendly** 사용자 친화적인 **cutting-edge** 첨단의 **align with** ~와 방향이 일치하다

발신: 마이클 트렌치, 운영부장
수신: 앱이즈 전 직원
날짜: 4월 15일
제목: 테크노바 인수
첨부: 현재의_초과 근무_정책

안녕하세요, 팀원 여러분,

여러분 대부분이 아시다시피, 테크노바의 최근 인수와 함께, 몇몇 회사 정책이 변경될 것입니다. 5월 1일부터 우리를 대상으로 시행될 테크노바의 초과 근무 정책 및 수당과 관련해 여러분께 알려 드리고자 이메일을 씁니다. 확인을 위해, 우리의 초과 근무 정책은 다음과 같을 것입니다.

- 초과 근무 수당은 주당 40시간을 초과해 근무하는 시간에 대해 1.5배로 계산될 것입니다.
- 주말 및 휴일 근무에 대해서는 2배의 지급액을 받으시게 될 것입니다.
- **10** **초과 근무 승인은 이틀 전에 미리 이뤄지는 직속 상관 결재를 필요로 할 것입니다.**

참고를 위해 우리 앱이즈의 현 정책을 첨부해 드렸습니다. 어떤 우려 사항이든 명확하게 하는 데 도움을 드리기 위해, **8** **9** **테크노바 본사의 멜리사 해스킨 운영부장님께서 4월**

20일 오전 10시에 가상 질의 응답 시간을 주최하실 것입니다. 여러분 모두 참석하시기를 기대합니다.

안녕히 계십시오.

마이클 트렌치
운영부장
앱이즈

어휘 take effect 시행되다 be as follows 다음과 같다 calculate ~을 계산하다 time-and-a-half 1.5배의 sign-off 결재, 서명을 통한 승인 clarify ~을 명확하게 하다 virtual 가상의

앱이즈
현 초과 근무 정책

- 초과 근무 시간이란 계약된 주당 40시간을 초과해 근무하는 모든 시간이다. 초과 근무 시간은 정상 시급의 1.5배에 해당하는 급여로 지급된다.
- 때때로, 직원들은 주말 동안에 걸쳐 또는 공휴일에 근무하도록 요청받는다. 이러한 경우의 초과 근무 시간은 주당 40시간을 바탕으로 정상 시급의 2배에 해당하는 급여로 지급된다.
- 10 **초과 근무를 계획하는 경우, 반드시 최소 하루 전에 미리 직속 관리자의 승인을 받아야 한다.** 직속 관리자는 직원들의 초과 근무 시간이 다음 급여 명세서에 반영되도록 회계팀에 승인서를 제출한다.

어휘 in excess of ~을 초과하는 contracted 계약된, 계약을 맺은 line manager 직속 관리자 pay slip 급여 명세서

6. 기사 내용에 따르면, 테크노바가 왜 앱이즈를 인수하는가?
(A) 유통망을 확장하기 위해
(B) 업무 현장 생산성을 향상시키기 위해
(C) 유럽의 소프트웨어 시장으로 진출하기 위해
(D) 더 다양한 종류의 제품을 제공하기 위해

해설 첫 지문 첫 단락에 앱이즈의 인수가 모바일 앱 시장으로 사업을 확장해 제품 포트폴리오를 다양화하려는 전략적 계획의 일환이라고 쓰여 있다. 제품 포트폴리오의 다양화는 결국 더 다양한 제품을 만든다는 뜻이므로 (D)가 정답이다.

어휘 break into ~로 진출하다

7. 앱이즈는 어떤 종류의 모바일 애플리케이션을 주로 만드는가?
(A) 인적 자원
(B) 재무 관리
(C) 그래픽 디자인
(D) 인스턴트 메시지 전송

해설 첫 지문 첫 단락에 인적 자원 애플리케이션 분야에서 앱이즈가 보유한 앱 개발 전문 지식이 언급되어 있으므로 (A)가 정답이다.

8. 해스킨 씨의 사무실은 어디에 있는가?
(A) 오스틴에
(B) 시애틀에
(C) 뉴욕에
(D) 샌프란시스코에

해설 두 번째 지문 세 번째 단락에 해스킨 씨가 테크노바의 본사에 근무한다는 정보가 제시되어 있고, 첫 지문 두 번째 단락에는 테크노바가 샌프란시스코에 본사를 두고 있다고 쓰여 있으므로 (D)가 정답이다.

9. 앱이즈의 직원들이 4월 20일에 무엇을 할 것으로 예상되는가?
(A) 테크노바의 본사를 방문하는 일
(B) 온라인 회의 시간에 참석하는 일
(C) 새 고용 계약서에 서명하는 일
(D) 교육 과정을 이수하는 일

해설 4월 20일이라는 시점이 제시된 두 번째 지문 세 번째 단락에 테크노바 본사의 멜리사 해스킨 운영부장이 4월 20일 오전 10시에 가상 질의 응답 시간을 주최한다는 사실과 함께 모두 참석하도록 당부하는 말이 쓰여 있으므로 (B)가 정답이다.

10. 앱이즈의 현 초과 근무 정책이 테크노바의 것과 어떻게 다른가?
(A) 더 짧은 통보가 초과 근무 승인을 위해 필요하다.
(B) 직원들이 매주 더 적은 시간을 근무하도록 계약되어 있다.
(C) 초과 근무 수당이 주말과 휴일에 대해 더 높다.
(D) 직원들이 계약된 시간을 초과하는 초과 근무 시간에 대해 비용을 덜 지급 받는다.

해설 두 번째 지문 두 번째 단락에 테크노바의 초과 근무 승인이 이틀 전에 미리 이뤄져야 한다고 쓰여 있는 반면, 세 번째 지문 세 번째 항목에는 앱이즈의 초과 근무 승인이 최소 하루 전에 미리 이뤄져야 한다고 언급되어 있다. 따라서, 앱이즈의 통보 기간이 더 짧다는 것을 알 수 있으므로 (A)가 정답이다.

어휘 exceed ~을 초과하다

LISTENING

Playlist 1
만점을 위한 사람사진&고난도 표현의 모든 것!

Practice

1. (A)	**2.** (D)	**3.** (B)	**4.** (D)	**5.** (B)
6. (D)	**7.** (B)	**8.** (B)		

1. **(A) The women are walking down a ramp.**
(B) A bicycle is parked near a railing.
(C) One of the women is searching in her bag.
(D) Some poles are lying on the ground.

(A) 여자들이 경사로를 걸어 내려가고 있다.
(B) 자전거 한 대가 난간 근처에 주차되어 있다.
(C) 여자들 중 한 명이 가방 안을 살피고 있다.
(D) 몇몇 막대기들이 바닥 위에 놓여 있다.

해설 여자 두 명이 공원에서 경사로를 걸어 내려가고 있는 모습에 초점을 맞춰 묘사한 (A)가 정답이다.

어휘 ramp 경사로 railing 난간 pole 막대기, 기둥

2. (A) A wall of a building is being repaired by a crew.
(B) A crane has been set up on a street corner.
(C) A worker is climbing up a ladder.
(D) A streetlamp is being repaired.

(A) 건물의 벽이 작업자에 의해 수리되고 있다.
(B) 크레인이 길거리 모퉁이에 설치되어 있다.
(C) 노동자가 사다리에 올라가고 있다.
(D) 가로등이 수리되고 있다.

해설 한 작업자에 의해 가로등이 수리되고 있는 모습에 초점을 맞춰 묘사한 (D)가 정답이다.

3. (A) He is adjusting his glasses.
(B) He is wearing safety gloves.
(C) He is reaching for a bottle on the table.
(D) He is moving a microscope out of a laboratory.

(A) 남자가 안경을 조절하고 있다.
(B) 남자가 보호 장갑을 착용하고 있다.
(C) 남자가 탁자 위에 있는 물병에 손을 뻗고 있다.
(D) 남자가 실험실 밖으로 현미경을 옮기고 있다.

해설 남자가 실험실에서 보호 장갑을 착용한 상태에 초점을 맞춰 묘사한 (B)가 정답이다.

어휘 adjust ~을 조절하다, 조정하다 microscope 현미경

4. (A) One of the women is holding a coffee mug.
(B) One of the women is picking up a file folder.
(C) They are speaking behind a podium.
(D) They are looking at some notes on a whiteboard.

(A) 여자들 중 한 명이 커피 머그를 잡고 있다.
(B) 여자들 중 한 명이 파일 폴더를 집어 올리고 있다.
(C) 사람들이 강단 뒤에서 말하고 있다.
(D) 사람들이 화이트보드에 있는 몇몇 메모를 보고 있다.

해설 회의실에서 사람들이 화이트보드에 붙어 있는 메모지를 보고 있는 상태에 초점을 맞춰 묘사한 (D)가 정답이다.

어휘 podium 강단, 연단

5. (A) She is checking the numbers on a meter box.
(B) She is holding a garden hose.
(C) She is looking out a window.
(D) She is clearing off an outdoor table.

(A) 여자가 계기 상자의 수치를 확인하고 있다.
(B) 여자가 정원용 호스를 잡고 있다.
(C) 여자가 창문 밖을 보고 있다.
(D) 여자가 야외 탁자를 치우고 있다.

해설 여자가 정원에서 호스를 잡고 있는 동작에 초점을 맞춰 묘사한 (B)가 정답이다.

어휘 meter box 계기 상자 clear off ~을 치우다

6. (A) She is loading some boxes into a fridge.
(B) She is walking along an aisle.
(C) She is putting some products into a shopping basket.
(D) She is reaching for some merchandise on a shelf.

(A) 여자가 냉장고에 몇몇 박스를 싣고 있다.
(B) 여자가 복도를 따라 걷고 있다.
(C) 여자가 쇼핑 바구니에 몇몇 제품들을 넣고 있다.
(D) 여자가 선반에 있는 몇몇 상품에 손을 뻗고 있다.

해설 여자가 마트 선반에 있는 상품에 손을 뻗고 있는 동작에 초점을 맞춰 묘사한 (D)가 정답이다.

어휘 fridge 냉장고 reach for ~에 손을 뻗다

7. (A) A brick chimney is being removed.
(B) A roof is under construction.
(C) One of the people is bending to pick up a helmet.
(D) Some workers are holding a piece of a wood panel.

(A) 벽돌 굴뚝이 제거되고 있다.
(B) 지붕이 공사 중이다.
(C) 사람들 중 한 명이 헬멧을 집어 올리기 위해 허리를 숙이고 있다.
(D) 몇몇 노동자들이 나무 판자 한 개를 잡고 있다.

해설 작업자들에 의해 지붕이 공사되고 있는 상태에 초점을 맞춰 묘사한 (B)가 정답이다.

어휘 chimney 굴뚝 under construction 공사 중인 bend 허리를 숙이다

8. (A) They are hanging up their shirts.
(B) They are strolling outside.
(C) They are boating on the ocean.
(D) They are packing up some luggage.

(A) 사람들이 셔츠를 걸고 있다.
(B) 사람들이 바깥에서 산책하고 있다.
(C) 사람들이 바다에서 보트를 타고 있다.
(D) 사람들이 몇몇 짐을 싸고 있다.

해설 해변가에서 사람 두 명이 산책하고 있는 모습에 초점을 맞춰 묘사한 (B)가 정답이다.

어휘 boat v. 보트를 타다 pack up (짐 등) ~을 싸다, 꾸리다

Check-up Test

1. (C)	**2.** (C)	**3.** (B)	**4.** (A)	**5.** (B)
6. (C)	**7.** (C)	**8.** (D)	**9.** (C)	**10.** (B)
11. (C)	**12.** (A)			

1. (A) She is wearing a pair of boots.
(B) She is grasping a garden tool.
(C) She is bending over some flowers.
(D) She is weaving a wicker basket.

(A) 여자가 부츠 한 켤레를 신고 있다.
(B) 여자가 정원 도구 하나를 잡고 있다.
(C) 여자가 몇몇 꽃들 위로 허리를 숙이고 있다.
(D) 여자가 라탄 바구니를 짜고 있다.

해설 여자가 정원에서 꽃 위로 허리를 숙인 동작에 초점을 맞춰 묘사한 (C)가 정답이다.

어휘 weave ~을 짜다 wicker 라탄

2. (A) The man is shutting a door.
(B) The man is wearing a safety vest.
(C) The man is kneeling to examine some tools.
(D) The man is placing a pipe on a wall.

(A) 남자가 문을 닫고 있다.
(B) 남자가 안전 조끼를 입고 있다.
(C) 남자가 몇몇 도구들을 자세히 보기 위해 무릎을 꿇고 있다.
(D) 남자가 벽에 파이프를 설치하고 있다.

해설 남자가 무릎을 꿇은 상태로 도구를 살펴보는 동작에 초점을 맞춰 묘사한 (C)가 정답이다.

3. (A) A woman is adjusting her eyeglasses with her hands.
(B) A woman is facing a bookshelf.
(C) A woman is piling some books into a cart.
(D) A woman is tying her hair up.

(A) 여자가 손으로 안경을 조절하고 있다.
(B) 여자가 책꽂이를 마주보고 있다.
(C) 여자가 카트에 몇몇 책들을 쌓고 있다.
(D) 여자가 머리를 위로 묶고 있다.

해설 여자가 책꽂이를 마주보고 있는 상태에 초점을 맞춰 묘사한 (B)가 정답이다.

4. **(A) A group of people is reviewing documents together.**
(B) One of the men is giving a file folder to his colleagues.
(C) A woman is typing on a laptop.
(D) People are gathered in a circle.

(A) 한 무리의 사람들이 함께 서류를 검토 중이다.
(B) 남자들 중 한 명이 동료에게 파일 폴더를 주고 있다.
(C) 여자가 노트북으로 타자를 치고 있다.
(D) 사람들이 원을 이루어 모여있다.

해설 여러 명의 사람들이 함께 서류를 보고 있는 상태에 초점을 맞춰 묘사한 (A)가 정답이다.

어휘 in a circle 원(모양)을 이루어

5. (A) Some windowpanes are being polished.
(B) A pillow is being placed on a seat.

(C) Wooden furniture has been propped against a wall.
(D) A plant is being carried into a seating area.

(A) 몇몇 창유리들이 닦이고 있다.
(B) 베개 하나가 의자에 놓이고 있다.
(C) 나무로 된 가구가 벽에 기대어져 있다.
(D) 한 식물이 좌석 구역으로 옮겨지고 있다.

해설 베개 한 개가 소파에 놓이고 있는 상태에 초점을 맞춰 묘사한 (B)가 정답이다.

어휘 windowpanes 창유리

6. (A) The woman is unplugging a cord from an outlet.
(B) The woman is pushing a button on an appliance.
(C) The woman is gripping a cupboard handle.
(D) The woman is wiping some kitchen tiles.

(A) 여자가 콘센트에서 코드를 빼고 있다.
(B) 여자가 가전기기의 버튼을 누르고 있다.
(C) 여자가 찬장 손잡이를 잡고 있다.
(D) 여자가 몇몇 주방 타일들을 닦고 있다.

해설 여자가 주방에서 찬장 손잡이를 잡고 있는 동작에 초점을 맞춰 묘사한 (C)가 정답이다.

어휘 unplug (플러그 등) ~을 뽑다 outlet 콘센트 cupboard 찬장

7. (A) Some luggage is being lifted from a conveyor belt.
(B) The engine of an airplane is being repaired by a technician.
(C) Some people are boarding an airplane.
(D) Passengers are seated in a waiting area.

(A) 몇몇 짐이 컨베이어 벨트에서 들어 올려지고 있다.
(B) 비행기의 엔진이 기술자에 의해 수리되고 있다.
(C) 몇몇 사람들이 비행기에 탑승하고 있다.
(D) 승객들이 대합실에 앉아 있다.

해설 사람들이 비행기에 탑승 중인 동작에 초점을 맞춰 묘사한 (C)가 정답이다.

8. (A) A person is swimming in the water.
(B) A boat is docked at a pier.
(C) A beach is crowded with visitors.
(D) A person is rowing a boat.

(A) 한 사람이 물에서 수영하고 있다.
(B) 보트가 부두에 정박해 있다.
(C) 해변이 방문객들로 붐빈다.
(D) 한 사람이 배의 노를 젓고 있다.

해설 남자가 물 위에서 배의 노를 젓고 있는 동작에 초점을 맞춰 묘사한 (D)가 정답이다.

어휘 dock ~에 정박하다 row 노를 젓다

9. (A) He is packing some items into his backpack.
(B) He is taking a picture of some flowers.
(C) He is climbing up an outdoor rocky path.
(D) He is walking out of a forest.

(A) 남자가 배낭에 몇몇 물건들을 싸고 있다.
(B) 남자가 몇몇 꽃 사진을 찍고 있다.
(C) 남자가 야외 돌길을 오르고 있다.
(D) 남자가 숲에서 걸어 나오고 있다.

해설 남자가 배낭을 매고 야외에서 돌로 된 길을 오르는 동작에 초점을 맞춰 묘사한 (C)가 정답이다.

어휘 rocky 돌로 된

10. (A) A woman is leaning against a fence.
(B) One of the people is standing right in front of the stairs.
(C) People are walking through a door.
(D) A man is picking up some boxes in front of an entrance.

(A) 여자가 울타리에 기대어 있다.
(B) 사람들 중 한 명이 계단 바로 앞에 서있다.
(C) 사람들이 문을 통과해서 걸어가고 있다.
(D) 남자가 입구 앞에서 몇몇 박스들을 들어올리고 있다.

해설 여자 한 명이 계단 바로 앞에 서 있는 상태에 초점을 맞춰 묘사한 (B)가 정답이다.

11. (A) A clerk is displaying some items in a store.
(B) A customer is paying for a purchase at a cash register.
(C) Some wine bottles are lined up on shelves.
(D) Some ceiling lights have been turned off.

(A) 점원이 가게에서 몇몇 물건들을 진열하고 있다.
(B) 고객이 계산대에서 구매품에 대해 지불하고 있다.
(C) 몇몇 와인병들이 선반에 줄지어져 있다.
(D) 몇몇 천장 조명이 꺼져 있다.

해설 선반에 일렬로 진열된 와인병의 상태에 초점을 맞춰 묘사한 (C)가 정답이다.

12. **(A) A shovel is being used.**
(B) Some posts have been installed along a walkway.
(C) The roof of a building is being painted.
(D) A bicycle is leaning against a metal surface.

(A) 삽이 사용되고 있는 중이다.
(B) 몇몇 기둥들이 보도를 따라 설치되어 있다.
(C) 건물 지붕이 페인트칠되고 있다.
(D) 자전거가 금속 표면에 기대어져 있다.

해설 삽이 사람에 의해 사용되고 있는 상태에 초점을 맞춰 묘사한 (A)가 정답이다.

▶ Playlist 2
만점을 위한 사물사진&고난도 표현의 모든 것!

Practice

1. (C)	**2.** (C)	**3.** (B)	**4.** (D)

1. (A) Workers are fixing some tires on a truck.
(B) Some wooden furniture has been set up outside.
(C) The door of a van have been left open.
(D) Some boxes are being stacked next to a truck.

(A) 작업자들이 트럭의 타이어 몇 개를 고치고 있다.
(B) 몇몇 나무로 된 가구가 야외에 설치되어 있다.
(C) 승합차의 문이 열린 상태로 놓여 있다.
(D) 몇몇 박스들이 트럭 옆에 쌓여지고 있다.

해설 차량의 문이 열려 있는 상태에 초점을 맞춰 묘사한 (C)가 정답이다.

어휘 van 승합차

2. (A) Some people are resting on a sandy beach.
(B) There are towels hanging on chairs.
(C) Some umbrellas are placed on a beach.
(D) A pathway runs parallel to the water.

(A) 몇몇 사람들이 모래 해변에서 휴식을 취하고 있다.
(B) 수건들이 의자에 걸려 있다.
(C) 몇몇 파라솔이 해변에 놓여 있다.
(D) 길이 물가와 평행하게 있다.

해설 파라솔들이 모래 해변에 놓여 있는 상태에 초점을 맞춰 묘사한 (C)가 정답이다.

어휘 sandy 모래로 된 parallel to ~와 평행하게

3. (A) Some kitchen tiles are being polished.
(B) Light fixtures are suspended from the ceiling.
(C) Several plates have been placed on a counter.
(D) Some eating utensils have been organized in a drawer.

(A) 몇몇 주방 타일들이 닦여지고 있다.
(B) 조명 기구들이 천장에 매달려 있다.
(C) 여러 개의 접시들이 조리대 위에 놓여 있다.
(D) 몇몇 식기가 서랍에 정리되어 있다.

해설 조명 기구들이 천장에 달려 있는 상태에 초점을 맞춰 묘사한 (B)가 정답이다.

어휘 suspend ~을 달다

4. (A) Lampposts are being repaired.
(B) Some vehicles are parked near a curb.
(C) Some trees are growing along the road.
(D) A sign has been installed in a parking area.

(A) 가로등들이 수리되고 있다.
(B) 몇몇 차량들이 연석 근처에 주차되어 있다.
(C) 몇몇 나무들이 도로를 따라 자라고 있다.
(D) 표지판이 주차 구역에 설치되어 있다.

해설 표지판 하나가 주차장에 설치되어 있는 상태에 초점을 맞춰 묘사한 (D)가 정답이다.

Check-up Test

1. (B)	**2.** (D)	**3.** (D)	**4.** (D)	**5.** (B)
6. (C)	**7.** (C)	**8.** (C)	**9.** (D)	**10.** (D)
11. (B)	**12.** (C)			

1. (A) Some bushes are on both sides of a door.
(B) Light fixtures are mounted on either side of the entrance.
(C) Some cushions have been arranged on the ground.
(D) There are some armchairs facing a window.

(A) 몇몇 관목들이 문의 양쪽에 있다.
(B) 조명 기구들이 입구 양쪽에 걸려 있다.
(C) 몇몇 쿠션이 바닥에 정리되어 있다.
(D) 몇몇 안락의자들이 창문을 향해 있다.

해설 입구의 출입문 벽 양쪽에 조명들이 걸려 있는 상태에 초점을 맞춰 묘사한 (B)가 정답이다.

어휘 mount ~을 (위에) 걸다

2. (A) Some trees are being trimmed.
(B) A walking trail leads to a pond.
(C) An umbrella has been left open in a grassy area.
(D) Some benches have been set up outside.

(A) 몇몇 나무들이 다듬어지고 있다.
(B) 산책로 하나가 연못으로 이어지고 있다.
(C) 파라솔이 잔디가 있는 공간에 펼쳐진 상태로 놓여있다.
(D) 몇몇 벤치들이 야외에 설치되어 있다.

해설 야외 공간에 벤치들이 설치되어 있는 상태에 초점을 맞춰 묘사한 (D)가 정답이다.

어휘 trim ~을 다듬다 grassy 잔디가 있는

3. (A) A forklift is parked near a curb.
(B) Some branches are being lifted by a truck.
(C) A garden path is paved with stones.
(D) Some leaves have been stacked into a pile.

(A) 지게차 한 대가 연석 근처에 주차되어 있다.
(B) 몇몇 나뭇가지들이 트럭에 의해 들어 올려지고 있다.
(C) 정원 길이 돌로 포장되어 있다.
(D) 몇몇 나뭇잎들이 더미로 쌓여 있다.

해설 공원 길 위에 나뭇잎들이 쌓여 있는 상태에 초점을 맞춰 묘사한 (D)가 정답이다.

어휘 forklift 지게차 be paved with ~로 포장되어 있다

4. (A) A rug has been placed in the middle of a hallway.
(B) Some drawers have been filled with items.
(C) A picture frame is being displayed on the wall.
(D) Some clothes are hanging on a rack.

(A) 러그 하나가 복도 한가운데에 놓여있다.
(B) 몇몇 서랍들이 물건들로 채워져 있다.
(C) 액자 하나가 벽에 전시되어 있다.
(D) 몇몇 옷들이 옷걸이에 걸려있다.

해설 옷들이 벽면에 설치된 옷걸이에 걸려있는 상태에 초점을 맞춰 묘사한 (D)가 정답이다.

5. (A) The curtains are pulled closed.
(B) A stool is positioned in front of a musical instrument.
(C) An outdoor place is full of people dining.
(D) Floral arrangements are put on a table.

(A) 커튼들이 닫혀져 있다.
(B) 의자가 악기 앞에 놓여져 있다.
(C) 야외 공간이 식사하는 사람들로 가득 차 있다.
(D) 꽃꽂이들이 탁자 위에 놓여있다.

해설 피아노 앞에 의자 하나가 놓여 있는 상태에 초점을 맞춰 묘사한 (B)가 정답이다.

6. (A) A ferry is sailing along a shore.
(B) There are passengers boarding a ship.
(C) Some boats are docked in a harbor.
(D) A platform is being built at a pier.

(A) 배 하나가 해안을 따라 항해 중이다.
(B) 배에 탑승 중인 승객들이 있다.
(C) 몇몇 배들이 항구에 정박해 있다.
(D) 부두에 승강장이 지어지고 있다.

해설 항구에 여러 척의 배들이 정박해 있는 상태에 초점을 맞춰 묘사한 (C)가 정답이다.

7. (A) The chair is being occupied.
(B) A lamp is illuminated near the seating area.
(C) A laptop is placed on a cluttered desk.
(D) Some cords are lying on the floor.

(A) 의자가 사용되고 있다.
(B) 램프가 좌석 구역 근처에서 비춰지고 있다.
(C) 노트북이 어수선한 책상 위에 놓여있다.
(D) 몇몇 선들이 바닥에 놓여있다.

해설 노트북이 여러 물건이 있는 책상 위에 올려진 상태에 초점을 맞춰 묘사한 (C)가 정답이다.

어휘 illuminate ~을 비추다 cluttered 어수선한

8. (A) A café is decorated with banners.
(B) Some diners are seated under a restaurant patio.
(C) Some awnings have been installed at a street corner.
(D) A streetlamp is being repaired behind a building.

(A) 카페가 현수막으로 장식되어 있다.
(B) 몇몇 식사하는 사람들이 식당의 야외 테라스 아래에 앉아 있다.
(C) 몇몇 차양들이 거리 모퉁이에 설치되어 있다.
(D) 가로등 하나가 건물 뒤에서 수리되고 있다.

해설 거리 모퉁이에 위치한 가게에 차양이 설치되어 있는 상태에 초점을 맞춰 묘사한 (C)가 정답이다.

어휘 banner 현수막 awning 차양

9. (A) Some cars are driving on a mountain road.
(B) Skyscrapers are lined up along the edge of the water.
(C) A boat is passing under a bridge.
(D) The sunset is being cast over the river.

(A) 몇몇 차량들이 산길을 달리고 있다.
(B) 고층 건물들이 물가를 따라 줄지어 있다.
(C) 배 한 척이 다리 아래를 지나고 있다.
(D) 노을이 강에 드리워져 있다.

해설 강물에 노을이 비친 상태에 초점을 맞춰 묘사한 (D)가 정답이다.

10. (A) A house is made of some bricks.
(B) A wooden structure is being removed by a crane.
(C) Landscaping workers are doing some maintenance.
(D) Some building materials are scattered on the ground.

(A) 집 한 채가 몇몇 벽돌들로 만들어져 있다.
(B) 나무로 된 구조물이 크레인에 의해 치워지고 있다.
(C) 조경 작업자들이 몇몇 유지보수 작업을 하고 있다.
(D) 몇몇 건축 자재들이 땅 위에 흩어져 있다.

해설 땅 바닥에 여러 건설 자재들이 흩어져 있는 상태에 초점을 맞춰 묘사한 (D)가 정답이다.

어휘 landscaping 조경 scatter ~을 흩어지게 하다

11. (A) Some poles are being taken out of the worksite.
(B) Some telephone wires are suspended over a road.
(C) Some country roads run along a hillside.
(D) A street sign is being placed at an intersection.

(A) 몇몇 기둥들이 작업 현장에서 뽑혀지고 있다.
(B) 몇몇 전화선들이 도로 위로 매달려 있다.
(C) 몇몇 시골 길들이 언덕을 따라 이어져 있다.
(D) 도로 표지판이 교차로에 놓여지고 있다.

해설 도로 위로 전화선들이 기둥에 매달려 있는 상태에 초점을 맞춰 묘사한 (B)가 정답이다.

어휘 pole 기둥, 막대기 intersection 교차로

12. (A) Some flower bushes are being watered.
(B) A tree has been planted in the middle of a park.
(C) Some potted plants are lined up in the backyard.
(D) There is a wooden bench covered in leaves.

(A) 몇몇 꽃 덤불들에 물이 주어지고 있다.
(B) 나무가 공원의 중앙에 심어져 있다.
(C) 뒷마당에 몇몇 화분에 심어진 식물들이 줄지어 있다.
(D) 나뭇잎으로 덮인 나무 벤치가 있다.

해설 뒷마당에 화분에 담긴 여러 식물들이 줄지어 있는 상태에 초점을 맞춰 묘사한 (C)가 정답이다.

▶ Playlist 3
시험 전 의문사 의문문 벼락치기 ①

Practice

1. (C)	**2.** (C)	**3.** (A)	**4.** (C)	**5.** (C)
6. (B)	**7.** (C)	**8.** (C)	**9.** (B)	

1. Who can I ask about processing a refund for this jacket?
(A) It didn't fit me well.
(B) By the cash register.
(C) I can take care of that for you.

이 자켓을 환불 처리하는 것에 대해 누구에게 물어볼 수 있나요?
(A) 그건 저한테 잘 맞지 않아요.
(B) 현금 등록기 옆에요.
(C) 제가 처리해 드릴 수 있어요.

해설 Who와 함께 환불 처리에 대해 문의할 수 있는 사람을 묻고 있으므로 자신이 처리해 주겠다고 답하는 (C)가 정답이다.

어휘 cash register 현금 등록기

2. Who's responsible for distributing everyone's training packets?
(A) No more than three hours.
(B) Some extra handouts.
(C) The HR intern.

누가 모두의 교육 자료집을 나눠주는 것을 담당하나요?
(A) 3시간 이내요.
(B) 몇몇 추가 유인물들이요.
(C) 인사부 인턴이요.

해설 Who와 함께 교육 자료를 나눠줄 담당자를 묻고 있으므로 인턴이라는 직책명으로 답하는 (C)가 정답이다.

어휘 no more than ~ 이내

3. Who's planning the keynote seminar?
(A) I believe it should be Ms. Monroe.
(B) We're excited for your speech.
(C) At the community center.

누가 기조 세미나를 기획하고 있나요?
(A) 제 생각엔 먼로 씨인 것 같아요.
(B) 당신의 연설에 대해 설렙니다.
(C) 커뮤니티 센터에서요.

해설 Who와 함께 세미나를 기획하는 사람을 묻고 있으므로 I believe 표현과 함께 담당자를 알려주는 (A)가 정답이다.

어휘 be excited for ~에 대해 설레다

4. When will you visit the new factory grounds?
(A) A spacious area.
(B) The visitors were impressed.
(C) I've decided to wait until next month.

새로운 공장 부지는 언제 방문하실 예정인가요?
(A) 넓은 구역이에요.
(B) 방문객들이 깊은 감명을 받았어요.
(C) 다음 달까지 기다리기로 결정했어요.

해설 When과 함께 새 부지에 방문하는 시기를 묻고 있으므로 현재완료시제를 사용해 다음 달까지 기다리기로 결정했다고 답하는 (C)가 정답이다.

어휘 ground 부지, 대지 spacious 넓은

5. When did we first apply for the construction permit?
(A) Yes. I was offered the position.
(B) The project is on schedule.
(C) Two weeks ago.

우리가 언제 처음으로 건축 허가를 신청했죠?
(A) 네. 그 직책을 제안 받았어요.
(B) 그 프로젝트는 일정대로예요.
(C) 2주 전에요.

해설 When과 함께 건축 허가를 처음 신청한 시점을 묻고 있으므로 동일한 과거시제를 사용해 특정 시점으로 답하는 (C)가 정답이다.

어휘 on schedule 일정대로, 예정대로

6. When can we receive the quote?
(A) An affordable hourly rate.
(B) No later than tomorrow evening.
(C) For the catering services.

견적서를 언제 받아볼 수 있나요?
(A) 적정한 가격의 시급이요.
(B) 늦어도 내일 저녁까지요.
(C) 출장 음식 제공 서비스를 위해서요.

해설 When과 함께 견적서를 받을 수 있는 시점을 묻고 있으므로 늦어도 내일 저녁까지라는 시점 표현으로 답하는 (B)가 정답이다.

어휘 quote 견적서 hourly rate 시급

7. Where are the forms for employee onboarding?
(A) Three new staff members.
(B) By 5 o'clock on Wednesday.
(C) Savannah would know.

직원 온보딩을 위한 양식들은 어디에 있나요?
(A) 세 명의 새로운 직원들이요.
(B) 수요일 5시 정각까지요.
(C) 사바나 씨가 알 거에요.

해설 Where과 함께 신입 교육을 위한 양식의 위치를 묻고 있으므로 사람 이름을 사용하여 담당자로 답하는 (C)가 정답이다.

어휘 onboarding 신입 교육, 신입 사원 적응 프로그램

8. Where's the soccer game being held?
(A) Mainly for local fans.
(B) Please have your tickets ready.
(C) Let's search it up online.

축구 경기는 어디에서 열리나요?
(A) 주로 지역 팬들을 위해서요.
(B) 입장권을 준비해 주세요.
(C) 온라인에서 찾아보죠.

해설 Where과 함께 축구 경기가 열리는 장소를 묻고 있으므로 해당 정보를 온라인에서 찾아보자고 답하는 (C)가 정답이다.

어휘 search A up A를 찾아보다

9. Where is the closest auto repair shop?
(A) No, I don't own a car.
(B) It's just around the corner.
(C) We'll prepare them tomorrow.

가장 가까운 자동차 수리점이 어디인가요?
(A) 아니요, 저는 차를 가지고 있지 않아요.
(B) 코너 돌면 바로 있어요.
(C) 그것들을 내일까지 준비할게요.

해설 Where과 함께 가장 가까운 수리점의 위치를 묻고 있으므로 「전치사 + 장소명사」로 답하는 (B)가 정답이다.

어휘 auto 자동차

Check-up Test

1. (B)	**2.** (B)	**3.** (A)	**4.** (A)	**5.** (A)
6. (C)	**7.** (A)	**8.** (C)	**9.** (A)	**10.** (C)
11. (C)	**12.** (A)	**13.** (C)	**14.** (C)	**15.** (B)
16. (C)	**17.** (A)	**18.** (A)	**19.** (C)	**20.** (A)

1. Who's the headlining act at tomorrow's festival?
(A) Can you remind me of the movie's name?
(B) Blue Lucy, a jazz singer from Italy.
(C) Our headquarters are there.

내일 축제에서 누가 주 공연팀인가요?
(A) 그 영화 제목 좀 다시 알려 주시겠어요?
(B) 이탈리아에서 온 재즈 가수 블루 루시요.
(C) 저희 본사가 거기 있습니다.

해설 내일 축제에서 주 공연팀이 누구인지 묻고 있으므로 사람 이름과 직업명을 언급하는 (B)가 정답이다.

어휘 headlining act 주 공연팀 remind A of B A에게 B를 다시 알려 주다, 상기시키다

2. When did you open your first credit card?
(A) There's a bank nearby.
(B) Right after I graduated from college.
(C) I'd like to pay with cash.

언제 첫 신용카드를 개설하셨나요?
(A) 근처에 은행이 하나 있어요.
(B) 대학교를 졸업한 직후에요.
(C) 현금으로 결제하겠습니다.

해설 언제 첫 신용카드를 개설했는지 묻고 있으므로 대략적인 과거 시점으로 답변하는 (B)가 정답이다.

3. When should I send the candidate a follow-up e-mail?
(A) No later than next week.
(B) As much as they want.
(C) I'll deliver the order later today.

제가 언제 그 지원자에게 후속 이메일을 보내야 하나요?
(A) 늦어도 다음 주까지요.
(B) 그들이 원하는 만큼 많이요.
(C) 오늘 이따가 그 주문품을 배송해 드릴게요.

해설 언제 특정 지원자에게 후속 이메일을 보내야 하는지 묻고 있으므로 대략적인 미래 시점으로 답변하는 (A)가 정답이다.

어휘 follow-up 후속적인, 후속 조치의 as A as B B만큼 A하게

4. Where are the brightness controls on this projector?
(A) Sorry, I'm not quite sure.
(B) Twelve hours on a full charge.
(C) We set the project deadline for next week.

이 프로젝터의 밝기 조절 기능은 어디에 있나요?
(A) 죄송하지만, 잘 모르겠습니다.
(B) 완전 충전 상태로 12시간이요.
(C) 우리는 다음 주로 프로젝트 마감 기한을 정했어요.

해설 프로젝터의 밝기 조절 기능 위치를 묻고 있으므로 잘 모르겠다는 말로 우회적으로 답변하는 (A)가 정답이다.

어휘 on a full charge 완전 충전 상태로

5. Who will sort the packages that came in yesterday?
(A) No one. We have a machine for that.
(B) Yes, around noontime.
(C) Loading dock 4B.

누가 어제 들어 온 물품들을 분류할 예정인가요?
(A) 아무도요. 그 일을 하는 기계가 있어요.
(B) 네, 정오쯤에요.
(C) 하역장 4B요.

해설 누가 어제 들어 온 물품들을 분류하는지 묻고 있으므로 No one이라는 부정대명사와 함께 그 일을 하는 기계가 있다는 사실을 덧붙인 (A)가 정답이다.

어휘 sort v. ~을 분류하다 noontime 정오 loading dock (짐을 싣고 내리는) 하역장

6. Where should we put this cactus plant?
(A) The brand that manufactures bags.
(B) A large clay flowerpot.
(C) Over there on the windowsill.

이 선인장 식물을 어디에 두어야 하나요?
(A) 가방을 제조하는 브랜드요.
(B) 큰 점토 화분이요.
(C) 저기 저쪽에 있는 창턱에요.

해설 선인장 식물을 어디에 두어야 하는지 묻고 있으므로 식물이 놓일 수 있는 특정 위치를 「전치사 + 장소명사」로 답변하는 (C)가 정답이다.

어휘 cactus 선인장 flowerpot 화분 windowsill 창턱

7. When is the networking event happening?
(A) It's sometime next month.
(B) Alright, I can work that day.
(C) The convention center downtown.

인적 교류 행사가 언제 열리나요?
(A) 다음 달 중으로요.
(B) 좋아요, 저는 그날 일할 수 있습니다.
(C) 시내에 있는 컨벤션 센터요.

해설 인적 교류 행사가 언제 열리는지 묻고 있으므로 대략적인 미래 시점을 나타내는 표현으로 답변하는 (A)가 정답이다.

8. Where did you first hear about our dental offices?
(A) Do you have any slots for this Friday?
(B) This building has two entrances.
(C) I pass by here on my way to work every day.

저희 치과에 대해 어디서 처음 들으셨나요?
(A) 이번 금요일에 어떤 시간대든 있나요?
(B) 이 건물에는 입구가 두 곳 있어요.
(C) 매일 출근하는 길에 이곳을 지나갑니다.

해설 치과에 대해 어디서 처음 들었는지 묻고 있으므로 매일 출근하는 길에 지나간다는 말로 치과에 대해 알게 된 방법을 알리는 (C)가 정답이다.

어휘 slot (예약 등의) 시간대, 자리 pass by ~을 지나가다

9. Who delivers our products to the clients?
(A) Kodai handles all the courier contracts.
(B) I'm very sorry for the delay.
(C) Those are our best-sellers!

누가 우리 제품을 고객들에게 배송하나요?
(A) 코다이 씨가 모든 택배 회사 계약을 처리합니다.
(B) 지연에 대해 대단히 죄송합니다.
(C) 그것들이 저희의 베스트셀러입니다!

해설 누가 자신들의 제품을 고객들에게 배송하는지 묻고 있으므로 코다이 씨가 모든 택배 회사 계약을 처리한다는 말로 담당자를 알려주는 (A)가 정답이다.

어휘 courier 택배 회사, 택배 기사

10. When will our pasta dishes be served?
(A) A catering service.
(B) Please set it down in the center.
(C) Let's ask the waiter.

저희 파스타 요리가 언제 제공될까요?
(A) 출장 요리 제공 서비스요.
(B) 그걸 중앙 부분에 내려 놓으세요.
(C) 웨이터에게 물어보죠.

해설 자신들의 파스타 요리가 언제 제공될지 묻는 것에 대해 웨이터에게 물어보자는 말로 관련 정보를 확인할 수 있는 방법을 제안하는 (C)가 정답이다.

어휘 set A down A를 내려 놓다

11. When should we pass out the training manuals to our staff?
(A) Well, I've made these repairs before.
(B) Past the nearest station.
(C) We still need to finalize some details.

우리가 언제 교육 설명서를 우리 직원들에게 나눠 줘야 하나요?
(A) 음, 제가 전에 이런 수리 작업을 한 적이 있습니다.
(B) 가장 가까운 역을 지나서요.
(C) 여전히 몇 가지 세부사항들을 마무리해야 할 필요가 있어요.

해설 언제 교육 설명서를 직원들에게 나눠 줘야 하는지 묻는 것에 대해 여전히 세부사항을 마무리해야 한다는 말로 아직 그 정확한 시점을 알 수 없다는 뜻을 나타내는 (C)가 정답이다.

어휘 pass out ~을 나눠 주다, 배포하다

12. Who can I talk to regarding my parking permit?
(A) Are you a visitor?
(B) Just for another month, please.
(C) Wow, the new parking structure is huge!

제 주차증과 관련해서 누구와 이야기할 수 있나요?
(A) 방문객이신가요?
(B) 한 달만 더 부탁 드립니다.
(C) 우와, 새 주차 건물이 엄청 크네요!

해설 자신의 주차증과 관련해서 누구와 이야기하면 되는지 묻는 것에 대해 방문객인지 되묻는 것으로 주차 자격과 관련된 신분을 확인하려는 (A)가 정답이다.

13. When will the sports competition be taking place?
(A) Our competitors had strong sales.
(B) A companywide event.
(C) I posted the announcement just now.

그 스포츠 경기 대회가 언제 개최되는 건가요?
(A) 우리 경쟁사들은 판매 실적이 뛰어났어요.
(B) 회사 전체에 걸친 행사입니다.
(C) 제가 그 공지를 방금 막 게시했습니다.

해설 스포츠 경기 대회가 언제 개최되는지 묻는 것에 대해 그 공지를 방금 막 게시했다는 과거시제로 답한 (C)가 정답이다.

어휘 companywide 회사 전체의

14. Where do you usually get your car washed?
(A) Once every two months.
(B) No, she walks to work.
(C) I do it myself at home.

평소에 어디서 자동차를 세차하시나요?
(A) 두 달에 한 번씩이요.
(B) 아니요, 그분은 걸어서 출근해요.
(C) 집에서 직접 합니다.

해설 평소에 어디서 자동차를 세차하는지 묻는 것에 대해 집에서 직접 한다는 말로 세차 장소를 언급하는 (C)가 정답이다.

15. Who do I submit this warranty form to?
(A) A brand-new refrigerator.
(B) The customer service department.
(C) For another year.

누구에게 이 품질 보증 서비스 양식을 제출하나요?
(A) 완전히 새로운 냉장고요.
(B) 고객 서비스부요.
(C) 1년 더요.

해설 누구에게 품질 보증 서비스 양식을 제출하는지 묻고 있으므로 담당 부서를 알리는 (B)가 정답이다.

16. Where's the wellness fair going to be located?
(A) Mainly doctors and physicians.
(B) Please sign your name on this line.
(C) Let me check the posting again.

건강 박람회가 어디에 위치하게 되나요?
(A) 주로 박사들과 내과 의사들이요.
(B) 이 선에 성함을 서명하세요.
(C) 제가 게시글을 다시 확인해 볼게요.

해설 건강 박람회가 어디에 위치하는지 묻는 것에 대해 게시글을 다시 확인해 보겠다는 말로 관련 정보를 확인할 수 있는 출처를 언급하는 (C)가 정답이다.

어휘 wellness 건강 physician 내과 의사

17. Who's performing the inspection for the heating unit?
(A) A technician from Grafter's Repair Shop.
(B) He lives in apartment 72A.
(C) Yes, the results have been reviewed.

그 난방 장치에 대해 누가 점검을 실시하나요?
(A) 그래프터스 수리점의 기사님이요.
(B) 그분은 아파트 72A에 살고 계세요.
(C) 네, 그 결과들이 검토되었습니다.

해설 난방 장치에 대해 누가 점검을 실시하는지 묻고 있으므로 특정 수리점의 이름과 함께 직업명을 언급하는 (A)가 정답이다.

어휘 heating unit 난방 장치

18. When will the decorations for the party be set up?
(A) We plan to have everything ready by tomorrow night.
(B) A skilled contractor.
(C) One hundred balloons.

그 파티에 필요한 장식물들이 언제 설치될까요?
(A) 우리가 내일 밤까지 모든 것을 준비해 둘 계획입니다.
(B) 능숙한 계약업체요.
(C) 풍선 100개요.

해설 특정 파티에 필요한 장식물이 언제 설치되는지 묻고 있으므로 기한을 나타내는 표현을 포함해 준비 계획을 밝히는 (A)가 정답이다.

19. Where should I place these boxes of samples?
(A) This place is very crowded.
(B) At the trade show.
(C) On the third floor.

샘플들이 담긴 이 상자들을 어디에 두어야 하나요?
(A) 이곳은 아주 붐비네요.
(B) 무역 박람회에서요.
(C) 3층에요.

해설 샘플을 담은 상자들을 어디에 두어야 하는지 묻고 있으므로 특정 위치를 나타내는 「전치사 + 장소명사」 표현으로 답변하는 (C)가 정답이다.

20. When will you look over the report I submitted?
(A) Once I finish my current task.
(B) For the first quarter.
(C) I drafted a statement.

제가 제출해 드린 보고서를 언제 살펴보실 건가요?
(A) 현재 하고 있는 제 업무를 끝마치는 대로요.
(B) 1분기를 대상으로요.
(C) 제가 성명서 초안을 작성했어요.

해설 자신이 제출한 보고서를 언제 살펴 볼 것인지 묻고 있으므로 접속사 Once와 함께 현재 하고 있는 업무를 끝마치는 대로 하겠다는 말로 대략적인 시점을 언급하는 (A)가 정답이다.

어휘 draft v. ~의 초안을 작성하다 statement 성명(서), 진술(서), 내역(서)

▶ Playlist 4
시험 전 의문사 의문문 벼락치기 ②

Practice

1. (A)	**2.** (B)	**3.** (B)	**4.** (C)	**5.** (C)
6. (A)	**7.** (A)	**8.** (C)	**9.** (C)	**10.** (B)
11. (C)	**12.** (B)			

1. What time is the building maintenance scheduled?
(A) At 2 P.M., according to the notice.
(B) Yes, the agenda has been set.
(C) Some electrical repairs.

건물 시설 관리 작업이 몇 시에 예정되어 있나요?
(A) 오후 2시요, 공지에 따르면요.
(B) 네, 안건이 정해졌습니다.
(C) 몇몇 전기 관련 수리 작업이요.

해설 건물 시설 관리 작업이 몇 시에 예정되어 있는지 묻고 있으므로 What time과 어울리는 시점 숫자 표현으로 답변하는 (A)가 정답이다.

어휘 agenda 안건, 의제, 일정(표) set 정해진, 계획된, 준비된, 고정된

2. What floor did you park on?
(A) Can I have a ride, too?
(B) I think the fourth.
(C) That car's the same as mine.

몇 층에 주차하셨나요?
(A) 저도 태워 주실 수 있으세요?
(B) 4층인 것 같아요.
(C) 저 차가 제 것과 같아요.

해설 몇 층에 주차했는지 묻고 있으므로 What floor와 어울리는 숫자 표현을 활용하여 층 높이로 답변하는 (B)가 정답이다.

어휘 ride (차량 등) 타고 가기

3. What do you want me to bring to the meeting?
(A) In the board room.
(B) Just a writing utensil.
(C) A sales promotion.

제가 회의 시간에 뭘 가져 가길 원하세요?
(A) 이사회실에서요.
(B) 필기구 하나면 됩니다.
(C) 판매 촉진 행사요.

해설 회의 시간에 무엇을 가져 가길 원하는지 의견을 묻고 있으므로 회의에 참석하는 데 필요한 물품의 종류를 언급하는 (B)가 정답이다.

어휘 writing utensil 필기구

4. Which consultant should we receive advice from?
(A) Did you print the receipt?
(B) I say we raise the price.
(C) Pamela knows more about consulting firms.

우리가 어느 상담 전문가로부터 조언을 받아야 하나요?
(A) 영수증을 출력하셨나요?
(B) 우리가 가격을 인상하는 게 좋겠어요.
(C) 파멜라 씨가 컨설팅 업체에 관해 더 많이 알고 있어요.

해설 어느 상담 전문가로부터 조언을 받아야 하는지 묻는 것에 대해 파멜라 씨가 컨설팅 업체에 관해 더 많이 알고 있다는 말로 사람 이름으로 답하는 (C)가 정답이다.

어휘 I say (that) (의견을 말할 때) ~하는 게 좋겠어요

5. Which training session do you want to go to?
(A) Kevin is our new hire.
(B) No, I've never been there before.
(C) I'm interested in the time management one.

어느 교육 시간에 가고 싶으신가요?
(A) 케빈 씨가 우리 신입 사원이에요.
(B) 아니요, 저는 전에 그곳에 한 번도 가 본 적이 없어요.
(C) 저는 시간 관리에 관한 것에 관심이 있어요.

해설 어느 교육 시간에 가고 싶은지 묻고 있으므로 training session을 대명사 one으로 대신해 관심이 있는 주제를 다루는 시간을 언급하는 (C)가 정답이다.

6. Which bus are you trying to catch?
(A) The express one.
(B) A monthly pass.
(C) Yes, my stop is over there.

어느 버스를 타시려고 하는 건가요?
(A) 고속 버스요.
(B) 월 정기 승차권이요.
(C) 네, 제 정류장은 저기 저쪽입니다.

해설 어느 버스를 타려고 하는지 묻고 있으므로 bus를 대명사 one으로 대신해 고속 버스를 가리키는 express one으로 답변하는 (A)가 정답이다.

어휘 catch (교통편) ~을 타다

7. Why is Jared working late?
(A) To fill a big order.
(B) On the latest budget report.
(C) I think it'll be worth it.

자레드 씨가 왜 늦게까지 일하는 건가요?
(A) 중요한 주문을 처리하기 위해서요.
(B) 최신 예산 보고서에 있어요.
(C) 그럴 만한 가치가 있을 것 같아요.

해설 자레드 씨가 왜 늦게까지 일하는 것인지 묻고 있으므로 '~하기 위해서'라는 의미로 Why와 어울리는 목적을 나타내는 to부정사구로 답변하는 (A)가 정답이다.

8. Why don't we have a team dinner today?
(A) No, next to the restaurant.
(B) I'll go with steamed rice, please.
(C) The video conference is at 7 o'clock.

오늘 팀 저녁 회식을 하면 어떨까요?
(A) 아니요, 그 레스토랑 옆에요.
(B) 저는 쌀밥으로 할게요.
(C) 화상 회의가 7시에 있습니다.

해설 오늘 팀 저녁 회식을 하면 어떨지 제안하는 질문에 대해 화상 회의가 7시에 있다는 말로 거절을 나타내는 (C)가 정답이다.

어휘 go with (결정할 때) ~로 하다 video conference 화상 회의

9. Why didn't you display the new ads yet?
(A) Nothing too long, no.
(B) Check the top shelves.
(C) Did you see the schedule update?

새 광고를 왜 아직 게시하지 않으셨나요?
(A) 그렇게 길지는 않아요, 전혀요.
(B) 맨 위쪽 선반을 확인해 보세요.
(C) 일정에 관한 업데이트를 확인해 보셨나요?

해설 새 광고를 왜 아직 게시하지 않았는지 이유를 묻는 것에 대해 업데이트된 일정표를 확인해 봤는지 되묻는 것으로 변동 사항이 있음을 뜻하는 (C)가 정답이다.

어휘 nothing too + **형용사** 그렇게 ~하지는 않은, 아주 ~한 것은 아닌

10. How would you like to mail this letter today?
(A) I included three stamps.
(B) With standard shipping.
(C) A mailman had contacted me.

이 편지를 오늘 어떻게 부치고 싶으신가요?
(A) 우표를 세 장 포함했습니다.
(B) 일반 배송으로요.
(C) 집배원 한 분이 제게 연락했어요.

해설 편지를 어떻게 부치기를 원하는지 묻고 있으므로 How와 어울리는 방법의 하나로서 전치사 With를 사용하여 일반 배송을 언급하는 (B)가 정답이다.

11. How long will the contract negotiations take?
(A) Forty dollars a month.
(B) I usually take the metro.
(C) It's hard for us to predict.

그 계약 협의가 얼마나 오래 걸릴까요?
(A) 한 달에 40달러입니다.
(B) 저는 보통 지하철을 탑니다.
(C) 저희가 예측하긴 어렵습니다.

해설 계약 협의가 얼마나 오래 걸릴지 묻는 것에 대해 자신들이 예측하기 어렵다는 말로 알 수 없다는 의미를 나타내는 (C)가 정답이다.

12. How about offering a variety of deals to invite more shoppers to join our rewards program?
(A) No. The Customer Assistance Department.
(B) We should. That's a great idea.
(C) Yes, it was a rewarding project.

더 많은 쇼핑객들에게 우리 보상 프로그램에 가입하도록 요청하기 위해 다양한 거래 조건을 제공하면 어떨까요?
(A) 아니요. 고객 지원부요.
(B) 그래야죠. 아주 좋은 생각입니다.
(C) 네, 보람 있는 프로젝트였어요.

해설 쇼핑객들에게 보상 프로그램에 가입하도록 요청하기 위해 다양한 거래 조건을 제공하면 어떨지 묻는 것에 대해 그렇게 해야 한다는 말로 승낙하면서 아주 좋은 생각이라는 의견을 덧붙인 (B)가 정답이다.

어휘 deal 거래 (조건), 거래 제품, 계약 rewarding 보람 있는

Check-up Test

1. (A)	**2.** (A)	**3.** (C)	**4.** (C)	**5.** (A)
6. (A)	**7.** (C)	**8.** (A)	**9.** (C)	**10.** (A)
11. (B)	**12.** (C)	**13.** (C)	**14.** (A)	**15.** (C)
16. (A)	**17.** (C)	**18.** (A)	**19.** (B)	**20.** (A)

1. How much will the processing fees be?
(A) Our company doesn't charge any.
(B) Sorry, we only accept credit.
(C) In two or three days.

처리 수수료가 얼마나 될까요?
(A) 저희 회사는 어떤 것도 청구하지 않습니다.
(B) 죄송하지만, 저희는 신용카드만 받습니다.
(C) 2~3일 후에요.

해설 처리 수수료가 얼마나 될지 묻고 있으므로 청구하지 않는다는 말로 수수료가 없다는 뜻을 나타내는 (A)가 정답이다.

2. Why don't we grab lunch at the café after the client meeting?
(A) Sure, I don't mind doing that.
(B) A hot cup of espresso.
(C) The presentation slides look good.

고객 회의 후에 카페에서 간단히 점심 식사하시는 게 어때요?
(A) 네, 그렇게 해도 상관없어요.
(B) 따뜻한 에스프레소 한 잔이요.
(C) 발표 슬라이드들이 좋아 보이네요.

해설 고객 회의 후에 카페에서 간단히 점심 식사하는 게 어떤지 제안하고 있으므로 수락을 나타내는 Sure와 함께 상관없다는 말을 덧붙인 (A)가 정답이다.

어휘 grab 간단히 ~을 먹다

3. Which version of the software have you seen?
(A) He's our senior developer.
(B) On the computer monitor.
(C) The most recent one.

그 소프트웨어의 어느 버전을 확인해 보신 건가요?
(A) 그분은 저희 선임 개발자이십니다.
(B) 컴퓨터 모니터에서요.
(C) 가장 최신 것이요.

해설 특정 소프트웨어의 어느 버전을 확인해 봤는지 묻고 있으므로 version을 대명사 one으로 지칭해 가장 최신 것이라는 말로 특징을 밝히는 (C)가 정답이다.

4. Why isn't Ms. Lopez in her office?
(A) No, I've never been there.
(B) Marrion Business Center.
(C) Because she's coming in late today.

로페즈 씨가 왜 사무실에 계시지 않는 거죠?
(A) 아니요, 저는 그곳에 한 번도 가 본 적이 없어요.
(B) 매리언 비즈니스 센터요.
(C) 그분이 오늘 늦게 오시기 때문입니다.

해설 로페즈 씨가 왜 사무실에 있지 않은지 묻고 있으므로 Why 의문문과 짝을 이루는 Because와 함께 오늘 늦게 온다는 말로 지금 자리에 없는 이유를 밝히는 (C)가 정답이다.

5. How did you adjust the budget allocations?
(A) By using last quarter's financial data.
(B) What's the total amount?
(C) I've never flown first class.

예산 할당액을 어떻게 조정하셨나요?
(A) 지난 분기의 재무 데이터를 이용해서요.
(B) 총액이 얼마인가요?
(C) 저는 한 번도 비행기 일등석을 타 본 적이 없어요.

해설 예산 할당액을 어떻게 조정했는지 묻고 있으므로 How 의문문과 어울리는 방법을 나타내는 「By + -ing」를 통해 지난 분기의 재무 데이터를 이용했음을 언급하는 (A)가 정답이다.

어휘 allocation 할당(되는 것)

6. What do you want me to do before closing the shop tonight?
(A) Please wipe down all the countertops.
(B) Sorry, I can't cover for you.
(C) Yes, we're open until 9 P.M.

오늘 밤에 매장을 닫기 전에 제가 뭘 하면 될까요?
(A) 모든 조리대를 말끔히 닦아 주세요.
(B) 죄송하지만, 저는 대신해 드릴 수 없습니다.
(C) 네, 저희는 오후 9시까지 영업합니다.

해설 오늘 밤에 매장을 닫기 전에 무엇을 할지 묻고 있으므로 모든 조리대를 말끔히 닦아 달라는 말로 완료해야 하는 일을 지시하는 (A)가 정답이다.

어휘 wipe down ~을 말끔히 닦다 countertop 조리대
cover for (근무 등) ~을 대신하다

7. How about launching the new ad campaigns on the same week?
(A) Alright, I'll deliver those.
(B) It was cheaper than we expected.
(C) We don't have enough resources for that.

같은 주에 새로운 광고 캠페인을 시작하는게 어때요?
(A) 좋습니다, 제가 그것들을 전달해 드릴게요.
(B) 우리가 예상한 것보다 더 저렴했어요.
(C) 우리는 그것을 위한 자원이 충분하지 않습니다.

해설 같은 주에 새로운 광고 캠페인을 시작하면 어떨지 제안하는 질문에 대해 그 일을 위한 자원이 충분하지 않다는 말로 거절 의사를 나타내는 (C)가 정답이다.

8. Why don't we ask our manager for help?
(A) This report needs to be submitted right now.

(B) No, just down the hall.
(C) I didn't get a service request.

우리 부장님께 도움을 요청해 보면 어떨까요?
(A) 이 보고서는 지금 바로 제출되어야 합니다.
(B) 아니요, 그냥 복도를 따라가서요.
(C) 저는 서비스 요청서를 받지 않았어요.

해설 소속 부서장에게 도움을 요청해 보면 어떨지 제안하는 질문에 대해 보고서가 지금 바로 제출되어야 한다는 말로 거절의 뜻을 나타내는 (A)가 정답이다.

9. Which of these data storage providers is best?
(A) The warehouse isn't open.
(B) At least ten copies, please.
(C) I work in the legal department.

이 데이터 저장 서비스 제공업체들 중 어느 곳이 최고인가요?
(A) 창고가 열려 있지 않아요.
(B) 최소 10부 부탁합니다.
(C) 저는 법무팀에서 일합니다.

해설 특정 데이터 저장 서비스 제공업체들 중 어느 곳이 최고인지 묻는 질문에 대해 자신은 법무팀에서 일한다는 말로 알지 못한다는 뜻을 나타내는 (C)가 정답이다.

10. Which author is holding a book signing tomorrow?
(A) The same writer who did one last year.
(B) Yes, I signed my name on the paper.
(C) Their best-selling novel.

어느 작가가 내일 도서 사인회를 개최하나요?
(A) 작년에 하셨던 분과 같은 작가요.
(B) 네, 저는 그 서류에 제 이름을 서명했어요.
(C) 그분들의 베스트셀러 소설이요.

해설 어느 작가가 내일 도서 사인회를 개최하는지 묻고 있으므로 a book signing을 대명사 one로 대신해 작년과 동일한 작가가 한다고 밝히는 (A)가 정답이다.

11. How many active patients visit your clinic?
(A) I attend fitness classes twice every week.
(B) About 1,000, I believe.
(C) It'll take 30 minutes maximum.

얼마나 많은 유효 환자들이 당신의 진료소를 방문하나요?
(A) 저는 매주 두 번씩 운동 강좌에 참석해요.
(B) 약 1,000명인 것 같아요.
(C) 최대 30분이 걸릴 겁니다.

해설 얼마나 많은 유효 환자들이 상대방의 진료소를 방문하는지 묻고 있으므로 How many 및 patients와 어울리는 대략적인 인원수로 대답하는 (B)가 정답이다.

12. Why haven't the videos been uploaded yet?
(A) Not too slow, no.
(B) Search up the file name.
(C) Didn't Ms. Garret mention the system error?

그 동영상들이 왜 아직 업로드되지 않은 거죠?
(A) 별로 느리진 않아요, 네.
(B) 파일명을 검색해 보세요.
(C) 가렛 씨가 시스템 오류를 언급하시지 않았나요?

해설 특정 동영상들이 왜 아직 업로드되지 않은 것인지 묻는 질문에 대해 가렛 씨가 시스템 오류를 언급하지 않았는지 되묻는 것으로 업로드되지 않은 이유를 밝히는 (C)가 정답이다.

어휘 not too + **형용사** 별로 ~하지 않은

13. How soon do we need to hire a contractor for the repairs?
(A) That material is higher quality.
(B) It would cost around $300.
(C) As soon as possible would be great.

우리가 얼마나 빨리 수리 작업에 필요한 계약업자를 고용해야 하나요?
(A) 그 자재가 품질이 더 높습니다.
(B) 약 300달러의 비용이 들 겁니다.
(C) 가능한 한 빨리 하면 아주 좋을 겁니다.

해설 얼마나 빨리 수리 작업에 필요한 계약업자를 고용해야 하는지 묻고 있으므로 가능한 한 빨리 하는 게 아주 좋을 것이라는 말로 How soon과 어울리는 시점과 관련해 알리는 (C)가 정답이다.

14. Why has the printer in the break room been taken apart?
(A) So that we can send it to a different branch.
(B) The huge electronics outlet.
(C) Sure, I can pack it up.

휴게실에 있는 프린터가 왜 분해된 건가요?
(A) 그래야 우리가 그걸 다른 지사에 보낼 수 있습니다.
(B) 대형 전자제품 할인점이요.
(C) 네, 제가 그걸 포장할 수 있습니다.

해설 휴게실에 있는 프린터가 왜 분해된 건지 묻고 있으므로 Why 의문문과 어울리는 So that과 함께 그래야 다른 지사에 보낼 수 있다는 말로 이유를 밝히는 (A)가 정답이다.

어휘 take apart ~을 분해하다

15. How did the panel discussion go?
(A) No, we installed solar panels.
(B) They say it's raining tomorrow.
(C) I had to leave halfway through for a meeting.

패널 토론회가 어떻게 진행되었나요?
(A) 아니요, 저희는 태양열 전지판을 설치했어요.
(B) 사람들이 그러는데 내일 비가 내린답니다.
(C) 저는 회의 때문에 중간쯤에 가야 했습니다.

해설 패널 토론회가 어떻게 진행되었는지 묻는 질문에 대해 회의 때문에 중간에 가야 했다는 말로 정확한 진행 상황을 알지 못한다는 뜻을 나타내는 (C)가 정답이다.

어휘 panel discussion 패널 토론회(전문가 등이 참석하는 토론회) halfway through 중간쯤에, 중도에

16. Which train do you normally take?
(A) The one that leaves at 8 A.M. sharp.
(B) A skills training program.
(C) Your seat is in car 9, 15A.

보통 어느 열차를 이용하세요?
(A) 오전 8시 정각에 출발하는 것이요.
(B) 기술 교육 프로그램이요.
(C) 고객님의 좌석은 9호차, 15A석입니다.

해설 보통 어느 열차를 이용하는지 묻고 있으므로 train을 대명사 one으로 대신해 오전 8시 정각에 출발하는 것이라는 말로 Which train과 어울리는 특정 열차를 언급하는 (A)가 정답이다.

어휘 sharp 정각에

17. What time does the exhibition open?
(A) In the main hall gallery.
(B) I like to go to history museums.
(C) At 11 A.M. on weekends.

그 전시회는 몇 시에 여나요?
(A) 중앙 홀 미술관에서요.
(B) 저는 역사 박물관에 가는 걸 좋아해요.
(C) 주말마다 오전 11시에요.

해설 특정 전시회가 몇 시에 여는지 묻고 있으므로 What time과 어울리는 시간 표현으로 답변하는 (C)가 정답이다.

18. How can we streamline operations in the warehouse?
(A) By reorganizing our interior layout.
(B) No, I've never used that machine.
(C) At the management meeting.

우리가 어떻게 창고에서의 운영을 간소화할 수 있나요?
(A) 우리의 실내 배치를 재구성하는 방법으로요.
(B) 아니요, 저는 한 번도 그 기계를 사용해 본 적이 없어요.
(C) 경영진 회의 시간에요.

해설 어떻게 창고에서의 운영을 간소화할 수 있는지 묻고 있으므로 How 의문문과 어울리는 방법을 나타내는 「By + -ing」를 통해 실내 배치를 재구성하는 일을 언급하는 (A)가 정답이다.

어휘 streamline ~을 간소화하다

19. What dates are you going on vacation?
(A) You can take public transportation.
(B) In the last week of November.
(C) I'm free in the evening, if that works.

며칠에 휴가를 떠나시나요?
(A) 대중교통을 이용하시면 됩니다.
(B) 11월 마지막 주에요.
(C) 저는 저녁에 시간이 됩니다, 괜찮으시면요.

해설 며칠에 휴가를 떠나는지 묻고 있으므로 11월 마지막 주라는 말로 What dates와 어울리는 시점 표현으로 답변하는 (B)가 정답이다.

어휘 if that works (앞서 언급된 것에 대해) 괜찮다면, 그래도 된다면

20. What do you think of the action plan I sent out yesterday?
(A) Oh, I haven't checked my inbox yet.
(B) My designs for the brochure came out better than expected.
(C) Because it got approved.

제가 어제 보내 드린 시행 계획에 대해 어떻게 생각하세요?
(A) 아, 제 수신함을 아직 확인해 보지 못했어요.
(B) 안내책자를 위한 제 디자인이 예상보다 더 잘 나왔어요.
(C) 그게 승인되었기 때문입니다.

해설 어제 보낸 시행 계획에 대한 생각을 묻는 질문에 대해 수신함을 아직 확인해 보지 못했다는 말로 의견을 알려 줄 수 없다는 뜻을 나타내는 (A)가 정답이다.

어휘 action plan 시행 계획 inbox (이메일의) 수신함

▶ Playlist 5
헷갈리기 쉬운 일반/선택/요청&제안 의문문 정리

Practice

1. (A)	**2.** (C)	**3.** (C)	**4.** (A)	**5.** (A)
6. (B)	**7.** (B)	**8.** (A)	**9.** (A)	**10.** (C)
11. (B)	**12.** (C)			

1. Didn't there use to be a post office on that corner?
(A) Yes, but it got relocated.
(B) You can place your box on this scale.
(C) My company is close by.

전에 저 모퉁이에 우체국이 하나 있지 않았나요?
(A) 네, 근데 이전했어요.
(B) 이 저울에 갖고 계신 상자를 올리시면 됩니다.
(C) 저희 회사가 근처에 있습니다.

해설 전에 특정 모퉁이에 우체국이 있지 않았는지 묻고 있으므로 긍정을 뜻하는 Yes와 함께 그 우체국이 이전했다는 사실을 덧붙인 (A)가 정답이다.

어휘 scale 저울 close by 근처에, 인근에

2. Is it best for me to reserve a ticket online?
(A) A popular Broadway musical.
(B) How much did you pay?
(C) That's what I do.

제가 온라인으로 티켓을 예약하는 게 최선인가요?
(A) 인기 있는 브로드웨이 뮤지컬이요.
(B) 얼마나 지불하셨어요?
(C) 저는 그렇게 합니다.

해설 온라인으로 티켓을 예약하는 게 최선인지 묻고 있으므로 답변자 자신도 그렇게 한다는 말로 Yes를 생략한 긍정의 의미를 나타내는 (C)가 정답이다.

어휘 It is best for A to do A가 ~하는 게 최선이다, 가장 좋다

3. Have you read the guest comment cards?
(A) Mostly positive feedback.
(B) Sure, go ahead.
(C) I've been busy with a big project.

고객 의견 카드를 읽어 보셨나요?
(A) 대부분 긍정적인 의견입니다.
(B) 물론이죠, 어서 하세요.
(C) 제가 중요한 프로젝트로 바빴습니다.

해설 고객 의견 카드를 읽어 봤는지 묻고 있으므로 중요한 프로젝트로 바빴다는 말로 No를 생략해 읽어 보지 못했다는 뜻을 나타내는 (C)가 정답이다.

4. Does Ms. Zhao prefer a window or aisle seat?
(A) She took care of her own flight.
(B) That's the right street.
(C) A beautiful view.

자오 씨가 창가 좌석을 선호하시나요, 아니면 통로 쪽 좌석을 선호하시나요?
(A) 그분이 본인의 항공편을 처리했어요.
(B) 그 거리가 맞습니다.
(C) 아름다운 경관이네요.

해설 자오 씨가 창가 좌석을 선호하는지, 아니면 통로 쪽 좌석을 선호하는지 묻는 것에 대해 자오 씨가 직접 항공편 문제를 처리했다는 말로 선호 좌석을 파악할 필요가 없어 둘 다 아님을 뜻하는 (A)가 정답이다.

5. Would it be better to send a text message or an e-mail?
(A) Texting isn't as professional.
(B) I received it just now.
(C) Here's the sender's name.

문자 메시지를 보내는 게 더 나을까요, 아니면 이메일이 더 나을까요?
(A) 문자 메시지는 그렇게 전문적이지 않습니다.
(B) 그걸 지금 막 받았습니다.
(C) 여기 발신인 이름입니다.

해설 문자 메시지를 보내는 게 더 나을지, 아니면 이메일이 더 나을지 묻고 있으므로 문자 메시지는 그렇게 전문적이지 않다는 말로 이메일이 더 낫다는 뜻을 나타내 둘 중 하나를 선택하는 (A)가 정답이다.

어휘 not as A 그렇게 A하지 않은

6. Should we discuss the issue right now or schedule a meeting?
(A) There's plenty of seating.
(B) I don't mind either way.
(C) Yes, you have a good point.

우리가 지금 바로 그 문제를 논의해야 하나요, 아니면 회의 일정을 잡아야 하나요?
(A) 좌석 공간이 많이 있습니다.
(B) 저는 어느 쪽이든 상관없습니다.
(C) 네, 좋은 지적입니다.

해설 지금 바로 특정 문제를 논의해야 하는지, 아니면 회의 일정을 잡아야 하는지 묻는 것에 대해 어느 쪽이든 상관없다는 말로 아무거나 괜찮다는 뜻을 나타내는 (B)가 정답이다.

어휘 you have a good point 좋은 지적입니다, 일리 있는 말입니다

7. Could you ask the candidates to wait in the lobby?
(A) It's for a managerial role.
(B) They're already ready in room 26.
(C) The front desk is over there.

지원자들에게 로비에서 대기해 달라고 요청해 주시겠어요?
(A) 관리자 직책을 위한 것입니다.
(B) 그분들은 이미 26호실에서 준비하고 있습니다.
(C) 프론트 데스크가 저기 저쪽에 있습니다.

해설 지원자들에게 로비에서 대기해 달라고 요청하라는 질문에 대해 그 사람들이 이미 26호실에서 준비하고 있다는 말로 로비에서 대기해 달라고 요청할 필요가 없음을 뜻하는 (B)가 정답이다.

8. Why don't we pick up some coffee before heading to the expo?
(A) OK, we can do that.
(B) One iced café latte, please.
(C) The main theme is sustainability.

박람회로 가기 전에 커피를 좀 사가는 게 어떨까요?
(A) 좋아요, 그래도 됩니다.
(B) 아이스 카페 라떼 한 잔 주세요.
(C) 주요 주제는 지속 가능성입니다.

해설 박람회로 가기 전에 커피를 사가는 게 어떨지 묻고 있으므로 수락을 나타내는 OK와 함께 그렇게 하는 것을 that으로 지칭해 그래도 된다는 말을 덧붙인 (A)가 정답이다.

어휘 head to ~로 가다, 향하다 theme 주제 sustainability 지속 가능성

9. Please confirm the inspection schedule with the contractor.
(A) I'll make sure to verify that soon.
(B) It's a safety protocol.
(C) I was offered a contract.

계약업체에 점검 일정을 확인해 주세요.
(A) 그 부분을 반드시 곧 확인하도록 하겠습니다.
(B) 하나의 안전 규약입니다.
(C) 제가 계약을 한 가지 제안 받았습니다.

해설 계약업체에 점검 일정을 확인해 달라는 요청에 대하여 일정을 that으로 지칭해 반드시 확인하겠다고 수락하는 (A)가 정답이다.

어휘 verify ~을 확인하다, 입증하다 protocol 규약, 협약

10. Should I add anything to the presentation?
(A) Probably only with the sales team.
(B) It'll take about ten minutes.
(C) Are there enough visuals?

제가 발표 내용에 무엇이든 추가해야 하나요?
(A) 아마 영업팀만 함께 할 겁니다.
(B) 약 10분 소요될 겁니다.
(C) 시각자료가 충분히 있나요?

해설 발표 내용에 무엇이든 추가해야 하는지 묻고 있으므로 시각자료가 충분히 있는지 되묻는 것으로 추가 가능한 요소를 우회적으로 확인하려는 (C)가 정답이다.

어휘 visuals 시각자료

11. Does the airline offer any compensation for delayed flights?
(A) Miriam arrived right on time.
(B) We can make exceptions in certain situations.
(C) He's a frequent flyer.

항공사에서 지연된 항공편에 대해 어떤 보상이든 제공해 주나요?
(A) 미리엄 씨는 정확히 제 시간에 도착했어요.
(B) 저희는 특정한 상황에서 예외로 해 드릴 수 있습니다.
(C) 그분은 항공편 단골 이용 고객이에요.

해설 항공사에서 지연된 항공편에 대해 어떤 보상이든 제공해 주는지 묻는 것에 대해 특정한 상황에서 예외로 해 줄 수 있다는 말로 별도의 보상 기준이 있음을 우회적으로 의미하는 (B)가 정답이다.

어휘 frequent flyer 항공편 단골 이용 고객

12. Would you like to try our new signature dish?
(A) Please sign your name here.
(B) At the Italian restaurant.
(C) I'll just go with my usual order.

저희 새로운 대표 요리를 한 번 드셔 보시겠어요?
(A) 여기에 서명을 해 주시기 바랍니다.
(B) 이탈리안 레스토랑에서요.
(C) 그냥 제가 평소에 주문하던 것으로 할게요.

해설 새로운 대표 요리를 한 번 먹어 볼 생각이 있는지 묻고 있으므로 평소에 주문하던 것으로 하겠다는 말로 우회적으로 거절을 나타내는 (C)가 정답이다.

어휘 signature 대표적인

Check-up Test

1. (B)	**2.** (B)	**3.** (B)	**4.** (C)	**5.** (A)
6. (C)	**7.** (B)	**8.** (C)	**9.** (C)	**10.** (B)
11. (C)	**12.** (A)	**13.** (A)	**14.** (B)	**15.** (B)
16. (C)	**17.** (A)	**18.** (A)	**19.** (B)	**20.** (C)

1. Are you going to post the notice or send each person a reminder?
(A) We noticed an issue.
(B) I'm planning to do both.
(C) About 50 people came in total.

그 공지를 게시하실 건가요, 아니면 각각의 사람에게 알림 메시지를 보내실 건가요?
(A) 저희가 한 가지 문제를 알아차렸습니다.
(B) 둘 다 할 계획을 세우고 있습니다.
(C) 전부 합쳐서 약 50명이 왔습니다.

해설 공지를 게시할 건지, 아니면 각각의 사람에게 알림 메시지를 보낼 건지 묻고 있으므로 둘 모두를 하려는 계획임을 언급하는 (B)가 정답이다.

어휘 reminder (상기시키는) 알림 메시지 in total 전부 합쳐서, 총

2. Could you restock the snack section?
(A) It's in the break room.
(B) The shelves are all filled.
(C) They requested something light.

간식 구역의 상품을 다시 채워 주시겠어요?
(A) 그건 휴게실에 있어요.
(B) 그 선반들이 모두 가득 차 있습니다.
(C) 그분들은 뭔가 가벼운 걸 요청하셨어요.

해설 간식 구역의 상품을 다시 채워 달라고 요청하는 질문에 대해 그곳 선반들이 모두 가득 차 있다는 말로 이미 채워 놓은 상태임을 밝히는 (B)가 정답이다.

3. Do you want your sandwich with or without pickles?
(A) The brunch café on Crystal Street.
(B) I'll just have a salad.
(C) We'll need to ask the caterer for more.

샌드위치에 피클을 넣어 드릴까요, 아니면 빼 드릴까요?
(A) 크리스탈 스트리트에 있는 브런치 카페요.
(B) 저는 그냥 샐러드로 할게요.
(C) 출장 요리 업체에 더 많이 요청해야 할 겁니다.

해설 샌드위치에 피클을 넣을지, 아니면 빼야 하는지 묻는 질문에 대해 샐러드로 하겠다는 말로 제3의 선택지를 선택함을 알리는 (B)가 정답이다.

4. Are the strawberries ready to be picked?
(A) I'll pick them up at the station.
(B) We expanded our farm last month.
(C) It's still a bit too early.

딸기가 수확될 준비가 되어 있나요?
(A) 제가 역에서 그분들을 차로 모시고 올게요.
(B) 저희는 지난달에 농장을 확장했습니다.
(C) 여전히 좀 너무 이릅니다.

해설 딸기가 수확될 준비가 되어 있는지 묻고 있으므로 여전히 좀 너무 이르다는 말로 수확될 준비가 되어 있지 않다는 뜻을 나타내는 (C)가 정답이다.

5. Does the agent want to meet us at the property or at the real estate office?
(A) She'll call us back soon.
(B) You can take pictures if you'd like.
(C) That's exactly right.

그 중개인이 우리를 그 건물에서 만나고 싶어 하나요, 아니면 부동산 중개소에서 만나고 싶어 하나요?
(A) 그분이 곧 다시 전화 주실 겁니다.
(B) 원하시면 사진을 찍으셔도 됩니다.
(C) 정확히 그렇습니다.

해설 중개인이 건물에서 만나고 싶어 하는지, 아니면 부동산 중개소에서 만나고 싶어 하는지 묻는 질문에 대해 곧 다시 전화할 것이라는 말로 관련 정보를 파악할 수 있는 방법을 언급하는 (A)가 정답이다.

6. Can you pull up some more chairs?
(A) Thank you for understanding.
(B) He's going to present the total figures.
(C) There shouldn't be anyone else joining us.

의자를 몇 개 더 끌고 와 주시겠어요?
(A) 이해해 주셔서 감사합니다.
(B) 그분이 전체 수치를 발표할 예정입니다.
(C) 우리와 함께 하는 다른 사람이 아무도 없을 겁니다.

해설 의자를 몇 개 더 끌고 와 달라고 요청하는 질문에 대해 함께 하는 다른 사람이 없을 것이라는 말로 의자를 더 갖고 올 필요가 없다는 뜻을 나타내는 (C)가 정답이다.

어휘 pull up ~을 끌고 오다

7. Would you like to renew your plan for another year?

(A) Because the older model stopped working.
(B) I heard the price might increase soon.
(C) Only one subscription.

약정을 1년 더 갱신하시겠어요?
(A) 더 오래된 모델이 작동을 멈췄기 때문입니다.
(B) 가격이 곧 오를지도 모른다는 얘기를 들었어요.
(C) 한 가지 구독만요.

해설 약정을 1년 더 갱신하고 싶은지 묻는 질문에 대해 가격이 곧 오를지도 모른다는 얘기를 들었다는 말로 갱신하고자 하는 의지가 크지 않다는 뜻을 나타내는 (B)가 정답이다.

어휘 plan (서비스 계약·보험 등의) 약정, 제도

8. Have you shown Na-yoon how to handle product returns?
(A) I'd rather exchange it.
(B) Thanks, that should be plenty.
(C) I haven't gotten any today.

나윤 씨에게 반품을 처리하는 방법을 알려 주셨나요?
(A) 저는 그걸 교환하고 싶어요.
(B) 고마워요, 그거면 충분할 거예요.
(C) 오늘 하나도 받지 못했습니다.

해설 나윤 씨에게 반품을 처리하는 방법을 알려 주었는지 묻는 질문에 대해 오늘 반품을 하나도 받지 못했다는 말로 알려 주지 못했다는 뜻을 나타내는 (C)가 정답이다.

9. Should we announce the results to the whole team?
(A) He had a great performance.
(B) The statement is four pages long.
(C) No, let's hold off for now.

우리가 그 결과들을 팀 전체에 알려야 하나요?
(A) 그분은 훌륭한 성과를 보여 주셨어요.
(B) 내역서는 4페이지 길이입니다.
(C) 아니요, 일단은 미뤄 둡시다.

해설 결과를 팀 전체에 알려야 하는지 묻고 있으므로 부정을 뜻하는 No와 함께 미뤄 두자는 말을 덧붙이는 (C)가 정답이다.

어휘 whole 전체의 hold off 미루다, 보류하다

10. Is there a list of complaints that have been resolved?
(A) My tracking number is 573A0.
(B) The customer service team would know.
(C) A 4-star hotel in Chicago.

해결된 불만사항들을 담은 목록이 있나요?
(A) 제 추적 번호는 573A0입니다.
(B) 고객 서비스팀이 알 거예요.
(C) 시카고에 있는 4성급 호텔이요.

해설 해결된 불만사항들을 담은 목록이 있는지 묻는 질문에 대해 고객 서비스팀이 알고 있을 것이라는 말로 관련 정보를 확인할 수 있는 방법을 알리는 (B)가 정답이다.

11. Shouldn't we put the presenters in order based on popularity?
(A) That item is almost out of stock.
(B) Here's a script of the introduction.
(C) No, it can't be changed anymore.

인기를 바탕으로 발표자들의 순서를 정해야 하지 않나요?
(A) 그 제품은 거의 품절된 상태입니다.
(B) 여기 소개문 원고입니다.
(C) 아니요, 더 이상 변경될 수 없습니다.

해설 인기를 바탕으로 발표자들의 순서를 정해야 하지 않는지 묻고 있으므로 부정을 뜻하는 No와 함께 더 이상 변경될 수 없다는 말로 그렇게 할 수 없다는 뜻을 나타내는 (C)가 정답이다.

어휘 put A in order A를 순서대로 놓다 script 원고

12. Will you be able to come in on Monday or Tuesday?
(A) Either is good for me.
(B) Yes, I had a great visit.
(C) An annual check-up.

월요일에 오실 수 있으세요, 아니면 화요일에 오실 수 있으세요?
(A) 둘 중 어느 쪽이든 좋습니다.
(B) 네, 훌륭한 방문이었습니다.
(C) 연례적인 검진이요.

해설 월요일에 올 수 있는지, 아니면 화요일에 올 수 있는지 묻는 질문에 대해 둘 중 어느 쪽이든 좋다는 말로 둘 중 어느 요일이든 상관 없다는 뜻을 나타내는 (A)가 정답이다.

13. Didn't there use to be a shopping complex in this area?
(A) Yes, but the land's been cleared now.
(B) You can park over there in that lot.
(C) Their clothes are reasonably priced.

예전에 이 지역에 쇼핑 복합건물이 있지 않았나요?
(A) 네, 하지만 그 부지가 지금은 정리되었습니다.
(B) 저기 저쪽에 있는 저 주차장에 주차하시면 됩니다.
(C) 그곳 의류는 합리적으로 가격이 책정되어 있어요.

해설 전에 한 특정 지역에 쇼핑 복합건물이 있지 않았는지 묻고 있으므로 긍정을 뜻하는 Yes와 함께 해당 부지의 현재 상태를 언급하는 (A)가 정답이다.

14. Are you planning to contact a garden expert or just any landscaper?
(A) I've used that company before.
(B) An expert in flowers.
(C) George no longer works here.

원예 전문가에게 연락하실 계획이신가요, 아니면 그냥 아무 조경사에게나 연락하실 건가요?
(A) 제가 전에 그 회사를 이용해 본 적이 있어요.
(B) 꽃 분야의 전문가요.
(C) 조지 씨는 더 이상 이곳에서 근무하지 않습니다.

해설 원예 전문가에게 연락할 계획인지, 아니면 아무 조경사에게나 연락할 계획인지 묻고 있으므로 꽃과 관련된 전문가에게 연락하겠다는 뜻을 나타내는 (B)가 정답이다.

15. Why don't we take a cab to the venue?
(A) There are three floors of seating.
(B) Traffic gets pretty bad around this time.
(C) Faster than expected.

행사장까지 택시를 타고 가는 건 어떠세요?
(A) 좌석 공간이 세 개의 층으로 되어 있어요.
(B) 교통량이 이 시간쯤에는 아주 안 좋아집니다.
(C) 예상보다 더 빨리요.

해설 행사장까지 택시를 타고 가는 건 어떨지 제안하는 질문에 대해 교통량이 이 시간쯤에 아주 안 좋다는 말로 거절의 의사를 나타내는 (B)가 정답이다.

16. Don't we sell Ridgebury coffee makers?
(A) Paper cups are in that cabinet.
(B) Sorry, home delivery will cost extra.
(C) I manage the hardware supplies.

우리가 리지버리 커피 메이커를 판매하지 않나요?
(A) 종이컵은 저 캐비닛 안에 있어요.
(B) 죄송하지만, 자택 배송은 추가 비용이 듭니다.
(C) 저는 철물 용품을 관리합니다.

해설 소속 업체가 리지버리 커피 메이커를 판매하지 않는지 묻는 질문에 대해 자신은 철물 용품을 관리한다는 말로 해당 제품과 관련해 알지 못한다는 뜻을 나타내는 (C)가 정답이다.

어휘 hardware 철물

17. Are you reserving a regular or a premium bus ticket?
(A) My budget is quite tight.
(B) I'd prefer a smaller size.
(C) To Brisbane, please.

일반 버스 승차권을 예약하시나요, 아니면 우등 버스 승차권을 예약하시나요?
(A) 제 예산이 꽤 빠듯합니다.
(B) 더 작은 사이즈로 하고 싶어요.
(C) 브리즈번행으로 부탁합니다.

해설 일반 버스 승차권을 예약하는지, 아니면 우등 버스 승차권을 예약하는지 묻는 질문에 대해 예산이 꽤 빠듯하다는 말로 일반 버스 승차권을 예약한다는 뜻을 나타내는 (A)가 정답이다.

어휘 tight (비용·일정 등이) 빠듯한, 빡빡한

18. Did you want to register to become a member with us?
(A) Does it cost money?
(B) At the front counter.
(C) Amanda is our best sales associate.

저희 회원이 되기 위해 등록하기를 원하셨나요?
(A) 돈이 드나요?
(B) 앞쪽 카운터에요.
(C) 아만다 씨가 우리 회사 최고의 영업사원입니다.

해설 회원이 될 수 있도록 등록하기를 원했는지 묻는 질문에 대해 돈이 드는지 되묻는 것으로 회원 가입 조건을 먼저 확인하려는 (A)가 정답이다.

어휘 associate n. 직원, 동업자, 동료

19. Would you like me to guide you through our loan options?
(A) I borrowed them yesterday.
(B) That would be helpful.
(C) A low interest rate.

저희 대출 선택사항들을 차근차근 설명해 드릴까요?
(A) 저는 어제 그것들을 빌렸어요.
(B) 그러면 도움이 될 겁니다.
(C) 낮은 이자율이요.

해설 대출 선택사항들을 차근차근 설명해 줄지 제안하는 질문에 대해 그렇게 설명하는 것을 That으로 지칭해 그러면 도움이 될 것이라는 말로 수락하는 (B)가 정답이다.

어휘 guide A through B A에게 B를 차근차근 설명해 주다
loan 대출, 융자

20. Isn't your speech going to be longer than the allotted time?

(A) There's only one hour left.
(B) The speakers are above the stage.
(C) I'll probably cut some information out.

당신의 연설이 배정된 시간보다 더 길어지지 않나요?
(A) 겨우 한 시간이 남아 있어요.
(B) 연사들이 무대 위쪽에 있습니다.
(C) 아마 일부 정보를 뺄 겁니다.

해설 연설이 배정된 시간보다 더 길어지지 않는지 묻고 있으므로 일부 정보는 빼겠다는 말로 배정된 시간에 맞춰 연설을 진행하겠다는 뜻을 나타내는 (C)가 정답이다.

어휘 allot ~을 배정하다, 할당하다 cut A out A를 빼다, 삭제하다, 잘라내다

Playlist 6
자꾸 어려워지는 평서문/부가 의문문/간접 의문문

Practice

1. (B) **2.** (B) **3.** (A) **4.** (C) **5.** (C)
6. (C)

1. I can give you a cost estimate for the repairs.
(A) No more than $1,000.
(B) Can you e-mail it to me after lunch?
(C) Yes, she's the operations manager.

수리 작업에 대해 비용 견적서를 제공해 드릴 수 있습니다.
(A) 겨우 1,000달러입니다.
(B) 제게 점심 시간 후에 그것을 이메일로 보내 주시겠어요?
(C) 네, 그분이 운영부장님입니다.

해설 수리 작업에 대해 비용 견적서를 제공해 줄 수 있다는 말에 대해 점심 시간 후에 이메일로 보내 달라고 요청하는 것으로 전달 방법을 언급하는 (B)가 정답이다.

2. The office camera is running low on battery.
(A) At least 30 photos.
(B) I'll go grab the charger for you.
(C) It's just regular maintenance.

사무실 카메라의 배터리가 다 떨어져 가고 있어요.
(A) 적어도 30장의 사진이요.
(B) 제가 가서 충전기를 갖다 드릴게요.
(C) 그냥 정기적인 유지 관리 작업입니다.

해설 사무실 카메라의 배터리가 다 떨어져 가고 있다는 문제 상황을 알리는 말에 대해 충전기를 갖고 오겠다는 말로 해결책을 언급하는 (B)가 정답이다.

어휘 run low 다 떨어지다, 부족해지다

3. You want these subtitles translated, right?
(A) Actually, I can do it.
(B) No, I transferred the call.
(C) I rewatched it several times.

이 자막들이 번역되기를 원하시죠, 맞죠?
(A) 사실, 제가 할 수 있습니다.
(B) 아니요, 제가 그 전화를 돌려 드렸습니다.
(C) 저는 그걸 여러 번 재시청했어요.

해설 자막이 번역되기를 원하는 게 맞는지 묻는 것에 대해 그렇게 하는 일을 it으로 지칭해 답변자 자신이 할 수 있다는 말로 번역해 줄 필요가 없음을 뜻하는 (A)가 정답이다.

어휘 subtitle 자막 transfer a call (다른 사람과 통화하도록) 전화를 돌려 주다

4. Do you think our workers will like the new interior?
(A) We're holding an indoor activity.
(B) The employee directory is up to date.
(C) Yes, it feels welcoming.

우리 직원들이 새로운 인테리어를 마음에 들어 할 거라고 생각하세요?
(A) 저희는 실내 활동을 개최합니다.
(B) 직원 안내책자가 최신 상태입니다.
(C) 네, 안락한 느낌이네요.

해설 직원들이 새로운 실내를 마음에 들어 할 거라고 생각하는지 의견을 묻고 있으므로 긍정을 뜻하는 Yes와 함께 안락한 느낌이라는 말로 그 이유를 덧붙인 (C)가 정답이다.

어휘 directory (이름·주소 등의 정보를 담은) 안내책자 up to date 최신의, 최근의 welcoming 안락한, 따뜻하게 맞이하는

5. Do you know if the hotel has a vacation package for families?
(A) You've signed up for parcel tracking.
(B) The luxury beach resort.
(C) I've seen that offer before, actually.

그 호텔에 가족용 휴가 패키지 상품이 있는지 아시나요?
(A) 귀하께서는 배송 조회 서비스에 등록하셨습니다.
(B) 그 고급 해변 리조트요.
(C) 실은, 전에 그 제공 서비스를 본 적이 있어요.

해설 특정 호텔에 가족용 휴가 패키지 상품이 있는지의 여부를 알고 있는지 묻고 있으므로 그 패키지 상품을 that offer로 지칭하고 Yes를 생략해 전에 그 제공 서비스를 본 적이 있다고 대답하는 (C)가 정답이다.

어휘 parcel 배송품, 소포 tracking 조회, 추적, 파악

6. Can you tell me about the latest software release?
(A) Yes, we went together.
(B) It's not too difficult to make.
(C) Our developers are still fixing it.

최신 소프트웨어 발매와 관련해 알려 주시겠어요?
(A) 네, 저희가 함께 갔습니다.
(B) 만들기 그렇게 어렵지 않습니다.
(C) 저희 개발 담당자들이 여전히 그것을 고치고 있습니다.

해설 최신 소프트웨어 발매와 관련해 알려 달라는 요청에 대해 개발 담당자들이 여전히 고치고 있다는 말로 아직 발매 준비가 되지 않은 상황임을 의미하는 (C)가 정답이다.

어휘 not too A to do ~하기 그렇게 A하지 않은

Check-up Test

1. (A)	**2.** (B)	**3.** (A)	**4.** (B)	**5.** (C)
6. (A)	**7.** (A)	**8.** (B)	**9.** (B)	**10.** (C)
11. (A)	**12.** (B)	**13.** (A)	**14.** (A)	**15.** (C)
16. (B)	**17.** (B)	**18.** (C)	**19.** (B)	**20.** (B)

1. Do you think we should follow up with the patient soon?
(A) We can give it some more time.
(B) The instructions have been printed.
(C) Nine appointments per day.

우리가 그 환자분에게 곧 후속 조치를 취해야 한다고 생각하시나요?
(A) 시간을 좀 더 두어도 됩니다.
(B) 안내사항이 인쇄되었어요.
(C) 하루에 아홉 건의 예약이요.

해설 특정 환자에게 곧 후속 조치를 취해야 한다고 생각하는지 묻는 질문에 대해 시간을 좀 더 두어도 된다는 말로 곧 후속 조치를 취하지는 않아도 된다는 뜻을 나타내는 (A)가 정답이다.

2. I'll be in a conference call all morning.
(A) A financial consultation.
(B) OK, I'll make a note of that.
(C) It was uploaded to our Web site.

제가 오전 내내 전화 회의 중일 겁니다.
(A) 재무 상담이요.
(B) 알겠습니다, 메모해 놓을게요.
(C) 그건 우리 웹 사이트에 업로드되었어요.

해설 오전 내내 전화 회의를 하고 있을 것이라는 사실을 알리고 있으므로 그 일정을 that으로 지칭해 메모해 놓겠다는 말로 정보를 기억할 방법을 언급하는 (B)가 정답이다.

어휘 conference call 전화 회의

3. Do you think we need bi-weekly project updates?
(A) Yes, they help keep us on track.
(B) No, save it for next time.
(C) Construction didn't take long.

격주로 하는 프로젝트 업데이트가 필요하다고 생각하세요?
(A) 네, 그게 우리가 정상 궤도를 유지하는 데 도움이 될 겁니다.
(B) 아니요, 다음 번을 위해 남겨 두세요.
(C) 건설 공사가 오래 걸리지 않았어요.

해설 격주로 하는 프로젝트 업데이트가 필요하다고 생각하는지 묻고 있으므로 긍정을 뜻하는 Yes와 함께 project updates를 they로 지칭해 그것이 업무에 미치는 긍정적인 영향을 언급하는 (A)가 정답이다.

어휘 bi-weekly 격주의 keep A on track (일의 진행 등) A를 정상 궤도로 유지하다, A가 순조롭게 진행되다

4. The aquarium on Walsh Avenue is being renovated.
(A) A brand new exhibit.
(B) Are there any other ones around here?
(C) Positive reviews have been increasing.

월시 애비뉴에 있는 수족관이 개조되고 있어요.
(A) 완전히 새로운 전시회요.
(B) 이 근처에 또 다른 곳이라도 있나요?
(C) 긍정적인 후기가 계속 늘어나고 있어요.

해설 월시 애비뉴에 있는 수족관이 개조되고 있다는 사실을 알리고 있으므로 aquarium을 대신하는 대명사 one을 복수형으로 사용해 근처에 다른 곳들이 있는지 묻는 것으로 해결책을 언급하는 (B)가 정답이다.

5. I'd like to propose an idea at the meeting.
(A) The agreement was very detailed.
(B) Kiran recommended a few people.
(C) Our agenda will be wide open.

제가 회의 시간에 아이디어를 하나 제안하고자 합니다.
(A) 그 합의서가 아주 상세했어요.
(B) 기란 씨가 몇몇 사람들을 추천해 주셨어요.
(C) 우리 안건은 활짝 열려 있을 겁니다.

해설 회의 시간에 아이디어를 하나 제안하고 싶다는 뜻을 밝히는 말에 대해 안건이 활짝 열려 있다는 말로 아이디어를 환영한다는 뜻을 나타내는 (C)가 정답이다.

어휘 wide open 활짝 열려 있는

6. You're attending a marketing course in the morning, aren't you?
(A) Actually, it's held at night.
(B) That room is down the hall.
(C) I finished making the flyers.

오전 시간에 마케팅 수업 과정에 참석하시죠, 그렇죠?
(A) 사실, 그건 야간에 열립니다.
(B) 그 방은 복도를 따라 가시면 있습니다.
(C) 저는 전단을 만드는 일을 끝마쳤습니다.

해설 오전 시간에 마케팅 수업 과정에 참석하지 않는지 묻는 질문에 대해 실제로는 밤에 열린다는 말로 오전에 가지 않는다는 뜻을 나타내는 (A)가 정답이다.

7. Can you tell me when my travel arrangements will be confirmed?
(A) Didn't you get the e-mail message?
(B) I believe it's a 5-hour flight.
(C) No, in the center.

제 여행 준비가 언제 확정될지 알려 주시겠어요?
(A) 이메일 메시지를 받지 못하셨나요?
(B) 5시간 비행인 것 같아요.
(C) 아니요, 중앙에서요.

해설 여행 준비가 언제 확정될지 알려 달라는 질문에 대해 이메일 메시지를 받지 못했는지 되묻는 것으로 관련 정보를 확인할 수 있는 방법을 언급하는 (A)가 정답이다.

8. There's a seafood section at the buffet, correct?
(A) She works at the fish market.
(B) Yes, it has a great selection.
(C) No, I didn't try any.

그 뷔페에 해산물 코너가 있죠, 맞죠?
(A) 그분은 어시장에서 일하세요.
(B) 네, 아주 다양한 종류가 있어요.
(C) 아니요, 저는 하나도 먹어 보지 않았어요.

해설 특정 뷔페에 해산물 코너가 있는 게 맞는지 묻고 있으므로 긍정을 뜻하는 Yes와 함께 선택 가능한 것이 아주 다양하게 있다는 사실을 언급하는 (B)가 정답이다.

9. The delivery is supposed to get here by noon, right?
(A) I dropped off the packages.
(B) No, the invoice said 3 P.M.
(C) Because the deliveryman got lost.

그 배송품이 정오까지 이곳에 오기로 되어 있죠, 맞죠?
(A) 제가 그 배송품들을 갖다 놨어요.
(B) 아니요, 거래 내역서에 오후 3시로 쓰여 있었어요.
(C) 배송 기사님이 길을 잃었기 때문입니다.

해설 배송품이 정오까지 오기로 되어 있는 게 맞는지 묻고 있으므로 부정을 뜻하는 No와 함께 거래 내역서에 기재된 시간을 밝히는 것으로 잘못 알고 있는 정보를 바로잡아 주는 (B)가 정답이다.

어휘 drop off (사물) ~을 갖다 놓다, (사람) ~을 차에서 내려 주다

10. I'm preparing a community outreach plan with the library.
(A) She's planning to retire soon.
(B) Right next to the large hospital.
(C) Is there anything I can do to help?

저는 도서관과 함께 지역 사회 봉사 계획을 준비하고 있습니다.
(A) 그분은 곧 은퇴하실 계획을 세우고 계세요.
(B) 그 대형 병원 바로 옆에요.
(C) 제가 도와 드리기 위해 할 수 있는 게 뭐라도 있을까요?

해설 도서관과 함께 지역 사회 봉사 계획을 준비하고 있다는 사실을 밝히고 있으므로 뭐라도 도울 수 있는 일이 있는지 되묻는 (C)가 정답이다.

어휘 outreach 봉사, 지원

11. It's a very useful device, isn't it?
(A) I heard that processing times have improved.
(B) The equipment rental service.
(C) Isn't maintenance still being done?

이거 아주 유용한 기기에요, 그렇죠?
(A) 처리 시간이 개선되었다는 얘기를 들었어요.
(B) 장비 대여 서비스요.
(C) 유지 관리 작업이 여전히 이뤄지고 있나요?

해설 특정 기기에 대해 아주 유용한 기기가 아닌지 묻는 질문에 대해 처리 시간이 개선되었다는 얘기를 들었다고 밝히는 것으로 유용하다는 점에 동의하는 의미를 나타내는 (A)가 정답이다.

12. Do you think you can draft the grant proposal by yourself?
(A) Did the manager grant you access?
(B) Of course, I certainly can.
(C) A fundraiser for a charity.

그 보조금 제안서 초안을 혼자 작성하실 수 있다고 생각하세요?
(A) 부장님께서 접근을 승인해 주었나요?
(B) 물론이죠, 분명히 할 수 있습니다.
(C) 한 자선 단체를 위한 모금 행사요.

해설 보조금 제안서 초안을 혼자 작성할 수 있다고 생각하는지 묻고 있으므로 긍정을 나타내는 Of course와 함께 분명히 할 수 있다는 뜻을 나타내는 (B)가 정답이다.

어휘 grant n. 보조금 v. ~을 승인하다, 주다

13. Do you know why Silvia missed the meeting yesterday?
(A) Yes, to deal with an urgent request.
(B) In the fourth-floor board room.
(C) That's when she will present.

실비아 씨가 왜 어제 회의 시간에 빠졌는지 아시나요?
(A) 네, 급한 요청을 처리하기 위해서요.
(B) 4층에 있는 이사회실이요.
(C) 그때 그분이 발표하실 겁니다.

해설 실비아 씨가 어제 회의 시간에 빠진 이유를 아는지 묻고 있으므로 Do you know에 대한 긍정을 뜻하는 Yes 및 why와 어울리는 목적을 나타내는 to부정사구를 이용해 급한 일이 있었음을 알리는 (A)가 정답이다.

14. The number of visitors to our museum has dropped lately.
(A) We have some extra funds in marketing left.
(B) A regular admission ticket.
(C) These are paintings from the Renaissance.

우리 박물관 방문객 숫자가 최근에 하락했습니다.
(A) 마케팅용 여유 자금이 좀 남아 있습니다.
(B) 일반 입장권이요.
(C) 이것들은 르네상스 시대의 그림들입니다.

해설 박물관 방문객 숫자가 최근에 하락했다는 문제를 알리고 있으므로 마케팅을 위한 자금이 좀 남아 있다는 말로 방문객을 끌어들이기 위한 해결책을 언급하는 (A)가 정답이다.

15. I had a chance to review our expenses from this quarter.
(A) Their rates are expensive.
(B) Later this month.
(C) What stood out to you?

제가 우리의 이번 분기 지출 비용을 살펴 볼 기회가 있었습니다.
(A) 그곳의 요금은 비쌉니다.
(B) 이달 말에요.
(C) 뭐가 당신의 눈에 띄었나요?

해설 이번 분기 지출 비용을 살펴 볼 기회가 있었다는 사실을 말하고 있으므로 무엇이 눈에 띄었는지 묻는 것으로 특이 사항이 있었는지 확인하려는 (C)가 정답이다.

어휘 stand out 눈에 띄다, 돋보이다, 두드러지다

16. Do you know whether the venue for the company dinner has been reserved?
(A) On January 27.
(B) Not that I'm aware of.
(C) A table for seven, please.

회사 저녁 만찬을 위한 행사장이 예약되었는지 알고 계신가요?
(A) 1월 27일에요.
(B) 제가 알기로는 되어 있지 않습니다.
(C) 7인 테이블로 부탁합니다.

해설 회사 저녁 만찬을 위한 행사장이 예약되었는지의 여부를 묻고 있으므로 자신이 알기로는 아니라는 의미로 예약 상태와 관련된 정보를 언급하는 (B)가 정답이다.

17. Taxi fares have gotten higher, haven't they?
(A) No, it hasn't arrived yet.
(B) Maybe we can just walk to the convention center.
(C) The job fair was quite helpful.

택시 요금이 더 높아졌죠, 그렇죠?
(A) 아니요, 그건 아직 도착하지 않았어요.
(B) 아마 우리가 컨벤션 센터까지 그냥 걸어가도 될 거예요.
(C) 그 취업 박람회가 꽤 도움이 되었어요.

해설 택시 요금이 더 높아지지 않았는지 묻는 질문에 대해 컨벤션 센터까지 걸어가는 방법을 말하는 것으로 높아진 택시 요금에 따른 조치를 언급하는 (B)가 정답이다.

18. Do you know where the networking event is happening?
(A) The Internet connection is weak.
(B) A business partnership.
(C) I'll forward you the information.

인적 교류 행사가 어디서 열리는지 알고 계신가요?
(A) 인터넷 연결 상태가 약합니다.
(B) 사업 제휴 관계요.
(C) 제가 그 정보를 전송해 드릴게요.

해설 인적 교류 행사가 열리는 장소를 알고 있는지 묻고 있으므

로 그 정보를 전송해 주겠다는 말로 관련 정보를 알고 있다는 뜻을 나타내는 (C)가 정답이다.

어휘 partnership 제휴 관계 forward A B A에게 B를 전송하다

19. I can show you around our factory if you'd like.
(A) The appliance manufacturer.
(B) My manager just called me in.
(C) A sample from the vendor.

원하시면 제가 저희 공장을 둘러 보시게 해 드릴 수 있습니다.
(A) 가전기기 제조사입니다.
(B) 저희 부장님께서 방금 저를 오라고 부르셨어요.
(C) 판매업체에서 보낸 샘플이요.

해설 상대방이 원할 경우에 공장을 둘러 보게 해 주겠다고 제안하는 말에 대해 부서장이 불렀다는 말로 둘러 볼 수 없는 상황임을 밝히는 (B)가 정답이다.

20. Can you tell me if the results from the lab test will be available this week?
(A) Is the clinic nearby?
(B) No, there's been a backlog.
(C) Yes, the figures were quite high.

실험실 테스트 결과가 이번 주에 이용 가능할지 말씀해 주시겠어요?
(A) 그 진료소가 근처에 있나요?
(B) 아니요, 밀린 업무가 있었습니다.
(C) 네, 그 수치는 꽤 높았습니다.

해설 실험실 테스트 결과가 이번 주에 이용 가능할지 말해 달라는 요청에 대해 부정을 뜻하는 No와 함께 밀린 업무가 있었다는 말로 이번 주에 이용할 수 없다는 뜻을 나타내는 (B)가 정답이다.

어휘 backlog 밀린 업무, 잔업

Playlist 7

1번 문제 단골 손님 주제&목적, 신분&직업, 장소

Practice

1. (B) **2.** (D) **3.** (A)

1.

W: Thank you for doing this interview with me today. **I'd like to know how you kick started your successful company** recently.
M: Yes, our business is still new, and we only operate online. But we've already received so much support from thousands of customers, so we hope to open our first physical store soon.
W: How exciting! What inspired you to start this brand?
M: Great question. It's all about sustainability. Our clothes are made from 100% recycled materials.

여: 오늘 저와 함께 하는 이 인터뷰에 응해 주셔서 감사합니다. 성공을 거두신 회사를 최근 어떻게 시작하시게 되셨는지 알고 싶습니다.
남: 네, 저희 업체는 여전히 새로운 곳이고, 오직 온라인으로만 운영합니다. 하지만 이미 수천 명의 고객들로부터 아주 많은 지지를 받아 왔기 때문에 곧 첫 번째 실제 매장을 개장하기를 바라고 있습니다.
여: 정말 흥미롭네요! 무엇이 이 브랜드를 시작하도록 영감을 주었나요?
남: 아주 좋은 질문입니다. 결국 관건은 지속 가능성입니다. 저희 의류는 100% 재활용된 소재로 만들어집니다.

어휘 kick start ~을 시작하다 physical 실제의, 물리적인 inspire A to do A에게 ~하도록 영감을 주다 It's all about A. 결국 관건은 A이다, 가장 중요한 것은 A이다 sustainability 지속 가능성

Q. 대화의 주제는 무엇인가?
(A) 몇몇 매장 재배치
(B) 브랜드의 출시
(C) 온라인 광고 캠페인
(D) 지속 가능한 소재

해설 여자가 남자에게 회사를 어떻게 시작했는지 알고 싶다고 밝힌 후, 그 브랜드를 시작하는 데 무엇이 영감을 주었는지 묻고 있으므로 (B)가 정답이다.

2.

M: Alright, **I've got the desserts for your table right here.** Tiramisu cake, caramel flan, and one vanilla milkshake.
W: We had a great meal. Please tell the chef that the chicken alfredo pasta was absolutely delicious!
M: Thanks, I'll pass that on to her. Chef Marie Torres is a top-tier cook who really cares about quality. She received her culinary

certification in Italy and worked at different restaurants all around Europe.

남: 자, 바로 여기 테이블에 놓아 드릴 디저트를 가져 왔습니다. 티라미수 케이크와 캐러멜 플랜, 그리고 바닐라 밀크쉐이크 한 잔입니다.
여: 저희는 훌륭한 식사를 했습니다. 주방장님께 치킨 알프레도 파스타가 굉장히 맛있었다고 말씀해 주세요!
남: 감사합니다, 그분께 전해 드리겠습니다. 마리 토레스 주방장님은 품질에 정말로 신경 쓰시는 일류 요리사이십니다. 그분은 이탈리아에서 요리 자격증을 받으셨으며, 유럽 전역의 여러 다른 레스토랑에서 근무하셨습니다.

어휘 **pass A on to B** A를 B에게 전하다 **top-tier** 일류의, 최고 수준의 **culinary** 요리의

Q. 남자는 누구일 것 같은가?
(A) 식품 공급업자
(B) 여행 가이드
(C) 항공기 승무원
(D) 웨이터

해설 남자가 디저트를 가져 왔다고 알리자, 여자가 식사를 칭찬하면서 주방장에게 파스타가 맛있었다는 말을 전해 달라고 요청하고 있어 식당 웨이터와 손님 사이의 대화임을 알 수 있으므로 (D)가 정답이다.

3.

M: Hi, Misaki. I know it's your first day at our center, but a delivery of chairs is coming in soon. **Would you like to see how shipments get unloaded?**
W: Sure. Can you explain how the inventory system works? **How exactly do you know where each container should go from the loading docks?**
M: We scan this barcode here and look at the index number. This indicates the designated storage zone. Each one corresponds to a certain type of office furniture.
W: Got it. I'll need to start memorizing the different sections of this facility!
M: Well, if you have any questions, just ask me. I know these aisles inside out.

남: 안녕하세요, 미사키 씨. 우리 센터에서 근무하시는 첫날이라는 건 알지만, 의자 배송품들이 곧 도착합니다. 배송 물품이 어떻게 내려지는지 확인해 주시겠어요?
여: 물론이죠. 재고 관리 시스템이 어떻게 운영되는지 설명해 주시겠어요? 각 컨테이너가 하역장에서 어디로 가야 하는지 정확히 어떻게 아시나요?
남: 여기 이 바코드를 스캔해서 목록 번호를 확인합니다. 이것이 지정 보관 구역을 나타냅니다. 각각의 것은 특정 유형의 사무용 가구와 일치합니다.
여: 알겠습니다. 이 시설의 여러 다른 구역들을 외우기 시작해야 할 필요가 있겠네요!
남: 음, 어떤 질문이든 있으시면, 그냥 저에게 물어 보세요. 제가 이 통로들을 훤히 알고 있습니다.

어휘 **loading dock** 하역장, 적재하는 곳 **index** 목록, 색인 **correspond to** ~와 일치하다 **know A inside out** A를 훤히 알고 있다

Q. 화자들이 어디에 근무하고 있을 것 같은가?
(A) 창고에
(B) 우체국에
(C) 서점에
(D) 철물점에

해설 대화 초반부에 남자와 여자가 배송 물품이 어떻게 내려지는지 확인하는 일과 컨테이너가 하역장에서 다른 곳으로 가는 것에 관해 이야기하고 있어 물류 창고에서 근무하는 사람들임을 알 수 있으므로 (A)가 정답이다.

Paraphrasing

1. (A) **2.** (A) **3.** (B) **4.** (A) **5.** (A)
6. (B)

1. 화자들은 무엇을 논의하고 있는가?

여: 우리는 최신 AI로 작동하는 우리 스마트 TV에 대해 고객들이 어떻게 생각하는지 물어보기 위해 설문조사를 보내야 합니다.
남: 사실, 멜리사 씨가 몇몇 사용자 의견들을 이미 모아서 요약본을 만들었습니다.

(A) 후기들을 모으는 것
(B) 설문조사를 완료하는 것

2. 남자는 왜 전화하고 있는가?

남: 안녕하세요, 휴잇 씨. 미네라 치과에서 전화드립니다. 리 선생님이 이번 주 금요일에는 더 이상 시간이 나지 않으셔서, 다음 주 월요일의 같은 시간대로 귀하의 예약을 옮길 수 있을지 여쭤보고 싶습니다.
여: 음, 제가 그 날 중요한 고객 미팅이 있지만, 가능하도록 할 수 있을 겁니다.

(A) 예약을 미루기 위해서
(B) 고객 견학 일정을 잡기 위해서

3. 여자는 누구인가?

> **여:** 페르세우스 항공사의 에이미입니다. 제가 오늘 어떻게 도와 드릴까요?
> **남:** 제가 6월 16일에 쿠알라 룸프르로 가는 항공권이 있는데, 캠핑 도구 몇 개를 가져갈 예정입니다. 이것이 규격 초과 수화물로 여겨질까요?

(A) 항공기 운전사
(B) 항공사 직원

4. 화자들은 어떤 업계에서 근무하고 있을 것 같은가?

> **남:** 수키 씨, 우리 봄 의류 신제품 라인의 디자이너들과의 미팅은 어땠어요? 특별히 당신의 눈에 띈 의상이 있었나요?
> **여:** 정말 마음에 든 뒤집어 입을 수 있는 바람막이가 하나 있었어요. 무게도 가볍고, 윤이 나는 단색들로 출시되어, 미니멀리스트 스타일을 좋아하는 사람들에게 좋을 거라고 확신해요.

(A) 패션
(B) 예술

5. 여자의 전화 통화의 목적은 무엇인가?

> **여:** 안녕하세요, 그레그 콜린스 씨인가요? 퀀텀 테크 사에서 전화 드리는 케이트 디아즈입니다. 귀하의 저희 재무 컨설턴트 직책에 대한 지원서를 살펴보았고, 저희는 귀하의 면접을 진행하고 싶다는 결정을 내렸습니다.
> **남:** 아, 연락 주셔서 감사합니다!

(A) 면접 일정을 잡기 위해서
(B) 상담을 준비하기 위해서

6. 화자들은 어디에서 근무하는가?

> **남:** 베가 씨, 예녹스 미디어사의 이사님이 방금 전화하셨어요. 저희의 법률 서비스를 논의하기 위해 화요일 오전 10시에 들릴 수 있다고 확인해 주셨어요.
> **여:** 좋네요! 예녹스 사는 온라인 광고의 주요 선두기업이라 우리에게 좋은 기회가 될거에요.

(A) 광고 대행사에서
(B) 법률 사무소에서

Check-up Test

1. (D)	**2.** (B)	**3.** (A)	**4.** (C)	**5.** (A)
6. (D)	**7.** (B)	**8.** (A)	**9.** (D)	**10.** (B)
11. (C)	**12.** (A)	**13.** (A)	**14.** (C)	**15.** (D)
16. (C)	**17.** (A)	**18.** (A)		

Questions 1-3 refer to the following conversation.

> **W:** Hey there, Danny. That flyer on our notice board that was put up this morning has gotten everyone talking. Did you read it?
> **M:** Not yet, but I heard we should expect some major changes to all of **1 our mail carriers.**
> **W:** Yep, the city has decided that **1 2 our postal delivery fleet will be entirely upgraded to electric vehicles.**
> **M:** Hopefully they don't need to be recharged every couple of hours. **3 I'm worried whether the battery can hold up for my entire trip.**
>
> **여:** 저, 있잖아요, 대니 씨. 우리 알림판에 오늘 오전에 게시된 그 전단 때문에 모두가 수군대고 있었어요. 읽어 보셨나요?
> **남:** 아직이요, 하지만 우리 우편 배달원 모두를 대상으로 몇몇 대대적인 변화를 예상해야 한다는 얘기를 들었어요.
> **여:** 네, 시에서 우리 우편 배달용 차량 전체가 전기 자동차로 완전히 업그레이드될 거라는 결정을 내렸어요.
> **남:** 그것들이 몇 시간마다 한 번씩 재충전되어야 하는 게 아니면 좋겠어요. 배터리가 제 전체 이동 시간을 견딜 수 있을지 걱정입니다.

어휘 **put up** ~을 게시하다, 내걸다 **get A -ing** A가 ~하게 되다 **mail carrier** 우편 배달원 **postal** 우편의 **fleet** (한 단체가 보유한) 전체 차량/선박/항공기 **hold up** 견디다

1. 화자들은 누구인가?
(A) 배송 트럭 기사들
(B) 프론트 데스크 안내 직원들
(C) 뉴스 기자들
(D) 우체국 직원들

해설 대화 중반부에 남자와 여자가 우편 배달원 모두를 대상으로 하는 변화 및 자신들의 우편 배달용 차량 전체가 전기 자동차로 업그레이드되는 것에 관해 이야기하고 있으므로 (D)가 정답이다.

2. 전단에 무엇이 공지되었는가?
(A) 몇몇 배선이 수리될 것이다.
(B) 몇몇 차량들이 교체될 것이다.
(C) 휴대전화 공급업체가 변경될 것이다.
(D) 시 관계자가 방문할 것이다.

해설 대화 중반부에 여자가 전단에 담긴 내용으로 우편 배달용 차량 전체가 전기 자동차로 완전히 업그레이드된다는 점을 언급하고 있으므로 (B)가 정답이다.

어휘 wiring 배선 cellular 휴대전화의

3. 남자는 무엇과 관련해 우려하는가?
(A) 배터리가 얼마나 오래 지속될지
(B) 목적지 한 곳이 얼마나 멀리 있는지
(C) 한 구역이 얼마나 붐빌지
(D) 한 가지 업무가 얼마나 까다로운지

해설 대화 후반부에 남자가 배터리가 자신의 전체 이동 시간을 견딜 수 있을지 걱정이라고 밝히고 있으므로 (A)가 정답이다.

Questions 4-6 refer to the following conversation.

M: Hello, Esther. **4** **How's it going with the applications from our sales associates who applied for the general manager role?** Any thoughts? We have to choose a candidate by next week.

W: **4** **Julianne Shin's application really stood out to me.** **5** **She's the employee who negotiated a deal with Linderman Incorporated.**

M: Yeah! **5** **That deal was crucial since Linderman has now become a primary client of ours.** I think Julianne would do a great job.

W: Same! Good to know our opinions align. **6** **I'll finalize the paperwork and pass it on to HR before lunchtime.**

남: 안녕하세요, 에스더 씨. 본부장 직책에 지원한 우리 영업 사원들의 지원서는 어떻게 진행되고 있나요? 어떻게 생각하세요? 다음 주까지 지원자를 한 명 선택해야 합니다.

여: 줄리앤 신 씨의 지원서가 정말로 제 눈에 띄었어요. 그분이 린더먼 주식회사와의 계약을 협상했던 직원입니다.

남: 네! 린더먼 사가 지금 우리의 주요 고객사가 되었기 때문에 그 계약은 아주 중요했죠. 줄리앤 씨가 아주 잘 해 주실 것 같아요.

여: 동감입니다! 우리 의견의 방향이 일치한다는 걸 알게 되어 다행이네요. 제가 점심 시간 전에 서류 작업을 마무리 짓고 인사부에 전달할게요.

어휘 align 방향이 일치하다, 어울리다 pass A on to B A를 B에게 전하다

4. 화자들은 주로 무엇을 이야기하고 있는가?
(A) 등록 과정
(B) 직원 복지 혜택
(C) 새로운 역할에 대한 지원자
(D) 계절 판매 촉진 행사

해설 남자가 대화를 시작하면서 본부장 직책에 지원한 소속 영업 사원들의 지원서를 살펴 봤는지 물은 뒤로 줄리앤 신이라는 지원자에 관해 이야기하고 있으므로 (C)가 정답이다.

5. 화자들의 말에 따르면, 줄리앤 신 씨가 무엇을 완수했는가?
(A) 한 가지 사업 계약을 따냈다.
(B) 특별 면허증을 취득했다.
(C) 회사의 수익성을 높여 주었다.
(D) 웹 사이트를 재디자인했다.

해설 대화 중반부에 줄리앤 신 씨가 린더먼 주식회사와의 계약을 협의한 사실과 함께 린더먼 사가 주요 고객이 된 사실을 언급하고 있어 계약을 따냈다는 것을 알 수 있으므로 (A)가 정답이다.

6. 여자는 무엇을 할 것이라고 말하는가?
(A) 추천서를 쓰는 일
(B) 회의를 마련하는 일
(C) 몇몇 손님용 출입증을 나눠 주는 일
(D) 몇몇 서류를 제출하는 일

해설 여자가 대화 마지막 부분에 점심 시간 전에 서류 작업을 마무리 짓고 인사부에 전달하겠다고 알리고 있으므로 (D)가 정답이다.

Questions 7-9 refer to the following conversation.

M: Welcome to your first day here. We're going to start off by walking along all the trails so you can familiarize yourself with the region. As we walk around, we'll also gather some water samples.

W: The water samples will get tested **7** **to monitor the condition of the preserve's streams and ponds**, right?

M: Yep. But **8** **we don't have our own laboratory, so we have to ship them**

elsewhere every month for testing. Also, since the weather's nice and sunny today, **9 I'd appreciate it if you took some pictures for our Web site.**

W: **9 Sure, I have my camera with me.**

남: 이곳에서의 첫째 날에 오신 것을 환영합니다. 이 지역에 익숙해지실 수 있도록 모든 산길을 따라 걷는 것으로 시작해 보겠습니다. 우리가 곳곳을 걸어 다니면서, 몇몇 물 샘플도 수집할 것입니다.

여: 그 물 샘플들이 보호 구역 내에 있는 개울과 연못들의 상태를 관찰하기 위해 테스트되는 게 맞나요?

남: 네. 하지만 우리가 자체 실험실이 없기 때문에, 테스트를 위해 매달 다른 곳으로 보내야 합니다. 그리고, 오늘 날씨가 맑고 화창하기 때문에, 우리 웹 사이트를 위해 몇몇 사진을 찍어 주시면 감사하겠습니다.

여: 물론이죠, 저한테 카메라가 있습니다.

어휘 **start off** 시작하다 **familiarize oneself with** ~에 익숙해지다, 숙지하다 **preserve** 보호 구역

7. 화자들은 어디에 근무하고 있을 것 같은가?
(A) 과수원에
(B) 자연 보호 구역에
(C) 공공 저수지에
(D) 식물원에

해설 대화 중반부에 여자가 물 샘플 수집의 목적으로 현재 두 사람이 있는 장소와 관련해 보호 구역 내의 개울과 연못들을 언급하고 있으므로 (B)가 정답이다.

8. 화자들이 몇몇 샘플로 무엇을 할 것인가?
(A) 실험실에 보내는 일
(B) 창고에 보관하는 일
(C) 다양한 고객들에게 할당하는 일
(D) 숫자로 라벨을 표기하는 일

해설 남자가 대화 중반부에 자체 실험실이 없어서 샘플을 다른 곳으로 보내야 한다고 알리고 있으므로 (A)가 정답이다.

어휘 **allocate** ~을 할당하다, 배정하다

9. 여자는 무엇을 하는 데 동의하는가?
(A) 한 장소를 조사하는 일
(B) 일기 예보를 확인하는 일
(C) 몇몇 메모를 적어 두는 일
(D) 몇몇 사진을 촬영하는 일

해설 대화 후반부에 남자가 웹 사이트를 위해 몇몇 사진을 찍어 달라고 요청하는 것에 대해 여자가 동의하고 있으므로 (D)가 정답이다.

Questions 10-12 refer to the following conversation.

W: Yuko, **10 we just got a catering order that I think you should start on.**

M: OK. What is it?

W: **10 Chicken Marsala for a party of 20. They also want a medium tray of stuffed mushrooms.** On their order, they wrote in a special request to add basil to the mushrooms.

M: Oh... but aren't we all out of fresh basil?

W: I believe you're right. But **11 I was thinking maybe we can use dried basil instead.**

M: That works.

W: **12 Let me check our storage room to see if we have enough of it.**

여: 유코 씨, 시작해 주셔야 한다고 생각하는 출장 요리 주문을 방금 받았어요.

남: 네, 뭔가요?

여: 20명의 일행을 위한 치킨 마르살라입니다. 이분들이 속을 채운 버섯들이 담긴 중간 크기의 트레이도 원하고 있어요. 주문서에, 바질을 버섯에 추가해 달라는 특별 요청 사항도 기재하셨어요.

남: 아... 하지만 신선한 바질이 다 떨어지지 않았나요?

여: 맞는 말씀인 것 같아요. 하지만 아마 건조된 바질을 대신 이용할 수 있을 거라고 생각하고 있었습니다.

남: 그럼 되겠네요.

여: 그게 충분히 있는지 알아 볼 수 있게 보관실을 확인해 보겠습니다.

어휘 **party** 일행, 당사자 **stuffed** 속을 채워 넣은 **have enough of** ~이 충분히 있다

10. 남자의 직업은 무엇일 것 같은가?
(A) 농부
(B) 요리사
(C) 상인
(D) 종업원

해설 여자가 대화 시작 부분에 남자가 시작해야 하는 출장 요리 주문을 언급하면서 치킨과 버섯이 들어가는 음식 이름을 말하고 있으므로 (B)가 정답이다.

11. 여자는 무엇을 제안하는가?

(A) 한 제품의 재고를 다시 채워 놓는 일
(B) 한 가지 배송 서비스를 이용해 보는 일
(C) 한 가지 재료를 대체하는 일
(D) 다른 도구를 이용하는 일

해설 여자가 대화 중반부에 다 떨어진 신선한 바질 대신 건조된 바질을 이용할 수 있을 거라고 생각했다는 사실을 밝히고 있으므로 (C)가 정답이다.

어휘 substitute ~을 대체하다

12. 여자는 곧이어 무엇을 할 것이라고 말하는가?
(A) 보관실을 확인해 보는 일
(B) 환불을 처리해 주는 일
(C) 한 고객의 의견을 요청하는 일
(D) 슈퍼마켓을 방문하는 일

해설 대화 후반부에 여자가 건조된 바질이 충분히 있는지 알아볼 수 있게 보관실을 확인해 보겠다고 알리고 있으므로 (A)가 정답이다.

Questions 13-15 refer to the following conversation.

W: Hello, 13 **I'm calling because my cell phone bill came out much more than I expected.** My name is Catherine Gee, and my account number is 984555.

M: Thanks. It looks like you have some international data charges. 14 **Did you travel recently?**

W: Oh, 14 **I was in Singapore last week.** I only used my phone to take pictures, though.

M: Well, 15 **unless you turn off the data roaming feature on your phone**, you will be automatically charged for mobile data usage abroad. So, if you had any apps running in the background, that's probably what happened.

W: Wow, I had no clue. Is there any way I can get these charges waived? I'm a long-time customer.

여: 안녕하세요, 제 휴대전화 요금 고지서가 제가 예상했던 것보다 훨씬 더 많이 나왔기 때문에 전화 드립니다. 제 이름은 캐서린 지이고, 제 계정 번호는 984555입니다.

남: 감사합니다. 몇몇 해외 데이터 청구 요금이 있는 것 같습니다. 최근에 여행하셨나요?

여: 아, 지난주에 싱가포르에 있었어요. 하지만, 제 전화기를 이용해 사진만 찍었어요.

남: 저, 전화기의 데이터 로밍 기능을 꺼 놓지 않으시면, 자동으로 해외에서 모바일 데이터 이용에 대해 요금이 청구됩니다. 그러니까, 배경에 어떤 앱이든 작동하게 해 놓으셨다면, 아마 그래서 그럴 겁니다.

여: 우와, 전혀 몰랐어요. 이 청구 요금이 면제되도록 할 수 있는 어떤 방법이라도 있나요? 제가 장기 이용 고객이거든요.

어휘 bill 고지서, 청구서, 계산서 abroad 해외에서, 해외로 run 작동하다 have no clue 전혀 모르다 waive ~을 면제해 주다, 철회하다

13. 여자는 왜 전화하는가?
(A) 고지서와 관련해 불만을 제기하기 위해
(B) 비용 견적서를 논의하기 위해
(C) 몇몇 서류를 요청하기 위해
(D) 자신의 계정 정보를 편집하기 위해

해설 여자가 대화를 시작하면서 휴대전화 요금 고지서와 관련해서 전화했다고 밝히면서 예상했던 것보다 훨씬 더 많이 나왔다는 사실을 말하고 있다. 이는 불만을 제기하는 것이므로 (A)가 정답이다.

14. 여자는 지난주에 무엇을 했는가?
(A) 새 휴대전화기를 구입했다.
(B) 아파트로 이사했다.
(C) 해외에서 여행했다.
(D) 한 가지 과정을 수강했다.

해설 대화 중반부에 남자가 여자에게 최근에 여행했는지 묻자, 여자가 지난주에 싱가포르에 있었다고 대답하고 있으므로 (C)가 정답이다.

15. 남자의 말에 따르면, 여자는 아마 무엇을 하지 못했을 것 같은가?
(A) 요청서를 제출하는 일
(B) 한 직원에게 연락하는 일
(C) 여러 사진들을 이메일로 보내는 일
(D) 기기의 한 가지 기능을 꺼 놓는 일

해설 남자가 대화 후반부에 전화기의 데이터 로밍 기능을 꺼 놓지 않았을 경우에 발생할 수 있는 요금 청구에 관해 알리고 있으므로 (D)가 정답이다.

Questions 16-18 refer to the following conversation with three speakers.

W: Welcome, Charlie, to our crew. 16 **We have a busy harvest season ahead!**
M1: I can't wait to get to work.
W: This is Austin. 16 **He's going to show you the watermelon fields** as part of your training.
M2: Nice to meet you, Charlie. 17 **This pair of gloves is for you.**
M1: Thanks!
M2: Picking watermelons is quite simple. 18 **The most important part is to drink lots of water** and stay hydrated in this hot weather.
M1: I always carry a large water bottle with me, so I'm prepared.

여: 저희 작업팀에 오신 것을 환영합니다, 찰리 씨. 저희가 바쁜 수확철을 앞두고 있습니다!
남1: 빨리 일을 시작하고 싶네요.
여: 이분은 오스틴 씨입니다. 교육의 일환으로 수박 밭을 보여 드릴 겁니다.
남2: 만나서 반갑습니다, 찰리 씨. 이 장갑 한 켤레를 드릴게요.
남1: 감사합니다!
남2: 수박을 따는 일은 꽤 간단합니다. 가장 중요한 부분은 물을 많이 마셔서 더운 날씨에 수분이 보충된 상태를 유지하는 겁니다.
남1: 저는 항상 큰 물병을 가지고 다니기 때문에, 준비되어 있습니다.

어휘 **have A ahead** A를 앞두고 있다 **harvest** 수확, 추수 **get to do** ~하기 시작하다 **as part of** ~의 일환으로 **pick** (과일·꽃 등) ~을 따다, 꺾다 **hydrated** 수분이 보충된

16. 대화가 어디에서 진행되고 있을 것 같은가?
(A) 해변에서
(B) 스포츠 경기장에서
(C) 농장에서
(D) 식료품 매장에서

해설 여자가 대화 초반부에 바쁜 수확철을 앞두고 있다고 말하는 부분과 오스틴이라는 남자가 수박 밭을 보여 줄 것이라고 알리는 부분을 통해 농장이 대화 장소임을 알 수 있으므로 (C)가 정답이다.

17. 오스틴 씨는 찰리 씨에게 무엇을 주는가?
(A) 장갑
(B) 선글라스
(C) 열쇠 꾸러미
(D) 공책

해설 여자가 대화 중반부에 한 남자를 오스틴이라고 소개하자, 그 남자가 장갑을 건네 주며 말을 하고 있으므로 (A)가 정답이다.

18. 오스틴 씨의 말에 따르면, 무엇이 중요한가?
(A) 물을 마시는 것
(B) 모자를 착용하는 것
(C) 적절한 위치를 고르는 것
(D) 한 구역 내에 머물러 있는 것

해설 여자가 오스틴이라고 소개한 남자가 장갑을 건넨 후에 가장 중요한 부분은 물을 많이 마시는 것이라고 알리고 있으므로 (A)가 정답이다.

Playlist 8

2번 문제는 주로 세부사항과 문제점!

Practice

1. (B) **2.** (D)

1.

M: Hey, Alice and Lauren, I walked around and inspected all the seating areas of the arena yesterday. Nothing needs major fixing, but **I did notice some paint starting to crack on many of the handrails.**
W1: It's been a while since those got repainted. And the dry weather hasn't been helping.
W2: **We should hire a painting company to take care of that.** Do we have the budget for it?
M: Yes, we still have extra surplus for maintenance repairs. While they're at it, we can have them repaint all the staircases, too. Lauren, can you figure out the exact paint colors we'll need for all this?
W2: Okay, sure. I can find that info in our inventory logs.

남: 안녕하세요, 앨리스 씨 그리고 로렌 씨, 제가 어제 경기장의 모든 좌석 구역 곳곳을 걸어 다니면서 점검했습니다. 어느 곳도 중요한 수리를 필요로 하지는 않은데, 일부 페인트가 대부분의 손잡이에서 갈라지기 시작하고 있다는 걸 알게 되었어요.

여1: 그것들이 다시 도색되지 좀 됐죠. 그리고 건조한 날씨도 계속 도움이 되지 않고 있어요.
여2: 그 일을 처리할 도색 전문 회사를 고용해야 합니다. 그에 대한 예산이 있나요?
남: 네, 유지보수용 수리 작업을 위한 추가 여유분이 여전히 있습니다. 그 사람들이 그 일을 하는 동안, 모든 계단도 다시 도색하도록 할 수 있습니다. 로렌 씨, 이 모든 작업에 필요한 정확한 페인트 색상을 파악해 주시겠어요?
여2: 네, 물론이죠. 우리 재고 기록에서 그 정보를 찾을 수 있어요.

어휘 **fixing** 수리, 설치, 고정 **notice A -ing** A가 ~하는 것을 알게 되다 **crack** 갈라지다, 금이 가다, 깨지다 **handrail** 손잡이 **surplus** 여유분, 나머지 **figure out** ~을 파악하다, 알아 보다 **log** 기록(지)

Q. 화자들은 무엇을 하는 데 동의하는가?
(A) 한 행사를 위해 더 많은 인력을 고용하는 것
(B) 일부 재단장 작업을 실시하는 것
(C) 좌석 배치를 재구성하는 것
(D) 새로운 안전 장비를 설치하는 것

해설 남자가 대화 초반부에 페인트가 손잡이에서 갈라지고 있는 문제를 지적하자 여자 중 한 명이 그 문제를 처리할 도색 전문 회사를 고용해야 한다고 제안하고 있으므로 (B)가 정답이다.

어휘 **refurbishment** 재단장 **reconfigure** ~을 재구성하다

2.

W: Hi, can you please take me to Monterey Bay Aquarium? It's next to City Hall on Shoreline Boulevard.
M: Okay, but **traffic through that part of Shoreline Boulevard is blocked off for the day. They're doing road repairs.**
W: Oh, no! I'm set to give a presentation there in 30 minutes, so I can't be late.
M: Alright, hold on now. I can take you to the corner of Halford and Mercado instead. You'll have to walk a bit more, but I think that's the closest I can get.

여: 안녕하세요, 몬테레이 베이 수족관으로 데려가 주실 수 있으세요? 쇼어라인 블리바드에 있는 시청 옆에 있습니다.
남: 네, 하지만 쇼어라인 블리바드의 그 구간을 통과하는 차량들이 오늘 하루 차단된 상태입니다. 도로 수리 작업을 하고 있거든요.
여: 아, 이런! 제가 30분 후에 그곳에서 발표를 할 예정이라서, 늦으면 안 됩니다.
남: 알겠습니다, 잠시만요. 핼포드와 메카도가 만나는 모퉁이로 대신 모셔다 드릴 수 있습니다. 조금 더 걸어 가셔야 하겠지만, 그곳이 제가 갈 수 있는 가장 가까운 곳인 것 같아요.

어휘 **block off** ~을 차단하다, 가로막다 **be set to do** ~할 예정이다 **hold on now** 잠시만요

Q. 무엇이 문제인가?
(A) 한 업체가 폐업했다.
(B) 다리 하나가 접근할 수 없다.
(C) 한 주문이 너무 오래 걸리고 있다.
(D) 도로 한 곳이 부분적으로 폐쇄되었다.

해설 대화 중반부에 남자가 쇼어라인 블리바드의 일부 구간이 오늘 차단된 상태임을 알리면서 도로 수리 작업을 하고 있다는 말로 이유를 언급하고 있으므로 (D)가 정답이다.

어휘 **shut down** 폐업하다, 폐쇄되다 **inaccessible** 접근할 수 없는, 이용할 수 없는

Check-up Test

1. (B)	**2.** (A)	**3.** (C)	**4.** (B)	**5.** (C)
6. (B)	**7.** (A)	**8.** (B)	**9.** (C)	**10.** (B)
11. (A)	**12.** (D)	**13.** (D)	**14.** (C)	**15.** (B)
16. (B)	**17.** (D)	**18.** (D)		

Questions 1-3 refer to the following conversation.

M: Welcome to Castro's Pasta. How many are in your party?
W: Quite a lot. There's ten of us, but 1 **I forgot to reserve a table.**
M: That's alright. I do want to let you know that 2 **because of a private reception, our dinner service will be ending earlier than normal tonight.** We have a spacious area on the patio that should be able to accommodate everyone. Is that okay? We'll set up the tables immediately.
W: Sure, that works for us – thanks. But 3 **we'd prefer to sit at a single table together**, if that's possible. We plan to have a big discussion.

남: 카스트로스 파스터에 오신 것을 환영합니다. 일행이 몇 분이신가요?
여: 꽤 많습니다. 저희가 10명이긴 하지만, 제가 테이블을 예약하는 걸 잊었어요.
남: 괜찮습니다. 개인 축하 연회 때문에, 저희 저녁 식사 서비스가 오늘 밤에 평소보다 더 일찍 종료될 것이라는 사실을 꼭 알려 드리고 싶습니다. 테라스 구역에 모든 분을 수용할 수 있을 널찍한 공간이 있습니다. 괜찮으신가요? 저희가 테이블을 즉시 마련해 드리겠습니다.
여: 네, 그렇게 해 주시면 됩니다, 감사합니다. 그런데 저희는 테이블 한 곳에 함께 앉고 싶어요, 가능하다면요. 저희가 중요한 논의를 할 계획이거든요.

어휘 party 일행, 당사자 reception 축하 연회 spacious 널찍한

1. 여자는 무엇을 하는 것을 잊었는가?
(A) 영수증을 받는 것
(B) 예약하는 것
(C) 쿠폰을 가져오는 것
(D) 자신의 이름을 적어 놓는 것

해설 대화 초반부에 여자가 테이블을 예약하는 것을 잊었다고 말하고 있으므로 (B)가 정답이다.

2. 남자는 레스토랑과 관련해 무슨 말을 하는가?
(A) 오늘 영업 시간에 변동이 있다.
(B) 인원이 많은 일행에 대해 추가 요금이 있다.
(C) 옥외에 있는 공간은 개인 행사 전용이다.
(D) 업체가 최근에 설립되었다.

해설 남자가 대화 중반부에 개인 축하 연회 때문에 저녁 식사 서비스가 오늘 밤에 평소보다 더 일찍 종료된다는 사실을 밝히고 있다. 이는 영업 시간의 변동을 뜻하므로 (A)가 정답이다.

3. 여자는 무엇을 요청하는가?
(A) 요리 추천
(B) 물 한 잔
(C) 한 테이블에 앉는 것
(D) 더 따뜻한 구역에 앉는 것

해설 대화 마지막 부분에 여자가 일행과 테이블 한 곳에 함께 앉고 싶다고 요청하고 있으므로 (C)가 정답이다.

Questions 4-6 refer to the following conversation.

W: Hey, Rishi, **4 I feel like our employees are in need of some extra training. What about having them try this mobile application I found?** The app provides a huge library of training modules, and our employees can access the materials on their phones whenever they want.
M: I think I've heard of those programs before. **5 Don't they tend to be expensive, though?**
W: It's not as bad as you might think. And **6 I read some reviews on the developers' Web site from other businesses that found it to be a helpful tool.**

여: 있잖아요, 리시 씨, 저는 우리 직원들이 일부 추가 교육이 필요한 것 같은 느낌이에요. 제가 찾은 이 모바일 애플리케이션을 한 번 이용하게 해 보면 어떨까요? 이 앱이 교육 이수 단위들로 구성된 엄청난 규모의 라이브러리를 제공하는데, 우리 직원들이 언제든 원할 때 각자의 전화기에서 그 자료에 접속할 수 있어요.
남: 전에 그런 프로그램들을 들어 본 것 같아요. 하지만, 그것들은 비싼 경향이 있지 않나요?
여: 그럴지도 모른다고 생각하시는 것만큼 나쁘지 않습니다. 그리고 제가 개발사 웹 사이트에서 다른 업체들이 도움이 되는 도구라고 생각했다는 후기들도 좀 읽어 봤습니다.

어휘 in need of ~을 필요로 하는 have A do A에게 ~하게 하다 module 이수 단위

4. 여자는 무엇을 하도록 제안하는가?
(A) 지역 도서관을 방문하는 일
(B) 교육 애플리케이션을 이용하는 일
(C) 마케팅 전략을 개발하는 일
(D) 더 많은 직원을 모집하는 일

해설 여자가 대화를 시작하면서 직원 교육과 관련해 자신이 찾은 모바일 애플리케이션을 한 번 이용하게 해 보면 어떨지 제안하고 있으므로 (B)가 정답이다.

5. 남자는 무엇에 대해 우려하는가?
(A) 처리 시간
(B) 예산 제한
(C) 제품 비용
(D) 제품 이용 가능성

해설 남자가 대화 중반부에 여자가 제안하는 모바일 애플리케이션에 대한 얘기를 들은 후, 그런 것들이 비싼 경향이 있지 않는지 묻고 있으므로 (C)가 정답이다.

6. 여자의 말에 따르면, 웹 사이트에서 무엇을 찾을 수 있는가?

(A) 직무 설명
(B) 고객 후기
(C) 토론용 포럼
(D) 영업 시간

해설 대화 맨 마지막 부분에 여자가 개발사 웹 사이트에서 다른 업체들이 도움이 되는 도구라고 생각했다는 후기를 읽은 사실을 밝히고 있으므로 (B)가 정답이다.

Questions 7-9 refer to the following conversation.

M: Mayu, since a lot of customers order their electronics online nowadays, 7 **we should brainstorm some ideas for boosting sales at our store.**

W: Remember that 8 **tech podcast I mentioned before? Actually, an episode I listened to recently** covered some interesting approaches to product presentation and visuals – for any kind of physical store.

M: What did they talk about?

W: They said 9 **to arrange packaged products to build displays that represent an image or an object**, almost like building blocks. That way, shoppers will be attracted to the eye-catching layout.

M: 9 **I like that!** It'll make them more curious and likely to purchase something.

남: 마유 씨, 많은 고객들이 요즘 온라인으로 전자 제품을 주문하기 때문에, 우리 매장에서 판매량을 촉진할 몇몇 아이디어를 떠올려 봐야 합니다.

여: 제가 전에 언급해 드렸던 기술 팟캐스트 기억하세요? 사실, 제가 최근에 들은 방송분에서 제품 발표 및 시각자료에 대한 몇몇 흥미로운 접근법을 다뤘는데, 모든 종류의 실제 매장이 대상이었어요.

남: 무엇에 관해 이야기하던가요?

여: 하나의 이미지 또는 물체를 표현하는 진열품을 만들 수 있도록 포장된 제품을 배치하라고 했어요, 거의 마치 건축용 블록처럼요. 그렇게 하면, 쇼핑객들이 그 시선을 사로잡는 배치에 이끌릴 겁니다.

남: 마음에 드네요! 사람들을 더 호기심 있게 만들어서 뭔가 구입할 가능성이 생길 거예요.

어휘 brainstorm (아이디어 등) ~을 떠올리다, 구상하다 episode 1회 방송분 physical 실제의, 물리적인 represent ~을 표현하다, ~에 해당하다 that way 그렇게 하면, 그런 방법으로 eye-catching 시선을 사로잡는

7. 대화가 무엇에 관한 것인가?
(A) 매장 내 판매량을 개선하는 일
(B) 제품 출시 행사를 마련하는 일
(C) 개조 공사를 준비하는 일
(D) 직원 생산성을 높이는 일

해설 대화 시작 부분에 남자가 매장에서 판매량을 촉진할 몇몇 아이디어를 떠올려 봐야 한다고 제안한 뒤로 판매량 촉진 방법과 관련해 이야기하고 있으므로 (A)가 정답이다.

8. 여자는 어떻게 아이디어를 얻었는가?
(A) 전문가와 상의함으로써
(B) 팟캐스트를 들음으로써
(C) 발표회를 봄으로써
(D) 온라인 과정을 수강함으로써

해설 여자가 대화 중반부에 자신이 전에 언급했던 기술 팟캐스트에 관해 이야기하면서 자신이 최근에 들은 방송분의 주제를 설명하고 있으므로 (B)가 정답이다.

9. 화자들이 무엇을 할 것 같은가?
(A) 안내 표지를 게시하는 일
(B) 일부 가구를 조립하는 일
(C) 일부 상품을 재배치하는 일
(D) 일부 이미지를 출력하는 일

해설 여자가 대화 후반부에 하나의 이미지 또는 물체를 표현하는 진열품을 만들 수 있도록 제품을 배치하는 방식을 언급하는 것에 대해 남자도 마음에 들어 하고 있으므로 (C)가 정답이다.

Questions 10-12 refer to the following conversation.

M: Morning, Ms. Boyle. This is Alan Dixon speaking, the operations supervisor of Renaldo Resorts. Lots of guests are loving 10 **the mural you painted** for the exterior of our entrance, so I wanted to ask if you'd like to do another one for our on-site restaurant.

W: Hi, Mr. Dixon. Wonderful to hear from you again. For that project, how soon would you need me to start? I'm getting ready for a big art exhibit this summer, so 11 **I'm afraid I won't be available until it's all set up.**

M: That's no problem. We're still currently remodeling the eatery, so you can only start painting after it's done anyway. For now, 12 **I can send you the dimensions of the wall** where the mural will be, so that you have a good idea of the space.

남: 안녕하세요, 보일 씨. 저는 레날도 리조트의 운영 책임자 앨런 딕슨입니다. 저희 입구 외부에 그려 주신 벽화를 많은 고객들께서 아주 마음에 들어 하고 계셔서, 저희 구내 레스토랑을 위해 하나 더 작업해 주실 수 있으신지 여쭤 보고 싶었습니다.
여: 안녕하세요, 딕슨 씨. 다시 연락 주셔서 반갑습니다. 그 프로젝트를 위해, 제가 얼마나 빨리 시작해야 하나요? 제가 올 여름에 중요한 미술 전시회 준비를 하고 있어서, 죄송하지만 그게 모두 준비되고 나서야 시간이 될 것 같아요.
남: 괜찮습니다. 저희가 현재 그 식당을 여전히 개조하고 있어서, 어쨌든 그게 완료된 후에야 그리기 시작하실 수 있습니다. 일단은, 그 공간에 대해 좋은 아이디어를 얻으시도록, 벽화가 있을 벽의 치수를 보내 드릴 수 있습니다.

어휘 mural 벽화 exterior (건물의) 외부, 외면 on-site 구내의, 부지 내의 dimension 치수, 규격, 크기

10. 여자는 누구일 것 같은가?
(A) 미술품 수집가
(B) 화가
(C) 건축가
(D) 레스토랑 소유주

해설 남자가 대화 초반부에 여자가 과거에 그려 준 벽화를 언급하고 있으므로 (B)가 정답이다.

11. 여자는 어떤 문제를 언급하는가?
(A) 즉시 작업을 시작할 수 없다.
(B) 교통편에 대해 지원이 필요할 것이다.
(C) 새로운 일자리를 제안받았다.
(D) 해외로 이주할 준비를 하고 있다.

해설 여자가 대화 중반부에 전시회 준비를 언급하면서 그것이 모두 준비된 후에야 시간이 될 것이라고 알리고 있으므로 (A)가 정답이다.

12. 남자는 무엇을 보내겠다고 하는가?
(A) 초대장
(B) 근로 계약서
(C) 사진
(D) 상세 치수 정보

해설 대화 후반부에 남자가 벽화를 그릴 벽의 치수를 보내 줄 수 있다고 언급하고 있으므로 (D)가 정답이다.

Questions 13-15 refer to the following conversation with three speakers.

M: Hi, 13 14 **I was trying on some clothes here a few hours ago, but I believe I left my phone in one of the fitting rooms.**
W1: Oh, okay. Let me ask Rhea, who's the associate for that section of the store today.
M: Thank you. I really can't afford to lose my phone.
W1: I understand. 15 **Hi, Rhea.** We have a customer here who says he might've left his cellphone in one of the fitting rooms earlier today.
W2: Oh, someone did turn one in not long ago. 15 **What color is it?**
M: The case is olive green.
W2: Oh, yes! Let me go grab that for you.

남: 안녕하세요, 제가 몇 시간 전에 이곳에서 몇몇 의류를 입어 보고 있었는데, 탈의실 중 한 곳에 제 전화기를 놓아 둔 것 같아요.
여1: 아, 네. 오늘 매장의 그 구역을 맡고 있는 직원인, 레아 씨에게 물어 보겠습니다.
남: 감사합니다. 제가 정말로 전화기를 분실할 여유가 없습니다.
여1: 알겠습니다. 있잖아요, 레아 씨. 오늘 아까 탈의실 중 한 곳에 전화기를 놓아 두셨을지 모른다고 말씀하시는 고객이 여기 한 분 계십니다.
여2: 아, 어떤 분께서 조금 전에 분명 하나 돌려 주셨어요. 무슨 색상이죠?
남: 케이스가 올리브 그린색입니다.
여2: 아, 네! 제가 가서 가져 오겠습니다.

어휘 turn A in A를 돌려 주다, 제출하다 not long ago 조금 전에, 얼마 전에 go do 가서 ~하다

13. 화자들은 어디에 있는가?
(A) 인쇄소에
(B) 전자 제품 매장에
(C) 맞춤 양복점에
(D) 의류 매장에

해설 남자가 대화 시작 부분에 몇몇 의류를 입어 보는 일과 탈의실을 언급하고 있으므로 탈의실에서 옷을 입어 볼 수 있는 곳인 (D)가 정답이다.

어휘 tailor (남성복) 재단사

14. 남자는 왜 해당 업체에 있는가?
(A) 온라인 주문품을 가져 가기 위해
(B) 결제 오류를 지적하기 위해
(C) 분실품을 찾기 위해
(D) 제품을 교환하기 위해

해설 대화 초반부에 남자가 탈의실 중 한 곳에 자신의 전화기를 놓아 둔 것 같다고 언급하고 있으므로 (C)가 정답이다.

15. 레아 씨는 무엇과 관련해 묻는가?
(A) 브랜드
(B) 색상
(C) 디자인
(D) 주소

해설 대화 중반부에 여자 한 명이 다른 여자에게 레아 씨라고 부르면서 고객의 상황을 설명하자, 그 여자가 대답하면서 무슨 색상인지 묻고 있으므로 (B)가 정답이다.

Questions 16-18 refer to the following conversation with three speakers.

M: Hello. I'm Javier Franco from Vivaldi Incorporated. I'm here to meet Ms. Huang to tour your campgrounds for 16 **an upcoming retreat that my company is holding.**
W1: I'm aware that you have an appointment with her, but 17 **she just took an urgent phone call. I think she should be coming now, though.**
W2: Hello, there. Mr. Franco, right? I'm Courtney Huang. Would you like to view our main dining hall first?
M: Sure. I'm looking forward to seeing all the different cabin options too. 18 **Your facilities have high-speed Internet, right?**
W2: Yes, even in the recreation areas.

남: 안녕하세요. 저는 비발디 주식회사의 하비에르 프랑코입니다. 저희 회사에서 곧 개최하는 야유회를 위해 이곳 캠핑장을 둘러 보기 위해 후앙 씨를 만나러 왔습니다.
여1: 약속이 되어 있으시다는 건 알고 있지만, 그분께서는 막 급한 전화를 받으셨습니다. 하지만, 지금 오시고 계시는 것 같습니다.
여2: 안녕하세요. 프랑코 씨 맞으시죠? 저는 코트니 후앙입니다. 저희 본관 식당 먼저 확인해 보시겠어요?
남: 네. 서로 다른 오두막 선택사항들도 모두 확인해 보기를 고대하고 있습니다. 이곳 시설에 초고속 인터넷이 있는 게 맞죠?
여2: 네, 심지어 오락 활동 구역에도 있습니다.

어휘 tour v. ~을 둘러 보다, 견학하다 retreat 야유회

16. 남자는 어떤 종류의 행사를 계획하고 있는가?
(A) 요리 경연 대회
(B) 회사 야유회
(C) 직원 오리엔테이션
(D) 전문 컨퍼런스

해설 남자가 대화를 시작하면서 소속 회사에서 곧 개최하는 야유회를 언급하고 있으므로 (B)가 정답이다.

17. 후앙 씨는 왜 지체되었는가?
(A) 급한 회의에 가 있었다.
(B) 출장에서 복귀하고 있었다.
(C) 보고서를 작성하고 있었다.
(D) 전화 통화를 하고 있었다.

해설 대화 중반부에 여자 한 명이 후앙 씨가 급한 전화를 받은 사실과 함께 지금 오고 있을 것이라고 말하고 있으므로 (D)가 정답이다.

18. 남자는 무엇에 관해 문의하는가?
(A) 시급
(B) 교통편 선택사항
(C) 에어컨
(D) 인터넷 접속

해설 남자가 대화 후반부에 초고속 인터넷이 있는지 묻고 있으므로 (D)가 정답이다.

Playlist 9
3번 문제는 요청&제안, 다음에 할 일만 기억하세요!

Practice

1. (B) **2.** (B)

1.

W: Nasir, I wanted to ask if we can edit the dress code section in our workbooks for tomorrow's new staff orientation.
M: Oh, but the materials have all been printed now.
W: Already? I found out that our CEO now wants to allow more casual attire in the office so that employees can feel more comfortable.

M: Hmm… In that case, **how about just pasting an extra page to the back of each workbook** so everyone's aware of the change?

여: 나시르 씨, 내일 있을 신입 직원 오리엔테이션을 위해 우리 업무 규정서의 복장 규정 부분을 편집할 수 있는지 여쭤 보고 싶었습니다.
남: 아, 하지만 그 자료들이 지금 모두 인쇄되었습니다.
여: 벌써요? 우리 대표이사님께서 직원들이 더 편하게 느낄 수 있도록 사무실 내에서 더 간편한 복장을 허용하고 싶어 하신다는 사실을 지금 알게 되었습니다.
남: 흠... 그런 경우라면, 모든 사람이 변동 사항을 알고 있도록 각 규정서의 뒤쪽에 추가 페이지만 붙이는 건 어떠세요?

어휘 attire 복장, 의복 in that case 그런 경우라면, 그렇다면 paste ~을 붙이다

Q. 남자는 무엇을 제안하는가?
(A) 색상 선택을 변경하는 것
(B) 책자에 페이지를 하나 추가하는 것
(C) 원고 편집자의 도움을 받는 것
(D) 온라인 카탈로그를 만드는 것

해설 남자가 대화 마지막 부분에 모든 사람이 변동 사항을 알고 있도록 각 규정서의 뒤쪽에 추가 페이지를 붙이는 방법을 제안하고 있으므로 (B)가 정답이다.

2.

M1: Hi, Calvin. How's your new place?
M2: Great so far. I want to start decorating my interior, so I've been thinking of getting houseplants.
M1: Victoria, you know a lot about growing indoor plants, right?
W: Yes, it's my hobby. I own a lot of plants myself.
M2: Cool! Can you recommend a place where I can buy some?
W: There's a massive garden center that I love shopping at, but **the roads around there are a bit confusing. Here, I can show you how to get there on this map.**

남1: 안녕하세요, 캘빈 씨. 새 집은 어떠신가요?
남2: 지금까지 아주 좋습니다. 제가 실내를 장식하기 시작하고 싶어서, 실내용 화초를 구입할 생각을 하고 있었습니다.
남1: 빅토리아 씨, 당신이 실내용 식물을 기르는 것에 관해 많이 알고 있는 게 맞죠?
여: 네, 그게 제 취미입니다. 제 자신도 식물을 많이 소유하고 있어요.
남2: 잘됐네요! 제가 몇 가지 구입할 수 있는 곳을 추천해 주시겠어요?
여: 제가 쇼핑하기 아주 좋아하는 엄청 큰 원예 용품점이 하나 있긴 한데, 그곳 주변 도로가 좀 헷갈려요. 여기, 이 지도에서 그곳으로 가는 방법을 알려 드릴 수 있어요.

어휘 houseplant 실내용 화초 massive 엄청나게 큰, 거대한 get there 그곳으로 가다

Q. 여자는 곧이어 무엇을 할 것인가?
(A) 웹 사이트 링크를 보내는 일
(B) 길 안내 정보를 제공하는 일
(C) 재고를 확인하는 일
(D) 판매업체에 전화하는 일

해설 여자가 대화 마지막 부분에 자신이 좋아하는 원예 용품점 주변 도로가 헷갈린다고 알리면서 지도에서 그곳으로 가는 방법을 알려 주겠다고 제안하고 있으므로 (B)가 정답이다.

Check-up Test

1. (B)	**2.** (C)	**3.** (A)	**4.** (C)	**5.** (B)
6. (B)	**7.** (C)	**8.** (D)	**9.** (A)	**10.** (B)
11. (D)	**12.** (A)	**13.** (A)	**14.** (A)	**15.** (B)
16. (D)	**17.** (B)	**18.** (A)		

Questions 1-3 refer to the following conversation.

M: 1 **The farm manager just reached out to me**, and 2 **he would like to install a ventilation system** in the greenhouse to improve airflow. He says 1 **the vegetables in there should grow in a balanced environment.**
W: Alright, we should get to work. Let's go over there now to measure the size of the work area so we know what tools we'll need to gather too.
M: OK. I think we might have 3 **parts we can use** from when we built a similar machine before. 3 **I can search for them** after we stop by the vegetable beds.

남: 농장 관리자님께서 막 제게 연락하셨는데, 공기 흐름을

개선하기 위해 온실 내에 환기 시스템을 설치하고 싶어 하세요. 그곳에 있는 채소들이 균형 잡힌 환경에서 자라야 한다고 말하고 계십니다.

여: 알겠어요, 작업에 착수해야겠네요. 우리가 어떤 도구들을 모아야 할지도 알도록 지금 그쪽으로 가서 작업 구역 크기를 측정해 봅시다.

남: 좋아요. 우리가 전에 유사한 기계를 조립했을 때 남은 것 중에서 이용할 수 있는 부품들이 있을 수도 있을 것 같아요. 우리가 채소 모판 구역에 들른 후에 제가 그것들을 찾아 볼 수 있어요.

어휘 ventilation 환기, 통풍 greenhouse 온실 airflow 공기 흐름 stop by ~에 들르다 bed (채소·꽃 등의) 모판, 화단

1. 화자들이 어디에 근무하고 있을 것 같은가?
(A) 지역 공원에
(B) 채소 농장에
(C) 과학 실험실에
(D) 자연 보호 구역에

해설 남자가 대화 초반부에 농장 관리자가 전화한 사실 및 채소를 균형 잡힌 환경에서 자라게 해 주는 방법을 언급하고 있으므로 (B)가 정답이다.

어휘 preserve n. 보호 구역

2. 화자들은 무엇을 하도록 요청 받았는가?
(A) 목재 구조물을 짓는 일
(B) 도구를 주문하는 일
(C) 환기 장치를 설치하는 일
(D) 일부 손상된 작물을 모으는 일

해설 남자가 대화 초반부에 농장 관리자가 환기 시스템을 설치하고 싶어 한다고 알린 뒤로 그 설치 작업의 진행과 관련해 이야기하고 있으므로 (C)가 정답이다.

어휘 crop 작물

3. 남자는 무엇을 하겠다고 하는가?
(A) 일부 물품을 찾아 보는 일
(B) 기계를 켜는 일
(C) 온라인으로 정보를 검색하는 일
(D) 수리소를 방문하는 일

해설 남자가 대화 후반부에 이용할 수 있는 부품을 언급하면서 자신이 그것들을 찾아 볼 수 있다고 알리고 있으므로 (A)가 정답이다.

Questions 4-6 refer to the following conversation.

M: Hey, excuse me. I've been waiting here at this platform for the past 10 minutes, but not a single train has come by.

W: Oh, yeah. Apparently, **4 the lights on one section of the track are being repaired, so this platform's closed.**

M: Well, I wish I had known earlier. **5 It's upsetting because now I'm late to my appointment!**

W: Sorry to hear that. **6 Why don't you use the free shuttle for the next few stations?** The stop is right outside the eastern exit.

남: 저, 실례합니다. 제가 지난 10분 동안 이곳 승강장에서 계속 기다리고 있는데, 단 한 대의 기차도 지나가지 않았습니다.

여: 아, 네. 분명, 선로의 한 구역에 있는 신호등이 수리되고 있어서, 이 승강장이 폐쇄되었을 겁니다.

남: 저, 더 일찍 알았다면 좋았을 거예요. 지금 제가 약속에 늦어서 속상하네요!

여: 그 말씀을 듣게 되어 유감입니다. 이후의 몇몇 역에 대한 무료 셔틀을 이용하시는 건 어떠세요? 그 정류장은 동쪽 출구 바로 바깥쪽에 있습니다.

어휘 come by 지나가다, 들렀다 가다 apparently 분명히, 보아하니 upsetting 속상하게 만드는, 화나게 만드는

4. 기차 승강장이 왜 폐쇄되어 있는가?
(A) 일부 열차 칸이 청소되고 있다.
(B) 화장실이 보수되고 있다.
(C) 신호등 수리 작업이 실시되고 있다.
(D) 정보 표시용 기기가 설치되고 있다.

해설 여자가 대화 중반부에 선로의 한 구역에 있는 신호등이 수리되고 있어서 승강장이 폐쇄되었다고 알리고 있으므로 (C)가 정답이다.

어휘 car (열차의) 칸 display 표시용 기기, 화면 표시 장치

5. 남자는 무엇에 대해 속상하다고 말하는가?
(A) 부정확한 길 안내 정보를 따라가는 것
(B) 약속에 늦은 것
(C) 승차권에 대해 과다 청구된 것
(D) 엉뚱한 역에서 환승하는 것

해설 대화 중반부에 남자가 약속 시간에 늦어서 속상하다고 말하고 있으므로 (B)가 정답이다.

6. 남자는 곧이어 무엇을 할 것 같은가?
(A) 안내 데스크를 방문하는 일
(B) 셔틀 버스를 타는 일
(C) 택시를 부르는 일
(D) 문제를 보고하는 일

해설 대화 후반부에 여자가 이후의 몇몇 역에 대한 무료 셔틀 버스를 이용하는 것을 제안하고 있으므로 (B)가 정답이다.

Questions 7-9 refer to the following conversation.

W: Hi, Eric. Our delivery driver who's usually assigned to go to Johnson's Wholesale is sick today. 7 **Could you make his 5 o'clock delivery instead?**
M: Sure, but I've never been there before, so 8 **I'll need directions to get to that store's loading dock.** Do you know the best way?
W: I suggest going through Benson Avenue to avoid customer traffic and then enter the back lot on Gerald Road. Oh, and 9 **make sure the store supervisor signs the delivery confirmation form when you arrive.**

여: 안녕하세요, 에릭 씨. 평소에 존슨즈 도매점으로 가도록 배정되시는 배송 기사님께서 오늘 몸이 편찮으십니다. 그 분의 5시 배송 작업을 대신 해 주시겠어요?
남: 네, 하지만 제가 전에 한 번도 그곳에 가 본 적이 없어서, 그 매장의 하역장으로 가는 길 안내 정보가 필요할 겁니다. 가장 좋은 길을 알고 계신가요?
여: 고객 차량들을 피할 수 있도록 벤슨 애비뉴를 통과해 가신 다음, 제럴드 로드에 있는 뒤쪽 주차장으로 들어가시기를 권해 드립니다. 아, 그리고 도착하시면 반드시 그곳 점장님께서 배송 확인서에 서명하시도록 해 주시기 바랍니다.

어휘 be assigned to do ~하도록 배정되다 loading dock 하역장 lot 주차장

7. 여자는 남자에게 무엇을 하도록 요청하는가?
(A) 차량에 짐을 싣는 일
(B) 공급업체에 연락하는 일
(C) 동료 직원의 업무를 맡는 일
(D) 배송 날짜를 변경하는 일

해설 여자가 대화 시작 부분에 몸이 아픈 한 배송 기사를 언급하면서 남자에게 그 사람의 5시 배송을 대신해 달라고 요청하고 있으므로 (C)가 정답이다.

8. 남자는 무엇이 필요하다고 말하는가?
(A) 제품 목록
(B) 인쇄된 거래 내역서
(C) 몇몇 연락 정보
(D) 매장으로 가는 길 안내 정보

해설 대화 중반부에 남자가 한 번도 가 본 적이 없다는 말과 함께 매장의 하역장으로 가는 길 안내 정보가 필요할 거라고 알리고 있으므로 (D)가 정답이다.

9. 여자는 남자에게 무엇을 하도록 상기시키는가?
(A) 서명을 받아 오는 일
(B) 다른 업체를 방문하는 일
(C) 특정 구역에서 대기하는 일
(D) 소속 부서장에게 알리는 일

해설 여자가 대화 후반부에 남자에게 매장에 도착해서 반드시 그곳 점장에게 배송 확인서에 서명하게 해달라고 당부하고 있으므로 (A)가 정답이다.

Questions 10-12 refer to the following conversation.

W: Hello, I just stumbled upon this place. It looks really nice! Seems like all your equipment is pretty new.
M: Welcome in. We opened about a month ago, and 10 **we have high-tech weight and cardio machines and lots of other workout accessories.**
W: Good to know! 11 **I might join since my workplace is close by.**
M: Here's a pamphlet with each level of membership we offer. Let me know if you have any questions.
W: Thank you. Do you offer yoga classes by any chance? I've been interested in yoga these days.
M: Yes, we have a studio for that. Actually, 12 **I'd be happy to show you around our facilities if you'd like.**

여: 안녕하세요, 제가 이곳을 막 우연히 발견했습니다. 정말 멋져 보이네요! 모든 장비가 꽤 새것인 것처럼 보여요.
남: 환영합니다. 저희가 약 한 달 전에 개장했는데, 최신 웨이트 운동 기계와 심장 강화 운동 기계, 그리고 많은 다른 운동 부대 용품을 보유하고 있습니다.
여: 알아두면 좋은 정보네요! 제 직장이 근처에 있어서 가입할지도 모릅니다.

남: 여기 저희가 제공해 드리는 각 수준별 회원 자격 정보가 담긴 안내 책자입니다. 어떤 질문이든 있으시면 제게 알려 주십시오.
여: 감사합니다. 혹시 요가 강좌도 제공하시나요? 제가 요즘 요가에 관심이 생겨서요.
남: 네, 저희가 그에 필요한 스튜디오를 보유하고 있습니다. 실은, 원하시면 기꺼이 저희 시설을 둘러 보시게 해 드리겠습니다.

어휘 stumble upon ~을 우연히 발견하다 high-tech 최신의, 첨단의 cardio 심장 강화 운동 by any chance 혹시

10. 남자는 어디에 근무하는가?
(A) 장비 대여 시설에
(B) 피트니스 센터에
(C) 가정 용품 매장에
(D) 컴퓨터 매장에

해설 남자가 대화 중반부에 최신 웨이트 운동 기계와 심장 강화 운동 기계, 그리고 많은 다른 운동 부대 용품을 보유하고 있다는 사실을 밝히고 있으므로 (B)가 정답이다.

11. 여자의 방문 목적은 무엇인가?
(A) 한 가지 과정에 등록하고 있다.
(B) 상담을 받고 싶어 한다.
(C) 한 제품을 수리 받아야 한다.
(D) 회원권에 관심이 있다.

해설 대화 중반부에 운동 장비에 관한 남자의 설명을 들은 여자가 직장이 근처에 있어서 가입할지도 모른다고 말하고 있으므로 (D)가 정답이다.

12. 여자는 곧이어 무엇을 할 것 같은가?
(A) 견학하는 일
(B) 동영상을 시청하는 일
(C) 무료 선물을 받는 일
(D) 회의를 연기하는 일

해설 남자가 대화 후반부에 여자에게 시설을 둘러 보게 해 줄 수 있다고 제안하고 있으므로 (A)가 정답이다.

Questions 13-15 refer to the following conversation with three speakers.

M1: Excuse me, Ms. Garland. **13 Our technician, Steven, is still inspecting the side fence**, but we'll be finished soon.
W: How's it looking so far?
M1: Oh, Steven's coming now, so he can explain in detail.
M2: Hello. I looked at the entire perimeter, and **14 a majority of the sections are still upright with no structural damage. Only about six planks of wood will need replacement** because of the fallen tree branches.
W: **14 What a relief!** I'm glad we won't need any major repairs then.
M2: **15 Why don't you close your shop for a few hours** while we do the work? It'll be noisy.
M1: **15 Is Thursday morning okay?**
W: **15 Yes, that works for me.**

남1: 실례합니다, 갈랜드 씨. 저희 기술자이신 스티븐 씨께서 여전히 측면 담장을 점검하고 계시는데, 곧 끝마칠 겁니다.
여: 지금까지 어때 보이시나요?
남1: 아, 스티븐 씨께서 지금 오시고 계셔서, 상세하게 설명해 드릴 수 있습니다.
남2: 안녕하세요. 제가 전체 경계면을 살펴 봤는데, 대부분의 구역이 구조적 손상 없이 여전히 똑바로 서 있는 상태입니다. 오직 약 6개의 목재 판자만 떨어진 나뭇가지들 때문에 교체가 필요할 겁니다.
여: 정말 다행입니다! 그럼 저희가 어떤 대대적인 수리 작업도 필요하지 않을 것이라는 사실이 기쁘네요.
남2: 저희가 그 작업을 하는 몇 시간 동안 매장 문을 닫으시면 어떨까요? 시끄러울 겁니다.
남1: 목요일 오전도 괜찮으신가요?
여: 네, 저는 좋습니다.

어휘 perimeter 경계(면) a majority of 대부분의 upright 똑바로 서 있는 plank 판자, 널빤지 relief 다행인 것, 안심인 것

13. 남자들이 어떤 종류의 업체에 근무하고 있을 것 같은가?
(A) 담장 설치 전문 회사
(B) 배관 서비스 업체
(C) 철물 공급업체
(D) 이사 전문 회사

해설 남자 한 명이 대화를 시작하면서 소속 업체의 기술자인 스티븐 씨가 측면 담장을 점검하고 있다는 사실을 언급하고 있으므로 (A)가 정답이다.

14. 여자는 왜 안심하는가?

(A) 일부 손상이 사소하다.

(B) 비용 견적이 감당할 수 있다.

(C) 일부 직원이 시간이 난다.

(D) 시에서 허가증을 발급했다.

해설 남자 한 명이 대화 중반부에 대부분의 구역이 구조적 손상 없이 여전히 똑바로 서 있는 상태라는 점과 오직 약 6개의 목재 판자만 교체하면 된다는 점을 알리자, 여자가 안도의 말을 하고 있다. 이는 손상이 심각하지 않다는 점에 대해 안도하는 것이므로 (A)가 정답이다.

15. 여자는 목요일에 무엇을 할 것인가?

(A) 출장을 떠나는 일

(B) 일시적으로 매장을 닫는 일

(C) 일부 전동 공구를 구입하는 일

(D) 새 장비를 설치하는 일

해설 대화 후반부에 남자 한 명이 작업하는 몇 시간 동안 매장 문을 닫도록 제안하는 것에 대해 다른 남자가 목요일 오전도 괜찮은지 묻자 여자가 좋다고 대답하고 있으므로 (B)가 정답이다.

Questions 16-18 refer to the following conversation with three speakers.

M1: Thanks for coming, everyone. I wanted to know **17** **how our sales have been going** after we launched **16** **our salted caramel chocolate bars**. Any comments, Jess?

W: So far, **17** **sales are up by seven percent compared to last quarter**, and we anticipate increasing numbers going into the holiday season.

M1: Jackson, do you have the exact figures for those chocolate bars?

M2: I do. We've sold about 17,000 units in the past two weeks.

M1: Awesome! I'm curious how our previous flavors have done in comparison. Jess, **18** **could you compile a list of all our special flavors we've released during the holidays, and bring it to our next meeting?**

W: Okay, sure thing!

남1: 와 주셔서 감사합니다, 여러분. 저는 우리가 솔티드 캐러멜 초콜릿 바를 출시한 뒤로 우리 판매량이 어떻게 되어 왔는지 알고 싶었습니다. 하실 말씀 있으신가요, 제스 씨?

여: 지금까지, 판매량이 지난 분기에 비해 7퍼센트 상승했는데, 휴가철로 접어 들면서 수치가 오를 것으로 예상하고 있습니다.

남1: 잭슨 씨, 그 초콜릿 바에 대한 정확한 수치 자료를 갖고 계신가요?

남2: 갖고 있습니다. 지난 2주 동안 약 17,000개를 판매했습니다.

남1: 아주 좋습니다! 우리의 이전 맛들과 비교해 볼 때 어땠는지 궁금하네요. 제스 씨, 우리가 휴가철에 출시했던 모든 특별 맛들에 대한 목록을 정리하신 다음, 다음 회의 시간에 가져와 주실 수 있나요?

여: 네, 알겠습니다!

어휘 anticipate ~을 예상하다, 기대하다 in comparison 비교해 (볼 때) compile (자료 등을 모아) ~을 정리하다

16. 해당 회사는 무엇을 생산하는가?

(A) 에너지 음료

(B) 쿠키

(C) 팝콘

(D) 초콜릿

해설 남자 한 명이 대화 초반부에 자사의 솔티드 캐러멜 초콜릿 바 제품을 언급하고 있으므로 (D)가 정답이다.

17. 화자들은 주로 무엇을 이야기하고 있는가?

(A) 생산 지연

(B) 판매 수치

(C) 계절 판촉 행사

(D) 연구 조사

해설 대화 초반부에 남자 한 명이 제품 판매량이 어떻게 되어 왔는지 알고 싶다고 말하자 여자가 판매량이 지난 분기에 비해 7퍼센트 상승한 사실을 언급하고 있으므로 (B)가 정답이다.

18. 여자는 다음 회의를 위해 무엇을 하도록 요청받는가?

(A) 제품 목록을 만드는 일

(B) 평면도를 수정하는 일

(C) 포스터 디자인을 만드는 일

(D) 재무제표를 검토하는 일

해설 대화 후반부에 남자가 한 명이 여자에게 휴가철에 출시했던 모든 특별 맛들에 대한 목록을 정리해서 다음 회의 시간에 가져오도록 요청하고 있으므로 (A)가 정답이다.

어휘 financial statement 재무제표

▶ Playlist 10

만점강사는 의도파악 문제를 어떻게 풀까?

의도파악

여: 당신의 실험실 실험에서 나온 긍정적인 결과에 대해 축하드립니다!
남: 감사합니다. 저는 저희가 적어도 8번 정도 테스트를 진행해야 할까봐 걱정했지만, 2차 시도에서 저희가 원했던 화학 반응을 얻어 냈습니다!
여: 그 결과물과 함께 제출하셔야 할 양식이 하나 있습니다. 그게 우리 네하 연구소장님께 전달되어야 할 것 같습니다.
남: 저, 네하 소장님의 마지막 날이 이번 주 금요일입니다.
여: 아, 정말인가요? 그분께서 떠나시는 걸 보는 게 슬프네요. 어느 분께서 후임자가 되실지 아시는 거라도 있으세요?
남: 아니요, 하지만 우리가 진행하고 있는 아주 많은 다양한 연구 프로젝트가 있기 때문에 우리의 모든 운영을 조정해 주실 수 있는 리더가 분명 필요합니다.

Q. 남자가 "네하 소장님의 마지막 날이 이번 주 금요일입니다" 라고 말할 때 무엇을 암시하는가?
(A) 네하 씨를 위한 파티에 참석할 계획이다.
(B) 자신이 새 리더 역할을 맡을 것이다.
(C) 네하 씨에게 양식을 제출하지 않을 것이다.
(D) 한 프로젝트 마감기한이 연장될 수 없다.

Practice

1. (B) **2.** (B)

1.

M: Hey, Simmone. Sorry I was late to the meeting this morning. Union Station was so chaotic today.
W: It's okay. You didn't miss much. Did something happen?
M: They were doing some emergency electrical work on one of the light rail tracks, so there was one less train operating. You see, **the train's my only way of crossing the Bay Bridge!**
W: Actually, the city does run a commuter shuttle.
M: **I didn't know that!** Do you know where I can find more information?
W: Sure, I'll send you a link to download the app for it.

남: 저, 시먼 씨. 오늘 아침에 회의 시간에 늦어서 죄송합니다. 유니언 역이 오늘 아주 혼잡했습니다.
여: 괜찮습니다. 놓치신 게 많지 않았습니다. 무슨 일이 있었나요?
남: 사람들이 경전철 선로들 중 한 곳에서 어떤 긴급 전기 작업을 하고 있어서, 운행하는 열차가 한 대 더 적었습니다. 그러니까, 그 열차가 베이 브리지를 건너는 제 유일한 방법입니다!
여: 사실, 시에서 통근자용 셔틀 버스를 운영하고 있습니다.
남: 그런 줄을 몰랐습니다! 제가 어디서 추가 정보를 찾을 수 있는지 아시나요?
여: 물론이죠, 그에 필요한 앱을 다운로드할 수 있는 링크를 보내 드릴게요.

어휘 chaotic 혼잡한, 혼란스러운 commuter 통근자

Q. 여자가 왜 "시에서 통근자용 셔틀 버스를 운영하고 있습니다"라고 말하는가?
(A) 한 가지 서비스가 무료임을 나타내기 위해
(B) 잘못 알고 있는 생각을 바로잡기 위해
(C) 격려를 제공하기 위해
(D) 한 가지 정부 정책을 칭찬하기 위해

해설 남자가 대화 중반부에 특정 열차가 자신이 베이 브리지를 건너는 유일한 방법이라고 언급하자, 여자가 '시에서 통근자용 셔틀 버스를 운영하고 있습니다'라고 말하는 흐름이다. 이는 또 다른 이동 방법이 있음을 알리는 것으로 남자가 잘못 알고 있음을 지적하는 말이므로 (B)가 정답이다.

어휘 mistaken 잘못 알고 있는 assumption 생각, 추정 encouragement 격려, 권장

2.

W: Hi, Mr. Addison. This is Ritta Griffin calling from Florence Farms. Regarding your order of organic peaches, I'm sorry to say that we can only give you three boxes.
M: Oh, no. That's unfortunate. Our bakery is catering for a big event this Friday, and we planned to serve peach cheesecake slices as one of the desserts.
W: Oh… Unfortunately, a larger order came in before yours, and our harvest just hasn't been strong this month. **We do have mangoes. Would you like those instead?**
M: Well, our clients personally requested that flavor.

W: Alright then. How about I call some other nearby farms in the area to see if they can send you more?
M: I'd really appreciate that. Thank you!

여: 안녕하세요, 애디슨 씨. 저는 플로렌스 팜즈에서 전화 드리는 리타 그리핀입니다. 귀하의 유기농 복숭아 주문과 관련해, 저희가 겨우 세 상자만 제공해 드릴 수 있다는 사실을 말씀 드리게 되어 죄송합니다.
남: 아, 이런. 안타깝네요. 저희 제과점이 이번 주 금요일에 중요한 행사를 위해 출장 음식을 제공하는데, 디저트들 중 하나로 복숭아 치즈 조각 케이크를 제공할 계획이었습니다.
여: 아... 유감스럽게도, 더 큰 주문이 귀하의 것에 앞서 들어왔는데, 저희 수확량이 단지 이번 달에 많지 않았습니다. 망고는 분명히 있습니다. 대신 이것으로 해 드릴까요?
남: 음, 저희 고객들께서 직접 그 맛을 요청하셨습니다.
여: 그럼, 알겠습니다. 제가 지역 내에 있는 근처의 몇몇 다른 농장에 전화해서 더 보내 드릴 수 있는지 알아 보면 어떨까요?
남: 그렇게 해 주시면 정말 감사하겠습니다. 고맙습니다!

어휘 cater for ~에 출장 음식을 제공하다 serve (음식 등) ~을 제공하다, 내오다 harvest 수확(량)

Q. 남자가 "저희 고객들께서 직접 그 맛을 요청하셨습니다"라고 말할 때 무엇을 의미하는가?
(A) 아직 승인을 받지 못했다.
(B) 변경이 불가능하다.
(C) 한 고객이 수년 동안 단골이었다.
(D) 한 가지 주문이 아주 급하다.

해설 대화 중반부에 여자가 망고는 분명히 있다고 언급하면서 대신 이것으로 할지 묻는 것에 대해 남자가 '저희 고객들께서 직접 그 맛을 요청하셨습니다'라고 반응하는 흐름이다. 이는 고객들의 요청으로 인해 여자가 제안하는 다른 재료로 바꾸는 것이 불가능하다는 뜻이므로 (B)가 정답이다.

어휘 loyal 단골인, 충성스러운

빈출 의도파악 연습

1. (B) **2.** (A) **3.** (A) **4.** (A)

1. 여자가 "이 자료는 세이델 박사님의 논문에서 온 것이 아닌가요?"라고 말할 때 암시하는 것은 무엇인가?

남: 저와 함께 제 슬라이드를 빠르게 검토해주실 수 있으신가요?
여: 물론이죠.
남: 제가 모든 그래프와 도표에 대한 적절한 인용을 포함했는지 확실히 하고 싶습니다.
여: 확인해보죠... 네... 아, 잠시만요! 이 자료는 세이델 박사님의 논문에서 온 것이 아닌가요?
남: 오! 네, 맞습니다. 그걸 발견해 주셔서 감사합니다.

(A) 연구 논문이 도움이 될 것이다.
(B) 슬라이드가 일부 정보를 포함해야 한다.

2. 남자가 "여름에는 이 곳이 무척 더워질 수도 있습니다"라고 말할 때 무엇을 의미하는가?

여: 새롭게 보수된 우리 회의실에 오신 것을 환영합니다. 어떠한 의견들이 있으신가요?
남1: 공간이 매우 넓어서 부서 회의에 완벽하다고 생각합니다. 큰 창들이 제공하는 풍경들도 좋아요.
남2: 흠... 아시다시피, 여름에는 이 곳이 무척 더워질 수도 있습니다.
여: 그건 사실입니다. 제가 건물 관리인에게 우리가 창문 블라인드를 설치할 수 있을지 물어보겠습니다.

(A) 공간이 너무 많은 햇빛을 받는다.
(B) 공간이 가끔 사용되어야 한다.

3. 남자는 왜 "저희 루프탑 좌석 중 일부는 이용 가능합니다." 라고 말하는가?

남: 안녕하세요, 엠브로스 비스트로에 오신 것을 환영합니다. 두 분이신가요?
여: 네. 대기 시간이 얼마나 긴가요? 저희가 몇 시간 후에 기차를 타야 해서요.
남: 내부 테이블에 앉으시려면 약 20분에서 30분정도 걸릴 겁니다. 저희 루프탑 좌석 중 일부는 이용 가능합니다.
여: 오... 하지만 오늘 밤은 조금 춥네요.

(A) 대안을 제시하기 위해
(B) 오해를 바로 잡기 위해

4. 남자가 "그건 저희 예약 시스템에 중대한 조정을 하는 것을 수반할 겁니다."라고 말할 때 암시하는 것은 무엇인가?

여: 많은 고객분들이 예약 시간에 의사들과 더 많은 시간을 갖고 싶다고 언급했습니다. 현재, 의사와 환자가 이야기할 시간은 약 15분뿐입니다. 환자 한 명당 할당 시간을 늘리는 것이 가능할까요?
남: 그건 저희 예약 시스템에 중대한 조정을 하는 것을 수반할 겁니다. 저희 기관의 이사진이 최종 승인도 해야 하고요.

(A) 변경사항이 시행될 것에 의문을 가진다.
(B) 기술적인 지원이 필요하다고 생각한다.

Check-up Test

1. (B)	**2.** (A)	**3.** (C)	**4.** (D)	**5.** (B)
6. (B)	**7.** (C)	**8.** (D)	**9.** (A)	**10.** (D)
11. (A)	**12.** (B)	**13.** (C)	**14.** (B)	**15.** (A)
16. (A)	**17.** (A)	**18.** (B)		

Questions 1-3 refer to the following conversation.

M: Hello. **1 Thanks for coming by my booth at this trade show.** I'm Novak from Fonta Systems.
W: Pleased to meet you. I'm Rebecca from Hylab Creative. May I ask what kind of products your company makes?
M: Sure. We develop software tools for project management, which helps all kinds of businesses streamline their operations. **2 The version I'm showcasing now is for a workforce of up to 30 people.**
W: Oh, we have over a hundred workers.
M: Well, **3 let me give you this chart here with our full product lineup.**

남: 안녕하세요. 이번 무역 박람회의 저희 부스에 들러 주셔서 감사합니다. 저는 폰타 시스템즈 사의 노박입니다.
여: 만나서 반갑습니다. 저는 하이랩 크리에이티브의 레베카입니다. 소속 회사에서 어떤 종류의 제품을 만드는지 여쭤 봐도 될까요?
남: 물론입니다. 저희는 프로젝트 관리에 필요한 소프트웨어 툴을 개발하는데, 모든 종류의 업체가 각자의 운영을 간소화하는 데 도움을 드립니다. 제가 지금 선보이고 있는 이 버전은 최대 30명의 직원들이 있는 곳을 위한 것입니다.
여: 아, 저희는 100명이 넘는 직원들이 있어요.
남: 그러시면, 여기 저희 전체 제품 목록이 있는 이 차트를 드리겠습니다.

어휘 come by ~에 들르다 streamline ~을 간소화하다 showcase ~을 선보이다 workforce 직원들, 인력

1. 화자들은 어디에 있는가?
(A) 취업 박람회에
(B) 무역 박람회에
(C) 워크숍에
(D) 모금 행사에

해설 남자가 대화 시작 부분에 무역 박람회에 있는 자사 부스에 들른 것에 대해 감사의 인사를 전하고 있으므로 (B)가 정답이다.

2. 여자가 "저희는 100명이 넘는 직원들이 있어요"라고 말할 때 무엇을 의미하는가?
(A) 한 제품이 자신의 회사에 유용하지 않을 수도 있다.
(B) 일부 직원이 충분한 교육을 받지 못했다.
(C) 자신의 회사 사무실이 곧 확장될 것이다.
(D) 자신이 최근 관리자로 선임되었다.

해설 대화 중반부에 남자가 제품의 한 가지 버전을 언급하면서 최대 30명의 직원들이 있는 곳을 위한 것이라고 알리자, 여자가 '저희는 100명이 넘는 직원들이 있어요'라고 말하는 흐름이다. 이는 인원 규모가 달라서 자신의 회사에 맞지 않는다는 의미를 나타내는 것이므로 (A)가 정답이다.

어휘 sufficient 충분한 appoint ~을 선임하다, 임명하다

3. 남자는 여자에게 무엇을 주는가?
(A) 신청서
(B) 명함
(C) 차트
(D) 지도

해설 대화 마지막 부분에 남자가 전체 제품 목록이 있는 차트를 주겠다고 알리고 있으므로 (C)가 정답이다.

Questions 4-6 refer to the following conversation.

M: Valerie, **4 after reviewing the production process for our brownies**, I noticed that there's a part we could try to modify for improvement.
W: As in, **5 to improve our manufacturing times?**
M: Yep. You know, once the brownies are done cooling, the trays are usually transferred one by one to the packaging area.
W: I see your point. If we use portable racks instead of stationary ones, we can move the brownies over more quickly.
M: Right! This minor adjustment can make a big impact on our output numbers.
W: But isn't that equipment expensive?
M: **6 I've already prepared some cost projections.**

남: 발레리 씨, 우리 브라우니 생산 과정을 살펴 본 끝에, 우리가 개선을 위해 변경하도록 노력해 볼 수 있는 부분이 하나 있다는 걸 알게 되었습니다.

여: 말하자면, 우리 제조 시간을 개선하기 위해서요?
남: 네. 그러니까, 일단 브라우니를 식히는 작업이 완료되는 대로, 그 쟁반들이 일반적으로 하나씩 포장 구역으로 옮겨집니다.
여: 무슨 말씀이신지 알겠어요. 고정되어 있는 것 대신 이동 가능한 받침대를 이용하면, 브라우니를 더 빨리 옮길 수 있죠.
남: 그렇습니다! 이 사소한 조정이 우리 생산량 수치에 큰 영향을 미칠 수 있습니다.
여: 하지만 그 장비가 비싸지 않나요?
남: 제가 이미 몇몇 비용 견적을 준비해 두었습니다

어휘 modify ~을 변경하다, 개조하다 as in 말하자면, 다시 말해서 be done -ing ~하는 것을 완료하다 I see your point 무슨 말인지 알겠습니다 portable 이동 가능한, 휴대용의 rack 받침대, 거치대 stationary 고정되어 있는, 정지된 output 생산량, 산출량 projection 견적, 예상

4. 화자들은 어디에 근무하고 있을 것 같은가?
(A) 사무실 구내식당에
(B) 소매 식품점에
(C) 창고에
(D) 공장에

해설 남자가 대화를 시작하면서 자사의 브라우니 생산 과정을 살펴 보는 일을 한 사실을 밝히고 있는데, 이는 제품을 생산하는 공장에서 할 수 있는 일이므로 (D)가 정답이다.

5. 남자가 "그 쟁반들이 일반적으로 하나씩 포장 구역으로 옮겨집니다"라고 말할 때 무엇을 암시하는가?
(A) 한 가지 기기가 이용하기에 실용적이지 않다.
(B) 한 가지 과정이 시간 소모적이다.
(C) 일부 배송비가 합리적이지 않다.
(D) 인력이 충분히 있지 않다.

해설 남자의 개선 방법을 들은 여자가 대화 중반부에 제조 시간을 개선하기 위한 것인지 묻자, 남자가 '그 쟁반들이 일반적으로 하나씩 포장 구역으로 옮겨집니다'라고 대답하는 흐름이다. 이는 제조 시간과 관련해 개선이 필요한 한 가지 과정을 구체적으로 언급한 것이므로 (B)가 정답이다.

어휘 practical 실용적인 time-consuming 시간 소모적인 unreasonable 합리적이지 않은

6. 남자가 여자에게 무엇을 보여 줄 것인가?
(A) 프로젝트 제안서
(B) 비용 견적서
(C) 설계도
(D) 달력

해설 대화 마지막 부분에 남자가 이미 몇몇 비용 견적을 준비해 두었다고 밝히고 있으므로 (B)가 정답이다.

Questions 7-9 refer to the following conversation.

W: Hey, Omar. Did you see our new post on social media?
M: I didn't. **7 I've been prepping for my kickboxing class.**
W: **7 8 Our gym is planning to open another location in the city next to us. But I feel like its too close to our facility here.**
M: Well, this region is heavily populated.
W: Yeah, that's true. **9 We should probably hire more people** though, since we definitely don't have enough staff to manage both locations.

여: 안녕하세요, 오마르 씨. 소셜 미디어에서 우리의 새 게시물을 보셨나요?
남: 보지 못했습니다. 제 킥복싱 수업을 계속 준비하고 있었습니다.
여: 우리 체육관이 도시 내에서 우리 옆에 지점을 하나 더 개장할 계획을 세우고 있어요. 하지만 저는 여기 있는 우리 시설과 너무 가까운 것 같아요.
남: 저, 이 지역은 인구가 밀집되어 있어요.
여: 네, 사실이에요. 하지만 우리가 아마 더 많은 사람을 고용해야 할 텐데, 우리는 분명히 두 지점 모두 관리할 직원이 충분히 있지 않기 때문입니다.

어휘 prep for ~을 준비하다 heavily populated 인구가 밀집된 definitely 분명히, 확실히

7. 화자들은 어디에 근무하고 있을 것 같은가?
(A) 서점에
(B) 병원에
(C) 피트니스 센터에
(D) 수상 스포츠 시설에

해설 대화 초반부에 남자는 자신의 킥복싱 수업을 준비하고 있었다고 말하고 있고, 여자는 소속 업체를 Our gym으로 지칭하고 있으므로 (C)가 정답이다.

8. 남자가 왜 "이 지역은 인구가 밀집되어 있어요"라고 말하는가?
(A) 비교를 하기 위해
(B) 한 정책에 동의하지 않기 위해
(C) 긴 대기 시간에 대해 주의를 주기 위해
(D) 한 가지 결정사항을 설명하기 위해

해설 여자가 대화 중반부에 바로 옆에 지점을 하나 더 개장하려는 계획과 관련해 너무 가까운 것 같다고 말하자, 남자가 '이 지역은 인구가 밀집되어 있어요'라고 반응하는 흐름이다. 이는 그만큼 수요가 많다는 뜻으로서 바로 옆에 지점을 하나 더 개장하려는 결정에 대한 이유에 해당하므로 (D)가 정답이다.

9. 여자는 업체가 무엇을 해야 한다고 생각하는가?
(A) 더 많은 직원을 고용하는 일
(B) 마케팅 전략을 변경하는 일
(C) 몇몇 자원 봉사자를 모집하는 일
(D) 새로운 차량을 구입하는 일

해설 대화 후반부에 여자가 더 많은 사람을 고용해야 한다는 의견을 밝히고 있으므로 (A)가 정답이다.

Questions 10-12 refer to the following conversation.

M: Candice, do you have time to discuss our amusement park's concession stands? 10 **I want to think of more snack options that our visitors might like.**
W: Sure. 11 12 **Maybe we can figure that out by giving customers a brief survey to complete** as part of the process for buying tickets online. It will show us what kinds of food people want to have.
M: 12 **I like that idea.**
W: Making a draft is pretty easy.
M: Okay, sounds good. Thank you!

남: 캔디스 씨, 우리 놀이공원의 매점들에 관해 이야기하실 시간이 있으신가요? 우리 방문객들께서 좋아하실 수도 있는 추가 간식 선택사항을 생각해 보고 싶습니다.
여: 물론입니다. 아마 온라인에서 입장권을 구입하는 것에 대한 과정의 일환으로 고객들께 작성 완료할 간단한 설문 조사지를 제공해서 그 부분을 파악할 수 있을 거예요. 그게 우리에게 어떤 종류의 식품을 사람들이 먹고 싶어 하는지 보여 줄 겁니다.
남: 그 생각이 마음에 들어요.
여: 초안을 작성하는 게 꽤 쉽습니다.
남: 네, 좋은 것 같아요. 감사합니다!

어휘 concession stand 매점 figure A out A를 파악하다, 알아내다 brief 간단한, 짧은 as part of ~의 일환으로

10. 남자는 무엇을 이야기하고 싶어 하는가?
(A) 손님 수
(B) 입장권 가격
(C) 예산 할당액
(D) 간식 선택사항

해설 대화 시작 부분에 남자가 매점에서 방문객들께서 좋아할 수도 있는 추가 간식 선택사항을 생각해 보고 싶다는 말로 대화 주제를 밝히고 있으므로 (D)가 정답이다.

어휘 allocation 할당(되는 것), 배정(되는 것)

11. 여자는 무엇을 제안하는가?
(A) 고객 의견을 얻는 것
(B) 결제 과정을 간소화하는 것
(C) 새로운 놀이기구를 짓는 것
(D) 특별 상품을 제공하는 것

해설 남자의 말을 들은 여자가 고객들에게 작성 완료할 간단한 설문 조사지를 제공해서 파악하는 방법을 제안하고 있다. 이는 고객들의 의견을 들어 보려는 것이므로 (A)가 정답이다.

어휘 simplify ~을 간소화하다

12. 여자가 "초안을 작성하는 게 꽤 쉽습니다"라고 말할 때 의미하는 것은 무엇인가?
(A) 이미 문제를 해결했다.
(B) 한 가지 일을 완료할 의향이 있다.
(C) 일부 정보가 곧 발송될 것이다.
(D) 보고서가 빠르게 만들어질 수 있다.

해설 대화 중반부에 여자가 설문 조사를 이용하는 방법을 제안하는 것에 대해 남자가 마음에 든다는 생각을 밝히자, 여자가 '초안을 작성하는 게 꽤 쉽습니다'라고 말하는 흐름이다. 이는 자신의 경험상 그렇게 하는 것이 쉽기 때문에 그 일을 돕고자 하는 의향을 나타내는 것이므로 (B)가 정답이다.

Questions 13-15 refer to the following conversation.

M: Hello there. Can I help you find anything here at our garden center?
W: 13 **I recently built a swimming pool in my backyard**, but I want to decorate the surrounding land with some nice plants.
M: 14 **What exactly are you looking for?**
W: I'm interested in desert plants, but this is my first time buying succulents.
M: I see. Well, in general, all succulents are very low-maintenance and perfect for brightening up any space. First off, have you decided if you want to display them in pots or containers?
W: No, not yet.

M: Alright then. **15 Here's a photo catalog with a huge variety of succulent arrangements.** Maybe it can give you some inspiration.

남: 안녕하세요, 이곳 저희 원예 센터에서 무엇이든 찾으시도록 도와 드릴까요?
여: 제가 최근에 저희 뒤뜰에 수영장을 하나 만들었는데, 몇몇 멋진 식물로 그 주변의 땅을 장식하고 싶습니다.
남: 정확히 무엇을 찾고 계신가요?
여: 제가 사막 식물에 관심이 있긴 한데, 이번이 다육 식물을 구입하는 게 처음입니다.
남: 알겠습니다. 저, 일반적으로, 모든 다육 식물은 손이 아주 많이 가지 않으며, 어떤 공간이든 활기를 더하기에 완벽합니다. 가장 먼저, 화분에 담아 진열하실 건지, 아니면 용기에 담아 진열하실 건지 결정하셨나요?
여: 아니요, 아직이요.
남: 그럼, 좋습니다. 여기 엄청나게 다양한 다육 식물 배치가 담긴 사진 카탈로그가 있습니다. 아마 이것이 영감을 좀 제공해 드릴 수 있을 겁니다.

어휘 surrounding 주변의 succulents (선인장 같은) 다육 식물 low-maintenance 손이 많이 가지 않는 brighten up ~에 활기를 더해 주다, ~을 밝게 만들어 주다 pot 화분 arrangement 배치, 조치, 조정 inspiration 영감(을 주는 것)

13. 여자는 최근에 무엇을 했는가?
(A) 취미로 수영을 다시 시작했다.
(B) 자신만의 농산물을 기르기 시작했다.
(C) 자신의 건물에 수영장을 지었다.
(D) 한 행사장을 장식하는 일이 배정되었다.

해설 여자가 대화 초반부에 최근 뒤뜰에 수영장을 하나 만들었다는 사실을 밝히고 있으므로 (C)가 정답이다.

어휘 pick up ~을 다시 시작하다 be assigned to do ~하는 일이 배정되다

14. 여자가 "이번이 다육 식물을 구입하는 게 처음입니다"라고 말할 때 암시하는 것은 무엇인가?
(A) 선택 가능한 종류에 깊은 인상을 받았다.
(B) 조언이 좀 필요하다.
(C) 특정 구역을 찾을 수 없다.
(D) 가격을 알고 싶어 한다.

해설 대화 중반부에 남자가 여자에게 정확히 무엇을 찾고 있는지 묻자, 여자가 '이번이 다육 식물을 구입하는 게 처음입니다'라고 대답하는 흐름이다. 이는 처음이기 때문에 도움이 필요하다는 뜻이므로 (B)가 정답이다.

15. 여자는 곧이어 무엇을 할 것 같은가?
(A) 카탈로그를 쭉 훑어 보는 일
(B) 몇몇 제품을 재배치하는 일
(C) 옥외 진열품을 확인해 보는 일
(D) 저장 용기를 가득 채우는 일

해설 남자가 대화 후반부에 여자에게 다양한 다육 식물 배치가 담긴 사진 카탈로그를 건네는 말을 하고 있으므로 (A)가 정답이다.

어휘 look through ~을 쭉 훑어 보다 rearrange ~을 재배치하다, 재조정하다 fill up ~을 가득 채우다

Questions 16-18 refer to the following conversation.

W: I'm really excited to hear Marvin Baker speak later today. I used to study lots of his articles and papers on quality assurance when I was a student. **16 This business innovation conference has been great so far.**
M: I agree. The turnout has been surprising. Look at how almost all the seats are already taken! **17 Why don't we just sit over there?**
W: In the back? We should try harder. **17 I want to see the presentation slides up close.**
M: Oh, but you don't have to worry too much about that. I saw that **18 the presentation handouts are being passed out by the entrance.** I can grab one for you right now.

여: 저는 오늘 이따가 마빈 베이커 씨가 연설하시는 것을 듣게 되어 정말 흥분돼요. 제가 학생이었을 때 품질 보증에 관한 이분의 기사와 논문을 많이 공부하곤 했거든요. 이 비즈니스 혁신 컨퍼런스가 지금까지 아주 좋았습니다.
남: 동감이에요. 참석률이 놀라울 정도였어요. 어떻게 거의 모든 좌석이 이미 차 있는지 보세요! 그냥 저기 저쪽에 앉으면 어떨까요?
여: 뒤쪽에요? 더 열심히 찾아 봐요. 저는 발표 슬라이드를 바로 가까이에서 보고 싶어요.
남: 아, 하지만 그 부분에 대해서는 너무 많이 걱정하실 필요가 없습니다. 발표 유인물이 입구 옆에서 배부되고 있는 것을 봤거든요. 제가 지금 바로 하나 가져 올 수 있어요.

어휘 turnout 참석률, 참석자 수 up close 바로 가까이에서 pass out ~을 배부하다, 나눠 주다

16. 화자들은 어떤 종류의 행사에 참석하고 있는가?
(A) 비즈니스 컨퍼런스
(B) 회사 기념 행사
(C) 무역 박람회
(D) 지역 축제 마당

해설 여자가 대화 초반부에 현재 참석 중인 행사를 This business innovation conference라고 밝히고 있으므로 (A)가 정답이다.

17. 여자가 왜 "더 열심히 찾아 봐요"라고 말하는가?
(A) 다른 선택사항을 시도해 보기를 선호한다.
(B) 남자를 격려해 주고 있다.
(C) 제안서의 일부를 변경하고 싶어 한다.
(D) 더 나은 결과를 달성할 수 있다고 생각한다.

해설 대화 중반부에 남자가 특정 위치를 언급하면서 그곳에 앉으면 어떨지 제안하자, 여자가 '더 열심히 찾아 봐요'라고 대답하면서 발표 슬라이드를 바로 가까이에서 보고 싶다고 밝히는 흐름이다. 이는 다른 곳에 앉을 수 있도록 시도해 보자는 뜻이므로 (A)가 정답이다.

18. 남자는 발표 유인물과 관련해 무슨 말을 하는가?
(A) 모든 참석자들에게 전자식으로 발송될 것이다.
(B) 입구 근처에서 이용 가능하다.
(C) 정보 책자 묶음과 함께 포함되어 있다.
(D) 오직 몇 부만 남아 있다.

해설 남자가 대화 후반부에 발표 유인물이 입구 옆에서 배부되고 있는 것을 봤다고 알리고 있으므로 (B)가 정답이다.

어휘 electronically 전자식으로, 컴퓨터로

Playlist 11

파트3에 꼭 나오는 시각자료 연계문제 총정리

시각자료

여: 안녕하세요, 프레드 씨. 혹시 공항에 도착하셨나요? 고속도로 교통량이 끔찍했어서, 저는 여전히 약 30분 거리에 있어요. 비행기를 놓치게 될 것 같은 느낌이에요!
남: 있잖아요, 질 씨. 제가 여기 5분 전에 도착했는데, 사실, 우리 비행기가 1시간 30분 지연되었습니다. 그래서 괜찮으실 것 같아요.
여: 아, 아주 운이 좋네요! 그러면, 우리의 새 도착 시간과 관련해서 공항 환승 기사님께 연락해 주시겠어요? 그렇게 하면, 그분께서 언제 우리를 태우러 오셔야 하는지 아실 거예요.

목적지	출발 시간	현황
시애틀	15:10	탑승 중
피닉스	15:30	정시 출발
앨버커키	16:00	지연 - 17:30
샌디에이고	17:30	지연 - 18:00

Q. 시각자료를 보시오. 화자들은 어디로 가는가?
(A) 시애틀로
(B) 피닉스로
(C) 앨버커키로
(D) 샌디에이고로

Practice

1. (B)

1.

M: Hi, do you have a schedule of the library's events?
W: Sure, here's a copy for this month. We have an event almost every day, except for this Thursday. We'll be closed for carpet cleaning.
M: Got it. Do you guys hold any movie screenings?
W: We do! There's one on Wednesday.
M: Oh, no. I'm going out of town that day.
W: I see. Well, **do you know director Calum Pardo? He's giving a talk on Tuesday.**
M: **I do like his films, so I'll be sure to check that out.** Thanks!

남: 안녕하세요, 도서관 행사 일정표를 가지고 계신가요?
여: 네, 여기 이번 달에 대한 사본입니다. 저희가 거의 매일 한 가지 행사가 있습니다, 이번 주 목요일만 제외하고요. 저희가 카펫 청소로 인해 문을 닫을 것입니다.
남: 알겠습니다. 영화 상영회도 개최하시는 것이 있나요?
여: 있습니다! 수요일에 한 차례 있습니다.
남: 아, 이런. 제가 그날 다른 지역으로 갑니다.
여: 그러시군요. 그럼, 칼럼 파르도 감독님을 아시나요? 그분께서 화요일에 강연을 하십니다.
남: 제가 그분 영화를 정말 좋아하기 때문에, 그 행사를 꼭 확인해 볼게요. 감사합니다!

월요일	오후 4시	아동 도서 낭독회
화요일	오후 7시	특별 강연: 영화 감독 칼럼 파르도
수요일	오후 6시	영화 상영회
목요일	휴무	---

어휘 except for ~은 제외하고 screening 상영(회) read-aloud 낭독회

Q. 시각자료를 보시오. 남자는 언제 도서관 행사에 참석할 것 같은가?
(A) 월요일에
(B) 화요일에
(C) 수요일에
(D) 목요일에

해설 여자가 대화 후반부에 칼럼 파르도 감독을 아는지 물으면서 그 사람이 화요일에 강연을 한다고 알리자, 남자가 꼭 확인해 보겠다고 대답하고 있다. 시각자료에서 영화 감독 칼럼 파르도의 이름이 표기된 두 번째 줄에 개최 요일이 Tuesday로 쓰여 있으므로 (B)가 정답이다.

빈출 시각자료 ①

시간표

비행편 번호	출발	도착
XZ6005	오전 6:20	오전 9:45
SQ5815	오전 7:05	오전 10:30
TY8903	오전 8:30	오전 11:15
GJ4752	오전 9:45	오후 12:30

여: 산호세에 약 오전 11시 30분에 도착하는한, 저는 특별히 선호하는 시간대는 없습니다.

Q. 시각자료를 보시오. 여자는 어느 비행편을 이용할 것 같은가?

정답 TY8903

가격표

가격 정보	
수량	가격
100	75달러
250	110달러
500	200달러
1,000	380달러 → 340달러 할인!

남: 안녕하세요, 봉투 500장을 주문하고 싶습니다. 봉투에 제 회사 로고를 새길 계획입니다.

Q. 시각자료를 보시오. 남자의 주문은 얼마가 들 것인가?

정답 200달러

막대 그래프

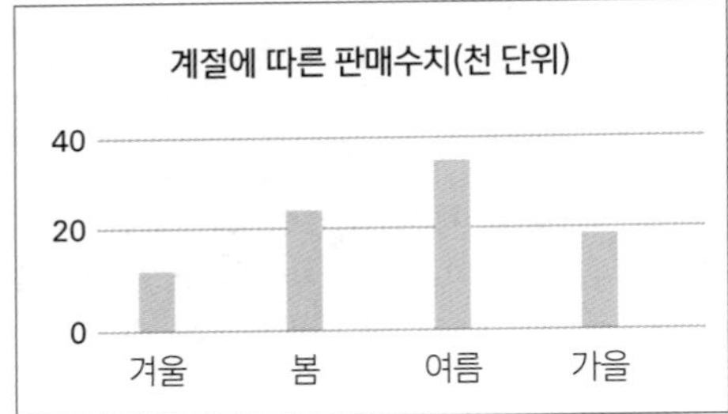

여: 레이저스핀 3A가 우리의 가장 유명한 스쿠터 모델 아닌가요? 그리고 우린 그 모델을 38,000대를 팔았습니다. 어떻게 이게 가능했나요?

Q. 시각자료를 보시오. 여자가 어떤 계절의 판매 수치에 대해 묻고 있는가?

정답 여름

스케줄

주간 배송 일정	
베닝턴 아파트 ·········	4월 2일
글래스온 무도회장 ·········	4월 4일
메르세데스 호텔 & 스위트 ·········	4월 5일
센터필드 테크 솔루션 ·········	4월 7일

남: 사실, 제가 글래스온 무도회장이 이번 주 말에 풍선을 받아도 된다고 언급한 것이 기억나요. 이 일정을 짬을 내어 4월 7일로 넣어보고, 하이퍼엔드 솔루션즈를 그 날에 배정합시다.

Q. 시각자료를 보시오. 하이퍼엔드 솔루션즈의 배송이 언제 이루어질 것 같은가?

정답 4월 4일

설명서

단계 1. 주 트레이에 종이를 채우십시오
단계 2. 전원을 연결하십시오
단계 3. 프린터 전원을 켜십시오
단계 4. 프린터 소프트웨어를 설치하십시오

여: 제가 여기 사용자 설명서를 가지고 있어요. 설명서에 최신 프린트 소프트웨어를 다운 받아 설치해야 한다고 적혀 있습니다. 그리고 나서, 우리가 바로 프린터기를 사용하는 것을 시작할 수 있을 겁니다.

Q. 시각자료를 보시오. 여자가 다음에 해야 할 단계는 무엇인가?

정답 단계 4

원 그래프

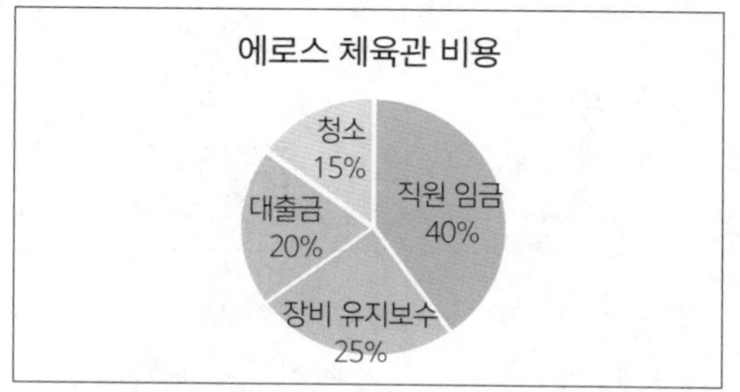

남: 하나 씨, 우리 체육관 예산에 관해 논의할 수 있을까요? 우리 지출 비용을 살펴보았는데, 우리가 장비 유지보수에 너무 많이 소비 중인 것 같아 걱정됩니다.

Q. 시각자료를 보시오. 남자는 예산의 어느 비중에 대해 걱정하는가?

정답 25%

빈출 시각자료 ②

지도

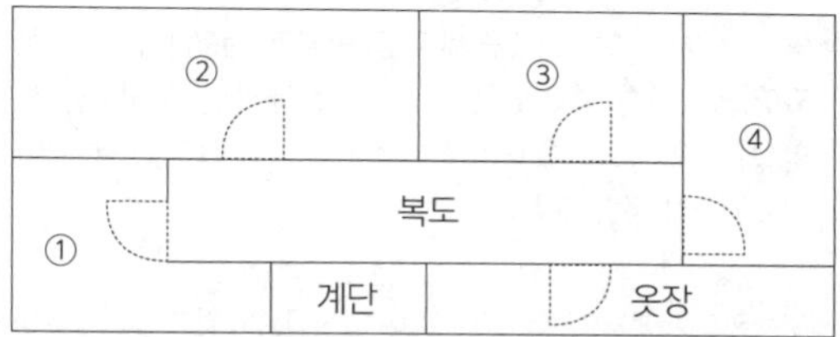

여: 가죽 소파부터 시작해 주세요. 그건 2층에 있어서 계단을 올라가신 후에 복도로 오른쪽으로 돌면 됩니다. 소파는 옷장 건너편에 있는 방에 있을 거에요.

Q. 시각자료를 보시오. 여자는 어느 방을 가리키는가?

정답 3번 방

일기예보

일기예보			
목요일	금요일	토요일	일요일
24도 흐림	25도 구름 조금	27도 대체로 맑음	30도 맑음

남: 일기예보를 확인해 볼게요. 다음 주 말에는 훨씬 나아보이네요.

여: 네, 27도는 꽤 따뜻하고, 구름도 너무 많지는 않을 거고요. 그때 활동을 개최할 수 있을 것 같아요!

Q. 시각자료를 보시오. 화자들은 어느 날을 선택하는가?

정답 토요일

층별 안내도

층	코너
5	명품 의류
4	전자기기
3	가정 용품
2	신발
1	화장품 & 미용

여: 안녕하세요, 노트북 컴퓨터 세일을 진행한다고 들었습니다. 제가 직접 몇 개를 보려고 하는데, 어떤 모델들이 전시 중인지 궁금합니다.

Q. 시각자료를 보시오. 여자는 몇 층을 방문할 예정인가?

정답 4층

제품 목록

40달러 48달러 34달러 52달러

남: 목이 가장 넓은 것이 많은 꽃을 전시해두기에 좋을 것 같아요!

Q. 시각자료를 보시오. 남자가 사고 싶어 하는 꽃병의 가격은 얼마인가?

정답 52달러

좌석 배치도

여: 잠시만요... 오, 서로의 바로 옆에 있는 마지막 좌석 한 쌍이 있네요! 귀하를 위해 즉시 예매해드릴 수 있습니다. 성함을 알 수 있을까요?

Q. 시각자료를 보시오. 남자는 어느 열의 티켓을 구입할 예정인가?

정답 B열

쿠폰

여름 파격 세일!

20% 할인 – 월요일 한정

25% 할인 – 수요일 한정

30% 할인 – 금요일 한정

남: 아시다시피, 그것을 사기 위해 금요일까지 기다리신다면, 30퍼센트를 절약하실 수 있어요.

여: 맞아요, 하지만 제가 이번 주에 출장이 있어요. 20퍼센트 할인으로 만족해야 할 것 같아요.

Q. 시각자료를 보시오. 여자는 어느 날에 물건을 구입하는가?

정답 월요일

Check-up Test

1. (C)	**2.** (A)	**3.** (D)	**4.** (A)	**5.** (C)
6. (D)	**7.** (B)	**8.** (C)	**9.** (B)	**10.** (A)
11. (D)	**12.** (B)			

Questions 1-3 refer to the following conversation and map.

W: Welcome to the French Museum of Art. How may I assist you?

M: [1] **I have a scheduled tour of the medieval art section**, but I'm running late. Can you show me how to get there?

W: Here's a pamphlet with all the information you'll need. The map shows you how to get to the medieval art exhibits. Any other questions?

M: Oh, and [2] **I'm interested in signing up for the stained glass-making workshop this fall.**

W: Sure. Registration can be done right here.

M: I'll come back for that after my tour then. I should probably get going.

W: No problem. Oh, and [3] **you should use the escalator at the back of the building since lots of people are always using the front entrance one.**

여: 프랑스 미술관에 오신 것을 환영합니다. 무엇을 도와 드릴까요?

남: 제가 중세 미술 구역에 대한 투어가 예정되어 있는데, 늦었습니다. 그곳으로 가는 방법을 알려 주시겠어요?

여: 여기 필요로 하실 모든 정보가 담긴 안내책자입니다. 이 지도에 중세 미술 전시회로 가시는 방법이 나와 있습니다. 다른 질문이 더 있으신가요?

남: 아, 그리고 올 가을에 스테인드 글라스 제작 워크숍에 등록하는 데 관심이 있습니다.

여: 네. 등록은 바로 이곳에서 하실 수 있습니다.

남: 그럼 투어 후에 하러 다시 오겠습니다. 저는 아마 가 봐야 할 것 같아요.

여: 알겠습니다. 아, 그리고 많은 분들께서 항상 정문 쪽에 있는 것을 이용하고 계시기 때문에 건물 뒤쪽에 있는 에스컬레이터를 이용해 보세요.

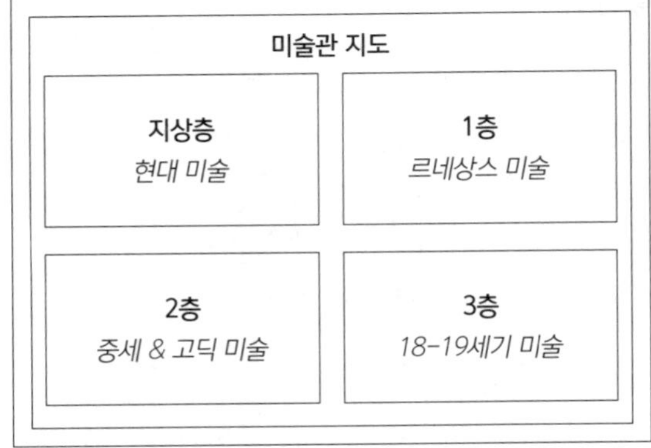

어휘 **medieval** 중세의 **run late** 늦다, 늦게 도착하다 **get going** 가다, 출발하다 **contemporary** 현대의, 동시대의

1. 시각자료를 보시오. 남자는 어느 층에서 투어를 할 것인가?
(A) 지상층
(B) 1층
(C) 2층
(D) 3층

해설 남자가 대화 초반부에 중세 미술 구역에 대한 투어가 예정되어 있다고 밝히고 있는데, 시각자료에서 중세 미술을 포함하는 Medieval & Gothic Art가 표기된 층이 Level 2이므로 (C)가 정답이다.

2. 미술관에서 올 가을에 무슨 일이 있을 것인가?
(A) 워크숍이 제공될 것이다.
(B) 컨퍼런스가 개최될 것이다.
(C) 특별 할인이 제공될 것이다.
(D) 몇몇 미술가들이 강연할 것이다.

해설 대화 중반부에 남자가 올 가을에 스테인드 글라스 제작 워크숍에 등록하는 데 관심이 있다는 말을 하고 있으므로 (A)가 정답이다.

3. 여자는 왜 미술관 뒤쪽에 있는 에스컬레이터를 이용하도록 권하는가?
(A) 로비에 가깝다.
(B) 최근에 지어졌다.
(C) 속도가 더 빠르다.
(D) 붐비지 않는다.

해설 여자가 대화 마지막 부분에 많은 사람들이 항상 정문 쪽에 있는 것을 이용하고 있기 때문에 건물 뒤쪽에 있는 에스컬레이터를 이용해 보라고 권하고 있으므로 (D)가 정답이다.

Questions 4-6 refer to the following conversation and price list.

W: Hello, I'm Dr. Naomi Parrino. I'm calling regarding the Cumberland Institute Health Fair. **4** **I've been trying to register online, but the Web site is acting up.**

M: I apologize for the difficulties, Dr. Parrino. I'm happy to help you register by phone. **5** **How many days of the fair will you be attending?**

W: **5** **Just the last day. And I am a member with Cumberland Institute.**

M: Great, thank you. **6** **If you can provide me with your membership ID number**, I can apply the discount for you.

W: Yeah, sure. One second, please... Let me get my ID card out.

여: 안녕하세요, 저는 나오미 패리노 박사입니다. 컴벌랜드 협회 건강 박람회와 관련해 전화 드립니다. 제가 온라인으로 계속 등록해 보려 하고 있지만, 웹 사이트가 말썽입니다.

남: 그 문제에 대해 사과 드립니다, 패리노 박사님. 제가 전화로 등록하시도록 기꺼이 도와 드리겠습니다. 박람회 기간 중 며칠 동안 참석하실 예정이신가요?

여: 마지막 날에만요. 그리고 제가 컴벌랜드 협회 회원입니다.

남: 아주 좋습니다, 감사합니다. 회원 ID 번호를 제게 제공해 주실 수 있다면, 할인을 적용해 드릴 수 있습니다.

여: 네, 물론입니다. 잠시만요... 제 ID 카드를 꺼낼게요.

컴벌랜드 협회 건강 박람회 요금		
1일차 한정	회원	20달러
	비회원	25달러
2일차 한정	회원	22달러
	비회원	30달러
3일차 한정	회원	27달러
	비회원	37달러

어휘 act up 말썽을 부리다, 제대로 기능하지 않다 apply ~을 적용하다

4. 여자는 어떤 문제를 언급하는가?
(A) 웹 사이트가 작동하지 않는다.
(B) 티켓이 발급되지 않았다.
(C) 몇몇 가격이 부정확하다.
(D) 몇몇 주문 사항이 접수되지 않았다.

해설 대화 초반부에 여자가 온라인으로 계속 등록해 보려고 하는데 웹 사이트가 말썽이라고 밝히고 있으므로 (A)가 정답이다.

5. 시각자료를 보시오. 여자는 얼마를 지불할 것 같은가?
(A) 20달러
(B) 22달러
(C) 27달러
(D) 37달러

해설 대화 중반부에 남자가 여자에게 참석 기간과 관련해 묻자, 여자가 마지막 날에만 참석한다는 말과 함께 컴벌랜드 협회 회원임을 밝히고 있다. 시각자료에서 마지막 날인 3일차 항목에 회원(Member) 요금이 $27로 표기되어 있으므로 (C)가 정답이다.

6. 남자는 여자에게 무엇을 제공하도록 요청하는가?
(A) 연락처
(B) 청구서 발송 주소
(C) 신용카드 번호
(D) 증명서 번호

해설 남자가 대화 후반부에 회원 ID 번호를 제공하도록 요청하고 있으므로 (D)가 정답이다.

Questions 7-9 refer to the following conversation and building directory.

W: Welcome to Grandview Tower Business Suites.

M: Good afternoon. **7** **I'm here for Packman Credit Union.** Can you tell me where their offices are?

W: They should be on the fifth floor. There'll be a directory on the wall right when you get off the elevator.

M: Thanks. **8** **I've been told the filters in their water dispensers need to be replaced.**

W: Yes. One of their employees notified me about your arrival earlier today. I think they were expecting you sooner, though.

M: Well, **9** **the specific parts I need for the models were hard to find**, so it took me slightly longer than normal to prepare for this request.

W: I see. I just need you to sign this visitors' form before you head up there.

여: 그랜드뷰 타워 비즈니스 스위트에 오신 것을 환영합니다.
남: 안녕하세요. 팩맨 신용 조합에 왔습니다. 사무실이 어디에 있는지 알려 주시겠어요?
여: 5층에 있을 겁니다. 엘리베이터에서 내리시자마자 보이는 벽에 안내판이 있습니다.
남: 감사합니다. 그곳 정수기의 필터가 교체되어야 한다는 말을 들었습니다.
여: 네. 오늘 아까 그곳 직원들 중 한 분께서 제게 당신이 도착하실 거라고 알려 주셨습니다. 하지만, 그분들은 당신이 더 일찍 오실 것으로 예상했던 것 같아요.
남: 그게, 그 모델들에 필요한 특정 부품들이 찾기 힘들었기 때문에, 이 요청에 대해 준비하는 데 평소보다 약간 더 시간이 걸렸습니다.
여: 알겠습니다. 그곳으로 올라 가시기 전에 이 방문객 양식에 서명만 해 주셨으면 합니다.

그랜드뷰 타워 비즈니스 스위트
5층 안내판

511호실	데이비슨 엔지니어링 & 건설
512호실	팩맨 신용 조합
513호실	칼리 & 레디코 법률 서비스
514호실	골든스타인 출판사

어휘 **directory** (건물의 층별 사무실 등이 표기된) 안내판, 안내도 **get off** ~에서 내리다 **water dispenser** 정수기, 급수기 **head up** 올라 가다, 위를 향해가다

7. 시각자료를 보시오. 남자는 어느 사무실을 방문할 것인가?
(A) 511호실
(B) 512호실
(C) 513호실
(D) 514호실

해설 대화 초반부에 남자가 팩맨 신용 조합에 왔다고 알리고 있으며, 시각자료에서 Packman Credit Union이 Office 512로 표기되어 있으므로 (B)가 정답이다.

8. 남자는 무엇을 할 예정인가?
(A) 관리자와 거래하는 일
(B) 보안 시스템을 설치하는 일
(C) 일부 정수 필터를 교체하는 일
(D) 일부 전구를 바꾸는 일

해설 남자가 대화 중반부에 자신이 하려는 일과 관련해 정수기의 필터가 교체되어야 한다는 말을 들었다는 사실을 밝히고 있으므로 (C)가 정답이다.

어휘 **make a deal** 거래하다

9. 남자는 왜 늦었는가?
(A) 일정표를 잘못 읽었다.
(B) 일부 물품을 찾을 수 없었다.
(C) 더 급한 요청이 있었다.
(D) 자동차가 고장 났다.

해설 대화 후반부에 남자가 특정 부품이 찾기 힘들었기 때문에 평소보다 더 오래 걸렸다는 말로 늦은 이유를 알리고 있으므로 (B)가 정답이다.

어휘 **misread** ~을 잘못 읽다 **break down** 고장 나다, 망가지다

Questions 10-12 refer to the following conversation and product list.

W: Hello there. 10 **Do you need help with anything?**
M: I do, actually. 10 **I want to buy some new shoes, but I can't decide what's best.**
W: Alright. What type do you have in mind?
M: Well, I go surfing at the beach often, so I want comfortable open-toe shoes, but nothing too heavy nor bulky.
W: There's actually a summer sale going on at our store right now, and 11 **these sandals might be just what you're looking for.** Here's a flyer for reference.
M: 11 **Oh, these look great.** Are there any available in size 12 for men?
W: 12 **I can look in the stockroom for you right now.** One moment, please.

여: 안녕하세요. 무엇이든 도움이 필요하신 게 있으신가요?
남: 실은, 있습니다. 제가 새 신발을 좀 구입하려고 하는데, 무엇이 가장 좋은지 결정하지 못하겠어요.
여: 알겠습니다. 어떤 종류를 염두에 두고 계신가요?
남: 저, 제가 해변으로 자주 서핑하러 가기 때문에, 앞부분이 트인 편한 신발을 원하기는 하지만, 너무 무겁거나 부피가 크지 않으면 좋겠습니다.
여: 실은 지금 바로 저희 매장에서 여름 세일 행사가 진행되고 있고, 이 샌들이 바로 고객님께서 찾고 계신 것일지도 모르겠습니다. 여기 참고를 위한 전단지가 있습니다.
남: 아, 아주 좋아 보여요. 남성용 사이즈 12로 구입 가능한 것이 있을까요?
여: 지금 바로 재고 창고를 살펴 봐 드릴 수 있습니다. 잠시만 기다려 주세요.

운동화 브랜드: 에어로노바	정장 구두 브랜드: 포시 벨
등산화 브랜드: 트레이블레이저스	**해변용 샌들** 브랜드: 베일리 워커

어휘 have A in mind A를 염두에 두다 open-toe 신발 앞부분이 트여 있는 bulky 부피가 큰 stockroom 재고 창고, 물품 보관실

10. 여자는 누구일 것 같은가?
(A) 영업 사원
(B) 제품 디자이너
(C) 신발 제작자
(D) 스포츠 코치

해설 대화 초반부에 여자는 도움이 필요한지 묻고 있고, 남자는 새 신발 구입과 관련해 무엇이 가장 좋은지 결정하지 못하겠다고 밝히고 있다. 따라서, 신발 매장 점원과 고객 사이의 대화임을 알 수 있으므로 (A)가 정답이다.

11. 시각자료를 보시오. 남자는 어느 브랜드가 마음에 든다고 말하는가?
(A) 에어로노바
(B) 포시 벨
(C) 트레이블레이저스
(D) 베일리 워커

해설 대화 중반부에 여자가 샌들 제품을 추천하자, 남자가 아주 좋아 보인다는 말로 반응하고 있다. 시각자료에서 샌들 그림이 있는 오른쪽 하단에 브랜드가 Bailey Walker로 표기되어 있으므로 (D)가 정답이다.

12. 여자는 무엇을 하겠다고 하는가?
(A) 물품을 포장하는 일
(B) 재고를 확인해 보는 일
(C) 할인 쿠폰을 제공하는 일
(D) 한 제품을 판매 보류하는 일

해설 여자가 대화 마지막 부분에 지금 바로 재고 창고를 살펴 봐 주겠다고 알리고 있으므로 (B)가 정답이다.

어휘 wrap up ~을 포장하다, 싸다 inventory 재고 (목록) put A on hold A를 보류하다

Playlist 12

최빈출 담화 유형 회의발췌/전화메시지

회의 발췌

이 레스토랑을 개장한 이후로 언제나 발생한 한 가지 문제에 대해 다루기 위해 이 시간을 쓰고자 합니다. 지역 및 각국의 손님들로부터 저희 음식에 대한 많은 솔직한 피드백을 온라인으로 받아왔습니다. 몇몇 분들이 저희의 동남 아시아 풍미가 진정성이 부족하다고 말씀하셔서, 저희에게 도움을 제공해 주고 전문적인 조언을 공유해 주시도록 태국 출신의 요리 전문가에게 연락했습니다. 그분이 다음 주 화요일 오전에 저희를 교육시키러 오실 것이며, 이는 모두의 근무 시간이 그 날에 오전 10시에 시작할 것임을 의미합니다. 여러분들의 일정에 표시해 놓는 것을 잊지 마십시오.

Practice

1. (D) **2.** (A) **3.** (B)

Question 1-3 refer to the following excerpt from a meeting.

Alright, let's review the product testing feedback for the Astrolink-22V, our **satellite TV system**. The Astrolink-22V is our first satellite dish that can broadcast channels from all over the world. Test users loved having access to a huge variety of content. But, some also reported that when there's **stormy weather**, the satellite's connection got **cut off** sometimes. I think we should create a dish cover that protects the reflector and antenna from any moisture and debris buildup. I'd like you each to take some time to **research some durable materials** that can act as a good barrier and, let's reconvene later.

좋습니다, 우리 위성 TV 시스템인 애스트로링크-22V에 대한 제품 테스트 의견을 살펴 보도록 하겠습니다. 애스트로링크-22V는 우리의 첫 접시형 위성 안테나로서, 전 세계 각지의 채널들을 방송할 수 있습니다. 테스트 사용자들께서 엄청날 정도로 다양한 콘텐츠를 이용할 수 있다는 점을 정말 마음에 들어 하셨습니다. 하지만, 어떤 분들은 험한 날씨가 있을 때, 위성 연결이 때때로 차단되었다는 사실을 알려 주시기도 했습니다. 저는 우리가 반사기와 안테나 부분을 모든 습기와 부스러기 축적으로부터 보호해 주는 접시 덮개를 만들어야 한다고 생각합니다. 저는 여러분 각자가 시간을 좀 갖고 좋은

장벽의 역할을 할 수 있는 몇몇 내구성이 뛰어난 소재들을 조사한 다음, 나중에 다시 모입시다.

어휘 satellite (인공) 위성 broadcast ~을 방송하다 cut off ~을 차단하다, 끊다 reflector 반사기, 반사 장치 debris 부스러기, 쓰레기 buildup 축적 durable 내구성이 좋은 act as ~의 역할을 하다 barrier 장벽, 장애물 reconvene 다시 모이다

1. 해당 팀이 어떤 종류의 제품을 개발했는가?
(A) 라디오 방송용 스피커
(B) 외국어 번역용 스캐너
(C) 날씨 업데이트용 디스플레이 모니터
(D) TV 프로그램용 접시형 위성 안테나

해설 화자가 담화를 시작하면서 애스트로링크-22V라는 이름의 접시형 위성 안테나를 소개하면서 제품 테스트 의견에 관해 이야기하고 있으므로 (D)가 정답이다.

2. 무엇이 일부 이용자들에게 문제를 초래했는가?
(A) 좋지 못한 기상 조건
(B) 제한적인 스트리밍 서비스
(C) 공간의 부족
(D) 복잡한 설정 절차

해설 화자가 담화 중반부에 험한 날씨가 있을 때 위성 연결이 차단된 사실을 알린 사람들이 있었다고 밝히고 있으므로 (A)가 정답이다.

3. 청자들은 다음에 무엇을 할 것 같은가?
(A) 한 구역을 측정하는 일
(B) 몇몇 제품을 찾아 보는 일
(C) 다른 공급업체에 연락하는 일
(D) 일부 데이터를 수집하는 일

해설 담화 후반부에 화자가 청자들에게 시간을 갖고 몇몇 내구성이 뛰어난 소재를 조사하도록 요청하고 있다. 이는 그러한 소재를 위해 제품을 찾아 보는 일에 해당하므로 (B)가 정답이다.

어휘 look up (정보 등을 위해) ~을 찾아 보다

전화메시지

안녕하세요, 램버트 씨. 귀하의 전기 서비스를 새로운 주소로 이전하시려는 요청과 관련해 전화 드립니다. 단지 확인을 위해서, 귀하께서는 현 거주지에서 9월 21일에 이사하실 예정이시며, 새 거주지 주소는 브라이언트 애비뉴 577번지입니다. 그리고, 자동 고지서 납부와 함께 종이 없는 고지서 발급 서비스에 등록되어 있으신 것으로 기록되어 있습니다. 이러한 설정들 중 어떤 것이든 변경하시고자 하는 경우, 저희 웹 사이트를 방문해 주시기 바랍니다. 555-6215번으로 제게 직접 연락하셔도 됩니다.

Practice

1. (B) **2.** (D) **3.** (B)

Question 1-3 refer to the following telephone message.

Hi, my name is Kyle Chen, and I'm calling to **see if the doctor can see me** today. I'm hoping a last-minute slot is available. I played in a **basketball tournament** this past weekend and had no issues the entire time. But, well, come Monday afternoon, I started feeling some discomfort in my right knee. I think I might need to get an x-ray. Could you return this call when you get the chance? I'll be **speaking at a conference** all morning, so if I'm unable to pick up my phone, please just leave a voicemail. Thank you.

안녕하세요, 제 이름은 카일 첸이며, 의사 선생님께서 오늘 저를 진찰하실 수 있는지 알아 보기 위해 전화 드립니다. 저는 마지막 순간의 시간대가 이용 가능하기를 바라고 있습니다. 제가 지난 주말에 농구 토너먼트에서 경기했는데, 그 전체 시간 동안 어떤 문제도 없었습니다. 하지만, 저, 월요일 오후가 되니까, 제 오른쪽 무릎에 불편함이 느껴지기 시작했습니다. 제 생각에 엑스레이를 찍어 봐야 할 수도 있을 것 같습니다. 기회가 되실 때 이 전화에 회신해 주시겠습니까? 제가 오전 내내 컨퍼런스에서 연설하고 있을 것이기 때문에, 제가 전화를 받을 수 없는 경우에는, 그냥 음성 메시지를 남겨 주시기 바랍니다. 감사합니다.

어휘 last-minute 마지막 순간의, 막바지의 slot (예약 등의) 시간대, 자리 discomfort 불편함

1. 화자는 왜 전화하는가?
(A) 예약을 확인해 주기 위해
(B) 예약과 관련해 문의하기 위해
(C) 서비스에 대해 불만을 표하기 위해
(D) 추천 사항을 요청하기 위해

해설 화자가 담화 시작 부분에 오늘 의사의 진찰을 받을 수 있는지 알아 보기 위해 전화한다고 알리면서 이용 가능한 시간대가 있기를 바란다고 말하고 있다. 이는 예약 가능 여부에 대한 바람을 나타내는 것이므로 (B)가 정답이다.

2. 화자는 최근 어떤 행사에 참가했는가?
(A) 댄스 공연
(B) 지역 사회 축제
(C) 회사 워크숍
(D) 운동 경기 대회

해설 담화 중반부에 화자가 지난 주말에 농구 토너먼트에서 경기한 사실을 말하고 있으므로 (D)가 정답이다.

어휘 athletic 운동의, 체육의

3. 화자는 오늘 오전에 무엇을 하고 있을 것이라고 말하는가?
(A) 몇몇 직원을 교육하는 일
(B) 연설을 하는 일
(C) 몇몇 건물을 방문하는 일
(D) 회의에 참석하는 일

해설 화자가 담화 후반부에 오전 내내 컨퍼런스에서 연설하고 있을 것이라고 알리고 있으므로 (B)가 정답이다.

Check-up Test

1. (D)	**2.** (B)	**3.** (B)	**4.** (B)	**5.** (A)
6. (C)	**7.** (C)	**8.** (B)	**9.** (D)	**10.** (C)
11. (C)	**12.** (A)	**13.** (A)	**14.** (D)	**15.** (A)
16. (B)	**17.** (C)	**18.** (D)		

Questions 1-3 refer to the following telephone message.

Hi, Marcus. 1 **I'm calling about the Mercado Hotel account — the one we're designing social media ads for.** I received a message from them, and they were complimenting you on how well you've been handling their project needs. 2 **Such positive feedback from our clients is always nice to hear**, and this assignment is your first. Oh, and they mentioned wanting to change 3 **some items on the project timeline. Could you send me the latest version of it via e-mail?** Thanks in advance!

안녕하세요, 마커스 씨. 우리가 소셜 미디어 광고를 디자인하고 있는 곳인, 메르카도 호텔 고객사와 관련해 연락 드립니다. 제가 그쪽에서 메시지를 하나 받았는데, 당신이 그쪽의 프로젝트 관련 요구 사항을 얼마나 잘 처리해 오고 있는지 칭찬해 주셨습니다. 우리 고객들께서 전해 주시는 이런 긍정적인 의견은 항상 듣기 좋은 일이며, 이 업무는 당신에게 처음 할당된 일입니다. 아, 그리고 그쪽에서 프로젝트 진행 일정에서 몇 사항들을 변경하고 싶다고 언급하셨습니다. 이메일을 통해 그 최신 버전을 제게 보내 주시겠어요? 미리 감사 드립니다!

어휘 reach out 연락하다 account 고객(사), 계정, 계좌 compliment A on B B에 대해 A를 칭찬하다 timeline 진행 일정(표), 추진 일정(표) via ~을 통해

1. 화자는 어떤 분야에서 일하고 있을 것 같은가?
(A) 회계
(B) 연예
(C) 관광
(D) 광고

해설 화자가 담화를 시작하면서 자신들이 소셜 미디어 광고를 디자인하고 있는 메르카도 호텔 고객사를 언급하고 있으므로 (D)가 정답이다.

2. 화자가 "이 업무는 당신에게 처음 할당된 일입니다"라고 말할 때 의미하는 것은 무엇인가?
(A) 필요 시에 도움을 제공해 줄 수 있다.
(B) 일부 업무에 대해 깊은 인상을 받았다.
(C) 한 가지 업무가 인내심을 필요로 할 것이다.
(D) 일부 정보가 부족해질 것이다.

해설 화자가 담화 중반부에 고객들이 전하는 긍정적인 의견이 항상 듣기 좋다고 언급하면서 '이 업무는 당신에게 처음 할당된 일입니다'라고 말하는 흐름이다. 이는 첫 번째 업무임에도 불구하고 고객들의 칭찬을 받은 것이 인상적이었음을 나타내는 말이므로 (B)가 정답이다.

3. 화자는 청자에게 무엇을 보내도록 요청하는가?
(A) 초대장
(B) 진행 일정표
(C) 보고서의 몇몇 초안
(D) 몇몇 비용 추정치

해설 담화 후반부에 화자가 프로젝트 진행 일정에서 몇몇 사항들을 변경하는 일을 언급하면서 이메일로 그 최신 버전을 보내 달라고 요청하고 있으므로 (B)가 정답이다.

어휘 draft 초안 projection 추정(치), 예측

Questions 4-6 refer to the following excerpt from a meeting.

The busy travel season has arrived. 4 **As you all know, we are short of ground staff, baggage handlers, and receptionists** to meet the increased demand. This has led to longer 4 **wait times and delays for** passengers. So, **5** **we're going to recruit additional staff as a top priority.** I'm sure you know about our incentive program that encourages employees to refer friends, so **6** **please spread the word about our open positions.** And starting this week, we'll be providing complimentary meals in all employee lounges for current staff. We want to express our gratitude and show that you are a highly valued worker.

바쁜 여행 시즌이 찾아 왔습니다. 여러분들 모두 아시다시피, 우리는 수요 증가를 충족할 지상 직원들과 수하물 처리 담당자들, 그리고 안내 담당자들이 부족한 상태입니다. 이는 탑승객들을 대상으로 더 긴 대기 시간과 지연 문제로 이어져 왔습니다. 따라서, 우리의 최우선 순위로서 추가 직원들을 모집할 예정입니다. 직원들에게 친구분들을 소개하도록 권장하는 우리의 장려 정책 프로그램에 관해 분명 알고 계실 것이므로, 우리의 공석에 관해 입소문을 내 주시기 바랍니다. 그리고 이번 주부터, 현재의 직원들을 대상으로 모든 직원 라운지에서 무료 식사를 제공하게 될 것입니다. 우리는 감사의 뜻을 표하고 여러분께서 대단히 소중한 직원임을 보여 드리고자 합니다.

어휘 arrive (때가) 찾아 오다, 도래하다 short of ~가 부족한 handler 처리 담당자 spread the word 입소문을 내다

4. 화자는 어떤 업계에 종사하고 있을 것 같은가?
(A) 정치
(B) 운송
(C) 소매
(D) 자동차

해설 화자가 담화 초반부에 지상 직원들과 수하물 처리 담당자들, 그리고 안내 담당자들의 부족 문제 및 그로 인한 탑승객들의 대기 시간과 지연 상황을 언급하고 있어 항공사 직원으로 볼 수 있으므로 (B)가 정답이다.

5. 화자는 무엇이 우선순위라고 말하는가?
(A) 더 많은 직원을 고용하는 것
(B) 영업 시간을 연장하는 것
(C) 더 많은 이용자를 끌어들이는 것
(D) 판매 수익을 늘리는 것

해설 담화 중반부에 화자가 최우선 순위는 추가 직원들을 모집하는 것이라고 밝히고 있으므로 (A)가 정답이다.

6. 화자는 청자에게 무엇을 하도록 요청하는가?
(A) 예산을 줄이기
(B) 일부 교대 근무를 재조정하기
(C) 공석에 대한 정보를 공유하기
(D) 특별 교육을 제공하기

해설 담화 중반부에 직원들에게 친구를 소개하도록 권장하는 장려 정책 프로그램에 대해 언급하며 공석에 대해 입소문을 내달라고 요청하고 있으므로 (C)가 정답이다.

Questions 7-9 refer to the following telephone message and seating plan.

Hello, Mr. Nguyen, **7** **this is Francesca Jansen calling from McKenzy Concert Hall. I have your name down as next on the theater's wait list.** According to your selection survey, **7** **you wanted three seats together** in either the orchestra or lower balcony sections. **8** **But unfortunately, it looks like those areas are all sold out for the day you marked. However, there are three seats available together in the mid-balcony on that date.** **9** **I can put those on hold for you if you'd like, but only for 48 hours. If you're still interested in attending the event, please call our box office** at your earliest convenience.

안녕하세요, 은구옌 씨, 저는 맥켄지 콘서트 홀에서 전화 드리는 프란체스카 잰슨입니다. 귀하의 성함이 저희 공연장 대기 명단의 다음 순서로 기재되어 있습니다. 귀하의 선택 사항 조사 내용에 따르면, 오케스트라 구역 또는 하단 발코니 구역의 좌석 세 개를 함께 원하셨습니다. 하지만 안타깝게도, 그 구역들은 표기해 주신 날짜에 모두 매진되어 있는 것처럼 보입니다. 하지만, 그 날짜에 중간 발코니 구역에 이용 가능하신 좌석이 세 개 있습니다. 원하실 경우에 그 좌석들을 대기 상태로 해 드릴 수 있지만, 오직 48시간 동안만입니다. 여전히 행사에 참석하시는 데 관심이 있으시면, 가급적 빨리 저희 매표소로 전화 주시기 바랍니다.

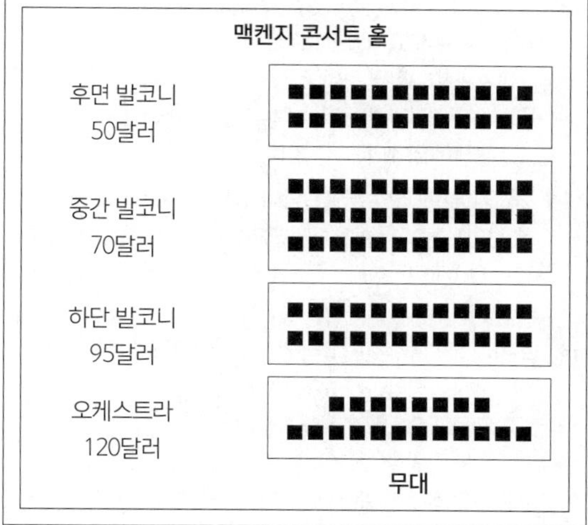

어휘 have A down A가 기재되어 있다, A를 적어 놓다 selection 선택, 선정 put A on hold A를 대기 상태에 두다, 보류하다

7. 화자는 누구일 것 같은가?
(A) 클래식 음악가
(B) 호텔 종업원
(C) 판매 담당 직원
(D) 뮤지컬 배우

해설 화자가 담화 초반부에 상대방이 대기 명단에 있고 세 개의 좌석을 원했다는 점을 밝히고 있어 입장권 판매 업무를 담당하는 직원으로 볼 수 있으므로 (C)가 정답이다.

8. 시각자료를 보시오. 이용 가능한 구역의 입장권 비용이 얼마인가?
(A) 50달러
(B) 70달러
(C) 95달러
(D) 120달러

해설 담화 중반부에 화자가 중간 발코니 구역에 이용 가능한 좌석이 있다고 밝히고 있다. 시각자료에서 중간 부분에 Mid-balcony로 표기된 구역에 $70로 쓰여 있으므로 (B)가 정답이다.

9. 청자는 48시간 내에 무엇을 해야 하는가?
(A) 계정에 로그인하는 일
(B) 프론트 데스크로 가는 일
(C) 이메일에 답장하는 일
(D) 전화를 거는 일

해설 화자가 담화 후반부에 입장권을 판매 대기 상태로 두는 것이 48시간 동안만 가능하다고 밝히면서 행사 참석에 관심이 있으면 가급적 빨리 전화해 달라고 요청하고 있으므로 (D)가 정답이다.

Questions 10-12 refer to the following excerpt from a meeting.

10 I want to give heartfelt thanks to our servers for their hard work since we opened. Our customers love both our dishes and our service, and we've been receiving many positive reviews. **11 I'm also delighted to share that we'll be adding cake slices to our dessert menu soon.** We just signed a deal with Karina's Cake Shop. **12 I'd love to hear your thoughts on which of their flavors would sell best with our customers. I've got some samples right here, so let me know your opinions.**

우리가 개장한 이후로 우리 서버 여러분의 노고에 대해 진심 어린 감사의 인사를 전하고 싶습니다. 우리 고객들께서 우리 요리와 서비스 둘 모두를 아주 좋아하고 계시며, 우리는 많은 긍정적인 평가를 받아 오고 있습니다. 곧 우리 디저트 메뉴에 조각 케이크들을 추가하게 될 것이라는 사실을 공유해 드리는 것도 기쁩니다. 우리가 막 카리나스 케이크 매장과 계약을 맺었습니다. 그곳의 제품 맛들 중 어느 것이 우리 고객들께 가장 잘 판매될지에 관한 여러분의 생각을 꼭 들어 보고 싶습니다. 바로 여기 몇몇 샘플들이 있으므로, 여러분의 의견을 알려 주시기 바랍니다.

어휘 heartfelt 진심 어린

10. 회의가 어디에서 진행되고 있을 것 같은가?
(A) 소매 식품점에서
(B) 카페에서
(C) 레스토랑에서
(D) 식품 생산 공장에서

해설 화자가 담화 초반부에 소속 업체의 특성과 관련해 our server와 our dishes 등을 언급하고 있으므로 (C)가 정답이다.

11. 화자는 무엇과 관련해 기쁘다고 말하는가?
(A) 신제품을 개발하는 일
(B) 전문가와 협업하는 일
(C) 선택 범위를 확대하는 일
(D) 한 과정을 개선하는 일

해설 담화 중반부에 화자가 디저트 메뉴에 조각 케이크들을 추가하는 것이 기쁘다고 말하고 있으며, 이는 제품 선택 범위를 확대하는 것이므로 (C)가 정답이다.

12. 화자는 청자들에게 무엇을 하기를 원하는가?
(A) 몇몇 의견을 제공하는 일
(B) 탁자 진열품을 옮기는 일
(C) 고객 맞이 인사를 연습하는 일
(D) 재고 목록을 업데이트하는 일

해설 화자가 담화 후반부에 어느 제품 맛이 고객들에게 가장 잘 판매될지에 관한 생각을 들어 보고 싶다는 뜻을 밝히고 있으므로 (A)가 정답이다.

어휘 greeting (맞이하거나 안부를 묻는) 인사

Questions 13-15 refer to the following telephone message.

Hello, I'm the building manager, Irina, and 13 **I'm calling to inform you that workers will be arriving tomorrow afternoon to replace a faulty water pipe** beneath the sidewalk next to your apartment unit. The job should be relatively quick, but 14 **I know you work remotely**, and the machinery will be noisy. I apologize for the short notice — since part of the pipe is near a utility pole, I had to request a permit to ensure everything is conducted safely. 15 **I expected the application to get approved in about a week, but approval was actually granted this morning.** Please leave a message for me if you need anything else.

안녕하세요. 저는 건물 관리 책임자인 이리나이며, 귀하의 아파트 세대 옆 보도 밑에 위치한 결함이 있는 수도관을 교체하기 위해 작업자들이 내일 오후에 도착할 예정이라는 사실을 알려 드리기 위해 전화 드립니다. 이 작업이 비교적 신속한 것이기는 하지만, 귀하께서 재택 근무를 하고 계신다는 사실을 알고 있으며, 기계가 시끄러울 것입니다. 촉박한 통보에 대해 사과 드리며, 이 수도관의 일부가 전봇대 근처에 있기 때문에, 반드시 모든 게 안전하게 실시되도록 허가증을 요청해야 했습니다. 저는 이 신청서가 약 일주일 후에 승인될 것으로 예상했지만, 승인이 실제로 오늘 아침에 이뤄졌습니다. 다른 어떤 것이든 필요하시면 제게 메시지 남겨 주시기 바랍니다.

어휘 faulty 결함이 있는 unit (아파트·상가 등의) 세대, 점포 work remotely 재택 근무를 하다 short notice 촉박한 통보 utility pole 전봇대

13. 화자는 내일 무슨 일이 있을 것이라고 말하는가?
(A) 파이프가 교체될 것이다.
(B) 기계가 수리될 것이다.
(C) 시 관계자가 방문할 것이다.
(D) 정책이 업데이트될 것이다.

해설 화자가 담화 초반부에 결함이 있는 수도관을 교체하기 위해 작업자들이 내일 오후에 도착한다는 사실을 알리고 있으므로 (A)가 정답이다.

14. 화자가 왜 "기계가 시끄러울 것입니다"라고 말하는가?
(A) 오해를 명확하게 하기 위해
(B) 도움을 요청하기 위해
(C) 문의 사항을 해결하기 위해
(D) 주의를 주기 위해

해설 담화 중반부에 화자가 상대방이 재택 근무를 하고 있다는 사실을 알고 있다고 밝히면서 '기계가 시끄러울 것입니다'라고 말하는 흐름이다. 이는 집에서 일하는 상대방에게 소음과 관련해 미리 주의를 주는 것이므로 (D)가 정답이다.

어휘 clarify ~을 명확하게 하다, 분명히 말하다

15. 화자는 허가증과 관련해 무슨 말을 하는가?
(A) 예상보다 더 빨리 발급되었다.
(B) 청자에게 전달될 것이다.
(C) 눈에 띄게 보여져야 한다.
(D) 한 달 동안 이용될 수 있다.

해설 화자가 담화 후반부에 허가증 신청서가 약 일주일 후에 승인될 것으로 예상했지만 실제로 오늘 아침에 승인 받았다는 사실을 밝히고 있다. 이는 예기치 못하게 더 빨리 승인 받은 것에 대한 놀라움을 나타내는 말이므로 (A)가 정답이다.

Questions 16-18 refer to the following excerpt from a meeting and chart.

16 **Before we end this sales meeting, let's review our second-quarter performance.** As you're aware, we've decided to discontinue the production of our speakers, so we already anticipated lower sales numbers in that area. Regardless, 17 **the five percent growth rate we can see here is quite unexpected.** Moving forward, we should certainly aim for even better quarterly progress. So, 18 **management has agreed to reduce the cost of these items to boost sales.** This price drop will be effective immediately across all our distribution channels.

우리의 2분기 성과를 살펴 보는 것으로 이 영업 회의를 끝마치고자 합니다. 여러분도 아시다시피, 우리 스피커의 생산을 중단하기로 결정했기 때문에, 우리는 이미 이 부문에서 더 낮은 판매 수치를 예상했습니다. 그럼에도 불구하고, 우리가 이 부분에서 볼 수 있는 5퍼센트의 성장률은 꽤 뜻밖입니다. 앞으로, 우리는 분명히 훨씬 더 나은 분기별 발전을 목표로 삼아야 합니다. 따라서, 경영진에서는 판매를 촉진하기 위해 이 제품들의 가격을 낮추는 데 합의했습니다. 이 가격 인하는 우리의 모든 유통 경로 전체에 걸쳐 즉시 시행될 것입니다.

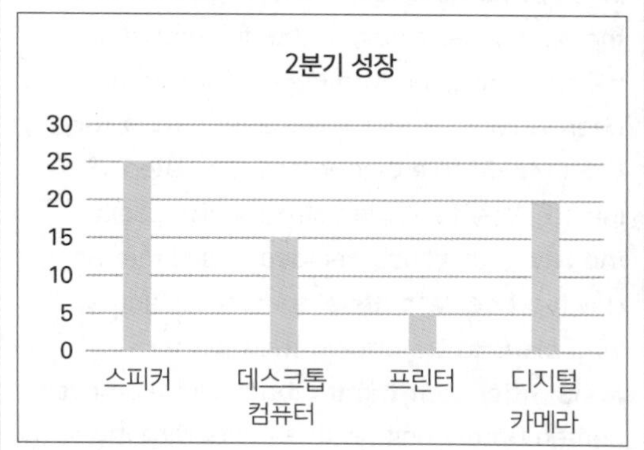

어휘 regardless 그럼에도 불구하고, 상관없이 moving forward 앞으로 effective 시행되는, 발효되는

16. 청자들은 누구일 것 같은가?
(A) 기술 지원 담당 직원들
(B) 영업 사원들
(C) 행사 기획자들
(D) 공장 직원들

해설 화자가 담화 시작 부분에 영업 회의임을 밝히고 있으므로 영업과 관련된 업무를 담당하는 사람들인 (B)가 정답이다.

17. 시각자료를 보시오. 화자는 어느 항목과 관련해 우려하는가?
(A) 스피커
(B) 데스크톱 컴퓨터
(C) 프린터
(D) 디지털 카메라

해설 담화 중반부에 화자가 5퍼센트의 성장률을 특별히 언급하면서 그것이 뜻밖이라고 밝히고 있다. 시각자료에서 5퍼센트로 표기된 항목이 왼쪽에서 세 번째에 위치한 Printers이므로 (C)가 정답이다.

18. 회사는 무엇을 하기로 결정했는가?
(A) 유명인 출연 광고를 이용하는 것
(B) 새로운 지점들을 개장하는 것
(C) 온라인 주문을 수용하는 것
(D) 몇몇 가격을 내리는 것

해설 화자가 담화 후반부에 경영진이 판매 촉진을 위해 제품들의 가격을 낮추는 데 합의한 사실을 언급하고 있으므로 (D)가 정답이다.

어휘 celebrity endorsement 유명인 출연 광고

Playlist 13
파트4가 좋아하는 담화/방송 공략법

담화

할링턴 대저택에 오신 것을 환영합니다. 이전의 소유주는 버니스 리우라는 성함의 유명 목수셨습니다. 이 건물의 한 가지 특별한 측면은 리우 씨께서 이 사유지 전체를 직접 개인적으로 디자인하셨다는 점입니다. 저희가 처음으로 이 대저택을 공원으로 개장할 준비를 하고 있기 때문에, 자원 봉사자들께서 정원 이동로에서 떨어진 나뭇가지와 쓰레기를 치우는 데 도움을 주셨으면 합니다. 봉지와 장갑은 제공됩니다. 그리고, 출발하시기 전에 저에게 확인 받으시는 것을 잊지 마시기 바라며, 여러분 각자가 무료 방문객 출입증을 받으셔야 하는데, 이것으로 여러분은 이 대저택 및 전체 여름 내내 개최되는 전체 행사에 대한 출입 권한을 얻으시게 됩니다.

Practice

1. (C) **2.** (D) **3.** (B)

Questions 1-3 refer to the following talk.

I'm really glad that we were able to get the exclusive interview with the governor earlier today. We managed to **broadcast** it before all the other **stations**! Just a quick reminder that next week we'll be **holding tours** for students and jobseekers interested in **our line of work**. They'll get to check out areas like the production planning desk, our recording studios, and the main operations center. I want to **gather a few volunteers** who can dedicate some of their time to help with this. If you'd like to participate, please send me an e-mail.

저희가 오늘 아까 주지사님과 독점 인터뷰를 할 수 있었던 것이 정말 기쁩니다. 저희는 다른 모든 방송국들보다 앞서 그 내용을 방송할 수 있었습니다! 다시 한 번 간단히 말씀 드리고 싶은 것은, 다음 주에 저희가 저희 분야의 일에 관심 있으신 학생 및 구직자들을 위해 견학 행사를 개최할 예정입니다. 제작 기획 데스크, 저희 녹음 스튜디오, 그리고 중앙 관제 센터

같은 구역들을 확인해 보시게 될 것입니다. 이 행사에 도움을 주시는 데 일부 시간을 할애해 주실 수 있는 몇몇 자원 봉사자를 모집하고자 합니다. 참여하고자 하시는 경우, 제게 이메일을 보내 주시기 바랍니다.

어휘 exclusive 독점적인, 전용의 governor 주지사 manage to do (어떻게든) ~할 수 있다, ~해내다

1. 화자는 어떤 업계에 종사하고 있을 것 같은가?
(A) 교육
(B) 의료
(C) 언론
(D) 통신

해설 화자가 담화 시작 부분에 채널 청취에 대한 감사의 인사를 전하면서 주지사와 가졌던 인터뷰를 언급하고 있어 방송국 직원임을 알 수 있으므로 (C)가 정답이다.

2. 무엇이 다음 주에 계획되어 있는가?
(A) 신입 사원 오리엔테이션
(B) 온라인 영상 생방송
(C) 보안 점검
(D) 시설 견학

해설 담화 중반부에 화자가 학생 및 구직자들을 위한 견학 행사를 개최한다고 알리면서 제작 기획 데스크, 녹음 스튜디오, 그리고 중앙 관제 센터 같은 구역들을 확인해 본다고 알리고 있으므로 (D)가 정답이다.

어휘 streaming 온라인 방송, 영상 재생

3. 누가 화자에게 이메일을 보내야 하는가?
(A) 세미나에 참석하는 사람들
(B) 자원 봉사할 의향이 있는 사람들
(C) 후보자를 추천해 주기를 원하는 사람들
(D) 출장을 떠나는 사람들

해설 화자가 담화 후반부에 행사에 도움을 주는 데 시간을 할애할 수 있는 자원 봉사자를 모집한다는 말과 함께 참여를 원하면 자신에게 이메일을 보내라고 요청하고 있으므로 (B)가 정답이다.

방송

지역 날씨 소식을 전해 드리겠습니다. 오늘 남은 하루 동안, 소노마 지역 전체에 걸쳐 건조하고 잔뜩 흐린 날씨가 예상되겠습니다. 내일은, 기온이 다시 내려갈 것으로 예상되는 가운데, 가볍게 흩날리는 강설량이 발생할 가능성이 있습니다. 따라서, 어떤 야외 활동 계획이든 있으실 경우에 반드시 따뜻하게 차려 입으시기 바랍니다. 다음 주를 내다보면, 마침내 약간의 봄 기운이 느껴질 것입니다. 이제, 잠시 후에 이어질 순서로, 중요한 축구 경기 승리를 포함해, 우리 지역 스포츠 팀들의 최근 결과를 살펴 보겠습니다.

Practice

1. (D) **2.** (C) **3.** (A)

Questions 1-3 refer to the following broadcast.

This is your host, Carl Kelly. In other news, the old textile factory in the downtown area is finally set to be torn down. The site has been vacant for four years after the **factory transferred** to a bigger facility located inland. After reviewing several proposals, the city council has decided to sell the run-down property to **developer** Alex Santos, who plans to **transform the land into residential apartments** that include a dozen contemporary units with an underground parking area. Next up, it seems like the rain is starting to ease up, meaning sunny skies this weekend. Stay tuned after the commercial break for the **weather forecast** with Hannah.

저는 여러분의 진행자, 칼 켈리입니다. 다른 소식으로, 시내 지역의 한 오래된 직물 공장이 마침내 철거될 예정입니다. 이 부지는 해당 공장이 내륙 지역에 위치한 더 큰 시설로 이전한 뒤로 4년 동안 비어 있는 상태였습니다. 여러 제안서들을 검토한 후에, 시의회가 이 노후한 건물을 개발업자 알렉스 산토스 씨에게 매각하기로 결정했으며, 산토스 씨는 해당 부지를 지하 주차장을 갖춘 십여 개의 현대적인 세대를 포함하는 주거용 아파트로 탈바꿈시킬 계획입니다. 다음 소식으로는, 비가 누그러지기 시작할 것으로 보이며, 이는 이번 주말 하늘이 쾌청할 것임을 의미합니다. 광고 후에 한나 씨와 함께 하는 일기 예보를 위해 채널 고정해 주시기 바랍니다.

어휘 textile 직물 tear down ~을 철거하다 inland ad. 내륙에, 내륙으로 a. 내륙의 run-down 노후한, 낡은 dozen 십여 개의, 12개의 contemporary 현대적인 ease up 누그러지다, 완화되다 stay tuned 채널을 고정해 놓다

1. 화자의 말에 따르면, 4년 전에 무슨 일이 있었는가?
(A) 한 건물이 심하게 손상되었다.
(B) 시 의회가 설립되었다.
(C) 한 건축 프로젝트가 시작되었다.

(D) 한 업체가 이전했다.

해설 담화 초반부에 화자가 오래된 공장 한 곳을 언급하면서 그 공장이 내륙 지역에 위치한 더 큰 시설로 이전한 뒤로 부지가 4년 동안 비어 있었다고 알리고 있으므로 (D)가 정답이다.

2. 알렉스 산토스 씨는 누구인가?
(A) 시 소속 점검 담당자
(B) 대출 담당 은행원
(C) 부동산 개발업자
(D) 행사 기획자

해설 화자가 담화 중반부에 시 의회가 노후한 건물을 개발업자 알렉스 산토스 씨에게 매각하기로 결정한 사실과 함께 산토스 씨가 그 건물을 주거용 아파트로 탈바꿈시킬 것이라고 알리고 있어 부동산 개발업자임을 알 수 있으므로 (C)가 정답이다.

3. 청자들은 곧이어 무엇에 관해 들을 것인가?
(A) 날씨
(B) 새로운 주차 법
(C) 음악 축제
(D) 교통 소식

해설 담화 후반부에 화자가 비와 관련된 이야기를 꺼내면서 광고 후에 일기 예보를 들을 수 있도록 채널 고정해 달라고 요청하고 있으므로 (A)가 정답이다.

Check-up Test

1. (A)	**2.** (C)	**3.** (B)	**4.** (D)	**5.** (D)
6. (B)	**7.** (D)	**8.** (A)	**9.** (D)	**10.** (A)
11. (A)	**12.** (B)	**13.** (B)	**14.** (C)	**15.** (A)
16. (C)	**17.** (C)	**18.** (D)		

Questions 1-3 refer to the following broadcast.

In this episode of the Business Spotlight, **1 we're exploring everything related to social media marketing.** The big question is, what steps can companies take to enhance their marketing approaches and connect more effectively with target customers? Well, we have Emma Gustavson, Chief Marketing Director at Morales Consulting, joining us to offer her insight. As you may know, Emma is a regular on our show because **2 she's great at simplifying complicated business concepts and providing straightforward advice.** Before we begin, though, **3 I'm going to go over my findings from a survey** I conducted where many of you shared creative product placement techniques.

비즈니스 스포트라이트의 이번 방송분에서는, 소셜 미디어 마케팅과 관련된 모든 것을 탐구합니다. 중요한 질문은, '회사들이 마케팅 접근법을 향상시키고 대상 고객들과 더욱 효과적으로 교류하기 위해 어떤 조치를 취할 수 있는가?'입니다. 자, 모랄레스 컨설팅 사의 최고 마케팅 이사이신 엠마 거스터브슨 씨께서 함께 자리하셔서 통찰력을 제공해 주시겠습니다. 아마 아시겠지만, 엠마 씨께서는 저희 프로그램의 단골 초대 손님이신데, 이분께서 복잡한 비즈니스 개념을 단순화해 간단한 조언을 제공해 주시는 데 탁월하시기 때문입니다. 하지만, 시작하기에 앞서, 여러분 중 많은 분들께서 창의적인 제품 배치 기술을 공유해 주셨던 것으로서 제가 실시했던 설문 조사의 결과물을 살펴 보겠습니다.

어휘 episode 1회 방송분 explore ~을 탐구하다, 살펴 보다 step 조치, 단계 insight 통찰력 simplify ~을 간소화하다 straightforward 간단한, 복잡하지 않은 go over ~을 살펴 보다, 검토하다 placement 배치, 놓아 두기

1. 팟캐스트 방송분은 무엇에 관한 것인가?
(A) 마케팅 전략
(B) 인터넷 보안
(C) 대중 연설
(D) 최근의 소비자 경향

해설 화자가 담화를 시작하면서 소셜 미디어 마케팅과 관련된 모든 것을 탐구한다는 말로 방송 주제를 밝히고 있으므로 (A)가 정답이다.

2. 화자는 거스터브슨 씨가 무엇에 탁월하다고 말하는가?
(A) 대규모 팀을 관리하는 일
(B) 직원 효율성을 개선하는 일
(C) 복잡한 아이디어들을 설명하는 일
(D) 회사들이 돈을 아끼도록 돕는 일

해설 담화 중반부에 화자가 거스터브슨 씨를 언급하면서 그 사람이 복잡한 비즈니스 개념을 단순화해 간단한 조언을 제공하는 데 탁월하다고 설명하고 있으므로 (C)가 정답이다.

3. 화자는 곧이어 무엇을 이야기할 것인가?
(A) 재정 관련 조언
(B) 설문 조사 결과
(C) 새로운 뉴스
(D) 지역 후원사

해설 화자가 담화 마지막 부분에 자신이 실시한 설문 조사의 결

과물을 먼저 살펴 보겠다고 알리고 있으므로 (B)가 정답이다.

Questions 4-6 refer to the following talk.

4 **If you're a beginner in travel photography, you've joined the right place!** I'm a professional photographer with years of experience working all over the world, and I have a few simple tips for taking great photos. Even when you're on the go, the fundamentals remain the same. But, **5** **always pay special attention to the lighting** — it dramatically affects the overall quality of your pictures. I notice people are already leaving comments in the live chat right now. If you'd like, **6** **please upload your photos there, because I'll be picking several to evaluate next month on my blog.**

여행 사진 촬영의 초보자이시라면, 제대로 찾아 오셨습니다! 저는 전 세계 모든 곳에서 수년 간의 작업 경험을 지닌 전문 사진 작가이며, 훌륭한 사진을 촬영하기 위한 몇 가지 간단한 팁이 있습니다. 심지어 바쁘게 움직이시는 경우에도, 기본 원칙은 동일하게 유지됩니다. 하지만, 항상 빛에 특별히 주의를 기울이셔야 하는데, 그것이 여러분 사진의 전반적인 수준에 극적으로 영향을 미치기 때문입니다. 여러분께서 지금 벌써 라이브 채팅창에 의견을 남겨 주시고 계시는 게 보이네요. 괜찮으시면, 여러분의 사진을 그곳에 업로드해 주셨으면 하는데, 제가 몇 개를 선별해서 다음 달에 제 블로그에서 평가할 것이기 때문입니다.

어휘 **photography** 사진 촬영(술) **on the go** 바쁘게 움직이는, 끊임없이 활동하는 **fundamental** n. 기본 원칙, 근본, 핵심 **remain the same** 동일하게 유지되다

4. 담화는 어떤 종류의 사진 촬영에 관한 것인가?
(A) 풍경
(B) 광고
(C) 행사
(D) 여행

해설 화자가 담화를 시작하면서 여행 사진 촬영의 초보자를 대상으로 하는 프로그램임을 밝히고 있으므로 (D)가 정답이다.

5. 화자의 말에 따르면, 무엇이 사진가가 좋은 사진을 촬영하는 데 도움을 주는가?
(A) 자동 플래시
(B) 카메라 스탠드
(C) 광각 렌즈
(D) 광원

해설 담화 중반부에 화자가 항상 빛에 특별히 주의를 기울이도록 당부하고 있으므로 (D)가 정답이다.

6. 화자가 다음 달에 무엇을 할 것이라고 말하는가?
(A) 몇몇 질문에 답변하는 일
(B) 몇몇 사진을 평가하는 일
(C) 동영상을 게시하는 일
(D) 시연회를 제공하는 일

해설 담화 맨 마지막 부분에 화자가 사진을 업로드하도록 권하면서 다음 달에 자신의 블로그에서 몇 개를 선별해 평가할 것이라고 알리고 있으므로 (B)가 정답이다.

Questions 7-9 refer to the following broadcast and map.

Hello, I'm Morris Li with updates for Westmont citizens. **7** **You probably noticed that taxes have risen this year**, and I'm sure you want to know how those funds are being utilized. Well, the city is launching four big projects to enhance our garden, city hall, sports arena, and airport. **8** **Construction at the sports arena is already under way**, with the other projects scheduled to begin soon. And don't forget that next month, the election for mayor is happening. Your vote will determine which community initiatives will be prioritized in the future. **9** **Candidates will be in our studio this Thursday to hold a debate**, so please tune in!

안녕하세요, 저는 웨스트몬트 시민 여러분께 새로운 소식을 전해 드리는 모리스 리입니다. 아마 올해 세금이 인상되었다는 사실을 아셨을 텐데, 분명 그 자금이 어떻게 활용되고 있는지 알고 싶으실 것입니다. 자, 시에서는 우리의 정원과 시청, 스포츠 경기장, 그리고 공항을 향상시키기 위한 네 가지 중요 프로젝트에 착수합니다. 스포츠 경기장 공사가 이미 진행 중이며, 나머지 프로젝트들도 곧 시작될 예정입니다. 그리고 다음 달에, 시장 선거가 있다는 사실을 잊지 마시기 바랍니다. 여러분의 표가 어느 지역 사회 계획들이 앞으로 우선시될지 결정할 것입니다. 후보자들께서 이번 주 목요일에 저희 스튜디오에 나오셔서 토론을 개최하실 것이므로, 채널을 고정해 주시기 바랍니다!

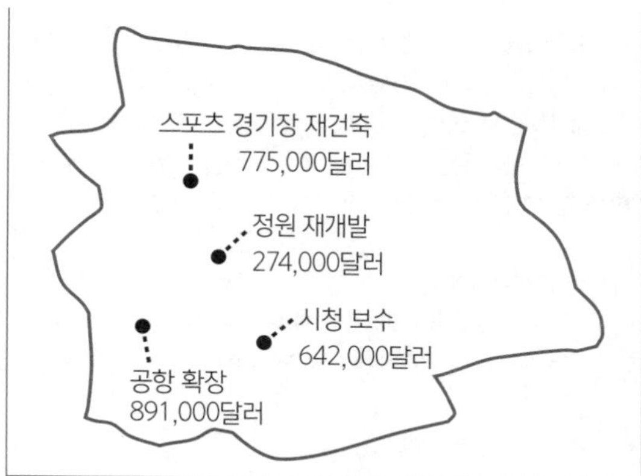

어휘 utilize ~을 활용하다 under way 진행 중인 election 선거 vote 표, 투표, 표결 determine ~을 결정하다 initiative n. 계획 prioritize ~을 우선시하다 tune in 채널을 고정하다

7. 화자는 주민들이 무엇을 알게 되었다고 말하는가?
(A) 더 높은 공과금
(B) 좋지 못한 도로 상태
(C) 더 많은 여가 시설
(D) 늘어난 지방세

해설 화자가 담화 초반부에 청자들이 올해 세금이 인상되었다는 사실을 알게 되었을 거라고 언급하고 있으므로 (D)가 정답이다.

어휘 utility (수도·전기 등의) 공익 사업

8. 시각자료를 보시오. 현재 작업이 이뤄지고 있는 프로젝트의 비용이 얼마인가?
(A) 775,000달러
(B) 274,000달러
(C) 642,000달러
(D) 891,000달러

해설 담화 중반부에 화자가 스포츠 경기장 공사가 이미 진행 중이라고 알리고 있으며, 시각자료에서 상단에 Sports Arena Reconstruction으로 표기된 공사의 비용이 $775,000로 쓰여 있으므로 (A)가 정답이다.

9. 무엇이 목요일로 예정되어 있는가?
(A) 경연 대회
(B) 포럼
(C) 세미나
(D) 토론

해설 화자가 담화 후반부에 시장 선거 후보자들이 이번 주 목요일에 스튜디오에서 토론을 개최할 것이라고 밝히고 있으므로 (D)가 정답이다.

Questions 10-12 refer to the following talk.

As the nutrition advisor commissioned by your company, 10 **I plan to assess your cafeteria's menu and make improvements.** 11 **Did you know that reducing meat consumption is not only beneficial for our health but also more environmentally friendly?** What's more, a recent study on thousands of cafeteria meals revealed something intriguing – when more vegetarian choices are available, the number of vegetarian dishes getting eaten rises considerably. 12 **I understand some of you worry that I might completely recreate your company's whole menu.** But even minor adjustments can make a huge impact!

귀사로부터 의뢰를 받은 영양 자문으로서, 저는 귀사 구내식당의 메뉴를 평가하고 개선할 계획입니다. 고기 소비를 줄이는 것이 우리의 건강에 유익할 뿐만 아니라 환경적으로도 더 친화적이라는 사실을 알고 계셨나요? 더욱이, 수천 곳의 구내식당에 대한 최근 연구에 따르면 아주 흥미로운 점이 드러났는데, 더 많은 채식주의 선택사항이 이용 가능할 때, 사람들이 먹는 채식주의 요리의 수도 상당히 증가합니다. 여러분 중 일부는 제가 귀사의 전체 메뉴를 완전히 다시 만들까 봐 걱정하고 계신다는 사실을 알고 있습니다. 하지만, 심지어 사소한 조정이 엄청난 영향을 미칠 수 있습니다!

어휘 nutrition 영양 (섭취) commission ~에게 의뢰하다, 위탁하다 consumption 소비, 먹음 What's more 더욱이 reveal ~을 드러내다 intriguing 아주 흥미로운 whole 전체의 adjustment 조정, 조절

10. 화자는 주로 무엇을 이야기하고 있는가?
(A) 선택 가능한 식사 종류를 업데이트하는 일
(B) 채식주의 식단을 권장하는 일
(C) 지속 가능성을 촉진하는 일
(D) 선호 음식 관련 정보를 수집하는 일

해설 화자가 담화 초반부에 구내식당의 메뉴를 평가하고 개선할 계획임을 먼저 밝힌 다음, 그러한 계획을 세운 이유 등과 관련해 이야기하고 있으므로 (A)가 정답이다.

어휘 selection 선택 (가능한 종류) sustainability 지속 가능성

11. 화자가 왜 최근의 연구를 언급하는가?
(A) 자신의 의견을 뒷받침하기 위해
(B) 한 가지 정책을 소개하기 위해

(C) 실수를 바로잡기 위해
(D) 비교하기 위해

해설 화자가 담화 중반부에 고기 소비를 줄이는 것이 건강에도 유익하고 더 환경 친화적이라는 사실을 알고 있었는지 물은 다음, 최근의 연구 결과에 나타난 채식주의 식사의 이점을 언급하고 있다. 이는 자신이 주장하는 바를 뒷받침하기 위한 일종의 증거를 제시하는 것이므로 (A)가 정답이다.

12. 화자가 왜 "심지어 사소한 조정이 엄청난 영향을 미칠 수 있습니다"라고 말하는가?
(A) 우려를 표하기 위해
(B) 청자들을 안심시키기 위해
(C) 회의를 개최하도록 제안하기 위해
(D) 직원들에게 상기시키는 메시지를 전하기 위해

해설 화자가 담화 후반부에 청자들이 전체 메뉴를 완전히 다시 만들까 걱정하고 있다는 사실을 알고 있다고 알리면서 '심지어 사소한 조정이 엄청난 영향을 미칠 수 있습니다'라고 말하는 흐름이다. 이는 메뉴 변화의 긍정적인 영향을 언급해 청자들이 걱정하지 않도록 안심시키려는 말이므로 (B)가 정답이다.

어휘 **reassure** ~을 안심시키다 **reminder** (상기시키는) 메시지, 안내, 말

Questions 13-15 refer to the following broadcast.

In today's local events, 13 **Fullerton Mart is hosting a party that's open to the public to commemorate its third year since opening.** Owner Sadia Klossner sat down with me to chat about the business's success. She explained that Fullerton Mart is known for 14 **providing a wide range of goods to cater to the city's multicultural community. Many shoppers clearly love having the opportunity to buy items that remind them of their home countries.** Looking ahead, Klossner mentioned that 15 **she's starting to raise funds from investors, with the hopes of establishing additional Fullerton Marts across the nation.**

오늘의 지역 행사 소식으로는, 풀러튼 마트가 개장 이후로 3주년을 기념하기 위해 일반인들에게 공개되는 파티를 주최합니다. 소유주 사디아 클로스너 씨가 이 업체의 성공에 관해 이야기해 주시기 위해 저와 함께 앉아 계셨습니다. 클로스너 씨는 풀러튼 마트가 우리 시에 있는 다문화 공동체의 구미에 맞춘 아주 다양한 상품을 제공하는 것으로 알려져 있다고 설명해 주셨습니다. 많은 쇼핑객들은 분명 고국을 떠올리게 해 주는 제품을 구입할 기회를 갖는 것을 아주 좋아합니다. 미래를 내다보면서, 클로스너 씨는 전국에 걸쳐 추가로 풀러튼 마트를 설립하기 위한 희망을 안고, 투자자들을 통해 자금을 마련하기 시작하는 중이라고 언급해 주셨습니다.

어휘 **commemorate** ~을 기념하다 **cater to** ~의 구미에 맞추다, ~을 충족시키다 **remind A of B** A에게 B를 떠올리게 하다, 상기시키다 **look ahead** 미래를 내다보다

13. 풀러튼 마트는 왜 파티를 주최하는가?
(A) 더 많은 고객을 끌어들이기 위해
(B) 기념일을 축하하기 위해
(C) 할인된 제품을 판매하기 위해
(D) 은퇴하는 직원을 기리기 위해

해설 화자가 담화를 시작하면서 풀러튼 마트가 개장 이후로 3주년을 기념하기 위해 일반인들에게 공개되는 파티를 주최한다고 밝히고 있으므로 (B)가 정답이다.

14. 사디아 클로스너 씨의 말에 따르면, 풀러튼 마트는 왜 성공했는가?
(A) 다국어 서비스를 제공한다.
(B) 널찍한 시설이 있다.
(C) 외국 제품을 제공한다.
(D) 다른 업체들과 협업한다.

해설 화자가 담화 중반부에 풀러튼 마트가 다문화 공동체의 구미에 맞춘 아주 다양한 상품을 제공하는 것으로 알려져 있다고 클로스너 씨가 말한 것을 언급하면서 많은 쇼핑객들이 고국을 떠올리게 해 주는 제품을 구입할 수 있다고 밝히고 있다. 이는 외국에서 들여 온 제품을 판매한다는 뜻이므로 (C)가 정답이다.

어휘 **multilingual** 다국어의

15. 사디아 클로스너 씨는 왜 자금을 마련하고 있는가?
(A) 더 많은 지점을 개장하기 위해
(B) 지역에 기부하기 위해
(C) 선택 가능한 종류를 확대하기 위해
(D) 해외로 여행하기 위해

해설 화자가 담화 마지막 부분에 클로스너 씨가 전국에 걸쳐 추가로 풀러튼 마트를 설립하기 위해 자금을 마련하기 시작하는 중이라고 언급한 사실을 전하고 있으므로 (A)가 정답이다.

Questions 16-18 refer to the following talk.

Here's the storage cabinet with all the supplies for our cleaning crew. **16 During today's training, you must become familiar** with which surface cleaners are used for different areas of our resort, like wooden or marble floors. **17 The large dispenser on the top shelf, Sparkle-X, is for bath tiles, and right below that is a new item that we implemented recently.** It's great for removing carpet stains. Also, please keep in mind that **18 a deliveryman comes every Wednesday at 11 A.M. to restock any low supplies**, so be sure to check inventory regularly.

여기 우리 청소팀을 위해 모든 용품이 담긴 보관용 캐비닛이 있습니다. 오늘 교육 시간 중에, 여러분께서는 반드시 어느 표면 세척제가 목재 바닥 또는 대리석 바닥 같이, 우리 리조트의 서로 다른 구역에 쓰이는지 숙지하신 상태가 되어야 합니다. 맨 위쪽 선반의 대용량 용기에 담긴 스파클-X는 욕실 타일용이며, 바로 그 아래에 있는 것은 우리가 최근 도입한 신제품입니다. 카펫 얼룩을 제거하는 데 아주 좋습니다. 또한, 배송 기사님께서 매주 수요일 오전 11시에 오셔서 모든 부족한 용품을 다시 채워 주시므로, 꼭 주기적으로 재고를 확인하셔야 한다는 점도 명심하시기 바랍니다.

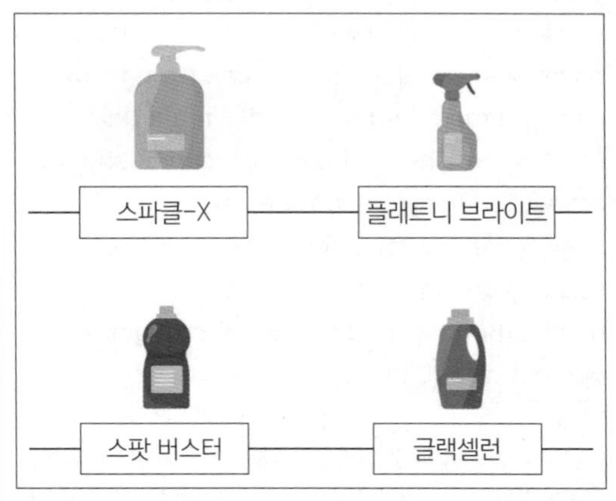

어휘 crew (함께 작업하는) 팀, 조 surface 표면 dispenser (버튼 등을 이용해 내용물을 꺼내 사용하는) 용기 stain 얼룩 keep in mind that ~임을 명심하다 restock (재고 등) ~을 다시 채우다 inventory 재고 (목록)

16. 담화의 목적은 무엇인가?
(A) 문제를 해결하는 것
(B) 몇몇 제품을 시연하는 것
(C) 일부 직원을 교육하는 것
(D) 행사를 준비하는 것

해설 화자가 담화 초반부에 교육 시간임을 밝히면서 청자들이 숙지해야 하는 부분을 알리고 있으므로 (C)가 정답이다.

17. 시각자료를 보시오. 화자가 어느 제품이 새 것이라고 말하는가?
(A) 스파클-X
(B) 플래트니 브라이트
(C) 스팟 버스터
(D) 글랙셀런

해설 담화 중반부에 화자가 맨 위쪽 선반의 대용량 용기에 담긴 스파클-X 바로 아래에 있는 것이 최근 도입한 신제품이라고 알리고 있다. 시각자료에서 왼쪽 상단에 Sparkle-X가 있고, 그 아래에 위치한 제품이 Spot Buster로 표기되어 있으므로 (C)가 정답이다.

18. 수요일마다 11시에 무슨 일이 있는가?
(A) 점검이 진행된다.
(B) 일정표가 게시된다.
(C) 책임자가 방문한다.
(D) 배송이 도착한다.

해설 화자가 담화 마지막 부분에 배송 기사가 매주 수요일 오전 11시에 와서 모든 부족한 용품을 다시 채워 준다고 알리고 있다. 이는 배송 물품이 온다는 뜻이므로 (D)가 정답이다.

Playlist 14
공지/광고 담화 절대 안 틀리는 방법

공지

승객 여러분, 주목해 주십시오. 이 안내 방송은 바르셀로나로 향하는 선스트림 항공사 DX42 항공편에 대한 것입니다. 유감스럽게도, 지역 내 강한 폭풍으로 인해 탑승하는데 지연을 겪고 있습니다. 우리 지역 기상 관측소는 상황이 한 시간 내에 개선될 것이라고 알렸습니다. 그 사이에, 저희가 검색 과정을 시작할 수 있도록 여러분의 탑승권을 꺼내 준비해 주시기 바랍니다. 여러분의 인내 및 선스트림 항공사를 선택해 주신 것에 대해 감사드립니다.

Practice

1. (B) **2.** (B) **3.** (C)

Questions 1-3 refer to the following announcement.

I'd like to kick off our team meeting with exciting news. I'm happy to announce that the International Marketing Association has chosen our agency to **receive an award**! As you may recall, we signed a contract with Big Smile Snacks, our first major client, earlier this year. Our 3D graphics team developed a set of animated **commercials** for them. The award will honor the creative animation style that was demonstrated in those **ads**. So, please join our **banquet** on February 9, where the award will be presented.

흥미로운 소식으로 우리 팀 회의를 시작하고자 합니다. 국제 마케팅 협회에서 우리 업체가 상을 받도록 선정했다는 소식을 전해 드리게 되어 기쁩니다! 기억하실지 모르겠지만, 우리는 올해 초에 우리의 첫 주요 고객사인 빅 스마일 스낵 사와 계약을 맺었습니다. 우리 3D 그래픽 팀이 그곳을 위해 일련의 애니메이션 광고들을 개발했습니다. 이 상은 그 광고들 속에서 보여진 창의적인 애니메이션 양식을 기릴 것입니다. 따라서, 2월 9일에 이 상이 수여될 우리 연회에 함께 해 주시기 바랍니다.

어휘 kick off ~을 시작하다 recall 기억하다, 떠올리다 honor ~을 기리다, ~에 영예를 주다 demonstrate ~을 보여 주다, 시연하다, 설명하다

1. 화자는 무엇과 관련해 기쁘다고 말하는가?
(A) 사무실 공간을 확장하는 일
(B) 상을 받는 일
(C) 세미나를 진행하는 일
(D) 한 출판물에 특집으로 실리는 일

해설 화자가 담화 초반부에 국제 마케팅 협회가 화자의 소속 업체를 상을 받는 곳으로 선정한 사실을 알리면서 기쁨을 표현하고 있으므로 (B)가 정답이다.

2. 화자가 어떤 종류의 업체에 근무하고 있는가?
(A) 영화 제작사
(B) 광고 회사
(C) 재무 컨설팅 업체
(D) 식품 제조사

해설 담화 중반부에 화자가 소속 업체의 3D 그래픽 팀이 고객사를 위해 애니메이션 광고를 만든 사실을 언급하고 있으므로 (B)가 정답이다.

3. 무엇이 2월 9일로 계획되어 있는가?
(A) 연례 저녁 만찬
(B) 제품 시연회
(C) 연회
(D) 공연

해설 화자가 담화 마지막 부분에 2월 9일에 있을 연회에 함께 하도록 권하는 말을 하고 있으므로 (C)가 정답이다.

광고

침실 하나짜리 아파트에 거주하고 계시면서 가구를 찾고 계신가요? CozyCorner.com으로 오셔서 저희 소형 안락 의자를 확인해 보십시오! 이 혁신적인 의자는 쿠션 처리된 상자에 깔끔하게 접혀 들어가므로, 여러분의 공간을 최대한 활용하시게 됩니다. 이용하실 준비가 되시면, 소파를 지탱할 수 있도록 손잡이 끈을 잡아 당겨 주시기만 하면 됩니다. 더욱이, 이번 달에는, 저희 청취자들을 위한 독점 제공 서비스가 있습니다! 저희 웹 사이트의 결제 코너에서 코드 921X를 사용하시면 귀하의 주문품과 함께 무료 베개 2개를 받으실 것입니다. 그러므로 오늘 CozyCorner.com을 방문하셔서 여러분의 단독 공간을 널찍한 아파트로 탈바꿈시켜 보시기 바랍니다!

Practice

1. (D) **2.** (B) **3.** (A)

Questions 1-3 refer to the following advertisement.

Tired of constantly misplacing items because your space is too messy? If this sounds like you, the Ultimate Storage Organizer is just what you need. Specifically created for busy office workers, this product can **transform** even the most **cluttered** table into a **tidy** workspace. The best part is, it can **easily adjust** to fit any amount of area on your desk. Whether you need it slim or wide, you can configure it in just seconds! **Call** us now **within the next 30 minutes** to get a 25 percent discount!

여러분의 공간이 너무 엉망이기 때문에 지속적으로 물품을 분실하시는 것이 지겨우신가요? 이것이 여러분의 이야기처럼 들리신다면, 얼티메이트 스토리지 오거나이저가 바로 여러분께 필요한 것입니다. 바쁜 사무직 직장인들을 위해 특별히 만들어진, 이 제품은 심지어 가장 어수선한 탁자도 말끔한 업무 공간으로 탈바꿈시켜 드릴 수 있습니다. 가장 뛰어난 부분은, 여러분 책상 위에서 어떤 크기의 공간에도 어울릴 수 있도록 손쉽게 조절될 수 있다는 점입니다. 슬림할 필요가 있든, 아니면 폭이 넓을 필요가 있든 상관없이, 불과 몇 초 만에 구성하실 수 있습니다! 앞으로 30분 내에 지금 저희에게 전화하셔서 25퍼센트 할인을 받아 보시기 바랍니다!

어휘 constantly 지속적으로, 끊임없이 misplace ~을 분실하다, 둔 곳을 잊다 messy 엉망인, 지저분한 specifically 특별히, 구체적으로 cluttered 어수선한 configure ~을 구성하다

1. 어떤 종류의 제품이 광고되고 있는가?
(A) 컴퓨터 모니터
(B) 보관 창고
(C) 식탁
(D) 책상 정리용품

해설 담화 시작 부분에 화자가 Ultimate Storage Organizer라는 제품명을 언급하고 있고, 이어서 가장 어수선한 탁자도 말끔한 업무 공간으로 탈바꿈시켜 줄 수 있다는 특징을 알리고 있으므로 (D)가 정답이다.

2. 화자는 어떤 특별 기능을 강조하는가?
(A) 무게가 가볍다.
(B) 조절 가능하다.
(C) 재활용 소재로 만들어진다.
(D) 다양한 디자인으로 나온다.

해설 화자가 담화 중반부에 책상 위에서 어떤 크기의 공간에도 어울릴 수 있도록 손쉽게 조절될 수 있다는 특징을 특별히 언급하고 있으므로 (B)가 정답이다.

어휘 lightweight 가벼운, 경량인 adjustable 조절 가능한, 조정 가능한

3. 청자들은 어떻게 할인을 받을 수 있는가?
(A) 제한 시간 내에 전화함으로써
(B) 특정 웹 페이지를 방문함으로써
(C) 한 소셜 미디어 계정을 팔로우함으로써
(D) 키워드를 한 번호에 문자메시지로 전송함으로써

해설 담화 마지막 부분에 화자가 30분 내로 전화하면 25퍼센트 할인을 받을 수 있다고 알리고 있으므로 (A)가 정답이다.

Check-up Test

1. (B)	**2.** (A)	**3.** (C)	**4.** (D)	**5.** (B)
6. (C)	**7.** (C)	**8.** (D)	**9.** (A)	**10.** (B)
11. (A)	**12.** (D)	**13.** (A)	**14.** (A)	**15.** (B)
16. (A)	**17.** (B)	**18.** (B)		

Questions 1-3 refer to the following advertisement.

Ever feel like you don't have enough time to read? 1 **ListenUp Audiobooks is your solution.** Whenever you're busy commuting, exercising, or doing chores, we help you make the most of your time. 1 **Using the ListenUp app,** you can easily select a publication from our wide range of options and save it directly to your phone or tablet. 2 **Our collection is so vast that we've even earned an award from the United Readers Association for our comprehensive mix of classic and modern texts.** Interested in giving us a try? 3 **Head over to ListenUp's official Web site to download your first audiobook for free** when you become a member.

독서할 시간이 충분하지 않은 것 같다고 항상 느끼시나요? 리슨업 오디오북이 여러분의 해결책입니다. 통근이나 운동, 또는 잡일을 하시느라 바쁘실 때마다, 저희가 여러분의 시간을 최대한 활용하시도록 도와 드립니다. 리슨업 앱을 이용하셔서, 손쉽게 아주 다양한 저희 선택사항들 중에서 출간물을 하나 고르신 다음, 곧바로 여러분의 전화기나 태블릿에 저장하실 수 있습니다. 저희 소장품이 너무 방대해서 저희는 심지어 고전 및 현대 도서의 포괄적인 조합에 대해 독서가 연합 협회로부터 상도 받은 바 있습니다. 한번 시도해 보시는 데 관심이 있으신가요? 저희 리슨업의 공식 웹 사이트로 찾아 오셔서 회원이 되실 때 무료로 첫 오디오북을 다운로드해 보시기 바랍니다.

어휘 commute 통근하다, 통학하다 chores 잡일 make the most of ~을 최대한 활용하다 vast 방대한, 막대한 head over to ~로 찾아 가다, 향하다

1. 어떤 업체가 광고되고 있는가?
(A) 출판사
(B) 오디오북 플랫폼
(C) 스포츠 아카데미
(D) 녹음 스튜디오

해설 화자가 담화 초반부에 '리슨업 오디오북'이라는 업체명과 함께 이곳의 앱을 이용하는 방법을 언급하고 있으므로 (B)가 정답이다.

2. 업체는 무엇에 대해 상을 받았는가?
(A) 다양한 선택 종류
(B) 합리적인 요금
(C) 제품 혁신
(D) 소비자 만족도

해설 담화 중반부에 화자가 소속 업체의 소장품이 너무 방대해서 고전 및 현대 도서의 포괄적인 조합에 대해 한 협회로부터 상을 받은 사실을 밝히고 있으므로 (A)가 정답이다.

3. 화자는 어떤 제공 서비스를 언급하는가?
(A) 환불 보장
(B) 무료 특급 배송
(C) 무료 제품
(D) 회원 카드

해설 화자가 담화 후반부에 회원이 될 때 무료로 첫 오디오북을 다운로드할 수 있는 혜택을 알리고 있으므로 (C)가 정답이다.

어휘 money-back 환불해 주는

Questions 4-6 refer to the following announcement.

We appreciate your attendance to our classical music concert tonight. **4 The performance was set to start at 6 o'clock**, but some of our speakers are having issues. **4 Our audio team is currently working hard to fix the problem.** Meanwhile, I'd like to share an opportunity to support our theater. **5 Did you know that our ushers are all volunteers? And, we're always open to more help. Ushers help** collect admission tickets and guide guests to their seats, all while getting to enjoy live shows at no cost. For those interested, **6 please see the back of your program for further information.**

오늘 밤 저희 클래식 음악 콘서트에 참석해 주셔서 감사 드립니다. 공연이 6시에 시작될 예정이었지만, 일부 스피커에 문제가 있습니다. 저희 오디오 담당팀이 현재 이 문제를 바로잡기 위해 열심히 노력하고 있습니다. 그 사이에, 저희 극장을 지원하실 수 있는 기회를 공유해 드리고자 합니다. 저희 안내원들이 모두 자원 봉사자라는 사실을 알고 계셨나요? 그리고, 저희는 항상 추가 도움에 대해 열려 있습니다. 안내원은 입장권을 걷고 손님들을 좌석으로 안내하는 데 도움을 드림과 동시에, 모두 무료로 라이브 공연을 즐기게 됩니다. 관심 있으신 분들께서는, 추가 정보를 위해 가지고 계신 프로그램 책자의 뒷면을 확인하시기 바랍니다.

어휘 be set to do ~할 예정이다 meanwhile 그 사이에, 그러는 동안 usher 안내원 get to do ~하게 되다 at no cost 무료로

4. 화자가 왜 "일부 스피커에 문제가 있습니다"라고 말하는가?
(A) 발표자의 변동을 설명하기 위해
(B) 제품 추천을 요청하기 위해
(C) 청자들에게 한 가지 정책을 상기시키기 위해
(D) 지연 문제에 대해 사과하기 위해

해설 화자가 담화 시작 부분에 공연이 6시에 시작될 예정이었다는 말과 함께 '일부 스피커에 문제가 있습니다'라고 언급하면서 그 문제를 바로잡기 위해 노력하고 있다고 밝히고 있다. 이는 공연 지연 문제에 대한 원인을 밝히고 사과의 말을 전하는 것이므로 (D)가 정답이다.

5. 청자들은 무엇을 하도록 요청받는가?
(A) 중고 물품을 기부하는 일
(B) 자원 봉사자가 되는 일
(C) 소식지를 신청하는 일
(D) 몇몇 다과를 즐기는 일

해설 담화 중반부에 화자가 안내원들이 모두 자원 봉사자라는 사실을 알고 있었는지 물으면서 항상 추가 도움에 대해 열려 있다고 밝힌 다음, 안내원들이 하는 일을 간략히 설명하고 있다. 이는 자원 봉사자로서 안내원의 역할을 하도록 요청하는 것과 같으므로 (B)가 정답이다.

6. 화자는 어디에서 일부 정보를 찾을 수 있다고 말하는가?
(A) 소셜 미디어 페이지에서
(B) 동사무소에서
(C) 프로그램 안내책자에서
(D) 게시판에서

해설 화자가 담화 후반부에 프로그램 책자 뒷면에서 추가 정보를 확인할 수 있다고 알리고 있으므로 (C)가 정답이다.

어휘 booklet 안내책자, 소책자

Questions 7-9 refer to the following advertisement and price list.

7 Looking to brighten up your front or backyard? Call us, Sunny Green Yard Services, today. Our experienced professionals have been providing top-notch garden and lawn care to homes and businesses in Fresno County for over 30 years. We provide a huge variety of maintenance services, such as lawn mowing, pest control, leaf blowing, and hedge trimming. And you won't want to miss out on some super savings! **8 For this month only, we're offering a 20% discount on all our service packages.** Visit our Web site at www.sunnygreenyards.ca to explore **9 our plans, which are arranged based on popularity.**

건물 정면 또는 뒤뜰을 화사하게 만들기를 바라고 계신가요? 저희 써니 그린 야드 서비스 사에 오늘 전화 주십시오. 경험 많은 저희 전문가들은 30년 넘게 프레스노 카운티의 주택 및 업체들을 대상으로 최고의 정원 및 잔디 관리 서비스를 제공해 오고 있습니다. 저희는 잔디 깎기와 병충해 방제, 나뭇잎 송풍 정리, 생울타리 손질 같은, 엄청나게 다양한 유지 관리 서비스를 제공해 드립니다. 그리고 몇몇 초특급 할인 혜택을 놓치고 싶지 않으실 것입니다! 이번 달에 한해, 모든 저희 서비스 패키지에 대해 20퍼센트 할인을 제공해 드립니다. 저희 웹 사이트 www.sunnygreenyards.ca를 방문하셔서 저희 서비스 약정을 살펴 보시기 바라며, 이는 인기도를 바탕으로 정렬되어 있습니다.

서비스 약정	가격
스탠다드	시간당 120달러
프리미엄	시간당 155달러
온고잉 케어	시간당 60달러
엘리트	시간당 210달러

어휘 look to do ~하기를 바라다 brighten up ~을 화사하게 만들다, 밝게 만들다 top-notch 최고의 mowing 풀 깎기, 풀 베기 pest control 병충해 방제 hedge 생울타리 trimming 손질, 다듬기 savings 할인, 절약

7. 어떤 종류의 업체가 광고되고 있는가?
(A) 지붕 공사
(B) 배관
(C) 조경
(D) 카펫 청소

해설 화자가 담화를 시작하면서 건물 정면 또는 뒤뜰을 화사하게 만드는 일과 관련해 소속 업체를 소개하고 있으므로 (C)가 정답이다.

8. 화자의 말에 따르면, 이달 말에 무슨 일이 일어날 것 같은가?
(A) 개조 공사가 완료될 것이다.
(B) 일련의 워크숍이 개최될 것이다.
(C) 새로운 장비가 설치될 것이다.
(D) 판촉 행사가 종료될 것이다.

해설 담화 후반부에 화자가 이번 달에 한해 모든 서비스 패키지에 대해 20퍼센트 할인을 제공한다는 사실을 밝히고 있다. 따라서, 이달 말에 판촉용 할인 행사가 종료된다는 것을 알 수 있으므로 (D)가 정답이다.

9. 시각자료를 보시오. 업체에서 가장 인기 있는 서비스 약정의 비용이 얼마인가?
(A) 시간당 120 달러
(B) 시간당 155 달러
(C) 시간당 60 달러
(D) 시간당 210 달러

해설 화자가 담화 후반부에 자사 웹 사이트에서 서비스 약정 정보를 살펴 보도록 권하면서 그것이 인기도를 바탕으로 정렬되어 있다고 알리고 있다. 따라서, 시각자료 첫 줄에 표기된 Standard가 가장 인기 있는 서비스이며, 그 금액이 시간당 $120로 쓰여 있으므로 (A)가 정답이다.

Questions 10-12 refer to the following announcement.

Attention, vendors. Welcome to the Electronic Displays Showcase! 10 **As sellers of digital signage, this is your chance to meet potential clients face-to-face.** The exhibition hall will open at 9 A.M. sharp. 11 **For the safety of all attendees, please ensure that the walkways and space around your booth are free of any boxes or clutter. Also, all structures should be securely fastened** using anchors or weights. Please keep in mind that 12 **the hall will close at 6 P.M. for the evening reception**, where exhibitors can network and mingle.

모든 판매업체에 알립니다. 일렉트로닉 디스플레이 쇼케이스에 오신 것을 환영합니다! 디지털 사이니지의 판매업체로서, 이 행사는 잠재 고객들을 대면해 만나실 수 있는 기회입니다. 전시홀은 오전 9시 정각에 개방될 것입니다. 모든 참석자들의 안전을 위해, 반드시 여러분 부스 주변의 통로 및 공간에 어떤 상자나 잡동사니도 있지 않도록 해 주시기 바랍니다. 또한, 모든 구조물은 고정 장치나 무거운 것을 이용해 단단히 고정되어야 합니다. 전시홀이 저녁 축하 연회를 위해 오후 6시에 닫는다는 점을 명심하시기 바라며, 이곳에서 전시 참가자들께서 교류하고 어울리실 수 있습니다.

어휘 digital signage 디지털 사이니지(공공 장소에서 마케팅이나 광고 등에 쓰이는 디지털 영상 장치) face-to-face 대면으로 sharp 정각에 clutter 잡동사니 anchor 고정 장치 reception 축하 행사 exhibitor 전시 참가자 mingle 어울리다

10. 청자들은 누구인가?
(A) 기술 지원 담당 직원들
(B) 무역 박람회 참가자들
(C) 행사 주최자들
(D) 시설 관리 팀원들

해설 화자가 담화 초반부에 청자들이 제품 판매와 관련해 잠재 고객들을 대면 방식으로 만날 수 있는 기회라고 언급하고 있다. 따라서, 제품을 선보이고 고객들과 만나는 기회를 얻을 수 있는 행사인 (B)가 정답이다.

어휘 trade show 무역 박람회 crew (함께 작업하는) 팀, 조

11. 화자는 청자들에게 무엇을 하도록 요청하는가?
(A) 안전 예방 조치를 취하는 일
(B) 방 한 곳에 상자를 보관하는 일
(C) 무료 선물을 가져 가는 일
(D) 특정 이동로를 이용하는 일

해설 화자가 담화 중반부에 참석자들의 안전을 위해 부스 주변의 통로 및 공간에 대한 주의 사항 및 모든 구조물의 고정과 관련된 조치를 당부하고 있으므로 (A)가 정답이다.

어휘 take safety precautions 안전 예방 조치를 취하다

12. 저녁 시간에 무슨 일이 있을 것인가?
(A) 음악 공연
(B) 연회 만찬
(C) 점검
(D) 축하 행사

해설 담화 후반부에 화자가 저녁 축하 연회를 위해 전시홀이 오후 6시에 닫는다고 알리고 있으므로 (D)가 정답이다.

Questions 13-15 refer to the following advertisement.

Want to build better habits this year? Located on Crestwood Avenue, 13 **Riverbend Wellness has finally opened its doors as the finest fitness complex in Danville.** Members can enjoy premium exercise classes and facilities while staying close to the city center. 14 **What sets us apart from other establishments is our heated outdoor pool, available all year long.** 15 **Check out our Web site to take a virtual tour of our spaces.** Get active and kick off the new year strong by becoming a member at Riverbend Wellness today.

올해는 더 나은 습관을 들이고 싶으신가요? 크레스트우드 애비뉴에 위치해 있는, 저희 리버벤드 웰니스가 마침내 댄빌에서 가장 훌륭한 피트니스 복합 건물로서 그 문을 열었습니다. 회원들께서는 도심 구역과 가까이 지내시면서 고급 운동 강좌와 시설을 즐기실 수 있습니다. 저희가 다른 시설들과 차별화되는 점은 일년 내내 이용 가능한, 옥외 온수 수영장입니다. 저희 웹 사이트를 확인하셔서 저희 공간들에 대한 가상 투어를 진행해 보십시오. 오늘 저희 리버벤드 웰니스의 회원이 되시는 것으로 적극성을 갖고 새해를 힘차게 시작해 보시기 바랍니다.

어휘 set A apart from B A를 B와 차별화시키다 establishment 시설, 설립(물) virtual 가상의 active 적극적인, 활동적인 kick off ~을 시작하다

13. 무엇이 광고되고 있는가?
(A) 피트니스 센터
(B) 고급 리조트
(C) 주택 관련 커뮤니티
(D) 워터 파크

해설 화자가 담화 초반부에 소속 업체인 리버벤드 웰니스가 댄빌에서 가장 훌륭한 피트니스 복합 건물로서 문을 열었다고 밝히고 있으므로 (A)가 정답이다.

14. 화자의 말에 따르면, 무엇이 리버벤드 웰니스를 다른 업체들과 차별화시키는가?
(A) 옥외 수영장
(B) 중심부 위치
(C) 초고속 인터넷
(D) 무료 사물함 이용

해설 담화 중반부에 화자가 다른 시설들과 차별화되는 점이 일년 내내 이용 가능한 옥외 온수 수영장이라고 언급하고 있으므로 (A)가 정답이다.

15. 화자는 청자들에게 온라인으로 무엇을 하도록 제안하는가?
(A) 할인 쿠폰을 받는 일
(B) 가상 투어를 하는 일
(C) 예약을 하는 일
(D) 회원 프로그램에 등록하는 일

해설 화자가 담화 후반부에 소속 업체 웹 사이트를 확인해서 그곳 공간들에 대한 가상 투어를 해 보도록 제안하고 있으므로 (B)가 정답이다.

Questions 16-18 refer to the following announcement and train information.

Attention, travelers. 16 **We are currently upgrading our train station and therefore apologize for any disturbance caused by the construction noise.** Fortunately, regional train times remain unchanged. Train BX34 to Munich will be arriving soon. At this moment, all passengers for Munich should proceed to platform 5A. **17 If you require help with your luggage, please ask a station agent at the ticketing counter. 18 The next stop for Train BX34 will be Dresden**, followed by Nuremberg, and then finally, Munich.

여행객 여러분께 알립니다. 저희가 현재 저희 기차역을 업그레이드하고 있으므로 공사 소음으로 인해 초래되는 모든 지장에 대해 사과 드립니다. 다행히, 지역 열차 시간은 변경되지 않은 상태로 유지됩니다. 뮌헨행 BX34 열차가 곧 도착할 예정입니다. 현재, 뮌헨으로 떠나시는 모든 승객들께서는 5A 승강장으로 이동해 주시기 바랍니다. 수하물에 대해 도움이 필요하신 경우, 매표 카운터에서 역무원에게 문의하시기 바랍니다. BX34 열차의 다음 정거장은 드레스덴이 될 것이며, 그 후로는 뉘른베르크, 그 다음으로는 마지막으로, 뮌헨이 될 것입니다.

열차 번호: BX34	
도시	도착 시간
함부르크	오후 4:30
베를린	오후 6:15
드레스덴	오후 7:45
뉘른베르크	오후 9:00
뮌헨	오후 10:30

어휘 disturbance 지장, 방해 at this moment 현재 proceed to ~로 이동하다, 나아가다 agent 직원, 대리인, 중개인 followed by A 그 다음이 A인

16. 화자가 왜 사과하는가?
(A) 일부 역내 작업이 소음을 만들어 내고 있다.
(B) 일부 도착 시간이 변경되었다.
(C) 안내 표지판이 오작동했다.
(D) 모든 기차가 야간 운행을 위해 출발했다.

해설 화자가 담화를 시작하면서 기차역을 업그레이드하고 있어서 그 공사 소음으로 인해 초래되는 모든 지장에 대해 사과의 말을 전하고 있으므로 (A)가 정답이다.

어휘 malfunction 오작동하다

17. 화자의 말에 따르면, 일부 청자들이 왜 직원을 만나야 할 수도 있는가?
(A) 티켓을 출력하기 위해
(B) 수하물 서비스를 요청하기 위해
(C) 분실물에 관해 문의하기 위해
(D) 연간 이용권을 구입하기 위해

해설 담화 중반부에 화자가 수하물에 대해 도움이 필요하면 역무원에게 문의하라고 알리고 있으므로 (B)가 정답이다.

18. 시각자료를 보시오. 열차 BX34가 언제 다음 정거장에 도착할 예정인가?
(A) 오후 6시 15분에
(B) 오후 7시 45분에
(C) 오후 9시에
(D) 오후 10시 30분에

해설 화자가 담화 후반부에 다음 정거장이 드레스덴이라고 밝히고 있다. 시각자료에서 Dresden이 표기된 세 번째 줄에 도착 시간이 7:45 P.M.으로 쓰여 있으므로 (B)가 정답이다.

Playlist 15

나오면 바로 점수 줍줍! 녹음메시지/소개

녹음메시지

프룬리지 아파트 관리소의 안내 전화입니다. 중앙 출입구 근처의 주차장이 5월 19일, 화요일에 재포장 공사를 거치게 될 것이라는 점에 유의하시기 바랍니다. 모든 프룬리지 주민들께 화요일 오전 10시 전에 각자의 배정된 주차 공간에서 자동차를 이동해 주시도록 요청 드립니다. 이 시간 후에 주차장 내에 남아 있는 모든 차량은 소유주 비용 부담으로 견인될 것입니다. 대체 주차 장소를 나타내는 지도가 지난주에 주민 여러분께 이메일로 전송되었습니다. 받지 못하셨다면, 출력본을 위해, 저희 프론트 데스크를 방문하시기 바랍니다.

Practice

1. (C) **2.** (A) **3.** (B)

Questions 1-3 refer to the following recorded message.

Hello there. You have reached Golden **Gas and Electric**, the leading **energy provider** in the Bay Area. Please stay on the line for the next available agent. If you're calling about the **power outages** in Santa Clara County, we can confirm that our technicians have been dispatched, and **services will be back to normal** by 2 P.M. If you've recently changed residences and need to start, stop, or transfer your service, please visit our Web site to **submit a form** for your **work order**. Thank you.

안녕하세요. 귀하께서는 베이 에어리어의 선도적인 에너지 공급업체인, 골든 가스 전기 회사에 연락 주셨습니다. 시간이 나는 다음 직원과 통화하시려면 끊지 말고 대기해 주시기 바

랍니다. 산타 클라라 카운티의 정전과 관련해 전화하시는 분인 경우, 저희 기술자들이 파견되어 서비스가 오후 2시까지 다시 정상화될 것이라는 사실을 확인해 드릴 수 있습니다. 최근에 주거지를 변경하셔서 서비스를 시작, 중단, 또는 이전하셔야 하는 경우에는, 저희 웹 사이트를 방문하셔서 여러분의 작업 주문에 필요한 양식을 제출해 주시기 바랍니다. 감사합니다.

어휘 **stay on the line** (전화상에서) 끊지 않고 대기하다 **power outage** 정전 **dispatch** (사람) ~을 파견하다, (사물 등) ~을 발송하다

1. 어떤 종류의 업체가 메시지를 녹음했는가?
(A) 전자제품 매장
(B) 소프트웨어 개발업체
(C) 공익 사업 회사
(D) 인터넷 서비스 제공업체

해설 화자가 담화 초반부에 베이 에어리어의 선도적인 에너지 공급업체인 골든 가스 전기 회사에 연락했다고 언급하고 있으므로 (C)가 정답이다.

어휘 **utility** (전기·가스·수도 등의) 공익 사업

2. 화자가 오후 2시까지 무슨 일이 있을 것이라고 말하는가?
(A) 한 가지 문제가 해결될 것이다.
(B) 새 웹 사이트 한 곳이 발표될 것이다.
(C) 일부 직원들이 사무실로 복귀할 것이다.
(D) 일부 구역들이 폐쇄된 상태가 될 것이다.

해설 담화 중반부에 화자가 산타 클라라 카운티의 정전과 관련해 기술자들이 파견되어 서비스가 오후 2시까지 다시 정상화될 것이라고 알리고 있다. 이는 정전 문제가 2시까지 해결된다는 뜻이므로 (A)가 정답이다.

어휘 **close off** ~을 폐쇄하다, 차단시키다

3. 화자는 웹 사이트에서 무엇이 이용 가능하다고 말하는가?
(A) 배송 정책
(B) 작업 주문서
(C) 요금 목록
(D) 의견 설문 조사지

해설 담화 후반부에 화자가 웹 사이트를 방문해 작업 주문에 필요한 양식을 제출해 달라고 요청하고 있으므로 (B)가 정답이다.

소개

오늘 컨퍼런스에 참석해 주신 여러분 모두에게 감사 드립니다! 여러분 대부분이 이 공간을 찾으실 수 있어서 다행입니다. 모든 혼란에 대해 사과 드리며, 저는 새로운 장소가 일정표에 업데이트되었다고 생각했지만, 그렇게 되지 못한 것 같습니다. 이제, 우리 첫 번째 연사이신 아멜리아 클레멘트 씨를 소개해 드리고자 합니다. 클레멘트 씨께서는 스트랫포드 대학교에서 의사 소통 수업을 가르치고 계십니다. 이분께서는 효과적인 협업 전략에 관한 전문가이시며, 이분의 강의들은 개인이 하나의 팀으로서 더 잘 일할 수 있는 여러 다른 방법을 집중 조명합니다. 저는 분명 우리 모두가 뛰어난 협업 능력이 얼마나 중요한지 알고 있다고 생각합니다. 클레멘트 씨를 무대로 맞이하겠습니다!

Practice

1. (C) **2.** (C) **3.** (B)

Questions 1-3 refer to the following introduction.

Welcome, everyone, to the 20th Global Marine Science **Symposium**. We're delighted to have Clara Griffin from the Port Costa Research Institute with us to give an opening statement. Dr. Griffin is **well-known** for her **studies** on **marine pollution** and has collaborated extensively with researchers across the globe to develop initiatives for ocean conservation. Before I let her start, please take a moment to **flip through your informational materials** to ensure you have a ticket for lunch. Several attendees have mentioned that their packets didn't have one.

제20회 세계 해양 과학 심포지엄에 오신 모든 분을 환영합니다. 개회사를 해 주실 포트 코스타 연구소의 클라라 그리핀 씨를 우리와 한 자리에 모시게 되어 기쁘게 생각합니다. 그리핀 박사님께서는 해양 오염에 관한 연구로 잘 알려진 분이시며, 해양 보존을 위한 계획을 개발하시기 위해 전 세계 각지의 연구가들과 광범위하게 협업해 오셨습니다. 이분께서 시작하시도록 해 드리기 전에, 반드시 여러분께서 점심 식권을 갖고 계시도록 해 드리기 위해 가지고 계신 안내 자료를 쭉 훑어 보실 시간을 가지시기 바랍니다. 여러 참석자들께서 안내책자 묶음에 들어 있지 않았다고 언급해 주신 바 있습니다.

어휘 **opening statement** 개회사 **extensively** 광범위하게, 폭넓게 **initiative** n. 계획, 솔선수범, 주도(권)

conservation 보존 flip through (페이지를 넘기면서) ~을 쭉 훑어 보다 packets 안내책자 묶음

1. 소개가 어디에서 진행되고 있는가?
(A) 과학 전시회에서
(B) 모금 행사에서
(C) 전문 컨퍼런스에서
(D) 회사 기념 행사에서

해설 화자가 담화를 시작하면서 제20회 세계 해양 과학 심포지엄에 온 청자들을 환영한다는 인사말을 전하고 있으므로 (C)가 정답이다.

2. 화자의 말에 따르면, 클라라 그리핀 씨가 무엇으로 알려져 있는가?
(A) 자연 보호 구역을 설립하는 일
(B) 마케팅 전략을 개발하는 일
(C) 해양 오염에 대한 연구
(D) 해외 여행 경험

해설 담화 중반부에 화자가 그리핀 박사의 이름을 언급하면서 해양 오염에 관한 연구로 잘 알려진 사람이라고 소개하고 있으므로 (C)가 정답이다.

3. 청자들은 무엇을 하도록 요청 받는가?
(A) 점심 식사를 선택하는 일
(B) 안내책자 묶음을 확인해 보는 일
(C) 뉴스 기사를 읽어 보는 일
(D) 각자의 버스 승차권을 예약하는 일

해설 화자가 담화 후반부에 청자들이 반드시 점심 식권을 갖고 있도록 하기 위해 각자의 안내 자료를 쭉 훑어 볼 시간을 가지라고 요청하고 있으므로 (B)가 정답이다.

Check-up Test

1. (A)	**2.** (B)	**3.** (C)	**4.** (C)	**5.** (A)
6. (B)	**7.** (A)	**8.** (D)	**9.** (B)	**10.** (D)
11. (B)	**12.** (D)	**13.** (D)	**14.** (B)	**15.** (D)
16. (A)	**17.** (B)	**18.** (A)		

Questions 1-3 refer to the following recorded message.

Hello, and thank you for contacting 1 **Harmond Industries, the UK's leading provider of printer paper.** Due to last week's severe snowstorm, 2 **the roadways around our distribution center were inaccessible. This may have prevented customers from receiving their orders on time.** The roads have reopened, and our deliveries have resumed service, but it may take several days to get fully up to speed. If you've been affected, we'll provide 30% off your next order as an apology for the inconvenience. Simply enter your invoice number on our Web site, and 3 **you'll receive a discount code via e-mail immediately.**

안녕하세요, 영국의 선도적인 프린터 용지 제공업체인, 저희 하먼드 인더스트리에 연락 주셔서 감사합니다. 지난주의 극심한 폭설로 인해, 저희 유통 센터 주변의 도로들이 접근 불가능한 상태였습니다. 이것으로 인해 고객들께서 제때 주문품을 받지 못하셨을 수도 있습니다. 도로도 재개방되었고, 저희 배송도 서비스를 재개했지만, 기대 수준에 완전히 이르려면 며칠 걸릴 것입니다. 귀하께서 영향을 받으신 경우, 불편함에 대한 사과의 의미로 다음 번 주문에 대해 30퍼센트 할인을 제공해 드리겠습니다. 저희 웹 사이트에 거래 내역서 번호를 입력하시기만 하면, 즉시 이메일을 통해 할인 코드를 받으실 것입니다.

어휘 leading 선도적인, 앞서 가는 severe 극심한, 가혹한 distribution 유통, 배부, 배급 inaccessible 접근 불가능한, 이용 불가능한 may have p.p. ~했을 수도 있다 on time 제때 resume ~을 재개하다 up to speed 기대 수준을 보이는, 최신 정보를 갖춘 via ~을 통해

1. 하먼드 인더스트리 사는 무엇을 판매하는가?
(A) 프린터 용지
(B) 식탁 의자
(C) 청소 용품
(D) 컴퓨터 부품

해설 화자가 담화를 시작하면서 하먼드 인더스트리라는 회사명과 함께 영국의 선도적인 프린터 용지 제공업체라는 말로 소개하고 있으므로 (A)가 정답이다.

2. 화자의 말에 따르면, 회사는 어떤 문제를 겪고 있는가?
(A) 공급 부족
(B) 배송 지연
(C) 웹 사이트 오류
(D) 정전

해설 담화 중반부에 화자가 폭설에 따른 도로 상태로 인해 고객들이 제때 주문품을 받지 못했을 것이라는 문제를 언급하고 있다. 이는 배송이 지연되는 문제를 의미하므로 (B)가 정답이다.

어휘 power outage 정전

3. 이메일을 통해 무엇이 도착할 것인가?
(A) 환불 양식
(B) 배송 일정표
(C) 할인 코드
(D) 수정된 거래 내역서

해설 화자가 담화 후반부에 사과의 의미로 다음 번 주문에 대해 30퍼센트 할인을 제공하겠다고 알리면서 이메일을 통해 할인 코드를 받는 방법을 설명하고 있으므로 (C)가 정답이다.

Questions 4-6 refer to the following introduction.

Good evening, everyone, and welcome to the Lakewood Business Leaders Banquet, 4 **where every year, we honor one local entrepreneur who has made significant contributions to our community. Our honoree for this year** certainly represents everything we value. 5 **Hayley Kim, owner of Peak Performance, has built an extensive shop that carries all sorts of sporting equipment.** Outside of business hours, Ms. Kim is also dedicated to promoting health and wellness. 6 **She offers fitness classes free of charge to the public three times a week,** in the morning and evening! So, please give a round of applause for this year's distinguished guest, Ms. Kim.

안녕하세요, 여러분, 그리고 매년, 저희가 우리 지역 사회에 상당히 공헌해 오신 지역 기업가 한 분을 기리는, 레이크우드 비즈니스 리더스 연회에 오신 것을 환영합니다. 올해의 수상자께서는 분명 저희가 가치 있게 여기는 모든 것을 대표하시는 분입니다. 피크 퍼포먼스의 소유주, 헤일리 김 씨께서는 모든 종류의 스포츠 장비를 취급하는 대규모 매장을 지으셨습니다. 영업 시간 외에, 김 씨께서는 보건 복지를 증진하시는 데에도 헌신하고 계십니다. 이분께서는 일주일에 세 차례, 아침과 저녁에 일반인들을 대상으로 무료로 피트니스 강좌를 제공해 주고 계십니다! 그럼, 올해의 훌륭한 초대 손님이신 김 씨께 뜨거운 박수 부탁 드립니다.

어휘 honor v. ~을 기리다, ~에게 영예를 주다 honoree 수상자 represent ~을 대표하다, ~에 해당하다 carry (상점 등이) ~을 취급하다 the public 일반인들 give a round of applause for ~에게 뜨거운 박수를 보내다 distinguished 훌륭한, 뛰어난, 저명한

4. 소개가 어디에서 진행되고 있을 것 같은가?
(A) 직원 야유회에서
(B) 스포츠 경기 대회에서
(C) 시상식에서
(D) 기업 축하 연회에서

해설 화자가 담화 초반부에 행사명과 함께 지역 사회에 상당히 공헌해 온 지역 기업가 한 명을 기리는 행사라고 밝히면서 올해의 수상자를 소개하고 있으므로 (C)가 정답이다.

어휘 retreat 야유회 reception 축하 연회, 기념 연회

5. 헤일리 김 씨가 어떤 종류의 업체를 소유하고 있는가?
(A) 스포츠 용품 매장
(B) 미용실
(C) 건강 식품 매장
(D) 헬스장

해설 담화 중반부에 화자가 헤일리 김 씨를 피크 퍼포먼스의 소유주로 소개하면서 스포츠 장비를 취급하는 대규모 매장을 지은 사실을 알리고 있으므로 (A)가 정답이다.

6. 김 씨는 어떻게 다른 이들이 건강을 유지하도록 돕는가?
(A) 영양에 관한 강연을 제공한다.
(B) 무료 강좌를 제공한다.
(C) 지역 공동체 텃밭을 운영한다.
(D) 건강 애플리케이션을 개발했다.

해설 화자가 담화 후반부에 헤일리 김 씨가 일주일에 세 차례 일반인들을 대상으로 무료로 피트니스 강좌를 제공한다고 언급하고 있으므로 (B)가 정답이다.

어휘 nutrition 영양

Questions 7-9 refer to the following recorded message and schedule.

Hi, Leila, this is Tom. 7 **The newest version of the marketing brochure came out,** so I just forwarded it to you. 7 **I want to talk about maybe including a picture of our manufacturing plant** so that buyers can really see where our soaps are made. 8 **I'm attending a sales conference after lunch** and 9 **originally had an in-person appointment with a customer in the morning, but that just got canceled.** So if you'll be in the office today, let me know if you're free to meet.

안녕하세요, 레일라 씨, 톰입니다. 최신 버전의 마케팅 안내 책자가 나왔기 때문에, 막 전송해 드렸습니다. 구매자들께서 우리 비누가 만들어지는 곳을 정말로 확인해 보실 수 있도록 아마 우리 제조 공장 사진을 한 장 포함하는 것에 관해 이야기하고 싶습니다. 제가 점심 식사 후에 영업 컨퍼런스에 참석하는데, 원래 오전에 고객 한 분을 직접 만나 뵙는 약속이 있었지만, 막 취소되었습니다. 그래서 오늘 사무실에 계시면, 만나 뵐 시간이 있으신지 제게 알려 주시기 바랍니다.

일일 일정 - 10월 11일, 월요일 직원: 톰 퀌비	
9:00	가을 판촉 행사 회의
10:10	고객 상담
11:00	화상 회의 (ARD Co.와 함께)
11:45	부서별 출근 기록 관련 회의
12:30	점심 식사 (마리사 B.와 함께)

어휘 **forward** ~을 전송하다 **in-person** 직접 가서 하는 **w/** ~와 함께 **check-in** (기기 등을 이용한) 출근 기록, (공항·호텔 등에서의) 수속

7. 화자가 무엇과 관련해 청자와 이야기하고 싶어 하는가?
(A) 안내 책자에 이미지를 포함하는 일
(B) 생산 공장을 방문하는 일
(C) 샘플을 지역 매장들에게 기증하는 일
(D) 마케팅 전략을 바꾸는 일

해설 화자가 담화 초반부에 최신 버전의 마케팅 안내 책자가 나온 사실과 함께 자사의 제조 공장 사진을 한 장 포함하는 것에 관해 이야기하고 싶다는 뜻을 밝히고 있으므로 (A)가 정답이다.

8. 화자가 점심 식사 후에 무엇에 참석할 것이라고 말하는가?
(A) 경영진 회의
(B) 비즈니스 세미나
(C) 교육 시간
(D) 영업 컨퍼런스

해설 담화 중반부에 화자가 점심 식사 후에 영업 컨퍼런스에 참석하는 일정을 언급하고 있으므로 (D)가 정답이다.

9. 시각자료를 보시오. 화자와 청자가 몇 시에 만날 것 같은가?
(A) 9시
(B) 10시 10분
(C) 11시
(D) 12시 30분

해설 화자가 담화 후반부에 오전에 고객 한 명을 직접 만나는 약속이 있었지만 막 취소되었다는 사실을 말하고 있다. 시각자료에서 고객과 만나는 약속에 해당하는 것이 Client consultation이며, 그 시간이 10:10으로 쓰여 있으므로 (B)가 정답이다.

Questions 10-12 refer to the following introduction.

Good morning, everyone. First off, thank you for attending our information session. 10 **We at Rosegold Solutions are excited to see so many people interested in our company. We're hoping to fill 22 job vacancies, so please do apply.** Now, I'd like to introduce our principal designer, Isaac Yamagishi, who has been with Rosegold for over a decade. In fact, just last month, 11 **Mr. Yamagishi was featured on HomeTrends.com as one of the top industrial designers in the nation!** We're so proud of his achievements. 12 **He'll be sharing his experiences of working at Rosegold. After that, there'll be time to ask us any questions about our hiring process.**

안녕하세요, 여러분. 가장 먼저, 저희 설명회에 참석해 주셔서 감사합니다. 저희 로즈골드 솔루션즈는 저희 회사에 관심을 갖고 계신 분을 이렇게 많이 뵙게 되어 기쁩니다. 저희가 22개의 공석을 충원할 수 있기를 희망하고 있으므로, 꼭 지원해 주시기 바랍니다. 이제, 저희 로즈골드 사와 10년 넘게 함께 해 오신 분으로서, 저희 수석 디자이너이신 아이작 야마기시 씨를 소개해 드리고자 합니다. 사실, 불과 지난달에, 야마기시 씨께서는 전국 최고의 산업 디자이너들 중 한 분으로 HomeTrends.com에 특별히 실리셨습니다! 저희는 이분의 업적을 정말 자랑스럽게 생각합니다. 이분께서 로즈골드에서의 근무 경험을 공유해 주실 예정입니다. 그 후에는, 저희에게 고용 과정에 관한 어떤 질문이든 하실 수 있는 시간이 있을 것입니다.

어휘 **first off** 가장 먼저, 우선 **job vacancy** 공석, 빈 자리 **feature** (잡지 등에) ~을 특별히 싣다, 특징으로 하다

10. 해당 시간의 목적이 무엇인가?
(A) 더 많은 고객들을 끌어들이는 것
(B) 업적을 축하하는 것
(C) 확장을 발표하는 것
(D) 신입 직원을 모집하는 것

해설 화자가 담화 초반부에 청자들이 자신의 회사에 관심을 갖고 있는 사람들임을 언급하면서 22개의 공석을 충원할 수 있기를 희망한다는 말과 함께 꼭 지원하도록 당부하고 있

으므로 (D)가 정답이다.

11. 야마기시 씨는 누구인가?
(A) 광고 제작 총감독
(B) 산업 디자이너
(C) 온라인 잡지 편집자
(D) 인사부장

해설 담화 중반부에 화자가 야마기시 씨를 소개하면서 전국 최고의 산업 디자이너들 중 한 명으로 선정된 사실을 밝히고 있으므로 (B)가 정답이다.

12. 야마기시 씨의 담화 후에 무슨 일이 있을 것인가?
(A) 패널 토론회
(B) 사인회
(C) 제품 시연회
(D) 문의 시간

해설 화자가 담화 후반부에 야마기시 씨가 근무 경험을 공유해 준 후에 고용 과정에 관한 어떤 질문이든 할 수 있는 시간이 있을 것이라고 밝히고 있으므로 (D)가 정답이다.

Questions 13-15 refer to the following recorded message.

Hi, you've reached Apex Style Central. 13 **From silk scarves to antique sunglasses to leather belts, we offer an unbeatable variety of products.** As a token of our gratitude to all our clients, 14 **we've decided to extend our holiday sale for three more days.** If you have a question about an order you've placed, please hold for the next available customer support agent. Due to a temporary staff shortage, 15 **we would like to apologize if you stay on hold for longer than normal.** We kindly ask for your patience.

안녕하세요, 귀하께서는 에이펙스 스타일 센트럴에 연락 주셨습니다. 실크 스카프에서부터 고풍스러운 선글라스와 가죽 벨트에 이르기까지, 저희는 타의 추종을 불허할 정도로 다양한 제품을 제공해 드리고 있습니다. 모든 저희 고객들께 전해 드리는 감사의 표시로, 저희는 휴일 세일 행사를 3일 더 연장하기로 결정했습니다. 귀하께서 주문하신 제품과 관련해 질문이 있으신 경우, 다음 고객 지원 담당 직원이 시간이 날 때까지 대기해 주시기 바랍니다. 일시적인 직원 부족 문제로 인해, 평소보다 더 오래 대기 상태로 유지되는 경우에 사과 드리고자 합니다. 인내심을 가져 주시기를 정중히 요청 드립니다.

어휘 **antique** 고풍스러운, 골동품의 **unbeatable** 타의 추종을 불허하는, 능가할 수 없는 **as a token of** ~의 표시로 **gratitude** 감사(의 뜻) **hold** (전화상에서 끊지 않고) 대기하다 **shortage** 부족 **patience** 인내(심)

13. 업체에서 어떤 종류의 제품을 판매할 것 같은가?
(A) 미술 공예 용품
(B) 미용 제품
(C) 파티용 장식품
(D) 의류 액세서리

해설 화자가 담화 초반부에 자사의 제품 종류와 관련해 실크 스카프와 선글라스, 가죽 벨트를 언급하고 있으므로 (D)가 정답이다.

14. 화자의 말에 따르면, 무엇이 연장되었는가?
(A) 제출 마감 기한
(B) 판촉 행사
(C) 무료 배송 제공 서비스
(D) 반품 정책

해설 담화 중반부에 화자가 휴일 세일 행사를 3일 더 연장하기로 결정한 사실을 밝히고 있으므로 (B)가 정답이다.

15. 화자가 왜 사과하는가?
(A) 일부 가격이 인상되었다.
(B) 일부 배송이 지연되었다.
(C) 주차 공간이 이용 불가능하다.
(D) 대기 시간이 길어질지도 모른다.

해설 화자가 담화 후반부에 일시적인 직원 부족 문제로 인해 평소보다 더 오래 대기 상태로 유지되는 경우에 사과한다고 말하고 있으므로 (D)가 정답이다.

Questions 16-18 refer to the following introduction and information.

Now, it's my pleasure 16 **to reveal the winner for Outstanding TV Commercial of the Year. The award goes to... Crescent Studio!** Their ad campaign for Sangwoo Systems' latest range of energy-efficient laptops made of sustainable materials is brilliantly imaginative. And to top it off, they are a corporation that truly demonstrates social responsibility. 17 **We want to commend Crescent Studio for contributing a share of its earnings to a foundation that's dedicated to preserving the environment.** Before we welcome the CEO of Crescent Studio up to the stage,

18 let's take a moment to watch a video showcasing the company's creative commercials.

자, 올해의 우수 TV 광고상 수상자를 공개해 드리게 되어 기쁩니다. 수상의 영광은... 크레센트 스튜디오에게 돌아갑니다! 지속 가능한 소재로 만들어진 상우 시스템즈 사의 에너지 효율적인 최신 노트북 컴퓨터 제품군에 대한 이곳의 광고 캠페인은 훌륭할 정도로 창의적이었습니다. 그리고 그 외에도, 이곳은 진정으로 사회적 책임감을 보여 주고 있는 기업입니다. 저희는 수익의 일부분을 환경을 보존하는 데 전념하고 있는 한 재단에 기부하는 것에 대해 크레센트 스튜디오를 칭찬해 드리고 싶습니다. 크레센트 스튜디오의 대표이사님을 무대로 맞이하기에 앞서, 잠시 이 회사의 창의적인 광고를 선보이는 동영상을 시청하는 시간을 갖겠습니다.

재단	사명
더 그레이트 디퍼	음악 교육
더 스프링타임 이니셔티브	생태계 보존
홈 이즈 히어	지역 사회 복구
블루밍 시즌	청소년 육성

어휘 reveal ~을 공개하다, 드러내다 sustainable 지속 가능한 brilliantly 훌륭하게 to top it off 그 외에도, 설상가상으로 commend A for B B에 대해 A를 칭찬하다 preserve ~을 보존하다 showcase ~을 선보이다 ecological 생태계의, 생태학의 conservation 보존, 유지 restoration 복구, 복원

16. 어떤 종류의 행사가 개최되고 있는가?
(A) 시상식
(B) 모금 행사
(C) 기자 회견
(D) 전사 워크숍

해설 화자가 담화를 시작하면서 올해의 우수 TV 광고상 수상자를 공개한다고 밝히면서 수상자를 알리고 있으므로 (A)가 정답이다.

어휘 companywide 전사의, 회사 전체적인

17. 시각자료를 보시오. 크레센트 스튜디오가 어느 재단과 협업했을 것 같은가?
(A) 더 그레이트 디퍼
(B) 더 스프링타임 이니셔티브
(C) 홈 이즈 히어
(D) 블루밍 시즌

해설 화자가 담화 중반부에 크레센트 스튜디오가 수익의 일부분을 환경을 보존하는 데 전념하고 있는 한 재단에 기부한 사실을 밝히고 있다. 시각자료에서 환경 보존에 해당하는 Ecological conservation으로 쓰여 있는 곳이 The Springtime Initiative이므로 (B)가 정답이다.

18. 청자들이 곧이어 무엇을 할 것 같은가?
(A) 동영상을 시청하는 일
(B) 서로 인사하는 일
(C) 몇몇 사진을 촬영하는 일
(D) 추첨 행사에 참가하는 일

해설 담화 맨 마지막 부분에 화자가 크레센트 스튜디오의 대표이사를 무대로 맞이하기 전에 잠시 그 회사의 창의적인 광고 동영상을 시청하는 시간을 갖겠다고 언급하고 있으므로 (A)가 정답이다.

어휘 greet ~에게 인사하다, ~을 맞이하다 raffle 추첨 행사

실전모의고사

TEST 1

Part 1

1. (D) **2.** (C) **3.** (D) **4.** (C) **5.** (C) **6.** (A)

Part 2

7. (C) **8.** (A) **9.** (A) **10.** (B) **11.** (C) **12.** (B) **13.** (A) **14.** (B) **15.** (B) **16.** (B)
17. (A) **18.** (B) **19.** (C) **20.** (A) **21.** (B) **22.** (C) **23.** (A) **24.** (C) **25.** (A) **26.** (C)
27. (C) **28.** (A) **29.** (A) **30.** (B) **31.** (B)

Part 3

32. (C) **33.** (D) **34.** (A) **35.** (D) **36.** (D) **37.** (C) **38.** (C) **39.** (B) **40.** (C) **41.** (B)
42. (A) **43.** (D) **44.** (D) **45.** (B) **46.** (C) **47.** (D) **48.** (C) **49.** (B) **50.** (C) **51.** (B)
52. (C) **53.** (C) **54.** (D) **55.** (D) **56.** (B) **57.** (D) **58.** (C) **59.** (C) **60.** (B) **61.** (C)
62. (B) **63.** (C) **64.** (D) **65.** (C) **66.** (C) **67.** (D) **68.** (D) **69.** (B) **70.** (C)

Part 4

71. (C) **72.** (D) **73.** (B) **74.** (C) **75.** (D) **76.** (B) **77.** (C) **78.** (B) **79.** (D) **80.** (B)
81. (B) **82.** (A) **83.** (D) **84.** (A) **85.** (D) **86.** (B) **87.** (A) **88.** (D) **89.** (B) **90.** (A)
91. (D) **92.** (A) **93.** (C) **94.** (B) **95.** (A) **96.** (C) **97.** (C) **98.** (C) **99.** (D) **100.** (B)

Part 5

101. (B) **102.** (B) **103.** (C) **104.** (A) **105.** (D) **106.** (D) **107.** (C) **108.** (C) **109.** (B) **110.** (A)
111. (A) **112.** (A) **113.** (D) **114.** (A) **115.** (D) **116.** (B) **117.** (D) **118.** (A) **119.** (C) **120.** (C)
121. (A) **122.** (C) **123.** (B) **124.** (D) **125.** (C) **126.** (B) **127.** (D) **128.** (A) **129.** (B) **130.** (B)

Part 6

131. (A) **132.** (C) **133.** (D) **134.** (C) **135.** (B) **136.** (D) **137.** (A) **138.** (D) **139.** (D) **140.** (C)
141. (D) **142.** (B) **143.** (B) **144.** (C) **145.** (A) **146.** (B)

Part 7

147. (D) **148.** (C) **149.** (C) **150.** (B) **151.** (A) **152.** (B) **153.** (C) **154.** (D) **155.** (C) **156.** (B)
157. (B) **158.** (D) **159.** (C) **160.** (D) **161.** (B) **162.** (C) **163.** (D) **164.** (D) **165.** (A) **166.** (C)
167. (B) **168.** (D) **169.** (C) **170.** (C) **171.** (C) **172.** (C) **173.** (A) **174.** (C) **175.** (C) **176.** (D)
177. (C) **178.** (A) **179.** (B) **180.** (C) **181.** (D) **182.** (C) **183.** (A) **184.** (D) **185.** (D) **186.** (C)
187. (D) **188.** (D) **189.** (B) **190.** (B) **191.** (C) **192.** (D) **193.** (C) **194.** (D) **195.** (B) **196.** (C)
197. (C) **198.** (D) **199.** (B) **200.** (D)

TEST 2

Part 1

1. (A)	**2.** (A)	**3.** (C)	**4.** (D)	**5.** (D)	**6.** (A)				

Part 2

7. (C)	**8.** (B)	**9.** (C)	**10.** (C)	**11.** (A)	**12.** (B)	**13.** (B)	**14.** (A)	**15.** (A)	**16.** (C)
17. (A)	**18.** (A)	**19.** (A)	**20.** (C)	**21.** (B)	**22.** (B)	**23.** (A)	**24.** (B)	**25.** (A)	**26.** (A)
27. (C)	**28.** (B)	**29.** (A)	**30.** (C)	**31.** (B)					

Part 3

32. (A)	**33.** (B)	**34.** (C)	**35.** (A)	**36.** (D)	**37.** (B)	**38.** (B)	**39.** (C)	**40.** (C)	**41.** (A)
42. (B)	**43.** (D)	**44.** (D)	**45.** (B)	**46.** (C)	**47.** (C)	**48.** (D)	**49.** (B)	**50.** (C)	**51.** (A)
52. (D)	**53.** (C)	**54.** (D)	**55.** (C)	**56.** (B)	**57.** (D)	**58.** (D)	**59.** (C)	**60.** (A)	**61.** (C)
62. (C)	**63.** (A)	**64.** (D)	**65.** (C)	**66.** (B)	**67.** (D)	**68.** (D)	**69.** (C)	**70.** (C)	

Part 4

71. (C)	**72.** (A)	**73.** (D)	**74.** (C)	**75.** (C)	**76.** (A)	**77.** (D)	**78.** (C)	**79.** (A)	**80.** (B)
81. (C)	**82.** (A)	**83.** (D)	**84.** (C)	**85.** (D)	**86.** (B)	**87.** (C)	**88.** (A)	**89.** (C)	**90.** (D)
91. (C)	**92.** (D)	**93.** (C)	**94.** (D)	**95.** (C)	**96.** (D)	**97.** (C)	**98.** (D)	**99.** (B)	**100.** (C)

Part 5

101. (D)	**102.** (A)	**103.** (B)	**104.** (C)	**105.** (C)	**106.** (C)	**107.** (C)	**108.** (B)	**109.** (A)	**110.** (B)
111. (D)	**112.** (B)	**113.** (D)	**114.** (B)	**115.** (B)	**116.** (A)	**117.** (A)	**118.** (C)	**119.** (C)	**120.** (A)
121. (D)	**122.** (B)	**123.** (C)	**124.** (D)	**125.** (C)	**126.** (B)	**127.** (D)	**128.** (B)	**129.** (D)	**130.** (D)

Part 6

131. (C)	**132.** (D)	**133.** (B)	**134.** (A)	**135.** (B)	**136.** (C)	**137.** (D)	**138.** (C)	**139.** (C)	**140.** (D)
141. (D)	**142.** (B)	**143.** (B)	**144.** (C)	**145.** (A)	**146.** (C)				

Part 7

147. (D)	**148.** (C)	**149.** (B)	**150.** (C)	**151.** (C)	**152.** (B)	**153.** (B)	**154.** (D)	**155.** (C)	**156.** (B)
157. (D)	**158.** (B)	**159.** (D)	**160.** (B)	**161.** (D)	**162.** (A)	**163.** (C)	**164.** (C)	**165.** (C)	**166.** (B)
167. (D)	**168.** (B)	**169.** (D)	**170.** (D)	**171.** (A)	**172.** (B)	**173.** (C)	**174.** (C)	**175.** (A)	**176.** (C)
177. (D)	**178.** (B)	**179.** (C)	**180.** (D)	**181.** (C)	**182.** (A)	**183.** (C)	**184.** (C)	**185.** (C)	**186.** (B)
187. (D)	**188.** (D)	**189.** (B)	**190.** (C)	**191.** (B)	**192.** (D)	**193.** (C)	**194.** (D)	**195.** (B)	**196.** (C)
197. (B)	**198.** (C)	**199.** (C)	**200.** (C)						

TEST 3

Part 1

1. (C) **2.** (C) **3.** (B) **4.** (A) **5.** (B) **6.** (C)

Part 2

7. (C) **8.** (C) **9.** (C) **10.** (B) **11.** (A) **12.** (A) **13.** (C) **14.** (C) **15.** (C) **16.** (A)
17. (A) **18.** (C) **19.** (A) **20.** (A) **21.** (A) **22.** (B) **23.** (C) **24.** (A) **25.** (A) **26.** (B)
27. (A) **28.** (B) **29.** (B) **30.** (C) **31.** (B)

Part 3

32. (D) **33.** (A) **34.** (A) **35.** (C) **36.** (D) **37.** (D) **38.** (B) **39.** (D) **40.** (D) **41.** (D)
42. (C) **43.** (D) **44.** (B) **45.** (A) **46.** (A) **47.** (C) **48.** (B) **49.** (A) **50.** (B) **51.** (C)
52. (D) **53.** (B) **54.** (D) **55.** (C) **56.** (C) **57.** (A) **58.** (D) **59.** (C) **60.** (A) **61.** (D)
62. (C) **63.** (B) **64.** (B) **65.** (D) **66.** (D) **67.** (C) **68.** (B) **69.** (C) **70.** (A)

Part 4

71. (B) **72.** (A) **73.** (B) **74.** (B) **75.** (C) **76.** (B) **77.** (B) **78.** (D) **79.** (C) **80.** (C)
81. (D) **82.** (C) **83.** (B) **84.** (D) **85.** (B) **86.** (A) **87.** (D) **88.** (B) **89.** (B) **90.** (B)
91. (D) **92.** (A) **93.** (A) **94.** (B) **95.** (B) **96.** (C) **97.** (A) **98.** (B) **99.** (C) **100.** (D)

Part 5

101. (C) **102.** (A) **103.** (D) **104.** (B) **105.** (C) **106.** (A) **107.** (B) **108.** (D) **109.** (C) **110.** (A)
111. (D) **112.** (C) **113.** (A) **114.** (C) **115.** (B) **116.** (D) **117.** (B) **118.** (A) **119.** (D) **120.** (C)
121. (A) **122.** (C) **123.** (B) **124.** (B) **125.** (A) **126.** (D) **127.** (A) **128.** (C) **129.** (C) **130.** (B)

Part 6

131. (A) **132.** (C) **133.** (D) **134.** (B) **135.** (B) **136.** (D) **137.** (A) **138.** (A) **139.** (B) **140.** (A)
141. (C) **142.** (C) **143.** (D) **144.** (A) **145.** (C) **146.** (C)

Part 7

147. (C) **148.** (C) **149.** (C) **150.** (A) **151.** (A) **152.** (C) **153.** (B) **154.** (D) **155.** (B) **156.** (B)
157. (B) **158.** (D) **159.** (B) **160.** (D) **161.** (D) **162.** (A) **163.** (B) **164.** (B) **165.** (B) **166.** (D)
167. (B) **168.** (C) **169.** (D) **170.** (B) **171.** (D) **172.** (C) **173.** (B) **174.** (D) **175.** (D) **176.** (C)
177. (C) **178.** (C) **179.** (A) **180.** (A) **181.** (D) **182.** (B) **183.** (A) **184.** (A) **185.** (D) **186.** (B)
187. (A) **188.** (D) **189.** (B) **190.** (C) **191.** (D) **192.** (B) **193.** (B) **194.** (D) **195.** (C) **196.** (A)
197. (D) **198.** (B) **199.** (B) **200.** (B)

★ ★ ★

서아쌤의 토익 비밀과외

온라인 강의

< RC/LC/실전모의고사 >

13만 유튜버 서아쌤!
유튜브를 인강에 녹여
말자막으로
편하게 학습!

토익시험을 매회 응시하는
토익 만점강사 서아쌤의
최신 고득점 기출포인트
집약!

RC+LC+실전모의고사
3주 완성
All-in-One 커리큘럼으로
토익 고득점 달성!

시원스쿨LAB(lab.siwonschool.com)에서 유료 강의를 수강하실 수 있습니다.

★Special Event★ 서아쌤의 토익 비밀과외 학습 지원!

SIWONSCHOOL LAB
서아쌤 토익
단과 1만원 할인쿠폰
쿠폰번호 : **서아쌤토익1**
COUPON

SIWONSCHOOL LAB
서아쌤 토익
프리패스 2만원 할인쿠폰
쿠폰번호 : **서아쌤토익2**
COUPON

* 시원스쿨LAB(lab.siwonschool.com)에서 쿠폰번호 등록 후 사용가능합니다. / *쿠폰 유효기간 : 등록일로부터 3일간

서아쌤만의 비밀과외 노하우 방출
초밀착 케어까지!

서아쌤 토익 프리패스

토익 3주 초단기 완성을 위한

서아쌤 토익 프리패스의 특별혜택

1

RC+LC 3주 종결 가능
서아쌤 토익 강의/교재 포함

2

기본기에 필요한 알짜 강의
처음토익 LC/RC 무료증정

3

토익 기초체력 마스터
기초영문법 토익 VOCA 교재 포함

4

점수 달성 보장
수강기간 90일씩 무한 연장
*목표점수 미달성시

토익 한 번에 끝내줄
서아쌤 스터디 자료 3종 무료 제공

6

토익+취업까지 책임지는
취업영어 강의 무료 제공

시원스쿨LAB(lab.siwonschool.com)에서 프리패스를 신청하실 수 있습니다.
제공하는 혜택은 기간에 따라 다를 수 있습니다.

과목별 스타 강사진 영입, 기대하세요!

시원스쿨LAB 강사 라인업

20년 노하우의 토익/토스/오픽/지텔프/텝스/아이엘츠/토플/SPA/듀오링고
기출 빅데이터 심층 연구로 빠르고 효율적인 목표 점수 달성을 보장합니다.

시험영어 전문 연구 조직

시원스쿨어학연구소

 시험영어 전문

 기출 빅데이터

 264,000시간

히트브랜드 토익·토스·오픽 인강 1위

시원스쿨LAB 교재 라인업

*2020-2024 5년 연속 히트브랜드대상 1위 토익·토스·오픽 인강

시원스쿨 토익 교재 시리즈

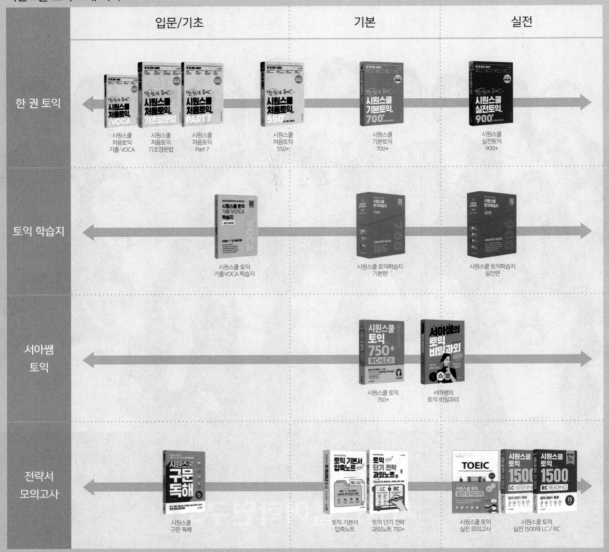

	입문/기초	기본	실전
한 권 토익	시원스쿨 처음토익 기출 VOCA 시원스쿨 처음토익 기초영문법 시원스쿨 처음토익 Part 7	시원스쿨 처음토익 550+ 시원스쿨 기본토익 700+	시원스쿨 실전토익 900+
토익 학습지	시원스쿨 토익 기출VOCA 학습지	시원스쿨 토익학습지 기본편	시원스쿨 토익학습지 실전편
서아쌤 토익		시원스쿨 토익 750+ 서아쌤의 토익 비밀과외	
전략서 모의고사	시원스쿨 구문 독해	토익 기본서 압축노트 토익 단기 전략 과외노트 750+	시원스쿨 토익 실전 모의고사 시원스쿨 토익 실전 1500제 LC / RC

시원스쿨 토익스피킹·오픽 교재 시리즈

10가지 문법으로 시작하는 토익스피킹 기초영문법

28시간에 끝내는 토익스피킹 START

5일 만에 끝내는 토익스피킹 실전모의고사

15개 템플릿으로 끝내는 토익스피킹 필수전략서

멀티캠퍼스X시원스쿨 오픽 진짜학습지 IM 실전

멀티캠퍼스X시원스쿨 오픽 진짜학습지 IH 실전

멀티캠퍼스X시원스쿨 오픽 진짜학습지 AL 실전

OPIc All in one PACKAGE IM-AL

어디서도 알려준 적 없는
토익 고득점 비밀과외

POINT 1 RC + LC + 실전모의고사를 한 권에!

[1권] RC 이론 + LC 이론 + 실전모의고사 3회분
[2권] 정답 및 해설

POINT 2 3주 완성 커리큘럼으로 고득점 획득

RC/LC(15일) + 실전모의고사 3회분(1일 1모의고사) ▸ 3주 완성
목표 점수 달성에 꼭 필요한 핵심포인트만 정리

POINT 3 최신 기출 트렌드 완벽 반영

최근 크게 어려워진 LC 난이도 반영
고득점을 위해 꼭 끝까지 풀어야 하는 Part 7 집중 학습

POINT 4 QR코드 스캔으로 편리하게 학습

QR코드만 찍으면 음원 및 강의(유료) 바로 재생
QR코드로 실전모의고사 모바일 해설 바로 보기

POINT 5 13만 토익 유튜버 서아쌤 저자 직강

토익 시험을 매회 응시하고 분석하는 만점강사 서아쌤이 유료 인강을 통해 고득점 비법과 전략 전수
강의 패키지 구매 시, 부교재 <서아쌤의 토익 비밀노트> 및 실시간 카톡 스터디 서비스 제공

정가 **18,800**원

ISBN 979-11-6150-914-3 13740